# with MyEconLab®

- **Learning Catalytics**—Generates classroom discussion, guides lectures, and promotes peer-to-peer learning with real-time analytics. Students can use any device to interact in the classroom, engage with content, and even draw and share graphs.

- **Real-Time Data Analysis Exercises**—Using current macro data to help students understand the impact of changes in economic variables, Real-Time Data Analysis Exercises communicate directly with the Federal Reserve Bank of St. Louis's FRED® site and update as new data are available.

- **Current News Exercises**—Every week, current microeconomic and macroeconomic news stories, with accompanying exercises, are posted to MyEconLab. Assignable and auto-graded, these multi-part exercises ask students to recognize and apply economic concepts to real-world events.

- **Experiments**—Flexible, easy-to-assign, auto-graded, and available in Single and Multiplayer versions, Experiments in MyEconLab make learning fun and engaging.

- **Reporting Dashboard**—View, analyze, and report learning outcomes clearly and easily. Available via the Gradebook and fully mobile-ready, the Reporting Dashboard presents student performance data at the class, section, and program levels in an accessible, visual manner.

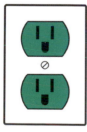

- **LMS Integration**—Link from any LMS platform to access assignments, rosters, and resources, and synchronize MyLab grades with your LMS gradebook. For students, new direct, single sign-on provides access to all the personalized learning MyLab resources that make studying more efficient and effective.

- **Mobile Ready**—Students and instructors can access multimedia resources and complete assessments right at their fingertips, on any mobile device.

**PEARSON**

# The Pearson Series in Economics

**Abel/Bernanke/Croushore**
*Macroeconomics**

**Acemoglu/Laibson/List**
*Economics**

**Bade/Parkin**
*Foundations of Economics**

**Berck/Helfand**
*The Economics of the Environment*

**Bierman/Fernandez**
*Game Theory with Economic Applications*

**Blanchard**
*Macroeconomics**

**Blau/Ferber/Winkler**
*The Economics of Women, Men, and Work*

**Boardman/Greenberg/Vining/Weimer**
*Cost-Benefit Analysis*

**Boyer**
*Principles of Transportation Economics*

**Branson**
*Macroeconomic Theory and Policy*

**Bruce**
*Public Finance and the American Economy*

**Carlton/Perloff**
*Modern Industrial Organization*

**Case/Fair/Oster**
*Principles of Economics**

**Chapman**
*Environmental Economics: Theory, Application, and Policy*

**Cooter/Ulen**
*Law & Economics*

**Daniels/VanHoose**
*International Monetary & Financial Economics*

**Downs**
*An Economic Theory of Democracy*

**Ehrenberg/Smith**
*Modern Labor Economics*

**Farnham**
*Economics for Managers*

**Folland/Goodman/Stano**
*The Economics of Health and Health Care*

**Fort**
*Sports Economics*

**Froyen**
*Macroeconomics*

**Fusfeld**
*The Age of the Economist*

**Gerber**
*International Economics**

**González-Rivera**
*Forecasting for Economics and Business*

**Gordon**
*Macroeconomics**

**Greene**
*Econometric Analysis*

**Gregory**
*Essentials of Economics*

**Gregory/Stuart**
*Russian and Soviet Economic Performance and Structure*

**Hartwick/Olewiler**
*The Economics of Natural Resource Use*

**Heilbroner/Milberg**
*The Making of the Economic Society*

**Heyne/Boettke/Prychitko**
*The Economic Way of Thinking*

**Holt**
*Markets, Games, and Strategic Behavior*

**Hubbard/O'Brien**
*Economics**

*Money, Banking, and the Financial System**

**Hubbard/O'Brien/Rafferty**
*Macroeconomics**

**Hughes/Cain**
*American Economic History*

**Husted/Melvin**
*International Economics*

**Jehle/Reny**
*Advanced Microeconomic Theory*

**Johnson-Lans**
*A Health Economics Primer*

**Keat/Young/Erfle**
*Managerial Economics*

**Klein**
*Mathematical Methods for Economics*

**Krugman/Obstfeld/Melitz**
*International Economics: Theory & Policy**

**Laidler**
*The Demand for Money*

**Leeds/von Allmen**
*The Economics of Sports*

**Leeds/von Allmen/Schiming**
*Economics**

**Lynn**
*Economic Development: Theory and Practice for a Divided World*

**Miller**
*Economics Today**

*Understanding Modern Economics*

**Miller/Benjamin**
*The Economics of Macro Issues*

**Miller/Benjamin/North**
*The Economics of Public Issues*

**Mills/Hamilton**
*Urban Economics*

**Mishkin**
*The Economics of Money, Banking, and Financial Markets**

*The Economics of Money, Banking, and Financial Markets, Business School Edition**

*Macroeconomics: Policy and Practice**

**Murray**
*Econometrics: A Modern Introduction*

**O'Sullivan/Sheffrin/Perez**
*Economics: Principles, Applications and Tools**

**Parkin**
*Economics**

**Perloff**
*Microeconomics**

*Microeconomics: Theory and Applications with Calculus**

**Perloff/Brander**
*Managerial Economics and Strategy**

**Phelps**
*Health Economics*

**Pindyck/Rubinfeld**
*Microeconomics**

**Riddell/Shackelford/Stamⁱ Schneider**
*Economics: A Tool for Criticallyⁱ Understanding Society*

**Roberts**
*The Choice: A Fable of Free Trⁱ and Protection*

**Rohlf**
*Introduction to Economic Reasoning*

**Roland**
*Development Economics*

**Scherer**
*Industry Structure, Strategy, aⁱ Public Policy*

**Schiller**
*The Economics of Poverty and Discrimination*

**Sherman**
*Market Regulation*

**Stock/Watson**
*Introduction to Econometrics*

**Studenmund**
*Using Econometrics: A Practicaⁱ Guide*

**Tietenberg/Lewis**
*Environmental and Natural Resource Economics*
*Environmental Economics and Policy*

**Todaro/Smith**
*Economic Development*

**Waldman/Jensen**
*Industrial Organization: Theory and Practice*

**Walters/Walters/Appel/Callahan/Centanni/Maex/O'Neill**
*Econversations: Today's Studenⁱ Discuss Today's Issues*

**Weil**
*Economic Growth*

**Williamson**
*Macroeconomics*

# Principles of
# **Macroeconomics**

TWELFTH EDITION

# Principles of
# Macroeconomics

## Karl E. Case
*Wellesley College*

## Ray C. Fair
*Yale University*

## Sharon M. Oster
*Yale University*

**PEARSON**

Boston   Columbus   Indianapolis   New York   San Francisco   Amsterdam   Cape Town   Dubai
London   Madrid   Milan   Munich   Paris   Montréal   Toronto   Delhi   Mexico City
São Paulo   Sydney   Hong Kong   Seoul   Singapore   Taipei   Tokyo

**Vice President, Business Publishing:** Donna Battista
**Editor-in-Chief:** Adrienne D'Ambrosio
**AVP/Executive Editor:** David Alexander
**Editorial Assistant:** Michelle Zeng
**Vice President, Product Marketing:** Maggie Moylan
**Director of Marketing, Digital Services and Products:** Jeanette Koskinas
**Executive Field Marketing Manager:** Adam Goldstein
**Executive Field Marketing Manager:** Ramona Elmer
**Product Marketing Assistant:** Jessica Quazza
**Team Lead, Program Management:** Ashley Santora
**Program Manager:** Lindsey Sloan
**Team Lead, Project Management:** Jeff Holcomb
**Project Manager:** Roberta Sherman
**Operations Specialist:** Carol Melville
**Creative Director:** Blair Brown
**Art Director:** Jon Boylan

**Vice President, Director of Digital Strategy and Assessment:** Paul Gentile
**Manager of Learning Applications:** Paul DeLuca
**Digital Editor:** Denise Clinton
**Director, Digital Studio:** Sacha Laustsen
**Digital Studio Manager:** Diane Lombardo
**Digital Studio Project Manager:** Melissa Honig
**Digital Studio Project Manager:** Robin Lazrus
**Digital Content Team Lead:** Noel Lotz
**Digital Content Project Lead:** Courtney Kamauf
**Full-Service Project Management and Composition:** Integra Software Services, Inc.
**Interior Designer:** Integra Software Services, Inc.
**Cover Designer:** Jon Boylan
**Cover Art:** Jon Boylan
**Printer/Binder:** LSC Communications
**Cover Printer:** LSC Communications

Microsoft® and Windows® are registered trademarks of the Microsoft Corporation in the U.S.A. and other countries. This book is not sponsored or endorsed by or affiliated with the Microsoft Corporation.

Acknowledgments of third-party content appear on the appropriate page within the text.

FRED® is a registered trademark and the FRED® Logo and ST. LOUIS FED are trademarks of the Federal Reserve Bank of St. Louis. http://research.st.louisfed.org/fred2/

PEARSON, ALWAYS LEARNING, and MYECONLAB® are exclusive trademarks owned by Pearson Education, Inc. or its affiliates in the U.S. and/or other countries.

Unless otherwise indicated herein, any third-party trademarks that may appear in this work are the property of their respective owners, and any references to third-party trademarks, logos, or other trade dress are for demonstrative or descriptive purposes only. Such references are not intended to imply any sponsorship, endorsement, authorization, or promotion of Pearson's products by the owners of such marks, or any relationship between the owner and Pearson Education, Inc. or its affiliates, authors, licensees, or distributors.

**Cataloging-in-Publication Data is on file at the LIbrary of Congress.**

ISBN 10:    0-13-407880-2
ISBN 13: 978-0-13-407880-9

# About the Authors

**Karl E. Case** is Professor of Economics Emeritus at Wellesley College where he has taught for 34 years and served several tours of duty as Department Chair. He is a Senior Fellow at the Joint Center for Housing Studies at Harvard University and a founding partner in the real estate research firm of Fiserv Case Shiller Weiss, which produces the S&P Case-Shiller Index of home prices. He serves as a member of the Index Advisory Committee of Standard and Poor's, and along with Ray Fair he serves on the Academic Advisory Board of the Federal Reserve Bank of Boston.

Before coming to Wellesley, he served as Head Tutor in Economics (director of undergraduate studies) at Harvard, where he won the Allyn Young Teaching Prize. He was Associate Editor of the *Journal of Economic Perspectives* and the *Journal of Economic Education,* and he was a member of the AEA's Committee on Economic Education.

Professor Case received his B.A. from Miami University in 1968; spent three years on active duty in the Army, and received his Ph.D. in Economics from Harvard University in 1976.

Professor Case's research has been in the areas of real estate, housing, and public finance. He is author or coauthor of five books, including *Principles of Economics, Economics and Tax Policy,* and *Property Taxation: The Need for Reform,* and he has published numerous articles in professional journals.

For the last 25 years, his research has focused on real estate markets and prices. He has authored numerous professional articles, many of which attempt to isolate the causes and consequences of boom and bust cycles and their relationship to regional and national economic performance.

**Ray C. Fair** is Professor of Economics at Yale University. He is a member of the Cowles Foundation at Yale and a Fellow of the Econometric Society. He received a B.A. in Economics from Fresno State College in 1964 and a Ph.D. in Economics from MIT in 1968. He taught at Princeton University from 1968 to 1974 and has been at Yale since 1974.

Professor Fair's research has primarily been in the areas of macroeconomics and econometrics, with particular emphasis on macroeconometric model building. He also has done work in the areas of finance, voting behavior, and aging in sports. His publications include *Specification, Estimation, and Analysis of Macroeconometric Models* (Harvard Press, 1984); *Testing Macroeconometric Models* (Harvard Press, 1994); *Estimating How the Macroeconomy Works* (Harvard Press, 2004), and *Predicting Presidential Elections and Other Things* (Stanford University Press, 2012).

Professor Fair has taught introductory and intermediate macroeconomics at Yale. He has also taught graduate courses in macroeconomic theory and macroeconometrics.

Professor Fair's U.S. and multicountry models are available for use on the Internet free of charge. The address is http://fairmodel.econ.yale.edu. Many teachers have found that having students work with the U.S. model on the Internet is a useful complement to an introductory macroeconomics course.

**Sharon M. Oster** is the Frederic Wolfe Professor of Economics and Management and former Dean of the Yale School of Management. Professor Oster joined Case and Fair as a coauthor in the ninth edition of this book. Professor Oster has a B.A. in Economics from Hofstra University and a Ph.D. in Economics from Harvard University.

Professor Oster's research is in the area of industrial organization. She has worked on problems of diffusion of innovation in a number of different industries, on the effect of regulations on business, and on competitive strategy. She has published a number of articles in these areas and is the author of several books, including *Modern Competitive Analysis* and *The Strategic Management of Nonprofits.*

Prior to joining the School of Management at Yale, Professor Oster taught for a number of years in Yale's Department of Economics. In the department, Professor Oster taught introductory and intermediate microeconomics to undergraduates as well as several graduate courses in industrial organization. Since 1982, Professor Oster has taught primarily in the Management School, where she teaches the core microeconomics class for MBA students and a course in the area of competitive strategy. Professor Oster also consults widely for businesses and nonprofit organizations and has served on the boards of several publicly traded companies and nonprofit organizations.

# Brief Contents

# Contents

## PART IV    Further Macroeconomics Issues    264

# Preface

Our goal in the 12th edition, as it was in the first edition, is to instill in students a fascination with both the functioning of the economy and the power and breadth of economics. The first line of every edition of our book has been "The study of economics should begin with a sense of wonder." We hope that readers come away from our book with a basic understanding of how market economies function, an appreciation for the things they do well, and a sense of the things they do poorly. We also hope that readers begin to learn the art and science of economic thinking and begin to look at some policy and even personal decisions in a different way.

## What's New in This Edition?

- The 12th edition has continued the changes in the *Economics in Practice* boxes that we began several editions ago. In these boxes, we try to bring economic thinking to the concerns of the typical student. In many cases, we do this by spotlighting recent research, much of it by young scholars. Some of the many new boxes include:
  - Chapter 3 uses behavioral economics to ask whether having unusually sunny weather increases consumer purchasess of convertible cars.
  - In Chapter 7 we look at new research on how individuals unemployed as a result of a recession spend their time. How much of that new time goes to job search versus other activities?
  - In Chapter 14 we describe recent research on how well recessions can be predicted.
  - In Chapter 20 we describe work that uses children's height in India to examine hunger and gender inequality.
  - Chapter 21, our new chapter, contains three boxes, examining the Moving to Opportunity program, birth weight and infant mortality, and the effects of the minimum wage.

  In other cases we use recent events or common situations to show the power and breadth of economic models. For example:
  - In Chapter 25 we illustrate the role of banks in creating money by describing bank runs in two classic movies and in the legend of Wyatt Earp.

  It is our hope that students will come to see both how broad the tools of economics are and how exciting is much of the new research in the field. For each box, we have also added questions to take students back from the box to the analytics of the textbook to reinforce the underlying economic principles of the illustrations.

- As in the previous edition, we have reworked some of the chapters to streamline them and to improve readability. In this edition, Chapter 20 has been revised to include more of the modern approach to economic development, including discussion of the millennium challenge.

- A major change in macro in the last edition was to replace the LM curve with a Fed interest rate rule, where the money supply now plays a smaller role in the analysis. Continuing in this spirit, in the current edition we have merged the supply of money and demand for money chapters into one chapter, Chapter 10. This streamlines the analysis and eliminates material that is no longer important.

- We have added a new chapter, Chapter 21, "Critical Thinking About Research," which we are quite excited about. It may be the first time a chapter like this has been included in an introductory economics text. This chapter covers the research methodology of economics. We highlight some of the key concerns of empirical economics: selection issues, causality, statistical significance, and regression analysis. Methodology is a key part of economics these days, and we have tried to give the introductory student a sense of what this methodology is.

- All of the macro data have been updated through 2014. The slow recovery from the 2008–2009 recession is still evident in these data, as it was in the 11<sup>th</sup> edition. This gives students a good idea of what has been happening to the economy since they left high school.
- Many new questions and problems at the end of the chapters have been added.

## The Foundation

The themes of *Principles of Macroeconomics*, 12<sup>th</sup> edition, are the same themes of the first eleven editions. The purposes of this book are to introduce the discipline of economics and to provide a basic understanding of how economies function. This requires a blend of economic theory, institutional material, and real-world applications. We have maintained a balance between these ingredients in every chapter. The hallmark features of our book are as follows:

1. Three-tiered explanations of key concepts (*stories-graphs-equations*)
2. Intuitive and accessible structure
3. International coverage

### Three-Tiered Explanations: Stories-Graphs-Equations

Professors who teach principles of economics are faced with a classroom of students with different abilities, backgrounds, and learning styles. For some students, analytical material is difficult no matter how it is presented; for others, graphs and equations seem to come naturally. The problem facing instructors and textbook authors is how to convey the core principles of the discipline to as many students as possible without selling the better students short. Our approach to this problem is to present most core concepts in the following three ways.

First, we present each concept in the context of a simple intuitive *story* or example in words often followed by a table. Second, we use a *graph* in most cases to illustrate the story or example. And finally, in many cases where appropriate, we use an *equation* to present the concept with a mathematical formula.

## Macroeconomic Structure

We remain committed to the view that it is a mistake simply to throw aggregate demand and aggregate supply curves at students in the first few chapters of a principles book. To understand the AS and AD curves, students need to know about the functioning of both the goods market and the money market. The logic behind the simple demand curve is wrong when it is applied to the relationship between aggregate demand and the price level. Similarly, the logic behind the simple supply curve is wrong when it is applied to the relationship between aggregate supply and the price level. We thus build up to the AS/AD model slowly.

The goods market is discussed in Chapters 8 and 9 (the IS curve). The money market is discussed in Chapter 10 (material behind the Fed rule). Everything comes together in Chapter 11, which derives the AD and AS curves and determines the equilibrium values of aggregate output, the price level, and the interest rate. This is the core chapter and where the Fed rule plays a major role. Chapter 12 then uses the model in Chapter 11 to analyze policy effects and cost shocks. Chapter 13 then brings in the labor market. The figure at the top of the next page (Figure III.1 on page 139) gives you an overview of this structure.

One of the big issues in the organization of the macroeconomic material is whether long-run growth issues should be taught before short-run chapters on the determination of national income and countercyclical policy. In the last four editions, we moved a significant discussion of growth to Chapter 7, "Unemployment, Inflation, and Long-Run

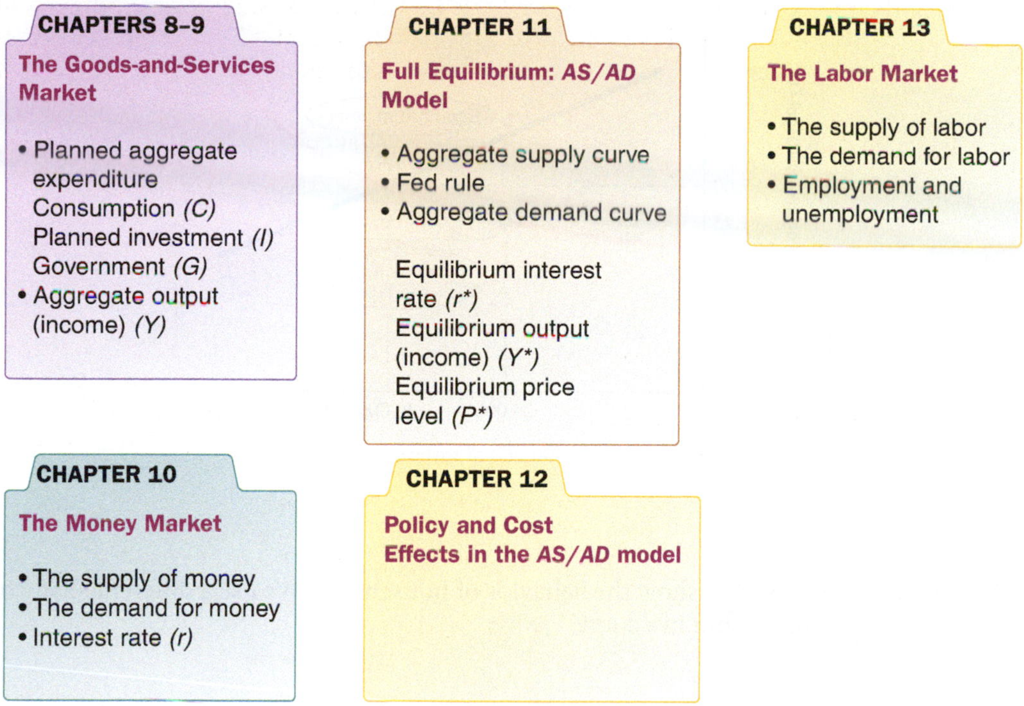

**CHAPTERS 8–9**

**The Goods-and-Services Market**

- Planned aggregate expenditure
  Consumption (C)
  Planned investment (I)
  Government (G)
- Aggregate output (income) (Y)

**CHAPTER 11**

**Full Equilibrium: AS/AD Model**

- Aggregate supply curve
- Fed rule
- Aggregate demand curve

  Equilibrium interest rate (r*)
  Equilibrium output (income) (Y*)
  Equilibrium price level (P*)

**CHAPTER 13**

**The Labor Market**

- The supply of labor
- The demand for labor
- Employment and unemployment

**CHAPTER 10**

**The Money Market**

- The supply of money
- The demand for money
- Interest rate (r)

**CHAPTER 12**

**Policy and Cost Effects in the AS/AD model**

▲ FIGURE III.1 **The Core of Macroeconomic Theory**

Growth," and highlighted it. However, while we wrote Chapter 16, the major chapter on long-run growth, so that it can be taught before or after the short-run chapters, we remain convinced that it is easier for students to understand the growth issue once they have come to grips with the logic and controversies of short-run cycles, inflation, and unemployment.

## International Coverage

As in previous editions, we continue to integrate international examples and applications throughout the text. This probably goes without saying: The days in which an introductory economics text could be written with a closed economy in mind have long since gone.

## Tools for Learning

As authors and teachers, we understand the challenges of the principles of economics course. Our pedagogical features are designed to illustrate and reinforce key economic concepts through real-world examples and applications.

### Economics in Practice

As described earlier, the *Economics in Practice* feature focuses on recent research or events that support a key concept in the chapter and help students think about the broad and exciting applications of economics to their lives and the world around them. Each box contains a question or two to further connect the material they are learning with their lives.

### Graphs

Reading and interpreting graphs is a key part of understanding economic concepts. The Chapter 1 Appendix, "How to Read and Understand Graphs," shows readers how to interpret the 200-plus graphs featured in this book. We use red curves to illustrate the behavior

▶ **FIGURE 3.9  Excess Demand, or Shortage**
At a price of $1.75 per bushel, quantity demanded exceeds quantity supplied. When excess *demand* exists, there is a tendency for price to rise. When quantity demanded equals quantity supplied, excess demand is eliminated and the market is in equilibrium. Here the equilibrium price is $2.00 and the equilibrium quantity is 40,000 bushels.

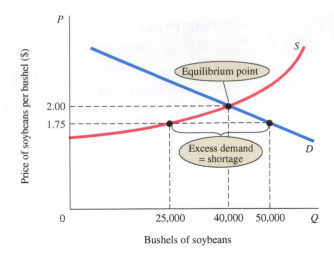

of firms and blue curves to show the behavior of households. We use a different shade of red and blue to signify a shift in a curve.

## Problems and Solutions

Each chapter and appendix ends with a problem set that asks students to think about and apply what they've learned in the chapter. These problems are not simple memorization questions. Rather, they ask students to perform graphical analysis or to apply economics to a real-world situation or policy decision. More challenging problems are indicated by an asterisk. Many problems have been updated. The solutions to all of the problems are available in the *Instructor's Manuals*. Instructors can provide the solutions to their students so they can check their understanding and progress.

# Digital features located in MyEconLab

MyEconLab is a unique online course management, testing, and tutorial resource. It is included with the eText version of the book or as a supplement to the print book. Students and instructors will find the following online resources to accompany the twelfth edition:

- **Concept Checks:** Each section of each learning objective concludes with an online Concept Check that contains one or two multiple choice, true/false, or fill-in questions. These checks act as "speed bumps" that encourage students to stop and check their understanding of fundamental terms and concepts before moving on to the next section. The goal of this digital resource is to help students assess their progress on a section-by-section basis, so they can be better prepared for homework, quizzes, and exams.

- **Animations:** Graphs are the backbone of introductory economics, but many students struggle to understand and work with them. Select numbered figures in the text have a supporting animated version online. The goal of this digital resource is to help students understand shifts in curves, movements along curves, and changes in equilibrium values. Having an animated version of a graph helps students who have difficulty interpreting the static version in the printed text. Graded practice exercises are included with the animations. Our experience is that many students benefit from this type of online learning.

- **Learning Catalytics:** Learning Catalytics is a "bring your own device" Web-based student engagement, assessment, and classroom intelligence system. This system generates classroom discussion, guides lectures, and promotes peer-to-peer learning with real-time analytics. Students can use any device to interact in the classroom, engage with content, and even draw and share graphs.

  To learn more, ask your local Pearson representative or visit www.learningcatalytics.com.

- **Digital Interactives:** Focused on a single core topic and organized in progressive levels, each interactive immerses students in an assignable and auto-graded activity. Digital Interactives are also engaging lecture tools for traditional, online, and hybrid courses, many incorporating real-time data, data displays, and analysis tools for rich classroom discussions.

- **Dynamic Study Modules:** With a focus on key topics, these modules work by continuously assessing student performance and activity in real time and using data and analytics, provide personalized content to reinforce concepts that target each student's particular strengths and weaknesses.

- **NEW: Math Review Exercises:** MyEconLab now offers a rich array of assignable and auto-graded exercises covering fundamental math concepts geared specifically to principles and intermediate economics students. Aimed at increasing student confidence and success, our new math skills review Chapter R is accessible from the assignment manager and contains over 150 graphing, algebra, and calculus exercises for homework, quiz, and test use. Offering economics students warm-up math assignments, math remediation, or math exercises as part of any content assignment has never been easier!

- **Graphs Updated with Real-Time Data from FRED:** Approximately 25 graphs are continuously updated online with the latest available data from FRED (Federal Reserve Economic Data), which is a comprehensive, up-to-date data set maintained by the Federal Reserve Bank of St. Louis. Students can display a pop-up graph that shows new data plotted in the graph. The goal of this digital feature is to help students understand how to work with data and understand how including new data affects graphs.

- **Interactive Problems and Exercises Updated with Real-Time Data from FRED:** The end-of-chapter problems in select chapters include real-time data exercises that use the latest data from FRED.

## MyEconLab for the Instructor

Instructors can choose how much or how little time to spend setting up and using MyEconLab. Here is a snapshot of what instructors are saying about MyEconLab:

> MyEconLab offers [students] a way to practice every week. They receive immediate feedback and a feeling of personal attention. As a result, my teaching has become more targeted and efficient.—Kelly Blanchard, Purdue University

> Students tell me that offering them MyEconLab is almost like offering them individual tutors.—Jefferson Edwards, Cypress Fairbanks College

> MyEconLab's eText is great—particularly in that it helps offset the skyrocketing cost of textbooks. Naturally, students love that.—Doug Gehrke, Moraine Valley Community College

Each chapter contains two preloaded homework exercise sets that can be used to build an individualized study plan for each student. These study plan exercises contain tutorial resources, including instant feedback, links to the appropriate learning objective in the eText,

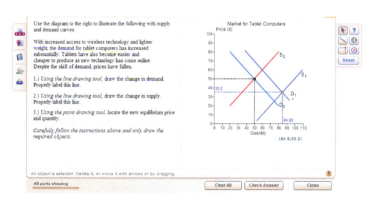

pop-up definitions from the text, and step-by-step guided solutions, where appropriate. After the initial setup of the course by the instructor, student use of these materials requires no further instructor setup. The online grade book records each student's performance and time spent on the tests and study plan and generates reports by student or chapter.

Alternatively, instructors can fully customize MyEconLab to match their course exactly, including reading assignments, homework assignments, video assignments, current news assignments, and quizzes and tests. Assignable resources include:

- Preloaded exercise assignments sets for each chapter that include the student tutorial resources mentioned earlier
- Preloaded quizzes for each chapter that are unique to the text and not repeated in the study plan or homework exercise sets
- Study plan problems that are similar to the end-of-chapter problems and numbered exactly like the book to make assigning homework easier
- *Real-Time-Data Analysis Exercises*, marked with ⬤, allow students and instructors to use the very latest data from FRED. By completing the exercises, students become familiar with a key data source, learn how to locate data, and develop skills in interpreting data.
- In the eText available in MyEconLab, select figures labeled MyEconLab Real-time data ⬤ allow students to display a pop-up graph updated with real-time data from FRED.
- *Current News Exercises*, provide a turnkey way to assign gradable news-based exercises in MyEconLab. Each week, Pearson scours the news, finds a current microeconomics and macroeconomics article, creates exercises around these news articles, and then automatically adds them to MyEconLab. Assigning and grading current news-based exercises that deal with the latest micro and macro events and policy issues has never been more convenient.
- *Experiments in MyEconLab* are a fun and engaging way to promote active learning and mastery of important economic concepts. Pearson's Experiments program is flexible, easy-to-assign, auto-graded, and available in single- and multiplayer versions.
  - Single-player experiments allow your students to play against virtual players from anywhere at any time so long as they have an Internet connection.
  - Multiplayer experiments allow you to assign and manage a real-time experiment with your class.
  - Pre- and post-questions for each experiment are available for assignment in MyEconLab.
  - For a complete list of available experiments, visit **www.myeconlab.com**.
- Test Item File questions that allow you to assign quizzes or homework that will look just like your exams
- Econ Exercise Builder, which allows you to build customized exercises

Exercises include multiple-choice, graph drawing, and free-response items, many of which are generated algorithmically so that each time a student works them, a different variation is presented.

MyEconLab grades every problem type except essays, even problems with graphs. When working homework exercises, students receive immediate feedback, with links to additional learning tools.

**Customization and Communication**   MyEconLab in MyLab/Mastering provides additional optional customization and communication tools. Instructors who teach distance-learning courses or very large lecture sections find the MyLab/Mastering format useful because they can upload course documents and assignments, customize the order of chapters, and use communication features such as Document Sharing, Chat, ClassLive, and Discussion Board.

# MyEconLab for the Student

MyEconLab puts students in control of their learning through a collection of testing, practice, and study tools tied to the online, interactive version of the textbook and other media resources. Here is a snapshot of what students are saying about MyEconLab:

- It was very useful because it had EVERYTHING, from practice exams to exercises to reading. Very helpful.—student, Northern Illinois University
- I would recommend taking the quizzes on MyEconLab because it gives you a true account of whether or not you understand the material.—student, Montana Tech
- It made me look through the book to find answers, so I did more reading.—student, Northern Illinois University

Students can study on their own or can complete assignments created by their instructor. In MyEconLab's structured environment, students practice what they learn, test their understanding, and pursue a personalized study plan generated from their performance on sample tests and from quizzes created by their instructors. In Homework or Study Plan mode, students have access to a wealth of tutorial features, including:

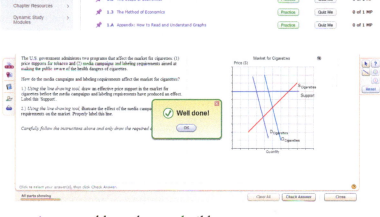

- Instant feedback on exercises that helps students understand and apply the concepts
- Links to the eText to promote reading of the text just when the student needs to revisit a concept or an explanation
- Step-by-step guided solutions that force students to break down a problem in much the same way an instructor would do during office hours
- Pop-up key term definitions from the eText to help students master the vocabulary of economics
- A graphing tool that is integrated into the various exercises to enable students to build and manipulate graphs to better understand how concepts, numbers, and graphs connect

**Additional MyEconLab Tools**  MyEconLab includes the following additional features:

- **Enhanced eText**—Students actively read and learn, and with more engagement than ever before, through embedded and auto-graded practice, real-time data-graph updates, animations, and more.
- **Print upgrade**—For students who wish to complete assignments in MyEconLab but read in print, Pearson offers registered MyEconLab users a loose-leaf version of the print text at a significant discount.
- **Glossary flashcards**—Every key term is available as a flashcard, allowing students to quiz themselves on vocabulary from one or more chapters at a time.

MyEconLab content has been created through the efforts of Chris Annala, State University of New York–Geneseo; Charles Baum, Middle Tennessee State University; Peggy Dalton, Frostburg State University; Carol Dole, Jacksonville University; David Foti, Lone Star College; Sarah Ghosh, University of Scranton; Satyajit Ghosh, University of Scranton; Woo Jung, University of Colorado; Chris Kauffman, University of Tennessee–Knoxville; Russell Kellogg, University of Colorado–Denver; Katherine McCann, University of Delaware; Daniel Mizak, Frostburg State University; Christine Polek, University of Massachusetts–Boston; Mark Scanlan, Stephen F. Austin State University; Leonie L. Stone, State University of New York–Geneseo; and Bert G. Wheeler, Cedarville University.

# Other Resources for the Instructor

The following supplements are designed to make teaching and testing flexible and easy and are available for *Micro, Macro,* and *Economics* volumes.

## Instructor's Manuals

Two *Instructor's Manuals*, one for *Principles of Microeconomics* and one for *Principles of Macroeconomics*, were prepared by Tony Lima of California State University, East Bay (Hayward, California). The *Instructor's Manuals* are designed to provide the utmost teaching support for instructors. They include the following content:

- Detailed *Chapter Outlines* include key terminology, teaching notes, and lecture suggestions.
- *Topics for Class Discussion* provide topics and real-world situations that help ensure that economic concepts resonate with students.
- Unique *Economics in Practice* features that are not in the main text provide extra real-world examples to present and discuss in class.
- *Teaching Tips* provide tips for alternative ways to cover the material and brief reminders on additional help to provide students. These tips include suggestions for exercises and experiments to complete in class.
- *Extended Applications* include exercises, activities, and experiments to help make economics relevant to students.
- *Excel Workbooks*, available for many chapters, make it easy to customize numerical examples and produce graphs.
- *Solutions* are provided for all problems in the book.

## Four Test Item Files

We have tailored the Test Item Files to help instructors easily and efficiently assess student understanding of economic concepts and analyses. Test questions are annotated with the following information:

- **Difficulty:** 1 for straight recall, 2 for some analysis, 3 for complex analysis
- **Type:** Multiple-choice, true/false, short-answer, essay
- **Topic:** The term or concept the question supports
- **Skill:** Fact, definition, analytical, conceptual
- **AACSB:** See description in the next section.

The Test Item Files include questions with tables that students must analyze to solve for numerical answers. The Test Item Files also contain questions based on the graphs that appear in the book. The questions ask students to interpret the information presented in the graph. Many questions require students to sketch a graph on their own and interpret curve movements.

**Microeconomics Test Item File,** by Randy Methenitis of Richland College: The Microeconomics Test Item File includes over 2,700 questions. All questions are machine gradable and are either multiple-choice or true/false. This Test Item File is for use with the 12th edition of *Principles of Microeconomics* in the first year of publication. It is available in a computerized format using TestGen EQ test-generating software and is included in MyEconLab.

**Microeconomics Test Item File Discussion and Short Answer,** by Richard Gosselin of Houston Community College: This second Test Item File includes 1,000 conceptual problems, essay questions, and short-answer questions. Application-type problems ask students to draw graphs and analyze tables. The Word files are available on the Instructor's Resource Center (www.pearsonhighered.com/educator).

**Macroeconomics Test Item File** by Randy Methenitis of Richland College: The Macroeconomics Test Item File includes over 2,900 questions. All questions are machine gradable and are either multiple-choice or true/false. This Test Item File is for use with the 12$^{th}$ edition of *Principles of Macroeconomics* in the first year of publication. This Test Item File is available in a computerized format using TestGen EQ test-generating software and included in MyEconLab.

**Macroeconomics Test Item File: Discussion and Short Answer,** by Richard Gosselin of Houston Community College: This second Test Item File includes 1,000 conceptual problems, essay questions, and short-answer questions. Application-type problems ask students to draw graphs and analyze tables. The Word files are available on the Instructor's Resource Center (www.pearsonhighered.com/educator).

The Test Item Files were checked for accuracy by the following professors:

Leon J. Battista, Bronx Community College; Margaret Brooks, Bridgewater State College; Mike Casey, University of Central Arkansas; Mike Cohick, Collin County Community College; Dennis Debrecht, Carroll College; Amrik Dua, California State Polytechnic University, Pomona; Mitchell Dudley, The College of William & Mary; Ann Eike, University of Kentucky; Connel Fullencamp, Duke University; Craig Gallet, California State University, Sacramento; Michael Goode, Central Piedmont Community College; Steve Hamilton, California State Polytechnic University; James R. Irwin, Central Michigan University; Aaron Jackson, Bentley College; Rus Janis, University of Massachusetts, Amherst; Jonatan Jelen, The City College of New York; Kathy A. Kelly, University of Texas, Arlington; Kate Krause, University of New Mexico; Gary F. Langer, Roosevelt University; Leonard Lardaro, University of Rhode Island; Ross LaRoe, Denison University; Melissa Lind, University of Texas, Arlington; Solina Lindahl, California State Polytechnic University; Pete Mavrokordatos, Tarrant County College; Roberto Mazzoleni, Hofstra University; Kimberly Mencken, Baylor University; Ida Mirzaie, Ohio State University; Shahruz Mohtadi, Suffolk University; Mary Pranzo, California State University, Fresno; Ed Price, Oklahoma State University; Robert Shoffner, Central Piedmont Community College; James Swofford, University of South Alabama; Helen Tauchen, University of North Carolina, Chapel Hill; Eric Taylor, Central Piedmont Community College; Henry Terrell, University of Maryland; John Tommasi, Bentley College; Mukti Upadhyay, Eastern Illinois University; Robert Whaples, Wake Forest University; and Timothy Wunder, University of Texas, Arlington.

**The Association to Advance Collegiate Schools of Business (AACSB)**    The authors of the Test Item File have connected select Test Item File questions to the general knowledge and skill guidelines found in the AACSB assurance of learning standards.

**What Is the AACSB?**    AACSB is a not-for-profit corporation of educational institutions, corporations, and other organizations devoted to the promotion and improvement of higher education in business administration and accounting. A collegiate institution offering degrees in business administration or accounting may volunteer for AACSB accreditation review. The AACSB makes initial accreditation decisions and conducts periodic reviews to promote continuous quality improvement in management education. Pearson Education is a proud member of the AACSB and is pleased to provide advice to help you apply AACSB Assurance of Learning Standards.

**What Are AACSB Assurance of Learning Standards?**    One of the criteria for AACSB accreditation is quality of the curricula. Although no specific courses are required, the AACSB expects a curriculum to include learning experiences in areas such as the following:

- Written and Oral Communication
- Ethical Understanding and Reasoning

- Analytic Thinking Skills
- Information Technology
- Diverse and Multicultural Work
- Reflective Thinking
- Application of Knowledge

Questions that test skills relevant to these guidelines are tagged with the appropriate standard. For example, a question testing the moral questions associated with externalities would receive the Ethical Understanding and Reasoning tag.

**How Can Instructors Use the AACSB Tags?**   Tagged questions help you measure whether students are grasping the course content that aligns with the AACSB guidelines noted earlier. This in turn may suggest enrichment activities or other educational experiences to help students achieve these skills.

### TestGen

The computerized TestGen package allows instructors to customize, save, and generate classroom tests. The test program permits instructors to edit, add, or delete questions from the Test Item Files; analyze test results; and organize a database of tests and student results. This software allows for extensive flexibility and ease of use. It provides many options for organizing and displaying tests, along with search and sort features. The software and the Test Item Files can be downloaded from the Instructor's Resource Center (www.pearsonhighered.com/educator).

### PowerPoint® Lecture Presentations

PowerPoint slides for *Principles of Microeconomics* and *Principles of Macroeconomics,* prepared by Jim Lee of Dickinson State University, are available:

- A comprehensive set of PowerPoint slides can be used by instructors for class presentations or by students for lecture preview or review. These slides include all the figures, photos, tables, key terms, and equations in the textbook. Instructors may download these PowerPoint presentations from the Instructor's Resource Center (www.pearsonhighered.com/educator).
- A student version of the PowerPoint slides are available as .pdf files. This version allows students to print the slides and bring them to class for note taking. Instructors can download these PowerPoint presentations from the Instructor's Resource Center. (www.pearsonhighered.com/educator).

## Acknowledgments

We are grateful to the many people who helped us prepare the 12th edition. We thank David Alexander, our editor, and Lindsey Sloan, our program manager, for their help and enthusiasm.

Roberta Sherman, project manager, and Jeffrey Holcomb, our Team Lead of Project Management, ensured that the production process of the book went smoothly. In addition, we also want to thank Stephanie Raga of Integra Software Services, Inc., who kept us on schedule, and Jenell Forschler, who managed the research of the many photographs that appear in the book.

We want to give special thanks to Patsy Balin, Murielle Dawdy, and Tracy Waldman for their research assistance.

We also owe a debt of gratitude to those who reviewed and checked the 12th edition for accuracy. They provided us with valuable insight as we prepared this edition and its supplement package.

## Reviewers of the 12<sup>th</sup> Edition

Bahram Adrangi, University of Portland
Anthony Andrews, Governors State
University
J Jeffrey Blais, Rhode Island College
Paula M. Cole, University of Denver
Karen Fitzner, DePaul University
James Frederick, UNC at Pembroke
Richard Gearhart, California State
University, Bakersfield
Wayne Hickenbottom, University of
Texas at Austin
Janet Koscianski, Shippensburg University
Tim Kwock, University of Hawaii
West Oahu
Sangjoon Lee, Alfred University
David Lehmkuhl, Lakeland College
Benjamin Liebman, St. Joseph's
University
Basel Mansour, New Jersey City University
Chris Phillips, Somerset Community
College
Sarah Quintanar, University of Arkansas
at Little Rock
Daniel Sichel, Wellesley College
John Solow, University of Iowa
Jadrian Wooten, Penn State University
Linus Yamane, Pitzer College

## Reviewers of Previous Editions

The following individuals were of
immense help in reviewing all or part of
previous editions of this book and the
teaching/learning package in various
stages of development:

Cynthia Abadie, Southwest Tennessee
Community College
Shawn Abbott, College of the Siskiyous
Fatma Abdel-Raouf, Goldey-Beacom
College
Lew Abernathy, University of North
Texas
Rebecca Abraham, Nova Southeastern
University
Basil Adams, Notre Dame de Namur
University
Jack Adams, University of Maryland
Douglas K. Adie, Ohio University
Douglas Agbetsiafa, Indiana University,
South Bend
Sheri Aggarwal, University of Virginia
Carlos Aguilar, El Paso Community
College
Ehsan Ahmed, James Madison University
Ferhat Akbas, Texas A&M University
Sam Alapati, Rutgers University

Terence Alexander, Iowa State
University
John W. Allen, Texas A&M University
Polly Allen, University of Connecticut
Stuart Allen, University of North
Carolina at Greensboro
Hassan Aly, Ohio State University
Alex Anas, University at Buffalo, The
State University of New York
David Anderson, Centre College
Joan Anderssen, Arapahoe Community
College
Jim Angresano, Hampton-Sydney
College
Kenneth S. Arakelian, University of
Rhode Island
Harvey Arnold, Indian River Community
College
Nick Apergis, Fordham University
Bevin Ashenmiller, Occidental College
Richard Ashley, Virginia Technical
University
Birjees Ashraf, Houston Community
College Southwest
Kidane Asmeron, Pennsylvania State
University
Musa Ayar, University of Texas, Austin
James Aylesworth, Lakeland Community
College
Moshen Bahmani, University of
Wisconsin—Milwaukee
Asatar Bair, City College of San
Francisco
Diana Bajrami, College of Alameda
Mohammad Bajwa, Northampton
Community College
Rita Balaban, University of North
Carolina, Chapel Hill
A. Paul Ballantyne, University of
Colorado, Colorado Springs
Richard J. Ballman, Jr., Augustana
College
King Banaian, St. Cloud State University
Nick Barcia, Baruch College
Henry Barker, Tiffin University
Robin Bartlett, Denison University
Laurie Bates, Bryant University
Kari Battaglia, University of North Texas
Leon Battista, Bronx Community College
Amanda Bayer, Swarthmore College
Klaus Becker, Texas Tech University
Richard Beil, Auburn University
Clive Belfield, Queens College
Willie J. Belton, Jr., Georgia Institute of
Technology
Daniel K. Benjamin, Clemson University
Charles A. Bennett, Gannon University
Emil Berendt, Siena Heights University
Daniel Berkowitz, University of
Pittsburgh

Kurt Beron, University of Texas, Dallas
Derek Berry, Calhoun Community
College
Tibor Besedes, Georgia Institute of
Technology
Thomas Beveridge, Durham Technical
Community College
Anoop Bhargava, Finger Lakes CC
Eugenie Bietry, Pace University
Kelly Blanchard, Purdue University
Mannie Bloemen, Houston Community
College
Mark Bock, Loyola College in Maryland
Howard Bodenhorn, Lafayette College
Bruce Bolnick, Northeastern University
Frank Bonello, University of
Notre Dame
Jeffrey Bookwalter, University of
Montana
Antonio Bos, Tusculum College
Maristella Botticini, Boston University
George Bowling, St. Charles Community
College
G. E. Breger, University of South Carolina
Dennis Brennan, William Rainey Harper
Junior College
Anne E. Bresnock, California State
Polytechnic University, Pomona,
and the University of California, Los
Angeles
Barry Brown, Murray State University
Bruce Brown, California State
Polytechnic University, Pomona
Jennifer Brown, Eastern Connecticut
State University
David Brownstone, University of
California, Irvine
Don Brunner, Spokane Falls Community
College
Jeff Bruns, Bacone College
David Bunting, Eastern Washington
University
Barbara Burnell, College of Wooster
Alison Butler, Willamette University
Charles Callahan, III, State University of
New York at Brockport
Fred Campano, Fordham University
Douglas Campbell, University of
Memphis
Beth Cantrell, Central Baptist College
Kevin Carlson, University of
Massachusetts, Boston
Leonard Carlson, Emory University
Arthur Schiller Casimir, Western New
England College
Lindsay Caulkins, John Carroll
University
Atreya Chakraborty, Boston College
Suparna Chakraborty, Baruch College of
the City University of New York

Winston W. Chang, University at Buffalo, The State University of New York

Janie Chermak, University of New Mexico

David Ching, University of Hawaii – Honolulu

Harold Christensen, Centenary College

Daniel Christiansen, Albion College

Susan Christoffersen, Philadelphia University

Samuel Kim-Liang Chuah, Walla Walla College

Dmitriy Chulkov, Indiana University, Kokomo

David Colander, Middlebury College

Daniel Condon, University of Illinois at Chicago; Moraine Valley Community College

Karen Conway, University of New Hampshire

Cesar Corredor, Texas A&M University

David Cowen, University of Texas, Austin

Tyler Cowen, George Mason University

Amy Cramer, Pima Community College, West Campus

Peggy Crane, Southwestern College

Barbara Craig, Oberlin College

Jerry Crawford, Arkansas State University

James Cunningham, Chapman University

Scott Cunningham, Baylor University

Elisabeth Curtis, Dartmouth

James D'Angelo, University of Cincinnati

David Dahl, University of St. Thomas

Sheryll Dahlke, Lees-McRae College

Joseph Dahms, Hood College

Sonia Dalmia, Grand Valley State University

Rosa Lea Danielson, College of DuPage

David Danning, University of Massachusetts, Boston

Minh Quang Dao, Eastern Illinois University

Amlan Datta, Cisco Junior College

David Davenport, McLennan Community College

Stephen Davis, Southwest Minnesota State University

Dale DeBoer, Colorado University, Colorado Springs

Dennis Debrecht, Carroll College

Juan J. DelaCruz, Fashion Institute of Technology and Lehman College

Greg Delemeester, Marietta College

Yanan Di, State University of New York, Stony Brook

Amy Diduch, Mary Baldwin College

Timothy Diette, Washington and Lee University

Vernon J. Dixon, Haverford College

Alan Dobrowolksi, Manchester Community College

Eric Dodge, Hanover College

Carol Dole, Jacksonville University

Michael Donihue, Colby College

Leslie Doss, University of Texas San Antonio

Shahpour Dowlatshahi, Fayetteville Technical Community College

Joanne M. Doyle, James Madison University

Robert Driskill, Ohio State University

James Dulgeroff, San Bernardino Valley College

Kevin Duncan, Colorado State University

Yvonne Durham, Western Washington University

Debra Sabatini Dwyer, State University of New York, Stony Brook

Gary Dymski, University of Southern California

David Eaton, Murray State University

Jay Egger, Towson State University

Erwin Ehrhardt, University of Cincinnati

Ann Eike, University of Kentucky

Eugene Elander, Plymouth State University

Ronald D. Elkins, Central Washington University

Tisha Emerson, Baylor University

Michael Enz, Western New England College

Erwin Erhardt III, University of Cincinnati

William Even, Miami University

Ali Faegh, Houston Community College

Noel J. J. Farley, Bryn Mawr College

Mosin Farminesh, Temple University

Dan Feaster, Miami University of Ohio

Susan Feiner, Virginia Commonwealth University

Getachew Felleke, Albright College

Lois Fenske, South Puget Sound Community College

William Field, DePauw University

Deborah Figart, Richard Stockton College

Barbara Fischer, Cardinal Stritch University

Mary Flannery, Santa Clara University

Bill Foeller, State University of New York, Fredonia

Fred Foldvary, Santa Clara University

Roger Nils Folsom, San Jose State University

Mathew Forstater, University of Missouri-Kansas City

Kevin Foster, The City College of New York

Richard Fowles, University of Utah

Sean Fraley, College of Mount Saint Joseph

Johanna Francis, Fordham University

Roger Frantz, San Diego State University

Mark Frascatore, Clarkson University

Amanda Freeman, Kansas State University

Morris Frommer, Owens Community College

Brandon Fuller, University of Montana

David Fuller, University of Iowa

Mark Funk, University of Arkansas, Little Rock

Alejandro Gallegos, Winona State University

Craig Gallet, California State University, Sacramento

N. Galloro, Chabot College

Bill Galose, Drake University

William Ganley, Buffalo State, SUNY

Martin A. Garrett, Jr., College of William and Mary

Tom Gausman, Northern Illinois University

Shirley J. Gedeon, University of Vermont

Jeff Gerlach, Sungkyunkwan Graduate School of Business

Lisa Giddings, University of Wisconsin, La Crosse

Gary Gigliotti, Rutgers University

Lynn Gillette, Spalding University

Donna Ginther, University of Kansas

James N. Giordano, Villanova University

Amy Glass, Texas A&M University

Sarah L. Glavin, Boston College

Roy Gobin, Loyola University, Chicago

Bill Godair, Landmark College

Bill Goffe, University of Mississippi

Devra Golbe, Hunter College

Roger Goldberg, Ohio Northern University

Joshua Goodman, New York University

Ophelia Goma, DePauw University

John Gonzales, University of San Francisco

David Gordon, Illinois Valley College

Richard Gosselin, Houston Community College

Eugene Gotwalt, Sweet Briar College

John W. Graham, Rutgers University

Douglas Greenley, Morehead State University

Thomas A. Gresik, University of Notre Dame

Lisa M. Grobar, California State University, Long Beach

Wayne A. Grove, Le Moyne College

Daryl Gruver, Mount Vernon Nazarene University

Osman Gulseven, North Carolina State University

Mike Gumpper, Millersville University

Benjamin Gutierrez, Indiana University, Bloomington

A. R. Gutowsky, California State University, Sacramento

Anthony Gyapong, Penn State University, Abington

David R. Hakes, University of Missouri, St. Louis

Bradley Hansen, University of Mary Washington

Stephen Happel, Arizona State University

Mehdi Haririan, Bloomsburg University of Pennsylvania

David Harris, Benedictine College

David Harris, San Diego State University

James Hartley, Mount Holyoke College

Bruce Hartman, California Maritime Academy of California State University

Mitchell Harwitz, University at Buffalo, The State University of New York

Dewey Heinsma, Mt. San Jacinto College

Sara Helms, University of Alabama, Birmingham

Brian Hill, Salisbury University

David Hoaas, Centenary College

Arleen Hoag, Owens Community College

Carol Hogan, University of Michigan, Dearborn

Harry Holzer, Michigan State University

Ward Hooker, Orangeburg-Calhoun Technical College

Bobbie Horn, University of Tulsa

John Horowitz, Ball State University

Ali Faegh, Houston Community College

Daniel Horton, Cleveland State University

Ying Huang, Manhattan College

Janet Hunt, University of Georgia

E. Bruce Hutchinson, University of Tennessee, Chattanooga

Creed Hyatt, Lehigh Carbon Community College

Ana Ichim, Louisiana State University

Aaron Iffland, Rocky Mountain College

Fred Inaba, Washington State University

Richard Inman, Boston College

Aaron Jackson, Bentley College

Brian Jacobsen, Wisconsin Lutheran College

Rus Janis, University of Massachusetts

Jonatan Jelen, The City College of New York

Eric Jensen, The College of William & Mary

Aaron Johnson, Missouri State University

Donn Johnson, Quinnipiac University

Paul Johnson, University of Alaska, Anchorage

Shirley Johnson, Vassar College

Farhoud Kafi, Babson College

R. Kallen, Roosevelt University

Arthur E. Kartman, San Diego State University

Hirshel Kasper, Oberlin College

Brett Katzman, Kennesaw State University

Bruce Kaufman, Georgia State University

Dennis Kaufman, University of Wisconsin, Parkside

Pavel Kapinos, Carleton College

Russell Kashian, University of Wisconsin, Whitewater

Amoz Kats, Virginia Technical University

David Kaun, University of California, Santa Cruz

Brett Katzman, Kennesaw State University

Fred Keast, Portland State University

Stephanie Kelton, University of Missouri, Kansas City

Deborah Kelly, Palomar College

Erasmus Kersting, Texas A&M University

Randall Kesselring, Arkansas State University

Alan Kessler, Providence College

Dominique Khactu, The University of North Dakota

Gary Kikuchi, University of Hawaii, Manoa

Hwagyun Kim, State University of New York, Buffalo

Keon-Ho Kim, University of Utah

Kil-Joong Kim, Austin Peay State University

Sang W. Kim, Hood College

Phillip King, San Francisco State University

Barbara Kneeshaw, Wayne County Community College

Inderjit Kohli, Santa Clara University

Heather Kohls, Marquette University

Janet Koscianski, Shippensburg University

Vani Kotcherlakota, University of Nebraska, Kearney

Barry Kotlove, Edmonds Community College

Kate Krause, University of New Mexico

David Kraybill, University of Georgia

David Kroeker, Tabor College

Stephan Kroll, California State University, Sacramento

Joseph Kubec, Park University

Jacob Kurien, Helzberg School of Management

Rosung Kwak, University of Texas at Austin

Sally Kwak, University of Hawaii-Manoa

Steven Kyle, Cornell University

Anil K. Lal, Pittsburg State University

Melissa Lam, Wellesley College

David Lang, California State University, Sacramento

Gary Langer, Roosevelt University

Anthony Laramie, Merrimack College

Leonard Lardaro, University of Rhode Island

Ross LaRoe, Denison University

Michael Lawlor, Wake Forest University

Pareena Lawrence, University of Minnesota, Morris

Daniel Lawson, Drew University

Mary Rose Leacy, Wagner College

Margaret D. Ledyard, University of Texas, Austin

Jim Lee, Fort Hays State University

Judy Lee, Leeward Community College

Sang H. Lee, Southeastern Louisiana University

Don Leet, California State University, Fresno

Robert J. Lemke, Lake Forest College

Gary Lemon, DePauw University

Alan Leonard, Wilson Technical Community College

Mary Lesser, Iona College

Ding Li, Northern State University

Zhe Li, Stony Brook University

Larry Lichtenstein, Canisius College

Benjamin Liebman, Saint Joseph's University

Jesse Liebman, Kennesaw State University

George Lieu, Tuskegee University

Stephen E. Lile, Western Kentucky University

Jane Lillydahl, University of Colorado at Boulder

Tony Lima, California State University, East Bay

Melissa Lind, University of Texas, Arlington

Al Link, University of North Carolina Greensboro

Charles R. Link, University of Delaware

Robert Litro, U.S. Air Force Academy

Samuel Liu, West Valley College

Jeffrey Livingston, Bentley College

Ming Chien Lo, St. Cloud State University

Burl F. Long, University of Florida

Alina Luca, Drexel University

Adrienne Lucas, Wellesley College

Nancy Lutz, Virginia Technical University

Kristina Lybecker, Colorado College

Gerald Lynch, Purdue University

Karla Lynch, University of North Texas

Ann E. Lyon, University of Alaska, Anchorage

Bruce Madariaga, Montgomery College

Michael Magura, University of Toledo

Marvin S. Margolis, Millersville University of Pennsylvania

Tim Mason, Eastern Illinois University

Don Mathews, Coastal Georgia Community College

Don Maxwell, Central State University

Nan Maxwell, California State University at Hayward

Roberto Mazzoleni, Hofstra University

Cynthia S. McCarty, Jacksonville State University

J. Harold McClure, Jr., Villanova University

Patrick McEwan, Wellesley College

Ronnie McGinness, University of Mississippi

Todd McFall, Wake Forest University

Rick McIntyre, University of Rhode Island

James J. McLain, University of New Orleans

Dawn McLaren, Mesa Community College

B. Starr McMullen, Oregon State University

K. Mehtaboin, College of St. Rose

Martin Melkonian, Hofstra University

Alice Melkumian, Western Illinois University

William Mertens, University of Colorado, Boulder

Randy Methenitis, Richland College

Art Meyer, Lincoln Land Community College

Carrie Meyer, George Mason University

Meghan Millea, Mississippi State University

Jenny Minier, University of Miami

Ida Mirzaie, The Ohio State University

David Mitchell, Missouri State University

Bijan Moeinian, Osceola Campus

Robert Mohr, University of New Hampshire

Shahruz Mohtadi, Suffolk University

Amyaz Moledina, College of Wooster

Gary Mongiovi, St. John's University

Terry D. Monson, Michigan Technological University

Barbara A. Moore, University of Central Florida

Joe L. Moore, Arkansas Technical University

Myra Moore, University of Georgia

Robert Moore, Occidental College

Norma C. Morgan, Curry College

W. Douglas Morgan, University of California, Santa Barbara

David Murphy, Boston College

John Murphy, North Shore Community College, Massachusetts

Ellen Mutari, Richard Stockton College of New Jersey

Steven C. Myers, University of Akron

Veena Nayak, University at Buffalo, The State University of New York

Ron Necoechea, Robert Wesleyan College

Doug Nelson, Spokane Community College

Randy Nelson, Colby College

David Nickerson, University of British Columbia

Sung No, Southern University and A&M College

Rachel Nugent, Pacific Lutheran University

Akorlie A. Nyatepe-Coo, University of Wisconsin LaCrosse

Norman P. Obst, Michigan State University

William C. O'Connor, Western Montana College

Constantin Ogloblin, Georgia Southern University

David O'Hara, Metropolitan State University

Albert Okunade, University of Memphis

Ronald Olive, University of Massachusetts, Lowell

Martha L. Olney, University of California, Berkeley

Kent Olson, Oklahoma State University

Jaime Ortiz, Florida Atlantic University

Theresa Osborne, Hunter College

Donald J. Oswald, California State University, Bakersfield

Mete Ozcan, Brooklyn College

Alexandre Padilla, Metropolitan State College of Denver

Aaron Pankratz, Fresno City College

Niki Papadopoulou, University of Cyprus

Walter Park, American University

Carl Parker, Fort Hays State University

Spiro Patton, Rasmussen College

Andrew Pearlman, Bard College

Charlie Pearson, Southern Maine Community College

Richard Peck, University of Illinois at Chicago

Don Peppard, Connecticut College

Elizabeth Perry, Randolph College

Nathan Perry, University of Utah

Joe Petry, University of Illinois-Urbana-Champaign

Joseph A. Petry, University of Illinois

Mary Ann Pevas, Winona State University

Chris Phillips, Somerset Community College

Jeff Phillips, Morrisville Community College

Frankie Pircher, University of Missouri, Kansas City

Tony Pizelo, Spokane Community College

Dennis Placone, Clemson University

Mike Pogodzinski, San Jose State University

Linnea Polgreen, University of Iowa

Elizabeth Porter, University of North Florida

Bob Potter, University of Central Florida

Ed Price, Oklahoma State University

Abe Qastin, Lakeland College

Kevin Quinn, St. Norbert College

Ramkishen S. Rajan, George Mason University

James Rakowski, University of Notre Dame

Amy Ramirez-Gay, Eastern Michigan University

Paul Rappoport, Temple University

Artatrana Ratha, St. Cloud State University

Michael Rendich, Westchester Community College

Lynn Rittenoure, University of Tulsa

Travis Roach, Texas Tech University

Brian Roberson, Miami University

Michael Robinson, Mount Holyoke College

Juliette Roddy, University of Michigan, Dearborn

Michael Rolleigh, University of Minnesota

Belinda Roman, Palo Alto College

S. Scanlon Romer, Delta College

Brian Rosario, University of California, Davis

Paul Roscelli, Canada College

David C. Rose, University of Missouri-St. Louis
Greg Rose, Sacramento City College
Richard Rosenberg, Pennsylvania State University
Robert Rosenman, Washington State University
Robert Rosenthal, Stonehill College
Howard Ross, Baruch College
Paul Rothstein, Washington University
Charles Roussel, Louisiana State University
Jeff Rubin, Rutgers University
Mark Rush, University of Florida
Dereka Rushbrook, Ripon College
Jerard Russo, University of Hawaii
Luz A. Saavedra, University of St. Thomas
William Samuelson, Boston University School of Management
Allen Sanderson, University of Chicago
David Saner, Springfield College – Benedictine University
Ahmad Saranjam, Bridgewater State College
David L. Schaffer, Haverford College
Eric Schansberg, Indiana University – Southeast
Robert Schenk, Saint Joseph's College
Ramon Schreffler, Houston Community College System (retired)
Adina Schwartz, Lakeland College
Jerry Schwartz, Broward Community College
Amy Scott, DeSales University
Gary Sellers, University of Akron
Atindra Sen, Miami University
Chad Settle, University of Tulsa
Jean Shackleford, Bucknell University
Ronald Shadbegian, University of Massachusetts, Dartmouth
Linda Shaffer, California State University, Fresno
Dennis Shannon, Southwestern Illinois College
Stephen L. Shapiro, University of North Florida
Paul Shea, University of Oregon
Geoff Shepherd, University of Massachusetts Amherst
Bih-Hay Sheu, University of Texas at Austin
David Shideler, Murray State University
Alden Shiers, California Polytechnic State University
Gerald Shilling, Eastfield College
Dongsoo Shin, Santa Clara University
Elias Shukralla, St. Louis Community College, Meramec

Anne Shugars, Harford Community College
Richard Sicotte, University of Vermont
William Simeone, Providence College
Scott Simkins, North Carolina Agricultural and Technical State University
Larry Singell, University of Oregon
Priyanka Singh, University of Texas, Dallas
Sue Skeath, Wellesley College
Edward Skelton, Southern Methodist University
Ken Slaysman, York College
John Smith, New York University
Paula Smith, Central State University, Oklahoma
Donald Snyder, Utah State University
Marcia Snyder, College of Charleston
David Sobiechowski, Wayne State University
John Solow, University of Iowa
Angela Sparkman, Itawamba Community College
Martin Spechler, Indiana University
David Spigelman, University of Miami
Arun Srinivasa, Indiana University, Southeast
David J. St. Clair, California State University at Hayward
Sarah Stafford, College of William & Mary
Richard Stahl, Louisiana State University
Rebecca Stein, University of Pennsylvania
Mary Stevenson, University of Massachusetts, Boston
Susan Stojanovic, Washington University, St. Louis
Courtenay Stone, Ball State University
Ernst W. Stromsdorfer, Washington State University
Edward Stuart, Northeastern Illinois University
Chris Stufflebean, Southwestern Oklahoma State University
Chuck Stull, Kalamazoo College
Kenneth Slaysman, York College of Pennsylvania
Della Sue, Marist College
Abdulhamid Sukar, Cameron University
Christopher Surfield, Saginaw Valley State University
Rodney B. Swanson, University of California, Los Angeles
James Swofford, University of Alabama
Bernica Tackett, Pulaski Technical College
Michael Taussig, Rutgers University

Samia Tavares, Rochester Institute of Technology
Timothy Taylor, Stanford University
William Taylor, New Mexico Highlands University
Sister Beth Anne Tercek, SND, Notre Dame College of Ohio
Henry Terrell, University of Maryland
Jennifer Thacher, University of New Mexico
Donna Thompson, Brookdale Community College
Robert Tokle, Idaho State University
David Tolman, Boise State University
Susanne Toney, Hampton University
Karen M. Travis, Pacific Lutheran University
Jack Trierweler, Northern State University
Brian M. Trinque, University of Texas at Austin
HuiKuan Tseng, University of North Carolina at Charlotte
Boone Turchi, University of North Carolina
Kristin Van Gaasbeck, California State University, Sacramento
Amy Vander Laan, Hastings College
Ann Velenchik, Wellesley College
Lawrence Waldman, University of New Mexico
Chris Waller, Indiana University, Bloomington
William Walsh, University of St. Thomas
Chunbei Wang, University of St. Thomas
John Watkins, Westminster
Janice Weaver, Drake University
Bruce Webb, Gordon College
Ross Weiner, The City College of New York
Elaine Wendt, Milwaukee Area Technical College
Walter Wessels, North Carolina State University
Christopher Westley, Jacksonville State University
Joan Whalen-Ayyappan, DeVry Institute of Technology
Robert Whaples, Wake Forest University
Leonard A. White, University of Arkansas
Alex Wilson, Rhode Island College
Wayne Winegarden, Marymount University
Jennifer Wissink, Cornell University
Arthur Woolf, University of Vermont
Paula Worthington, Northwestern University
Bill Yang, Georgia Southern University

Ben Young, University of Missouri,
  Kansas City
Darrel Young, University of Texas
Michael Youngblood, Rock Valley
  College
Jay Zagorsky, Boston University

Alexander Zampieron, Bentley
  College
Sourushe Zandvakili, University of
  Cincinnati
Walter J. Zeiler, University of
  Michigan

Abera Zeyege, Ball State
  University
James Ziliak, Indiana University,
  Bloomington
Jason Zimmerman, South Dakota State
  University

We welcome comments about the 12th edition. Please write to us care of David Alexander, Executive Editor, Pearson Economics, 501 Boylston Street, Boston, MA 02116.

**Karl E. Case**

**Ray C. Fair**

**Sharon M. Oster**

Save a Tree!

Many of the components of the teaching and learning package are available online. Online supplements conserve paper and allow you to select and print only the material you plan to use. For more information, please contact your Pearson sales representative.

TWELFTH EDITION

# Principles of
# **Macroeconomics**

# The Scope and Method of Economics

The study of economics should begin with a sense of wonder. Pause for a moment and consider a typical day in your life. It might start with a bagel made in a local bakery with flour produced in Minnesota from wheat grown in Kansas. After class you drive with a friend on an interstate highway that is part of a system that took 20 years and billions of dollars to build. You stop for gasoline refined in Louisiana from Saudi Arabian crude oil. Later, you log onto the Web with a laptop assembled in Indonesia from parts made in China and Skype with your brother in Mexico City. You use or consume tens of thousands of things. Somebody organized men and women and materials to produce and distribute them. Thousands of decisions went into their completion, and somehow they got to you.

In the United States, about 150 million people—almost half the total population—work at hundreds of thousands of different jobs producing nearly $18 trillion worth of goods and services every year. Some cannot find work; some choose not to work. The United States imports more than $300 billion worth of automobiles and parts and more than $350 billion worth of petroleum and petroleum products each year; it exports around $140 billion worth of agricultural products, including food. In the modern economy, consumers' choices include products made all over the globe.

**Economics** is the study of how individuals and societies choose to use the scarce resources that nature and previous generations have provided. The key word in this definition is *choose*. Economics is a behavioral, or social, science. In large measure, it is the study of how people make choices. The choices that people make, when added up, translate into societal choices.

**economics** The study of how individuals and societies choose to use the scarce resources that nature and previous generations have provided.

The purpose of this chapter and the next is to elaborate on this definition and to introduce the subject matter of economics. What is produced? How is it produced? Who gets it? Why? Is the result good or bad? Can it be improved?

Identify three key reasons to study economics. Think of an example from your life in which understanding opportunity costs or the principle of efficient markets could make a difference in your decision making.

# Why Study Economics?

There are three main reasons to study economics: to learn a way of thinking, to understand society, and to be an informed citizen.

## To Learn a Way of Thinking

Probably the most important reason for studying economics is to learn a way of thinking. Economics has three fundamental concepts that, once absorbed, can change the way you look at everyday choices: opportunity cost, marginalism, and the working of efficient markets.

**Opportunity Cost**  What happens in an economy is the outcome of thousands of individual decisions. People must decide how to divide their incomes among all the goods and services available in the marketplace. They must decide whether to work, whether to go to school, and how much to save. Businesses must decide what to produce, how much to produce, how much to charge, and where to locate. Economic analysis provides a structured way of thinking about these types of decisions.

**opportunity cost** The best alternative that we forgo, or give up, when we make a choice or a decision.

Nearly all decisions involve trade-offs. A key concept that recurs in analyzing the decision-making process is the notion of *opportunity cost*. The full "cost" of making a specific choice includes what we give up by not making the best alternative choice. The best alternative that we forgo, or give up, when we make a choice or a decision is called the **opportunity cost** of that decision.

When asked how much a movie costs, most people cite the ticket price. For an economist, this is only part of the answer: to see a movie takes not only a ticket but also time. The opportunity cost of going to a movie is the value of the other things you could have done with the same money and time. If you decide to take time off from work, the opportunity cost of your leisure is the pay that you would have earned had you worked. Part of the cost of a college education is the income you could have earned by working full-time instead of going to school.

**scarce** Limited.

Opportunity costs arise because resources are scarce. **Scarce** simply means limited. Consider one of our most important resources—time. There are only 24 hours in a day, and we must live our lives under this constraint. A farmer in rural Brazil must decide whether it is better to continue to farm or to go to the city and look for a job. A hockey player at the University of Vermont must decide whether to play on the varsity team or spend more time studying.

**marginalism** The process of analyzing the additional or incremental costs or benefits arising from a choice or decision.

**Marginalism**  A second key concept used in analyzing choices is the notion of **marginalism**. In weighing the costs and benefits of a decision, it is important to weigh only the costs and benefits that arise from the decision. Suppose, for example, that you live in New Orleans and that you are weighing the costs and benefits of visiting your mother in Iowa. If business required that you travel to Kansas City anyway, the cost of visiting Mom would be only the additional, or *marginal*, time and money cost of getting to Iowa from Kansas City.

There are numerous examples in which the concept of marginal cost is useful. For an airplane that is about to take off with empty seats, the marginal cost of an extra passenger is essentially zero; the total cost of the trip is roughly unchanged by the addition of an extra passenger. Thus, setting aside a few seats to be sold at big discounts through www.priceline.com or other Web sites can be profitable even if the fare for those seats is far below the average cost per seat of making the trip. As long as the airline succeeds in filling seats that would otherwise have been empty, doing so is profitable.

**Efficient Markets—No Free Lunch** Suppose you are ready to check out of a busy grocery store on the day before a storm and seven checkout registers are open with several people in each line. Which line should you choose? Clearly you should go to the shortest line! But if everyone thinks this way—as is likely—all the lines will be equally long as people move around. Economists often loosely refer to "good deals" or risk-free ventures as *profit opportunities*. Using the term loosely, a profit opportunity exists at the checkout lines when one line is shorter than the others. In general, such profit opportunities are rare. At any time, many people are searching for them; as a consequence, few exist. Markets like this, where any profit opportunities are eliminated almost instantaneously, are said to be **efficient markets**. (We discuss *markets*, the institutions through which buyers and sellers interact and engage in exchange, in detail in Chapter 2.)

> **efficient market** A market in which profit opportunities are eliminated almost instantaneously.

The common way of expressing the efficient markets concept is "there's no such thing as a free lunch." How should you react when a stockbroker calls with a hot tip on the stock market? With skepticism. Thousands of individuals each day are looking for hot tips in the market. If a particular tip about a stock is valid, there will be an immediate rush to buy the stock, which will quickly drive up its price. This view that very few profit opportunities exist can, of course, be carried too far. There is a story about two people walking along, one an economist and one not. The non-economist sees a $20 bill on the sidewalk and says, "There's a $20 bill on the sidewalk." The economist replies, "That is not possible. If there were, somebody would already have picked it up."

There are clearly times when profit opportunities exist. Someone has to be first to get the news, and some people have quicker insights than others. Nevertheless, news travels fast, and there are thousands of people with quick insights. The general view that large profit opportunities are rare is close to the mark and is powerful in helping to guide decision making.

> The study of economics teaches us a way of thinking and helps us make decisions.

## To Understand Society

Another reason for studying economics is to understand society better. Past and present economic decisions have an enormous influence on the character of life in a society. The current state of the physical environment, the level of material well-being, and the nature and number of jobs are all products of the economic system.

At no time has the impact of economic change on a society been more evident than in England during the late eighteenth and early nineteenth centuries, a period that we now call the **Industrial Revolution**. Increases in the productivity of agriculture, new manufacturing technologies, and development of more efficient forms of transportation led to a massive movement of the British population from the countryside to the city. At the beginning of the eighteenth century, approximately 2 out of 3 people in Great Britain worked in agriculture. By 1812, only 1 in 3 remained in agriculture; by 1900, the figure was fewer than 1 in 10. People jammed into overcrowded cities and worked long hours in factories. England had changed completely in two centuries—a period that in the run of history was nothing more than the blink of an eye.

> **Industrial Revolution** The period in England during the late eighteenth and early nineteenth centuries in which new manufacturing technologies and improved transportation gave rise to the modern factory system and a massive movement of the population from the countryside to the cities.

The discipline of economics began to take shape during this period. Social critics and philosophers looked around and knew that their philosophies must expand to accommodate the changes. Adam Smith's *Wealth of Nations* appeared in 1776. It was followed by the writings of David Ricardo, Karl Marx, Thomas Malthus, and others. Each tried to make sense out of what was happening. Who was building the factories? Why? What determined the level of wages paid to workers or the price of food? What would happen in the future, and what *should* happen? The people who asked these questions were the first economists.

Societal changes are often driven by economics. Consider the developments in the early years of the World Wide Web. Changes in the ways people communicate with one another and with the rest of the world, largely created by private enterprise seeking profits, have affected almost every aspect of our lives, from the way we interact with friends and family to the jobs that we have and the way cities and governments are organized.

> The study of economics is an essential part of the study of society.

## To Be an Informed Citizen

A knowledge of economics is essential to being an informed citizen. Between 2008 and 2013 much of the world struggled with a major recession and slow recovery, leaving millions of people around the world out of work. Understanding what happens in a recession and what the government can and cannot do to help in a recovery is an essential part of being an informed citizen.

Economics is also essential in understanding a range of other everyday government decisions at the local and federal levels. Why do governments pay for public schools and roads, but not cell phones? The federal government under President Barack Obama moved toward universal health care for U.S. citizens. What are the pros and cons of this policy? In some states, scalping tickets to a ball game is illegal. Is this a good policy or not? Every day, across the globe, people engage in political decision making around questions like these, questions that depend on an understanding of economics.

> To be an informed citizen requires a basic understanding of economics.

**1.2 LEARNING OBJECTIVE**

Describe microeconomics, macroeconomics, and the diverse fields of economics.

# The Scope of Economics

Most students taking economics for the first time are surprised by the breadth of what they study. Some think that economics will teach them about the stock market or what to do with their money. Others think that economics deals exclusively with problems such as inflation and unemployment. In fact, it deals with all those subjects, but they are pieces of a much larger puzzle. Economists use their tools to study a wide range of topics.

The easiest way to get a feel for the breadth and depth of what you will be studying is to explore briefly the way economics is organized. First of all, there are two major divisions of economics: microeconomics and macroeconomics.

## Microeconomics and Macroeconomics

**microeconomics** The branch of economics that examines the functioning of individual industries and the behavior of individual decision-making units—that is, firms and households.

**Microeconomics** deals with the functioning of individual industries and the behavior of individual economic decision-making units: firms and households. Firms' choices about what to produce and how much to charge and households' choices about what and how much to buy help to explain why the economy produces the goods and services it does.

Another big question addressed by microeconomics is who gets the goods and services that are produced? Understanding the forces that determine the distribution of output is the province of microeconomics. Microeconomics helps us to understand how resources are distributed among households. What determines who is rich and who is poor?

**macroeconomics** The branch of economics that examines the economic behavior of aggregates—income, employment, output, and so on—on a national scale.

**Macroeconomics** looks at the economy as a whole. Instead of trying to understand what determines the output of a single firm or industry or what the consumption patterns are of a single household or group of households, macroeconomics examines the factors that determine national output, or national product. Microeconomics is concerned with *household* income; macroeconomics deals with *national income*.

Whereas microeconomics focuses on individual product prices and relative prices, macroeconomics looks at the overall price level and how quickly (or slowly) it is rising (or falling). Microeconomics questions how many people will be hired (or fired) this year in a particular industry or in a certain geographic area and focuses on the factors that determine how much labor a firm or an industry will hire. Macroeconomics deals with *aggregate* employment and unemployment: how many jobs exist in the economy as a whole and how many people who are willing to work are not able to find work.

## ECONOMICS IN PRACTICE

### iPod and the World

It is impossible to understand the workings of an economy without first understanding the ways in which economies are connected across borders. The United States was importing goods and services at a rate of more than $2.8 trillion per year in 2014 and was exporting at a rate of more than $2.3 trillion per year.

For literally hundreds of years, the virtues of free trade have been the subject of heated debate. Opponents have argued that buying foreign-produced goods costs Americans jobs and hurts U.S. producers. Proponents argue that there are gains from trade—that all countries can gain from specializing in the production of the goods and services they produce best.

In the modern world, it is not always easy to track where products are made. A sticker that says "Made in China" can often be misleading. Recent studies of two iconic U.S. products, the iPod and the Barbie doll, make this complexity clear.

The Barbie doll is one of Mattel's best and longest selling products. The Barbie was designed in the United States. It is made of plastic fashioned in Taiwan, which came originally from the Mideast in the form of petroleum. Barbie's hair comes from Japan, while the cloth for her clothes mostly comes from China. Most of the assembly of the Barbie is also done in China, using, as we see, pieces from across the globe. A doll that sells for $10 in the United States carries an export value when leaving Hong Kong of $2, of which only 35 cents is for Chinese labor, with most of the rest covering transportation and raw materials. Because the Barbie comes to the United States from assembly in China and transport from Hong Kong, some would count it as being produced in China. Yet, for this Barbie, $8 of its retail value of $10 is captured by the United States![1]

The iPod is similar. A recent study by three economists, Greg Linden, Kenneth Kraemer, and Jason Dedrick, found that once one includes Apple's payment for its intellectual property, distribution costs, and production costs for some components, almost 80 percent of the retail price of the iPod is captured by the United States.[2] Moreover, for some of the

other parts of the iPod, it is not easy to tell exactly where they are produced. The hard drive, a relatively expensive component, was produced in Japan by Toshiba, but some of the components of that hard drive were actually produced elsewhere in Asia. Indeed, for the iPod, which is composed of many small parts, it is almost impossible to accurately tell exactly where each piece was produced without pulling it apart.

So, next time you see a label saying "Made in China" keep in mind that from an economics point of view, one often has to dig a little deeper to see what is really going on.

#### THINKING PRACTICALLY

1. What do you think accounts for *where* components of the iPod and Barbie are made?

[1] For a discussion of the Barbie see Robert Feenstra, "Integration of Trade and Disintegration of Production in the Global Economy," *Journal of Economic Perspectives*, Fall 1998: 31–50.

[2] Greg Linden, Kenneth Kraemer, and Jason Dedrick, "Who Profits from Innovation in Global Value Chains?" *Industrial and Corporate Change*, 2010: 81–116.

To summarize:

> Microeconomics looks at the individual unit—the household, the firm, the industry. It sees and examines the "trees." Macroeconomics looks at the whole, the aggregate. It sees and analyzes the "forest."

Table 1.1 summarizes these divisions of economics and some of the subjects with which they are concerned.

## The Diverse Fields of Economics

Individual economists focus their research and study in many different areas. The subfields of economics are listed in Table 1.2 along with a sample research or policy question that an economist in this subfield might study.

**TABLE 1.1    Examples of Microeconomic and Macroeconomic Concerns**

| Division of Economics | Production | Prices | Income | Employment |
|---|---|---|---|---|
| Microeconomics | *Production/output in individual industries and businesses* <br> How much steel <br> How much office space <br> How many cars | *Prices of individual goods and services* <br> Price of medical care <br> Price of gasoline <br> Food prices <br> Apartment rents | *Distribution of income and wealth* <br> Wages in the auto industry <br> Minimum wage <br> Executive salaries <br> Poverty | *Employment by individual businesses and industries* <br> Jobs in the steel industry <br> Number of employees in a firm <br> Number of accountants |
| Macroeconomics | *National production/output* <br> Total industrial output <br> Gross domestic product <br> Growth of output | *Aggregate price level* <br> Consumer prices <br> Producer prices <br> Rate of inflation | *National income* <br> Total wages and salaries <br> Total corporate profits | *Employment and unemployment in the economy* <br> Total number of jobs <br> Unemployment rate |

**TABLE 1.2    The Fields of Economics**

| | |
|---|---|
| *Behavioral economics* | Do aggregate household savings increase when we automatically enroll people in savings programs and let them opt out as opposed to requiring them to sign up? |
| *Comparative economic systems* | How does the resource allocation process differ in market versus command and control systems? |
| *Econometrics* | What inferences can we make based on conditional moment inequalities? |
| *Economic development* | Does increasing employment opportunities for girls in developing nations increase their educational achievement? |
| *Economic history* | How did the growth of railroads and improvement in transportation more generally change the U.S. banking systems in the nineteenth century? |
| *Environmental economics* | What effect would a tax on carbon have on emissions? Is a tax better or worse than rules? |
| *Finance* | Is high frequency trading socially beneficial? |
| *Health economics* | Do co-pays by patients change the choice and use of medicines by insured patients? |
| *The history of economic thought* | How did Aristotle think about just prices? |
| *Industrial organization* | How do we explain price wars in the airline industry? |
| *International economics* | What are the benefits and costs of free trade? Does concern about the environment change our views of free trade? |
| *Labor economics* | Will increasing the minimum wage decrease employment opportunities? |
| *Law and economics* | Does the current U.S. patent law increase or decrease the rate of innovation? |
| *Public economics* | Why is corruption more widespread in some countries than in others? |
| *Urban and regional economics* | Do enterprise zones improve employment opportunities in central cities? |

# The Method of Economics

Economics asks and attempts to answer two kinds of questions: positive and normative. **Positive economics** attempts to understand behavior and the operation of economic systems *without making judgments* about whether the outcomes are good or bad. It strives to describe what exists and how it works. What determines the wage rate for unskilled workers? What would happen if we abolished the corporate income tax? The answers to such questions are the subject of positive economics.

In contrast, **normative economics** looks at the outcomes of economic behavior and asks whether they are good or bad and whether they can be made better. Normative economics involves judgments and prescriptions for courses of action. Should the government subsidize or regulate the cost of higher education? Should the United States allow importers to sell foreign-produced goods that compete with U.S.-made products? Should we reduce or eliminate inheritance taxes? Normative economics is often called *policy economics*.

Of course, most normative questions involve positive questions. To know whether the government *should* take a particular action, we must know first if it *can* and second what the consequences are likely to be.

## Theories and Models

In many disciplines, including physics, chemistry, meteorology, political science, and economics, theorists build formal models of behavior. A **model** is a formal statement of a theory. It is usually a mathematical statement of a presumed relationship between two or more variables.

A **variable** is a measure that can change from time to time or from observation to observation. Income is a variable—it has different values for different people and different values for the same person at different times. The price of a quart of milk is a variable; it has different values at different stores and at different times. There are countless other examples.

Because all models simplify reality by stripping part of it away, they are abstractions. Critics of economics often point to abstraction as a weakness. Most economists, however, see abstraction as a real strength.

The easiest way to see how abstraction can be helpful is to think of a map. A map is a representation of reality that is simplified and abstract. A city or state appears on a piece of paper as a series of lines and colors. The amount of reality that the mapmaker can strip away before the map loses something essential depends on what the map will be used for. If you want to drive from St. Louis to Phoenix, you need to know only the major interstate highways and roads. However, to travel around Phoenix, you may need to see every street and alley.

Like maps, economic models are abstractions that strip away detail to expose only those aspects of behavior that are important to the question being asked. The principle that irrelevant detail should be cut away is called the principle of **Ockham's razor** after the fourteenth-century philosopher William of Ockham.

Be careful—although abstraction is a powerful tool for exposing and analyzing specific aspects of behavior, it is possible to oversimplify. Economic models often strip away a good deal of social and political reality to get at underlying concepts. When an economic theory is used to help formulate actual government or institutional policy, political and social reality must often be reintroduced if the policy is to have a chance of working.

The appropriate amount of simplification and abstraction depends on the use to which the model will be put. To return to the map example: You do not want to walk around San Francisco with a map made for drivers—there are too many very steep hills.

**All Else Equal** It is usually true that whatever you want to explain with a model depends on more than one factor. Suppose, for example, that you want to explain the total number of miles driven by automobile owners in the United States. Many things might affect total miles driven. More or fewer people may be driving. This number, in turn, can be affected by changes in the driving age, by population growth, or by changes in state laws. Other factors might include the price of gasoline, the household's income, the number and age of children in the household, the distance from home to work, the location of shopping facilities, and the availability and

**1.3 LEARNING OBJECTIVE**

Think about an example of bad causal inference leading to erroneous decision making. Identify the four main goals of economic policy.

**positive economics** An approach to economics that seeks to understand behavior and the operation of systems without making judgments. It describes what exists and how it works.

**normative economics** An approach to economics that analyzes outcomes of economic behavior, evaluates them as good or bad, and may prescribe courses of action. Also called *policy economics*.

**model** A formal statement of a theory, usually a mathematical statement of a presumed relationship between two or more variables.

**variable** A measure that can change from time to time or from observation to observation.

**Ockham's razor** The principle that irrelevant detail should be cut away.

quality of public transport. When any of these variables change, the members of the household may drive more or less. If changes in any of these variables affect large numbers of households across the country, the total number of miles driven will change.

Very often we need to isolate or separate these effects. For example, suppose we want to know the impact on driving of a higher tax on gasoline. This increased tax would raise the price of gasoline at the pump, and this could reduce driving.

**ceteris paribus, or all else equal**  A device used to analyze the relationship between two variables while the values of other variables are held unchanged.

To isolate the impact of one single factor, we use the device of **ceteris paribus, or all else equal**. We ask, "What is the impact of a change in gasoline price on driving behavior, ceteris paribus, or assuming that nothing else changes?" If gasoline prices rise by 10 percent, how much less driving will there be, assuming no simultaneous change in anything else—that is, assuming that income, number of children, population, laws, and so on, all remain constant? Using the device of ceteris paribus is one part of the process of abstraction. In formulating economic theory, the concept helps us simplify reality to focus on the relationships that interest us.

**Expressing Models in Words, Graphs, and Equations**  Consider the following statements: Lower airline ticket prices cause people to fly more frequently. Higher gasoline prices cause people to drive less and to buy more fuel-efficient cars. By themselves, these observations are of some interest. But for a firm, government, or an individual to make good decisions, oftentimes they need to know more. How much does driving fall when prices rise? Quantitative analysis is an important part of economics as well. Throughout this book, we will use both graphs and equations to capture the quantitative side of our economic observations and predictions. The appendix to this chapter reviews some graphing techniques.

**Cautions and Pitfalls**  In formulating theories and models, it is especially important to seperate causation from correlation.

**What Is Really Causal?**  In much of economics, we are interested in cause and effect. But cause and effect are often difficult to figure out. Recently, many people in the United States have begun to worry about consumption of soda and obesity. Some areas have begun taxing soda, trying to raise the price so that people will drink less of it. Is this working? Answering this question turns out to be hard. Suppose we see that one city raises the tax and at more or less the same time, soda consumption falls. Did the increased tax and price really *cause* all or most of the change in behavior? Or perhaps the city that voted the soda tax increase is more health conscious than its neighbors and it is that health consciousness that accounts for both the town's decision to raise taxes *and* its reduction in soda purchases. In this case, raising taxes in the neighboring towns will not necessarily reduce soda consumption. Sorting out causality from correlation is not always easy, particularly when one wants a quantitative answer to a question.

**post hoc, ergo propter hoc**  Literally, "after this (in time), therefore because of this." A common error made in thinking about causation: If Event A happens before Event B, it is not necessarily true that A caused B.

In our everyday lives, we often confuse causality. When two events occur in a sequence, it seems natural to think A caused B. I walked under a ladder and subsequently stubbed my toe. Did the ladder cause my bad luck? Most of us would laugh at this. But everyday we hear stock market analysts make a similar causal jump. "Today the Dow Jones industrial average rose 100 points on heavy trading due to progress in talks between Israel and Syria." How do they know this? Investors respond to many news events on any given day. Figuring out which one, if any, causes the stock market to rise is not easy. The error of inferring causality from two events happening one after the other is called the **post hoc, ergo propter hoc** fallacy ("after this, therefore because of this"). The *Economics in Practice* box describes a causality confusion in looking at peer effects.

**empirical economics**  The collection and use of data to test economic theories.

**Testing Theories and Models: Empirical Economics**  In science, a theory is rejected when it fails to explain what is observed or when another theory better explains what is observed. The collection and use of data to test economic theories is called **empirical economics**.

Numerous large data sets are available to facilitate economic research. For example, economists studying the labor market can now test behavioral theories against the actual working experiences of thousands of randomly selected people who have been surveyed continuously since the 1960s. Macroeconomists continuously monitoring and studying the behavior of the national economy at the National Bureau of Economic Research (NBER), analyze thousands of items of data, collected by both government agencies and private companies, over the Internet. Firms like Google, Uber, and Amazon have an enormous amount of data about individual consumers that they analyze with the help of PhD economists to understand consumers' buying

## ECONOMICS IN PRACTICE

### Does Your Roommate Matter for Your Grades?

Most parents are concerned about their children's friends. Often they worry that if one of their children has a misbehaving friend, their own child will be led astray. And, in fact, in many areas of life, there are strong indications that *peer effects* matter. The likelihood that a child will be obese, have difficulties in school, or engage in criminal activity all seem to be higher if their friends also have these issues. And yet, in looking at peer effects, it is not hard to see the problem of causality we described in the text. At least to some extent, children choose their own friends. The father worried about the bad influence of his son's friends on his own son should perhaps be equally worried about what his son's choice of friends says about that son's inclinations. Did the friends cause the misbehavior or did an inclination toward mischief cause the son's choice of friends?

Sorting out causality in peer effects, given that peer groups are oftentimes partially a matter of choice, is difficult. But several recent economics studies of the effect of roommates on college grades do a nice job of sorting out the causality puzzle. Dartmouth college, in common with many other schools, randomly assigns roommates to freshmen. In this case, part of a student's peer group—his or her roommate— is not a matter of choice, but a matter of chance. Bruce Sacerdote, a professor at Dartmouth, used data on freshmen academic and social performance, combined with their background data, to test the peer effects from different types of roommates.[1] Sacerdote found that after taking into account many background characteristics, there were strong roommate effects both on grade point average, effort in school, and fraternity membership.

Of course, a roommate is only part of one's peer group. At the U.S. Air Force Academy, students are assigned to 30-person squadrons with whom they eat, study, live, and do intramural sports. Again, these groups were randomly assigned, so one did not have the problem of similarly inclined people choosing one another. Scott Carrell, Richard Fullerton, and James West found that for this intense peer group, there were strong peer effects on academic effort and performance.[2] The bottom line: Choose your friends wisely!

#### THINKING PRACTICALLY

1. Would you expect college seniors who choose their own roommates to have more or less similar grades than college freshmen who are assigned as roommates? Why or why not?

[1] Bruce Sacerdote, "Peer Effects with Random Assignment: Results for Dartmouth Roommates," *Quarterly Journal of Economics,* 2001: 681–704.
[2] Scott E. Carrell, Richard L. Fullerton, and James E. West, "Does Your Cohort Matter? Measuring Peer Effects in College Achievement," *Journal of Labor Economics,* 2009: 439–464.

behavior and improve the profitability of their businesses. In doing this analysis, economicsts have learned to be especially careful about causality issues.

In the natural sciences, controlled experiments, typically done in the lab, are a standard way of testing theories. In recent years, economics has seen an increase in the use of experiments, both in the field and in the lab, as a tool to test its theories. One economist, John List of Chicago, tested the effect on prices of changing the way auctions for rare baseball cards were run by sports memorabilia dealers in trade shows. (The experiment used a standard Cal Ripkin Jr. card.) Another economist, Keith Chen of UCLA, has used experiments with monkeys to investigate the deeper biological roots of human decision making.

## Economic Policy

Economic theory helps us understand how the world works, but the formulation of *economic policy* requires a second step. We must have objectives. What do we want to change? Why? What is good and what is bad about the way the system is operating? Can we make it better?

Such questions force us to be specific about the grounds for judging one outcome superior to another. What does it mean to be better? Four criteria are frequently applied in judging economic outcomes:

1. Efficiency
2. Equity
3. Growth
4. Stability

**Efficiency**   In physics, "efficiency" refers to the ratio of useful energy delivered by a system to the energy supplied to it. An efficient automobile engine, for example, is one that uses a small amount of fuel per mile for a given level of power.

**efficiency**   In economics, "efficiency" means "allocative efficiency." An efficient economy is one that produces what people want at the least possible cost.

In economics, **efficiency** means *allocative efficiency*. An efficient economy is one that produces what people want at the least possible cost. If the system allocates resources to the production of goods and services that nobody wants, it is inefficient. If all members of a particular society were vegetarians and somehow half of all that society's resources were used to produce meat, the result would be inefficient.

The clearest example of an efficient change is a voluntary exchange. If you and I each want something that the other has and we agree to exchange, we are both better off and no one loses. When a company reorganizes its production or adopts a new technology that enables it to produce more of its product with fewer resources, without sacrificing quality, it has made an efficient change. At least potentially, the resources saved could be used to produce more of something else.

Inefficiencies can arise in numerous ways. Sometimes they are caused by government regulations or tax laws that distort otherwise sound economic decisions. Suppose that land in Ohio is best suited for corn production and that land in Kansas is best suited for wheat production. A law that requires Kansas to produce only corn and Ohio to produce only wheat would be inefficient. If firms that cause environmental damage are not held accountable for their actions, the incentive to minimize those damages is lost and the result is inefficient.

**equity**   Fairness.

**Equity**   While efficiency has a fairly precise definition that can be applied with some degree of rigor, **equity** (fairness) lies in the eye of the beholder. To many, fairness implies a more equal distribution of income and wealth. For others, fairness involves giving people what they earn. In 2013, French economist Thomas Piketty's popular new book *Capital in the Twenty-First Century*, brought new historical data to our attention on the extent of inequality across the Western world.

**Growth**   As the result of technological change, the building of machinery, and the acquisition of knowledge, societies learn to produce new goods and services and to produce old ones better. In the early days of the U.S. economy, it took nearly half the population to produce the required food supply. Today less than 2 percent of the country's population works in agriculture.

**economic growth**   An increase in the total output of an economy.

When we devise new and better ways of producing the goods and services we use now and when we develop new goods and services, the total amount of production in the economy increases. **Economic growth** is an increase in the total output of an economy. If output grows faster than the population, output per person rises and standards of living increase. Rural and agrarian societies become modern industrial societies as a result of economic growth and rising per capita output.

Some policies discourage economic growth, and others encourage it. Tax laws, for example, can be designed to encourage the development and application of new production techniques. Research and development in some societies are subsidized by the government. Building roads, highways, bridges, and transport systems in developing countries may speed up the process of economic growth. If businesses and wealthy people invest their wealth outside their country rather than in their country's industries, growth in their home country may be slowed.

**stability**   A condition in which national output is growing steadily, with low inflation and full employment of resources.

**Stability**   Economic **stability** refers to the condition in which national output is growing steadily, with low inflation and full employment of resources. During the 1950s and 1960s, the U.S. economy experienced a long period of relatively steady growth, stable prices, and low unemployment. The decades of the 1970s and 1980s, however, were not as stable. The United States experienced two periods of rapid price inflation (more than 10 percent) and two periods of severe unemployment. In 1982, for example, 12 million people (10.8 percent of the workforce) were looking for work. The beginning of the 1990s was another period of instability, with a recession occurring in 1990–1991. In 2008–2009, much of the world, including the United States, experienced a large contraction in output and rise in unemployment, the effects of which lasted until 2013. This was clearly an unstable period.

The causes of instability and the ways in which governments have attempted to stabilize the economy are the subject matter of macroeconomics.

# An Invitation

This chapter has prepared you for your study of economics. The first part of the chapter invited you into an exciting discipline that deals with important issues and questions. You cannot begin to understand how a society functions without knowing something about its economic history and its economic system.

The second part of the chapter introduced the method of reasoning that economics requires and some of the tools that economics uses. We believe that learning to think in this powerful way will help you better understand the world.

As you proceed, it is important that you keep track of what you have learned in previous chapters. This book has a plan; it proceeds step-by-step, each section building on the last. It would be a good idea to read each chapter's table of contents at the start of each chapter and scan each chapter before you read it to make sure you understand where it fits in the big picture.

## ———— S U M M A R Y ————

1. *Economics* is the study of how individuals and societies choose to use the scarce resources that nature and previous generations have provided.

### 1.1 WHY STUDY ECONOMICS? *p. 2*

2. There are many reasons to study economics, including (a) to learn a way of thinking, (b) to understand society, and (c) to be an informed citizen.

3. The best alternative that we forgo when we make a choice or a decision is the *opportunity cost* of that decision.

### 1.2 THE SCOPE OF ECONOMICS *p. 4*

4. *Microeconomics* deals with the functioning of individual markets and industries and with the behavior of individual decision-making units: business firms and households.

5. *Macroeconomics* looks at the economy as a whole. It deals with the economic behavior of aggregates—national output, national income, the overall price level, and the general rate of inflation.

6. Economics is a broad and diverse discipline with many special fields of inquiry. These include economic history, international economics, and urban economics.

### 1.3 THE METHOD OF ECONOMICS *p. 7*

7. Economics asks and attempts to answer two kinds of questions: positive and normative. *Positive economics* attempts to understand behavior and the operation of economies without making judgments about whether the outcomes are good or bad. *Normative economics* looks at the results of economic behavior and asks whether they are good or bad and whether they can be improved.

8. An economic *model* is a formal statement of an economic theory. Models simplify and abstract from reality.

9. It is often useful to isolate the effects of one variable on another while holding "all else constant." This is the device of *ceteris paribus*.

10. Models and theories can be expressed in many ways. The most common ways are in words, in graphs, and in equations.

11. Figuring out causality is often difficult in economics. Because one event happens before another, the second event does not necessarily happen as a result of the first. To assume that "after" implies "because" is to commit the fallacy of *post hoc, ergo propter hoc*.

12. *Empirical economics* involves the collection and use of data to test economic theories. In principle, the best model is the one that yields the most accurate predictions.

13. To make policy, one must be careful to specify criteria for making judgments. Four specific criteria are used most often in economics: *efficiency, equity, growth, and stability*.

---
# REVIEW TERMS AND CONCEPTS
---

*ceteris paribus, or all else equal, p. 8*

economic growth, *p. 10*

economics, *p. 1*

efficiency, *p. 10*

efficient market, *p. 3*

empirical economics, *p. 8*

equity, *p. 10*

Industrial Revolution, *p. 3*

macroeconomics, *p. 4*

marginalism, *p. 2*

microeconomics, *p. 4*

model, *p. 7*

normative economics, *p. 7*

Ockham's razor, *p. 7*

opportunity cost, *p. 2*

positive economics, *p. 7*

*post hoc, ergo propter hoc, p. 8*

scarce, *p. 2*

stability, *p. 10*

variable, *p. 7*

---
# PROBLEMS
---

All problems are available on MyEconLab.

## 1.1 WHY STUDY ECONOMICS

LEARNING OBJECTIVE: Identify three key reasons to study economics. Think of an example from your life in which understanding opportunity costs or the principle of efficient markets could make a difference in your decision making.

**1.1** One of the scarce resources that constrain our behavior is time. Each of us has only 24 hours in a day. How do you go about allocating your time in a given day among competing alternatives? How do you go about weighing the alternatives? Once you choose a most important use of time, why do you not spend all your time on it? Use the notion of opportunity cost in your answer.

**1.2** Every Friday night, Gustavo pays $39.99 to eat nothing but crab legs at the all-you-can-eat seafood buffet at the M Resort in Las Vegas. On average, he consumes 28 crab legs each Friday. What is the average cost of each crab leg to Gustavo? What is the marginal cost of an additional crab leg?

**1.3** For each of the following situations, identify the full cost (opportunity cost) involved:
  **a.** Monique quits her $50,000 per-year job as an accountant to become a full-time volunteer at a women's shelter.
  **b.** The Agrizone Corporation invests $12 million in a new inventory tracking system.
  **c.** Taylor receives $500 from his grandmother for his birthday and uses it all to buy shares of stock in Harley-Davidson, Inc.
  **d.** Hector decides to spend the summer backpacking across Europe after he graduates from Tulane University.
  **e.** After receiving her master's degree, Molly chooses to enter the doctoral program in Behavioral Science at the University of Texas.
  **f.** Sanjay chooses to use his vacation time to paint the exterior of his house.
  **g.** After a night of karaoke, Tiffany forgets to set her alarm and sleeps through her Calculus final exam.

**1.4** On the *Forbes* 2015 list of the World's Billionaires, Bill Gates ranks at the top with a net worth of $79.2 billion.

Does this "richest man in the world" face scarcity, or does scarcity only affect those with more limited incomes and lower net worth?

*Source:* "The World's Billionaires," *Forbes*, March 2, 2015.

## 1.2 THE SCOPE OF ECONOMICS

LEARNING OBJECTIVE: Describe microeconomics, macroeconomics, and the diverse fields of economics.

**2.1** [**Related to the *Economics in Practice* on p. 5**] Log onto www.census.gov/foreign-trade/statistics/state/. In the State Trade by Commodity and Country section, click on "Exports and Imports", then click on "Exports" for your state. There you will find a list of the top 25 commodities produced in your state which are exported around the world. In looking over that list, are you surprised by anything? Do you know any of the firms that produce these items? Search the Internet to find a company that does. Do some research and write a paragraph about this company: what it produces, how many people it employs, and whatever else you can learn about the firm. You might even call the company to obtain the information.

**2.2** Explain whether each of the following is an example of a macroeconomic concern or a microeconomic concern.
  **a.** The Federal Aviation Administration (FAA) is considering increasing the number of takeoff and landing slots available at Ronald Reagan Washington National Airport.
  **b.** The president has proposed increasing the marginal tax rate for people whose annual earnings exceed $275,000 and lowering the marginal tax rate for those who earn less than $275,000.
  **c.** Walmart announced that it will increase its starting wage for employees to $10 per hour by February 2016.
  **d.** Congress extends the maximum duration for the collection of unemployment benefits from 26 weeks to 52 weeks.

## 1.3 THE METHOD OF ECONOMICS

LEARNING OBJECTIVE: Think about an example of bad causal inference leading to erroneous decision making. Identify the four main goals of economic policy.

**3.1** In the summer of 2007, the housing market and the mortgage market were both in decline. Housing prices in most U.S. cities began to decline in mid-2006. With prices falling and the inventory of unsold houses rising, the production of new homes fell to around 1.5 million in 2007 from 2.3 million in 2005. With new construction falling dramatically, it was expected that construction *employment* would fall and that this would have the potential of slowing the national economy and increasing the general unemployment rate. Go to www.bls.gov and check out the recent data on total employment and construction employment. Have they gone up or down from their levels in August 2007? What has happened to the unemployment rate? Go to www.fhfa.gov and look at the housing price index. Have home prices risen or fallen since August 2007? Finally, look at the latest GDP release at www.bea.gov. Look at residential and nonresidential investment (Table 1.1.5) during the last 2 years. Do you see a pattern? Does it explain the employment numbers? Explain your answer

**3.2** Which of the following statements are examples of positive economic analysis? Which are examples of normative analysis?

  **a.** A devaluation of the U.S. dollar would increase exports from the United States.
  **b.** Increasing the federal tax on gasoline would cause shipping costs in the United States to increase.
  **c.** Florida should devote all revenues from its state lottery to improving public education.
  **d.** Eliminating the trade embargo with Cuba would increase the number of Cuban cigars available in the United States.
  **e.** As a public safety measure, the state of Texas should not pass legislation that allows people with concealed handgun permits to carry concealed weapons on college campuses.

**3.3** In 2012, Colorado and Washington became the first states to legalize marijuana for recreational use, and have since been joined by Oregon, Alaska and Washington, D.C. In 2014, Colorado is reported to have received more than $50 million in tax revenue from the sale of recreational marijuana, much of which was slated to be used for school construction. The potential for increased tax revenues and the benefits these revenues can provide has a number of other states contemplating the possible legalization of recreational-use marijuana.

  **a.** Recall that efficiency means producing what people want at the least cost. Can you make an efficiency argument in favor of states allowing the recreational use of marijuana?
  **b.** What nonmonetary costs might be associated with legalizing marijuana use? Would these costs have an impact on the efficiency argument you presented in part a?
  **c.** Using the concept of equity, argue for or against the legalization of recreational-use marijuana.
  **d.** What do you think would happen to the flow of tax revenue to state governments if all 50 states legalized marijuana?

**3.4** [**Related to the *Economics in Practice* on p. 9**] Most college students either currently have, or at one time have had, roommates or housemates. Think about a time when you have shared your living space with one or more students, and describe the effect this person (or people) had on your college experience, such as your study habits, the classes you took, your grade point average, and the way you spent time away from the classroom. Now describe the effect you think you had on your roommate(s). Were these roommates or housemates people you chose to live with, or were they assigned randomly? Explain if you think this made a difference in your or their behavior?

**3.5** Explain the pitfalls in the following statements.

  **a.** People who eat kale on a regular basis are more likely to exercise every day than people who do not eat kale. Therefore, exercising daily causes people to eat kale.
  **b.** Whenever the Chicago Cubs are down by 2 runs in the eighth inning, they usually come back to win whenever self-proclaimed Cubs fanatic Cassandra decides to watch the game with her pet ferret Bobo. Last night with the Cubs down by 2 runs in the eighth, Cassandra rushed to grab Bobo and as she expected, the Cubs won the game. Obviously, the Cubs won because Cassandra watched the game with Bobo by her side.
  **c.** The manager of a large retail furniture store found that sending his least productive salespeople to a week-long motivational training workshop resulted in a 15 percent increase in sales for those employees. Based on this success, the manager decided to spend the money to send all of his other salespeople to this workshop so sales would increase for everyone.

# CHAPTER 1 APPENDIX: How to Read and Understand Graphs

**LEARNING OBJECTIVE**

Understand how data can be graphically represented.

**graph** A two-dimensional representation of a set of numbers or data.

**time series graph** A graph illustrating how a variable changes over time.

Economics is the most quantitative of the social sciences. If you flip through the pages of this or any other economics text, you will see countless tables and graphs. These serve a number of purposes. First, they illustrate important economic relationships. Second, they make difficult problems easier to understand and analyze. Finally, they can show patterns and regularities that may not be discernible in simple lists of numbers.

A **graph** is a two-dimensional representation of a set of numbers, or data. There are many ways that numbers can be illustrated by a graph.

## Time Series Graphs

It is often useful to see how a single measure or variable changes over time. One way to present this information is to plot the values of the variable on a graph, with each value corresponding to a different time period. A graph of this kind is called a **time series graph**. On a time series graph, time is measured along the horizontal scale and the variable being graphed is measured along the vertical scale. Figure 1A.1 is a time series graph that presents the total disposable personal income in the U.S. economy for each year between 1975 and 2014.[1] This graph is based on

▶ **FIGURE 1A.1** **Total Disposable Personal Income in the United States: 1975–2014 (in billions of dollars)**

*Source*: See Table 1A.1.

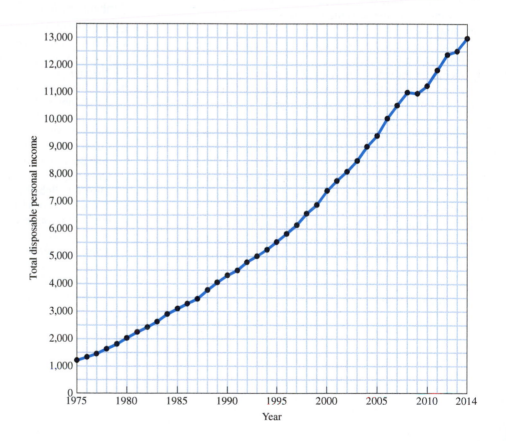

---

[1] The measure of income presented in Table 1A.1 and in Figure 1A.1 is disposable personal income in billions of dollars. It is the total personal income received by all households in the United States minus the taxes that they pay.

| TABLE 1A.1 | Total Disposable Personal Income in the United States, 1975–2014 (in billions of dollars) | | |
|---|---|---|---|
| Year | Total Disposable Personal Income | Year | Total Disposable Personal Income |
| 1975 | 1,219 | 1995 | 5,533 |
| 1976 | 1,326 | 1996 | 5,830 |
| 1977 | 1,457 | 1997 | 6,149 |
| 1978 | 1,630 | 1998 | 6,561 |
| 1979 | 1,809 | 1999 | 6,876 |
| 1980 | 2,018 | 2000 | 7,401 |
| 1981 | 2,251 | 2001 | 7,752 |
| 1982 | 2,425 | 2002 | 8,099 |
| 1983 | 2,617 | 2003 | 8,486 |
| 1984 | 2,904 | 2004 | 9,002 |
| 1985 | 3,099 | 2005 | 9,401 |
| 1986 | 3,288 | 2006 | 10,037 |
| 1987 | 3,466 | 2007 | 10,507 |
| 1988 | 3,770 | 2008 | 10,994 |
| 1989 | 4,052 | 2009 | 10,943 |
| 1990 | 4,312 | 2010 | 11,238 |
| 1991 | 4,485 | 2011 | 11,801 |
| 1992 | 4,800 | 2012 | 12,384 |
| 1993 | 5,000 | 2013 | 12,505 |
| 1994 | 5,244 | 2014 | 12,981 |

*Source:* U.S. Department of Commerce, Bureau of Economic Analysis.

the data found in Table 1A.1. By displaying these data graphically, we can see that total disposable income has increased every year between 1975 and 2014 except for a small dip in 2009.

## Graphing Two Variables

More important than simple graphs of one variable are graphs that contain information on two variables at the same time. The most common method of graphing two variables is a graph constructed by drawing two perpendicular lines: a horizontal line, or **X-axis**, and a vertical line, or **Y-axis**. The axes contain measurement scales that intersect at 0 (zero). This point is called the **origin**. On the vertical scale, positive numbers lie above the horizontal axis (that is, above the origin) and negative numbers lie below it. On the horizontal scale, positive numbers lie to the right of the vertical axis (to the right of the origin) and negative numbers lie to the left of it. The point at which the graph intersects the Y-axis is called the **Y-intercept**. The point at which the graph intersects the X-axis is called the **X-intercept**. When two variables are plotted on a single graph, each point represents a pair of numbers. The first number is measured on the X-axis, and the second number is measured on the Y-axis.

## Plotting Income and Consumption Data for Households

Table 1A.2 presents data from the Bureau of Labor Statistics (BLS) for 2012. This table shows average income and average spending for households ranked by income. For example, the average income for the top fifth (20 percent) of the households was $167,010 in 2012. The average spending for the top 20 percent was $99,368.

Figure 1A.2 presents the numbers from Table 1A.2 graphically. Along the horizontal scale, the X-axis, we measure average income. Along the vertical scale, the Y-axis, we measure average consumption spending. Each of the five pairs of numbers from the table is represented by a

**X-axis** The horizontal line against which a variable is plotted.

**Y-axis** The vertical line against which a variable is plotted.

**origin** The point at which the horizontal and vertical axes intersect.

**Y-intercept** The point at which a graph intersects the Y-axis.

**X-intercept** The point at which a graph intersects the X-axis.

▶ **FIGURE 1A.2**

## Household Consumption and Income

A graph is a simple two-dimensional geometric representation of data. This graph displays the data from Table 1A.2. Along the horizontal scale (X-axis), we measure household income. Along the vertical scale (Y-axis), we measure household consumption.

*Note:* At point A, consumption equals $22,154 and income equals $9,988. At point B, consumption equals $32,632 and income equals $27,585.

*Source:* See Table 1A.2.

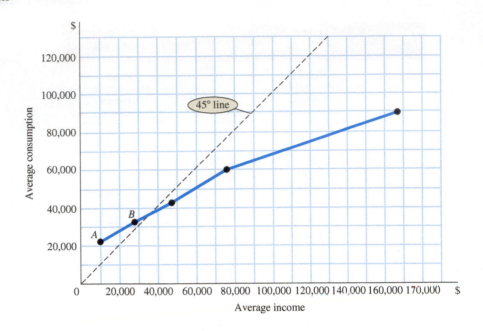

| TABLE 1A.2 | Consumption Expenditures and Income, 2012 | |
| --- | --- | --- |
| | Average Income Before Taxes | Average Consumption Expenditures |
| Bottom fifth | $  9,988 | $ 22,154 |
| 2nd fifth | 27,585 | 32,632 |
| 3rd fifth | 47,265 | 43,004 |
| 4th fifth | 75,952 | 59,980 |
| Top fifth | 167,010 | 99,368 |

*Source: Consumer Expenditures in 2012*, U.S. Bureau of Labor Statistics.

**positive relationship**
A relationship between two variables, X and Y, in which a decrease in X is associated with a decrease in Y, and an increase in X is associated with an increase in Y.

**negative relationship**
A relationship between two variables, X and Y, in which a decrease in X is associated with an increase in Y and an increase in X is associated with a decrease in Y.

**slope** A measurement that indicates whether the relationship between variables is positive or negative and how much of a response there is in Y (the variable on the vertical axis) when X (the variable on the horizontal axis) changes.

point on the graph. Because all numbers are positive numbers, we need to show only the upper right quadrant of the coordinate system.

To help you read this graph, we have drawn a dotted line connecting all the points where consumption and income would be equal. *This 45-degree line does not represent any data.* Instead, it represents the line along which all variables on the X-axis correspond exactly to the variables on the Y-axis, for example, (10,000, 10,000), (20,000, 20,000), and (37,000, 37,000). The heavy blue line traces the data; the purpose of the dotted line is to help you read the graph.

There are several things to look for when reading a graph. The first thing you should notice is whether the line slopes upward or downward as you move from left to right. The blue line in Figure 1A.2 slopes upward, indicating that there seems to be a **positive relationship** between income and spending: The higher a household's income, the more a household tends to consume. If we had graphed the percentage of each group receiving welfare payments along the Y-axis, the line would presumably slope downward, indicating that welfare payments are lower at higher income levels. The income level/welfare payment relationship is thus a **negative relationship**.

## Slope

The **slope** of a line or curve is a measure that indicates whether the relationship between the variables is positive or negative and how much of a response there is in Y (the variable on the vertical axis) when X (the variable on the horizontal axis) changes. The slope of a line between two points is

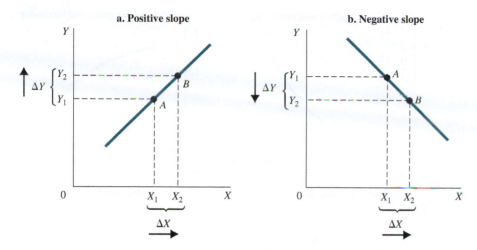

▲ **FIGURE 1A.3**   **A Curve with (a) Positive Slope and (b) Negative Slope**
A *positive* slope indicates that increases in *X* are associated with increases in *Y* and that decreases in *X* are associated with decreases in *Y*. A *negative* slope indicates the opposite—when *X* increases, *Y* decreases; and when *X* decreases, *Y* increases.

the change in the quantity measured on the *Y*-axis divided by the change in the quantity measured on the *X*-axis. We will normally use $\Delta$ (the Greek letter *delta*) to refer to a change in a variable. In Figure 1A.3, the slope of the line between points *A* and *B* is $\Delta Y$ divided by $\Delta X$. Sometimes it is easy to remember slope as "the rise over the run," indicating the vertical change over the horizontal change.

To be precise, $\Delta X$ between two points on a graph is simply $X_2$ minus $X_1$, where $X_2$ is the *X* value for the second point and $X_1$ is the *X* value for the first point. Similarly, $\Delta Y$ is defined as $Y_2$ minus $Y_1$, where $Y_2$ is the *Y* value for the second point and $Y_1$ is the *Y* value for the first point. Slope is equal to

$$\frac{\Delta Y}{\Delta X} = \frac{Y_2 - Y_1}{X_2 - X_1}$$

As we move from *A* to *B* in Figure 1A.3(a), both *X* and *Y* increase; the slope is thus a positive number. However, as we move from *A* to *B* in Figure 1A.3(b), *X* increases [$(X_2 - X_1)$ is a positive number], but *Y* decreases [$(Y_2 - Y_1)$ is a negative number]. The slope in Figure 1A.3(b) is thus a negative number because a negative number divided by a positive number results in a negative quotient.

To calculate the numerical value of the slope between points *A* and *B* in Figure 1A.2, we need to calculate $\Delta Y$ and $\Delta X$. Because consumption is measured on the *Y*-axis, $\Delta Y$ is 10,478 [$(Y_2 - Y_1) = (32,632 - 22,154)$]. Because income is measured along the *X*-axis, $\Delta X$ is 17,597 [$(X_2 - X_1) = (27,585 - 9,988)$]. The slope between *A* and *B* is

$$\frac{\Delta Y}{\Delta X} = \frac{10,478}{17,597} = +0.60.$$

Another interesting thing to note about the data graphed in Figure 1A.2 is that all the points lie roughly along a straight line. (If you look very closely, however, you can see that the slope declines as you move from left to right; the line becomes slightly less steep.) A straight line has a constant slope. That is, if you pick any two points along it and calculate the slope, you will always get the same number. A horizontal line has a zero slope ($\Delta Y$ is zero); a vertical line has an "infinite" slope because $\Delta Y$ is too big to be measured.

Unlike the slope of a straight line, the slope of a *curve* is continually changing. Consider, for example, the curves in Figure 1A.4. Figure 1A.4(a) shows a curve with a positive slope that decreases as you move from left to right. The easiest way to think about the concept of increasing

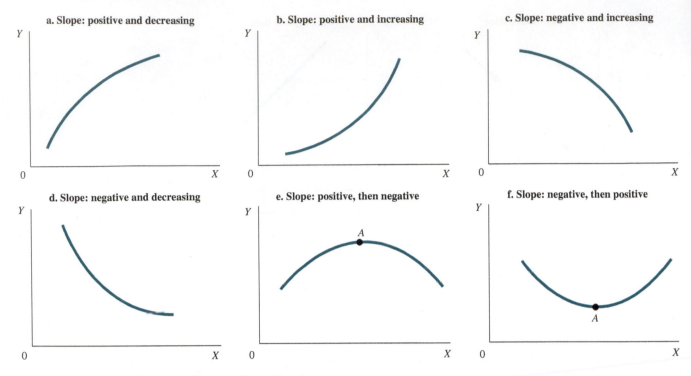

▲ **FIGURE 1A.4    Changing Slopes Along Curves**

or decreasing slope is to imagine what it is like walking up a hill from left to right. If the hill is steep, as it is in the first part of Figure 1A.4(a), you are moving more in the Y direction for each step you take in the X direction. If the hill is less steep, as it is further along in Figure 1A.4(a), you are moving less in the Y direction for every step you take in the X direction. Thus, when the hill is steep, slope $(\Delta Y/\Delta X)$ is a larger number than it is when the hill is flatter. The curve in Figure 1A.4(b) has a positive slope, but its slope *increases* as you move from left to right.

The same analogy holds for curves that have a negative slope. Figure 1A.4(c) shows a curve with a negative slope that increases (in absolute value) as you move from left to right. This time think about skiing down a hill. At first, the descent in Figure 1A.4(c) is gradual (low slope), but as you proceed down the hill (to the right), you descend more quickly (high slope). Figure 1A.4(d) shows a curve with a negative slope that *decreases* (in absolute value) as you move from left to right.

In Figure 1A.4(e), the slope goes from positive to negative as X increases. In Figure 1A.4(f), the slope goes from negative to positive. At point A in both, the slope is zero. (Remember, slope is defined as $\Delta Y/\Delta X$. At point A, Y is not changing ($\Delta Y = 0$). Therefore, the slope at point A is zero.)

## Some Precautions

When you read a graph, it is important to think carefully about what the points in the space defined by the axes represent. Table 1A.3 and Figure 1A.5 present a graph of consumption and income that is different from the one in Table 1A.2 and Figure 1A.2. First, each point in Figure 1A.5 represents a different year; in Figure 1A.2, each point represented a different group of households at the *same* point in time (2012). Second, the points in Figure 1A.5 represent *aggregate* consumption and income for the whole nation measured in *billions* of dollars; in Figure 1A.2, the points represented average *household* income and consumption measured in dollars.

It is interesting to compare these two graphs. All points on the aggregate consumption curve in Figure 1A.5 lie below the 45-degree line, which means that aggregate consumption is always less than aggregate income. However, the graph of average household income and consumption in Figure 1A.2 crosses the 45-degree line, implying that for some households, consumption is larger than income.

| TABLE 1A.3 | Aggregate Disposable Personal Income and Consumption for the United States, 1930–2014 (in billions of dollars) | |
|---|---|---|
| | Aggregate Disposable Personal Income | Aggregate Consumption |
| 1930 | 75 | 70 |
| 1940 | 78 | 71 |
| 1950 | 215 | 192 |
| 1960 | 377 | 332 |
| 1970 | 762 | 648 |
| 1980 | 2,018 | 1,755 |
| 1990 | 4,312 | 3,826 |
| 2000 | 7,401 | 6,792 |
| 2010 | 11,238 | 10,202 |
| 2011 | 11,801 | 10,689 |
| 2012 | 12,384 | 11,083 |
| 2013 | 12,505 | 11,484 |
| 2014 | 12,981 | 11,928 |

*Source:* U.S. Department of Commerce, Bureau of Economic Analysis.

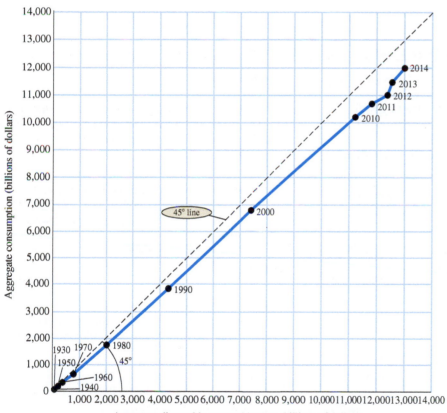

▲ **FIGURE 1A.5   Disposable Personal Income and Consumption**
It is important to think carefully about what is represented by points in the space defined by the axes of a graph. In this graph, we have graphed income with consumption, as in Figure 1A.2, but here each observation point is national income and aggregate consumption in *different years*, measured in billions of dollars.
*Source:* See Table 1A.3.

—————————— A P P E N D I X   S U M M A R Y ——————————

1. A *graph* is a two-dimensional representation of a set of numbers, or data. A *time series graph* illustrates how a single variable changes over time.

2. A graph of two variables includes an X (horizontal)-*axis* and a Y (vertical)-*axis*. The points at which the two axes intersect is called the *origin*. The point at which a graph intersects the Y-axis is called the *Y-intercept*. The point at which a graph intersects the X-axis is called the *X-intercept*.

3. The *slope* of a line or curve indicates whether the relationship between the two variables graphed is positive or negative and how much of a response there is in Y (the variable on the vertical axis) when X (the variable on the horizontal axis) changes. The slope of a line between two points is the change in the quantity measured on the Y-axis divided by the change in the quantity measured on the X-axis.

——— A P P E N D I X   R E V I E W   T E R M S   A N D   C O N C E P T S ———

graph, *p. 14*

negative relationship, *p. 16*

origin, *p. 15*

positive relationship, *p. 16*

slope, *p. 16*

time series graph, *p. 14*

X-axis, *p. 15*

X-intercept, *p. 15*

Y-axis, *p. 15*

Y-intercept, *p. 15*

——————————— A P P E N D I X   P R O B L E M S ———————————

All problems are available on MyEconLab.

### CHAPTER 1 APPENDIX: HOW TO READ AND UNDERSTAND GRAPHS

LEARNING OBJECTIVE: Understand how data can be graphically represented.

1A.1 Graph each of the following sets of numbers. Draw a line through the points and calculate the slope of each line.

| 1 | | 2 | | 3 | | 4 | | 5 | | 6 | |
|---|---|---|---|---|---|---|---|---|---|---|---|
| X | Y | X | Y | X | Y | X | Y | X | Y | X | Y |
| 1 | 5 | 1 | 25 | 0 | 0 | 0 | 40 | 0 | 0 | 0.1 | 100 |
| 2 | 10 | 2 | 20 | 10 | 10 | 10 | 30 | 10 | 10 | 0.2 | 75 |
| 3 | 15 | 3 | 15 | 20 | 20 | 20 | 20 | 20 | 20 | 0.3 | 50 |
| 4 | 20 | 4 | 10 | 30 | 30 | 30 | 10 | 30 | 10 | 0.4 | 25 |
| 5 | 25 | 5 | 5 | 40 | 40 | 40 | 0 | 40 | 0 | 0.5 | 0 |

1A.2 Plot the income and consumption data in the following table on a graph, with income on the X-axis. Does the data indicate a positive or negative relationship between income and consumption?

| Households by Percentage | Average Income Before Taxes | Average Consumption Expenditures |
|---|---|---|
| Bottom fifth | $ 5,500 | $ 16,000 |
| 2nd fifth | 12,000 | 22,500 |
| 3rd fifth | 37,800 | 35,000 |
| 4th fifth | 59,000 | 46,800 |
| Top fifth | 95,000 | 72,500 |

1A.3 For each of the graphs in Figure 1, determine whether the curve has a positive or negative slope. Give an intuitive explanation for what is happening with the slope of each curve.

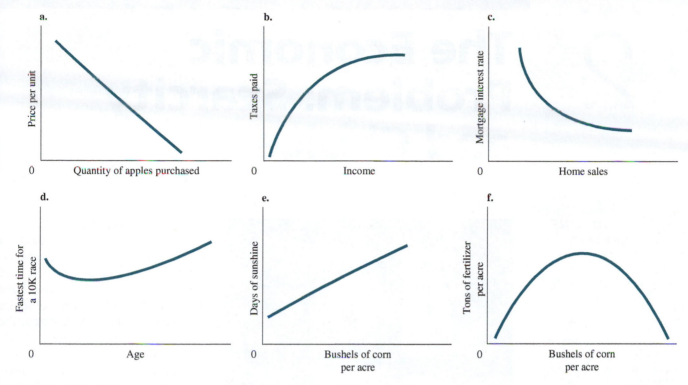

▲ FIGURE 1

1A.4 The following table shows the relationship between the price of organic turkeys and the number of turkeys sold by Godfrey's Free-Range Gobblers.
a. Is the relationship between the price of turkeys and the number of turkeys sold by Godfrey's Free-Range Gobblers a positive relationship or a negative relationship? Explain.
b. Plot the data from the table on a graph, draw a line through the points, and calculate the slope of the line.

| Price per Turkey | Quantity of Turkeys | Month |
|---|---|---|
| $ 16 | 70 | September |
| 20 | 80 | October |
| 52 | 160 | November |
| 36 | 120 | December |
| 8 | 50 | January |

1A.5 Calculate the slope of the demand curve at point A and at point B in the following figure.

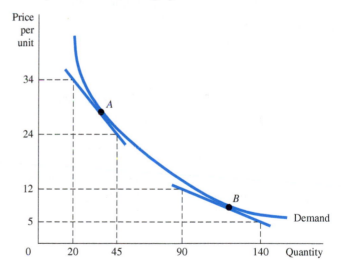

# 2

# The Economic Problem: Scarcity and Choice

In the last chapter we provided you with some sense of the questions asked by economists and the broad methods that they use. As you read that chapter, some of you may have been surprised by the range of topics covered by economics. A look at the work done by the economists teaching at your own university will likely reveal a similarly broad range of interests. Some of your faculty will study how Apple and Samsung compete in smartphones. Others will look at discrimination in labor markets. Still others may be exploring the effects of microfinance in India. On the surface, these issues seem quite different from one another. But fundamental to each of these inquiries is the concern with choice in a world of scarcity. Economics explores how individuals make choices in a world of scarce resources and how those individual's choices come together to determine three key features of their society:

- What gets produced?
- How is it produced?
- Who gets what is produced?

This chapter explores these questions in detail. In a sense, this entire chapter *is* the definition of economics. It lays out the central problems addressed by the discipline and presents a framework that will guide you through the rest of the book. The starting point is the presumption that *human wants are unlimited but resources are not*. Limited or scarce resources force individuals and societies to choose among competing uses of resources—alternative combinations of produced goods and services—and among alternative final distributions of what is produced among households.

These questions are *positive or descriptive*. Understanding how a system functions is important before we can ask the normative questions of whether the system produces good or bad outcomes and how we might make improvements.

Economists study choices in a world of scarce resources. What do we mean by resources? If you look at Figure 2.1, you will see that resources are broadly defined. They include products of nature like minerals and timber, but also the products of past generations like buildings and factories. Perhaps most importantly, resources include the time and talents of the human population.

Things that are produced and then used in the production of other goods and services are called capital resources, or simply **capital**. Buildings, equipment, desks, chairs, software, roads, bridges, and highways are a part of the nation's stock of capital.

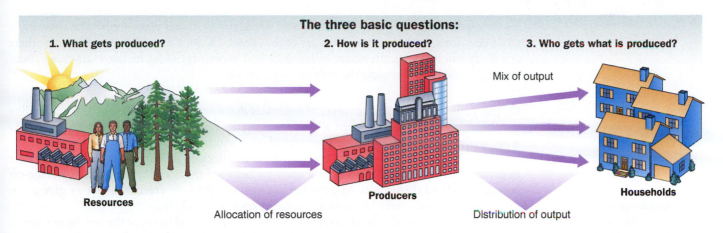

▲ **FIGURE 2.1** **The Three Basic Questions**
Every society has some system or process that transforms its scarce resources into useful goods and services. In doing so, it must decide what gets produced, how it is produced, and to whom it is distributed. The primary resources that must be allocated are land, labor, and capital.

The basic resources available to a society are often referred to as **factors of production, or simply factors**. The three key factors of production are land, labor, and capital. The process that transforms scarce resources into useful goods and services is called **production**. In many societies, most of the production of goods and services is done by private firms. Private airlines in the United States use land (runways), labor (pilots and mechanics), and capital (airplanes) to produce transportation services. But in all societies, some production is done by the public sector, or government. Examples of government-produced or government-provided goods and services include national defense, public education, police protection, and fire protection.

Resources or factors of production are the **inputs** into the process of production; goods and services of value to households are the **outputs** of the process of production.

**capital** Things that are produced and then used in the production of other goods and services.

**factors of production (or factors)** The inputs into the process of production. Another term for resources.

**production** The process that transforms scarce resources into useful goods and services.

# Scarcity, Choice, and Opportunity Cost

In the second half of this chapter we discuss the global economic landscape. Before you can understand the different types of economic systems, it is important to master the basic economic concepts of scarcity, choice, and opportunity cost.

## Scarcity and Choice in a One-Person Economy

The simplest economy is one in which a single person lives alone on an island. Consider Bill, the survivor of a plane crash, who finds himself cast ashore in such a place. Here individual and society are one; there is no distinction between social and private. *Nonetheless, nearly all the same basic decisions that characterize complex economies must also be made in a simple economy.* That is, although Bill will get whatever he produces, he still must decide how to allocate the island's resources, what to produce, and how and when to produce it.

First, Bill must decide *what* he wants to produce. Notice that the word *needs* does not appear here. Needs are absolute requirements; but beyond just enough water, basic nutrition, and shelter to survive, needs are very difficult to define. In any case, Bill must put his wants in some order of priority and make some choices.

Next, he must look at the *possibilities*. What can he do to satisfy his wants given the limits of the island? In every society, no matter how simple or complex, people are constrained in what they can do. In this society of one, Bill is constrained by time, his physical condition, his knowledge, his skills, and the resources and climate of the island.

Given that resources are limited, Bill must decide *how* to best use them to satisfy his hierarchy of wants. Food would probably come close to the top of his list. Should he spend

Understand why even in a society in which one person is better than a second at all tasks, it is still beneficial for the two to specialize and trade.

**inputs or resources** Anything provided by nature or previous generations that can be used directly or indirectly to satisfy human wants.

**outputs** Goods and services of value to households.

his time gathering fruits and berries? Should he clear a field and plant seeds? The answers to those questions depend on the character of the island, its climate, its flora and fauna (*are there any fruits and berries?*), the extent of his skills and knowledge (*does he know anything about farming?*), and his preferences (he may be a vegetarian).

**Opportunity Cost**  The concepts of *constrained choice* and *scarcity* are central to the discipline of economics. They can be applied when discussing the behavior of individuals such as Bill and when analyzing the behavior of large groups of people in complex societies.

Given the scarcity of time and resources, if Bill decides to hunt, he will have less time to gather fruits and berries. He faces a trade-off between meat and fruit. There is a trade-off between food and shelter, too. As we noted in Chapter 1, the best alternative that we give up, or forgo, when we make a choice is the **opportunity cost** of that choice.

Bill may occasionally decide to rest, to lie on the beach, and to enjoy the sun. In one sense, that benefit is free—he does not have to buy a ticket to lie on the beach. In reality, however, relaxing does have an opportunity cost. The true cost of that leisure is the value of the other things Bill could have otherwise produced, but did not, during the time he spent on the beach.

The trade-offs that are made in this kind of society are vividly and often comically portrayed in the reality television shows that show groups of strangers competing on some deserted island, all trying to choose whether it is better to fish, hunt for berries, build a hut, or build an alliance. Making one of these choices involves giving up an opportunity to do another, and in many episodes we can see the consequences of those choices.

## Scarcity and Choice in an Economy of Two or More

Now suppose that another survivor of the crash, Colleen, appears on the island. Now that Bill is not alone, things are more complex and some new decisions must be made. Bill's and Colleen's preferences about what things to produce are likely to be different. They will probably not have the same knowledge or skills. Perhaps Colleen is good at tracking animals and Bill has a knack for building things. How should they split the work that needs to be done? Once things are produced, the two castaways must decide how to divide them. How should their products be distributed?

The mechanism for answering these fundamental questions is clear when Bill is alone on the island. The "central plan" is his; he simply decides what he wants and what to do about it. The minute someone else appears, however, a number of decision-making arrangements immediately become possible. One or the other may take charge, in which case that person will decide for both of them. The two may agree to cooperate, with each having an equal say, and come up with a joint plan; or they may agree to split the planning as well as the production duties. Finally, they may go off to live alone at opposite ends of the island. Even if they live apart, however, they may take advantage of each other's presence by specializing and trading.

Modern industrial societies must answer the same questions that Colleen and Bill must answer, but the mechanics of larger economies are more complex. Instead of two people living together, the United States has more than 300 million people. Still, decisions must be made about what to produce, how to produce it, and who gets it.

**Specialization, Exchange, and Comparative Advantage**  The idea that members of society benefit by specializing in what they do best has a long history and is one of the most important and powerful ideas in all of economics. David Ricardo, a major nineteenth-century British economist, formalized the point precisely. According to Ricardo's **theory of comparative advantage**, specialization and free trade will benefit all trading parties, even when some are "absolutely" more efficient producers than others. Ricardo's basic point applies just as much to Colleen and Bill as it does to different nations.

To keep things simple, suppose that Colleen and Bill have only two tasks to accomplish each week: gathering food to eat and cutting logs to burn. If Colleen could cut more logs than Bill in one day and Bill could gather more nuts and berries than Colleen could, specialization would clearly lead to more total production. Both would benefit if Colleen only cuts logs and Bill only gathers nuts and berries, as long as they can trade.

---

**opportunity cost**  The best alternative that we give up, or forgo, when we make a choice or decision.

**theory of comparative advantage**  Ricardo's theory that specialization and free trade will benefit all trading parties, even those that may be "absolutely" more efficient producers.

## ECONOMICS IN PRACTICE

### Frozen Foods and Opportunity Costs

In 2012, $44 billion of frozen foods were sold in U.S. grocery stores, one quarter of it in the form of frozen dinners and entrées. In the mid-1950s, sales of frozen foods amounted to only $1 billion, a tiny fraction of the overall grocery store sales. One industry observer attributes this growth to the fact that frozen food tastes much better than it did in the past. Can you think of anything else that might be occurring?

The growth of the frozen dinner entrée market in the last 50 years is a good example of the role of opportunity costs in our lives. One of the most significant social changes in the U.S. economy in this period has been the increased participation of women in the labor force. In 1950, only 24 percent of married women worked; by 2013, that fraction had risen to 58 percent. Producing a meal takes two basic ingredients: food and time. When both husbands and wives work, the opportunity cost of time for housework—including making meals—goes up. This tells us that making a home-cooked meal became more expensive in the last 50 years. A natural result is to shift people toward labor-saving ways to make meals. Frozen foods are an obvious solution to the problem of increased opportunity costs.

Another, somewhat more subtle, opportunity cost story is at work encouraging the consumption of frozen foods. In 1960, the first microwave oven was introduced. The spread of this device into America's kitchens was rapid. The microwave turned out to be a quick way to defrost and cook those frozen entrées. So this technology lowered the opportunity cost of making frozen dinners, reinforcing the advantage these meals had over home-cooked meals. Microwaves made cooking with frozen foods cheaper once opportunity cost was considered while home-cooked meals were becoming more expensive.

The entrepreneurs among you also might recognize that the rise we described in the opportunity cost of the home-cooked meal *contributed* in part to the spread of the microwave, creating a reinforcing cycle. In fact, many entrepreneurs find that the simple tools of economics—like the

idea of opportunity costs—help them anticipate what products will be profitable for them to produce in the future. The growth of the two-worker family has stimulated many entrepreneurs to search for labor-saving solutions to family tasks.

The public policy students among you might be interested to know that some researchers attribute part of the growth in obesity in the United States to the lower opportunity costs of making meals associated with the growth of the markets for frozen foods and the microwave. (See David M. Cutler, Edward L. Glaeser, and Jesse M. Shapiro, "Why Have Americans Become More Obese?" *Journal of Economic Perspectives*, Summer 2003: 93–118.)

#### THINKING PRACTICALLY

1. Many people think that soda consumption also leads to increased obesity. Many schools have banned the sale of soda in vending machines. Use the idea of opportunity costs to explain why some people think these bans will reduce consumption. Do you agree?

---

Suppose instead that Colleen is better than Bill both at cutting logs *and* gathering food. In particular, whereas Colleen can gather 10 bushels of food per day, Bill can gather only 8 bushels. Further, while Colleen can cut 10 logs per day, Bill can cut only 4 per day. In this sense, we would say Colleen has an **absolute advantage** over Bill in both activities.

Thinking about this situation and focusing just on the productivity levels, you might conclude that it would benefit Colleen to move to the other side of the island and be by herself. Since she is more productive both in cutting logs and gathering food, would she not be better off on her own? How could she benefit by hanging out with Bill and sharing what they produce? One of Ricardo's lasting contributions to economics has been his analysis of exactly this situation. His analysis, which is illustrated in Figure 2.2, shows both how Colleen and Bill should divide the work of the island and how much they will gain from specializing and exchanging even if, as in this example, one party is absolutely better at everything than the other party.

**absolute advantage**
A producer has an absolute advantage over another in the production of a good or service if he or she can produce that product using fewer resources (a lower absolute cost per unit).

The key to this question is remembering that Colleen's time is limited: this limit creates an opportunity cost. Though Bill is less able at all tasks than Colleen, having him spend time producing something frees up Colleen's time and this has value. The value from Bill's time depends on his comparative advantage. A producer has a **comparative advantage** over another in the production of a good or service if he or she can produce the good or service at a lower opportunity cost. First, think about Bill. He can produce 8 bushels of food per day, or he can cut 4 logs. To get 8 additional bushels of food, he must give up cutting 4 logs. Thus, *for Bill, the opportunity cost of 8 bushels of food is 4 logs.* Think next about Colleen. She can produce 10 bushels of food per day, or she can cut 10 logs. She thus gives up 1 log for each additional bushel; so *for Colleen, the opportunity cost of 8 bushels of food is 8 logs.* Bill has a comparative advantage over Colleen in the production of food because he gives up only 4 logs for an additional 8 bushels, whereas Colleen gives up 8 logs.

Think now about what Colleen must give up in terms of food to get 10 logs. To produce 10 logs she must work a whole day. If she spends a day cutting 10 logs, she gives up a day of gathering 10 bushels of food. Thus, *for Colleen, the opportunity cost of 10 logs is 10 bushels of food.* What must Bill give up to get 10 logs? To produce 4 logs, he must work 1 day. For each day he cuts logs, he gives up 8 bushels of food. He thus gives up 2 bushels of food for each log; so *for Bill, the opportunity cost of 10 logs is 20 bushels of food.* Colleen has a comparative advantage over Bill in the production of logs because she gives up only 10 bushels of food for an additional 10 logs, whereas Bill gives up 20 bushels.

Ricardo argued that two parties can benefit from specialization and trade even if one party has an absolute advantage in the production of both goods if each party takes advantage of his or her comparative advantage. Let us see how this works in the current example.

Suppose Colleen and Bill both want equal numbers of logs and bushels of food. If Colleen goes off on her own and splits her time equally, in one day she can produce 5 logs and 5 bushels of food. Bill, to produce equal amounts of logs and food, will have to spend more time on the wood than the food, given his talents. By spending one third of his day producing food and two thirds chopping wood, he can produce $2\frac{2}{3}$ units of each. In sum, when acting alone $7\frac{2}{3}$ logs and bushels of food are produced by our pair of castaways, most of them by Colleen. Clearly Colleen is a better producer than Bill. Why should she ever want to join forces with clumsy, slow Bill?

The answer lies in the gains from specialization, as we can see in Figure 2.2. In block a, we show the results of having Bill and Colleen each working alone chopping logs and gathering food: $7\frac{2}{3}$ logs and an equal number of food bushels. Now, recalling our calculations indicating that Colleen has a comparative advantage in wood chopping, let's see what happens if we assign Colleen to the wood task and have Bill spend all day gathering food. This system is described in block b of Figure 2.2. At the end of the day, the two end up with 10 logs, all gathered by Colleen and 8 bushels of food, all produced by Bill. By joining forces and specializing, the two have increased their production of both goods. This increased production provides an incentive for Colleen and Bill to work together. United, each can receive a bonus over what he or she could produce separately. This bonus—here $2\frac{1}{3}$ extra logs and $\frac{1}{3}$ bushel of food—represent the gains from specialization. Of course if both Bill and Colleen really favor equal amounts of the two goods, they could adjust their work time to get to this outcome; the main point here is that the total production increases with some specialization.

The simple example of Bill and Colleen should begin to give you some insight into why most economists see value in free trade. Even if one country is absolutely better than another country at producing everything, our example has shown that there are gains to specializing and trading.

*A Graphical Presentation of the Production Possibilities and Gains from Specialization*  Graphs can also be used to illustrate the production possibilities open to Colleen and Bill and the gains they could achieve from specialization and trade.

Figure 2.3(a) shows all of the possible combinations of food and wood Colleen can produce given her skills and the conditions on the island, acting alone. Panel (b) does the same for Bill. If Colleen spends all of her time producing wood, the best she can do is 10 logs, which we show where the line crosses the vertical axis. Similarly, the line crosses the horizontal axis at 10 bushels of food, because that is what Colleen could produce spending full time producing food. We

◀ **FIGURE 2.2**
**Comparative Advantage and the Gains from Trade**
Panel (a) shows the best Colleen and Bill can do each day, given their talents and assuming they each wish to consume an equal amount of food and wood. Notice Colleen produces by splitting her time equally during the day, while Bill must devote two thirds of his time to wood production if he wishes to equalize his amount produced of the two goods. Panel (b) shows what happens when both parties specialize. Notice more units are produced of each good.

**a. Daily production with no specialization, assuming Colleen and Bill each want to consume an equal number of logs and food**

|  | Wood (logs) | Food (bushels) |
|---|---|---|
| Colleen | 5 | 5 |
| Bill | $2\frac{2}{3}$ | $2\frac{2}{3}$ |
| Total | $7\frac{2}{3}$ | $7\frac{2}{3}$ |

**b. Daily Production with Specialization**

|  | Wood (logs) | Food (bushels) |
|---|---|---|
| Colleen | 10 | 0 |
| Bill | 0 | 8 |
| Total | 10 | 8 |

have also marked on the graph possibility C, where she divides her time equally, generating 5 bushels of food and 5 logs of wood.

Bill in panel (b) can get as many as 4 logs of wood or 8 bushels of food by devoting himself full time to either wood or food production. Again, we have marked on his graph a point F, where he produces $2\frac{2}{3}$ bushels of food and $2\frac{2}{3}$ logs of wood. Notice that Bill's production line is lower down than is Colleen's. The further to the right is the production line, the more productive is the individual; that is, the more he or she can produce of the two goods. Also notice that the slope of the two lines is not the same. Colleen trades off one bushel of food for one log of wood, while Bill gives up 2 bushels of food for one log of wood. These differing slopes show

**a. Colleen's production possibilities**

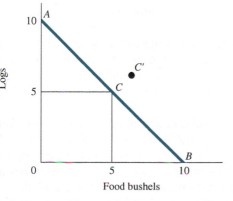

**b. Bill's production possibilities**

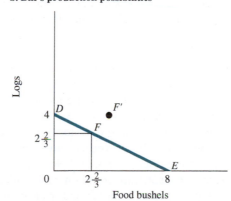

▲ **FIGURE 2.3    Production Possibilities with and without Trade**
This figure shows the combinations of food and wood that Colleen and Bill can each generate in one day of labor, working by themselves. Colleen can achieve independently any point along line ACB, whereas Bill can generate any combination of food and wood along line DFE. Specialization and trade would allow both Bill and Colleen to move to the right of their original lines, to points like C′ and F′. In other words, specialization and trade allow both people to be better off than they were acting alone.

the differing opportunity costs faced by Colleen and Bill. They also open up the possibility of gains from specialization. Try working through an example in which the slopes are the same to convince yourself of the importance of differing slopes.

What happens when the possibility of working together and specializing in either wood or food comes up? In Figure 2.2 we have already seen that specialization would allow the pair to go from production of $7\frac{2}{3}$ units of food and wood to 10 logs and 8 bushels of food. Colleen and Bill can split the $2\frac{1}{3}$ extra logs and the $\frac{1}{3}$ extra bushel of food to move to points like $C'$ and $F'$ in Figure 2.3, which were unachievable without cooperation. In this analysis we do not know how Bill and Colleen will divide the surplus food and wood they have created. But because there is a surplus means that both of them can do better than either would alone.

### Weighing Present and Expected Future Costs and Benefits

Very often we find ourselves weighing benefits available today against benefits available tomorrow. Here, too, the notion of opportunity cost is helpful.

While alone on the island, Bill had to choose between cultivating a field and just gathering wild nuts and berries. Gathering nuts and berries provides food now; gathering seeds and clearing a field for planting will yield food tomorrow if all goes well. Using today's time to farm may well be worth the effort if doing so will yield more food than Bill would otherwise have in the future. By planting, Bill is trading present value for future value.

The simplest example of trading present for future benefits is the act of saving. When you put income aside today for use in the future, you give up some things that you could have had today in exchange for something tomorrow. Because nothing is certain, some judgment about future events and expected values must be made. What will your income be in 10 years? How long are you likely to live?

We trade off present and future benefits in small ways all the time. If you decide to study instead of going to the dorm party, you are trading present fun for the expected future benefits of higher grades. If you decide to go outside on a very cold day and run 5 miles, you are trading discomfort in the present for being in better shape later.

### Capital Goods and Consumer Goods

A society trades present for expected future benefits when it devotes a portion of its resources to research and development or to investment in capital. As we said previously in this chapter, *capital* in its broadest definition is anything that has already been produced that will be used to produce other valuable goods or services over time.

Building capital means trading present benefits for future ones. Bill and Colleen might trade gathering berries or lying in the sun for cutting logs to build a nicer house in the future. In a modern society, resources used to produce capital goods could have been used to produce **consumer goods**

**consumer goods** Goods produced for present consumption.

—that is, goods for present consumption. Heavy industrial machinery does not directly satisfy the wants of anyone, but producing it requires resources that could instead have gone into producing things that do satisfy wants directly—for example, food, clothing, toys, or golf clubs.

Capital is everywhere. A road is capital. Once a road is built, we can drive on it or transport goods and services over it for many years to come. A house is also capital. Before a new manufacturing firm can start up, it must put some capital in place. The buildings, equipment, and inventories that it uses comprise its capital. As it contributes to the production process, this capital yields valuable services over time.

Capital does not need to be tangible. When you spend time and resources developing skills or getting an education, you are investing in human capital—your own human capital. This capital will continue to exist and yield benefits to you for years to come. A computer program produced by a software company and available online may cost nothing to distribute, but its true intangible value comes from the ideas embodied in the program itself. It too is capital.

**investment** The process of using resources to produce new capital.

The process of using resources to produce new capital is called **investment**. (In everyday language, the term *investment* often refers to the act of buying a share of stock or a bond, as in "I invested in some Treasury bonds." In economics, however, investment *always* refers to the creation of capital: the purchase or putting in place of buildings, equipment, roads, houses, and the like.) A wise investment in capital is one that yields future benefits that are more valuable than the present cost. When you spend money for a house, for example, presumably you value its future benefits. That is, you expect to gain more in shelter services than you would from the things you could buy today with the same money. Because resources are scarce, the opportunity cost of every investment in capital is forgone present consumption.

# The Production Possibility Frontier

A simple graphic device called the **production possibility frontier (ppf)** illustrates the principles of constrained choice, opportunity cost, and scarcity. The ppf is a graph that shows all the combinations of goods and services that can be produced if all of a society's resources are used efficiently. Figure 2.4 shows a ppf for a hypothetical economy. We have already seen a simplified version of a ppf in looking at the choices of Colleen and Bill in Figure 2.3. Here we will look more generally at the ppf.

On the Y-axis, we measure the quantity of capital goods produced. On the X-axis, we measure the quantity of consumer goods. All points below and to the left of the curve (the shaded area) represent combinations of capital and consumer goods that are possible for the society given the resources available and existing technology. Points above and to the right of the curve, such as point G, represent combinations that cannot currently be realized. You will recall in our example of Colleen and Bill that new trade and specialization possibilities allowed them to expand their collective production possibilities and move to a point like G. If an economy were to end up at point A on the graph, it would be producing no consumer goods at all; all resources would be used for the production of capital. If an economy were to end up at point B, it would be devoting all its resources to the production of consumer goods and none of its resources to the formation of capital.

While all economies produce some of each kind of good, different economies emphasize different things. About 13 percent of gross output in the United States in 2012 was new capital. In Japan, capital has historically accounted for a much higher percent of gross output, while in the Congo, the figure is about 7 percent. Japan is closer to point A on its ppf, the Congo is closer to B, and the United States is somewhere in between.

Points that are actually on the ppf are points of both full resource employment and production efficiency. (Recall from Chapter 1 that an efficient economy is one that produces the things that people want at the least cost. *Production efficiency* is a state in which a given mix of outputs is produced at the least cost.) Resources are not going unused, and there is no waste. Points that lie within the shaded area but that are not on the frontier represent either unemployment of resources or production inefficiency. An economy producing at point D in Figure 2.4 can produce more capital goods and more consumer goods, for example, by moving to point E. This is possible because resources are not fully employed at point D or are not being used efficiently.

**production possibility frontier (ppf)**   A graph that shows all the combinations of goods and services that can be produced if all of society's resources are used efficiently.

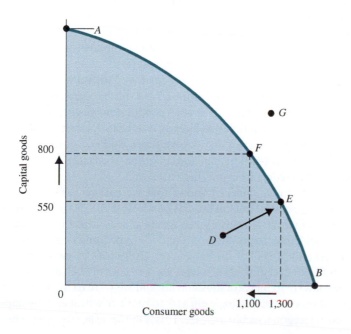

◀ **FIGURE 2.4**
**Production Possibility Frontier**
The ppf illustrates a number of economic concepts. One of the most important is *opportunity cost*. The opportunity cost of producing more capital goods is fewer consumer goods. Moving from *E* to *F*, the number of capital goods increases from 550 to 800, but the number of consumer goods decreases from 1,300 to 1,100.

**Negative Slope and Opportunity Cost**   Just as we saw with Colleen and Bill, the slope of the ppf is negative. Because a society's choices are constrained by available resources and existing technology, when those resources are fully and efficiently employed, it can produce more capital goods only by reducing production of consumer goods. The opportunity cost of the additional capital is the forgone production of consumer goods.

The fact that scarcity exists is illustrated by the negative slope of the ppf. (If you need a review of slope, see the Appendix to Chapter 1.) In moving from point E to point F in Figure 2.4, capital production *increases* by 800 − 550 = 250 units (a positive change), but that increase in capital can be achieved only by shifting resources out of the production of consumer goods. Thus, in moving from point E to point F in Figure 2.4, consumer goods production *decreases* by 1,300 − 1,100 = 200 units (a negative change). The slope of the curve, the ratio of the change in capital goods to the change in consumer goods, is negative.

| marginal rate of transformation (MRT) |
|---|
| The slope of the production possibility frontier (ppf). |

The value of the slope of a society's ppf is called the **marginal rate of transformation (MRT)**. In Figure 2.4, the MRT between points E and F is simply the ratio of the change in capital goods (a positive number) to the change in consumer goods (a negative number). It tells us how much society has to give up of one output to get a unit of a second.

**The Law of Increasing Opportunity Cost**   The negative slope of the ppf indicates the trade-off that a society faces between two goods. In the example of Colleen and Bill, we showed the ppf as a straight line. What does it mean that the ppf here is bowed out?

In our simple example, Bill gave up two bushels of food for every one log of wood he produced. Bill's per-hour ability to harvest wood or produce food didn't depend on how many hours he spent on that activity. Similarly Colleen faced the same trade off of food for wood regardless of how much of either she was producing. In the language we have just introduced, the marginal rate of transformation was constant for Bill and Colleen; hence the straight line ppf. But that is not always true. Perhaps the first bushel of food is easy to produce, low-hanging fruit for example. Perhaps it is harder to get the second log than the first because the trees are farther away. The bowed out ppf tells us that the more society tries to increase production of one good rather than another, the harder it is. In the example in Figure 2.4, the opportunity cost of using society's resources to make capital goods rather than consumer goods increases as we devote more and more resources to capital goods. Why might that be? A common explanation is that when society tries to produce only a small amount of a product, it can use resources—people, land and so on—most well-suited to those goods. As a society spends a larger portion of its resources on one good versus all others, getting more production of that good often becomes increasingly hard.

Let's look at the trade-off between corn and wheat production in Ohio and Kansas as an example. In a recent year, Ohio and Kansas together produced 510 million bushels of corn and 380 million bushels of wheat. Table 2.1 presents these two numbers, plus some hypothetical combinations of corn and wheat production that might exist for Ohio and Kansas together. Figure 2.5 graphs the data from Table 2.1.

Suppose that society's demand for corn dramatically increases. If this happens, farmers would probably shift some of their acreage from wheat production to corn production. Such a shift is represented by a move from point C (where corn = 510 and wheat = 380) up and to the left along the ppf toward points A and B in Figure 2.5. As this happens, it becomes more difficult to produce additional corn. The best land for corn production was presumably already in corn, and the best land for wheat production was already in wheat. As we try to produce more corn, the land is less well-suited to that crop. As we take more land out of wheat production, we are taking increasingly better wheat-producing land. In other words, the opportunity cost of more corn, measured in terms of wheat foregone, increases.

Moving from point E to D, Table 2.1 shows that we can get 100 million bushels of corn (400 − 300) by sacrificing only 50 million bushels of wheat (550 − 500)—that is, we get 2 bushels of corn for every bushel of wheat. However, when we are already stretching the ability of the land to produce corn, it becomes harder to produce more and the opportunity cost increases. Moving from point B to A, we can get only 50 million bushels of corn (700 − 650) by sacrificing 100 million bushels of wheat (200 − 100). For every bushel of wheat, we now get only half a bushel of corn. However, if the demand for *wheat* were to increase substantially and we were to move down and to the right along the ppf, it would become increasingly difficult to produce wheat and the opportunity cost of wheat, in terms of corn foregone, would increase. This is the *law of increasing opportunity cost*.

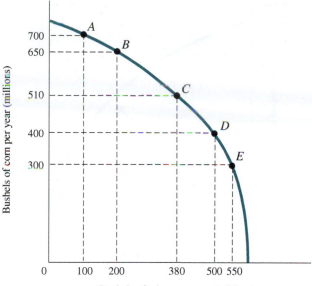

▲ **FIGURE 2.5   Corn and Wheat Production in Ohio and Kansas**
The ppf illustrates that the opportunity cost of corn production increases as we shift resources from wheat production to corn production. Moving from point E to D, we get an additional 100 million bushels of corn at a cost of 50 million bushels of wheat. Moving from point B to A, we get only 50 million bushels of corn at a cost of 100 million bushels of wheat. The *cost per bushel* of corn—measured in lost wheat—has increased.

| TABLE 2.1 | Production Possibility Schedule for Total Corn and Wheat Production in Ohio and Kansas | |
| --- | --- | --- |
| Point on ppf | Total Corn Production (Millions of Bushels per Year) | Total Wheat Production (Millions of Bushels per Year) |
| A | 700 | 100 |
| B | 650 | 200 |
| C | 510 | 380 |
| D | 400 | 500 |
| E | 300 | 550 |

**Unemployment**   During the Great Depression of the 1930s, the U.S. economy experienced prolonged unemployment. Millions of workers found themselves without jobs. In 1933, 25 percent of the civilian labor force was unemployed. This figure stayed above 14 percent until 1940. More recently, between the end of 2007 and 2010, the United States lost more than 8 million payroll jobs and unemployment rose to higher than 15 million.

In addition to the hardship that falls on the unemployed, unemployment of labor means unemployment of capital. During economic downturns or recessions, industrial plants run at less than their total capacity. When there is unemployment of labor and capital, we are not producing all that we can.

Periods of unemployment correspond to points inside the ppf, points such as D in Figure 2.4. Moving onto the frontier from a point such as D means achieving full employment of resources.

**Inefficiency**   Although an economy may be operating with full employment of its land, labor, and capital resources, it may still be operating inside its ppf (at a point such as D in Figure 2.4). It could be using those resources *inefficiently*.

Waste and mismanagement are the results of a firm operating below its potential. If you are the owner of a bakery and you forget to order flour, your workers and ovens stand idle while you figure out what to do.

Sometimes inefficiency results from mismanagement of the economy instead of mismanagement of individual private firms. Suppose, for example, that the land and climate in Ohio are

▶ **FIGURE 2.6**
**Inefficiency from Misallocation of Land in Farming**
Inefficiency always results in a combination of production shown by a point inside the ppf, like point *A*. Increasing efficiency will move production possibilities toward a point on the ppf, such as point *B*.

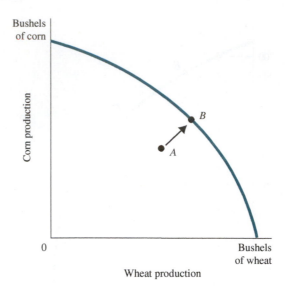

best-suited for corn production and that the land and climate in Kansas are best-suited for wheat production. If Congress passes a law forcing Ohio farmers to plant 50 percent of their acreage with wheat and Kansas farmers to plant 50 percent with corn, neither corn nor wheat production will be up to potential. The economy will be at a point such as *A* in Figure 2.6—inside the ppf. Allowing each state to specialize in producing the crop that it produces best increases the production of both crops and moves the economy to a point such as *B* in Figure 2.6.

**The Efficient Mix of Output**   To be efficient, an economy must produce what people want. This means that in addition to operating *on* the ppf, the economy must be operating at the *right point* on the ppf. This is referred to as *output efficiency*, in contrast to production efficiency. Suppose that an economy devotes 100 percent of its resources to beef production and that the beef industry runs efficiently using the most modern techniques. If everyone in the society were a vegetarian and there were no trade, resources spent on producing beef would be wasted.

It is important to remember that the ppf represents choices available within the constraints imposed by the current state of agricultural technology. In the long run, technology may improve, and when that happens, we have *growth*.

**economic growth**   An increase in the total output of an economy. Growth occurs when a society acquires new resources or when it learns to produce more using existing resources.

**Economic Growth**   **Economic growth** is characterized by an increase in the total output of an economy. It occurs when a society acquires new resources or learns to produce more with existing resources. New resources may mean a larger labor force or an increased capital stock. The production and use of new machinery and equipment (capital) increase workers' productivity. (Give a man a shovel, and he can dig a bigger hole; give him a steam shovel, and wow!) Improved productivity also comes from technological change and *innovation*, the discovery and application of new, more efficient production techniques.

In the past few decades, the productivity of U.S. agriculture has increased dramatically. Based on data compiled by the Department of Agriculture, Table 2.2 shows that yield per acre in corn production has increased sixfold since the late 1930s, and the labor required to produce it has dropped significantly. Productivity in wheat production has also increased, at only a slightly less remarkable rate: Output per acre has more than tripled, whereas labor requirements are down nearly 90 percent. These increases are the result of more efficient farming techniques, more and better capital (tractors, combines, and other equipment), and advances in scientific knowledge and technological change (hybrid seeds, fertilizers, and so on). As you can see in Figure 2.7, changes such as these shift the ppf up and to the right.

**Sources of Growth and the Dilemma of Poor Countries**   Economic growth arises from many sources. The two most important over the years have been the accumulation of capital and technological advances. For poor countries, capital is essential; they must build

| TABLE 2.2 | Increasing Productivity in Corn and Wheat Production in the United States, 1935–2009 | | | |
|---|---|---|---|---|
| | Corn | | Wheat | |
| | Yield per Acre (Bushels) | Labor Hours per 100 Bushels | Yield per Acre (Bushels) | Labor Hours per 100 Bushels |
| 1935–1939 | 26.1 | 108 | 13.2 | 67 |
| 1945–1949 | 36.1 | 53 | 16.9 | 34 |
| 1955–1959 | 48.7 | 20 | 22.3 | 17 |
| 1965–1969 | 78.5 | 7 | 27.5 | 11 |
| 1975–1979 | 95.3 | 4 | 31.3 | 9 |
| 1981–1985 | 107.2 | 3 | 36.9 | 7 |
| 1985–1990 | 112.8 | NA[a] | 38.0 | NA[a] |
| 1990–1995 | 120.6 | NA[a] | 38.1 | NA[a] |
| 1998 | 134.4 | NA[a] | 43.2 | NA[a] |
| 2001 | 138.2 | NA[a] | 43.5 | NA[a] |
| 2006 | 145.6 | NA[a] | 42.3 | NA[a] |
| 2007 | 152.8 | NA[a] | 40.6 | NA[a] |
| 2008 | 153.9 | NA[a] | 44.9 | NA[a] |
| 2009 | 164.9 | NA[a] | 44.3 | NA[a] |

[a] Data not available.

*Source: U.S. Department of Agriculture, Economic Research Service, Agricultural Statistics, Crop Summary.*

the communication networks and transportation systems necessary to develop industries that function efficiently. They also need capital goods to develop their agricultural sectors.

Recall that capital goods are produced only at a sacrifice of consumer goods. The same can be said for technological advances. Technological advances come from research and development that use resources; thus, they too must be paid for. The resources used to produce capital

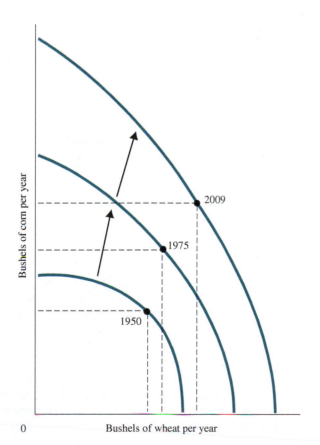

◀ **FIGURE 2.7** **Economic Growth Shifts the PPF Up and to the Right**
Productivity increases have enhanced the ability of the United States to produce both corn and wheat. As Table 2.2 shows, productivity increases were more dramatic for corn than for wheat. Thus, the shifts in the ppf were not parallel.

goods—to build a road, a tractor, or a manufacturing plant—*and* to develop new technologies could have been used to produce consumer goods.

When a large part of a country's population is poor, taking resources out of the production of consumer goods (such as food and clothing) is difficult. In addition, in some countries, people wealthy enough to invest in domestic industries choose instead to invest abroad because of political turmoil at home. As a result, it often falls to the governments of poor countries to generate revenues for capital production and research out of tax collections.

All these factors have contributed to the growing gap between some poor and rich nations. Figure 2.8 shows the result using ppfs. On the bottom left, the rich country devotes a larger portion of its production to capital, whereas the poor country on the top left produces mostly consumer goods. On the right, you see the results: The ppf of the rich country shifts up and out further and faster.

The importance of capital goods and technological developments to the position of workers in less-developed countries is well-illustrated by Robert Jensen's study of South India's industry. Conventional telephones require huge investments in wires and towers and, as a result, many less developed areas are without landlines. Mobile phones, on the other hand, require a lower investment; thus, in many areas, people upgraded from no phones directly to cell phones. Jensen found that in small fishing villages, the advent of cell phones allowed fishermen to determine on any given day where to take their catch to sell, resulting in a large decrease in fish wasted and an increase in fishing profits. The ability of newer communication technology to aid development is one of the exciting features of our times. (See Robert Jensen, "The Digital Provide: Information Technology, Market Performance, and Welfare in the South Indian Fisheries Sector," *Quarterly Journal of Economics*, 2007: 879–924.)

Although it exists only as an abstraction, the ppf illustrates a number of important concepts that we will use throughout the rest of this book: scarcity, unemployment, inefficiency, opportunity cost, the law of increasing opportunity cost, economic growth, and the gains from trade.

▶ **FIGURE 2.8** **Capital Goods and Growth in Poor and Rich Countries**
Rich countries find it easier than poor countries to devote resources to the production of capital, and the more resources that flow into capital production, the faster the rate of economic growth. Thus, the gap between poor and rich countries has grown over time.

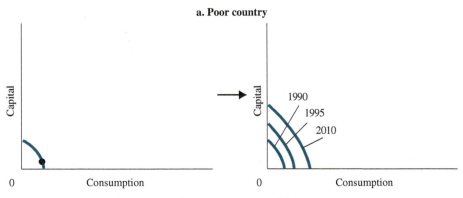

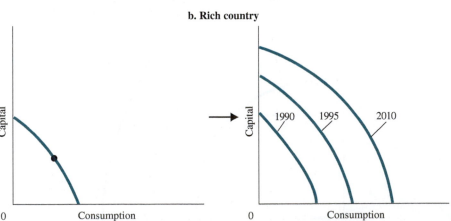

## ECONOMICS IN PRACTICE

### Trade-Offs among the Rich and Poor

In all societies, for all people, resources are limited relative to people's demands. There are, however, quite large differences in the kinds of trade-offs individuals face in rich versus poor countries.

In 1990, the World Bank defined the extremely poor people of the world as those earning less than $1 a day. Among development economists and policy makers, this figure continues to be used as a rough rule of thumb. In a recent survey, Abhijit Banerjee and Esther Duflo, two MIT economists, surveyed individuals living at this level in 13 countries across the world.[1] What did they learn about the consumption trade-offs faced by these individuals versus consumers in the United States?

It should not surprise you to learn that for the extremely poor, food is a much larger component of the budget. On average over the 13 countries, between 56 percent and 78 percent of consumption was spent on food. In the United States, just under 10 percent of the average budget goes to food. Even for the poorest consumers, however, biological need is not all determining. The Banerjee and Duflo study finds that in Udaipur, India, almost 10 percent of the typical food budget goes to sugar and processed foods rather than more nutritionally valuable grains. So even at these low levels of income, some choice remains. Perhaps more interestingly, almost 10 percent of the budget of those surveyed goes to weddings, funerals, and other festivals. In societies with very few entertainment outlets, Banerjee and Duflo suggest we

may see more demand for festivals, indicating that even in extremely poor societies, household choice plays a role.

#### THINKING PRACTICALLY

1. Why might we see a greater demand for festivals in poor countries than in rich ones? How might this be affected by choices available?

[1] Abhijit Banerjee and Esther Duflo, "The Economic Lives of the Poor," *Journal of Economic Perspective*, Winter 2007: 141–167.

## The Economic Problem

Recall the three basic questions facing all economic systems: (1) What gets produced? (2) How is it produced? and (3) Who gets it?

When Bill was alone on the island, the mechanism for answering those questions was simple: He thought about his own wants and preferences, looked at the constraints imposed by the resources of the island and his own skills and time, and made his decisions. As Bill set about his work, he allocated available resources quite simply, more or less by dividing up his available time. Distribution of the output was irrelevant. Because Bill was the society, he got it all.

Introducing even one more person into the economy—in this case, Colleen—changed all that. Cooperation and coordination may give rise to gains that would otherwise not be possible. When a society consists of millions of people, coordination and cooperation become more challenging, but the potential for gain also grows. In large, complex economies, specialization can grow dramatically. The range of products available in a modern industrial society is beyond anything that could have been imagined a hundred years ago, and so is the range of jobs. Specialization plays a role in this.

The amount of coordination and cooperation in a modern industrial society is almost impossible to imagine. Yet something seems to drive economic systems, if sometimes clumsily and inefficiently, toward producing the goods and services that people want. Given scarce resources, how do large, complex societies go about answering the three basic economic questions? This is the economic problem, which is what this text is about.

# Economic Systems and the Role of Government

Thus far we have described the questions that the economic system must answer. Now we turn to the mechanics of the system. What is the role played by government in deciding what and how things are produced? There are many circumstances in which the government may be able to improve the functioning of the market.

## Command Economies

**command economy** An economy in which a central government either directly or indirectly sets output targets, incomes, and prices.

In a pure **command economy**, like the system in place in the Soviet Union or China some years ago, the basic economic questions are answered by a central government. Through a combination of government ownership of state enterprises and central planning, the government, either directly or indirectly, sets output targets, incomes, and prices.

At present, for most countries in the world, private enterprise plays at least some role in production decisions. The debate today is instead about the extent and the character of government's role in the economy. Government involvement, in theory, may improve the efficiency and fairness of the allocation of a nation's resources. At the same time, a poorly functioning government can destroy incentives, lead to corruption, and result in the waste of a society's resources.

## Laissez-Faire Economies: The Free Market

**laissez-faire economy** Literally from the French: "allow [them] to do." An economy in which individual people and firms pursue their own self-interest without any government direction or regulation.

**market** The institution through which buyers and sellers interact and engage in exchange.

At the opposite end of the spectrum from the command economy is the **laissez-faire economy**. The term *laissez-faire*, which translated literally from French means "allow [them] to do," implies a complete lack of government involvement in the economy. In this type of economy, individuals and firms pursue their own self-interest without any central direction or regulation; the sum total of millions of individual decisions ultimately determines all basic economic outcomes. The central institution through which a laissez-faire system answers the basic questions is the **market**, a term that is used in economics to mean an institution through which buyers and sellers interact and engage in exchange.

In short:

> Some markets are simple and others are complex, but they all involve buyers and sellers engaging in exchange. The behavior of buyers and sellers in a laissez-faire economy determines what gets produced, how it is produced, and who gets it.

The following chapters explore market systems in great depth. A quick preview is worthwhile here, however.

**Consumer Sovereignty** In a free, unregulated market, goods and services are produced and sold only if the supplier can make a profit. In simple terms, making a *profit* means selling goods or services for more than it costs to produce them. You cannot make a profit unless someone wants the product that you are selling. This logic leads to the notion of **consumer sovereignty**: The mix of output found in any free market system is dictated ultimately by the tastes and preferences of consumers who "vote" by buying or not buying. Businesses rise and fall in response to consumer demands. No central directive or plan is necessary.

**consumer sovereignty** The idea that consumers ultimately dictate what will be produced (or not produced) by choosing what to purchase (and what not to purchase).

**Individual Production Decisions: Free Enterprise** Under a free market system, individual producers must also determine how to organize and coordinate the actual production of their products or services. In a free market economy, producers may be small or large. One person who is good with computers may start a business designing Web sites. On a larger scale, a group of furniture designers may put together a large portfolio of sketches, raise several million dollars, and start a bigger business. At the extreme are huge corporations such as Microsoft, Mitsubishi, Apple, and Intel, each of which sells tens of billions of dollars' worth of products every year. Whether the firms are large or small, however, production decisions in a market economy are made by separate private organizations acting in what they perceive to be their own interests.

Proponents of free market systems argue that the use of markets leads to more efficient production and better response to diverse and changing consumer preferences. If a producer is inefficient, competitors will come along, fight for the business, and eventually take it away. Thus, in a free market economy, competition forces producers to use efficient techniques of production and to produce goods that consumers want.

**Distribution of Output** In a free market system, the distribution of output—who gets what—is also determined in a decentralized way. To the extent that income comes from working for a wage, it is at least in part determined by individual choice. You will work for the wages available in the market only if these wages (and the products and services they can buy) are sufficient to compensate you for what you give up by working. You may discover that you can increase your income by getting more education or training.

**Price Theory** The basic coordinating mechanism in a free market system is price. A price is the amount that a product sells for per unit, and it reflects what society is willing to pay. Prices of inputs—labor, land, and capital—determine how much it costs to produce a product. Prices of various kinds of labor, or *wage rates*, determine the rewards for working in different jobs and professions. Many of the independent decisions made in a market economy involve the weighing of prices and costs, so it is not surprising that much of economic theory focuses on the factors that influence and determine prices. This is why microeconomic theory is often simply called *price theory*.

In sum:

> In a free market system, the basic economic questions are answered without the help of a central government plan or directives. This is what the "free" in free market means—the system is left to operate on its own with no outside interference. Individuals pursuing their own self-interest will go into business and produce the products and services that people want. Other individuals will decide whether to acquire skills; whether to work; and whether to buy, sell, invest, or save the income that they earn. The basic coordinating mechanism is price.

# Mixed Systems, Markets, and Governments

The differences between command economies and laissez-faire economies in their pure forms are enormous. In fact, these pure forms do not exist in the world; all real systems are in some sense "mixed." That is, individual enterprise exists and independent choice is exercised even in economies in which the government plays a major role.

Conversely, no market economies exist without government involvement and government regulation. The United States has basically a free market economy, but government purchases accounted for slightly more than 18 percent of the country's total production in 2014 Governments in the United States (local, state, and federal) directly employ about 14 percent of all workers (15 percent including active duty military). They also redistribute income by means of taxation and social welfare expenditures, and they regulate many economic activities.

One of the major themes in this book, and indeed in economics, is the tension between the advantages of free, unregulated markets and the desire for government involvement. Identifying what the market does well, and where it potentially fails, and exploring the role of government in dealing with market failure is a key topic in policy economics. We return to this debate many times throughout this text.

## Looking Ahead

This chapter described the economic problem in broad terms. We outlined the questions that all economic systems must answer. We also discussed broadly the two kinds of economic systems. In the next chapter, we analyze the way market systems work.

### — S U M M A R Y —

1. Every society has some system or process for transforming into useful form what nature and previous generations have provided. Economics is the study of that process and its outcomes.

2. *Producers* are those who take resources and transform them into usable products, or *outputs*. Private firms, households, and governments all produce something.

#### 2.1 SCARCITY, CHOICE, AND OPPORTUNITY COST *p. 23*

3. All societies must answer *three basic questions*: What gets produced? How is it produced? Who gets what is produced? These three questions make up the *economic problem*.

4. One person alone on an island must make the same basic decisions that complex societies make. When a society consists of more than one person, questions of distribution, cooperation, and specialization arise.

5. Because resources are scarce relative to human wants in all societies, using resources to produce one good or service implies *not* using them to produce something else. This concept of *opportunity cost* is central to understanding economics.

6. Using resources to produce *capital* that will in turn produce benefits in the future implies *not* using those resources to produce consumer goods in the present.

7. Even if one individual or nation is absolutely more efficient at producing goods than another, all parties will gain if they specialize in producing goods in which they have a *comparative advantage*.

8. A *production possibility frontier* (ppf) is a graph that shows all the combinations of goods and services that can be produced if all of society's resources are used efficiently. The ppf illustrates a number of important economic concepts: scarcity, unemployment, inefficiency, increasing opportunity cost, and economic growth.

9. *Economic growth* occurs when society produces more, either by acquiring more resources or by learning to produce more with existing resources. Improved productivity may come from additional capital or from the discovery and application of new, more efficient techniques of production.

#### 2.2 ECONOMIC SYSTEMS AND THE ROLE OF GOVERNMENT *p. 36*

10. In some modern societies, government plays a big role in answering the three basic questions. In pure *command economies*, a central authority directly or indirectly sets output targets, incomes, and prices.

11. A *laissez-faire economy* is one in which individuals independently pursue their own self-interest, without any central direction or regulation, and ultimately determine all basic economic outcomes.

12. A *market* is an institution through which buyers and sellers interact and engage in exchange. Some markets involve simple face-to-face exchange; others involve a complex series of transactions, often over great distances or through electronic means.

13. There are no purely planned economies and no pure laissez-faire economies; all economies are mixed. Individual enterprise, independent choice, and relatively free markets exist in centrally planned economies; there is significant government involvement in market economies such as that of the United States.

14. One of the great debates in economics revolves around the tension between the advantages of free, unregulated markets and the desire for government involvement in the economy. Free markets produce what people want, and competition forces firms to adopt efficient production techniques. The need for government intervention arises because free markets are characterized by inefficiencies and an unequal distribution of income and experience regular periods of inflation and unemployment.

### — R E V I E W   T E R M S   A N D   C O N C E P T S —

absolute advantage, *p. 25*

capital, *p. 22*

command economy, *p. 36*

comparative advantage, *p. 26*

consumer goods, *p. 28*

consumer sovereignty, *p. 36*

economic growth, *p. 32*

factors of production (or factors), *p. 23*

inputs *or* resources, *p. 23*

investment, *p. 28*

laissez-faire economy, *p. 36*

marginal rate of transformation (MRT), *p. 30*

market, *p. 36*

opportunity cost, *p. 24*

outputs, *p. 23*

production, *p. 23*

production possibility frontier (ppf), *p. 29*

theory of comparative advantage, *p. 24*

**MyEconLab** Visit **www.myeconlab.com** to complete these exercises online and get instant feedback. Exercises that update with real-time data are marked with art 🔴.

# PROBLEMS

All problems are available on MyEconLab.

## 2.1 SCARCITY, CHOICE, AND OPPORTUNITY COST

**LEARNING OBJECTIVE:** Understand why even in a society in which one person is better than a second at all tasks, it is still beneficial for the two to specialize and trade.

1.1 For each of the following, describe some of the potential opportunity costs:
  a. Going home for Thanksgiving vacation
  b. Riding your bicycle 20 miles every day
  c. The federal government using tax revenue to purchase 10,000 acres in Florida for use as a bird sanctuary
  d. A foreign government subsidizes its national airline to keep airfares down
  e. Upgrading to a balcony suite for your cruise around the Mediterranean Sea
  f. Staying up all night to watch season 5 of *Game of Thrones*

1.2 "As long as all resources are fully employed and every firm in the economy is producing its output using the best available technology, the result will be efficient." Do you agree or disagree with this statement? Explain your answer.

1.3 You are an intern to the editor of a small-town newspaper in Mallsburg, Pennsylvania. Your boss, the editor, asks you to write the first draft of an editorial for this week's paper. Your assignment is to describe the costs and the benefits of building a new bridge across the railroad tracks in the center of town. Currently, most people who live in this town must drive 2 miles through thickly congested traffic to the existing bridge to get to the main shopping and employment center. The bridge will cost the citizens of Mallsburg $25 million, which will be paid for with a tax on their incomes over the next 20 years. What are the opportunity costs of building this bridge? What are the benefits that citizens will likely receive if the bridge is built? What other factors might you consider in writing this editorial?

1.4 Alexi and Tony own a food truck that serves only two items, street tacos and Cuban sandwiches. As shown in the table, Alexi can make 80 street tacos per hour but only 20 Cuban sandwiches. Tony is a bit faster and can make 100 street tacos or 30 Cuban sandwiches in an hour. Alexi and Tony can sell all the street tacos and Cuban sandwiches that they are able to produce.

### Output Per Hour

|        | Street Tacos | Cuban Sandwiches |
|--------|--------------|------------------|
| Alexi  | 80           | 20               |
| Tony   | 100          | 30               |

  a. For Alexi and for Tony, what is the opportunity cost of a street taco? Who has a comparative advantage in the production of street tacos? Explain your answer.
  b. Who has a comparative advantage in the production of Cuban sandwiches? Explain your answer.
  c. Assume that Alexi works 20 hours per week in the business. Assuming Alexi is in business on his own, graph the possible combinations of street tacos and Cuban sandwiches that he could produce in a week. Do the same for Tony.
  d. If Alexi devoted half of his time (10 out of 20 hours) to making street tacos and half of his time to making Cuban sandwiches, how many of each would he produce in a week? If Tony did the same, how many of each would he produce? How many street tacos and Cuban sandwiches would be produced in total?
  e. Suppose that Alexi spent all 20 hours of his time on street tacos and Tony spent 17 hours on Cuban Sandwiches and 3 hours on street tacos. How many of each item would be produced?
  f. Suppose that Alexi and Tony can sell all their street tacos for $2 each and all their Cuban Sandwiches for $7.25 each. If each of them worked 20 hours per week, how should they split their time between the production of street tacos and Cuban sandwiches? What is their maximum joint revenue?

1.5 Briefly describe the trade-offs involved in each of the following decisions. Specifically, list some of the opportunity costs associated with each decision, paying particular attention to the trade-offs between present and future consumption.
  a. After a stressful senior year in high school, Sherice decides to take the summer off instead of working before going to college.
  b. Frank is overweight and decides to work out every day and to go on a diet.
  c. Mei is diligent about taking her car in for routine maintenance even though it takes 2 hours of her time and costs $100 four times each year.
  d. Jim is in a hurry. He runs a red light on the way to work.

*1.6 The countries of Orion and Scorpius are small mountainous nations. Both produce granite and blueberries. Each nation has a labor force of 800. The following table gives production per month for each worker in each country. Assume productivity is constant and identical for each worker in each country.

|                  | Tons of Granite | Bushels of Blueberries |
|------------------|-----------------|------------------------|
| Orion workers    | 6               | 18                     |
| Scorpius workers | 3               | 12                     |

Productivity of one worker for one month

  a. Which country has an absolute advantage in the production of granite? Which country has an absolute advantage in the production of blueberries?
  b. Which country has a comparative advantage in the production of granite? of blueberries?
  c. Sketch the ppf's for both countries.

   **d.** Assuming no trading between the two, if both countries wanted to have equal numbers of tons of granite and bushels of blueberries, how would they allocate workers to the two sectors?

   **e.** Show that specialization and trade can move both countries beyond their ppf's.

*1.7 Match each diagram in Figure 1 with its description here. Assume that the economy is producing or attempting to produce at point *A* and that most members of society like meat and not fish. Some descriptions apply to more than one diagram, and some diagrams have more than one description.

   **a.** Inefficient production of meat and fish
   **b.** Productive efficiency
   **c.** An inefficient mix of output
   **d.** Technological advances in the production of meat and fish
   **e.** The law of increasing opportunity cost
   **f.** An impossible combination of meat and fish

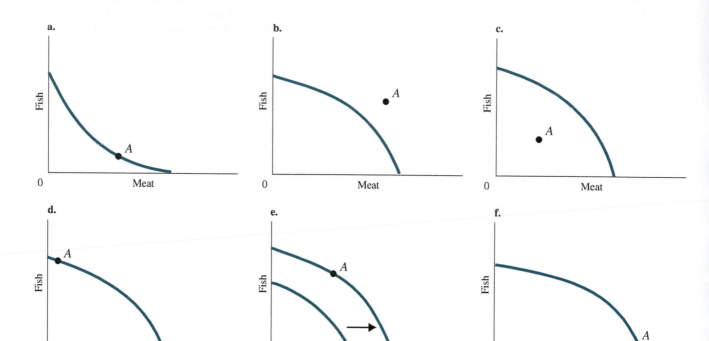

▲ **FIGURE 1**

1.8 A nation with fixed quantities of resources is able to produce any of the following combinations of carpet and carpet looms:

| Yards of carpet (Millions) | Carpet looms (Thousands) |
| --- | --- |
| 0 | 45 |
| 12 | 42 |
| 24 | 36 |
| 36 | 27 |
| 48 | 15 |
| 60 | 0 |

These figures assume that a certain number of previously produced looms are available in the current period for producing carpet.

   **a.** Using the data in the table, graph the ppf (with carpet on the vertical axis).

   **b.** Does the principle of "increasing opportunity cost" hold in this nation? Explain briefly. (*Hint:* What happens to the opportunity cost of carpet—measured in number of looms—as carpet production increases?)

   **c.** If this country chooses to produce both carpet and looms, what will happen to the ppf over time? Why?

Now suppose that a new technology is discovered that allows an additional 50 percent of yards of carpet to be produced by each existing loom.

   **d.** Illustrate (on your original graph) the effect of this new technology on the ppf.

   **e.** Suppose that before the new technology is introduced, the nation produces 15 thousand looms. After the new technology is introduced, the nation produces 27 thousand looms. What is the effect of the new technology on the production of carpet? (Give the number of yards before and after the change.)

*Note: Problems with an asterisk are more challenging.*

**1.9** [Related to the *Economics in Practice* on p. 25] An analysis of a large-scale survey of consumer food purchases by Mark Aguiar and Erik Hurst indicates that retired people spend less for the same market basket of food than working people do. Use the concept of opportunity cost to explain this fact.

*1.10 Betty Lou has a car washing and detailing business. She charges $20 to wash a car, a process that takes her 20 minutes and requires no help or materials. For car detailing, a process requiring 1 hour, she charges $50 net of materials. Again, no help is required. Is anything puzzling about Betty Lou's pricing pattern? Explain your answer.

**1.11** At the end of the 2014 NFL regular season, the Louisiana Lottery allowed customers to enter their non-winning New Orleans Saints scratch-off lottery game tickets in a final second-chance drawing, with a chance to win the 2015 Saints Season Prize Package Experience. This package includes 4 Plaza Sideline tickets and field passes to every 2015 Saints home game, a season parking pass, and overnight accommodations for each home game. Suppose you entered this second-chance drawing and won this Season Prize Package Experience for the Saints' 2015 season. Would there be a cost to you to attend the Saints' games during the 2015 season?

**1.12** High school football is arguably more popular in West Texas than in any other region of the country. During football season, small towns seem to shut down on Friday nights as local high school teams take to the field, and for the following week the results of the games are the talk of each town. Taking into consideration that many of these towns are one hundred or more miles away from any medium-sized or large cities, what might be an economic explanation for the extreme popularity of high school football in these small West Texas towns?

**1.13** The nation of Billabong is able to produce surfboards and kayaks in combinations represented by the data in the following table. Each number represents thousands of units. Plot this data on a production possibilities graph and explain why the data shows that Billabong experiences increasing opportunity costs.

|            | A  | B  | C  | D  | E  |
|------------|----|----|----|----|----|
| Surfboards | 0  | 20 | 40 | 60 | 80 |
| Kayaks     | 28 | 24 | 18 | 10 | 0  |

**1.14** Explain how each of the following situations would affect a nation's production possibilities curve.
  a. A law is passed which makes community college tuition-free for all U.S. citizens.
  b. An unexpectedly mild spring results in a bumper crop of citrus fruit in both Florida and California.
  c. A change in immigration laws significantly increases the number of immigrant workers entering the country.
  d. The amount of time that unemployed workers can collect unemployment insurance is increased from 26 weeks to 96 weeks during a recession, resulting in workers remaining unemployed for a longer period of time.
  e. An innovation in desalinization technology allows for the more efficient conversion of salt water to fresh water.
  f. A radiation leak at a nuclear power plant results in the long-term evacuation of a 10,000 square-mile area, which significantly reduces the nation's productive capacity.

## 2.2 ECONOMIC SYSTEMS AND THE ROLE OF GOVERNMENT

LEARNING OBJECTIVE:  Understand the central difference in the way command economies and market economies decide what is produced.

**2.1** Describe a command economy and a laissez-faire economy. Do any economic systems in the world reflect the purest forms of command or laissez-faire economies? Explain.

**2.2** Suppose that a simple society has an economy with only one resource, labor. Labor can be used to produce only two commodities—X, a necessity good (food), and Y, a luxury good (music and merriment). Suppose that the labor force consists of 100 workers. One laborer can produce either 5 units of necessity per month (by hunting and gathering) or 10 units of luxury per month (by writing songs, playing the guitar, dancing, and so on).
  a. On a graph, draw the economy's ppf. Where does the ppf intersect the Y-axis? Where does it intersect the X-axis? What meaning do those points have?
  b. Suppose the economy produced at a point *inside* the ppf. Give at least two reasons why this could occur. What could be done to move the economy to a point *on* the ppf?
  c. Suppose you succeeded in lifting your economy to a point on its ppf. What point would you choose? How might your small society decide the point at which it wanted to be?
  d. Once you have chosen a point on the ppf, you still need to decide how your society's production will be divided. If you were a dictator, how would you decide? What would happen if you left product distribution to the free market?

# 3

# Demand, Supply, and Market Equilibrium

Chapters 1 and 2 introduced the discipline, methodology, and subject matter of economics. We now begin the task of analyzing how a market economy actually works. This chapter and the next present an overview of the way individual markets work, introducing concepts used in both microeconomics and macroeconomics.

In the simple island society discussed in Chapter 2, Bill and Colleen solved the economic problem directly. They allocated their time and used the island's resources to satisfy their wants. Exchange occurred in a relatively simple way. In larger societies, with people typically operating at some distance from one another, exchange can be more complex. *Markets* are the institutions through which exchange typically takes place.

This chapter begins to explore the basic forces at work in market systems. The purpose of our discussion is to explain how the individual decisions of households and firms together, without any central planning or direction, answer the three basic questions: What gets produced? How is it produced? Who gets what is produced? We begin with some definitions.

# Firms and Households: The Basic Decision-Making Units

Throughout this book, we discuss and analyze the behavior of two fundamental decision-making units: *firms*—the primary producing units in an economy—and *households*—the consuming units in an economy. Both are made up of people performing different functions and playing different roles. Economics is concerned with how those people behave, and the interaction among them.

A **firm** exists when a person or a group of people decides to produce a product or products by transforming *inputs*—that is, resources in the broadest sense—into *outputs*, the products that are sold in the market. Some firms produce goods; others produce services. Some are large, many are small, and some are in between. All firms exist to transform resources into goods and services that people want. The Colorado Symphony Orchestra takes labor, land, a building, musically talented people, instruments, and other inputs and combines them to produce concerts. The production process can be extremely complicated. For example, the first flautist in the orchestra combines training, talent, previous performance experience, score, instrument, conductor's interpretation, and personal feelings about the music to produce just one contribution to an overall performance.

**firm** An organization that transforms resources (inputs) into products (outputs). Firms are the primary producing units in a market economy.

Most firms exist to make a profit for their owners, but some do not. Columbia University, for example, fits the description of a firm: It takes inputs in the form of labor, land, skills, books, and buildings and produces a service that we call *education*. Although the university sells that service for a price, it does not exist to make a profit; instead, it exists to provide education and research of the highest quality possible.

Still, most firms exist to make a profit. They engage in production because they can sell their product for more than it costs to produce it. The analysis of a firm's behavior that follows rests on the assumption that *firms make decisions to maximize profits*. Sometimes firms suffer losses instead of earning profits. When firms suffer losses, we will assume that they act to minimize those losses.

An **entrepreneur** is someone who organizes, manages, and assumes the risks of a firm. When a new firm is created, someone must organize the new firm, arrange financing, hire employees, and take risks. That person is an entrepreneur. Sometimes existing firms introduce new products, and sometimes new firms develop or improve on an old idea, but at the root of it all is entrepreneurship.

**entrepreneur** A person who organizes, manages, and assumes the risks of a firm, taking a new idea or a new product and turning it into a successful business.

The consuming units in an economy are **households**. A household may consist of any number of people: a single person living alone, a married couple with four children, or 15 unrelated people sharing a house. Household decisions are based on individual tastes and preferences. The household buys what it wants and can afford. In a large, heterogeneous, and open society such as the United States, wildly different tastes find expression in the marketplace. A six-block walk in any direction on any street in Manhattan or a drive from the Chicago Loop south into rural Illinois should be enough to convince anyone that it is difficult to generalize about what people do and do not like.

**households** The consuming units in an economy.

Even though households have wide-ranging preferences, they also have some things in common. All—even the very rich—have ultimately limited incomes, and all must pay in some way for the goods and services they consume. Although households may have some control over their incomes—they can work more hours or fewer hours—they are also constrained by the availability of jobs, current wages, their own abilities, and their accumulated and inherited wealth (or lack thereof).

# Input Markets and Output Markets: The Circular Flow

Households and firms interact in two basic kinds of markets: product (or output) markets and input (or factor) markets. Goods and services that are intended for use by households are

**product *or* output markets**
The markets in which goods and services are exchanged.

**input *or* factor markets**
The markets in which the resources used to produce goods and services are exchanged.

**labor market** The input/factor market in which households supply work for wages to firms that demand labor.

**capital market** The input/factor market in which households supply their savings, for interest or for claims to future profits, to firms that demand funds to buy capital goods.

**land market** The input/factor market in which households supply land or other real property in exchange for rent.

**factors of production**
The inputs into the production process. Land, labor, and capital are the three key factors of production.

exchanged in **product *or* output markets**. In output markets, firms *supply* and households *demand*.

To produce goods and services, firms must buy resources in **input *or* factor markets**. Firms buy inputs from households, which supply these inputs. When a firm decides how much to produce (supply) in output markets, it must simultaneously decide how much of each input it needs to produce the desired level of output. To produce smart phones Samsung and Apple need many inputs, including hardware and software and a variety of types of labor, both skilled and unskilled.

Figure 3.1 shows the *circular flow* of economic activity through a simple market economy. Note that the flow reflects the direction in which goods and services flow through input and output markets. For example, real goods and services flow from firms to households through output—or product—markets. Labor services flow from households to firms through input markets. Payment (most often in money form) for goods and services flows in the opposite direction.

In input markets, households *supply* resources. Most households earn their incomes by working—they supply their labor in the **labor market** to firms that demand labor and pay workers for their time and skills. Households may also loan their accumulated or inherited savings to firms for interest or exchange those savings for claims to future profits, as when a household buys shares of stock in a corporation. In the **capital market**, households supply the funds that firms use to buy capital goods. Households may also supply land or other real property in exchange for rent in the **land market**.

Inputs into the production process are also called **factors of production**. Land, labor, and capital are the three key factors of production. Throughout this text, we use the terms *input* and *factor of production* interchangeably. Thus, input markets and factor markets mean the same thing.

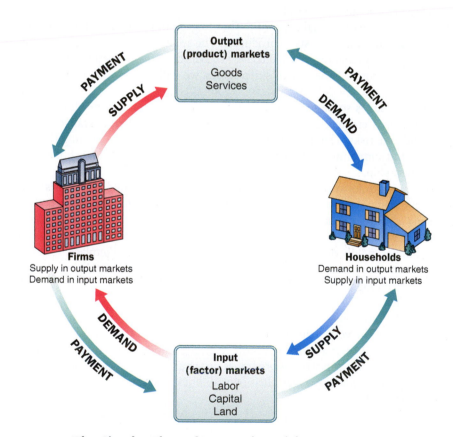

▲ **FIGURE 3.1 The Circular Flow of Economic Activity**
Diagrams like this one show the circular flow of economic activity, hence the name *circular flow diagram*. Here goods and services flow clockwise: Labor services supplied by households flow to firms, and goods and services produced by firms flow to households. Payment (usually money) flows in the opposite (counterclockwise) direction: Payment for goods and services flows from households to firms, and payment for labor services flows from firms to households.

*Note:* Color Guide-In Figure 3.1 households are depicted in *blue* and firms are depicted in *red*. From now on all diagrams relating to the behavior of households will be blue or shades of blue and all diagrams relating to the behavior of firms will be red or shades of red. The green color indicates a monetary flow.

The supply of inputs and their prices ultimately determine household income. Thus, the amount of income a household earns depends on the decisions it makes concerning what types of inputs it chooses to supply. Whether to stay in school, how much and what kind of training to get, whether to start a business, how many hours to work, whether to work at all, and how to invest savings are all household decisions that affect income.

As you can see:

> Input and output markets are connected through the behavior of both firms and households. Firms determine the quantities and character of outputs produced and the types and quantities of inputs demanded. Households determine the types and quantities of products demanded and the quantities and types of inputs supplied.[1]

In 2015 a 12-pack of 12 oz. soda costs about $5, and many of you likely have one somewhere in your dormitory room. What determines the price of that soda? How can I explain how much soda you will buy in a given month or year? By the end of this chapter you will see the way in which prices in the market are determined by the interaction of buyers like you and suppliers like soda manufacturers. The model of supply and demand covered in this chapter is the most powerful tool of economics. By the time you finish this chapter we hope you will look at shopping in a different way.

# Demand in Product/Output Markets

**3.3 LEARNING OBJECTIVE**
Understand what determines the position and shape of the demand curve and what factors move you along a demand curve and what factors shift the demand curve.

Every week you make hundreds of decisions about what to buy. Your choices likely look different from those of your friends or your parents. For all of you, however, the decision about what to buy and how much of it to buy ultimately depends on six factors:

- The *price of the product* in question.
- The *income available* to the household.
- The household's *amount of accumulated wealth*.
- The *prices of other products* available to the household.
- The household's *tastes and preferences*.
- The household's *expectations* about future income, wealth, and prices.

**Quantity demanded** is the amount (number of units) of a product that a household would buy in a given period *if it could buy all it wanted at the current market price*. Of course, the amount of a product that households finally purchase depends on the amount of product actually available in the market. The expression *if it could buy all it wanted* is critical to the definition of quantity demanded because it allows for the possibility that quantity supplied and quantity demanded are unequal.

**quantity demanded** The amount (number of units) of a product that a household would buy in a given period if it could buy all it wanted at the current market price.

## Changes in Quantity Demanded versus Changes in Demand

In our list of what determines how much you buy of a product the price of that product comes first. This is no accident. The most important relationship in individual markets is between market price and quantity demanded. So that is where we will start our work. In fact, we begin by looking

---

[1] Our description of markets begins with the behavior of firms and households. Modern orthodox economic theory essentially combines two distinct but closely related theories of behavior. The "theory of household behavior," or "consumer behavior," has its roots in the works of nineteenth-century utilitarians such as Jeremy Bentham, William Jevons, Carl Menger, Leon Walras, Vilfredo Parcto, and F. Y. Edgeworth. The "theory of the firm" developed out of the earlier classical political economy of Adam Smith, David Ricardo, and Thomas Malthus. In 1890, Alfred Marshall published the first of many editions of his *Principles of Economics*. That volume pulled together the main themes of both the classical economists and the utilitarians into what is now called *neoclassical economics*. Although there have been many changes over the years, the basic structure of the model that we build can be found in Marshall's work.

at what happens to the quantity a typical individual demands of a product when all that changes is its price. Economists refer to this device as *ceteris paribus*, or "all else equal." We will be looking at the relationship between quantity demanded of a good by an individual or household when its price changes, holding income, wealth, other prices, tastes, and expectations constant. If the price of that 12-pack of soda were cut in half, how many more cases would you buy in a given week?

In thinking about this question it is important to focus on the price change alone and to maintain the all else equal assumption. If next week you suddenly found yourself with more money than you expected (perhaps a windfall from an aunt), you might well find yourself buying an extra 12-pack of soda even if the price did not change at all. To be sure that we distinguish clearly between changes in price and other changes that affect demand, throughout the rest of the text we will be precise about terminology. Specifically:

> Changes in the price of a product affect the *quantity demanded* per period. Changes in any other factor, such as income or preferences, affect *demand*. Thus, we say that an increase in the price of Coca-Cola is likely to cause a decrease in the *quantity of Coca-Cola demanded*. However, we say that an increase in income is likely to cause an increase in the *demand* for most goods.

## Price and Quantity Demanded: The Law of Demand

**demand schedule** Shows how much of a given product a household would be willing to buy at different prices for a given time period.

A **demand schedule** shows how much of a product a person or household is willing to purchase per time period (each week or each month) at different prices. Clearly that decision is based on numerous interacting factors. Consider Alex who just graduated from college with an entry-level job at a local bank. During her senior year, Alex got a car loan and bought a used Mini Cooper. The Mini gets 25 miles per gallon of gasoline. Alex lives with several friends in a house 10 miles from her workplace and enjoys visiting her parents 50 miles away.

How often Alex will decide to drive herself to work and parties, visit her family, or even go joy riding depends on many things, including her income and whether she likes to drive. But the price of gasoline also plays an important role, and it is this relationship between price and quantity demanded that we focus on in the law of demand. With a gasoline price of $3.00 a gallon, Alex might decide to drive herself to work every day, visit her parents once a week, and drive another 50 miles a week for other activities. This driving pattern would add up to 250 miles a week, which would use 10 gallons of gasoline in her Mini. The demand schedule in Table 3.1 thus shows that at a price of $3.00 per gallon, Alex is willing to buy 10 gallons of gasoline. We can see that this demand schedule reflects a lot of information about Alex including where she lives and works and what she likes to do in her spare time.

Now suppose an international crisis in the Middle East causes the price of gasoline at the pump to rise to $5.00 per gallon. How does this affect Alex's demand for gasoline, assuming that everything else remains the same? Driving is now more expensive, and we would not be surprised if Alex decided to take the bus some mornings or share a ride with friends. She might visit her parents less frequently as well. On the demand schedule given in Table 3.1, Alex cuts her desired consumption of gasoline by half to 5 gallons when the price goes to $5.00. If,

| TABLE 3.1 | Alex's Demand Schedule for Gasoline |
| --- | --- |
| Price (per Gallon) | Quantity Demanded (Gallons per Week) |
| $ 8.00 | 0 |
| 7.00 | 2 |
| 6.00 | 3 |
| 5.00 | 5 |
| 4.00 | 7 |
| 3.00 | 10 |
| 2.00 | 14 |
| 1.00 | 20 |
| 0.00 | 26 |

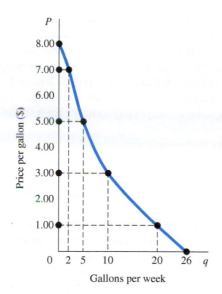

◀ **FIGURE 3.2 Alex's Demand Curve**
The relationship between price (P) and quantity demanded (q) presented graphically is called a demand curve. Demand curves have a negative slope, indicating that lower prices cause quantity demanded to increase. Note that Alex's demand curve is blue; demand in product markets is determined by household choice.

instead, the price of gasoline fell substantially, Alex might spend more time driving, and that is in fact the pattern we see in the table. This same information presented graphically is called a **demand curve**. Alex's demand curve is presented in Figure 3.2. You will note in Figure 3.2 that *quantity* (q) is measured along the horizontal axis and *price* (P) is measured along the vertical axis. This is the convention we follow throughout this book.

**demand curve** A graph illustrating how much of a given product a household would be willing to buy at different prices.

### Demand Curves Slope Downward

The data in Table 3.1 show that at lower prices, Alex buys more gasoline; at higher prices, she buys less. Thus, there is a *negative, or inverse, relationship between quantity demanded and price*. When price rises, quantity demanded falls, and when price falls, quantity demanded rises. Thus, demand curves always slope downward. This negative relationship between price and quantity demanded is often referred to as the **law of demand**, a term first used by economist Alfred Marshall in his 1890 textbook.

**law of demand** The negative relationship between price and quantity demanded: *Ceteris paribus*, as price rises, quantity demanded decreases; as price falls, quantity demanded increases during a given period of time, all other things remaining constant.

Some people are put off by the abstraction of demand curves. Of course, we do not actually draw our own demand curves for products. When we want to make a purchase, we usually face only a single price and how much we would buy at other prices is irrelevant. However, demand curves help analysts understand the kind of behavior that households are *likely* to exhibit if they are actually faced with a higher or lower price. We know, for example, that if the price of a good rises enough, the quantity demanded must ultimately drop to zero. The demand curve is thus a tool that helps us explain economic behavior and predict reactions to possible price changes.

Marshall's definition of a social "law" captures the idea:

The term "law" means nothing more than a general proposition or statement of tendencies, more or less certain, more or less definite...a *social law* is a statement of social tendencies; that is, that a certain course of action may be expected from the members of a social group under certain conditions.[2]

It seems reasonable to expect that consumers will demand more of a product at a lower price and less of it at a higher price. Households must divide their incomes over a wide range of goods and services. At $3.00 per gallon and 25 miles to a gallon, driving the 20 miles round trip to work costs Alex $2.40. It may look like a good deal relative to taking a bus. At $5.00 per gallon, the trip now costs $4.00. With the higher prices, Alex may have to give up her morning latte if she drives, and that may turn out to be too big a sacrifice for her. Now the bus may look better. As the price of gasoline rises, the opportunity cost of driving in terms of other types of consumption also rises and that is why Alex ends up driving less as the price of gasoline rises. Goods compete with one another for our spending.

---

[2] Alfred Marshall, *Principles of Economics*, 8th ed. (New York: Macmillan, 1948), p. 33. (The first edition was published in 1890.)

Economists use the concept of *utility* to explain the slope of the demand curve. We consume goods and services because they give us utility or satisfaction. As we consume more of a product within a given period of time, it is likely that each additional unit consumed will yield successively less satisfaction. The utility you gain from a second ice cream cone is likely to be less than the utility you gained from the first, the third is worth even less, and so on. This *law of diminishing marginal utility* is an important concept in economics. If each successive unit of a good is worth less to you, you are not going to be willing to pay as much for it. Thus, it is reasonable to expect a downward slope in the demand curve for that good.

Thinking about the ways that people are affected by price changes also helps us see what is behind the law of demand. Consider this example: Luis lives and works in Mexico City. His elderly mother lives in Santiago, Chile. Last year the airlines servicing South America got into a price war, and the price of flying between Mexico City and Santiago dropped from 20,000 pesos to 10,000 pesos. How might Luis's behavior change?

First, he is better off. Last year he flew home to Chile three times at a total cost of 60,000 pesos. This year he can fly to Chile the same number of times, buy exactly the same combination of other goods and services that he bought last year, and have 30,000 pesos left over. Because he is better off—his income can buy more—he may fly home more frequently. Second, the opportunity cost of flying home has changed. Before the price war, Luis had to sacrifice 20,000 pesos worth of other goods and services each time he flew to Chile. After the price war, he must sacrifice only 10,000 pesos worth of other goods and services for each trip. The trade-off has changed. Both of these effects are likely to lead to a higher quantity demanded in response to the lower price.

In sum:

> It is reasonable to expect quantity demanded to fall when price rises, ceteris paribus, and to expect quantity demanded to rise when price falls, ceteris paribus. Demand curves have a negative slope.

**Other Properties of Demand Curves**  Two additional things are notable about Alex's demand curve. First, it intersects the *Y*, or price, axis. This means that there is a price above which she buys no gasoline. In this case, Alex simply stops driving when the price reaches $8 per gallon. As long as households have limited incomes and wealth, all demand curves will intersect the price axis. For any commodity, there is always a price above which a household will not or cannot pay. Even if the good or service is important, all households are ultimately constrained, or limited, by income and wealth.

Second, Alex's demand curve intersects the *X*, or quantity, axis. Even at a zero price, there is a limit to how much she will drive. If gasoline were free, she would use 26 gallons, but not more. That demand curves intersect the quantity axis is a matter of common sense. Demand in a given period of time is limited, if only by time, even at a zero price.

To summarize what we know about the shape of demand curves:

1. They have a negative slope. An increase in price is likely to lead to a decrease in quantity demanded, and a decrease in price is likely to lead to an increase in quantity demanded.
2. They intersect the quantity (*X*) axis, a result of time limitations and diminishing marginal utility.
3. They intersect the price (*Y*) axis, a result of limited income and wealth.

That is all we can say; it is not possible to generalize further. The actual shape of an individual household demand curve—whether it is steep or flat, whether it is bowed in or bowed out—depends on the unique tastes and preferences of the household and other factors. Some households may be sensitive to price changes; other households may respond little to a change in price. In some cases, plentiful substitutes are available; in other cases, they are not. Thus, to fully understand the shape and position of demand curves, we must turn to the other determinants of household demand.

# Other Determinants of Household Demand

Of the many factors likely to influence a household's demand for a specific product, we have considered only the price of the product. But household income and wealth, the prices of other goods and services, tastes and preferences, and expectations also matter to demand.

**Income and Wealth**  Before we proceed, we need to define two terms that are often confused, *income* and *wealth*. A household's **income** is the sum of all the wages, salaries, profits, interest payments, rents, and other forms of earnings received by the household *in a given period of time*. Income is thus a *flow* measure: We must specify a time period for it—income *per month* or *per year*. You can spend or consume more or less than your income in any given period. If you consume less than your income, you save. To consume more than your income in a period, you must either borrow or draw on savings accumulated from previous periods.

**Wealth** is the total value of what a household owns minus what it owes. Another word for wealth is **net worth**—the amount a household would have left if it sold all of its possessions and paid all of its debts. Wealth is a *stock* measure: It is measured at a given point in time. If, in a given period, you spend less than your income, you save; the amount that you save is added to your wealth. Saving is the flow that affects the stock of wealth. When you spend more than your income, you *dissave*—you reduce your wealth.

Households with higher incomes and higher accumulated savings or inherited wealth can afford to buy more goods and services. In general, we would expect higher demand at higher levels of income/wealth and lower demand at lower levels of income/wealth. Goods for which demand goes up when income is higher and for which demand goes down when income is lower are called **normal goods**. Movie tickets, restaurant meals, and shirts are all normal goods.

However, generalization in economics can be hazardous. Sometimes demand for a good falls when household income rises. When a household's income rises, it is likely to buy higher-quality meats—its demand for filet mignon is likely to rise—but its demand for lower-quality meats—chuck steak, for example—is likely to fall. At higher incomes, people can afford to fly. People who can afford to fly are less likely to take the bus long distances. Thus, higher income may *reduce* the number of times someone takes a bus. Goods for which demand tends to fall when income rises are called **inferior goods**.

**Prices of Other Goods and Services**  No consumer decides in isolation on the amount of any one commodity to buy. Instead, each decision is part of a larger set of decisions that are made simultaneously. Households must apportion their incomes over many different goods and services. As a result, the price of any one good can and does affect the demand for other goods. This is most obviously the case when goods are substitutes for one another. For Alex the bus is an alternative that she uses when gasoline gets expensive.

When an *increase* in the price of one good causes demand for another good to *increase* (a positive relationship), we say that the goods are **substitutes**. A *fall* in the price of a good causes a *decline* in demand for its substitutes. Substitutes are goods that can serve as replacements for one another.

To be substitutes, two products do not need to be identical. Identical products are called **perfect substitutes**. Japanese cars are not identical to American cars. Nonetheless, all have four wheels, are capable of carrying people, and use fuel. Thus, significant changes in the price of one country's cars can be expected to influence demand for the other country's cars. Restaurant meals are substitutes for meals eaten at home, and flying from New York to Washington, D.C., is a substitute for taking the train. The *Economics in Practice* box describes substitution in the textbook market.

Often two products "go together"—that is, they complement each other. Bacon and eggs are **complementary goods**, as are cars and gasoline. When two goods are **complements**, a *decrease* in the price of one results in an *increase* in demand for the other and vice versa. For iPads and Kindles, for example, the availability of content at low prices stimulates demand for the devices.

**Tastes and Preferences**  Income, wealth, and prices of goods available are the three factors that determine the combinations of goods and services that a household is *able* to buy. You know that you cannot afford to rent an apartment at $1,200 per month if your monthly income is only

**income**  The sum of all a household's wages, salaries, profits, interest payments, rents, and other forms of earnings in a given period of time. It is a flow measure.

**wealth *or* net worth**  The total value of what a household owns minus what it owes. It is a stock measure.

**normal goods**  Goods for which demand goes up when income is higher and for which demand goes down when income is lower.

**inferior goods**  Goods for which demand tends to fall when income rises.

**substitutes**  Goods that can serve as replacements for one another; when the price of one increases, demand for the other increases.

**perfect substitutes**  Identical products.

**complements, complementary goods**  Goods that "go together"; a decrease in the price of one results in an increase in demand for the other and vice versa.

## ECONOMICS IN PRACTICE

### Have You Bought This Textbook?

As all of you know full well, college textbooks are expensive. And, at first, it may seem as though there are few substitutes available for the cash-strapped undergraduate. After *all*, if your professor assigns Smith's *Principles of Biology* to you, you cannot go out and see if Jones' *Principles of Chemistry* is perhaps cheaper and buy it instead. As it turns out, as some recent work by Judy Chevalier and Austan Goolsbee[1] discovered, even when instructors require particular texts, when prices are high students have found substitutes. Even in the textbook market student demand does slope down!

Chevalier and Goolsbee collected data on textbooks from more than 1600 colleges for the years 1997–2001 to do their research. For that period, the lion's share of both new and used college textbooks was sold in college bookstores. Next, they looked at class enrollments for each college in the large majors, economics, biology, and psychology. In each of those classes they were able to learn which textbook had been assigned. At first, one might think that the total number of textbooks, used plus new, should match the class enrollment. After all, the text is required! In fact, what they found was the higher the textbook price, the more text sales fell below class enrollments.

So what substitutes did students find for the required text? While the paper has no hard evidence on this, students themselves gave them lots of suggestions. Many decide to share books with roommates. Others use the library more. These solutions are not perfect, but when the price is high enough, students find it worth their while to walk to the library!

#### THINKING PRACTICALLY

1. If you were to construct a demand curve for a required text in a course, where would that demand curve intersect the horizontal axis?

2. And this much harder question: In the year before a new edition of a text is published, many college bookstores will not buy the older edition. Given this *fact*, what do you think happens to the gap between enrollments and new plus used book sales in the year before a new edition of a text is expected?

[1] Judith Chevalier and Austan Goolsbee, "Are Durable Goods Consumers Forward Looking? Evidence From College Textbooks," *Quarterly Journal of Economics*, 2009: 1853–1884.

$400, but within these constraints, you are more or less free to choose what to buy. Your final choice depends on your individual tastes and preferences.

Changes in preferences can and do manifest themselves in market behavior. Thirty years ago the major big-city marathons drew only a few hundred runners. Now tens of thousands enter and run. The demand for running shoes, running suits, stopwatches, and other running items has greatly increased.

Within the constraints of prices and incomes, preference shapes the demand curve, but it is difficult to generalize about tastes and preferences. First, they are volatile: Five years ago more people smoked cigarettes and fewer people had smartphones. Second, tastes are idiosyncratic: Some people like to text, whereas others still prefer to use e-mail; some people prefer dogs, whereas others are crazy about cats. The diversity of individual demands is almost infinite.

One of the interesting questions in economics is why, in some markets, diverse consumer tastes give rise to a variety of styles, whereas in other markets, despite a seeming diversity in tastes, we find only one or two varieties. All sidewalks in the United States are a similar gray color, yet houses are painted a rainbow of colors. Yet it is not obvious on the face of it that people would not prefer as much variety in their sidewalks as in their houses. To answer this type of question, we need to move beyond the demand curve. We will revisit this question in a later chapter.

## ECONOMICS IN PRACTICE

### On Sunny Days People Buy Convertibles!

Cars are a durable good. Most people who buy new cars expect to keep them for a number of years. Cars also have many different features, including size, power, and styling. These features in turn influence consumer demand for one type of car or another. As economists we might well expect people to choose the type of car they buy thinking about which features of those cars they will enjoy over the next few years. A four-wheel-drive car is likely to be more attractive if I expect a lot of snow in the next months or years. A convertible would be fun if it is likely to be clear and sunny on average in my region of the country.

On the other hand, given that cars are durable, we would be surprised if the weather *on a particular day* influenced car purchases. If a potential car buyer wakes up to an unseasonably warm and sunny day in November, we might be surprised if he or she all of a sudden decides to buy a convertible. A sunny day is a good reason to take a hike, but not a good reason to buy a durable good like a convertible that depends for its enjoyment on a string of sunny days. And, yet, in recent work, Meghan Busse, an economist at Northwestern, and her co-authors found after examining more than 40 million car transactions that car purchasers were heavily influenced in their choice of cars by temporary weather fluctuations at the time of purchase.[1] A snow storm increased the likelihood of buying a four-wheel drive vehicle within the next week by 6 percent, holding constant the average snow in that area of the country. An increase of 10 degrees on a fall or spring day over the norm increased purchase of convertibles by almost 3 percent.

Behavioral economists looking at this case would argue that the snow or sun makes one feature of a car—its four-wheel drive feature or soft top—more **salient** or important to the consumer's decision to purchase.

**THINKING PRACTICALLY**

1. Economists predict that my interest in purchasing a convertible also depends on how much I think other people like convertibles. How is this prediction related to the durability of cars?

[1] Meghan Busse, Devon Pope, Jaron Pope, and Jorge Silva-Russo, "The Psychological Effect of Weather on Car Purchases," *Quarterly Journal of Economics*, February, 2015.

**Expectations**   What you decide to buy today certainly depends on today's prices and your current income and wealth. You also have expectations about what your position will be in the future. You may have expectations about future changes in prices too, and these may affect your decisions today.

There are many examples of the ways expectations affect demand. When people buy a house or a car, they often must borrow part of the purchase price and repay it over a number of years. In deciding what kind of house or car to buy, they presumably must think about their income today, as well as what their income is likely to be in the future.

As another example, consider a student in the final year of medical school living on a scholarship of $25,000. Compare that student with another person earning $12 an hour at a full-time job, with no expectation of a significant change in income in the future. The two have virtually identical incomes. But even if they have the same tastes, the medical student is likely to demand different goods and services, simply because of the expectation of a major increase in income later on.

Increasingly, economic theory has come to recognize the importance of expectations. We will devote a good deal of time to discussing how expectations affect more than just demand. For the time being, however, it is important to understand that demand depends on more than just *current* incomes, prices, and tastes.

| Price (per Gallon) | Schedule $D_0$ Quantity Demanded (Gallons per Week at an Income of $500 per Week) | Schedule $D_1$ Quantity Demanded (Gallons per Week at an Income of $700 per Week) |
|---|---|---|
| $ 8.00 | 0 | 3 |
| 7.00 | 2 | 5 |
| 6.00 | 3 | 7 |
| 5.00 | 5 | 10 |
| 4.00 | 7 | 12 |
| 3.00 | 10 | 15 |
| 2.00 | 14 | 19 |
| 1.00 | 20 | 24 |
| 0.00 | 26 | 30 |

**TABLE 3.2** Shift of Alex's Demand Schedule Resulting from an Increase in Income

## Shift of Demand versus Movement along a Demand Curve

Recall that a demand curve shows the relationship between quantity demanded and the price of a good. Demand curves are constructed while holding income, tastes, and other prices constant. If income, tastes, or other prices change, we would have to derive an entirely new relationship between price and quantity.

Let us return once again to Alex. (See Table 3.1 and Figure 3.2 on pp. 46 and 47.) Suppose that when we derived the demand curve in Figure 3.2 Alex was receiving a salary of $500 per week after taxes. If Alex faces a price of $3.00 per gallon and chooses to drive 250 miles per week, her total weekly expenditure works out to be $3.00 per gallon times 10 gallons or $30 per week. That amounts to 6.0 percent of her income.

Suppose now she were to receive a raise to $700 per week after taxes. Alex's higher income may well raise the amount of gasoline being used by Alex *regardless* of what she was using before. The new situation is listed in Table 3.2 and graphed in Figure 3.3. Notice in Figure 3.3 that Alex's entire curve has shifted to the right—at $3.00 a gallon the curve shows an increase in the quantity demanded from 10 to 15 gallons. At $5.00, the quantity demanded by Alex increases from 5 gallons to 10 gallons.

The fact that demand *increased* when income increased implies that gasoline is a *normal good* to Alex.

▶ **FIGURE 3.3** **Shift of a Demand Curve Following a Rise in Income**

When the price of a good changes, we move *along* the demand curve for that good. When any other factor that influences demand changes (income, tastes, and so on), the demand curve shifts, in this case from $D_0$ to $D_1$. Gasoline is a normal good so an income increase shifts the curve to the right.

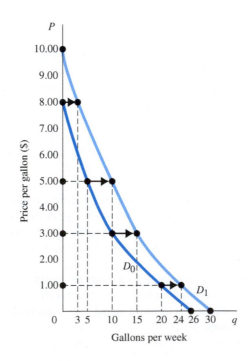

The conditions under which we drew Alex's original demand curve have now changed. One of the factors affecting Alex's demand for gasoline (in this case, her income) has changed, creating a new relationship between price and quantity demanded. This is referred to as a **shift of a demand curve.**

It is important to distinguish between a change in quantity demanded—that is, some movement *along* a demand curve—and a shift of demand. Demand schedules and demand curves show the relationship between the price of a good or service and the quantity demanded per period, ceteris paribus. If price changes, quantity demanded will change—this is a **movement along a demand curve.** When any of the *other* factors that influence demand change, however, a new relationship between price and quantity demanded is established—this is a *shift of a demand curve.* The result, then, is a *new demand curve.* Changes in income, preferences, or prices of other goods cause a demand curve to shift:

Change in price of a good or service leads to
└──▶ change in *quantity demanded* (**movement along a demand curve**).
Change in income, preferences, or prices of other goods or services leads to
└──▶ change in *demand* (**shift of a demand curve**).

Figure 3.4 illustrates the differences between movement along a demand curve and shifting demand curves. In Figure 3.4(a), an increase in household income causes demand for hamburger (an inferior good) to decline, or shift to the left from $D_0$ to $D_1$. (Because quantity is measured on the horizontal axis, a decrease means a *shift to the left.*) In contrast, demand for steak (a normal good) increases, or *shifts to the right*, when income rises.

In Figure 3.4(b), an increase in the price of hamburger from $1.49 to $3.09 a pound causes a household to buy less hamburger each month. In other words, the higher price causes the *quantity demanded* to decline from 10 pounds to 5 pounds per month. This change represents a movement *along* the demand curve for hamburger. In place of hamburger, the household buys more chicken. The household's demand for chicken (a substitute for hamburger) rises—the demand curve shifts to the right. At the same time, the demand for ketchup (a good that complements hamburger) declines—its demand curve shifts to the left.

## From Household Demand to Market Demand

So far we have been talking about what determines an individual's demand for a product. We ask the question: How many 12-packs of soda are you willing to buy per week when the price of that 12-pack is $5. This is a question you answer often in your life, whenever you go to the local store. We see the answer depends on how much money you have, how much you like soda, and what else is available to you at what price. Next time you go to the store and see a price change, we hope you think a bit more about your buying reaction.

Individual reactions to price changes are interesting, especially to the individual. But for us to be able to say something more general about prices in the market, we need to know about market demand.

**Market demand** is simply the sum of all the quantities of a good or service demanded per period by all the households buying in the market for that good or service. Figure 3.5 shows the derivation of a market demand curve from three individual demand curves. (Although this market demand curve is derived from the behavior of only three people, most markets have thousands, or even millions, of demanders.) As the table in Figure 3.5 shows, when the price of a pound of coffee is $3.50, both household A and household C would purchase 4 pounds per month, while household B would buy none. At that price, presumably, B drinks tea. Market demand at $3.50 would thus be a total of 4 + 4, or 8 pounds. At a price of $1.50 per pound, however, A would purchase 8 pounds per month; B, 3 pounds; and C, 9 pounds. Thus, at $1.50 per pound, market demand would be 8 + 3 + 9, or 20 pounds of coffee per month.

The total quantity demanded in the marketplace at a given price is the sum of all the quantities demanded by all the individual households shopping in the market *at that price.* A market demand curve shows the total amount of a product that would be sold at each price if

**shift of a demand curve** The change that takes place in a demand curve corresponding to a new relationship between quantity demanded of a good and price of that good. The shift is brought about by a change in the original conditions.

**movement along a demand curve** The change in quantity demanded brought about by a change in price.

**market demand** The sum of all the quantities of a good or service demanded per period by all the households buying in the market for that good or service.

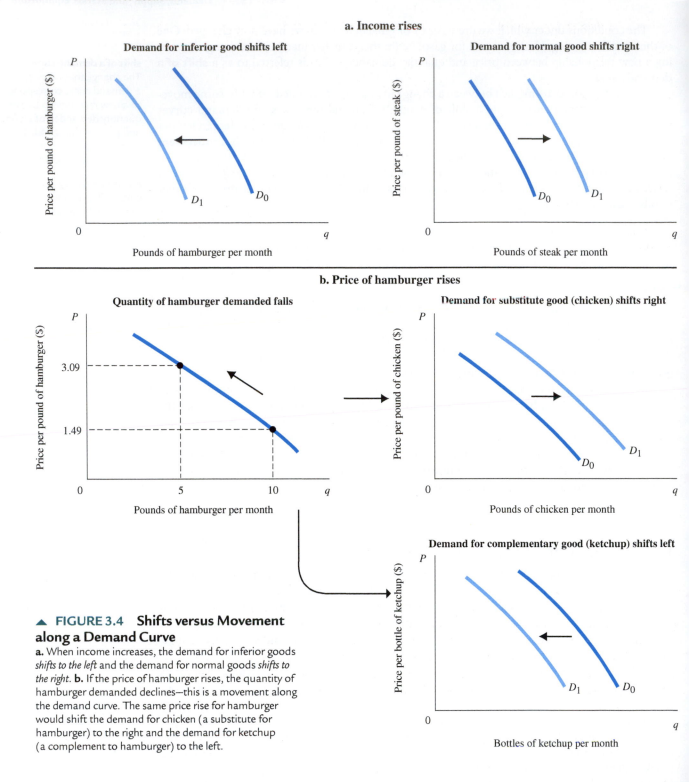

**▲ FIGURE 3.4** **Shifts versus Movement along a Demand Curve**

**a.** When income increases, the demand for inferior goods *shifts to the left* and the demand for normal goods *shifts to the right*. **b.** If the price of hamburger rises, the quantity of hamburger demanded declines—this is a movement along the demand curve. The same price rise for hamburger would shift the demand for chicken (a substitute for hamburger) to the right and the demand for ketchup (a complement to hamburger) to the left.

households could buy all they wanted at that price. As Figure 3.5 shows, the market demand curve is the sum of all the individual demand curves—that is, the sum of all the individual quantities demanded at each price. Thus, the market demand curve takes its shape and position from the shapes, positions, and number of individual demand curves. If more people are in a market, more demand curves must be added and the market demand curve will shift to the right. Market demand curves may also shift as a result of preference changes, income changes, or changes in the price of substitutes or complements.

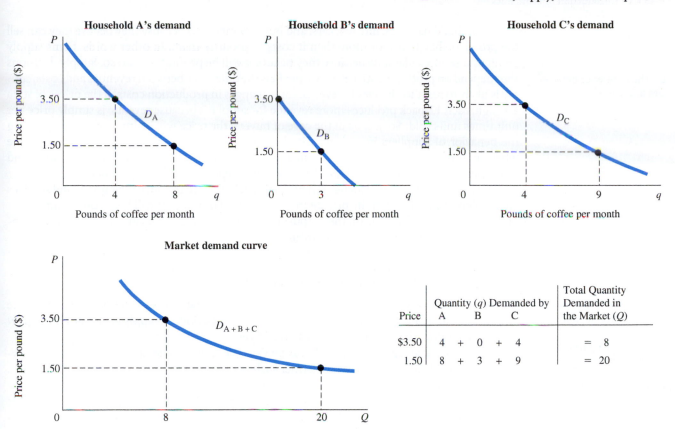

▲ FIGURE 3.5 **Deriving Market Demand from Individual Demand Curves**
Total demand in the marketplace is simply the sum of the demands of all the households shopping in a particular market. It is the sum of all the individual demand curves—that is, the sum of all the individual quantities demanded at each price.

As a general rule throughout this book, capital letters refer to the entire market and lowercase letters refer to individual households or firms. Thus, in Figure 3.5, Q refers to total quantity demanded in the market, while q refers to the quantity demanded by individual households.

An interesting feature of the demand curve in Figure 3.5 is that at different prices, the *type* of people demanding the product may change. When Apple halved the price of its iPhone in fall 2007, it announced that it wanted to make the iPhone available to a broader group of people. When prices fall, people like those in household B in Figure 3.5 move into markets that are otherwise out of their reach. When Apple introduced a new, improved, but much more expensive iPhone in the fall of 2014, its first sales were likely made to people who both had more resources and were more tech-savvy than the average old model iPhone user. Early adopters of products often look different from later users.

# Supply in Product/Output Markets

**3.4 LEARNING** OBJECTIVE
Be able to distinguish between forces that shift a supply curve and changes that cause a movement along a supply curve.

We began our exploration of supply and demand some pages back with a simple question: Why is the average price of a 12-pack of soda $5 in 2015? So far we have seen one side of the answer: Given the tastes, incomes, and substitute products available in the United States, there are a lot of people willing to pay at least $5 for a 12-pack of soda! Now we turn to the other half of the market: How can we understand the behavior of the many firms selling that soda? What determines their willingness to sell soda? We refer to this as the supply side of the market.

Firms build factories, hire workers, and buy raw materials because they believe they can sell the products they make for more than it costs to produce them. In other words, firms supply goods and services like soda because they believe it will be profitable to do so. Supply decisions thus depend on profit potential. Because **profit** is the difference between revenues and costs, supply is likely to react to changes in revenues and changes in production costs. If the prices of soda are high, each 12-pack produces more revenue for suppliers because revenue is simply price per unit times units sold. So, just as in the case of buyers, the price will be important in explaining the behavior of suppliers in a market. It also typically costs suppliers something to produce whatever product they are bringing to market. They have to hire workers, build factories, and buy inputs. So the supply behavior of firms will also depend on costs of production.

In later chapters, we will focus on how firms decide *how* to produce their goods and services and explore the cost side of the picture more formally. For now, we will begin our examination of firm behavior by focusing on the output supply decision and the relationship between quantity supplied and output price, *ceteris paribus*.

## Price and Quantity Supplied: The Law of Supply

**Quantity supplied** is the amount of a particular product that firms would be willing and able to offer for sale at a particular price during a given time period. A **supply schedule** shows how much of a product firms will sell at alternative prices.

Let us look at an agricultural market as an example. Table 3.3 itemizes the quantities of soybeans that an individual representative farmer such as Clarence Brown might sell at various prices. If the market paid $1.50 or less for a bushel for soybeans, Brown would not supply any soybeans: When Farmer Brown looks at the costs of growing soybeans, including the opportunity cost of his time and land, $1.50 per bushel will not compensate him for those costs. At $1.75 per bushel, however, at least some soybean production takes place on Brown's farm, and a price increase from $1.75 to $2.25 per bushel causes the quantity supplied by Brown to increase from 10,000 to 20,000 bushels per year. The higher price may justify shifting land from wheat to soybean production or putting previously fallow land into soybeans, or it may lead to more intensive farming of land already in soybeans, using expensive fertilizer or equipment that was not cost-justified at the lower price.

Generalizing from Farmer Brown's experience, we can reasonably expect an increase in market price, ceteris paribus, to lead to an increase in quantity supplied for Brown and farmers like him. In other words, there is a positive relationship between the quantity of a good supplied and price. This statement sums up the **law of supply**: An increase in market price will lead to an increase in quantity supplied, and a decrease in market price will lead to a decrease in quantity supplied.

The information in a supply schedule may be presented graphically in a **supply curve**. Supply curves slope upward. The upward, or positive, slope of Brown's curve in Figure 3.6 reflects this positive relationship between price and quantity supplied.

Note in Brown's supply schedule, however, that when price rises from $4 to $5, quantity supplied no longer increases. Often an individual firm's ability to respond to an increase in price is constrained by its existing scale of operations, or capacity, in the short run. For example, Brown's ability to produce more soybeans depends on the size of his farm, the fertility of his soil, and the types of equipment he has. The fact that output stays constant at 45,000 bushels per year suggests that he is running up against the limits imposed by the size of his farm, the quality of his soil, and his existing technology.

**profit** The difference between revenues and costs.

**quantity supplied** The amount of a particular product that a firm would be willing and able to offer for sale at a particular price during a given time period.

**supply schedule** Shows how much of a product firms will sell at alternative prices.

**law of supply** The positive relationship between price and quantity of a good supplied: An increase in market price, ceteris paribus, will lead to an increase in quantity supplied, and a decrease in market price will lead to a decrease in quantity supplied.

**supply curve** A graph illustrating how much of a product a firm will sell at different prices.

| TABLE 3.3 | Clarence Brown's Supply Schedule for Soybeans |
|---|---|
| Price (per Bushel) | Quantity Supplied (Bushels per Year) |
| $ 1.50 | 0 |
| 1.75 | 10,000 |
| 2.25 | 20,000 |
| 3.00 | 30,000 |
| 4.00 | 45,000 |
| 5.00 | 45,000 |

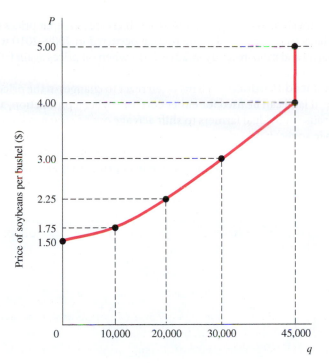

Bushels of soybeans produced per year

◀ **FIGURE 3.6   Clarence Brown's Individual Supply Curve**
A producer will supply more when the price of output is higher. The slope of a supply curve is positive. Note that the supply curve is red: Supply is determined by choices made by firms.

In the longer run, however, Brown may acquire more land or technology may change, allowing for more soybean production. The terms *short run and long run* have precise meanings in economics; we will discuss them in detail later. Here it is important only to understand that time plays a critical role in supply decisions. When prices change, firms' immediate response may be different from what they are able to do after a month or a year. Short-run and long-run supply curves are often different.

## Other Determinants of Supply

Of the factors we have listed that are likely to affect the quantity of output supplied by a given firm, we have thus far discussed only the price of output. Other factors that affect supply include the cost of producing the product and the prices of related products.

**The Cost of Production**    For a firm to make a profit, its revenue must exceed its costs. As an individual producer, like Farmer Brown, thinks about how much to supply at a particular price, the producer will be looking at his or her costs. Brown's supply decision is likely to change in response to changes in the cost of production. Cost of production depends on a number of factors, including the available technologies and the prices and quantities of the inputs needed by the firm (labor, land, capital, energy, and so on).

Technological change can have an enormous impact on the cost of production over time. The introduction of fertilizers, the development of complex farm machinery, and the use of bioengineering to increase the yield of individual crops have all powerfully affected the cost of producing agricultural products. Technology has similarly decreased the costs of producing flat screen televisions. When a technological advance lowers the cost of production, output is likely to increase. When yield per acre increases, individual farmers can and do produce more. The production of electronic calculators, and later personal computers and smartphones, boomed with the development of inexpensive techniques to produce microprocessors.

Cost of production is also directly affected by the price of the factors of production. In the spring of 2008, the world price of oil rose to more than $100 per barrel from below $20 in 2002. As a result, cab drivers faced higher gasoline prices, airlines faced higher fuel costs, and manufacturing firms faced higher heating bills. The result: Cab drivers probably spent less time driving around looking for customers, airlines cut a few low-profit routes, and some manufacturing plants stopped running extra shifts. The moral of this story: Increases in input prices raise costs of production and are likely to reduce supply. The reverse occurred in 2009–2010 when oil prices fell back to $75 per barrel and more recently in 2014-2015 when oil prices again fell.

**The Prices of Related Products**   Firms often react to changes in the prices of related products. For example, if land can be used for either corn or soybean production, an increase in soybean prices may cause individual farmers to shift acreage out of corn production into soybeans. Thus, an increase in soybean prices actually affects the amount of corn supplied.

Similarly, if beef prices rise, producers may respond by raising more cattle. However, leather comes from cowhide. Thus, an increase in beef prices may actually increase the supply of leather.

To summarize:

> Assuming that its objective is to maximize profits, a firm's decision about what quantity of output, or product, to supply depends on:
>
> 1. The price of the good or service.
> 2. The cost of producing the product, which in turn depends on:
>    - the price of required inputs (labor, capital, and land), and
>    - the technologies that can be used to produce the product.
> 3. The prices of related products.

## Shift of Supply versus Movement along a Supply Curve

A supply curve shows the relationship between the quantity of a good or service supplied by a firm and the price that good or service brings in the market. Higher prices are likely to lead to an increase in quantity supplied, ceteris paribus. Remember: The supply curve is derived holding everything constant except price. When the price of a product changes ceteris paribus, a change in the quantity supplied follows—that is, a **movement along a supply curve** takes place. As you have seen, supply decisions are also influenced by factors other than price. New relationships between price and quantity supplied come about when factors other than price change, and the result is a **shift of a supply curve**. When factors other than price cause supply curves to shift, we say that there has been a *change in supply*.

Recall that the cost of production depends on the price of inputs and the technologies of production available. Now suppose that a major breakthrough in the production of soybeans has occurred: Genetic engineering has produced a superstrain of disease- and pest-resistant seed. Such a technological change would enable individual farmers to supply more soybeans at *any* market price. Table 3.4 and Figure 3.7 describe this change. At $3 a bushel, farmers would have produced 30,000 bushels from the old seed (schedule $S_0$ in Table 3.4); with the lower cost of production and higher yield resulting from the new seed, they produce 40,000 bushels (schedule $S_1$ in Table 3.4). At $1.75 per bushel, they would have produced 10,000 bushels from the old seed; but with the lower costs and higher yields, output rises to 23,000 bushels.

**movement along a supply curve**   The change in quantity supplied brought about by a change in price.

**shift of a supply curve**   The change that takes place in a supply curve corresponding to a new relationship between quantity supplied of a good and the price of that good. The shift is brought about by a change in the original conditions.

| TABLE 3.4 | Shift of Supply Schedule for Soybeans following Development of a New Disease-Resistant Seed Strain | |
|---|---|---|
| | Schedule $S_0$ | Schedule $S_1$ |
| Price (per Bushel) | Quantity Supplied (Bushels per Year Using Old Seed) | Quantity Supplied (Bushels per Year Using New Seed) |
| $ 1.50 | 0 | 5,000 |
| 1.75 | 10,000 | 23,000 |
| 2.25 | 20,000 | 33,000 |
| 3.00 | 30,000 | 40,000 |
| 4.00 | 45,000 | 54,000 |
| 5.00 | 45,000 | 54,000 |

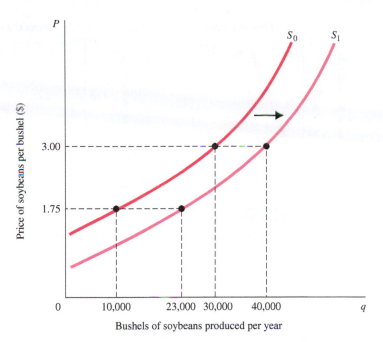

◀ **FIGURE 3.7** **Shift of the Supply Curve for Soybeans Following Development of a New Seed Strain**
When the price of a product changes, we move *along* the supply curve for that product; the quantity supplied rises or falls. When any other factor affecting supply changes, the supply curve *shifts*.

Increases in input prices may also cause supply curves to shift. If Farmer Brown faces higher fuel costs, for example, his supply curve will shift to the left—that is, he will produce less at any given market price. As Brown's soybean supply curve shifts to the left, it intersects the price axis at a higher point, meaning that it would take a higher market price to induce Brown to produce any soybeans at all.

As with demand, it is important to distinguish between *movements along* supply curves (changes in quantity supplied) and *shifts in* supply curves (changes in supply):

Change in price of a good or service leads to
   ⟶ change in *quantity supplied* (**movement along a supply curve**).
Change in costs, input prices, technology, or prices of related goods and services leads to
   ⟶ change in *supply* (**shift of a supply curve**).

# From Individual Supply to Market Supply

So far we have focused on the supply behavior of a single producer. For most markets many, many suppliers bring product to the consumer, and it is the behavior of all of those producers together that determines supply.

**Market supply** is determined in the same fashion as market demand. It is simply the sum of all that is supplied each period by all producers of a single product. Figure 3.8 derives a market supply curve from the supply curves of three individual firms. (In a market with more firms, total market supply would be the sum of the amounts produced by each of the firms in that market.) As the table in Figure 3.8 shows, at a price of $3, farm A supplies 30,000 bushels of soybeans, farm B supplies 10,000 bushels, and farm C supplies 25,000 bushels. At this price, the total amount supplied in the market is 30,000 + 10,000 + 25,000, or 65,000 bushels. At a price of $1.75, however, the total amount supplied is only 25,000 bushels (10,000 + 5,000 + 10,000). Thus, the market supply curve is the simple addition of the individual supply curves of all the firms in a particular market—that is, the sum of all the individual quantities supplied at each price.

The position and shape of the market supply curve depends on the positions and shapes of the individual firms' supply curves from which it is derived. The market supply curve also depends on the number of firms that produce in that market. If firms that produce for a particular market are earning high profits, other firms may be tempted to go into that line of business. The popularity and profitability of professional football has, three times, led to the formation of new leagues. When new firms enter an industry, the supply curve shifts to the right. When firms go out of business, or "exit" the market, the supply curve shifts to the left.

**market supply** The sum of all that is supplied each period by all producers of a single product.

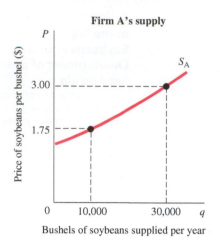

**Firm A's supply**

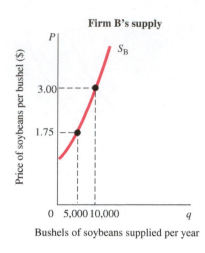

**Firm B's supply**

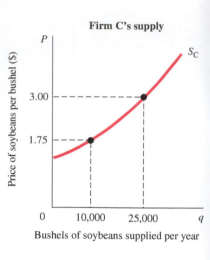

**Firm C's supply**

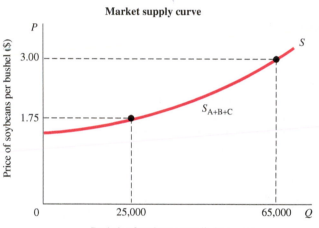

**Market supply curve**

| Price | Quantity (*q*) Supplied by | | | | Total Quantity Supplied in the Market (*Q*) |
|-------|------|------|------|---|--------|
| | A | B | C | | |
| $3.00 | 30,000 + | 10,000 + | 25,000 | = | 65,000 |
| 1.75 | 10,000 + | 5,000 + | 10,000 | = | 25,000 |

▲ **FIGURE 3.8** **Deriving Market Supply from Individual Firm Supply Curves**
Total supply in the marketplace is the sum of all the amounts supplied by all the firms selling in the market.
It is the sum of all the individual quantities supplied at each price.

---

Be able to explain how a market that is not in equilibrium responds to restore an equilibrium.

**equilibrium** The condition that exists when quantity supplied and quantity demanded are equal. At equilibrium, there is no tendency for price to change.

**excess demand or shortage** The condition that exists when quantity demanded exceeds quantity supplied at the current price.

# Market Equilibrium

So far, we have identified a number of factors that influence the amount that households demand and the amount that firms supply in product (output) markets. The discussion has emphasized the role of market price as a determinant of both quantity demanded and quantity supplied. We are now ready to see how supply and demand in the market interact to determine the final market price.

In our discussions, we have separated household decisions about how much to demand from firm decisions about how much to supply. The operation of the market, however, clearly depends on the interaction between suppliers and demanders. At any moment, one of three conditions prevails in every market: (1) The quantity demanded exceeds the quantity supplied at the current price, a situation called *excess demand*; (2) the quantity supplied exceeds the quantity demanded at the current price, a situation called *excess supply*; or (3) the quantity supplied equals the quantity demanded at the current price, a situation called **equilibrium**. At equilibrium, no tendency for price to change exists.

## Excess Demand

**Excess demand, or a shortage**, exists when quantity demanded is greater than quantity supplied at the current price. Figure 3.9, which plots both a supply curve and a demand curve on the same graph, illustrates such a situation. As you can see, market demand at

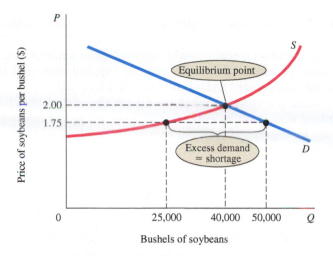

▲ **FIGURE 3.9   Excess Demand, or Shortage**
At a price of $1.75 per bushel, quantity demanded exceeds quantity supplied. When *excess demand* exists, there is a tendency for price to rise. When quantity demanded equals quantity supplied, excess demand is eliminated and the market is in equilibrium. Here the equilibrium price is $2.00 and the equilibrium quantity is 40,000 bushels.

$1.75 per bushel (50,000 bushels) exceeds the amount that farmers are currently supplying (25,000 bushels).

When excess demand occurs in an unregulated market, there is a tendency for price to rise as demanders compete against each other for the limited supply. The adjustment mechanisms may differ, but the outcome is always the same. For example, consider the mechanism of an auction. In an auction, items are sold directly to the highest bidder. When the auctioneer starts the bidding at a low price, many people bid for the item. At first, there is a shortage: Quantity demanded exceeds quantity supplied. As would-be buyers offer higher and higher prices, bidders drop out until the one who offers the most ends up with the item being auctioned. Price rises until quantity demanded and quantity supplied are equal.

At a price of $1.75 (see Figure 3.9 again), farmers produce soybeans at a rate of 25,000 bushels per year, but at that price, the demand is for 50,000 bushels. Most farm products are sold to local dealers who in turn sell large quantities in major market centers, where bidding would push prices up if quantity demanded exceeded quantity supplied. As price rises above $1.75, two things happen: (1) The quantity demanded falls as buyers drop out of the market and perhaps choose a substitute, and (2) the quantity supplied increases as farmers find themselves receiving a higher price for their product and shift additional acres into soybean production.[4]

This process continues until the shortage is eliminated. In Figure 3.9, this occurs at $2.00, where quantity demanded has fallen from 50,000 to 40,000 bushels per year and quantity supplied has increased from 25,000 to 40,000 bushels per year. When quantity demanded and quantity supplied are equal and there is no further bidding, the process has achieved an equilibrium, a situation in which *there is no natural tendency for further adjustment*. Graphically, the point of equilibrium is the point at which the supply curve and the demand curve intersect.

Increasingly, items are auctioned over the Internet. Companies such as eBay connect buyers and sellers of everything from automobiles to wine and from computers to airline tickets. Auctions are occurring simultaneously with participants located across the globe. The principles

---

[4] Once farmers have produced in any given season, they cannot change their minds and produce more, of course. When we derived Clarence Brown's supply schedule in Table 3.3, we imagined him reacting to prices that existed at the time he decided how much land to plant in soybeans. In Figure 3.9, the upward slope shows that higher prices justify shifting land from other crops. Final price may not be determined until final production figures are in. For our purposes here, however, we have ignored this timing problem. The best way to think about it is that demand and supply are *flows*, or *rates*, of production—that is, we are talking about the number of bushels produced *per production period*. Adjustments in the rate of production may take place over a number of production periods.

through which prices are determined in these auctions are the same: When excess demand exists, prices rise.

When quantity demanded exceeds quantity supplied, price tends to rise. When the price in a market rises, quantity demanded falls and quantity supplied rises until an equilibrium is reached at which quantity demanded and quantity supplied are equal.

This process is called *price rationing*. When the market operates without interference, price increases will distribute what is available to those who are willing and able to pay the most. As long as there is a way for buyers and sellers to interact, those who are willing to pay more will make that fact known somehow. (We discuss the nature of the price system as a rationing device in detail in Chapter 4.)

## Excess Supply

**excess supply *or* surplus**
The condition that exists when quantity supplied exceeds quantity demanded at the current price.

**Excess supply, *or* a surplus**, exists when the quantity supplied exceeds the quantity demanded at the current price. As with a shortage, the mechanics of price adjustment in the face of a surplus can differ from market to market. For example, if automobile dealers find themselves with unsold cars in the fall when the new models are coming in, you can expect to see price cuts. Sometimes dealers offer discounts to encourage buyers; sometimes buyers themselves simply offer less than the price initially asked. After Christmas, most stores have big sales during which they lower the prices of overstocked items. Quantities supplied exceeded quantities demanded at the current prices, so stores cut prices. Many Web sites exist that do little more than sell at a discount clothing and other goods that failed to sell at full price during the past season.

Figure 3.10 illustrates another excess supply/surplus situation. At a price of $3 per bushel, suppose farmers are supplying soybeans at a rate of 65,000 bushels per year, but buyers are demanding only 25,000. With 40,000 bushels of soybeans going unsold, the market price falls. As price falls from $3.00 to $2.00, quantity supplied decreases from 65,000 bushels per year to 40,000. The lower price causes quantity demanded to rise from 25,000 to 40,000. At $2.00, quantity demanded and quantity supplied are equal. For the data shown here, $2.00 and 40,000 bushels are the equilibrium price and quantity, respectively.

Although the mechanism by which price is adjusted differs across markets, the outcome is the same:

> When quantity supplied exceeds quantity demanded at the current price, the price tends to fall. When price falls, quantity supplied is likely to decrease and quantity demanded is likely to increase until an equilibrium price is reached where quantity supplied and quantity demanded are equal.

▶ **FIGURE 3.10** **Excess Supply or Surplus**
At a price of $3.00, quantity supplied exceeds quantity demanded by 40,000 bushels. This excess supply will cause the price to fall.

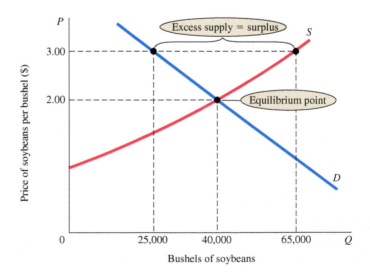

# Changes in Equilibrium

When supply and demand curves shift, the equilibrium price and quantity change. The following example will help to illustrate this point and show us how equilibrium is restored in markets in which either demand or supply changes.

South America is a major producer of coffee beans. In the mid-1990s, a major freeze hit Brazil and Colombia and drove up the price of coffee on world markets to a record $2.40 per pound. Bad weather in Colombia in 2005 and more recently in 2012 caused similar shifts in supply.

Figure 3.11 illustrates how the freezes pushed up coffee prices. Initially, the market was in equilibrium at a price of $1.20. At that price, the quantity demanded was equal to quantity supplied (13.2 billion pounds). At a price of $1.20 and a quantity of 13.2 billion pounds, the demand curve (labeled $D$) intersected the initial supply curve (labeled $S_0$). (Remember that equilibrium exists when quantity demanded equals quantity supplied—the point at which the supply and demand curves intersect.)

The freeze caused a decrease in the supply of coffee beans. That is, the freeze caused the supply curve to shift to the left. In Figure 3.11, the new supply curve (the supply curve that shows the relationship between price and quantity supplied after the freeze) is labeled $S_1$.

At the initial equilibrium price, $1.20, there is now a shortage of coffee. If the price were to remain at $1.20, quantity demanded would not change; it would remain at 13.2 billion pounds. However, at that price, quantity supplied would drop to 6.6 billion pounds. At a price of $1.20, quantity demanded is greater than quantity supplied.

When excess demand exists in a market, price can be expected to rise, and rise it did. As the figure shows, price rose to a new equilibrium at $2.40. At $2.40, quantity demanded is again equal to quantity supplied, this time at 9.9 billion pounds—the point at which the new supply curve ($S_1$) intersects the demand curve.

Notice that as the price of coffee rose from $1.20 to $2.40, two things happened. First, the quantity demanded declined (a movement along the demand curve) as people shifted to substitutes such as tea and hot cocoa. Second, the quantity supplied began to rise, but within the limits imposed by the damage from the freeze. (It might also be that some countries or areas with high costs of production, previously unprofitable, came into production and shipped to

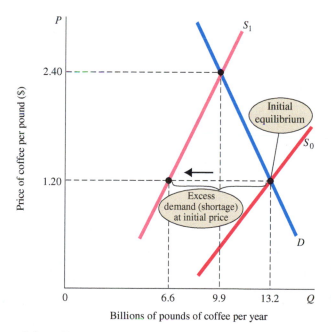

▲ **FIGURE 3.11** **The Coffee Market: A Shift of Supply and Subsequent Price Adjustment**
Before the freeze, the coffee market was in equilibrium at a price of $1.20 per pound. At that price, quantity demanded equaled quantity supplied. The freeze shifted the supply curve to the left (from $S_0$ to $S_1$), increasing the equilibrium price to $2.40.

the world market at the higher price.) That is, the quantity supplied increased in response to the higher price *along* the new supply curve, which lies to the left of the old supply curve. The final result was a higher price ($2.40), a smaller quantity finally exchanged in the market (9.9 billion pounds), and coffee bought only by those willing to pay $2.40 per pound.

Figure 3.12 summarizes the possible supply and demand shifts that have been discussed and the resulting changes in equilibrium price and quantity. Study the graphs carefully to ensure that you understand them.

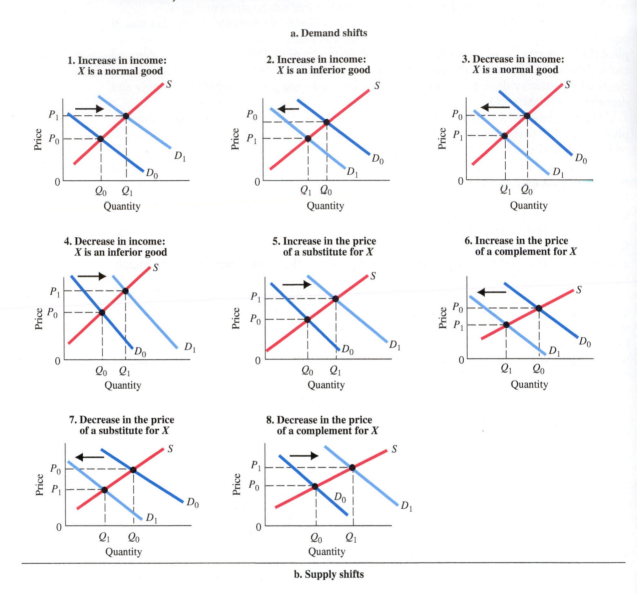

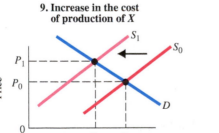

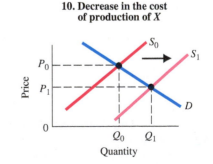

▲ **FIGURE 3.12** **Examples of Supply and Demand Shifts for Product X**

# ECONOMICS IN PRACTICE

## Quinoa

Those of you who follow a vegetarian diet, or even those of you who are foodies, likely have had quinoa sometime within the last few months. Once eaten mostly by people in Peru and Bolivia, and a reputed favorite of the Incas, quinoa, a high-protein grain, has found a large market among food aficionados. Growth in vegetarianism effectively shifted the demand curve for quinoa to the right.

With an upward sloping supply curve, this shift in demand resulted in increased prices. Farmers grew richer, whereas some local consumers found themselves facing higher prices for a staple product. Over time, these higher prices encouraged more farmers to enter the quinoa market. This shifted the supply curve to the right, helping to moderate the price increases. But quinoa growing turns out to be a tricky affair. Quinoa grows best in high altitudes with cold climates. It thrives on soil fertilized by the dung of herds of llama and sheep. Thus, while supply clearly shifted with new farmer entry, the particular nature of the production process limited that shift and in the end, despite the supply response, prices increased.

### THINKING PRACTICALLY

1. Use a graph to show the movement in prices and quantities described in the quinoa market.

# Demand and Supply in Product Markets: A Review

As you continue your study of economics, you will discover that it is a discipline full of controversy and debate. There is, however, little disagreement about the basic way that the forces of supply and demand operate in free markets. If you hear that a freeze in Florida has destroyed a good portion of the citrus crop, you can bet that the price of oranges will rise. If you read that the weather in the Midwest has been good and a record corn crop is expected, you can bet that corn prices will fall. When fishermen in Massachusetts go on strike and stop bringing in the daily catch, you can bet that the price of local fish will go up.

Here are some important points to remember about the mechanics of supply and demand in product markets:

1. A demand curve shows how much of a product a household would buy if it could buy all it wanted at the given price. A supply curve shows how much of a product a firm would supply if it could sell all it wanted at the given price.
2. Quantity demanded and quantity supplied are always per time period—that is, per day, per month, or per year.
3. The demand for a good is determined by price, household income and wealth, prices of other goods and services, tastes and preferences, and expectations.
4. The supply of a good is determined by price, costs of production, and prices of related products. Costs of production are determined by available technologies of production and input prices.
5. Be careful to distinguish between movements along supply and demand curves and shifts of these curves. When the price of a good changes, the quantity of that good demanded or supplied changes—that is, a movement occurs along the curve. When any other factor that affects supply or demand changes, the curve shifts, or changes position.
6. Market equilibrium exists only when quantity supplied equals quantity demanded at the current price.

## ECONOMICS IN PRACTICE

# Why Do the Prices of Newspapers Rise?

In 2006, the average price for a daily edition of a Baltimore newspaper was $0.50. In 2007, the average price had risen to $0.75. Three different analysts have three different explanations for the higher equilibrium price.

Analyst 1: The higher price for Baltimore newspapers is good news because it means the population is better informed about public issues. These data clearly show that the citizens of Baltimore have a new, increased regard for newspapers.

Analyst 2: The higher price for Baltimore newspapers is bad news for the citizens of Baltimore. The higher cost of paper, ink, and distribution reflected in these higher prices will further diminish the population's awareness of public issues.

Analyst 3: The higher price for Baltimore newspapers is an unfortunate result of newspapers trying to make money as many consumers have turned to the Internet to access news coverage for free.

As economists, we are faced with two tasks in looking at these explanations: Do they make sense based on what we know about economic principles? And if they do make sense, can we figure out which explanation applies to the case of rising newspaper prices in Baltimore?

What is Analyst 1 saying? Her observation about consumers' new increased regard for newspapers tells us something about the demand curve. Analyst 1 seems to be arguing that tastes have changed in favor of newspapers, which would mean a shift in the demand curve to the right. With upward-sloping supply, such a shift would produce a price increase. So Analyst 1's story is plausible.

Analyst 2 refers to an increased cost of newsprint. This would cause production costs of newspapers to rise, shifting the supply curve to the left. A downward-sloping demand curve also results in increased prices. So Analyst 2 also has a plausible story.

Since Analyst 1 and Analyst 2 have plausible stories based on economic principles, we can look at evidence to see who is in fact right. If you go back to the graphs in Figure 3.12 on p. 64, you will find a clue. When demand shifts to the right (as in Analyst 1's story) the price rises, but so does the quantity as shown in Figure (a). When supply shifts to the left (as in Analyst 2's story) the price rises, but the quantity falls as shown in Figure (b). So we would look at what happened to newspaper circulation during this period to see whether the price increase is from the demand side or the supply side. In fact, in most markets, including Baltimore, quantities of newspapers bought have been falling, so Analyst 2 is most likely correct.

But be careful. Both analysts may be correct. If demand shifts to the right and supply shifts to the left by a greater amount, the price will rise and the quantity sold will fall.

What about Analyst 3? Analyst 3 clearly never had an economics course! Free Internet access to news is a substitute for print media. A decrease in the price of this substitute should shift the demand for newspapers to the left. The result should be a lower price, not a price increase. The fact that the newspaper publishers are "trying to make money" faced with this new competition does not change the laws of supply and demand.

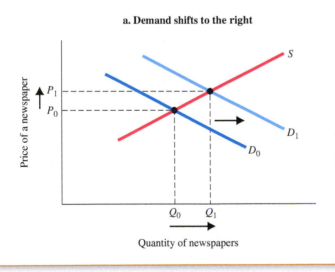

**a. Demand shifts to the right**

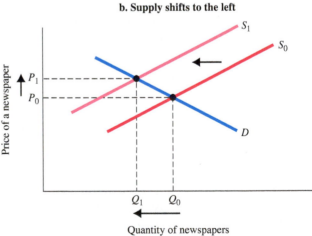

**b. Supply shifts to the left**

# Looking Ahead: Markets and the Allocation of Resources

You can already begin to see how markets answer the basic economic questions of what is produced, how it is produced, and who gets what is produced. A firm will produce what is profitable to produce. If the firm can sell a product at a price that is sufficient to ensure a profit after production costs are paid, it will in all likelihood produce that product. Resources will flow in the direction of profit opportunities.

■ Demand curves reflect what people are willing and able to pay for products; demand curves are influenced by incomes, wealth, preferences, prices of other goods, and expectations. Because product prices are determined by the interaction of supply and demand, prices reflect what people are willing to pay. If people's preferences or incomes change, resources will be allocated differently. Consider, for example, an increase in demand—a shift in the market demand curve. Beginning at an equilibrium, households simply begin buying more. At the equilibrium price, quantity demanded becomes greater than quantity supplied. When there is excess demand, prices will rise, and higher prices mean higher profits for firms in the industry. Higher profits, in turn, provide existing firms with an incentive to expand and new firms with an incentive to enter the industry. Thus, the decisions of independent private firms responding to prices and profit opportunities determine *what* will be *produced*. No central direction is necessary.

   Adam Smith saw this self-regulating feature of markets more than 200 years ago:

   > Every individual…by pursuing his own interest…promotes that of society. He is led…by an invisible hand to promote an end which was no part of his intention.[5]

   The term Smith coined, the *invisible hand*, has passed into common parlance and is still used by economists to refer to the self-regulation of markets.

■ Firms in business to make a profit have a good reason to choose the best available technology—lower costs mean higher profits. Thus, individual firms determine *how* to produce their products, again with no central direction.

■ So far, we have barely touched on the question of distribution—*who* gets what is produced? You can see part of the answer in the simple supply and demand diagrams. When a good is in short supply, price rises. As they do, those who are willing and able to continue buying do so; others stop buying.

   The next chapter begins with a more detailed discussion of these topics. How, exactly, is the final allocation of resources (the mix of output and the distribution of output) determined in a market system?

---

[5] Adam Smith, *The Wealth of Nations*, Modern Library Edition (New York: Random House, 1937), p. 456 (1st ed., 1776).

---

# SUMMARY

1. In societies with many people, production must satisfy wide-ranging tastes and preferences, and producers must therefore specialize.

## 3.1 FIRMS AND HOUSEHOLDS: THE BASIC DECISION-MAKING UNITS *p. 43*

2. A *firm* exists when a person or a group of people decides to produce a product or products by transforming resources, or *inputs*, into *outputs*—the products that are sold in the market. Firms are the primary producing units in a market economy. We assume that firms make decisions to try to maximize profits.

3. *Households* are the primary consuming units in an economy. All households' incomes are subject to constraints.

## 3.2 INPUT MARKETS AND OUTPUT MARKETS: THE CIRCULAR FLOW *p. 43*

4. Households and firms interact in two basic kinds of markets: *product or output markets* and *input or factor markets*. Goods and services intended for use by households are exchanged in output markets. In output markets, competing firms supply and competing households demand. In input markets, competing firms demand and competing households supply.

**MyEconLab** Visit **www.myeconlab.com** to complete these exercises online and get instant feedback. Exercises that update with real-time data are marked with art 🔴.

5. Ultimately, firms choose the quantities and character of outputs produced, the types and quantities of inputs demanded, and the technologies used in production. Households choose the types and quantities of products demanded and the types and quantities of inputs supplied.

## 3.3 DEMAND IN PRODUCT/OUTPUT MARKETS  *p. 45*

6. The quantity demanded of an individual product by an individual household depends on (1) price, (2) income, (3) wealth, (4) prices of other products, (5) tastes and preferences, and (6) expectations about the future.

7. *Quantity demanded* is the amount of a product that an individual household would buy in a given period if it could buy all that it wanted at the current price.

8. A *demand schedule* shows the quantities of a product that a household would buy at different prices. The same information can be presented graphically in a *demand curve.*

9. The *law of demand* states that there is a negative relationship between price and quantity demanded *ceteris paribus*: As price rises, quantity demanded decreases and vice versa. Demand curves slope downward.

10. All demand curves eventually intersect the price axis because there is always a price above which a household cannot or will not pay. Also, all demand curves eventually intersect the quantity axis because demand for most goods is limited, if only by time, even at a zero price.

11. When an increase in income causes demand for a good to rise, that good is a *normal good*. When an increase in income causes demand for a good to fall, that good is an *inferior good.*

12. If a rise in the price of good X causes demand for good Y to increase, the goods are *substitutes*. If a rise in the price of X causes demand for Y to fall, the goods are *complements.*

13. *Market demand* is simply the sum of all the quantities of a good or service demanded per period by all the households buying in the market for that good or service. It is the sum of all the individual quantities demanded at each price.

## 3.4 SUPPLY IN PRODUCT/OUTPUT MARKETS  *p. 55*

14. *Quantity supplied* by a firm depends on (1) the price of the good or service; (2) the cost of producing the product, which includes the prices of required inputs and the technologies that can be used to produce the product; and (3) the prices of related products.

15. *Market supply* is the sum of all that is supplied in each period by all producers of a single product. It is the sum of all the individual quantities supplied at each price.

16. It is important to distinguish between *movements* along demand and supply curves and *shifts* of demand and supply curves. The demand curve shows the relationship between price and quantity demanded. The supply curve shows the relationship between price and quantity supplied. A change in price is a movement along the curve. Changes in tastes, income, wealth, expectations, or prices of other goods and services cause demand curves to shift; changes in costs, input prices, technology, or prices of related goods and services cause supply curves to shift.

## 3.5 MARKET EQUILIBRIUM  *p. 60*

17. When quantity demanded exceeds quantity supplied at the current price, *excess demand* (or a *shortage*) exists and the price tends to rise. When prices in a market rise, quantity demanded falls and quantity supplied rises until an equilibrium is reached at which quantity supplied and quantity demanded are equal. At *equilibrium*, there is no further tendency for price to change.

18. When quantity supplied exceeds quantity demanded at the current price, *excess supply* (or a *surplus*) exists and the price tends to fall. When price falls, quantity supplied decreases and quantity demanded increases until an equilibrium price is reached where quantity supplied and quantity demanded are equal.

—————— **REVIEW TERMS AND CONCEPTS** ——————

capital market, *p. 44*
complements, complementary goods, *p. 49*
demand curve, *p. 47*
demand schedule, *p. 46*
entrepreneur, *p. 43*
equilibrium, *p. 60*
excess demand *or* shortage, *p. 60*
excess supply *or* surplus, *p. 62*
factors of production, *p. 44*
firm, *p. 43*
households, *p. 43*
income, *p. 49*

inferior goods, *p. 49*
input *or* factor markets, *p. 44*
labor market, *p. 44*
land market, *p. 44*
law of demand, *p. 47*
law of supply, *p. 56*
market demand, *p. 53*
market supply, *p. 59*
movement along a demand curve, *p. 53*
movement along a supply curve, *p. 58*
normal goods, *p. 49*
perfect substitutes, *p. 49*

product *or* output markets, *p. 44*
profit, *p. 56*
quantity demanded, *p. 45*
quantity supplied, *p. 56*
shift of a demand curve, *p. 53*
shift of a supply curve, *p. 58*
substitutes, *p. 49*
supply curve, *p. 56*
supply schedule, *p. 56*
wealth *or* net worth, *p. 49*

**MyEconLab** Visit **www.myeconlab.com** to complete these exercises online and get instant feedback. Exercises that update with real-time data are marked with art 🔴 .

# PROBLEMS

All problems are available on MyEconLab.

## 3.1 FIRMS AND HOUSEHOLDS: THE BASIC DECISION-MAKING UNITS

LEARNING OBJECTIVE: Understand the roles of firms, entrepreneurs, and households in the market.

1.1 List three examples of entrepreneurs in the tech industry and the firms they created. Explain how these people fit the definition of entrepreneur.

## 3.2 INPUT MARKETS AND OUTPUT MARKETS: THE CIRCULAR FLOW

LEARNING OBJECTIVE: Understand the role of households as both suppliers to firms and buyers of what firms produce.

2.1 Identify whether each of the following transactions will take place in an input market or in an output market, and whether firms or households are demanding the good or service or supplying the good or service.
   a. Anderson works 37 hours each week as a clerk at the county courthouse.
   b. Mei Lin purchases a 3-week Mediterranean cruise vacation for her parents.
   c. Caterpillar doubles employment at its Huntsville, Alabama factory.
   d. The Greyson family sells their 250-acre ranch to Marriott so it can build a new resort and golf course.

## 3.3 DEMAND IN PRODUCT/ OUTPUT MARKETS

LEARNING OBJECTIVE: Understand what determines the position and shape of the demand curve and what factors move you along a demand curve and what factors shift the demand curve.

3.1 [Related to the *Economics in Practice* on p. 50] Merchandise sales for professional sports leagues is a multibillion dollar business, and leagues such as the NBA, NFL, and MLB have strict licensing rules for official league merchandise. Suppose you are a huge NBA fan and wish to purchase an authentic NBA jersey in large. Go to the NBA Store's Website at store.nba.com and click on "Jerseys." Select a team and then click on "Authentic" and find the price of the jerseys. Do the same for two other teams. Would the jerseys you found be considered perfect substitutes or just substitutes? Why? Do you think there are other products available that would be considered substitute products for the authentic jerseys you looked up? Briefly explain.

3.2 Explain whether each of the following statements describes a change in demand or a change in quantity demanded, and specify whether each change represents an increase or a decrease.
   a. Julio believes the price of tires will rise next month, so he purchases a set of 4 for his pickup truck today.

   b. After an article is published asserting that eating kale causes hair loss, sales of kale drop by 75 percent.
   c. The Oink-N-Chew company experiences a significant decline in sales when it doubles the price of its bacon-flavored bubblegum.
   d. An increase in the federal minimum wage results in a decline in sales of fast food.
   e. An unexpected decrease in the price of peanut butter results in an increase in banana sales.

3.3 For each of the five statements (a–e) in the previous question, draw a demand graph representing the appropriate change in quantity demanded or change in demand.

3.4 [Related to the *Economics in Practice* on p. 51] In the town of Hurley, Wisconsin, an unseasonably warm summer saw temperatures rising into the mid-90s for a weeklong stretch in July. This was almost 20 degrees above the average high temperature of 77 degrees for this hottest month of the year. This unexpected heat wave resulted in a significant increase in household purchases of central air conditioning systems, which are uncommon in this part of the country. Which determinant or determinants of demand were most likely factors in the households' decisions to purchase these air conditioning systems, and how would these purchases affect the demand curve for central air conditioning systems?

## 3.4 SUPPLY IN PRODUCT/OUTPUT MARKETS

LEARNING OBJECTIVE: Be able to distinguish between forces that shift a supply curve and changes that cause a movement along a supply curve.

4.1 The market for fitness trackers is made up of five firms, and the data in the following table represents each firm's quantity supplied at various prices. Fill in the column for the quantity supplied in the market, and draw a supply graph showing the market data.

| | | Quantity supplied by: | | | | |
|---|---|---|---|---|---|---|
| PRICE | FIRM A | FIRM B | FIRM C | FIRM D | FIRM E | MARKET |
| $25 | 5 | 3 | 2 | 0 | 5 | |
| 50 | 7 | 5 | 5 | 3 | 6 | |
| 75 | 9 | 7 | 8 | 6 | 7 | |
| 100 | 11 | 10 | 11 | 9 | 8 | |

4.2 The following sets of statements contain common errors. Identify and explain each error:
   a. Supply decreases, causing prices to rise. Higher prices cause supply to increase. Therefore, prices fall back to their original levels.

**MyEconLab** Visit **www.myeconlab.com** to complete these exercises online and get instant feedback. Exercises that update with real-time data are marked with art 🔴.

**b.** The supply of pineapples in Hawaii increases, causing pineapple prices to fall. Lower prices mean that the demand for pineapples in Hawaiian households will increase, which will reduce the supply of pineapples and increase their price.

## 3.5 MARKET EQUILIBRIUM

**LEARNING OBJECTIVE:** Be able to explain how a market that is not in equilibrium responds to restore an equilibrium.

5.1 Illustrate the following with supply and demand curves:
  **a.** With increased access to wireless technology and lighter weight, the demand for tablet computers has increased substantially. Tablets have also become easier and cheaper to produce as new technology has come online. Despite the shift of demand, prices have fallen.
  **b.** Cranberry production in Massachusetts totaled 1.85 million barrels in 2013, a 15 percent decrease from the 2.12 million barrels produced in 2012. Demand decreased by even more than supply, dropping 2013 prices to $32.30 per barrel from $47.90 in 2012.
  **c.** During the high-tech boom in the late 1990s, San Jose office space was in high demand and rents were high. With the national recession that began in March 2001, however, the market for office space in San Jose (Silicon Valley) was hit hard, with rents per square foot falling. In 2005, the employment numbers from San Jose were rising slowly and rents began to rise again. Assume for simplicity that no new office space was built during the period.
  **d.** Before economic reforms were implemented in the countries of Eastern Europe, regulation held the price of bread substantially below equilibrium. When reforms were implemented, prices were deregulated and the price of bread rose dramatically. As a result, the quantity of bread demanded fell and the quantity of bread supplied rose sharply.
  **e.** The steel industry has been lobbying for high taxes on imported steel. Russia, Brazil, and Japan have been producing and selling steel on world markets at $610 per metric ton, well below what equilibrium would be in the United States with no imports. If no imported steel was permitted into the country, the equilibrium price would be $970 per metric ton. Show supply and demand curves for the United States, assuming no imports; then show what the graph would look like if U.S. buyers could purchase all the steel that they wanted from world markets at $610 per metric ton; label the portion of the graph that represents the quantity of imported steel.

5.2 On Saturday, September 13, the Los Angeles Dodgers and the San Francisco Giants played baseball at AT&T Park in San Francisco. Both teams were in pursuit of league championships. Tickets to the game were sold out, and many more fans would have attended if additional tickets had been available. On that same day, the Miami Marlins and the Philadelphia Phillies played each other and sold tickets to only 26,163 people in Philadelphia.
  The Phillies stadium, Citizens Bank Park, holds 43,651. AT&T Park in San Francisco holds 41,915. Assume for simplicity that tickets to all regular-season games are priced at $40.
  **a.** Draw supply and demand curves for the tickets to each of the two games. (*Hint:* Supply is fixed. It does not change with price.) Draw one graph for each game.
  **b.** Is there a pricing policy that would have filled the ballpark for the Phillies game?
  **c.** The price system was not allowed to work to ration the San Francisco tickets when they were initially sold to the public. How do you know? How do you suppose the tickets were rationed?

5.3 Do you agree or disagree with each of the following statements? Briefly explain your answers and illustrate each with supply and demand curves.
  **a.** The price of a good rises, causing the demand for another good to fall. Therefore, the two goods are substitutes.
  **b.** A shift in supply causes the price of a good to fall. The shift must have been an increase in supply.
  **c.** During 2009, incomes fell sharply for many Americans. This change would likely lead to a decrease in the prices of both normal and inferior goods.
  **d.** Two normal goods cannot be substitutes for each other.
  **e.** If demand increases and supply increases at the same time, price will clearly rise.
  **f.** The price of good A falls. This causes an increase in the price of good B. Therefore, goods A and B are complements.

5.4 Through October 2014, the U.S. government administered two programs that affected the market for cigarettes. Media campaigns and labeling requirements, which are still in place, aim at making the public aware of the health dangers of cigarettes, and until 2014 the Department of Agriculture also maintained price supports for tobacco. Under this program, the supported price was above the market equilibrium price and the government limited the amount of land that could be devoted to tobacco production. Were these two programs at odds with the goal of reducing cigarette consumption? As part of your answer, illustrate graphically the effects of both policies on the market for cigarettes.

5.5 During the period 2006 through 2010, housing production in the United States fell from a rate of more than 2.27 million housing starts per year to a rate of less than 500,000, a decrease of greater than 80 percent. At the same time, the number of new households slowed to a trickle. Students without a job moved in with their parents, fewer immigrants came to the United States, and more of those already here went home. If there are fewer households, it is a decline in demand. If fewer new units are built, it is a decline in supply.
  **a.** Draw a standard supply and demand diagram, which shows the demand for new housing units that are purchased each month, and the supply of new units built and put on the market each month. Assume that the quantity supplied and quantity demanded are equal at 45,000 units and at a price of $200,000.
  **b.** On the same diagram show a decline in demand. What would happen if this market behaved like most markets?
  **c.** Now suppose that prices did not change immediately. Sellers decided not to adjust price even though demand is below supply. What would happen to the number of homes for sale (the inventory of unsold new homes) if prices stayed the same following the drop in demand?

d. Now suppose that the supply of new homes put on the market dropped, but price still stayed the same at $200,000. Can you tell a story that brings the market back to equilibrium without a drop in price?

e. Go to www.census.gov/newhomesales. Look at the current press release, which contains data for the most recent month and the past year. What trends can you observe?

5.6 For each of the following statements, draw a diagram that illustrates the likely effect on the market for eggs. Indicate in each case the impact on equilibrium price and equilibrium quantity.

a. The surgeon general warns that high-cholesterol foods cause heart attacks.

b. The price of bacon, a complementary product, decreases.

c. The price of chicken feed increases.

d. Caesar salads become trendy at dinner parties. (The dressing is made with raw eggs.)

e. A technological innovation reduces egg breakage during packing.

*5.7 Suppose the demand and supply curves for eggs in the United States are given by the following equations:

$$Q_d = 100 - 20P$$
$$Q_s = 10 + 40P$$

where $Q_d$ = millions of dozens of eggs Americans would like to buy each year; $Q_s$ = millions of dozens of eggs U.S. farms would like to sell each year; and $P$ = price per dozen eggs.

a. Fill in the following table:

| Price (Per Dozen) | Quantity Demanded ($Q_d$) | Quantity Supplied ($Q_s$) |
|---|---|---|
| $ .50 | ___ | ___ |
| $ 1.00 | ___ | ___ |
| $ 1.50 | ___ | ___ |
| $ 2.00 | ___ | ___ |
| $ 2.50 | ___ | ___ |

b. Use the information in the table to find the equilibrium price and quantity.

c. Graph the demand and supply curves and identify the equilibrium price and quantity.

5.8 Housing policy analysts debate the best way to increase the number of housing units available to low-income households. One strategy—the demand-side strategy—is to provide people with housing vouchers, paid for by the government, that can be used to rent housing supplied by the private market. Another—a supply-side strategy—is to have the government subsidize housing suppliers or to build public housing.

a. Illustrate these supply- and demand-side strategies using supply and demand curves. Which results in higher rents?

b. Critics of housing vouchers (the demand-side strategy) argue that because the supply of housing to low-income households is limited and does not respond to higher rents, demand vouchers will serve only to drive up rents

and make landlords better off. Illustrate their point with supply and demand curves.

*5.9 Suppose the market demand for pizza is given by

$Q_d = 300 - 20P$ and the market supply for pizza is given by
$Q_s = 20P - 100$, where $P$ = price (per pizza).

a. Graph the supply and demand schedules for pizza using $5 through $15 as the value of $P$.

b. In equilibrium, how many pizzas would be sold and at what price?

c. What would happen if suppliers set the price of pizza at $15? Explain the market adjustment process.

d. Suppose the price of hamburgers, a substitute for pizza, doubles. This leads to a doubling of the demand for pizza. (At each price, consumers demand twice as much pizza as before.) Write the equation for the new market demand for pizza.

e. Find the new equilibrium price and quantity of pizza.

5.10 [Related to the *Economics in Practice* on p. 65] The growing popularity of quinoa has had an impact on the market for brown rice. With its higher fiber, protein, and iron content, quinoa is replacing brown rice as a staple food for many health-conscious individuals. Draw a supply and demand graph that shows how this increase in demand for quinoa has affected the market for brown rice. Describe what has happened to the equilibrium price and quantity of brown rice. What could brown rice producers do to return the price or quantity to the initial equilibrium price or quantity? Briefly explain if it is possible for brown rice producers to return both the price and quantity to the initial equilibriums without a change in consumer behavior.

5.11 The following table represents the market for solar wireless keyboards. Plot this data on a supply and demand graph and identify the equilibrium price and quantity. Explain what would happen if the market price is set at $60, and show this on the graph. Explain what would happen if the market price is set at $30, and show this on the graph.

| Price | Quantity Demanded | Quantity Supplied |
|---|---|---|
| $ 10.00 | 28 | 0 |
| 20.00 | 24 | 3 |
| 30.00 | 20 | 6 |
| 40.00 | 16 | 9 |
| 50.00 | 12 | 12 |
| 60.00 | 8 | 15 |
| 70.00 | 4 | 18 |

5.12 [Related to the *Economics in Practice* on p. 66] Analyst 1 suggested that the demand curve for newspapers in Baltimore might have shifted to the right because people were becoming more literate. Think of two other plausible stories that would result in this demand curve shifting to the right.

*Note: Problems with an asterisk are more challenging.

**MyEconLab** Visit **www.myeconlab.com** to complete these exercises online and get instant feedback. Exercises that update with real-time data are marked with art ●.

# 4

# Demand and Supply Applications

Every society has a system of institutions that determines what is produced, how it is produced, and who gets what is produced. In some societies, these decisions are made centrally, through planning agencies or by government directive. However, in every society, many decisions are made in a *decentralized* way, through the operation of markets.

Markets exist in all societies, and Chapter 3 provided a bare-bones description of how markets operate. In this chapter, we continue our examination of demand, supply, and the price system.

# The Price System: Rationing and Allocating Resources

The market system, also called the *price system*, performs two important and closely related functions. First, it provides an automatic mechanism for distributing scarce goods and services. That is, it serves as a **price rationing** device for allocating goods and services to consumers when the quantity demanded exceeds the quantity supplied. Second, the price system ultimately determines both the allocation of resources among producers and the final mix of outputs.

**4.1 LEARNING** OBJECTIVE
Understand how price floors and price ceilings work in the market place.

**price rationing** The process by which the market system allocates goods and services to consumers when quantity demanded exceeds quantity supplied.

## Price Rationing

Consider the simple process by which the price system eliminates a shortage. Figure 4.1 shows hypothetical supply and demand curves for wheat. Wheat is produced around the world, with large supplies coming from Russia and from the United States. Wheat is sold in a world market and used to produce a range of food products, from cereals and breads to processed foods, which line the kitchens of the average consumer. Wheat is thus demanded by large food companies as they produce breads, cereals, and cake for households.

As Figure 4.1 shows, the equilibrium price of wheat was $160 per metric ton in the spring of 2010. At this price, farmers from around the world were expected to bring 61.7 million metric tons to market. Supply and demand were equal. Market equilibrium existed at a price of $160 per metric ton because at that price, quantity demanded was equal to quantity supplied. (Remember that equilibrium occurs at the point where the supply and demand curves intersect. In Figure 4.1, this occurs at point C.)

In the summer of 2010, Russia experienced its warmest summer on record. Fires swept through Russia, destroying a substantial portion of the Russian wheat crop. With almost a third of the world wheat normally produced in Russia, the effect of this environmental disaster on world wheat supply was substantial. In the figure, the supply curve for wheat, which had been drawn in expectation of harvesting all the wheat planted in Russia along with the rest of the world, now shifted to the left, from $S_{\text{spring 2010}}$ to $S_{\text{fall 2010}}$. This shift in the supply curve created a situation of excess demand at the old price of $160. At that price, the quantity demanded is 61.7 million metric tons, but the burning of much of the Russia supply left the world with only 35 millions of metric tons expected to be supplied. Quantity demanded exceeded quantity supplied at the original price by 26.7 million metric tons.

The reduced supply caused the price of wheat to rise sharply. As the price rises, the available supply is "rationed." Those who are willing and able to pay the most get it. You can see the market's rationing function clearly in Figure 4.1. As the price rises from $160, the quantity

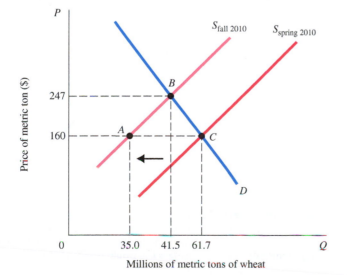

P

Price of metric ton ($)

$S_{\text{fall 2010}}$  $S_{\text{spring 2010}}$

247 — — — — — B

160 — — A — — C

D

0      35.0   41.5  61.7      Q

Millions of metric tons of wheat

◀ **FIGURE 4.1** **The Market for Wheat**
Fires in Russia in the summer of 2010 caused a shift in the world's supply of wheat to the left, causing the price to increase from $160 per metric ton to $247. The equilibrium moved from C to B.

demanded declines along the demand curve, moving from point C (61.7 million tons) toward point B (41.5 million tons). The higher prices mean that prices for products like Pepperidge Farm bread and Shredded Wheat cereal, which use wheat as an essential ingredient, also rise. People bake fewer cakes and begin to eat more rye bread and switch from Shredded Wheat to Corn Flakes in response to the price changes.

As prices rise, wheat farmers also change their behavior, though supply responsiveness is limited in the short term. Farmers outside of Russia, seeing the price rise, harvest their crops more carefully, getting more precious grains from each stalk. Perhaps some wheat is taken out of storage and brought to market. Quantity supplied increases from 35 million metric tons (point A) to 41.5 million tons (point B). The price increase has encouraged farmers who can to make up for part of the Russia wheat loss.

A new equilibrium is established at a price of $247 per metric ton, with 41.5 million tons transacted. The market has determined who gets the wheat: *The lower total supply is rationed to those who are willing and able to pay the higher price.*

This idea of "willingness to pay" is central to the distribution of available supply, and willingness depends on both desire (preferences) and income/wealth. Willingness to pay does not necessarily mean that only the rich will continue to buy wheat when the price increases. For anyone to continue to buy wheat at a higher price, his or her enjoyment comes at a higher cost in terms of other goods and services.

In sum:

> The adjustment of price is the rationing mechanism in free markets. Price rationing means that whenever there is a need to ration a good—that is, when a shortage exists—in a free market, the price of the good will rise until quantity supplied equals quantity demanded—that is, until the market clears.

There is some price that will clear any market you can think of. Consider the market for a famous painting such as Jackson Pollock's *No. 5, 1948*, illustrated in Figure 4.2. At a low price, there would be an enormous excess demand for such an important painting. The price would be bid up until there was only one remaining demander. Presumably, that price would be very high. In fact, the Pollock painting sold for a record $140 million in 2006. If the product is in strictly scarce supply, as a single painting is, its price is said to be *demand-determined*. That is, its price is determined solely and exclusively by the amount that the highest bidder or highest bidders are willing to pay.

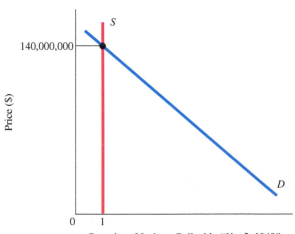

▲ **FIGURE 4.2** **Market for a Rare Painting**
There is some price that will clear any market, even if supply is strictly limited. In an auction for a unique painting, the price (bid) will rise to eliminate excess demand until there is only one bidder willing to purchase the single available painting. Some estimate that the *Mona Lisa* would sell for $600 million if auctioned.

One might interpret the statement that "there is some price that will clear any market" to mean "everything has its price," but that is not exactly what it means. Suppose you own a small silver bracelet that has been in your family for generations. It is quite possible that you would not sell it for *any* amount of money. Does this mean that the market is not working, or that quantity supplied and quantity demanded are not equal? Not at all. It simply means that *you* are the highest bidder. By turning down all bids, you must be willing to forgo what anybody offers for it.

# Constraints on the Market and Alternative Rationing Mechanisms

On occasion, both governments and private firms decide to use some mechanism other than the market system to ration an item for which there is excess demand at the current price. Policies designed to stop price rationing are commonly justified in a number of ways.

The rationale most often used is fairness. It is not "fair" to let landlords charge high rents, not fair for oil companies to run up the price of gasoline, not fair for insurance companies to charge enormous premiums, and so on. After all, the argument goes, we have no choice but to pay—housing and insurance are necessary, and one needs gasoline to get to work. The Economics in Practice box on page 76 describes complaints against price increases following Hurricane Sandy in 2012. Regardless of the rationale for controlling prices, the following examples will make it clear that trying to bypass the pricing system is often more difficult and more costly than it at first appears.

**Oil, Gasoline, and OPEC** One of the most important prices in the world is the price of crude oil. Millions of barrels of oil are traded every day. It is a major input into virtually every product produced. It heats our homes, and it is used to produce the gasoline that runs our cars. Its production has led to massive environmental disasters as well as wars. Its price has fluctuated wildly, leading to major macroeconomic problems. But oil is like other commodities in that its price is determined by the basic forces of supply and demand. Oil provides a good example of how markets work and how markets sometimes fail.

The Organization of the Petroleum Exporting Countries (OPEC) is an organization of twelve countries (Algeria, Angola, Ecuador, Iran, Iraq, Kuwait, Libya, Nigeria, Qatar, Saudi Arabia, the United Arab Emirates, and Venezuela) that together had about one-third of the global market share of oil sales in 2015, although the supply of oil produced in the United States has been growing as a result of new developments in hydraulic fracturing (fracking). In 1973 and 1974, OPEC imposed an embargo on shipments of crude oil to the United States. What followed was a drastic reduction in the quantity of gasoline available at local gas pumps, given the large market share of OPEC at the time.

Had the market system been allowed to operate, refined gasoline prices would have increased dramatically until quantity supplied was equal to quantity demanded. However, the government decided that rationing gasoline only to those who were willing and able to pay the most was unfair, and Congress imposed a **price ceiling**, or maximum price, of $0.57 per gallon of leaded regular gasoline. That price ceiling was intended to keep gasoline "affordable," but it also perpetuated the shortage. At the restricted price, quantity demanded remained greater than quantity supplied, and the available gasoline had to be divided up somehow among all potential demanders.

**price ceiling** A maximum price that sellers may charge for a good, usually set by government.

You can see the effects of the price ceiling by looking carefully at Figure 4.3. If the price had been set by the interaction of supply and demand, it would have increased to approximately $1.50 per gallon. Instead, Congress made it illegal to sell gasoline for more than $0.57 per gallon. At that price, quantity demanded exceeded quantity supplied and a shortage existed. Because the price system was not allowed to function, an alternative rationing system had to be found to distribute the available supply of gasoline.

Several devices were tried. The most common of all nonprice rationing systems is **queuing**, a term that means waiting in line. During 1974, long lines formed daily at gas stations, starting

**queuing** Waiting in line as a means of distributing goods and services: a nonprice rationing mechanism.

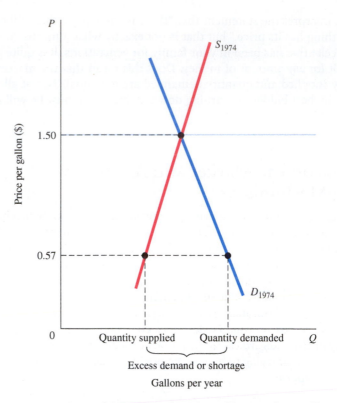

▲ **FIGURE 4.3** **Excess Demand (Shortage) Created by a Price Ceiling**
In 1974, a ceiling price of $0.57 cents per gallon of leaded regular gasoline was imposed. If the price had been set by the interaction of supply and demand instead, it would have increased to approximately $1.50 per gallon. At $0.57 per gallon, the quantity demanded exceeded the quantity supplied. Because the price system was not allowed to function, an alternative rationing system had to be found to distribute the available supply of gasoline.

as early as 5 AM. Under this system, gasoline went to those people who were willing to pay the most, but the sacrifice was measured in hours and aggravation instead of dollars.[1]

**favored customers** Those who receive special treatment from dealers during situations of excess demand.

A second nonprice rationing device used during the gasoline crisis was that of **favored customers**. Many gas station owners decided not to sell gasoline to the general public, but to reserve their scarce supplies for friends and favored customers. Not surprisingly, many customers tried to become "favored" by offering side payments to gas station owners. Owners also charged high prices for service. By doing so, they increased the actual price of gasoline but hid it in service overcharges to get around the ceiling.

**ration coupons** Tickets or coupons that entitle individuals to purchase a certain amount of a given product per month.

Yet another method of dividing up available supply is the use of **ration coupons**. It was suggested in both 1974 and 1979 that families be given ration tickets or coupons that would entitle them to purchase a certain number of gallons of gasoline each month. That way, everyone would get the same amount regardless of income. Such a system had been employed in the United States during the 1940s when wartime price ceilings on meat, sugar, butter, tires, nylon stockings, and many other items were imposed.

When ration coupons are used with no prohibition against trading them, however, the result is almost identical to a system of price rationing. Those who are willing and able to pay the most buy up the coupons and use them to purchase gasoline, chocolate, fresh eggs, or anything else that

---

[1] You can also show formally that the result is inefficient—that there is a resulting net loss of total value to society. First, there is the cost of waiting in line. Time has a value. With price rationing, no one has to wait in line and the value of that time is saved. Second, there may be additional lost value if the gasoline ends up in the hands of someone who places a lower value on it than someone else who gets no gas. Suppose, for example, that the market price of gasoline if unconstrained would rise to $2 but that the government has it fixed at $1. There will be long lines to get gas. Imagine that to motorist A, 10 gallons of gas is worth $35 but that she fails to get gas because her time is too valuable to wait in line. To motorist B, 10 gallons is worth only $15, but his time is worth much less, so he gets the gas. In the end, A could pay B for the gas and both would be better off. If A pays B $30 for the gas, A is $5 better off and B is $15 better off. In addition, A does not have to wait in line. Thus, the allocation that results from nonprice rationing involves a net loss of value. Such losses are called *deadweight losses*. See p. 84 of this chapter.

# ECONOMICS IN PRACTICE

## Why Is My Hotel Room So Expensive? A Tale of Hurricane Sandy

In October 2012 Hurricane Sandy hit the northeastern United States. In New York, New Jersey, and Connecticut flooding in particular caused disruption. In the aftermath of the storm, as individuals and public workers began to clean up, prices for a number of items began to rise. At this point, you should be able to predict which prices likely rose the most.

Before Sandy struck we would expect that most of the markets in these states, as in other areas, were more or less in equilibrium. The only merchants who actually *could* raise prices after the storm are ones who face either a large shift to the right of the demand curve facing them or a shift to the left of the supply curve in their market. Otherwise, if merchants post Sandy raised prices, they would simply end up with surplus goods on the shelf. So if we want to predict which prices rose after Sandy, all we need to do is to look at those businesses facing large shifts in either their demand or supply curves after the storm. With many people forced out of their homes, hotel rooms became scarce. With power out, generators became more valuable. With trees down, tree removal services heard from many more customers. In other words, all of these businesses saw a large shift out of demand curves in their markets and none would find it easy to quickly increase their output levels. One can't really build a Holiday Inn overnight! Higher prices were now possible.

As it turned out, gas prices at the pump also rose. Yet one might well have thought that following Sandy, people would drive less, given the conditions of roads and business closings. Here, the more likely problem was a shift in the supply curve, as delivery trucks found it hard to restock gas stations. A shift in the supply curve made higher prices possible, particularly given the fact that those people who did need to go to work really needed that gas!

As we suggest in the text, in some cases government policy controls how much prices *are allowed* to rise after an emergency. In the case of Hurricane Sandy, all three states lodged

complaints of price gouging against numerous businesses, virtually all in the hotel, tree removal, gas station, or generator sales business. In New Jersey, a law against gouging prohibits price increases of more than 10 percent in an emergency situation. Connecticut and New York are more graphic in their definitions, but less precise. In these states, price gouging involves price increases in emergencies which are "unconscionably excessive." Economics will not be much help in translating that definition into a number. But at this point we hope you can see that economics can very much help us predict what kinds of businesses are likely to be charged with the offense.

### THINKING PRACTICALLY

1. Gas prices rose after Sandy as supply shifted to the left, or inward, given transport problems. Transport problems likely also affected the delivery of Cheerios. Do you expect the price of Cheerios to also rise substantially? Why or why not?

---

is sold at a restricted price.[2] This means that the price of the restricted good will effectively rise to the market-clearing price. For instance, suppose that you decide not to sell your ration coupon. You are then forgoing what you would have received by selling the coupon. Thus, the "effective" price of the good you purchase will be higher (if only in opportunity cost) than the restricted price. Even when trading coupons is declared illegal, it is virtually impossible to stop black markets from developing. In a **black market**, illegal trading takes place at market-determined prices.

**black market**  A market in which illegal trading takes place at market-determined prices.

## Rationing Mechanisms for Concert and Sports Tickets

Tickets for sporting events such as the World Series, the Super Bowl, and the World Cup command huge prices in the open market. In many cases, the prices are substantially above the original issue price. One of the

---

[2] Of course, if you are assigned a number of tickets and you sell them, you are better off than you would be with price rationing. Ration coupons thus serve as a way of redistributing income.

hottest basketball tickets ever was one to the Boston Celtics and Los Angeles Lakers' NBA final series in 2010 that LA won in seven games. The online price for a courtside seat to one of the games in Los Angeles was $19,000.

You might ask why a profit-maximizing enterprise would not charge the highest price it could? The answer depends on the event. If the Chicago Cubs got into the World Series, the people of Chicago would buy all the tickets available for thousands of dollars each. But if the Cubs actually *charged* $2,000 a ticket, the hard-working fans would be furious: "Greedy Cubs Gouge Fans" the headlines would scream. Ordinary loyal fans earning reasonable salaries would not be able to afford those prices. Next season, perhaps some of those irate fans would change loyalties, supporting the White Sox over the Cubs. In part to keep from alienating loyal fans, prices for championship games are held down. It is interesting to look at this case to see how charging a ticket price lower than market plays out.

Let's consider a concert at the Staples Center, which has 20,000 seats. The supply of tickets is thus fixed at 20,000. Of course, there are good seats and bad seats, but to keep things simple, let's assume that all seats are the same and that the promoters charge $50 per ticket for all tickets. This is illustrated in Figure 4.4. Supply is represented by a vertical line at 20,000. Changing the price does not change the supply of seats. In the figure the quantity demanded at the price of $50 is 38,000, so at this price there is excess demand of 18,000.

Who would get to buy the $50 tickets? As in the case of gasoline, a variety of rationing mechanisms might be used. The most common is queuing, waiting in line. The tickets would go on sale at a particular time, and people would show up and wait. Now ticket sellers have virtual waiting rooms online. Tickets for the World Series go on sale at a particular time in September, and the people who log on to team Web sites at the right moment get into an electronic queue and can buy tickets. Often tickets are sold out in a matter of minutes.

There are also, of course, favored customers. Those who get tickets without queuing are local politicians, sponsors, and friends of the artist or friends of the players.

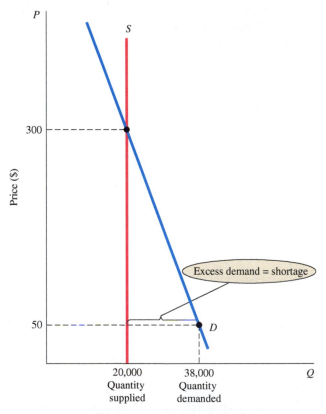

Tickets to a concert at the Staples Center

▲ **FIGURE 4.4** **Supply of and Demand for a Concert at the Staples Center**
At the face-value price of $50, there is excess demand for seats to the concert. At $50 the quantity demanded is greater than the quantity supplied, which is fixed at 20,000 seats. The diagram shows that the quantity demanded would equal the quantity supplied at a price of $300 per ticket.

But "once the dust settles," the power of technology and the concept of *opportunity cost* take over. Even if you get the ticket for the (relatively) low price of $50, that is not the true cost. The true cost is what you give up to sit in the seat. If people on eBay, StubHub, or Ticketmaster are willing to pay $300 for your ticket, that's what you must pay, or sacrifice, to go to the concert. Many people—even strong fans—will choose to sell that ticket. Once again, it is difficult to stop the market from rationing the tickets to those people who are willing and able to pay the most.

No matter how good the intentions of private organizations and governments, it is difficult to prevent the price system from operating and to stop people's willingness to pay from asserting itself. Every time an alternative is tried, the price system seems to sneak in the back door. With favored customers and black markets, the final distribution may be even more unfair than what would result from simple price rationing.

## Prices and the Allocation of Resources

Thinking of the market system as a mechanism for allocating scarce goods and services among competing demanders is revealing, but the market determines more than just the distribution of final outputs. It also determines what gets produced and how resources are allocated among competing uses.

Consider a change in consumer preferences that leads to an increase in demand for a specific good or service. During the 1980s, for example, people began going to restaurants more frequently than before. Researchers think that this trend, which continues today, is partially the result of social changes (such as a dramatic rise in the number of two-earner families) and partially the result of rising incomes. The market responded to this change in demand by shifting resources, both capital and labor, into more and better restaurants.

With the increase in demand for restaurant meals, the price of eating out rose and the restaurant business became more profitable. The higher profits attracted new businesses and provided old restaurants with an incentive to expand. As new capital, seeking profits, flowed into the restaurant business, so did labor. New restaurants need chefs. Chefs need training, and the higher wages that came with increased demand provided an incentive for them to get it. In response to the increase in demand for training, new cooking schools opened and existing schools began to offer courses in the culinary arts. This story could go on and on, but the point is clear:

Price changes resulting from shifts of demand in output markets cause profits to rise or fall. Profits attract capital; losses lead to disinvestment. Higher wages attract labor and encourage workers to acquire skills. At the core of the system, supply, demand, and prices in input and output markets determine the allocation of resources and the ultimate combinations of goods and services produced.

## Price Floor

As we have seen, price ceilings, often imposed because price rationing is viewed as unfair, result in alternative rationing mechanisms that are inefficient and may be equally unfair. Some of the same arguments can be made for price floors. A **price floor** is a minimum price below which exchange is not permitted. If a price floor is set above the equilibrium price, the result will be excess supply; quantity supplied will be greater than quantity demanded.

**price floor** A minimum price below which exchange is not permitted.

The most common example of a price floor is the **minimum wage**, which is a floor set for the price of labor. Employers (who demand labor) are not permitted under federal law to pay a wage less than $7.25 per hour (in 2015) to workers (who supply labor). Many states have much higher minimum wages; Washington, for example, had a minimum wage in 2015 of $9.47 per hour. Critics of the minimum wage argue that since it is above equilibrium, it may result in less labor hired.

**minimum wage** A price floor set for the price of labor.

**4.2 LEARNING** OBJECTIVE

Analyze the economic impact of an oil import tax.

# Supply and Demand Analysis: An Oil Import Fee

The basic logic of supply and demand is a powerful tool of analysis. As an extended example of the power of this logic, we will consider a proposal to impose a tax on imported oil. The idea of taxing imported oil is hotly debated, and the tools we have learned thus far will show us the effects of such a tax.

In 2012 the United States imported 45 percent of its oil. Of the imports, 22 percent come from the Persian Gulf States. Given the political volatility of that area of the world, many politicians have advocated trying to reduce our dependence on foreign oil. One tool often suggested by both politicians and economists to accomplish this goal has been an import oil tax or tariff.

Supply and demand analysis makes the arguments of the import tax proponents easier to understand. Figure 4.5(a) shows the U.S. market for oil as of late 2012. The world price of oil is at slightly more than $80, and the United States is assumed to be able to buy *all the oil that it wants* at this price. This means that domestic producers cannot charge any more than $80 per barrel. The curve labeled *Supply* US shows the amount that domestic suppliers will produce at each price level. At a price of $80, domestic production is 7 million barrels per day. U.S. producers will produce at point A on the supply curve. The total quantity of oil demanded in the United States in 2012 was approximately 13 million barrels per day. At a price of $80, the quantity demanded in the United States is point B on the demand curve.

The difference between the total quantity demanded (13 million barrels per day) and domestic production (7 million barrels per day) is total imports (6 million barrels per day).

▶ **FIGURE 4.5** **The U.S. Market for Crude Oil, 2012**

In 2012 the world market price for crude oil was approximately $80 per barrel. Domestic production in the United States that year averaged about 7 million barrels per day, whereas crude oil demand averaged just under 13 million barrels per day. The difference between production and consumption were made up of net imports of approximately 6 million barrels per day, as we see in panel (a).

If the government imposed a tax in this market of 33..33 percent, or $26.64, that would increase the world price to $106.64. That higher price causes quantity demanded to fall below its original level of 13 million barrels, while the price increase causes domestic production to rise above the original level. As we see in panel b, the effect is a reduction in import levels.

a. U.S. market, 2012

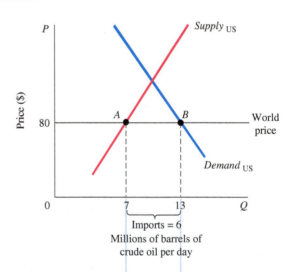

b. Effects of an oil import fee in the United States

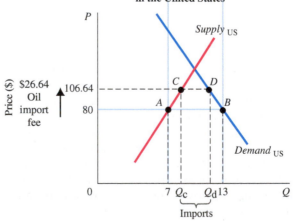

## ECONOMICS IN PRACTICE

### The Price Mechanism at Work for Shakespeare

Every summer, New York City puts on free performances of Shakespeare in the Park. Tickets are distributed on a first-come-first-serve basis at the Delacorte Theatre in the park beginning at 1 PM on the day of the show. People usually begin lining up at 6 AM when the park opens; by 10 AM the line has typically reached a length sufficient to give away all available tickets.

When you examine the people standing in line for these tickets, most of them seem to be fairly young. Many carry book bags identifying them as students in one of New York's many colleges. Of course, all college students may be fervent Shakespeare fans, but can you think of another reason for the composition of the line? Further, when you attend one of the plays and look around, the audience appears much older and much sleeker than the people who were standing in line. What is going on?

Although the tickets are "free" in terms of financial costs, their true price includes the value of the time spent standing in line. Thus, the tickets are cheaper for people (for example, students) whose time value is lower than they are for high-wage earners, like an investment banker from Goldman Sachs. The true cost of a ticket is $0 plus the opportunity cost of the time spent in line. If the average person spends 4 hours in line, as is done in the Central Park case, for someone with a high wage, the true cost of the ticket might be very high. For example, a lawyer who earns $300 an hour would be giving up $1,200 to wait in line. It should not surprise you to see more people waiting in line for whom the tickets are inexpensive.

What about the people who are at the performance? Think about our discussion of the power of entrepreneurs. In this case, the students who stand in line as consumers of the tickets also can play a role as producers. In fact, the students can produce tickets relatively cheaply by waiting in line. They

can then turn around and sell those tickets to the high-wage Shakespeare lovers. These days eBay is a great source of tickets to free events, sold by individuals with low opportunity costs of their time who queued up. Craigslist even provides listings for people who are willing to wait in line for you.

Of course, now and again we do encounter a busy businessperson in one of the Central Park lines. Recently, one of the authors encountered one and asked him why he was waiting in line rather than using eBay, and he replied that it reminded him of when he was young, waiting in line for rock concerts.

#### THINKING PRACTICALLY

1. Many museums offer free admission one day a week, on a weekday. On that day we observe that museum-goers are more likely to be senior citizens than on a typical Saturday. Why?

---

Now suppose that the government levies a tax of $33\frac{1}{3}$ percent on imported oil. Because the import price is $80, this tax rate translates into a tax of $26.64, which increases the price per barrel paid by U.S. importers to $106.64 ($80 + $26.64). This new, higher price means that U.S. producers can also charge up to $106.64 for a barrel of crude. Note, however, that the tax is paid only on imported oil. Thus, the entire 106.64 paid for domestic crude goes to domestic producers.

Figure 4.5(b) shows the result of the tax. First, because of a higher price, the quantity demanded drops. This is a movement *along* the demand curve from point B to point D. At the same time, the quantity supplied by domestic producers increases. This is a movement *along* the supply curve from point A to point C. With an increase in domestic quantity supplied and a decrease in domestic quantity demanded, imports decrease, as we can see clearly as $Q_d$-$Q_c$ is smaller than the original 6 billions barrels per day.

The tax also generates revenues for the federal government. The total tax revenue collected is equal to the tax per barrel ($26.64) times the number of imported barrels ($Q_d$-$Q_c$).

What does all of this mean? In the final analysis, an oil import fee would increase domestic production and reduce overall consumption. To the extent that one believes that Americans are consuming too much oil, the reduced consumption may be a good thing. We also see that the tax increases the price of oil in the United States.

**4.3 LEARNING OBJECTIVE**

Explain how consumer and producer surplus are generated.

# Supply and Demand and Market Efficiency

Clearly, supply and demand curves help explain the way that markets and market prices work to allocate scarce resources. Recall that when we try to understand "how the system works," we are doing "positive economics."

Supply and demand curves can also be used to illustrate the idea of market efficiency, an important aspect of "normative economics." To understand the ideas, you first must understand the concepts of consumer and producer surplus.

## Consumer Surplus

If we think hard about the lessons of supply and demand, we can see that the market forces us to reveal a great deal about our personal preferences. If you are free to choose within the constraints imposed by prices and your income and you decide to buy a hamburger for $2.50, you have "revealed" that a hamburger is worth at least $2.50 to you. Consumers reveal who they are by what they choose to buy and do.

This idea of purchases as preference revelation underlies a lot of the valuation economists do. Look at the demand curve in Figure 4.6(a). At the current market price of $2.50, consumers will purchase 7 million hamburgers per month. In this market, consumers who value a hamburger at $2.50 or more will buy it, and those who have lower values will do without.

As the figure shows, however, some people value hamburgers at more than $2.50. At a price of $5.00, for example, consumers would still buy 1 million hamburgers. These million hamburgers have a value to their buyers of $5.00 each. If consumers can buy these burgers for only $2.50, they would earn a **consumer surplus** of $2.50 per burger. Consumer surplus is the difference between the maximum amount a person is willing to pay for a good and its current market price. The consumer surplus earned by the people willing to pay $5.00 for a hamburger is approximately equal to the shaded area between point A and the price, $2.50.

**consumer surplus** The difference between the maximum amount a person is willing to pay for a good and its current market price.

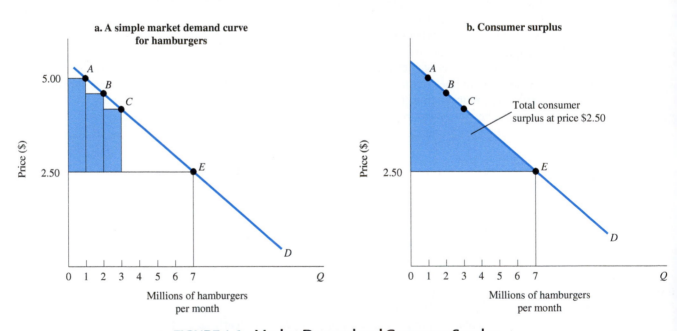

**a. A simple market demand curve for hamburgers**

**b. Consumer surplus**

Total consumer surplus at price $2.50

Millions of hamburgers per month

Millions of hamburgers per month

▲ **FIGURE 4.6** **Market Demand and Consumer Surplus**

As illustrated in Figure 4.6(a), some consumers (see point A) are willing to pay as much as $5.00 each for hamburgers. Since the market price is just $2.50, they receive a consumer surplus of $2.50 for each hamburger that they consume. Others (see point B) are willing to pay something less than $5.00 and receive a slightly smaller surplus. Because the market price of hamburgers is just $2.50, the area of the shaded triangle in Figure 4.6(b) is equal to total consumer surplus.

The second million hamburgers in Figure 4.6(a) are valued at more than the market price as well, although the consumer surplus gained is slightly less. Point *B* on the market demand curve shows the maximum amount that consumers would be willing to pay for the second million hamburgers. The consumer surplus earned by these people is equal to the shaded area between *B* and the price, $2.50. Similarly, for the third million hamburgers, maximum willingness to pay is given by point *C*; consumer surplus is a bit lower than it is at points *A* and *B*, but it is still significant.

The total value of the consumer surplus suggested by the data in Figure 4.6(a) is roughly equal to the area of the shaded triangle in Figure 4.6(b). To understand why this is so, think about offering hamburgers to consumers at successively lower prices. If the good were actually sold for $2.50, those near point *A* on the demand curve would get a large surplus; those at point *B* would get a smaller surplus. Those at point *E* would get no surplus.

## Producer Surplus

Similarly, the supply curve in a market shows the amount that firms willingly produce and supply to the market at various prices. Presumably it is because the price is sufficient to cover the costs or the opportunity costs of production and give producers enough profit to keep them in business. When speaking of cost of production, we include everything that a producer must give up to produce a good.

A simple market supply curve like the one in Figure 4.7(a) illustrates this point quite clearly. At the current market price of $2.50, producers will produce and sell 7 million hamburgers. There is only one price in the market, and the supply curve tells us the quantity supplied at each price.

Notice, however, that if the price were just $0.75 (75 cents), although production would be much lower—most producers would be out of business at that price—a few producers would actually be supplying burgers. In fact, producers would supply about 1 million burgers to the market. These firms must have lower costs: They are more efficient or they have access to raw beef at a lower price or perhaps they can hire low-wage labor.

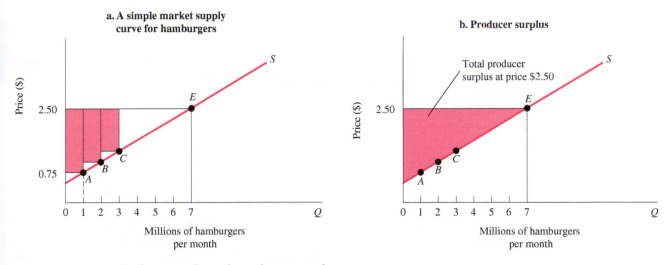

a. A simple market supply curve for hamburgers

b. Producer surplus

▲ **FIGURE 4.7** **Market Supply and Producer Surplus**
As illustrated in Figure 4.7(a), some producers are willing to produce hamburgers for a price of $0.75 each. Because they are paid $2.50, they earn a producer surplus equal to $1.75. Other producers are willing to supply hamburgers at prices less than $2.50, and they also earn producers surplus. Because the market price of hamburgers is $2.50, the area of the shaded triangle in Figure 4.7(b) is equal to total producer surplus.

▶ **FIGURE 4.8** **Total Producer and Consumer Surplus**
Total producer and consumer surplus is greatest where supply and demand curves intersect at equilibrium.

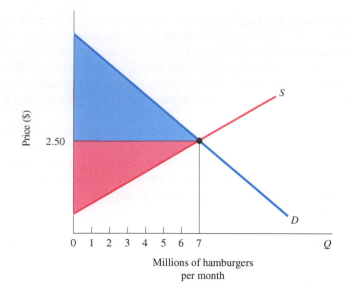

**producer surplus** The difference between the current market price and the cost of production for the firm.

If these efficient, low-cost producers are able to charge $2.50 for each hamburger, they are earning what is called a **producer surplus**. Producer surplus is the difference between the current market price and the cost of production for the firm. The first million hamburgers would generate a producer surplus of $2.50 minus $0.75, or $1.75 per hamburger: a total of $1.75 million. The second million hamburgers would also generate a producer surplus because the price of $2.50 exceeds the producers' total cost of producing these hamburgers, which is above $0.75 but much less than $2.50.

The total value of the producer surplus received by producers of hamburgers at a price of $2.50 per burger is roughly equal to the shaded triangle in Figure 4.7(b). Those producers just able to make a profit producing burgers will be near point E on the supply curve and will earn very little in the way of surplus.

## Competitive Markets Maximize the Sum of Producer and Consumer Surplus

In the preceding example, the quantity of hamburgers supplied and the quantity of hamburgers demanded are equal at $2.50. Figure 4.8 shows the total net benefits to consumers and producers resulting from the production of 7 million hamburgers. Consumers receive benefits in excess of the price they pay and equal to the blue shaded area between the demand curve and the price line at $2.50; the area is equal to the amount of consumer surplus being earned. Producers receive compensation in excess of costs and equal to the red-shaded area between the supply curve and the price line at $2.50; the area is equal to the amount of producer surplus being earned.

**deadweight loss** The total loss of producer and consumer surplus from underproduction or overproduction.

Now consider the result to consumers and producers if production were to be reduced to 4 million burgers. Look carefully at Figure 4.9(a). At 4 million burgers, consumers are willing to pay $3.75 for hamburgers and there are firms whose costs make it worthwhile to supply at a price as low as $1.50, yet something is stopping production at 4 million. The result is a loss of both consumer and producer surplus. You can see in Figure 4.9(a) that if production were expanded from 4 million to 7 million, the market would yield more consumer surplus and more producer surplus. The total loss of producer and consumer surplus from *underproduction* and, as we will see shortly, from overproduction is referred to as a **deadweight loss**. In Figure 4.9(a) the deadweight loss is equal to the area of triangle *ABC* shaded in yellow.

Figure 4.9(b) illustrates how a deadweight loss of both producer and consumer surplus can result from *overproduction* as well. For every hamburger produced above 7 million, consumers are willing to pay less than the cost of production. The cost of the resources needed to produce

**a. Deadweight loss from underproduction**

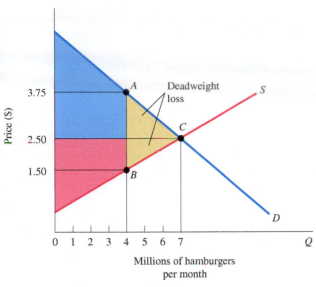

**b. Deadweight loss from overproduction**

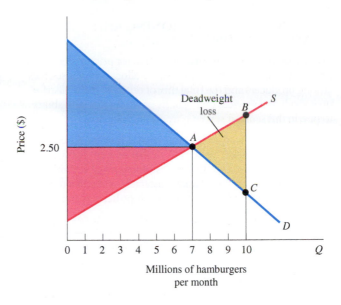

▲ **FIGURE 4.9    Deadweight Loss**

Figure 4.9(a) shows the consequences of producing 4 million hamburgers per month instead of 7 million hamburgers per month. Total producer and consumer surplus is reduced by the area of triangle *ABC* shaded in yellow. This is called the deadweight loss from underproduction. Figure 4.9(b) shows the consequences of producing 10 million hamburgers per month instead of 7 million hamburgers per month. As production increases from 7 million to 10 million hamburgers, the full cost of production rises above consumers' willingness to pay, resulting in a deadweight loss equal to the area of triangle *ABC*.

hamburgers above 7 million exceeds the benefits to consumers, resulting in a net loss of producer and consumer surplus equal to the yellow shaded area *ABC*.

# Potential Causes of Deadweight Loss From Under- and Overproduction

Most of the next few chapters will discuss perfectly competitive markets in which prices are determined by the free interaction of supply and demand. As you will see, when supply and demand interact freely, competitive markets produce what people want at the least cost, that is, they are efficient. Beginning in Chapter 13, however, we will begin to relax assumptions and will discover a number of naturally occurring sources of market failure. Monopoly power gives firms the incentive to underproduce and overprice, taxes and subsidies may distort consumer choices, external costs such as pollution and congestion may lead to over- or underproduction of some goods, and artificial price floors and price ceilings may have the same effects.

# Looking Ahead

We have now examined the basic forces of supply and demand and discussed the market/price system. These fundamental concepts will serve as building blocks for what comes next. Whether you are studying microeconomics or macroeconomics, you will be studying the functions of markets and the behavior of market participants in more detail in the following chapters.

Because the concepts presented in the first four chapters are so important to your understanding of what is to come, this might be a good time for you to review this material.

# SUMMARY

## 4.1 THE PRICE SYSTEM: RATIONING AND ALLOCATING RESOURCES *p. 73*

1. In a market economy, the market system (or price system) serves two functions. It determines the allocation of resources among producers and the final mix of outputs. It also distributes goods and services on the basis of willingness and ability to pay. In this sense, it serves as a *price rationing* device.

2. Governments as well as private firms sometimes decide not to use the market system to ration an item for which there is excess demand. Examples of nonprice rationing systems include *queuing, favored customers, and ration coupons.* The most common rationale for such policies is "fairness."

3. Attempts to bypass the market and use alternative nonprice rationing devices are more difficult and costly than it would seem at first glance. Schemes that open up opportunities for favored customers, black markets, and side payments often end up less "fair" than the free market. A supply curve shows the relationship between the quantity producers are willing to supply to the market and the price of a good.

## 4.2 SUPPLY AND DEMAND ANALYSIS: AN OIL IMPORT FEE *p. 80*

4. The basic logic of supply and demand is a powerful tool for analysis. For example, supply and demand analysis shows that an oil import tax will reduce quantity of oil demanded, increase domestic production, and generate revenues for the government.

## 4.3 SUPPLY AND DEMAND AND MARKET EFFICIENCY *p. 82*

5. Supply and demand curves can also be used to illustrate the idea of market efficiency, an important aspect of normative economics.

6. *Consumer surplus* is the difference between the maximum amount a person is willing to pay for a good and the current market price.

7. *Producer surplus* is the difference between the current market price and the cost of production for the firm.

8. At free market equilibrium with competitive markets, the sum of consumer surplus and producer surplus is maximized.

9. The total loss of producer and consumer surplus from underproduction or overproduction is referred to as a *deadweight loss.*

# REVIEW TERMS AND CONCEPTS

black market, *p. 77*
consumer surplus, *p. 82*
deadweight loss, *p. 84*
favored customers, *p. 76*
minimum wage, *p. 79*
price ceiling, *p. 75*
price floor, *p. 79*
price rationing, *p. 73*
producer surplus, *p. 84*
queuing, *p. 75*
ration coupons, *p. 76*

# PROBLEMS

All problems are available on MyEconLab.

## 4.1 THE PRICE SYSTEM: RATIONING AND ALLOCATING RESOURCES

LEARNING OBJECTIVE: Understand how price floors and price ceilings work in the market place.

1.1 Illustrate the following with supply and demand curves:
  a. In November 2014, Andy Warhol's silkscreen artwork *Triple Elvis [Ferus Type]* was sold at Christie's Auction House in New York for $81.9 million.
  b. In March 2015, hogs in the United States were selling for 62 cents per pound, down from 98 cents per pound a year before. This was due primarily to the fact that supply had increased during the period.
  c. In 2015, the demand for organic produce continued to rise, and represented 11 percent of all produce purchased in U.S. supermarkets. At the same time, the number of farmers growing organic crops had increased by 119 percent since 2007. The overall result was a drop in the

average price of organic produce and an increase in the quantity of organic produce sold.

1.2 Every demand curve must eventually hit the quantity axis because with limited incomes, there is always a price so high that there is no demand for the good. Do you agree or disagree? Why?

1.3 When excess demand exists for tickets to a major sporting event or a concert, profit opportunities exist for scalpers. Explain briefly using supply and demand curves to illustrate. Some argue that scalpers work to the advantage of everyone and are "efficient." Do you agree or disagree? Explain briefly.

1.4 In an effort to "support" the price of some agricultural goods, the Department of Agriculture pays farmers a subsidy in cash for every acre that they leave *unplanted*. The Agriculture Department argues that the subsidy increases the "cost" of planting and that it will reduce supply and increase the price of competitively produced agricultural goods. Critics argue that because the subsidy is a payment to farmers, it will reduce costs and lead to lower prices. Which argument is correct? Explain.

1.5 The rent for 2-bedroom apartments in Detroit has fallen from an average of $796 in September 2014 to $717 in March 2015. Demand for 2-bedroom apartments in Detroit was falling during this period as well. This is hard to explain because the law of demand says that lower prices should lead to higher demand. Do you agree or disagree? Explain your answer.

1.6 Illustrate the following with supply or demand curves:
   a. In Joseph Heller's iconic novel, *Catch 22*, one of the characters was paid by the government to not grow alfalfa. According to the story's narrator, "The more alfalfa he did not grow, the more money the government gave him, and he spent every penny he didn't earn on new land to increase the amount of alfalfa he did not produce."
   b. In 2015, Chipotle suspended the sale of pork at one-third of its restaurants due to animal welfare concerns, and this had a significant impact on the amount of chicken entrees it sold to customers.
   c. From 2007 to 2014, median income in the United States fell by 8 percent, shifting the demand for gasoline. During that same time period, crude oil prices fell 35 percent, shifting the supply of gasoline. At the new equilibrium, the quantity of gasoline sold is less than it was before. (Crude oil is used to produce gasoline.)

1.7 Illustrate the following with supply or demand curves:
   a. A situation of excess labor demand caused by a salary cap in the National Basketball Association (NBA).
   b. The effect of a sharp decrease in gasoline prices on the demand for electric vehicles.

1.8 [**Related to the *Economics in Practice* on p. 77**] The feature states that in New Jersey, a law against price gouging prohibits price increases of more than 10 percent in an emergency situation. Assume that prior

to Sandy the equilibrium price for portable generators was $100 and the equilibrium quantity was 200 units per month. After Sandy, demand increased to 500 units per month and generator sellers raised prices to the maximum amount allowed by law. Do you think that the new higher price will be high enough to meet the increased demand? Use a supply and demand graph to explain your answer.

1.9 In April 2015, the U.S. Energy Information Administration projected that the average retail price for regular-grade gasoline would be $2.45 per gallon for the remainder of the year. Do some research on the price of gasoline. Has this projection been accurate? What is the price of regular-grade gasoline today in your city or town? If it is below $2.45 per gallon, what are the reasons? Similarly, if it is higher than $2.45, what has happened to drive up the price? Illustrate with supply and demand curves.

1.10 Many cruise lines offer 5-day trips. A disproportionate number of these trips leave port on Thursday and return late Monday. Why might this be true?

1.11 [**Related to the *Economics in Practice* on p. 81**] Lines for free tickets to see free Shakespeare in Central Park are often long. A local politician has suggested that it would be a great service if the park provided music to entertain those who are waiting in line. What do you think of this suggestion?

1.12 The following graph represents the market for wheat. The equilibrium price is $20 per bushel and the equilibrium quantity is 14 million bushels.

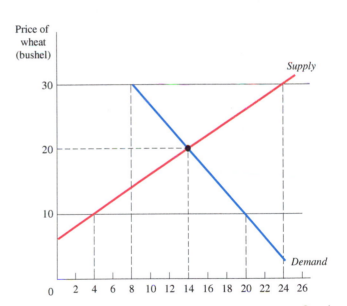

**a.** Explain what will happen if the government establishes a price ceiling of $10 per bushel of wheat in this market? What if the price ceiling was set at $30?

**b.** Explain what will happen if the government establishes a price floor of $30 per bushel of wheat in this market. What if the price floor was set at $10?

## 4.2 SUPPLY AND DEMAND ANALYSIS: AN OIL IMPORT FEE

LEARNING OBJECTIVE: Analyze the economic impact of an oil import tax.

**2.1** Suppose that the world price of oil is $60 per barrel and that the United States can buy all the oil it wants at this price. Suppose also that the demand and supply schedules for oil in the United States are as follows:

| Price ($ Per Barrel) | U.S. Quantity Demanded | U.S. Quantity Supplied |
|---|---|---|
| 55 | 26 | 14 |
| 60 | 24 | 16 |
| 65 | 22 | 18 |
| 70 | 20 | 20 |
| 75 | 18 | 22 |

**a.** On graph paper, draw the supply and demand curves for the United States.

**b.** With free trade in oil, what price will Americans pay for their oil? What quantity will Americans buy? How much of this will be supplied by American producers? How much will be imported? Illustrate total imports on your graph of the U.S. oil market.

**c.** Suppose the United States imposes a tax of $5 per barrel on imported oil. What quantity would Americans buy? How much of this would be supplied by American producers? How much would be imported? How much tax would the government collect?

**d.** Briefly summarize the impact of an oil import tax by explaining who is helped and who is hurt among the following groups: domestic oil consumers, domestic oil producers, foreign oil producers, and the U.S. government.

**2.2** Use the data in the preceding problem to answer the following questions. Now suppose that the United States allows no oil imports.

**a.** What are the equilibrium price and quantity for oil in the United States?

**b.** If the United States imposed a price ceiling of $65 per barrel on the oil market and prohibited imports, would there be an excess supply or an excess demand for oil? If so, how much?

**c.** Under the price ceiling, quantity supplied and quantity demanded differ. Which of the two will determine how much oil is purchased? Briefly explain why.

## 4.3 SUPPLY AND DEMAND AND MARKET EFFICIENCY

LEARNING OBJECTIVE: Explain how consumer and producer surplus are generated.

**3.1** Use the following diagram to calculate total consumer surplus at a price of $12 and production of 500 thousand flu vaccinations per day. For the same equilibrium, calculate total producer surplus. Assuming price remained at $12 but production was cut to 200 thousand vaccinations per day, calculate producer surplus and consumer surplus. Calculate the deadweight loss from underproduction.

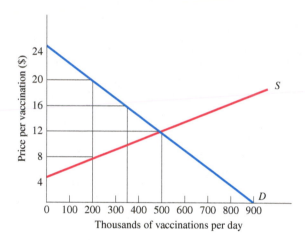

**3.2** Suppose the market demand for a cup of cappuccino is given by $Q_D = 24 - 4P$ and the market supply for a cup of cappuccino is given by $Q_S = 8P - 12$, where $P$ = price (per cup).

**a.** Graph the supply and demand schedules for cappuccino.

**b.** What is the equilibrium price and equilibrium quantity?

**c.** Calculate consumer surplus and producer surplus, and identify these on the graph.

**3.3** On April 20, 2010, an oil-drilling platform owned by British Petroleum exploded in the Gulf of Mexico, causing oil to leak into the gulf at estimates of 1.5 to 2.5 million gallons per day for well more than 2 months. As a result of the oil spill, the government closed more than 25 percent of federal waters, which devastated the commercial fishing industry in the area. Explain how the reduction in supply from the reduced fishing waters either increased or decreased consumer surplus and producer surplus, and show these changes graphically.

3.4 The following graph represents the market for DVDs.

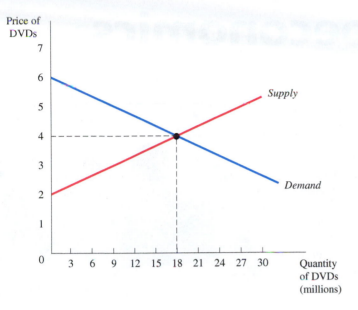

a. Find the values of consumer surplus and producer surplus when the market is in equilibrium, and identify these areas on the graph.

b. If underproduction occurs in this market, and only 9 million DVDs are produced, what happens to the amounts of consumer surplus and producer surplus? What is the value of the deadweight loss? Identify these areas on the graph.

c. If overproduction occurs in this market, and 27 million DVDs are produced, what happens to the amounts of consumer surplus and producer surplus? Is there a deadweight loss with overproduction? If so, what is its value? Identify these areas on the graph.

# 5

# Introduction to Macroeconomics

When the macroeconomy is doing well, jobs are easy to find, incomes are generally rising, and profits of corporations are high. On the other hand, if the macroeconomy is in a slump, new jobs are scarce, incomes are not growing well, and profits are low. Students who entered the job market in the boom of the late 1990s in the United States, on average, had an easier time finding a job than did those who entered in the recession of 2008–2009. The sluggish economy that continued into 2013 had negative effects on millions of people. Given the large effect that the macroeconomy can have on our lives, it is important that we understand how it works.

We begin by discussing the differences between microeconomics and macroeconomics that we glimpsed in Chapter 1. **Microeconomics** examines the functioning of individual industries and the behavior of individual decision-making units, typically firms and households. With a few assumptions about how these units behave (firms maximize profits; households maximize utility), we can derive useful conclusions about how markets work and how resources are allocated.

Instead of focusing on the factors that influence the production of particular products and the behavior of individual industries, **macroeconomics** focuses on the determinants of total national output. Macroeconomics studies not household income but *national* income, not individual prices but the *overall* price level. It does not analyze the demand for labor in the automobile industry but instead total employment in the economy.

Both microeconomics and macroeconomics are concerned with the decisions of households and firms. Microeconomics deals with individual decisions; macroeconomics deals with the sum of these individual decisions. *Aggregate* is used in macroeconomics to refer to sums. When we speak of **aggregate behavior**, we mean the behavior of all households as well as the behavior of all firms. We also speak of aggregate consumption and aggregate investment, which refer to total consumption and total investment in the economy, respectively.

Because microeconomists and macroeconomists look at the economy from different perspectives, you might expect that they would reach somewhat different conclusions about the way the economy behaves. This is true to some extent. Microeconomists generally conclude that markets work well. They see prices as flexible, adjusting to maintain equality between quantity supplied and quantity demanded. Macroeconomists, however, observe that important prices in the economy—for example, the wage rate (or price of labor)—often seem "sticky." **Sticky prices** are prices that do not always adjust rapidly to maintain equality between quantity supplied and quantity demanded. Microeconomists do not expect to see the quantity of apples supplied exceeding the quantity of apples demanded because the price of apples is not sticky. On the other hand, macroeconomists—who analyze aggregate behavior—examine periods of high unemployment, where the quantity of labor supplied appears to exceed the quantity of labor demanded. At such times, it appears that wage rates do not fall fast enough to equate the quantity of labor supplied and the quantity of labor demanded.

# Macroeconomic Concerns

Three of the major concerns of macroeconomics are

- Output growth
- Unemployment
- Inflation and deflation

Government policy makers would like to have high output growth, low unemployment, and low inflation. We will see that these goals may conflict with one another and that an important point in understanding macroeconomics is understanding these conflicts.

## Output Growth

Instead of growing at an even rate at all times, economies tend to experience short-term ups and downs in their performance. The technical name for these ups and downs is the **business cycle**. The main measure of how an economy is doing is **aggregate output**, the total quantity of goods and services produced in the economy in a given period. When less is produced (in other words, when aggregate output decreases), there are fewer goods and services to go around and the average standard of living declines. When firms cut back on production, they also lay off workers, increasing the rate of unemployment.

**Recessions** are periods during which aggregate output declines. It has become conventional to classify an economic downturn as a "recession" when aggregate output declines for two consecutive quarters. A prolonged and deep recession is called a **depression**, although economists do not agree on when a recession becomes a depression. Since the 1930s the United States has experienced one depression (during the 1930s) and eight recessions: 1946, 1954, 1958, 1974–1975, 1980–1982, 1990–1991, 2001, and 2008–2009. Other countries also experienced recessions in the twentieth century, some roughly coinciding with U.S. recessions and some not.

A typical business cycle is illustrated in Figure 5.1. Because most economies, on average, grow over time, the business cycle in Figure 5.1 shows a positive trend—the *peak* (the highest point) of a new business cycle is higher than the peak of the previous cycle. The period from a

### 5.1 LEARNING OBJECTIVE

Describe the three primary concerns of macroeconomics.

**microeconomics**    Examines the functioning of individual industries and the behavior of individual decision-making units—firms and households.

**macroeconomics**    Deals with the economy as a whole. Macroeconomics focuses on the determinants of total national income, deals with aggregates such as aggregate consumption and investment, and looks at the overall level of prices instead of individual prices.

**aggregate behavior**    The behavior of all households and firms together.

**sticky prices**    Prices that do not always adjust rapidly to maintain equality between quantity supplied and quantity demanded.

**business cycle**    The cycle of short-term ups and downs in the economy.

**aggregate output**    The total quantity of goods and services produced in an economy in a given period.

**recession**    A period during which aggregate output declines. Conventionally, a period in which aggregate output declines for two consecutive quarters.

**depression**    A prolonged and deep recession.

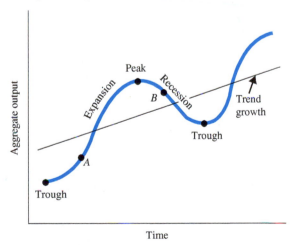

▲ **FIGURE 5.1    A Typical Business Cycle**
In this business cycle, the economy is expanding as it moves through point *A* from the trough to the peak. When the *economy* moves from a peak down to a trough, through point *B*, the economy is in recession.

**expansion or boom** The period in the business cycle from a trough up to a peak during which output and employment grow.

**contraction, recession, or slump** The period in the business cycle from a peak down to a trough during which output and employment fall.

*trough*, or bottom of the cycle, to a peak is called an **expansion or a boom**. During an expansion, output and employment grow. The period from a peak to a trough is called a **contraction, recession, *or* slump**, when output and employment fall.

In judging whether an economy is expanding or contracting, note the difference between the level of economic activity and its rate of change. If the economy has just left a trough (point A in Figure 5.1), it will be growing (rate of change is positive), but its level of output will still be low. If the economy has just started to decline from a peak (point B), it will be contracting (rate of change is negative), but its level of output will still be high. The business cycle drawn in Figure 5.1 is symmetrical, which means that the length of an expansion is the same as the length of a contraction. Most business cycles are not symmetrical, however. It is possible, for example, for the expansion phase to be longer than the contraction phase. When contraction comes, it may be fast and sharp, whereas expansion may be slow and gradual. Moreover, the economy is not nearly as regular as the business cycle in Figure 5.1 indicates. The ups and downs in the economy tend to be erratic.

Figure 5.2 shows the actual business cycles in the United States between 1900 and 2014. Although many business cycles have occurred in the last 115 years, each is unique. The economy is not so simple that it has regular cycles.

The periods of the Great Depression and World War I and II show the largest fluctuations in Figure 5.2, although other large contractions and expansions have taken place. Note the expansion in the 1960s and the five recessions since 1970. Some of the cycles have been long; some have been short. Note also that aggregate output actually increased between 1933 and 1937, even though it was still quite low in 1937. The economy did not come out of the Depression until the defense buildup prior to the start of World War II. Note also that business cycles were more extreme before World War II than they have been since then. Finally, note that the recovery from the 2008–2009 recession was unusually slow.

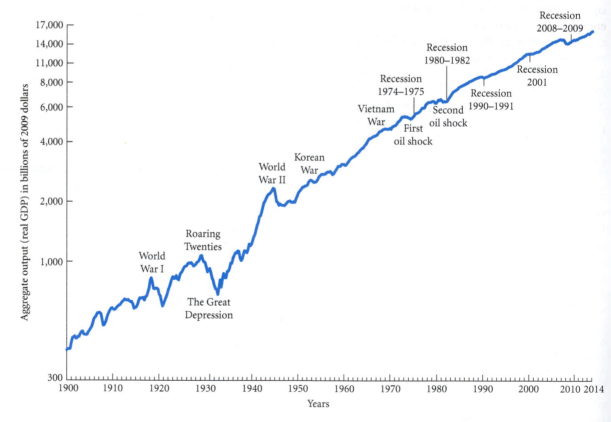

▲ **FIGURE 5.2** **U.S. Aggregate Output (Real GDP),** **1900–2014**     MyEconLab Real-time data

The periods of the Great Depression and World War I and II show the largest fluctuations in aggregate output.

# Unemployment

You cannot listen to the news or read a newspaper without noticing that data on the unemployment rate are released each month. The **unemployment rate**—the percentage of the labor force that is unemployed—is a key indicator of the economy's health. Because the unemployment rate is usually closely related to the economy's aggregate output, announcements of each month's new figure are followed with great interest by economists, politicians, and policy makers.

Although macroeconomists are interested in learning why the unemployment rate has risen or fallen in a given period, they also try to answer a more basic question: Why is there any unemployment at all? Part of the answer to this question is straightforward, coming from the fact that adjustments in labor markets generally take some time. At times people decide to quit their jobs and look for something better. Until they find a new job, they will be unemployed. At any time, some firms may go bankrupt because of competition from rivals, bad management, or bad luck. Employees of such firms typically are not able to find new jobs immediately, and while they are looking for work, they will be unemployed. Also, workers entering the labor market for the first time may require a few weeks or months to find a job. All of these factors tell us that some positive rate of unemployment is inevitable in a dynamic economy.

A key question in macroeconomics is how the economy adjusts when the unemployment rate rises beyond this base level. Supply and demand analysis leads us to expect a market response to the existence of unemployed workers. Specifically, when there is unemployment beyond some minimum amount, there is an excess supply of workers—at the going wage rates, there are people who want to work who cannot find work. Microeconomic theory tells us that excess supply causes a decrease in the price of the commodity in question. As prices fall, quantity demanded rises and the quantity supplied falls. In the end prices fall enough so that quantity supplied equals the quantity demanded, and equilibrium is restored as the market clears.

The existence of unemployment seems to imply that the aggregate labor market is not in equilibrium—that something prevents the quantity supplied and the quantity demanded from equating. Why do labor markets not clear when other markets do, or is it that labor markets are clearing and the unemployment data reflect something different? This is one of the ongoing debates in macroeconomics.

> **unemployment rate** The percentage of the labor force that is unemployed.

# Inflation and Deflation

**Inflation** is an increase in the overall price level. Keeping inflation low has long been a goal of government policy. Especially problematic are **hyperinflations**, or periods of very rapid increases in the overall price level.

Most Americans are unaware of what life is like under high inflation. In some countries at some times, people were accustomed to prices rising by the day, by the hour, or even by the minute. During the hyperinflation in Bolivia in 1984 and 1985, the price of one egg rose from 3,000 pesos to 10,000 pesos in 1 week. In 1985, three bottles of aspirin sold for the same price as a luxury car had sold for in 1982. At the same time, the problem of handling money became a burden. Bolivia's currency, printed in West Germany and England, was the country's third biggest import in 1984, surpassed only by wheat and mining equipment. In December 2014 the inflation rate in Venezuela reached 68 percent, and the country experienced numerous street protests against the policies of the relatively new president, Nicolas Maduro. Very high inflation can destabilize economies and governments. Hyperinflations are rare. Nonetheless, economists have devoted much effort to identifying the costs and consequences of even moderate inflation. Does anyone gain from inflation? Who loses? What costs does inflation impose on society? How severe are they? What causes inflation? What is the best way to stop it? Here too we find debate. A decrease in the overall price level is called **deflation**. In some periods in U.S. history and recently in Japan, deflation has occurred over an extended period of time. In 2015 the European Union began to take steps to fight what was seen as the early stages of deflation in that region. The goal of policy makers is to avoid prolonged periods of deflation as well as inflation to pursue the macroeconomic goal of stability.

> **inflation** An increase in the overall price level.

> **hyperinflation** A period of very rapid increases in the overall price level.

> **deflation** A decrease in the overall price level.

# The Components of the Macroeconomy

Understanding how the macroeconomy works can be challenging because a great deal is going on at one time. Everything seems to affect everything else. To see the big picture, it is helpful to divide the participants in the economy into four broad groups: (1) *households*, (2) *firms*, (3) the *government*, and (4) the *rest of the world*. Households and firms make up the private sector, the government is the public sector, and the rest of the world is the foreign sector. These four groups interact in the economy in a variety of ways, many involving either receiving or paying income.

## The Circular Flow Diagram

A useful way of seeing the economic interactions among the four groups in the economy is a **circular flow** diagram, which shows the income received and payments made by each group. A simple circular flow diagram is pictured in Figure 5.3.

> Let us walk through the circular flow step by step. Households work for firms and the government, and they receive wages for their work. Our diagram shows a flow of wages *into* households as payment for those services. Households also receive interest on corporate and government bonds and dividends from firms. Many households receive other payments from the government, such as Social Security benefits, veterans' benefits, and welfare payments. Economists call these kinds of payments from the government (for which the recipients do not supply goods, services, or labor) **transfer payments**. Together, these receipts make up the total income received by the households.

> Households buy goods and services from firms and pay taxes to the government. These items make up the total amount paid out by the households. The difference between the total receipts and the total payments of the households is the amount that the households save or dissave. If households receive more than they spend, they *save* during the period. If they receive

**circular flow** A diagram showing the flows in and out of the sectors in the economy.

**transfer payments** Cash payments made by the government to people who do not supply goods, services, or labor in exchange for these payments. They include Social Security benefits, veterans' benefits, and welfare payments.

▶ **FIGURE 5.3** **The Circular Flow of Payments**

Households receive income from firms and the government, purchase goods and services from firms, and pay taxes to the government. They also purchase foreign-made goods and services (imports). Firms receive payments from households and the government for goods and services; they pay wages, dividends, interest, and rents to households and taxes to the government. The government receives taxes from firms and households, pays firms and households for goods and services—including wages to government workers—and pays interest and transfers to households. Finally, people in other countries purchase goods and services produced domestically (exports).

*Note:* Although not shown in this diagram, firms and governments also purchase imports.

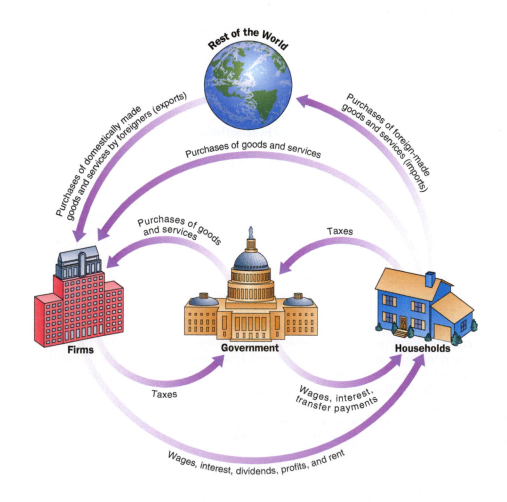

less than they spend, they *dissave*. A household can dissave by using up some of its previous savings or by borrowing. In the circular flow diagram, household spending is shown as a flow *out* of households. Saving by households is sometimes termed a "leakage" from the circular flow because it withdraws income, or current purchasing power, from the system.

Firms sell goods and services to households and the government earning revenue, which shows up in the circular flow diagram as a flow *into* the firm sector. Firms pay wages, interest, and dividends to households, and firms pay taxes to the government. These payments are shown flowing *out* of firms.

The government collects taxes from households and firms. The government also makes payments. It buys goods and services from firms, pays wages and interest to households, and makes transfer payments to households. If the government's revenue is less than its payments, the government is dissaving.

Finally, households spend some of their income on *imports*—goods and services produced in the rest of the world. Similarly, people in foreign countries purchase *exports*—goods and services produced by domestic firms and sold to other countries.

One lesson of the circular flow diagram is that everyone's expenditure is someone else's receipt. If you buy a personal computer from Dell, you make a payment to Dell, and Dell receives revenue. If Dell pays taxes to the government, it has made a payment and the government has received revenue. Everyone's expenditures go somewhere. It is impossible to sell something without there being a buyer, and it is impossible to make a payment without there being a recipient. Every transaction must have two sides.

## The Three Market Arenas

Another way of looking at the ways households, firms, the government, and the rest of the world relate to one another is to consider the markets in which they interact. We divide the markets into three broad arenas: (1) the goods-and-services market, (2) the labor market, and (3) the money (financial) market.

**Goods-and-Services Market**   Households and the government purchase goods and services from firms in the *goods-and-services market*. In this market, firms also purchase goods and services from each other. For example, Levi Strauss buys denim from other firms to make its blue jeans. In addition, firms buy capital goods from other firms. If General Motors needs new robots on its assembly lines, it may buy them from another firm instead of making them. The *Economics in Practice* in Chapter 1 describes how Apple, in constructing its iPod, buys parts from a number of other firms.

Firms *supply* to the goods-and-services market. Households, the government, and firms *demand* from this market. Finally, the rest of the world buys from and sells to the goods-and-services market. The United States imports hundreds of billions of dollars' worth of automobiles, DVDs, oil, and other goods. In the case of Apple's iPod, inputs come from other firms located in countries all over the world. At the same time, the United States exports hundreds of billions of dollars' worth of computers, airplanes, and agricultural goods.

**Labor Market**   Interaction in the *labor market* takes place when firms and the government purchase labor from households. In this market, households *supply* labor and firms and the government *demand* labor. In the U.S. economy, firms are the largest demanders of labor, although the government is also a substantial employer. The total supply of labor in the economy depends on the sum of decisions made by households. Individuals must decide whether to enter the labor force (whether to look for a job at all) and how many hours to work.

Labor is also supplied to and demanded from the rest of the world. In recent years, the labor market has become an international market. For example, vegetable and fruit farmers in California would find it difficult to bring their product to market if it were not for the labor of migrant farm workers from Mexico. For years, Turkey has provided Germany with "guest workers" who are willing to take low-paying jobs that more prosperous German workers avoid. Call centers run by major U.S. corporations are sometimes staffed by labor in India and other developing countries.

**Money Market**  In the *money market*—sometimes called the *financial market*—households purchase stocks and bonds from firms. Households *supply* funds to this market in the expectation of earning income in the form of dividends on stocks and interest on bonds. Households also *demand* (borrow) funds from this market to finance various purchases. Firms borrow to build new facilities in the hope of earning more in the future. The government borrows by issuing bonds to fund public programs. Much of the borrowing and lending of households, firms, the government, and the rest of the world are coordinated by financial institutions—commercial banks, savings and loan associations, insurance companies, and the like. These institutions take deposits from one group and lend them to others, often moving funds from one part of the world to another.

When a firm, a household, or the government borrows to finance a purchase, it has an obligation to pay that loan back, usually at some specified time in the future. Most loans also involve payment of interest as a fee for the use of the borrowed funds. When a loan is made, the borrower usually signs a "promise to repay," or *promissory note*, and gives it to the lender. When the federal government borrows, it issues "promises" called **Treasury bonds, notes, or bills** in exchange for money. Firms can borrow from banks, or in the case of corporations, they can issue **corporate bonds**.

Instead of issuing bonds to raise funds, corporations can also issue shares of stock. A **share of stock** is a financial instrument that gives the holder a share in the firm's ownership and therefore the right to share in the firm's profits. If the firm does well, the value of the stock increases and the stockholder receives a *capital gain*[1] on the initial purchase. In addition, the stock may pay **dividends**—that is, the firm may return some of its profits directly to its stockholders instead of retaining the profits to buy capital. If the firm does poorly, so does the stockholder. The capital value of the stock may fall, and dividends may not be paid. Stocks are traded in exchanges in many parts of the world, with the largest exchanges located in New York, London, and Tokyo.

Stocks and bonds are simply contracts, or agreements, between parties. I agree to loan you a certain amount, and you agree to repay me this amount plus something extra at some future date, or I agree to buy part ownership in your firm, and you agree to give me a share of the firm's future profits.

A critical variable in the money market is the *interest rate*. Although we sometimes talk as if there is only one interest rate, there is never just one interest rate at any time. Instead, the interest rate on a given loan reflects the length of the loan and the perceived risk to the lender. A business that is just getting started must pay a higher rate than General Motors pays. A 30-year mortgage has a different interest rate than a 90-day loan. Nevertheless, interest rates tend to move up and down together, and their movement reflects general conditions in the financial market.

## The Role of the Government in the Macroeconomy

The government plays a major role in the macroeconomy, so a useful way of learning how the macroeconomy works is to consider how the government uses policy to affect the economy. The two main policy instruments of the government are (1) fiscal policy and (2) monetary policy. Much of the study of macroeconomics is learning how fiscal and monetary policies work.

**Fiscal policy** refers to the government's decisions about how much to tax and spend. The federal government collects taxes from households and firms and spends those funds on goods and services ranging from missiles to parks to social security payments to interstate highways. Taxes take the form of personal income taxes, social security taxes, and corporate profits taxes, among others. An *expansionary* fiscal policy is a policy in which taxes are cut or government spending increases. A *contractionary* fiscal policy is the reverse.

**Monetary policy** in the United States is conducted by the Federal Reserve, the nation's central bank. The Fed, as it is usually called, controls short-term interest rates in the economy. The Fed's decisions have important effects on the economy. In fact, the task of trying to smooth out business cycles in the United States has historically been left to the Fed (that is, to monetary

**Treasury bonds, notes, or bills**  Promissory notes issued by the federal government when it borrows money.

**corporate bonds**  Promissory notes issued by corporations when they borrow money.

**shares of stock**  Financial instruments that give to the holder a share in the firm's ownership and therefore the right to share in the firm's profits.

**dividends**  The portion of a firm's profits that the firm pays out each period to its shareholders.

**fiscal policy**  Government policies concerning taxes and spending.

**monetary policy**  The tools used by the Federal Reserve to control short term interest rates.

---

[1] A *capital gain* occurs whenever the value of an asset increases. If you bought a stock for $1,000 and it is now worth $1,500, you have earned a capital gain of $500. A capital gain is "realized" when you sell the asset. Until you sell, the capital gain is *accrued* but not *realized*.

policy). The chair of the Federal Reserve, currently Janet Yellen, is sometimes said to be the second-most powerful person in the United States after the president. As we will see later in the text, the Fed played a more active role in the 2008–2009 recession than it had in previous recessions. Fiscal policy, however, also played an active role in the 2008–2009 recession and its aftermath.

# A Brief History of Macroeconomics

The severe economic contraction and high unemployment of the 1930s, the decade of the **Great Depression**, spurred a great deal of thinking about macroeconomic issues, especially unemployment. Figure 5.2 shows that this period had the largest and longest aggregate output contraction in the twentieth century in the United States. The 1920s had been prosperous years for the U.S. economy. Virtually everyone who wanted a job could get one, incomes rose substantially, and prices were stable. Beginning in late 1929, things took a sudden turn for the worse. In 1929, 1.5 million people were unemployed. By 1933, that had increased to 13 million out of a labor force of 51 million. In 1933, the United States produced about 27 percent fewer goods and services than it had in 1929. In October 1929, when stock prices collapsed on Wall Street, billions of dollars of personal wealth were lost. Unemployment remained above 14 percent of the labor force until 1940. (See the *Economics in Practice*, p. 98, "Macroeconomics in Literature," for Fitzgerald's and Steinbeck's take on the 1920s and 1930s.)

Before the Great Depression, economists applied microeconomic models, sometimes referred to as "classical" or "market clearing" models, to economy-wide problems. As we suggested, classical supply and demand analysis assumed that an excess supply of labor would drive down wages to a new equilibrium level. The decline in the wage rate would in turn raise the quantity of labor demanded by firms, erasing the unemployment. The prediction was clear: unemployment could not persist. But, during the Great Depression, unemployment levels remained high for nearly 10 years. In large measure, the failure of simple classical models to explain the prolonged existence of high unemployment provided the impetus for the development of macroeconomics. It is not surprising that what we now call macroeconomics was born in the 1930s.

One of the most important works in the history of economics, *The General Theory of Employment, Interest and Money*, by John Maynard Keynes, was published in 1936. Building on what was already understood about markets and their behavior, Keynes set out to construct a theory that would explain the confusing economic events of his time.

Much of macroeconomics has roots in Keynes's work. According to Keynes, it is not prices and wages alone that determine the level of employment, as classical models had suggested, but that the level of aggregate demand (sometimes called "total spending") for goods and services also plays a role. Moreover, Keynes believed that governments could intervene in the economy and affect the level of output and employment. When private demand is low, Keynes argued, governments could stimulate aggregate demand and, by so doing, lift the economy out of recession. (Keynes was a larger-than-life figure, one of the Bloomsbury group in England that included, among others, Virginia Woolf and Clive Bell.)

After World War II and especially in the 1950s, Keynes's views began to gain increasing influence over both professional economists and government policy makers. Governments came to believe that they could intervene in their economies to attain specific employment and output goals. They began to use their powers to tax and spend as well as their ability to affect interest rates and the money supply for the explicit purpose of controlling the economy's level of spending and therefore its ups and downs. This view of government policy became firmly established in the United States with the passage of the Employment Act of 1946. This act established the President's Council of Economic Advisers, a group of economists who advise the president on economic issues. The act also committed the federal government to intervening in the economy to prevent large declines in output and employment.

The notion that the government could and should act to stabilize the macroeconomy reached the height of its popularity in the 1960s. During these years, Walter Heller, the chairman of the Council of Economic Advisers under both President John Kennedy and President Lyndon B. Johnson, alluded to **fine-tuning** as the government's role in regulating inflation and

**5.3 LEARNING** OBJECTIVE

Summarize the macroeconomic history of the United States between 1929 and 1970.

**Great Depression** The period of severe economic contraction and high unemployment that began in 1929 and continued throughout the 1930s.

**fine-tuning** The phrase used by Walter Heller to refer to the government's role in regulating inflation and unemployment.

# ECONOMICS IN PRACTICE

## Macroeconomics in Literature

As you know, the language of economics includes a heavy dose of graphs and equations. But the underlying phenomena that economists study are the stuff of novels as well as graphs and equations. The following two passages, from *The Great Gatsby* by F. Scott Fitzgerald and *The Grapes of Wrath* by John Steinbeck, capture in graphic, although not graphical, form the economic growth and spending of the Roaring Twenties and the human side of the unemployment of the Great Depression. *The Great Gatsby*, written in 1925, is set in the 1920s, whereas *The Grapes of Wrath*, written in 1939, is set in the early 1930s. If you look at Figure 5.2 for these two periods, you will see the translation of Fitzgerald and Steinbeck into macroeconomics.

### From *The Great Gatsby*

At least once a fortnight a corps of caterers came down with several hundred feet of canvas and enough colored lights to make a Christmas tree of Gatsby's enormous garden. On buffet tables, garnished with glistening hors d'œuvre, spiced baked hams crowded against salads of harlequin designs and pastry pigs and turkeys bewitched to a dark gold. In the main hall a bar with a real brass rail was set up, and stocked with gins and liquors and with cordials so long forgotten that most of his female guests were too young to know one from another.

By seven o'clock the orchestra has arrived—no thin five piece affair but a whole pit full of oboes and trombones and saxophones and viols and cornets and piccolos and low and high drums. The last swimmers have come in from the beach now and are dressing upstairs; the cars from New York are parked five deep in the drive, and already the halls and salons and verandas are gaudy with primary colors and hair shorn in strange new ways and shawls beyond the dreams of Castile.

### From *The Grapes of Wrath*

The moving, questing people were migrants now. Those families who had lived on a little piece of land, who had lived and died on forty acres, had eaten or starved on the produce of forty acres, had now the whole West to rove in. And they scampered about, looking for work; and the highways were streams of people, and the ditch banks were lines of people. Behind them more were coming. The great highways streamed with moving people.

### THINKING PRACTICALLY

1. As we indicate in the introduction to this chapter, macroeconomics focuses on three concerns. Which of these concerns is covered in *The Grapes of Wrath* excerpt?
2. What economics textbook is featured in *The Great Gatsby*?
   *Hint*: Go to fairmodel.econ.yale.edu/rayfair/pdf /2000c.pdf.

*Source*: From *The Grapes of Wrath* by John Steinbeck, copyright 1939, renewed © 1967 by John Steinbeck. Used by permission of Viking Penguin, a division of Penguin Group (USA) Inc. and Penguin Group (UK) Ltd.

---

unemployment. During the 1960s, many economists believed the government could use the tools available to manipulate unemployment and inflation levels fairly precisely.

The optimism about the government's ability to finely manage the economy was short-lived. In the 1970s and early 1980s, the U.S. economy had wide fluctuations in employment, output, and inflation. In 1974–1975 and again in 1980–1982, the United States experienced a severe recession. Although not as catastrophic as the Great Depression of the 1930s, these two recessions left millions without jobs and resulted in billions of dollars of lost output and income. In 1974–1975 and again in 1979–1981, the United States also saw high rates of inflation.

The 1970s was thus a period of stagnation and high inflation, which came to be called stagflation. **Stagflation** is defined as a situation in which there is high inflation at the same time

**stagflation** A situation of both high inflation and high unemployment.

there are slow or negative output growth and high unemployment. Until the 1970s, high inflation had been observed only in periods when the economy was prospering and unemployment was low. The problem of stagflation was vexing both for macroeconomic theorists and policy makers concerned with the health of the economy.

It was clear by 1975 that the macroeconomy was more difficult to control than Heller's words or textbook theory had led economists to believe. The events of the 1970s and early 1980s had an important influence on macroeconomic theory. Much of the faith in the simple Keynesian model and the "conventional wisdom" of the 1960s was lost. Although we are now 45 years past the 1970s, the discipline of macroeconomics is still in flux and there is no agreed-upon view of how the macroeconomy works. Many important issues have yet to be resolved. This makes macroeconomics hard to teach but exciting to study.

# The U.S. Economy Since 1970

**5.4 LEARNING** OBJECTIVE

Describe the U.S. economy since 1970.

In the following chapters, it will be useful to have a picture of how the U.S. economy has performed recently. Since 1970, the U.S. economy has experienced five recessions and two periods of high inflation. The period since 1970 is illustrated in Figures 5.4, 5.5, and 5.6. These figures are based on quarterly data (that is, data for each quarter of the year). The first quarter consists of January, February, and March; the second quarter consists of April, May, and June; and so on. The Roman numerals I, II, III, and IV denote the four quarters. For example, 1972 III refers to the third quarter of 1972.

Figure 5.4 plots aggregate output for 1970 I–2014 IV. The five recessionary periods are 1974 I–1975 I, 1980 II–1982 IV, 1990 III–1991 I, 2001 I–2001 III, and 2008 I–2009 II.[2] These five periods are shaded in the figure. Figure 5.5 plots the unemployment rate for the same overall period with the same shading for the recessionary periods. Note that unemployment rose in all

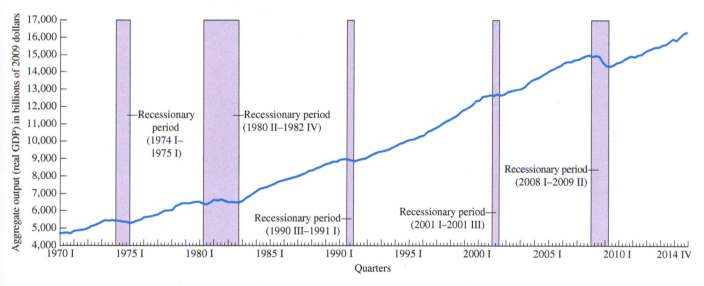

▲ **FIGURE 5.4**  **Aggregate Output (Real GDP), 1970 I–2014 IV**  MyEconLab Real-time data
Aggregate output in the United States since 1970 has risen overall, but there have been five recessionary periods: 1974 I–1975 I, 1980 II–1982 IV, 1990 III–1991 I, 2001 I–2001 III, and 2008 I–2009 II.

---

[2] Regarding the 1980 II–1982 IV period, output rose in 1980 IV and 1981 I before falling again in 1981 II. Given this fact, one possibility would be to treat the 1980 II–1982 IV period as if it included two separate recessionary periods: 1980 II–1980 III and 1981 I–1982 IV. Because the expansion was so short-lived, however, we have chosen not to separate the period into two parts. These periods are close to but are not exactly the recessionary periods defined by the National Bureau of Economic Research (NBER). The NBER is considered the "official" decider of recessionary periods. One problem with the NBER definitions is that they are never revised, but the macro data are, sometimes by large amounts. This means that the NBER periods are not always those that would be chosen using the latest revised data. In November 2008 the NBER declared that a recession began in December 2007. In September 2010 it declared that the recession ended in June 2009.

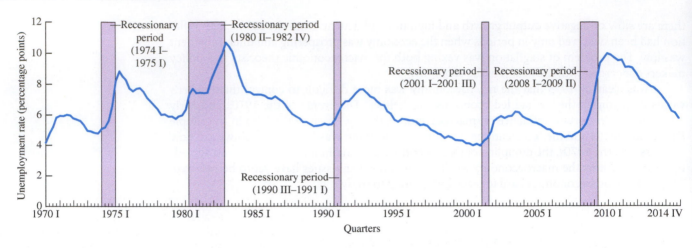

▲ **FIGURE 5.5** **Unemployment Rate, 1970 I–2014 IV**      MyEconLab Real-time data

The U.S. unemployment rate since 1970 shows wide variations. The five recessionary reference periods show increases in the unemployment rate.

five recessions. In the 1974–1975 recession, the unemployment rate reached a maximum of 8.8 percent in the second quarter of 1975. During the 1980–1982 recession, it reached a maximum of 10.7 percent in the fourth quarter of 1982. The unemployment rate continued to rise after the 1990–1991 recession and reached a peak of 7.6 percent in the third quarter of 1992. In the 2008-2009 recession it reached a peak of 9.9 percent in the fourth quarter of 2009. By 2015 the unemployment rate was 5.5 percent.

Figure 5.6 plots the inflation rate for 1970 I–2014 IV. The two high inflation periods are 1973 IV–1975 IV and 1979 I–1981 IV, which are shaded. In the first high inflation period, the inflation rate peaked at 11.1 percent in the first quarter of 1975. In the second high inflation period, inflation peaked at 10.2 percent in the first quarter of 1981. Since 1983, the inflation rate has been quite low by the standards of the 1970s. Since 1992, it has been between about 1 and 3 percent.

In the following chapters, we will explain the behavior of and the connections among variables such as output, unemployment, and inflation. When you understand the forces at work in creating the movements shown in Figures 5.4, 5.5, and 5.6, you will have come a long way in understanding how the macroeconomy works.

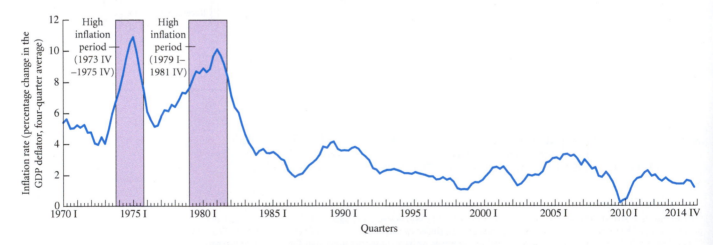

▲ **FIGURE 5.6** **Inflation Rate (Percentage Change**      MyEconLab Real-time data
**in the GDP Deflator, Four-Quarter Average), 1970 I–2014 IV**

Since 1970, inflation has been high in two periods: 1973 IV-1975 IV and 1979 I-1981 IV. Inflation between 1983 and 1992 was moderate. Since 1992, it has been fairly low.

## — SUMMARY —

1. *Microeconomics* examines the functioning of individual industries and the behavior of individual decision-making units. *Macroeconomics* is concerned with the sum, or aggregate, of these individual decisions—the consumption of *all* households in the economy, the amount of labor supplied and demanded by *all* individuals and firms, and the total amount of *all* goods and services produced.

### 5.1 MACROECONOMIC CONCERNS *p. 91*

2. The three topics of primary concern to macroeconomists are the growth rate of aggregate output, the level of unemployment, and increases in the overall price level, or *inflation*.

### 5.2 THE COMPONENTS OF THE MACROECONOMY *p. 94*

3. The *circular flow* diagram shows the flow of income received and payments made by the four groups in the economy—households, firms, the government, and the rest of the world. Everybody's expenditure is someone else's receipt—every transaction must have two sides.

4. Another way of looking at how households, firms, the government, and the rest of the world relate is to consider the markets in which they interact: the goods-and-services market, labor market, and money (financial) market.

5. Among the tools that the government has available for influencing the macroeconomy are *fiscal policy* (decisions on taxes and government spending) and *monetary policy* (control of short term interest rates).

### 5.3 A BRIEF HISTORY OF MACROECONOMICS *p. 97*

6. Macroeconomics was born out of the effort to explain the *Great Depression* of the 1930s. Since that time, the discipline has evolved, concerning itself with new issues as the problems facing the economy have changed. Through the late 1960s, it was believed that the government could fine-tune the economy to keep it running on an even keel at all times. The poor economic performance of the 1970s, however, showed that *fine-tuning* does not always work.

### 5.4 THE U.S. ECONOMY SINCE 1970 *p. 99*

7. Since 1970, the U.S. economy has seen five *recessions* and two periods of high inflation.

## — REVIEW TERMS AND CONCEPTS —

aggregate behavior, *p. 90*
aggregate output, *p. 91*
business cycle, *p. 91*
circular flow, *p. 94*
contraction, recession, *or slump, p. 92*
corporate bonds, *p. 96*
deflation, *p. 93*
depression, *p. 91*
dividends, *p. 96*

expansion *or boom, p. 92*
fine-tuning, *p. 97*
fiscal policy, *p. 96*
Great Depression, *p. 97*
hyperinflation, *p. 93*
inflation, *p. 93*
macroeconomics, *p. 90*
microeconomics, *p. 90*
monetary policy, *p. 96*

recession, *p. 91*
shares of stock, *p. 96*
stagflation, *p. 98*
sticky prices, *p. 90*
transfer payments, *p. 94*
Treasury bonds, notes, *or bills, p. 96*
unemployment rate, *p. 93*

## — PROBLEMS —

All problems are available on MyEconLab.

### 5.1 MACROECONOMIC CONCERNS

LEARNING OBJECTIVE: Describe the three primary concerns of macroeconomics.

1.1 Define inflation. Assume that you live in a simple economy in which only three goods are produced and traded: cashews, pecans, and almonds. Suppose that on January 1, 2015, cashews sold for $12.50 per pound, pecans were $4.00 per pound, and almonds were $5.50 per pound. At the end of the year, you discover that the cashew crop was lower than expected and that cashew prices had increased to $17.00 per pound, but pecan prices stayed at $4.00 and almond prices had actually fallen to $3.00. Can you say what happened to the overall "price level"? How might you construct a measure of the "change in the price level"? What additional information might you need to construct your measure?

1.2 Define *unemployment*. Should everyone who does not hold a job be considered "unemployed"? To help with your answer, draw a supply and demand diagram depicting the labor market. What is measured along the demand curve? What factors determine the quantity of labor demanded during a given period? What is measured along the labor supply curve? What factors determine the quantity of labor supplied by households during a given period? What is the opportunity cost of holding a job?

1.3 According to the National Bureau of Economic Research (NBER), what has been dubbed the Great Recession officially began in December, 2007 and ended in June, 2009. During this recession, national output of goods and services fell from the second quarter of 2008 until the end of the recession in the second quarter of 2009, and then slowly began to increase. When the recession was officially declared as being over, the unemployment rate continued to rise, reaching 10 percent in October, 2009 and remained close to that level until April, 2010 when it slowly started to decline. During that 10-month period, the net loss in jobs in the U.S. economy was close to 1.4 million. How is it possible that output can rise while at the same time employment falls?

1.4 Describe the economy of your state. What is the most recently reported unemployment rate? How has the number of payroll jobs changed over the last 3 months and over the last year? How does your state's performance compare to the U.S. economy's performance over the last year? What explanations have been offered in the press? How accurate are they?

1.5 Explain briefly how macroeconomics is different from microeconomics. How can macroeconomists use microeconomic theory to guide them in their work, and why might they want to do so?

1.6 In 1974, the price of a first-class postage stamp was 10 cents, a loaf of bread averaged 28 cents, gasoline was 53 cents per gallon, and the average price of a new car was $3,500. In 2014, the postage stamp cost 49 cents, a loaf of bread was $2.46, gasoline averaged $3.36 per gallon, and the average new car cost $32,531. From this statement, it follows that consumers today are worse off than consumers in 1975. Comment.

## 5.2 THE COMPONENTS OF THE MACROECONOMY

LEARNING OBJECTIVE: Discuss the interaction between the four components of the macroeconomy.

2.1 During 1993 when the economy was growing slowly, President Clinton recommended a series of spending cuts and tax increases designed to reduce the deficit. These were passed by Congress in the Omnibus Budget Reconciliation Act of 1993. Some who opposed the bill argued that the United States was pursuing a "contractionary fiscal policy" at precisely the wrong time. Explain their logic.

2.2 In which of the three market arenas is each of the following goods traded?
a. The athletic skills of the Green Bay Packers' quarterback Aaron Rodgers
b. Shares of Nike stock
c. The hair-braiding abilities of a hair stylist in Akron, Ohio
d. A Gibson Les Paul Custom guitar
e. Corporate bonds issued by Verizon
f. An Apple Watch

## 5.3 A BRIEF HISTORY OF MACROECONOMICS

LEARNING OBJECTIVE: Summarize the macroeconomic history of the United States between 1929 and 1970.

3.1 Many of the expansionary periods during the twentieth century occurred during wars. Why do you think this is true?

3.2 John Maynard Keynes was the first to show that government policy could be used to change aggregate output and prevent recession by stabilizing the economy. Describe the economy of the world at the time Keynes was writing. Describe the economy of the United States today. What measures are being proposed by potential presidential candidates for the election of 2016 to stimulate growth in the economy? Do any of these proposed policies follow the policies proposed by John Maynard Keynes? If so, which policies and from which candidates?

3.3 Assume that the demand for flight attendants increases significantly as a result of an increase in demand for air travel. Explain what will happen to unemployment using both classical and Keynesian reasoning.

3.4 Explain why the length and severity of the Great Depression necessitated a fundamental rethinking of the operations of the macroeconomy.

## 5.4 THE U.S. ECONOMY SINCE 1970

LEARNING OBJECTIVE: Describe the U.S. Economy Since 1970.

4.1 [**Related to the *Economics in Practice* on p. 98**] The *Economics in Practice* describes prosperity and recession as they are depicted in literature. In mid-2009, there was a debate about whether the U.S. economy had entered an economic expansion. Look at the data on real GDP growth and unemployment and describe the pattern since 2007. You can find raw data on employment and unemployment at www.bls.gov, and you can find raw data on real GDP growth at www.bea.gov. Summarize what happened in mid-2009. Did the United States enter an economic expansion? Explain.

# Measuring National Output and National Income

We saw in the last chapter that macroeconomics is concerned with aggregate output, unemployment, and inflation. In this chapter, we discuss the measurement of aggregate output and inflation. In the next chapter, we discuss the measurement of unemployment. Accurate measures of these variables are critical for understanding the economy. Without good measures, economists would have a hard time analyzing how the economy works and policy makers would have little to guide them on which policies are best for the economy.

Much of the macroeconomic data we use come from the **national income and product accounts**, which are compiled by the Bureau of Economic Analysis (BEA) of the U.S. Department of Commerce. It is hard to overestimate the importance of these accounts. They are, in fact, one of the great inventions of the twentieth century. (See the *Economics in Practice*, p. 112.) They not only convey data about the performance of the economy but also provide a conceptual framework that macroeconomists use to think about how the pieces of the economy fit together. When economists think about the macroeconomy, the categories and vocabulary they use come from the national income and product accounts.

The national income and product accounts can be compared with the mechanical or wiring diagrams for an automobile engine. The diagrams do not explain how an engine works, but they identify the key parts of an engine and show how they are connected. Trying to understand the macroeconomy without understanding national income accounting is like trying to fix an engine without a mechanical diagram and with no names for the engine parts.

**national income and product accounts** Data collected and published by the government describing the various components of national income and output in the economy.

There are literally thousands of variables in the national income and product accounts. In this chapter, we discuss only the most important. This chapter is meant to convey the way the national income and product accounts represent or organize the economy and the *sizes* of the various pieces of the economy.

**6.1 LEARNING OBJECTIVE**

Describe GDP fundamentals and differentiate between GDP and GNP.

# Gross Domestic Product

The key concept in the national income and product accounts is **gross domestic product (GDP)**.

**gross domestic product (GDP)** The total market value of all final goods and services produced within a given period by factors of production located within a country.

> GDP is the total market value of a country's output. It is the market value of all final goods and services produced within a given period of time by factors of production located within a country.

U.S. GDP for 2014—the value of all output produced by factors of production in the United States in 2014—was $17,418.9 billion.

GDP is a critical concept. Just as an individual firm needs to evaluate the success or failure of its operations each year, so the economy as a whole needs to assess itself. GDP, as a measure of the total production of an economy, provides us with a country's economic report card. Because GDP is so important, we need to take time to explain exactly what its definition means.

## Final Goods and Services

**final goods and services** Goods and services produced for final use.

**intermediate goods** Goods that are produced by one firm for use in further processing or for resale by another firm.

First, note that the definition refers to **final goods and services**. Many goods produced in the economy are not classified as *final* goods, but instead as intermediate goods. **Intermediate goods** are produced by one firm for use in further processing or for resale by another firm. For example, tires sold to automobile manufacturers are intermediate goods. The chips that go in Apple's iPhone are also intermediate goods. The value of intermediate goods is not counted in GDP.

Why are intermediate goods not counted in GDP? Suppose that in producing a car, General Motors (GM) pays $200 to Goodyear for tires. GM uses these tires (among other components) to assemble a car, which it sells for $24,000. The value of the car (including its tires) is $24,000, not $24,000 + $200. The final price of the car already reflects the value of all its components. To count in GDP both the value of the tires sold to the automobile manufacturers and the value of the automobiles sold to the consumers would result in double counting. It would also lead us to conclude that a decision by GM to produce its own tires rather than buy them from Goodyear leads to a reduction in the value of goods produced by the economy.

**value added** The difference between the value of goods as they leave a stage of production and the cost of the goods as they entered that stage.

Double counting can also be avoided by counting only the value added to a product by each firm in its production process. The **value added** during some stage of production is the difference between the value of goods as they leave that stage of production and the cost of the goods as they entered that stage. Value added is illustrated in Table 6.1. The four stages of the production of a gallon of gasoline are: (1) oil drilling, (2) refining, (3) shipping, and (4) retail sale. In the first stage, value added is the value of the crude oil. In the second stage, the refiner purchases the oil from the driller, refines it into gasoline, and sells it to the shipper. The refiner pays the driller $3.00 per gallon and charges the shipper $3.30. The value added by the refiner is thus

| TABLE 6.1 | Value Added in the Production of a Gallon of Gasoline (Hypothetical Numbers) | |
|---|---|---|
| **Stage of Production** | **Value of Sales** | **Value Added** |
| (1) Oil drilling | $3.00 | $3.00 |
| (2) Refining | 3.30 | 0.30 |
| (3) Shipping | 3.60 | 0.30 |
| (4) Retail sale | 4.00 | 0.40 |
| Total value added | | $4.00 |

$0.30 per gallon. The shipper then sells the gasoline to retailers for $3.60. The value added in the third stage of production is $0.30. Finally, the retailer sells the gasoline to consumers for $4.00. The value added at the fourth stage is $0.40, and the total value added in the production process is $4.00, the same as the value of sales at the retail level. Adding the total values of sales at each stage of production ($3.00 + $3.30 + $3.60 + $4.00 = $13.90) would significantly overestimate the value of the gallon of gasoline.

> In calculating GDP, we can sum up the value added at each stage of production or we can take the value of final sales. We do not use the value of total sales in an economy to measure how much output has been produced.

## Exclusion of Used Goods and Paper Transactions

GDP is concerned only with new, or current, production. Old output is not counted in current GDP because it was already counted when it was produced. It would be double counting to count sales of used goods in current GDP. If someone sells a used car to you, the transaction is not counted in GDP because no new production has taken place. Similarly, a house is counted in GDP only at the time it is built, not each time it is resold. In short:

> GDP does not count transactions in which money or goods changes hands and in which no new goods and services are produced.

Sales of stocks and bonds are not counted in GDP. These exchanges are transfers of ownership of assets, either electronically or through paper exchanges, and do not correspond to current production. What if you sell the stock or bond for more than you originally paid for it? Profits from the stock or bond market have nothing to do with current production, so they are not counted in GDP. However, if you pay a fee to a broker for selling a stock of yours to someone else, this fee is counted in GDP because the broker is performing a service for you. This service is part of current production. Be careful to distinguish between exchanges of stocks and bonds for money (or for other stocks and bonds), which do not involve current production, and fees for performing such exchanges, which do.

## Exclusion of Output Produced Abroad by Domestically Owned Factors of Production

> GDP is the value of output produced by factors of production *located within a country*.

The three basic factors of production are land, labor, and capital. The output produced by U.S. citizens abroad—for example, U.S. citizens working for a foreign company—is *not* counted in U.S. GDP because the output is not produced within the United States. Likewise, profits earned abroad by U.S. companies are not counted in U.S. GDP. However, the output produced by foreigners working in the United States is counted in U.S. GDP because the output is produced within the United States. Also, profits earned in the United States by foreign-owned companies are counted in U.S. GDP.

It is sometimes useful to have a measure of the output produced by factors of production owned by a country's citizens regardless of where the output is produced. This measure is called **gross national product (GNP)**. For most countries, including the United States, the difference between GDP and GNP is small. In 2014, GNP for the United States was $17,630.6 billion, which is close to the $17,418.9 billion value for U.S. GDP.

The distinction between GDP and GNP can be tricky. Consider the Honda plant in Marysville, Ohio. The plant is owned by the Honda Corporation, a Japanese firm, but most

**gross national product (GNP)** The total market value of all final goods and services produced within a given period by factors of production owned by a country's citizens, regardless of where the output is produced.

of the workers employed at the plant are U.S. workers. Although all the output of the plant is included in U.S. GDP, only part of it is included in U.S. GNP. The wages paid to U.S. workers are part of U.S. GNP, whereas the profits from the plant are not. The profits from the plant are counted in Japanese GNP because this is output produced by Japanese-owned factors of production (Japanese capital in this case). The profits, however, are not counted in Japanese GDP because they were not earned in Japan.

# Calculating GDP

**6.2 LEARNING** OBJECTIVE

Explain two methods for calculating GDP.

**expenditure approach** A method of computing GDP that measures the total amount spent on all final goods and services during a given period.

**income approach** A method of computing GDP that measures the income—wages, rents, interest, and profits—received by all factors of production in producing final goods and services.

GDP can be computed two ways. One way is to add up the total amount spent on all final goods and services during a given period. This is the **expenditure approach** to calculating GDP. The other way is to add up the income—wages, rents, interest, and profits—received by all factors of production in producing final goods and services. This is the **income approach** to calculating GDP. These two methods lead to the same value for GDP for the reason we discussed in the previous chapter: *Every payment (expenditure) by a buyer is at the same time a receipt (income) for the seller.* We can measure either income received or expenditures made, and we will end up with the same total output.

Suppose the economy is made up of just one firm and the firm's total output this year sells for $1 million. Because the total amount spent on output this year is $1 million, this year's GDP is $1 million. (Remember: The expenditure approach calculates GDP on the basis of the total amount spent on final goods and services in the economy.) However, *every one* of the million dollars of GDP either is paid to someone or remains with the owners of the firm as profit. Using the income approach, we add up the wages paid to employees of the firm, the interest paid to those who lent money to the firm, and the rents paid to those who leased land, buildings, or equipment to the firm. What is left over is profit, which is, of course, income to the owners of the firm. If we add up the incomes of all the factors of production, including profits to the owners, we get a GDP of $1 million.

## The Expenditure Approach

Recall from the previous chapter the four main groups in the economy: households, firms, the government, and the rest of the world. There are also four main categories of expenditure:

- Personal consumption expenditures (*C*): household spending on consumer goods
- Gross private domestic investment (*I*): spending by firms and households on new capital, that is, plant, equipment, inventory, and new residential structures
- Government consumption and gross investment (*G*)
- Net exports (*EX* − *IM*): net spending by the rest of the world, or exports (*EX*) minus imports (*IM*)

The expenditure approach calculates GDP by adding together these four components of spending. It is shown here in equation form:

$$GDP = C + I + G + (EX - IM)$$

**personal consumption expenditures (C)** Expenditures by consumers on goods and services.

**durable goods** Goods that last a relatively long time, such as cars and household appliances.

**nondurable goods** Goods that are used up fairly quickly, such as food and clothing.

**services** The things we buy that do not involve the production of physical things, such as legal and medical services and education.

U.S. GDP was $17,418.9 billion in 2014. The four components of the expenditure approach are shown in Table 6.2, along with their various categories.

**Personal Consumption Expenditures (C)** The largest part of GDP consists of **personal consumption expenditures (C)**. Table 6.2 shows that in 2014, the amount of personal consumption expenditures accounted for 68.5 percent of GDP. These are expenditures by consumers on goods and services.

There are three main categories of consumer expenditures: durable goods, nondurable goods, and services. **Durable goods**, such as automobiles, furniture, and household appliances, last a relatively long time. **Nondurable goods**, such as food, clothing, gasoline, and cigarettes, are used up fairly quickly. Payments for **services**—those things we buy that do not involve the

## ECONOMICS IN PRACTICE

### Where Does eBay Get Counted?

eBay runs an online marketplace with more than 220 million registered users who buy and sell 2.4 billion items a year, ranging from children's toys to oil paintings. In December 2007, one eBay user auctioned off a 1933 Chicago World's Fair pennant. The winning bid was slightly more than $20.

eBay is traded on the New York Stock Exchange, employs hundreds of people, and has a market value of about $40 billion. With regard to eBay, what do you think gets counted as part of current GDP?

That 1933 pennant, for example, does not get counted. The production of that pennant was counted back in 1933. The many cartons of K'nex bricks sent from one home to another don't count either. Their value was counted when the bricks were first produced. What about a newly minted Scrabble game? One of the interesting features of eBay is that it has changed from being a market in which individuals market their hand-me-downs to a place that small and even large businesses use as a sales site. The value of the new Scrabble game would be counted as part of this year's GDP if it were produced this year.

So do any of eBay's services count as part of GDP? eBay's business is to provide a marketplace for exchange. In doing so, it uses labor and capital and creates value. In return for creating this value, eBay charges fees to the sellers that use its site. The value of these fees does enter into GDP. So although the old knickknacks that people sell on eBay do

not contribute to current GDP, the cost of finding an interested buyer for those old goods does indeed get counted.

#### THINKING PRACTICALLY

1. John has a 2009 Honda Civic. In 2013, he sells it to Mary for $10,000. Is that $10,000 counted in the GDP for 2013?
2. If John is an automobile dealer, does that change your answer to Question 1 at all?

production of physical items—include expenditures for doctors, lawyers, and educational institutions. As Table 6.2 shows, in 2014, durable goods expenditures accounted for 7.5 percent of GDP, nondurables for 15.3 percent, and services for 45.7 percent. Almost half of GDP is now service consumption.

**TABLE 6.2   Components of U.S. GDP, 2014: The Expenditure Approach**

|  | Billions of Dollars ($) | | Percentage of GDP (%) | |
| --- | --- | --- | --- | --- |
| Personal consumption expenditures (C) | 11,930.3 | | 68.5 | |
|   Durable goods | | 1,302.5 | | 7.5 |
|   Nondurable goods | | 2,666.2 | | 15.3 |
|   Services | | 7,961.7 | | 45.7 |
| Gross private domestic investment (I) | 2,851.6 | | 16.4 | |
|   Nonresidential | | 2,210.5 | | 12.7 |
|   Residential | | 559.1 | | 3.2 |
|   Change in business inventories | | 82.0 | | 0.5 |
| Government consumption and gross investment (G) | 3,175.2 | | 18.2 | |
|   Federal | | 1,219.2 | | 7.0 |
|   State and local | | 1,956.1 | | 11.2 |
| Net exports (EX − IM) | −538.2 | | −3.1 | |
|   Exports (EX) | | 2,337.0 | | 13.4 |
|   Imports (IM) | | 2,875.2 | | 16.5 |
| Gross domestic product | 17,418.9 | | 100.0 | |

*Note:* Numbers may not add exactly because of rounding.
*Source:* U.S. Bureau of Economic Analysis, March 27, 2015.

**Gross Private Domestic Investment (*I*)** *Investment*, as we use the term in economics, refers to the purchase of new capital—housing, plants, equipment, and inventory. The economic use of the term is in contrast to its everyday use, where *investment* often refers to purchases of stocks, bonds, or mutual funds.

**gross private domestic invest-ment (*I*)** Total investment in capital—that is, the purchase of new housing, plants, equipment, and inventory by the private (or nongovern-ment) sector.

Total investment in capital by the private sector is called **gross private domestic investment (*I*)**. Expenditures by firms for machines, tools, plants, and so on make up **nonresidential investment**.[1] Because these are goods that firms buy for their own final use, they are part of "final sales" and counted in GDP. Expenditures for new houses and apartment buildings constitute **residential investment**. The third component of gross private domestic investment, the **change in business inventories**, is the amount by which firms' inventories change during a period. Business inventories can be looked at as the goods that firms produce now but intend to sell later. In 2014, gross private domestic investment accounted for 16.4 percent of GDP. Of that, 12.7 percent was nonresidential investment, 3.2 percent was residential investment, and 0.5 percent was change in business inventories.

**nonresidential investment** Expenditures by firms for machines, tools, plants, and so on.

**residential investment** Expenditures by households and firms on new houses and apartment buildings.

**change in business inventories** The amount by which firms' inventories change during a period. Inventories are the goods that firms produce now but intend to sell later.

*Change in Business Inventories* Why is the change in business inventories considered a component of investment—the purchase of new capital? To run a business most firms hold inventories, in part because they cannot predict exactly how much will be sold each day and want to avoid losing sales by running out of a product. Inventories—goods produced for later sale—are counted as capital because they produce value in the future. An increase in inventories is an increase in capital.

Regarding GDP, remember that it is not the market value of total final *sales* during the period, but rather the market value of total final *production*. The relationship between total production and total sales is as follows:

$$GDP = \text{Final sales} + \text{Change in business inventories}$$

Total production (GDP) equals final sales of domestic goods plus the change in business inventories. In 2014, production in the United States was larger than sales by $82.0 billion. The stock of inventories at the end of 2014 was $82.0 billion *larger* than it was at the end of 2013—the change in business inventories was $82.0 billion.

*Gross Investment versus Net Investment* During the process of production, capital (especially machinery and equipment) produced in previous periods gradually wears out. GDP includes newly produced capital goods but does not take account of capital goods "consumed" in the production process. As a result, GDP overstates the real production of an economy because it does not account for the part of that production that serves just to replace worn out capital.

**depreciation** The amount by which an asset's value falls in a given period.

The amount by which an asset's value falls each period is called its **depreciation**.[2] A personal computer purchased by a business today may be expected to have a useful life of 4 years before becoming worn out or obsolete. Over that period, the computer steadily depreciates.

**gross investment** The total value of all newly produced capital goods (plant, equipment, housing, and inventory) produced in a given period.

What is the relationship between gross investment (*I*) and depreciation? **Gross investment** is the total value of all newly produced capital goods (plant, equipment, housing, and inventory) produced in a given period. It takes no account of the fact that some capital wears out and must be replaced. **Net investment** is equal to gross investment minus depreciation. Net investment is a measure of how much the stock of capital *changes* during a period. Positive net investment means that the amount of new capital produced exceeds the amount that wears out, and negative net investment means that the amount of new capital produced is less than the amount that wears out. Therefore, if net investment is positive, the capital stock has increased, and if net

**net investment** Gross investment minus depreciation.

---

[1] The distinction between what is considered investment and what is considered consumption is sometimes fairly arbitrary. A firm's purchase of a car or a truck is counted as investment, but a household's purchase of a car or a truck is counted as consumption of durable goods. In general, expenditures by firms for items that last longer than a year are counted as investment expenditures. Expenditures for items that last less than a year are seen as purchases of intermediate goods.
[2] This is the formal definition of economic depreciation. Because depreciation is difficult to measure precisely, accounting rules allow firms to use shortcut methods to approximate the amount of depreciation that they incur each period. To complicate matters even more, the U.S. tax laws allow firms to deduct depreciation for tax purposes under a different set of rules.

investment is negative, the capital stock has decreased. Put another way, the capital stock at the end of a period is equal to the capital stock that existed at the beginning of the period plus net investment:

$$capital_{end\ of\ period} = capital_{beginning\ of\ period} + net\ investment$$

**Government Consumption and Gross Investment (G)** **Government consumption and gross investment (G)** include expenditures by federal, state, and local governments for final goods (bombs, pencils, school buildings) and services (military salaries, congressional salaries, school teachers' salaries). Some of these expenditures are counted as government consumption, and some are counted as government gross investment. Government transfer payments (Social Security benefits, veterans' disability stipends, and so on) are not included in *G* because these transfers are not purchases of anything currently produced. The payments are not made in exchange for any goods or services. Because interest payments on the government debt are also counted as transfers, they are excluded from GDP on the grounds that they are not payments for current goods or services.

As Table 6.2 shows, government consumption and gross investment accounted for $3,175.2 billion, or 18.2 percent of U.S. GDP, in 2014. Federal government consumption and gross investment accounted for 7.0 percent of GDP, and state and local government consumption and gross investment accounted for 11.2 percent.

**Net Exports (EX − IM)** The value of **net exports (EX − IM)** is the difference between *exports* (sales to foreigners of U.S.-produced goods and services) and *imports* (U.S. purchases of goods and services from abroad). This figure can be positive or negative. In 2014, the United States exported less than it imported, so the level of net exports was negative (−$538.2 billion). Before 1976, the United States was generally a net exporter—exports exceeded imports, so the net export figure was positive.

The reason for including net exports in the definition of GDP is simple. Consumption, investment, and government spending (*C, I,* and *G,* respectively) include expenditures on goods produced at home and abroad. Therefore, *C + I + G* overstates domestic production because it contains expenditures on foreign-produced goods—that is, imports (*IM*), which have to be subtracted from GDP to obtain the correct figure. At the same time, *C + I + G* understates domestic production because some of what a nation produces is sold abroad and therefore is not included in *C, I,* or *G*—exports (*EX*) have to be added in. If a U.S. firm produces computers and sells them in Germany, the computers are part of U.S. production and should be counted as part of U.S. GDP.

## The Income Approach

We now turn to calculating GDP using the income approach, which looks at GDP in terms of who receives it as income rather than as who purchases it.

We begin with the concept of **national income**, which is defined in Table 6.3. National income is the sum of eight income items. **Compensation of employees**, the largest of the eight items by far, includes wages and salaries paid to households by firms and by the government, as well as various supplements to wages and salaries such as contributions that employers make to social insurance and private pension funds. **Proprietors' income** is the income of unincorporated businesses. **Rental income**, a minor item, is the income received by property owners in the form of rent. **Corporate profits**, the second-largest item of the eight, is the income of corporations. **Net interest** is the interest paid by business. (Interest paid by households and the government is not counted in GDP because it is not assumed to flow from the production of goods and services.)

The sixth item, **indirect taxes minus subsidies**, includes taxes such as sales taxes, customs duties, and license fees less subsidies that the government pays for which it receives no goods or services in return. (Subsidies are like negative taxes.) The value of indirect taxes minus subsidies is thus net revenue received by the government. **Net business transfer payments** are net transfer

**government consumption and gross investment (G)** Expenditures by federal, state, and local governments for final goods and services.

**net exports (EX − IM)** The difference between exports (sales to foreigners of U.S.-produced goods and services) and imports (U.S. purchases of goods and services from abroad). The figure can be positive or negative.

**national income** The total income earned by the factors of production owned by a country's citizens.

**compensation of employees** Includes wages, salaries, and various supplements—employer contributions to social insurance and pension funds, for example—paid to households by firms and by the government.

**proprietors' income** The income of unincorporated businesses.

**rental income** The income received by property owners in the form of rent.

**corporate profits** The income of corporations.

**net interest** The interest paid by business.

**indirect taxes minus subsidies** Taxes such as sales taxes, customs duties, and license fees less subsidies that the government pays for which it receives no goods or services in return. Is net revenue received by the government.

**net business transfer payments** Net transfer payments by businesses to others.

**TABLE 6.3   National Income, 2014**

|  | Billions of Dollars ($) | Percentage of National Income (%) |
|---|---|---|
| National income | 15,070.4 | 100.0 |
| Compensation of employees | 9,221.6 | 61.2 |
| Proprietors' income | 1,380.2 | 9.2 |
| Rental income | 640.2 | 4.2 |
| Corporate profits | 2,089.8 | 13.9 |
| Net interest | 486.3 | 3.2 |
| Indirect taxes minus subsidies | 1,145.8 | 7.6 |
| Net business transfer payments | 140.6 | 0.9 |
| Surplus of government enterprises | −34.2 | −0.2 |

*Source:* U.S. Bureau of Economic Analysis, March 27, 2015.

**surplus of government enterprises**   Income of government enterprises.

payments by businesses to others and are thus income of others. The final item is the **surplus of government enterprises**, which is the income of government enterprises. Table 6.3 shows that this item was negative in 2014: government enterprises on net ran at a loss.

National income is the total income of the country, but it is not quite GDP. Table 6.4 shows what is involved in going from national income to GDP. Table 6.4 first shows that in moving from GDP to GNP, we need to add receipts of factor income from the rest of the world and subtract payments of factor income to the rest of the world. National income is income of the country's citizens, not the income of the residents of the country. So we first need to move from GDP to GNP. This, as discussed previously, is a minor adjustment.

We then need to subtract depreciation from GNP, which is a large adjustment. GNP less depreciation is called **net national product (NNP)**. Why is depreciation subtracted? To see why, go back to the example previously in this chapter in which the economy is made up of just one firm and total output (GDP) for the year is $1 million. Assume that after the firm pays wages, interest, and rent, it has $100,000 left. Assume also that its capital stock depreciated by $40,000 during the year. National income includes corporate profits (see Table 6.3), and in calculating corporate profits, the $40,000 depreciation is subtracted from the $100,000, leaving profits of $60,000. So national income does not include the $40,000. When we calculate GDP using the expenditure approach, however, depreciation is not subtracted. We simply add consumption, investment, government spending, and net exports. In our simple example, this is just $1 million. We thus must subtract depreciation from GDP (actually GNP when there is a rest-of-the-world sector) to get national income.

**net national product (NNP)** Gross national product minus depreciation; a nation's total product minus what is required to maintain the value of its capital stock.

Table 6.4 shows that net national product and national income are the same except for a **statistical discrepancy**, a data measurement error. If the government were completely accurate in its data collection, the statistical discrepancy would be zero. The data collection, however, is not perfect, and the statistical discrepancy is the measurement error in each period. Table 6.4 shows that in 2014, this error was $176.0 billion, which is small compared to national income of $15,070.4 billion.

**statistical discrepancy**   Data measurement error.

**TABLE 6.4   GDP, GNP, NNP, and National Income, 2014**

|  | Dollars ($, Billions) |
|---|---|
| **GDP** | 17,418.9 |
| Plus: Receipts of factor income from the rest of the world | +827.7 |
| Less: Payments of factor income to the rest of the world | −616.0 |
| Equals: **GNP** | 17,630.6 |
| Less: Depreciation | −2,736.2 |
| Equals: **Net national product (NNP)** | 14,894.4 |
| Less: Statistical discrepancy | −176.0 |
| Equals: **National income** | 15,070.4 |

*Source:* U.S. Bureau of Economic Analysis, March 27, 2015.

| TABLE 6.5   National Income, Personal Income, Disposable Personal Income, and Personal Saving, 2014 | Dollar (Billions, $) |
|---|---|
| National income | 15,070.4 |
| Less: Amount of national income not going to households | −341.8 |
| Equals: **Personal income** | 14,728.6 |
| Less: Personal income taxes | −1,742.9 |
| Equals: **Disposable personal income** | 12,985.8 |
| Less: Personal consumption expenditures | −11,930.3 |
| Personal interest payments | −256.8 |
| Transfer payments made by households | −170.3 |
| Equals: **Personal saving** | 628.3 |
| Personal saving as a percentage of disposable personal income: | 4.8% |

*Source:* U.S. Bureau of Economic Analysis, March 27, 2015.

We have so far seen from Table 6.3 the various income items that make up total national income, and we have seen from Table 6.4 how GDP and national income are related. A useful way to think about national income is to consider how much of it goes to households. The total income of households is called **personal income**, and it turns out that almost all of national income is personal income. Table 6.5 shows that of the $15,070.4 billion in national income in 2014, $14,728.6 billion was personal income. The second line in Table 6.5, the amount of national income not going to households, includes the profits of corporations not paid to households in the form of dividends, called the *retained earnings* of corporations. This is income that stays inside corporations for some period rather than going to households, and so it is part of national income but not personal income.

Personal income is the income received by households before they pay personal income taxes. The amount of income that households have to spend or save is called **disposable personal income, or after-tax income** . It is equal to personal income minus personal income taxes, as shown in Table 6.5.

Because disposable personal income is the amount of income that households can spend or save, it is an important income concept. Table 6.5 shows there are three categories of spending: (1) personal consumption expenditures, (2) personal interest payments, and (3) transfer payments made by households. The amount of disposable personal income left after total personal spending is **personal saving.** If your monthly disposable income is $500 and you spend $450, you have $50 left at the end of the month. Your personal saving is $50 for the month. Your personal saving level can be negative: If you earn $500 and spend $600 during the month, you have *dissaved* $100. To spend $100 more than you earn, you will have to borrow the $100 from someone, take the $100 from your savings account, or sell an asset you own.

The **personal saving rate** is the percentage of disposable personal income saved, an important indicator of household behavior. A low saving rate means households are spending a large fraction of their income. As Table 6.5 shows, the U.S. personal saving rate in 2014 was 4.8 percent. Saving rates tend to rise during recessionary periods, when consumers become anxious about their future, and fall during boom times, as pent-up spending demand gets released. In 2005 the saving rate got down to 2.5 percent.

**personal income**   The total income of households.

**disposable personal income or after-tax income**   Personal income minus personal income taxes. The amount that households have to spend or save.

**personal saving**   The amount of disposable income that is left after total personal spending in a given period.

**personal saving rate**   The percentage of disposable personal income that is saved. If the personal saving rate is low, households are spending a large amount relative to their incomes; if it is high, households are spending cautiously.

**current dollars**   The current prices that we pay for goods and services.

# Nominal versus Real GDP

We have thus far looked at GDP measured in **current dollars**, or the current prices we pay for goods and services. When we measure something in current dollars, we refer to it as a *nominal* value. **Nominal GDP** is GDP measured in current dollars—all components of GDP valued at their current prices.

In most applications in macroeconomics, however, nominal GDP is not what we are after. It is not a good measure of aggregate output over time. Why? Assume that there is only one

**6.3 LEARNING OBJECTIVE**

Discuss the difference between real GDP and nominal GDP.

**nominal GDP**   Gross domestic product measured in current dollars.

## ECONOMICS IN PRACTICE

## GDP: One of the Great Inventions of the 20th Century

As the 20th century drew to a close, the U.S. Department of Commerce embarked on a review of its achievements. At the conclusion of this review, the Department named the development of the national income and product accounts as "its achievement of the century."

J. Steven Landefeld *Director, Bureau of Economic Analysis*

While the GDP and the rest of the national income accounts may seem to be arcane concepts, they are truly among the great inventions of the twentieth century.

Paul A. Samuelson and William D. Nordhaus

GDP! The right concept of economy-wide output, accurately measured. The U.S. and the world rely on it to tell where we are in the business cycle and to estimate long-run growth. It is the centerpiece of an elaborate and indispensable system of social accounting, the national income and product accounts. This is surely the single most innovative achievement of the Commerce Department in the 20th century. I was fortunate to become an economist in the 1930's when Kuznets, Nathan, Gilbert, and Jaszi were creating this most important set of economic time series. In economic theory, macroeconomics was just beginning at the same time. Complementary, these two innovations deserve much credit for the improved performance of the economy in the second half of the century.

James Tobin

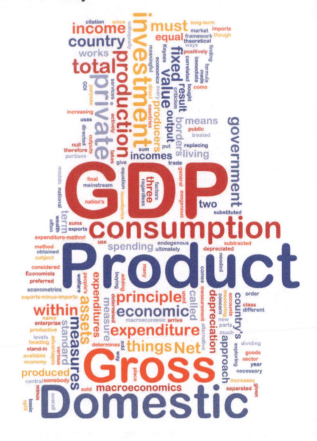

### FROM THE *SURVEY OF CURRENT BUSINESS*

Prior to the development of the NIPAs [national income and product accounts], policy makers had to guide the economy using limited and fragmentary information about the state of the economy. The Great Depression underlined the problems of incomplete data and led to the development of the national accounts:

One reads with dismay of Presidents Hoover and then Roosevelt designing policies to combat the Great Depression of the 1930s on the basis of such sketchy data as stock price indices, freight car loadings, and incomplete indices of industrial production. The fact was that comprehensive measures of national income and output did not exist at the time. The Depression, and with it the growing role of government in the economy, emphasized the need for such measures and led to the development of a comprehensive set of national income accounts.

Richard T. Froyen

In response to this need in the 1930s, the Department of Commerce commissioned Nobel laureate Simon Kuznets of the National Bureau of Economic Research to develop a set of national economic accounts.... Professor Kuznets coordinated the work of researchers at the National Bureau of Economic Research in New York and his staff at Commerce. The original set of accounts was presented in a report to Congress in 1937 and in a research report, *National Income, 1929–35*....

The national accounts have become the mainstay of modern macroeconomic analysis, allowing policy makers, economists, and the business community to analyze the impact of different tax and spending plans, the impact of oil and other price shocks, and the impact of monetary policy on the economy as a whole and on specific components of final demand, incomes, industries, and regions.

### THINKING PRACTICALLY

1. The articles emphasize the importance of being able to measure an economy's output to improve government policy. Looking at recent news, can you identify one economic policy debate or action that referenced GDP?

*Source: U.S. Department of Commerce, Bureau of Economics, "GDP: One of the Great Inventions of the 20th Century," Survey of Current Business, January 2000, pp. 6–9.*

good—say, pizza, which is the same quality year after year. In each year 1 and 2, one hundred units (slices) of pizza were produced. Production thus remained the same for year 1 and year 2. Suppose the price of pizza increased from $1.00 per slice in year 1 to $1.10 per slice in year 2. Nominal GDP in year 1 is $100 (100 units × $1.00 per unit), and nominal GDP in year 2 is $110 (100 units × $1.10 per unit). Nominal GDP has increased by $10 even though no more slices of pizza were produced and the quality of the pizza did not improve. If we use nominal GDP to measure growth, we can be misled into thinking production has grown when all that has really happened is a rise in the price level (inflation).

If there were only one good in the economy—for example, pizza—it would be easy to measure production and compare one year's value to another's. We would add up all the pizza slices produced each year. In the example, production is 100 in both years. If the number of slices had increased to 105 in year 2, we would say production increased by 5 slices between year 1 and year 2, which is a 5 percent increase. Alas, however, there is more than one good in the economy which makes adjusting for price changes more complex.

The following is a discussion of how the BEA adjusts nominal GDP for price changes. As you read the discussion, you will see that this adjustment is not easy. Even in an economy of just apples and oranges, it would not be obvious how to add up apples and oranges to get an overall measure of output. The BEA's task is to add up thousands of goods, each of whose price is changing over time.

In the following discussion, we will use the concept of a **weight**, either price weights or quantity weights. What is a weight? It is easiest to define the term by an example. Suppose in your economics course there is a final exam and two other tests. If the final exam counts for one-half of the grade and the other two tests for one-fourth each, the "weights" are one-half, one-fourth, and one-fourth. If instead the final exam counts for 80 percent of the grade and the other two tests for 10 percent each, the weights are 0.8, 0.1, and 0.1. The more important an item is in a group, the larger its weight.

**weight** The importance attached to an item within a group of items.

## Calculating Real GDP

Nominal GDP adjusted for price changes is called *real GDP*. All the main issues involved in computing real GDP can be discussed using a simple three-good economy and 2 years. Table 6.6 presents all the data that we will need. The table presents price and quantity data for 2 years and three goods. The goods are labeled *A, B,* and *C,* and the years are labeled 1 and 2. *P* denotes price, and *Q* denotes quantity. Keep in mind that everything in the following discussion, including the discussion of the GDP deflation, is based on the numbers in Table 6.6. Nothing has been brought in from the outside. The table is the entire economy.

The first thing to note from Table 6.6 is that *nominal output*—in current dollars—in year 1 for good *A* is the number of units of good *A* produced in year 1 (6) times the price of good *A* in year 1 ($0.50), which is $3.00. Similarly, nominal output in year 1 is 7 × $0.30 = $2.10 for good *B* and 10 × $0.70 = $7.00 for good *C*. The sum of these three amounts, $12.10 in column 5, is nominal GDP in year 1 in this simple economy. Nominal GDP in year 2—calculated by

**TABLE 6.6 A Three-Good Economy**

| | (1) | (2) | (3) | (4) | (5) | (6) | (7) | (8) |
|---|---|---|---|---|---|---|---|---|
| | | | | | GDP in Year 1 in Year 1 Prices | GDP in Year 2 in Year 1 Prices | GDP in Year 1 in Year 2 Prices | GDP in Year 2 in Year 2 Prices |
| | Production | | Price per Unit | | | | | |
| | Year 1 $Q_1$ | Year 2 $Q_2$ | Year 1 $P_1$ | Year 2 $P_2$ | $P_1 \times Q_1$ | $P_1 \times Q_2$ | $P_2 \times Q_1$ | $P_2 \times Q_2$ |
| Good *A* | 6 | 11 | $0.50 | $0.40 | $ 3.00 | $ 5.50 | $ 2.40 | $ 4.40 |
| Good *B* | 7 | 4 | 0.30 | 1.00 | 2.10 | 1.20 | 7.00 | 4.00 |
| Good *C* | 10 | 12 | 0.70 | 0.90 | 7.00 | 8.40 | 9.00 | 10.80 |
| Total | | | | | $12.10 Nominal GDP in year 1 | $15.10 | $18.40 | $19.20 Nominal GDP in year 2 |

using the year 2 quantities and the year 2 prices—is $19.20 (column 8). Nominal GDP has risen from $12.10 in year 1 to $19.20 in year 2, an increase of 58.7 percent.[3]

You can see that the price of each good changed between year 1 and year 2—the price of good A fell (from $0.50 to $0.40) and the prices of goods B and C rose (B from $0.30 to $1.00; C from $0.70 to $0.90). Some of the change in nominal GDP between years 1 and 2 is as a result of price changes and not production changes. How much can we attribute to price changes and how much to production changes? Here things get tricky. The procedure that the BEA used before 1996 was to pick a **base year** and to use the prices in that base year as weights to calculate real GDP. This is a **fixed-weight procedure** because the weights used, which are the prices, are the same for all years—namely, the prices that prevailed in the base year.

Let us use the fixed-weight procedure and year 1 as the base year, which means using year 1 prices as the weights. Then in Table 6.6, real GDP in year 1 is $12.10 (column 5) and real GDP in year 2 is $15.10 (column 6). Note that both columns use year 1 prices and that nominal and real GDP are the same in year 1 because year 1 is the base year. Real GDP has increased from $12.10 to $15.10, an increase of 24.8 percent.

Let us now use the fixed-weight procedure and year 2 as the base year, which means using year 2 prices as the weights. In Table 6.6, real GDP in year 1 is $18.40 (column 7) and real GDP in year 2 is $19.20 (column 8). Note that both columns use year 2 prices and that nominal and real GDP are the same in year 2, because year 2 is the base year. Real GDP has increased from $18.40 to $19.20, an increase of 4.3 percent.

This example shows that growth rates can be sensitive to the choice of the base year—24.8 percent using year 1 prices as weights and 4.3 percent using year 2 prices as weights. For many policy decisions, the growth rates play a role so that large differences coming from a seemingly arbitrary choice of base year is troubling. The old BEA procedure simply picked one year as the base year and did all the calculations using the prices in that year as weights. The new BEA procedure makes two important changes. The first (using the current example) is to take the average of the two years' price changes, in other words, to "split the difference" between 24.8 percent and 4.3 percent. What does "splitting the difference" mean? One way is to take the average of the two numbers, which is 14.55 percent. What the BEA does is to take the *geometric* average, which for the current example is 14.09 percent.[4] These two averages (14.55 percent and 14.09 percent) are quite close, and the use of either would give similar results. The point here is not that the geometric average is used, but that the first change is to split the difference using some average. When prices are going up, this procedure will lower the estimates of real growth rates relative to the use of year 1 as a base year, and conversely when prices are falling. Note that this new procedure requires two "base" years because 24.8 percent was computed using year 1 prices as weights and 4.3 percent was computed using year 2 prices as weights.

The second BEA change is to use years 1 and 2 as the base years when computing the percentage change between years 1 and 2, then use years 2 and 3 as the base years when computing the percentage change between years 2 and 3, and so on. The two base years change as the calculations move through time. The series of percentage changes computed this way is taken to be the series of growth rates of real GDP. So in this way, nominal GDP is adjusted for price changes. To make sure you understand this, review the calculations in Table 6.6, which provides all the data you need to see what is going on.

## Calculating the GDP Deflator

We now switch gears from real GDP, a quantity measure, to the GDP deflator, a price measure. One of economic policy makers' goals is to keep changes in the overall price level small. For this reason, policy makers not only need good measures of how real output is changing but also good measures of how the overall price level is changing. The GDP deflator is one measure of the overall price level. We can use the data in Table 6.6 to show how the BEA computes the GDP deflator.

In Table 6.6, the price of good A fell from $0.50 in year 1 to $0.40 in year 2, the price of good B rose from $0.30 to $1.00, and the price of good C rose from $0.70 to $0.90. If we are interested

**base year** The year chosen for the weights in a fixed-weight procedure.

**fixed-weight procedure** A procedure that uses weights from a given base year.

---

[3] The percentage change is calculated as $[(19.20 - 12.10)/12.10] \times 100 = .587 \times 100 = 58.7$ percent.
[4] The geometric average is computed as the square root of $124.8 \times 104.3$, which is 114.09.

only in how individual prices change, this is all the information we need. However, if we are interested in how the overall price *level* changes, we need to weight the individual prices in some way. Is it getting more expensive to live in this economy or less expensive? In this example that clearly depends on how people spend their incomes. So, the obvious weights to use are the quantities produced, but which quantities—those of year 1 or year 2? The same issues arise here for the quantity weights as for the price weights in computing real GDP.

Let us first use the fixed-weight procedure and year 1 as the base year, which means using year 1 quantities as the weights. Then in Table 6.6, the "bundle" price in year 1 is $12.10 (column 5) and the bundle price in year 2 is $18.40 (column 7). Both columns use year 1 quantities. The bundle price has increased from $12.10 to $18.40, an increase of 52.1 percent.

Next, use the fixed-weight procedure and year 2 as the base year, which means using year 2 quantities as the weights. Then the bundle price in year 1 is $15.10 (column 6), and the bundle price in year 2 is $19.20 (column 8). Both columns use year 2 quantities. The bundle price has increased from $15.10 to $19.20, an increase of 27.2 percent.

This example shows that overall price increases can be sensitive to the choice of the base year: 52.1 percent using year 1 quantities as weights and 27.2 percent using year 2 quantities as weights. Again, the old BEA procedure simply picked one year as the base year and did all the calculations using the quantities in the base year as weights. First, the new procedure splits the difference between 52.1 percent and 27.2 percent by taking the geometric average, which is 39.1 percent. Second, it uses years 1 and 2 as the base years when computing the percentage change between years 1 and 2, years 2 and 3 as the base years when computing the percentage change between years 2 and 3, and so on. The series of percentage changes computed this way is taken to be the series of percentage changes in the GDP deflator, that is, a series of inflation rates.

## The Problems of Fixed Weights

To see why the BEA switched to the new procedure, let us consider a number of problems using fixed-price weights to compute real GDP. First, 1987 price weights, the last price weights the BEA used before it changed procedures, are not likely to be accurate for, say, 2014. Many structural changes took place in the U.S. economy between 1987 and 2014, and it seems unlikely that 1987 prices are good weights to use for this much later period.

Another problem is that the use of fixed-price weights does not account for the responses in the economy to supply shifts. Perhaps bad weather leads to a lower production of oranges in year 2. In a simple supply-and-demand diagram for oranges, this corresponds to a shift of the supply curve to the left, which leads to an increase in the price of oranges and a decrease in the quantity demanded. As consumers move up the demand curve, they are substituting away from oranges. If technical advances in year 2 result in cheaper ways of producing computers, the result is a shift of the computer supply curve to the right, which leads to a decrease in the price of computers and an increase in the quantity demanded. Consumers are substituting toward computers. (You should be able to draw supply-and-demand diagrams for both cases.) Table 6.6 shows this tendency. The quantity of good A rose between years 1 and 2 and the price decreased (the computer case), whereas the quantity of good B fell and the price increased (the orange case). The computer supply curve has been shifting to the right over time, primarily because of technical advances. The result has been large decreases in the price of computers and large increases in the quantity demanded.

To see why these responses pose a problem for the use of fixed-price weights, consider the data in Table 6.6. Because the price of good A was higher in year 1, the increase in production of good A is weighted more if we use year 1 as the base year than if we used year 2 as the base year. Also, because the price of good B was lower in year 1, the decrease in production of good B is weighted less if we use year 1 as the base year. These effects make the overall change in real GDP larger if we use year 1 price weights than if we use year 2 price weights. Using year 1 price weights ignores the kinds of substitution responses discussed in the previous paragraph and leads to what many believe are too-large estimates of real GDP changes. In the past, the BEA tended to move the base year forward about every 5 years, resulting in the past estimates of real GDP growth being revised downward. It is undesirable to have past growth estimates change simply because of the change to a new base year. The new BEA procedure avoids many of these fixed-weight problems.

Similar problems arise when using fixed-quantity weights to compute price indexes. For example, the fixed-weight procedure ignores the substitution away from goods whose prices are increasing and toward goods whose prices are decreasing or increasing less rapidly. The procedure tends to overestimate the increase in the overall price level. As discussed in the next chapter, there are still a number of price indexes that are computed using fixed weights. The GDP deflator differs because it does not use fixed weights. It is also a price index for all the goods and services produced in the economy. Other price indexes cover fewer domestically produced goods and services but also include some imported (foreign-produced) goods and services.

It should finally be stressed that there is no "right" way of computing real GDP. The economy consists of many goods, each with its own price, and there is no exact way of adding together the production of the different goods. We can say that the BEA's new procedure for computing real GDP avoids the problems associated with the use of fixed weights, and it seems to be an improvement over the old procedure. We will see in the next chapter, however, that the consumer price index (CPI)—a widely used price index—is still computed using fixed weights.

**6.4 LEARNING OBJECTIVE**

Discuss the limitations of using GDP to measure well-being.

# Limitations of the GDP Concept

We generally think of increases in GDP as good. Increasing GDP (or preventing its decrease) is usually considered one of the chief goals of the government's macroeconomic policy. But there are some limitations to the use of GDP as a measure of welfare.

## GDP and Social Welfare

If crime levels went down, society would be better off, but a decrease in crime is not an increase in output and is not reflected in GDP. Neither is an increase in leisure time. Yet to the extent that households want extra leisure time (instead of having it forced on them by a lack of jobs in the economy), an increase in leisure is also an increase in social welfare. Furthermore, some increases in social welfare are associated with a *decrease* in GDP. An increase in leisure during a time of full employment, for example, leads to a decrease in GDP because less time is spent on producing output.

Most nonmarket and domestic activities, such as housework and child care, are not counted in GDP even though they amount to real production. However, if I decide to send my children to day care or hire someone to clean my house or drive my car for me, GDP increases. The salaries of day care staff, cleaning people, and chauffeurs are counted in GDP, but the time I spend doing the same things is not counted. A mere change of institutional arrangements, even though no more output is being produced, can show up as a change in GDP.

Furthermore, GDP seldom reflects losses or social ills. GDP accounting rules do not adjust for production that pollutes the environment. The more production there is, the larger the GDP, regardless of how much pollution results in the process. The *Economics in Practice* box on the next page 117 discusses how counting for pollution affects GDP measures. GDP also has nothing to say about the distribution of output among individuals in a society. It does not distinguish, for example, between the case in which most output goes to a few people and the case in which output is evenly divided among all people.

## The Informal Economy

**informal economy** The part of the economy in which transactions take place and in which income is generated that is unreported and therefore not counted in GDP.

Many transactions are missed in the calculation of GDP even though, in principle, they should be counted. Most illegal transactions are missed unless they are "laundered" into legitimate business. Income that is earned but not reported as income for tax purposes is usually missed, although some adjustments are made in the GDP calculations to take misreported income into account. The part of the economy that should be counted in GDP but is not is sometimes called the **informal economy.**

## ECONOMICS IN PRACTICE

### Green Accounting

The national income and product accounts include all market activities. So purchased child care is included, but child care provided by parents is not. Recently many economists and policy makers have become concerned about the exclusion of one particularly large and important non-market activity from the national income accounts: the environment.

Many industries when they produce goods also produce air pollution as a by-product. The market goods these firms produce go into the national income and product accounts, but the environmental costs of air pollution are not subtracted. How much difference does not counting of this by-product make? Recent work by Nick Muller, Robert Mendelsohn, and Bill Nordhaus estimates that for some industries in the United States, like stone mining and coal-powered electricity generation, including properly valued air pollution in the national income and product accounts as an offset to the value of the marketed goods produced by these industries would make the contribution of these industries to our nation's GDP negative![1]

#### THINKING PRACTICALLY

1. Why do you think we have not counted pollution in GDP measures in the past?

[1] Nicholas Muller, Robert Mendelsohn and William Nordhaus, "Environmental Accounting for Pollution in the United States Economy," *American Economics Review* August 2011, 1649–1675.

---

Tax evasion is usually thought to be one of the major incentives for people in developed countries to participate in the informal economy. Studies estimate the size of the U.S. informal economy at about 10 percent, whereas Europe is closer to 20 percent. In the developing world, for a range of reasons, the informal economy is much larger, particularly for women workers. In Latin America and Africa, it is estimated that the informal economy comprises well more than a third of GDP in many nations.[5]

Why should we care about the informal economy? To the extent that GDP reflects only a part of economic activity instead of a complete measure of what the economy produces, it is misleading. Unemployment rates, for example, may be lower than officially measured if people work in the informal economy without reporting this fact to the government. Also, if the size of the informal economy varies among countries—as it does—we can be misled when we compare GDP among countries. For example, Italy's GDP would be much higher if we considered its informal sector as part of the economy, and Switzerland's GDP would change very little.

## Gross National Income per Capita

Making comparisons across countries is difficult because such comparisons need to be made in a single currency, generally U.S. dollars. Converting GNP numbers for Japan into dollars requires converting from yen into dollars. Because exchange rates can change quite dramatically in short periods of time, such conversions are tricky. Recently, the World Bank adopted a new measuring system for international comparisons. The concept of **gross national income (GNI)** is GNP converted into dollars using an average of currency exchange rates over several years adjusted

**gross national income (GNI)** GNP converted into dollars using an average of currency exchange rates over several years adjusted for rates of inflation.

---

[5] Jacques Chermes, "The Informal Economy," *Journal of Applied Economic Research*, 2012.

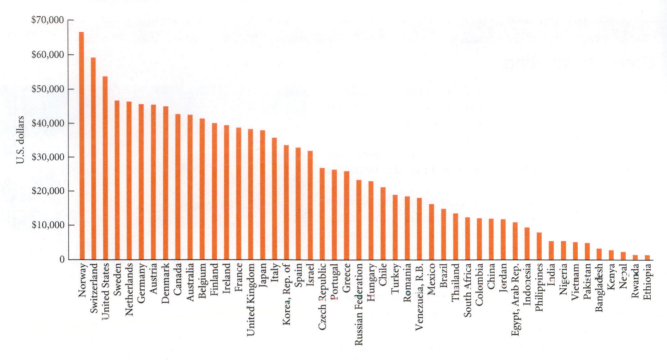

▲ **FIGURE 6.1** **National Income for Selected Countries, 2013**

*Source:* Data from GNI per capita, PPP (current international $), The World Bank Group, Retrieved from http://data.worldbank.org/indicator/NY.GNP.PCAP.PP.CD/countries/1W?display=default

for rates of inflation. Figure 6.1 lists the gross national income per capita (GNI divided by population) for various countries in 2013. Of the countries in the figure, Norway had the highest per capita GNI, followed by Switzerland, the United States, and the Netherlands. Ethiopia was estimated to have per capita GNI of only $1,380 in 2013. This compares to $66,520 for Norway.

## Looking Ahead

This chapter has introduced many key variables in which macroeconomists are interested, including GDP and its components. There is much more to be learned about the data that macroeconomists use. In the next chapter, we will discuss the data on employment, unemployment, and the labor force. In Chapter 10, we will discuss the data on money and interest rates. Finally, in Chapter 19, we will discuss in more detail the data on the relationship between the United States and the rest of the world.

# SUMMARY

1. One source of data on the key variables in the macroeconomy is the *national income and product accounts*. These accounts provide a conceptual framework that macroeconomists use to think about how the pieces of the economy fit together.

## 6.1 GROSS DOMESTIC PRODUCT *p. 104*

2. *Gross domestic product (GDP)* is the key concept in national income accounting. GDP is the total market value of all final goods and services produced within a given period by factors of production located within a country. GDP excludes *intermediate goods*. To include goods when they are purchased as inputs and when they are sold as final products would be double counting and would result in an overstatement of the value of production.

3. GDP excludes all transactions in which money or goods change hands but in which no new goods and services are produced. GDP includes the income of foreigners working in the United States and the profits that foreign companies earn in the United States. GDP excludes the income of U.S. citizens working abroad and profits earned by U.S. companies in foreign countries.

4. *Gross national product (GNP)* is the market value of all final goods and services produced during a given period by factors of production owned by a country's citizens.

## 6.2 CALCULATING GDP  *p. 106*

5. The *expenditure approach* to GDP adds up the amount spent on all final goods and services during a given period. The four main categories of expenditures are *personal consumption expenditures (C)*, *gross private domestic investment (I)*, *government consumption and gross investment (G)*, and *net exports (EX − IM)*. The sum of these categories equals GDP.

6. The three main components of *personal consumption expenditures (C)* are *durable goods*, *nondurable goods*, and *services*.

7. *Gross private domestic investment (I)* is the total investment made by the private sector in a given period. There are three kinds of investment: *nonresidential investment*, *residential investment*, and *changes in business inventories*. Gross investment does not take *depreciation*—the decrease in the value of assets—into account. *Net investment* is equal to gross investment minus depreciation.

8. *Government consumption and gross investment (G)* include expenditures by state, federal, and local governments for final goods and services. The value of *net exports (EX − IM)* equals the differences between exports (sales to foreigners of U.S.-produced goods and services) and imports (U.S. purchases of goods and services from abroad).

9. Because every payment (expenditure) by a buyer is a receipt (income) for the seller, GDP can be computed in terms of who receives it as income—the *income approach* to calculating gross domestic product.

10. GNP minus depreciation is *net national product (NNP)*. *National income* is the total amount earned by the factors of production in the economy. It is equal to NNP except for a statistical discrepancy. *Personal income* is the total income of households. *Disposable personal income* is what households have to spend or save after paying their taxes. The *personal saving rate* is the percentage of disposable personal income saved instead of spent.

## 6.3 NOMINAL VERSUS REAL GDP  *p. 111*

11. GDP measured in current dollars (the current prices that one pays for goods) is *nominal GDP*. If we use nominal GDP to measure growth, we can be misled into thinking that production has grown when all that has happened is a rise in the price level, or inflation. A better measure of production is *real GDP*, which is nominal GDP adjusted for price changes.

12. The GDP deflator is a measure of the overall price level.

## 6.4 LIMITATIONS OF THE GDP CONCEPT  *p. 116*

13. We generally think of increases in GDP as good, but some problems arise when we try to use GDP as a measure of happiness or well-being. The peculiarities of GDP accounting mean that institutional changes can change the value of GDP even if real production has not changed. GDP ignores most social ills, such as pollution. Furthermore, GDP tells us nothing about what kinds of goods are being produced or how income is distributed across the population. GDP also ignores many transactions of the *informal economy*.

14. The concept of *gross national income (GNI)* is GNP converted into dollars using an average of currency exchange rates over several years adjusted for rates of inflation.

## REVIEW TERMS AND CONCEPTS

base year, *p. 114*

change in business inventories, *p. 108*

compensation of employees, *p. 109*

corporate profits, *p. 109*

current dollars, *p. 111*

depreciation, *p. 108*

disposable personal income, *or* after-tax income, *p. 111*

durable goods, *p. 106*

expenditure approach, *p. 106*

final goods and services, *p. 104*

fixed-weight procedure, *p. 114*

government consumption and gross investment (G), *p. 109*

gross domestic product (GDP), *p. 104*

gross investment, *p. 108*

gross national income (GNI), *p. 117*

gross national product (GNP), *p. 105*

gross private domestic investment (I), *p. 108*

income approach, *p. 106*

indirect taxes minus subsidies, *p. 109*

informal economy, *p. 116*

intermediate goods, *p. 104*

national income, *p. 109*

national income and product accounts, *p. 103*

net business transfer payments, *p. 109*

net exports (EX − IM), *p. 109*

net interest, *p. 109*

net investment, *p. 108*

net national product (NNP), *p. 110*

nominal GDP, *p. 111*

nondurable goods, *p. 106*

nonresidential investment, *p. 108*

personal consumption expenditures (C), *p. 106*

personal income, *p. 111*

personal saving, *p. 111*

personal saving rate, *p. 111*

proprietors' income, *p. 109*

rental income, *p. 109*

residential investment, *p. 108*

services, *p. 106*

statistical discrepancy, *p. 110*

surplus of government enterprises, *p. 110*

value added, *p. 104*

weight, *p. 113*

Equations:

Expenditure approach to GDP:

$GDP = C + I + G + (EX − IM)$, *p. 106*

$GDP = $ Final sales $+$ Change in business inventories, *p. 108*

$capital_{end\ of\ period} = capital_{beginning\ of\ period} +$ net investment, *p. 109*

**MyEconLab** Visit **www.myeconlab.com** to complete these exercises online and get instant feedback. Exercises that update with real-time data are marked with art ●.

# PROBLEMS

All problems are available on MyEconLab.

## 6.1 GROSS DOMESTIC PRODUCT

LEARNING OBJECTIVE: Describe GDP fundamentals and differentiate between GDP and GNP.

**1.1** Explain what double counting is and discuss why GDP is not equal to total sales.

**1.2** [**Related to the** *Economics in Practice* **on p. 107**] Which of the following transactions would not be counted in GDP? Explain your answers.
  a. You buy a new pair of Lucchese Cowboy boots at the Lucchese factory in El Paso, Texas.
  b. You buy a vintage pair of Lucchese cowboy boots from a used clothing store in Jackson Hole, Wyoming.
  c. You take a day of vacation to work in your yard.
  d. A cat burglar sells $50,000 of stolen jewelry to an unscrupulous pawn shop.
  e. Amazon.com, Inc. issues new shares of stock to finance a new distribution warehouse.
  f. Amazon.com, Inc. builds a new distribution warehouse.
  g. Oralia buys 200 ostrich feathers that she uses to embellish the custom hats that she makes and sells.
  h. A private company builds a toll road to connect Nashville and Memphis.
  i. The government pays out unemployment benefits.
  j. AT&T purchases all the assets of DirecTV and takes over the company.
  k. You win $100,000 playing a slot machine at a casino in Reno, Nevada.

**1.3** Tobias, a classic car enthusiast in Phoenix, occasionally offers for sale one of his classic automobiles at the Barrett-Jackson collector car auction in neighboring Scottsdale. In January 2016, Tobias put a 1929 Cadillac 341B in the auction, and it sold to a buyer in Riyadh, Saudi Arabia for $167,500. What part, if any, of this transaction will be included as a part of U.S. GDP in 2016?

**1.4** Anissa makes custom bird houses in her garage and she buys all her supplies from a local lumber yard. Last year she purchased $3,500 worth of supplies and produced 250 bird houses. She sold all 250 bird houses to a local craft store for $25 each. The craft store sold all the bird houses to customers for $55 each. For the total bird house production, calculate the value added of Anissa and of the craft store.

## 6.2 CALCULATING GDP

LEARNING OBJECTIVE: Explain two methods for calculating GDP.

**2.1** [**Related to the** *Economics in Practice* **on p. 112**] In a simple economy, suppose that all income is either compensation of employees or profits. Suppose also that there are no indirect taxes. Calculate gross domestic product from the following set of numbers. Show that the expenditure approach and the income approach add up to the same figure.

| | |
|---|---|
| Consumption | $9,500 |
| Investment | 3,000 |
| Depreciation | 1,750 |
| Profits | 2,400 |
| Exports | 850 |
| Compensation of employees | 11,500 |
| Government purchases | 3,200 |
| Direct taxes | 1,200 |
| Saving | 1,600 |
| Imports | 900 |

**2.2** How do we know that calculating GDP by the expenditure approach yields the same answer as calculating GDP by the income approach?

**2.3** During 2002, real GDP in Japan rose about 1.3 percent. During the same period, retail sales in Japan fell 1.8 percent in real terms. What are some possible explanations for retail sales to consumers falling when GDP rises? (*Hint:* Think of the composition of GDP using the expenditure approach.)

**2.4** If you buy a new car, the entire purchase is counted as consumption in the year in which you make the transaction. Explain briefly why this is in one sense an "error" in national income accounting. (*Hint:* How is the purchase of a car different from the purchase of a pizza?) How might you correct this error? How is housing treated in the National Income and Product Accounts? Specifically how does owner-occupied housing enter into the accounts? (Hint: Do some Web searching on "imputed rent on owner-occupied housing.")

**2.5** Explain why imports are subtracted in the expenditure approach to calculating GDP.

**2.6** Beginning in 2005, the housing market, which had been booming for years, turned. Housing construction dropped sharply in 2006. Go to www.bea.gov. Look at the GDP release and at past releases from 2005 to 2015. In real dollars, how much private residential fixed investment (houses, apartments, condominiums, and cooperatives) took place in each quarter from 2005 to 2015? What portion of GDP did housing construction represent? After 2006, residential fixed investment was declining sharply, yet GDP was growing until the end of 2007. What categories of aggregate spending kept things moving between 2006 and the end of 2007?

# 6.3 NOMINAL VERSUS REAL GDP

LEARNING OBJECTIVE: Discuss the difference between real GDP and nominal GDP.

3.1 As the following table indicates, GNP and real GNP were almost the same in 1972, but there was a $300 billion difference by mid-1975. Explain why. Describe what the numbers here suggest about conditions in the economy at the time. How do the conditions compare with conditions today?

| Date (Year and Quarter) | GNP (Billions, $) | Real GNP (Billions, $) | Real GNP (% Change) | GNP Deflator (% Change) |
|---|---|---|---|---|
| 72:2 | 1,172 | 1,179 | 7.62 | 2.93 |
| 72:3 | 1,196 | 1,193 | 5.11 | 3.24 |
| 72:4 | 1,233 | 1,214 | 7.41 | 5.30 |
| 73:1 | 1,284 | 1,247 | 10.93 | 5.71 |
| 73:2 | 1,307 | 1,248 | .49 | 7.20 |
| 73:3 | 1,338 | 1,256 | 2.44 | 6.92 |
| 73:4 | 1,377 | 1,266 | 3.31 | 8.58 |
| 74:1 | 1,388 | 1,253 | −4.00 | 7.50 |
| 74:2 | 1,424 | 1,255 | .45 | 10.32 |
| 74:3 | 1,452 | 1,247 | −2.47 | 10.78 |
| 74:4 | 1,473 | 1,230 | −5.51 | 12.03 |
| 75:1 | 1,480 | 1,204 | −8.27 | 10.86 |
| 75:2 | 1,517 | 1,219 | 5.00 | 5.07 |

3.2 What are some of the problems in using fixed weights to compute real GDP and the GDP deflator? How does the BEA's approach attempt to solve these problems?

3.3 The following table gives some figures from forecasts of real GDP (in 2005 dollars) and population done in mid-2014. According to the forecasts, approximately how much real growth will there be between 2018 and 2019? What is the per-capita real GDP projected to be in 2018 and in 2019? Compute the forecast rate of change in real GDP and per-capita real GDP between 2018 and 2019.

| | |
|---|---|
| Real GDP 2018 (billions) | $18,121 |
| Real GDP 2019 (billions) | $18,375 |
| Population 2018 (millions) | 329.3 |
| Population 2019 (millions) | 331.9 |

3.4 Look at a recent edition of *The Economist*. Go to the section on economic indicators. Go down the list of countries and make a list of the ones with the fastest and slowest GDP growth. Look also at the forecast rates of GDP growth. Go back to the table of contents at the beginning of the journal to see if there are articles about any of these countries. Write a paragraph or two describing the events or the economic conditions in one of the countries. Explain why they are growing or not growing rapidly.

3.5 By mid-2009, many economists believed that the recession had ended and the U.S. economy had entered

an economic expansion. Define *recession* and *expansion*. Go to www.bea.gov and look at the growth of GDP during 2009. In addition, go to www.bls.gov and look at payroll employment and the unemployment rate. Had the recession ended and had the U.S. economy entered an expansion? What do you see in the data? Can you tell by reading newspapers or watching cable news whether the country had entered an expansion? Explain.

3.6 Gorgonzola is a small island nation with a simple economy that produces only six goods: sugar cane, yo-yos, rum, peanuts, harmonicas, and peanut butter. Assume that one-quarter of all the sugar cane is used to produce rum and one-half of all the peanuts are used to produce peanut butter.
   a. Use the production and price information in the table to calculate nominal GDP for 2015.
   b. Use the production and price information in the table to calculate real GDP for 2013, 2014, and 2015 using 2013 as the base year. What is the growth rate of real GDP from 2013 to 2014 and from 2014 to 2015?
   c. Use the production and price information in the table to calculate real GDP for 2013, 2014, and 2015 using 2014 as the base year. What is the growth rate of real GDP from 2013 to 2014 and from 2014 to 2015?

| | 2013 | | 2014 | | 2015 | |
|---|---|---|---|---|---|---|
| Product | Quantity | Price | Quantity | Price | Quantity | Price |
| Sugar cane | 240 | $0.80 | 240 | $1.00 | 300 | $1.15 |
| Yo-yos | 600 | 2.50 | 700 | 3.00 | 750 | 4.00 |
| Rum | 150 | 10.00 | 160 | 12.00 | 180 | 15.00 |
| Peanuts | 500 | 2.00 | 450 | 2.50 | 450 | 2.50 |
| Harmonicas | 75 | 25.00 | 75 | 30.00 | 85 | 30.00 |
| Peanut butter | 100 | 4.50 | 85 | 4.50 | 85 | 5.00 |

3.7 The following table contains nominal and real GDP data, in billions of dollars, from the U.S. Bureau of Economic Analysis for 2013 and 2014. The data is listed per quarter, and the real GDP data was calculated using 2009 as the base year. Fill in the columns for the GDP deflator and for the percent increase in price level.

| Quarter | Nominal GDP | Real GDP | GDP Deflator | Percent Increase in Price Level |
|---|---|---|---|---|
| $2013_q1$ | 16,502.4 | 15,538.4 | | |
| $2013_q2$ | 16,619.2 | 15,606.6 | | |
| $2013_q3$ | 16,872.3 | 15,779.9 | | |
| $2013_q4$ | 17,078.3 | 15,916.2 | | |
| $2014_q1$ | 17,044.0 | 15,831.7 | | |
| $2014_q2$ | 17,328.2 | 16,010.4 | | |
| $2014_q3$ | 17,599.8 | 16,205.6 | | |
| $2014_q4$ | 17,703.7 | 16,294.7 | | |

3.8 Evaluate the following statement: Even if the prices of a large number of goods and services in the economy increase dramatically, the real GDP for the economy can still fall, but if the prices of a large number of goods and services in the economy decrease dramatically, the real GDP for the economy cannot rise.

## 6.4  LIMITATIONS OF THE GDP CONCEPT

**LEARNING OBJECTIVE:**  Discuss the limitations of using GDP to measure well-being.

4.1  GDP calculations do not directly include the economic costs of environmental damage—for example, global warming and acid rain. Do you think these costs should be included in GDP? Why or why not? How could GDP be amended to include environmental damage costs?

4.2  [**Related to the *Economics in Practice* on p. 117**] A World Bank brief entitled *Natural Capital Accounting* contains the following statement: "(A) major limitation of GDP is the limited representation of natural capital. The full contribution of natural capital like forests, wetlands, and agricultural land does not show up." Identify some additional examples of natural capital and explain how limited representation of these types of natural capital could affect the measurement of gross domestic product.

Source: *Natural Capital Accounting*, World Bank brief, May 20, 2015.

# Unemployment, Inflation, and Long-Run Growth

# 7

Each month the U.S. Bureau of Labor Statistics (BLS) announces the value of the unemployment rate for the previous month. For example, on April 3, 2015, it announced that the unemployment rate for March 2015 was 5.5 percent. The unemployment rate is a key measure of how the economy is doing. This announcement is widely watched, and if the announced unemployment rate is different from what the financial markets expect, there can be large movements in those markets. It is thus

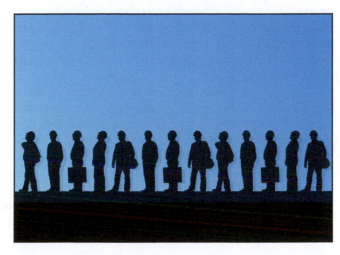

important to know how the BLS computes the unemployment rate. The first part of this chapter describes how the unemployment rate is computed and discusses its various components.

Inflation is another key macroeconomic variable. The previous chapter discussed how the GDP deflator, the price deflator for the entire economy, is computed. The percentage change in the GDP deflator is a measure of inflation. There are, however, other measures of inflation, each pertaining to some part of the economy. The most widely followed price index is the consumer price index (CPI), and its measurement is discussed in this chapter. The CPI is also announced monthly by the BLS, and this announcement is widely followed by the financial markets as well. For example, on March 24, 2015, the BLS announced that the percentage change in the CPI for February 2015 was 0.2 percent for the month. After discussing the measurement of the CPI, this chapter discusses various costs of inflation as well as the concerns policy makers might have when there is deflation (a fall in the price level).

The last topic considered in this chapter is long-run growth. Although much of macroeconomics is concerned with explaining business cycles, long-run growth is also a major concern. The average yearly growth rate of U.S. real GDP depicted in Figure 5.2 in Chapter 5 is 3.3 percent. Although there were many ups and downs during the 115 years depicted in Figure 5.2, on average, the economy was growing at an annual 3.3 percent rate. In the last part of this chapter, we discuss the sources of this growth.

Keep in mind that this chapter is still descriptive. We begin our analysis of how the economy works in the next chapter.

# Unemployment

We begin our discussion of unemployment with its measurement.

## Measuring Unemployment

The unemployment data released each month by the BLS are based on a survey of 60,000 households. Each interviewed household answers questions concerning the work activity of household members 16 years of age or older during the calendar week that contains the 12th of the month. (The survey is conducted in the week that contains the 19th of the month.)

If a household member 16 years of age or older worked 1 hour or more as a paid employee, either for someone else or in his or her own business or farm, the person is classified as **employed**. A household member is also considered employed if he or she worked 15 hours or more without pay in a family enterprise. Finally, a household member is counted as employed if the person held a job from which he or she was temporarily absent because of illness, bad weather, vacation, labor-management disputes, or personal reasons, regardless of whether he or she was paid.

Those who are not employed fall into one of two categories: (1) unemployed or (2) not in the labor force. To be considered **unemployed**, a person must be 16 years old or older, available for work, and have made specific efforts to find work during the previous 4 weeks. A person not looking for work because he or she does not want a job or has given up looking is classified as **not in the labor force**. People not in the labor force include full-time students, retirees, individuals in institutions, those staying home to take care of children, and discouraged job seekers.

The total **labor force** in the economy is the number of people employed plus the number of unemployed:

$$\text{labor force} = \text{employed} + \text{unemployed}$$

The total population 16 years of age or older is equal to the number of people in the labor force plus the number not in the labor force:

$$\text{population} = \text{labor force} + \text{not in labor force}$$

With these numbers, several ratios can be calculated. The **unemployment rate** is the ratio of the number of people unemployed to the total number of people in the labor force:

$$\text{unemployment rate} = \frac{\text{unemployed}}{\text{employed} + \text{unemployed}}$$

In March 2015, the labor force contained 156.906 million people, 148.331 million of whom were employed and 8.575 million of whom were unemployed and looking for work. The unemployment rate was 5.5 percent:

$$\frac{8.575}{148.331 + 8.575} = 5.5\%$$

The ratio of the labor force to the population 16 years old or over is called the **labor force participation rate**:

$$\text{labor force participation rate} = \frac{\text{labor force}}{\text{population}}$$

**employed**　Any person 16 years old or older (1) who works for pay, either for someone else or in his or her own business for 1 or more hours per week, (2) who works without pay for 15 or more hours per week in a family enterprise, or (3) who has a job but has been temporarily absent with or without pay.

**unemployed**　A person 16 years old or older who is not working, is available for work, and has made specific efforts to find work during the previous 4 weeks.

**not in the labor force**　A person who is not looking for work because he or she does not want a job or has given up looking.

**labor force**　The number of people employed plus the number of unemployed.

**unemployment rate**　The ratio of the number of people unemployed to the total number of people in the labor force.

**labor force participation rate**　The ratio of the labor force to the total population 16 years old or older.

# ECONOMICS IN PRACTICE

## Time Use for the Unemployed in a Recession

During the recession of 2008—2009, aggregate market work hours in the United States decreased substantially. A recent paper uses interesting new survey data to explore what the unemployed population did with these hours lost to the formal market.[1]

What would an economist expect to see in time use change for someone newly unemployed in a recession? First, we might expect people to spend some time looking for new jobs. Aguiar and his co-authors find that between 2 percent and 6 percent of the lost market hours go to job search. But clearly there are diminishing returns to job search, especially in a recession when new job opportunities are limited. What else did the survey reveal about time allocation? Twelve percent of the newly opened time went to activities tied to longer-run job placement, increased education, civic involvement, and health care. Other time, 35 percent of the hours lost, went to nonmarket work, cleaning, home maintenance, and child care. Clearly here the unemployed were substituting their own work for services they used to buy in the marketplace. For the unemployed worker, the opportunity cost of producing one's own home services is lower, so this change makes good economic sense. The remaining time, just under half the hours lost to the market, went to leisure activities, including sleeping.

### THINKING PRACTICALLY

1. How would you expect the time use of the unemployed to differ in a boom time?

[1] Mark Aguiar, Erik Hurst, Louokas Karabarbounis,"""Time Use During the Great Recession," *American Economic Review* 2013, 1664–1696

---

In March 2015, the population of 16 years old or older was 250.080 million. So the labor force participation rate was .63 (= 156.906/250.080).

Table 7.1 shows values of these variables for selected years since 1950. Although the unemployment rate has gone up and down over this period, the labor force participation rate grew steadily. Much of this increase was the result of the growth in the participation rate of women between the ages of 25 and 54. Column 3 in Table 7.1 shows how many new workers the U.S. economy has absorbed since 1950. The number of employed workers increased by 40.4 million between 1950 and 1980 and by 47.0 million between 1980 and 2014.

### TABLE 7.1   Employed, Unemployed, and the Labor Force, 1950–2014

|  | (1) | (2) | (3) | (4) | (5) | (6) |
|---|---|---|---|---|---|---|
|  | Population 16 Years Old or Over (Millions) | Labor Force (Millions) | Employed (Millions) | Unemployed (Millions) | Labor Force Participation Rate (Percentage Points) | Unemployment Rate (Percentage Points) |
| 1950 | 105.0 | 62.2 | 58.9 | 3.3 | 59.2 | 5.3 |
| 1960 | 117.2 | 69.6 | 65.8 | 3.9 | 59.4 | 5.5 |
| 1970 | 137.1 | 82.8 | 78.7 | 4.1 | 60.4 | 4.9 |
| 1980 | 167.7 | 106.9 | 99.3 | 7.6 | 63.8 | 7.1 |
| 1990 | 189.2 | 125.8 | 118.8 | 7.0 | 66.5 | 5.6 |
| 2000 | 212.6 | 142.6 | 136.9 | 5.7 | 67.1 | 4.0 |
| 2010 | 232.8 | 153.9 | 139.1 | 14.8 | 64.7 | 9.6 |
| 2014 | 247.9 | 155.9 | 146.3 | 9.6 | 62.9 | 6.2 |

*Note:* Figures are civilian only (military excluded).
*Source:* Economic Report of the President, 2015 and U.S. Bureau of Labor Statistics.

# Components of the Unemployment Rate

To get a better picture of unemployment in the United States, it is useful to look at unemployment rates across groups of people.

**Unemployment Rates for Different Demographic Groups**   There are large differences in rates of unemployment across demographic groups. Table 7.2 shows the unemployment rate for November 1982—the worst month of the recession in 1982—and for March 2015—a month of fairly low unemployment—broken down by race, sex, and age. In March 2015, when the overall unemployment rate was 5.5 percent, the rate for whites was 4.7 percent, whereas the rate for African Americans was more than twice that—10.1 percent.

During the recession of 1982, men fared worse than women. For African Americans, 19.3 percent of men 20 years and older and 16.5 percent of women 20 years and older were unemployed. Teenagers between 16 and 19 years of age fared worst. African Americans between 16 and 19 experienced an unemployment rate of 49.5 percent in November 1982. For whites between 16 and 19, the unemployment rate was 21.3 percent. The unemployment rate for teenagers was also high in March 2015, and African American men and women continue to have unemployment rates higher than their white counterparts.

**Discouraged-Worker Effects**   Many people believe that the unemployment rate underestimates the fraction of people who are involuntarily out of work. People who stop looking for work are classified as having dropped out of the labor force instead of being unemployed. During recessions, people may become discouraged about finding a job and stop looking. This lowers the unemployment rate as calculated by the BLS because those no longer looking for work are no longer counted as unemployed.

**discouraged-worker effect**
The decline in the measured unemployment rate that results when people who want to work but cannot find jobs grow discouraged and stop looking, thus dropping out of the ranks of the unemployed and the labor force.

To demonstrate how this **discouraged-worker effect** lowers the unemployment rate, suppose there are 10 million unemployed out of a labor force of 100 million. This means an unemployment rate of $10/100 = .10$, or 10 percent. If 1 million of these 10 million unemployed people stopped looking for work and dropped out of the labor force, 9 million would be unemployed out of a labor force of 99 million. The unemployment rate would then drop to $9/99 = .091$, or 9.1 percent.

The BLS survey provides some evidence on the size of the discouraged-worker effect. Respondents who indicate that they have stopped searching for work are asked why they stopped. If the respondent cites inability to find employment as the sole reason for not searching, that person might be classified as a discouraged worker.

The number of discouraged workers seems to hover around 1 percent of the size of the labor force in normal times. During the 1980–1982 recession, the number of discouraged workers increased steadily to a peak of 1.5 percent. In March 2015 discouraged workers were estimated to comprise about 0.5 percent of the size of the labor force. Some economists argue that adding the number of discouraged workers to the number who are now classified as unemployed gives a better picture of the unemployment situation.

**The Duration of Unemployment**   The unemployment rate measures unemployment at a given point in time. It tells us nothing about how long the average unemployed worker is out

| TABLE 7.2   Unemployment Rates by Demographic Group, 1982 and 2015 | | | |
|---|---|---|---|
| | Years | November 1982 | March 2015 |
| *Total* | | 10.8 | 5.5 |
| White | | 9.6 | 4.7 |
|    Men | 20+ | 9.0 | 4.4 |
|    Women | 20+ | 8.1 | 4.2 |
|    Both sexes | 16–19 | 21.3 | 15.7 |
| African American | | 20.2 | 10.1 |
|    Men | 20+ | 19.3 | 10.0 |
|    Women | 20+ | 16.5 | 9.2 |
|    Both sexes | 16–19 | 49.5 | 25.0 |

*Source:* U.S. Bureau of Labor Statistics. Data are seasonally adjusted.

## ECONOMICS IN PRACTICE

### A Quiet Revolution: Women Join the Labor Force

Table 7.1 shows that the labor force participation rate in the United States increased from 59.2 percent in 1950 to 62.9 percent in 2014. Much of this increase was as a result of the increased participation of women in the labor force. In 1955, the labor force participation rate of women was 36 percent. For married women, the rate was even lower at 29 percent. By the 1990s, these numbers shifted considerably. In 1996, the labor force participation rate was 60 percent for all women and 62 percent for married women. The reasons for these changes are complex. Certainly, in the 1960s, there was a change in society's attitude toward women and paid work. In addition, the baby boom became the baby bust as greater availability of birth control led to fewer births.

By comparison, the participation rate for men declined over this period—from 85 percent in 1955 to 75 percent in 1996. Why the labor force participation rate for men fell is less clear than why the women's rate rose. No doubt, some men dropped out to assume more traditional women's roles, such as child care. Whatever the causes, the economy grew in a way that absorbed virtually all the new entrants during the period in question.

As women began joining the labor force in greater numbers in the 1970s and 1980s, their wages relative to men's wages actually fell. Most economists attribute this decline to the fact that less experienced women were entering the labor force, pointing out the importance of correcting for factors such as experience and education when we analyze labor markets.

At least some of the women entering the labor force at this time hired housecleaners and child care workers to perform tasks they had once done themselves. As we learned in

Chapter 6, the salaries of daycare staff and cleaning people are counted in GDP, whereas the value of these tasks when done by a husband or wife in a household is not part of GDP.

If you are interested in learning more about the economic history of American women, read the book *Understanding the Gender Gap: An Economic History of American Women* by Harvard University economist Claudia Goldin.

#### THINKING PRACTICALLY

1. When a household decides to hire someone else to clean their house and uses their extra time to watch television, the wages paid to that household worker increase GDP. Is economic output in fact larger?

of work. With a labor force of 1,000 people and an annual unemployment rate of 10 percent, we know that at any moment 100 people are unemployed. But a different picture emerges if it turns out that the same 100 people are unemployed all year, as opposed to a situation in which each of the 1,000 people has a brief spell of unemployment of a few weeks during the year. The duration statistics give us information on this feature of unemployment. Table 7.3 shows that during recessionary periods, the average duration of unemployment rises. Between 1979 and 1983, the average duration of unemployment rose from 10.8 weeks to 20.0 weeks. The slow growth following the 1990–1991 recession resulted in an increase in duration of unemployment to 17.7 weeks in 1992 and to 18.8 weeks in 1994. In 2000, average duration was down to 12.7 weeks, which then rose to 19.6 weeks in 2004. Between 2007 and 2009 average duration rose sharply from 16.9 weeks to 24.3 weeks. Following the recession it rose even more—to 39.5 weeks in 2012. Average duration was still high in 2014, at 33.7 weeks. This reflects the slow overall recovery from the recession.

## The Costs of Unemployment

In the Employment Act of 1946, Congress declared that it was the continuing policy and responsibility of the federal government to use all practicable means . . . to promote maximum employment, production, and purchasing power.

In the years since, full employment has remained an important target of federal policy. Why should full employment be a policy objective of the federal government? What costs does unemployment impose on society?

## ECONOMICS IN PRACTICE

### The Consequences of Unemployment Persist

Throughout the recession of 2008–2009 and the slow recovery afterward many young college graduates found themselves unemployed, many for a number of months. As painful as that experience was, economists had more bad news for them. The negative effect of early unemployment on your career lasts for many years!

Lisa Kahn, a Yale economist, followed graduates of colleges from the period 1979–1989 over the subsequent 17 years.[1] You know from Chapter 5 that within this overall period there was one recession in 1980–1982. Kahn finds that even 15 years later, wage rates of those with post-college unemployment lagged substantially. Not only did low wages persist, but fewer graduates in recessionary periods were able to enter high prestige jobs, even when the economy recovered.

**THINKING PRACTICALLY**

1. Describe a mechanism that might help explain the persistence of wage-effects from a recession.

[1]Lisa Kahn, "The Long-Term Labor Consequences of Graduating from College in a Bad Economy," *Labour Economics*, April 2010.

**Frictional, Structural, and Cyclical Unemployment**   When we consider the various costs of unemployment, it is useful to categorize unemployment into three types:

- Frictional unemployment
- Structural unemployment
- Cyclical unemployment

In thinking about the social costs of unemployment, all unemployment is not created equal! When the BLS does its survey about work activity for the week containing the 12th of each month, it interviews many people who are involved in the normal search for work. Some are either newly entering the labor force, whereas others are switching jobs. This unemployment is both natural and beneficial for the economy. The portion of unemployment resulting from the

| TABLE 7.3 | Average Duration of Unemployment, 1970–2014 | | | | |
|---|---|---|---|---|---|
| | Weeks | | Weeks | | Weeks |
| 1970 | 8.6 | 1985 | 15.6 | 2000 | 12.7 |
| 1971 | 11.3 | 1986 | 15.0 | 2001 | 13.1 |
| 1972 | 12.0 | 1987 | 14.5 | 2002 | 16.7 |
| 1973 | 10.0 | 1988 | 13.5 | 2003 | 19.2 |
| 1974 | 9.8 | 1989 | 11.9 | 2004 | 19.6 |
| 1975 | 14.2 | 1990 | 12.0 | 2005 | 18.4 |
| 1976 | 15.8 | 1991 | 13.7 | 2006 | 16.8 |
| 1977 | 14.3 | 1992 | 17.7 | 2007 | 16.9 |
| 1978 | 11.9 | 1993 | 18.0 | 2008 | 17.8 |
| 1979 | 10.8 | 1994 | 18.8 | 2009 | 24.3 |
| 1980 | 11.9 | 1995 | 16.6 | 2010 | 33.1 |
| 1981 | 13.7 | 1996 | 16.7 | 2011 | 39.4 |
| 1982 | 15.6 | 1997 | 15.8 | 2012 | 39.5 |
| 1983 | 20.0 | 1998 | 14.5 | 2013 | 36.6 |
| 1984 | 18.2 | 1999 | 13.4 | 2014 | 33.7 |

*Source:* U.S. Bureau of Labor Statistics.

normal turnover in the labor market is called **frictional unemployment**. As long as job search takes some time, the frictional unemployment rate will not be zero.

The industrial structure of the U.S. economy is continually changing. Manufacturing, for instance, has yielded part of its share of total employment to services and to finance, insurance, and real estate. Within the manufacturing sector, the steel and textile industries have contracted sharply, whereas high-technology sectors have expanded. The unemployment that arises from such structural shifts is usually called **structural unemployment**. Thus, the term *frictional unemployment* is used to denote short-run job/skill-matching problems, problems that last a few weeks, and *structural unemployment* denotes longer-run adjustment problems—those that tend to last for years. Although structural unemployment is an indication of a dynamic economy, it also brings with it cost to those who lose their jobs because their skills are obsolete.

Economists sometimes use the term **natural rate of unemployment** to refer to the unemployment rate that occurs in a normal functioning economy, subject to some frictional and structural unemployment. Estimates of the natural rate vary from 4 percent to 6 percent.

Between 2007 and 2009 the actual unemployment rate rose from 4.6 percent to 9.3 percent, and it seems unlikely that all of this rise was simply because of a rise in frictional and structural unemployment. Any unemployment that is above frictional plus structural is called **cyclical unemployment**. It seems likely that much of the unemployment in 2009, during the 2008–2009 recession, and during earlier recessions, was cyclical unemployment.

**Social Consequences**   The costs of unemployment are neither evenly distributed across the population nor easily quantified. The social consequences of the Depression of the 1930s are perhaps the hardest to comprehend. Few emerged from this period unscathed. At the bottom were the poor and the fully unemployed, about 25 percent of the labor force. Even those who kept their jobs found themselves working part-time. Many people lost all or part of their savings as the stock market crashed and thousands of banks failed. Re-reading the excerpt from John Steinbeck's *The Grapes of Wrath* in Chapter 5 will give you a flavor for the social costs of the unemployment of that period. Many of you may also have seen friends or families lose valued jobs in the more recent recession of 2008–2009.

**frictional unemployment**   The portion of unemployment that is as a result of the normal turnover in the labor market; used to denote short-run job/skill-matching problems.

**structural unemployment**   The portion of unemployment that is as a result of changes in the structure of the economy that result in a significant loss of jobs in certain industries.

**natural rate of unemployment**   The unemployment rate that occurs as a normal part of the functioning of the economy. Sometimes taken as the sum of the frictional unemployment rate and the structural unemployment rate.

**cyclical unemployment**   Unemployment that is above frictional plus structural unemployment.

# Inflation and Deflation

**7.2 LEARNING** OBJECTIVE

Describe the tools used to measure inflation and discuss the costs and effects of inflation.

In a market economy like the U.S. economy, prices of individual goods continually change as supply and demand shift. Indeed, a major concern of microeconomics is understanding the way in which relative prices change—why, for example, have computers become less expensive over time and dental services more expensive? In macroeconomics, we are concerned not with relative price changes, but with changes in the *overall* price level of goods and services. Inflation is defined as an increase in the overall price level, whereas deflation is a decrease in the overall price level.

The fact that all prices for the multitude of goods and services in our economy do not rise and fall together at the same rate makes measurement of inflation difficult. We have already explored measurement issues in Chapter 6 in defining the GDP deflator, which measures the price level for all goods and services in an economy. We turn now to look at a second, commonly used measure of the price level, the consumer price index.

## The Consumer Price Index

The **consumer price index (CPI)** is the most widely followed price index. Unlike the GDP deflator, it is a fixed-weight index. It was first constructed during World War I as a basis for adjusting shipbuilders' wages, which the government controlled during the war. Currently, the CPI is computed by the BLS each month using a bundle of goods meant to represent the "market basket" purchased monthly by the typical urban consumer. The quantities of each good in the bundle that are used for the weights are based on extensive surveys of consumers. In fact, the BLS collects prices each month for about 71,000 goods and services from about 22,000 outlets in 44 geographic areas. For example, the cost of housing is included in the data

**consumer price index (CPI)**   A price index computed each month by the Bureau of Labor Statistics using a bundle that is meant to represent the "market basket" purchased monthly by the typical urban consumer.

collection by surveying about 5,000 renters and 1,000 homeowners each month. Figure 7.1 shows the CPI market basket for December 2007.

Table 7.4 shows values of the CPI since 1950. The base period for this index is 1982–1984, which means that the index is constructed to have a value of 100.0 when averaged across these three years. The percentage change for a given year in the table is a measure of inflation in that year. For example, from 1970 to 1971, the CPI increased from 38.8 to 40.5, a percentage change of 4.4 percent. [The percentage change is (40.5 − 38.8) / 38.8 times 100.] The table shows the high inflation rates in the 1970s and early 1980s and the fairly low inflation rates since 1992.

Because the CPI is a fixed-weight price index (with the current base period 1982–1984), it suffers from the substitution problem discussed in the last chapter. With fixed weights, it does not account for consumers' substitution away from high-priced goods. The CPI thus has a tendency to overestimate the rate of inflation. This problem has important policy implications because government transfers such as Social Security payments are tied to the CPI. If inflation as measured by percentage changes in the CPI is biased upward, Social Security payments will grow more rapidly than they would with a better measure: The government is spending more than it otherwise would.

In response to the fixed-weight problem, in August 2002, the BLS began publishing a version of the CPI called the Chained Consumer Price Index, which uses changing weights. Although this version is not yet the main version, it may be that within a few years the BLS completely moves away from the fixed-weight version of the CPI. Remember, however, that even if this happens, the CPI will still differ in important ways from the GDP deflator, discussed in the last chapter. The CPI covers only consumer goods and services—those listed in Figure 7.1—whereas the GDP deflator covers all goods and services produced in the economy. Also, the CPI includes prices of imported goods, which the GDP deflator does not.

**producer price indexes (PPIs)** Measures of prices that producers receive for products at various stages in the production process.

Other popular price indexes are **producer price indexes (PPIs)**, once called *wholesale price indexes*. These are indexes of prices that producers receive for products at various stages in the production process, not just the final stage. The indexes are calculated separately for various stages in the production process. The three main categories are *finished goods, intermediate materials,* and *crude materials,* although there are subcategories within each of these categories.

One advantage of some of the PPIs is that they detect price increases early in the production process. Because their movements sometimes foreshadow future changes in consumer prices, they are considered to be leading indicators of future consumer prices.

▶ **FIGURE 7.1** **The CPI Market Basket**

The CPI market basket shows how a typical consumer divides his or her money among various goods and services. Most of a consumer's money goes toward housing, transportation, and food and beverages.

*Source:* The Bureau of Labor Statistics

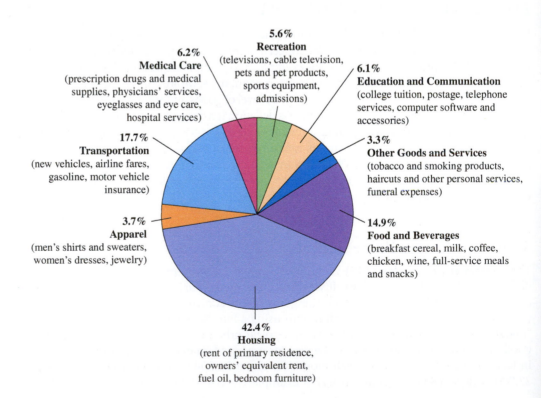

6.2% **Medical Care** (prescription drugs and medical supplies, physicians' services, eyeglasses and eye care, hospital services)

5.6% **Recreation** (televisions, cable television, pets and pet products, sports equipment, admissions)

6.1% **Education and Communication** (college tuition, postage, telephone services, computer software and accessories)

3.3% **Other Goods and Services** (tobacco and smoking products, haircuts and other personal services, funeral expenses)

14.9% **Food and Beverages** (breakfast cereal, milk, coffee, chicken, wine, full-service meals and snacks)

17.7% **Transportation** (new vehicles, airline fares, gasoline, motor vehicle insurance)

3.7% **Apparel** (men's shirts and sweaters, women's dresses, jewelry)

42.4% **Housing** (rent of primary residence, owners' equivalent rent, fuel oil, bedroom furniture)

| TABLE 7.4   The CPI, 1950–2014 |
|---|

| | Percentage Change in CPI | CPI | | Percentage Change in CPI | CPI |
|---|---|---|---|---|---|
| 1950 | 1.3 | 24.1 | 1982 | 6.2 | 96.5 |
| 1951 | 7.9 | 26.0 | 1983 | 3.2 | 99.6 |
| 1952 | 1.9 | 26.5 | 1984 | 4.3 | 103.9 |
| 1953 | 0.8 | 26.7 | 1985 | 3.6 | 107.6 |
| 1954 | 0.7 | 26.9 | 1986 | 1.9 | 109.6 |
| 1955 | −0.4 | 26.8 | 1987 | 3.6 | 113.6 |
| 1956 | 1.5 | 27.2 | 1988 | 4.1 | 118.3 |
| 1957 | 3.3 | 28.1 | 1989 | 4.8 | 124.0 |
| 1958 | 2.8 | 28.9 | 1990 | 5.4 | 130.7 |
| 1959 | 0.7 | 29.1 | 1991 | 4.2 | 136.2 |
| 1960 | 1.7 | 29.6 | 1992 | 3.0 | 140.3 |
| 1961 | 1.0 | 29.9 | 1993 | 3.0 | 144.5 |
| 1962 | 1.0 | 30.2 | 1994 | 2.6 | 148.2 |
| 1963 | 1.3 | 30.6 | 1995 | 2.8 | 152.4 |
| 1964 | 1.3 | 31.0 | 1996 | 3.0 | 156.9 |
| 1965 | 1.6 | 31.5 | 1997 | 2.3 | 160.5 |
| 1966 | 2.9 | 32.4 | 1998 | 1.6 | 163.0 |
| 1967 | 3.1 | 33.4 | 1999 | 2.2 | 166.6 |
| 1968 | 4.2 | 34.8 | 2000 | 3.4 | 172.2 |
| 1969 | 5.5 | 36.7 | 2001 | 2.8 | 177.1 |
| 1970 | 5.7 | 38.8 | 2002 | 1.6 | 179.9 |
| 1971 | 4.4 | 40.5 | 2003 | 2.3 | 184.0 |
| 1972 | 3.2 | 41.8 | 2004 | 2.7 | 188.9 |
| 1973 | 6.2 | 44.4 | 2005 | 3.4 | 195.3 |
| 1974 | 11.0 | 49.3 | 2006 | 3.2 | 201.6 |
| 1975 | 9.1 | 53.8 | 2007 | 2.8 | 207.3 |
| 1976 | 5.8 | 56.9 | 2008 | 3.9 | 215.3 |
| 1977 | 6.5 | 60.6 | 2009 | −0.4 | 214.5 |
| 1978 | 7.6 | 65.2 | 2010 | 1.7 | 218.1 |
| 1979 | 11.3 | 72.6 | 2011 | 3.1 | 224.9 |
| 1980 | 13.5 | 82.4 | 2012 | 2.1 | 229.6 |
| 1981 | 10.3 | 90.9 | 2013 | 1.5 | 233.0 |
| | | | 2014 | 1.6 | 236.7 |

*Sources*: U.S. Bureau of Labor Statistics.

# The Costs of Inflation

If you asked most people why inflation is bad, they would tell you that it lowers the overall standard of living by making goods and services more expensive. That is, it cuts into people's purchasing power. People are fond of recalling the days when a bottle of Coca-Cola cost a dime and a hamburger cost a quarter. Just think what we could buy today if prices had not changed. What people usually do not think about is what their incomes were in the "good old days." The fact that the cost of a Coke has increased from 10 cents to a dollar does not mean anything in real terms if people who once earned $5,000 now earn $50,000. During inflations, most prices—including input prices like wages—tend to rise together, and input prices determine both the incomes of workers and the incomes of owners of capital and land. So inflation by itself does not *necessarily* reduce one's purchasing power.

**Inflation May Change the Distribution of Income**   Whether you gain or lose during a period of inflation depends on whether your income rises faster or slower than the prices of the things you buy. The group most often mentioned when the impact of inflation is discussed is people living on fixed incomes. If your income is fixed and prices rise, your ability to purchase goods and services falls proportionately.

Although the elderly are often thought of as living on fixed incomes, many pension plans pay benefits that are *indexed* to inflation, as we describe in the *Economics in Practice* on the next page. The benefits these plans provide automatically increase when the general price level rises. If prices rise 10 percent, benefits also rise 10 percent. The biggest source of income for many elderly people is Social Security. These benefits are fully indexed; when prices rise—that is, when the CPI rises—by 5 percent, Social Security benefits also increase by 5 percent.

Wages are also sometimes indexed to inflation through cost-of-living adjustments (COLAs) written into labor contracts. These contracts usually stipulate that future wage increases will be larger the larger is the rate of inflation. If wages are fully indexed, workers do not suffer a fall in real income when inflation rises, although wages are not always fully indexed.

One way of thinking about the effects of inflation on the distribution of income is to distinguish between *anticipated* and *unanticipated* inflation. If inflation is anticipated and contracts are made and agreements written with the anticipated value of inflation in mind, there need not be any effects of inflation on income distribution. Consider an individual who is thinking about retiring and has a pension that is not indexed to the CPI. If she knew what inflation was going to be for the next 20 or 30 years of her retirement, there would be no problem. She would just wait to retire until she had enough money to pay for her anticipated growing expenses. The problem occurs if, after she has retired, inflation is higher than she expected. At that point, she may face the prospect of having to return to work. Similarly, if I as a landlord expect inflation to be 2 percent per year over the next 3 years and offer my tenants a 3-year lease with a 2 percent rent increase each year, I will be in bad shape if inflation turns out to be 10 percent per year and causes all my costs to rise by 10 percent per year.

For another example, consider debtors versus creditors. It is commonly believed that debtors benefit at the expense of creditors during an inflation because with inflation they pay back less in the future in real terms than they borrowed. But this is not the case if the inflation is anticipated and the loan contract is written with this in mind.

Suppose that you want to borrow $100 from me to be paid back in a year and that we both agree that if there is no inflation the appropriate interest rate is 5 percent. Suppose also that we both anticipate that the inflation rate will be 10 percent. In this case we will agree on a 15 percent interest rate—you will pay me back $115 at the end of the year. By charging you 15 percent I have taken into account the fact that you will be paying me back with dollars worth 10 percent less in real terms than when you borrowed them. I am then not hurt by inflation and you are not helped if the actual inflation rate turns out to equal our anticipated rate. I am earning a 5 percent **real interest rate**—the difference between the interest rate on a loan and the inflation rate.

Unanticipated inflation, on the other hand, is a different story. If the actual inflation rate during the year turns out to be 20 percent, I as a creditor will be hurt. I charged you 15 percent interest, expecting to get a 5 percent real rate of return, when I needed to charge you 25 percent to get the same 5 percent real rate of return. Because inflation was higher than anticipated, I got a negative real return of 5 percent. Inflation that is higher than anticipated benefits debtors; inflation that is lower than anticipated benefits creditors.

To summarize, the effects of anticipated inflation on the distribution of income are likely to be fairly small because people and institutions will adjust to the anticipated inflation. Unanticipated inflation, on the other hand, may have large effects, depending, among other things, on how much indexing to inflation there is. If many contracts are not indexed and are based on anticipated inflation rates that turn out to be wrong, there can be big winners and losers. In general, there is more uncertainty and risk when inflation is unanticipated. This uncertainty may prevent people from signing long-run contracts that would otherwise be beneficial for both parties.

**real interest rate** The difference between the interest rate on a loan and the inflation rate.

### Administrative Costs and Inefficiencies
There may be costs associated even with anticipated inflation. One is the administrative cost associated with simply keeping up. During the rapid inflation in Israel in the early 1980s, a telephone hotline was set up to give the hourly price index. In Zimbabwe, where the inflation rate in June 2008 was estimated by some to be more than 1 million percent at an annual rate, the government was forced to print ever-increasing denominations of money. In 2009 Zimbabwe abandoned its currency and started using the U.S. dollar and the South African Rand to conduct business.

## ECONOMICS IN PRACTICE

### Chain-Linked Consumer Price Index in the News

The calculations described in Chapter 6 on how to construct a chain-linked price index may seem complicated and a bit arcane to you. But throughout the last months of 2012 and into early 2013, as Republicans and Democrats argued over the federal budget, chain linking became a hot topic.

As we know from the discussion of fixed weights in Chapter 6, chain linking a price index accounts for product substitution that people make in response to relative price changes. Fixed-weight price indices, which do not take into account this substitution, tend to overestimate inflation. There are two versions of the consumer price index (CPI), one using fixed weights and one using chain linking. The fixed-weight version is the one that is used to adjust social security benefits and veteran benefits to price changes. If, say, the CPI increases by 2 percent in a year, benefits are increased by 2 percent. If the chain-linked CPI were used instead, benefits would tend to increase more slowly because in general the chain-linked CPI increases less than does the fixed-weight CPI (because of product substitution). You may see where this is going. One way to decrease expenditures on social security and veteran benefits in the future would be to use the chain-linked CPI rather than the fixed-weight CPI. The nonpartisan Congressional Budget Office estimated that if the chain-linked CPI were adopted, it would save

the federal government about $145 billion over a 10-year period from the lower benefits.

**THINKING PRACTICALLY**

1. Tax brackets are also tied to the fixed-weight CPI. How would tax revenue be affected if the chain-linked CPI were used instead?

## What about Deflation?

In 2015 most of the developed world experienced very little inflation. Indeed, the United States has not seen high inflation since the 1970s. Instead, governments in a number of countries have begun to worry about deflation hitting their economies. Why might we worry about price declines?

Part of the answer, of course, parallels the discussion of price increases. If prices fall and the fall is unanticipated, borrowers will gain at the expense of lenders, whereas those on fixed pensions will gain at the expense of the governments and firms paying those pensions. But deflation also brings with it another worry. It may be a signal that aggregate demand is too low to support full employment. We will have much to say about aggregate demand in future chapters.

# Long-Run Growth

In discussing long-run growth, it will be useful to begin with a few definitions. **Output growth** is the growth rate of the output of the entire economy. **Per-capita output growth** is the growth rate of output per person in the economy. If the population of a country is growing at the same rate as output, then per-capita output is not growing: Output growth is simply keeping up with population growth. Not everyone in a country works, and so output per worker is not the same as output per person. Output per worker is larger than output per person, and it is called productivity. **Productivity growth** is thus the growth rate of *output per worker*.

One measure of the economic welfare of a country is its per-capita output. Per-capita output can increase because productivity increases, as each worker now produces more than he or she did previously, or because there are more workers relative to nonworkers in the population. In the United States, both forces have been at work in increasing per-capita output.

**output growth**   The growth rate of the output of the entire economy.

**per-capita output growth**   The growth rate of output per person in the economy.

**productivity growth**   The growth rate of output per worker.

## Output and Productivity Growth

We have pointed out that aggregate output in the United States has grown at an annual rate of 3.3 percent since 1900, with year-to-year fluctuations. An area of economics called *growth theory* is concerned with the question of what determines this rate. Why 3.3 percent and not 2 percent or 4 percent? We take up this question in Chapter 16, but a few points are useful to make now.

In a simplified economy, machines (capital) and workers (labor) are needed to produce output. How can output increase in this economy? There are a number of ways. One way is to add more workers. With more workers, more output can be produced per machine per hour. Another way is to add more machines, so that each worker has more capital to work with. A third way is to increase the length of the work week. With workers and machines working more hours, more output can be produced. Output can thus increase if labor or capital increases or if the amount of time that labor and capital are working per week increases.

Another way for output to increase in our economy is for the quality of the workers to increase, perhaps through education, experience, or even better health. If workers become more physically fit by exercising more and eating less fat and more whole grains and fresh fruits and vegetables, their greater fitness may increase their output on the machines. People are sometimes said to be adding to their *human capital* when they increase their mental or physical skills.

The quality of the machines used in the workplace may also increase. In particular, new machines that replace old machines may allow more output to be produced per hour with the same number of workers. An obvious example is the replacement of an old computer with a new, faster one that allows more to be done per minute of work on the computer.

To summarize, output can increase when there are more workers, more skills per worker, more machines, better machines, or a longer workweek.

Output per worker hour is called *labor productivity* or sometimes just *productivity*. Output per worker hour is plotted in Figure 7.2 for the 1952 I–2014 IV period. Two features are immediately clear from the figure. First, there is an upward trend. Second, there are fairly sizable short-run fluctuations around the trend. Chapter 16 will discuss these short-run fluctuations, linking them to underutilization of an employed work force. For now, however, our main interest is the long-run trend.

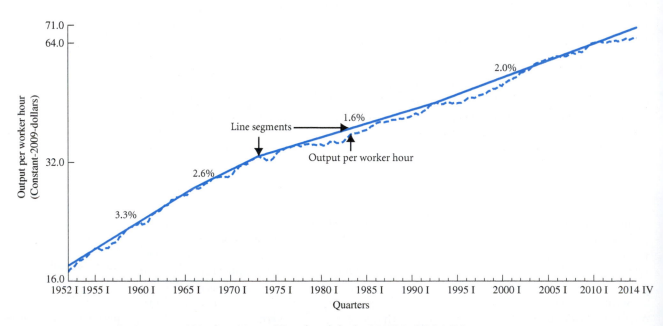

▲ **FIGURE 7.2** **Output per Worker Hour (Productivity), 1952 I–2014 IV**
Productivity grew much faster in the 1950s and 1960s than since.

▲ **FIGURE 7.3 Capital per Worker, 1952 I–2014 IV**
Capital per worker grew until about 1980 and then leveled off somewhat.

To smooth out the short-run fluctuations in Figure 7.2, we have added straight-line segments to the figure, where the segments roughly go through the high values. The slope of each line segment is the growth rate of productivity along the segment. The growth rates are listed in the figure. The different productivity growth rates in the figure tell an interesting story. From the 1950s through the mid-1960s, the growth rate was 3.3 percent. The rate then fell to 2.6 percent in the last half of the 1960s and early 1970s. Between the early 1970s and the early 1990s, the growth rate was much lower at 1.6 percent. Since the early 1990s, it has been 2.0 percent.

Why are the growth rates positive in Figure 7.2? Why has the amount of output that a worker can produce per hour risen in the last half-century? Part of the answer is that the amount of capital per worker has increased. In Figure 7.3 capital per worker is plotted for the same 1952 I–2014 IV period. It is clear from the figure that the amount of capital per worker has generally been rising. Therefore, with more capital per worker, more output can be produced per worker. The other part of the answer is that the quality of labor and capital has been increasing. Both the average skill of workers and the average quality of capital have been increasing. This means that more output can be produced per worker for a given quantity of capital because both workers and capital are getting better.

A harder question to answer concerning Figure 7.2 is why the growth rate of productivity was much higher in the 1950s and 1960s than it has been since the early 1970s. Again, part of the answer is that the amount of capital per worker rose more rapidly in the 1950s and 1960s than it has since then. This can be seen in Figure 7.3. The other part of the answer is, of course, that the quality of labor and capital must have increased more in the 1950s and 1960s than later, although this is difficult to explain or to get direct evidence on. Interestingly, it has been difficult to find big productivity gains from recent technological innovations in the communications area.

## Looking Ahead

This ends our introduction to the basic concepts and problems of macroeconomics. The first chapter of this part introduced the field; the second chapter discussed the measurement of national product and national income; and this chapter discussed unemployment, inflation, and long-run growth. We are now ready to begin the analysis of how the macroeconomy works.

# SUMMARY

## 7.1 UNEMPLOYMENT *p. 124*

1. The *unemployment rate* is the ratio of the number of *unemployed* people to the number of people in the *labor force*. To be considered unemployed and in the labor force, a person must be looking for work.

2. Big differences in rates of unemployment exist across demographic groups, regions, and industries. African Americans, for example, experience much higher unemployment rates than whites.

3. A person who decides to stop looking for work is considered to have dropped out of the labor force and is no longer classified as unemployed. People who stop looking because they are discouraged about finding a job are sometimes called *discouraged workers*.

4. Some unemployment is inevitable. Because new workers are continually entering the labor force, because industries and firms are continuously expanding and contracting, and because people switch jobs, there is a constant process of job search as workers and firms try to match the best people to the available jobs. This unemployment is both natural and beneficial for the economy.

5. The unemployment that occurs because of short-run job/skill-matching problems is called *frictional unemployment*. The unemployment that occurs because of longer-run structural changes in the economy is called *structural unemployment*. The *natural rate of unemployment* is the sum of the frictional rate and the structural rate. The increase in unemployment that

occurs during recessions and depressions is called *cyclical unemployment*.

## 7.2 INFLATION AND DEFLATION *p. 129*

6. The *consumer price index (CPI)* is a fixed-weight price index. It represents the "market basket" purchased by the typical urban consumer.

7. Whether people gain or lose during a period of inflation depends on whether their income rises faster or slower than the prices of the things they buy. The elderly are more insulated from inflation than most people think because Social Security benefits and many pensions are indexed to inflation.

8. Inflation is likely to have a larger effect on the distribution of income when it is unanticipated than when it is anticipated.

## 7.3 LONG-RUN GROWTH *p. 133*

9. Output growth depends on: (1) the growth rate of the capital stock, (2) the growth rate of output per unit of the capital stock, (3) the growth rate of labor, and (4) the growth rate of output per unit of labor.

10. Output per worker hour (labor productivity) rose faster in the 1950s and 1960s than it rose from the 1970s to 2014. An interesting question is whether labor productivity will rise faster in the future because of the Internet.

# REVIEW TERMS AND CONCEPTS

consumer price index (CPI), *p. 129*
cyclical unemployment, *p. 129*
discouraged-worker effect, *p. 126*
employed, *p. 124*
frictional unemployment, *p. 129*
labor force, *p. 124*
labor force participation rate, *p. 124*
natural rate of unemployment, *p. 129*
not in the labor force, *p. 124*

output growth, *p. 133*
per-capita output growth, *p. 133*
producer price indexes (PPIs), *p. 130*
productivity growth, *p. 133*
real interest rate, *p. 132*
structural unemployment, *p. 129*
unemployed, *p. 124*
unemployment rate, *p. 124*

Equations:
labor force = employed + unemployed, *p. 124*
population = labor force + not in labor force, *p. 124*

$$\text{unemployment rate} = \frac{\text{unemployed}}{\text{employed} + \text{unemployed}},$$
*p. 124*

$$\text{labor force participation rate} = \frac{\text{labor force}}{\text{population}}, p. 124$$

# PROBLEMS

All problems are available on MyEconLab.

## 7.1 UNEMPLOYMENT

LEARNING OBJECTIVE: Explain how unemployment is measured.

1.1 In late 2010 economists were debating whether the U.S. economy was in a recession. GDP seemed to be rising, yet the unemployment rate was stuck at close to 10 percent.

In thinking about the economic distress experienced during a recession, which is the most important: high unemployment or falling GDP? Defend your answer.

1.2 When an inefficient firm or a firm producing a product that people no longer want goes out of business, people are unemployed, but that is part of the normal process of

MyEconLab Visit www.myeconlab.com to complete these exercises online and get instant feedback. Exercises that update with real-time data are marked with art ⓦ.

economic growth and development. The unemployment is part of the natural rate and need not concern policy makers. Discuss that statement and its relevance to the economy today.

1.3 What is the unemployment rate in your state today? What was it in 1970, 1975, 1982, and 2008? How has your state done relative to the national average? Do you know or can you determine why?

1.4 **[Related to the *Economics in Practice* on p. 127]** For each of the following events, explain what is likely to happen to the labor force participation rate:
   a. The federal minimum wage is abolished.
   b. The minimum legal working age is lowered from 16 to 14.
   c. The economy is in the midst of a prolonged period of economic growth.
   d. The federal government decreases the duration of unemployment benefits from a high of 99 weeks back to a maximum of 26 weeks.
   e. The federal government lowers the minimum age requirement for collecting Social Security benefits.

1.5 **[Related to the *Economics in Practice* on p. 128]** According to the National Bureau of Economic Research (NBER), the United States experienced five recessions from 1980 to 2010. Following is the NBER's list of the start and end dates for each of these recessions:
   January 1980 – July 1980
   July 1981 – November 1982
   July 1990 – March 1991
   March 2001 – November 2001
   December 2007 – June 2009

   Go to the Bureau of Labor Statistics Web site (www.bls.gov) and look up the monthly unemployment data since 1980. (Find BLS series number LNS14000000 and choose 1980 as the "from" date.) What were the unemployment rates for the starting and ending months for each of the five recessions? How long after each recession ended did it take for the unemployment rate to start to decrease, and how long did it take for the unemployment rate to return to the pre-recession level?

1.6 Go to www.bls.gov and click on the links for state and area employment and unemployment. Look at your home state and describe what changes have taken place in the workforce. Has the labor force participation rate gone up or down? Provide an explanation for the rate change. Are your state's experiences the same as the rest of the country? Provide an explanation of why your state's experiences are the same as or different from the rest of the country.

1.7 Consider the following statements:
   a. Fewer people are employed in Freedonia now than at any time in the past 75 years.
   b. The unemployment rate in Freedonia is lower now than it has been in 75 years.
   Can both of those statements be true at the same time? Explain.

1.8 Suppose the number of employed people in an economy is 312,545,372. The unemployment rate in this economy is 7.4 percent, or .074, and the labor force participation rate is 80 percent, or .80.
   a. What is the size of the labor force?
   b. How many people are unemployed?
   c. What is the size of the working-age population?

1.9 On average, nations in Europe pay higher unemployment benefits for longer periods of time than does the United States. How do you suppose this would impact the unemployment rates in these nations? Explain which type of unemployment you think is most directly affected by the size and duration of unemployment benefits.

1.10 In each of the following cases, classify the person as cyclically unemployed, structurally unemployed, frictionally unemployed, or not in the labor force. Explain your answers.
   a. Samuel quit his job as a bank teller to work full-time on his master's degree.
   b. Charmaine lost her job as a customer service representative when her employer outsourced the work to India.
   c. Lucy just graduated from law school and is deciding which job offer she will accept.
   d. Carlos got laid off from his job as a limo driver six months ago and gave up looking for a new job two months later.
   e. Byron quit his teaching job in Atlanta six weeks ago to look for a higher-paying job in Miami. He is still looking for a job.
   f. Arlisha lost her job as a restaurant manager due to a recession.

## 7.2 INFLATION AND DEFLATION

**LEARNING OBJECTIVE:** Describe the tools to measure inflation and discuss the costs and effects of inflation.

2.1 Suppose all wages, salaries, welfare benefits, and other sources of income were indexed to inflation. Would inflation still be considered a problem? Why or why not?

2.2 What do the CPI and PPIs measure? Why do we need both of these types of price indexes? (Think about what purpose you would use each one for.)

2.3 The CPI is a fixed-weight index. It compares the price of a fixed bundle of goods in one year with the price of the same bundle of goods in some base year. Calculate the price of a bundle containing 50 units of good X, 125 units of good Y, and 100 units of good Z in 2013, 2014, and 2015. Convert the results into an index by dividing each bundle price figure by the bundle price in 2013 and multiplying by 100. Calculate the percentage change in your index between 2013 and 2014 and again between 2014 and 2015. Was there inflation between 2014 and 2015?

| Good | Quantity Consumed | 2013 Prices | 2014 Prices | 2015 Prices |
|------|-------------------|-------------|-------------|-------------|
| X | 50 | $2.00 | $1.50 | $2.00 |
| Y | 125 | 3.00 | 3.00 | 2.50 |
| Z | 100 | 0.75 | 1.25 | 1.50 |

2.4 [**Related to the *Economics in Practice* on p. 133**] In his 2015 State of the Union speech, President Barack Obama urged Congress to raise the federal minimum wage from $7.25 to $10.10 per hour, and stated that future minimum wage increases should be tied to the cost of living. Explain how tying the minimum wage to an index like the CPI could impact the economy? Do you suppose the impact would be different if the minimum wage was tied to the chain-linked CPI as opposed to the fixed-weight CPI? Explain.

2.5 Consider the following five situations. In which situation would a borrower be best off and in which situation would a lender be best off?
  **a.** The nominal interest rate is 6 percent and the inflation rate is 3 percent.
  **b.** The nominal interest rate is 13 percent and the inflation rate is 11 percent.
  **c.** The nominal interest rate is 3 percent and the inflation rate is −1 percent.
  **d.** The real interest rate is 8 percent and the inflation rate is 7 percent.
  **e.** The real interest rate is 5 percent and the inflation rate is 9 percent.

2.6 The CPI is 120 in year 1 and 150 in year 2. All inflation is anticipated. If the Gringotts Bank charges an interest rate of 30 percent in year 2, what is the bank's real interest rate?

## 7.3 LONG-RUN GROWTH

**LEARNING OBJECTIVE:** Discuss the components and implications of long-run growth.

3.1 Policy makers talk about the "capacity" of the economy to grow. What specifically is meant by the "capacity" of the economy? How might capacity be measured? In what ways is capacity limited by labor constraints and by capital constraints? What are the consequences if demand in the economy exceeds capacity? What signs would you look for?

3.2 What was the rate of growth in real GDP during the most recent quarter? You can find the answer in publications such as the *Survey of Current Business, The Economist, and Business Week*. Has growth been increasing or decreasing? What policies might you suggest for increasing the economy's potential long-run rate of growth?

3.3 An article in the *Gotham Times* states that the stock of capital and the workforce in Gotham are both increasing at an annual rate of 7 percent. The same article states that real output is growing by 11 percent. Explain if this is possible in the short run and in the long run.

# PART III

# The Core of Macroeconomic Theory

We now begin our discussion of the theory of how the macroeconomy works. We know how to calculate gross domestic product (GDP), but what factors *determine* it? We know how to define and measure inflation and unemployment, but what circumstances *cause* inflation and unemployment? What, if anything, can government do to reduce unemployment and inflation?

Analyzing the various components of the macroeconomy is a complex undertaking. The level of GDP, the overall price level, and the level of employment—three chief concerns of macroeconomists—are influenced by events in three broadly defined "markets":

■ Goods-and-services market

■ Financial (money) market

■ Labor market

We will explore each market, as well as the links between them, in our discussion of macroeconomic theory. Figure III.1 presents the plan of the next seven chapters, which form the core

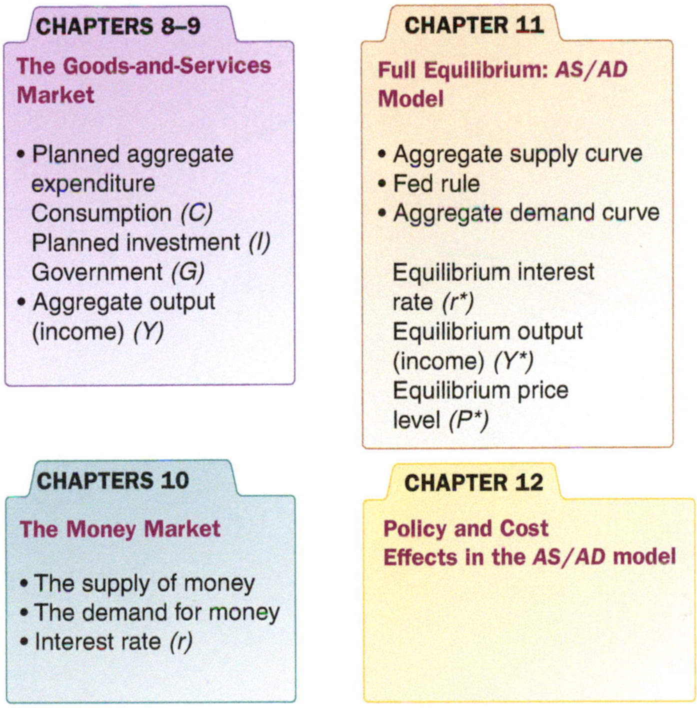

**CHAPTERS 8–9**

**The Goods-and-Services Market**

- Planned aggregate expenditure
  Consumption (C)
  Planned investment (I)
  Government (G)
- Aggregate output (income) (Y)

**CHAPTER 11**

**Full Equilibrium: AS/AD Model**

- Aggregate supply curve
- Fed rule
- Aggregate demand curve

Equilibrium interest rate (r*)
Equilibrium output (income) (Y*)
Equilibrium price level (P*)

**CHAPTER 13**

**The Labor Market**

- The supply of labor
- The demand for labor
- Employment and unemployment

**CHAPTERS 10**

**The Money Market**

- The supply of money
- The demand for money
- Interest rate (r)

**CHAPTER 12**

**Policy and Cost Effects in the AS/AD model**

▲ **FIGURE III.1** **The Core of Macroeconomic Theory**

We build up the macroeconomy slowly. In Chapters 8 and 9, we examine the market for goods and services. In Chapter 10, we examine the money market. Chapter 11 introduces the aggregate supply (AS) curve and the Fed rule and derives the aggregate demand (AD) curve. Chapter 12 uses the AS/AD model to examine policy and cost effects, and Chapter 13 discusses the labor market.

of macroeconomic theory. In Chapters 8 and 9, we describe the market for goods and services, often called the *goods market*. In Chapter 8, we explain several basic concepts and show how the equilibrium level of output is determined in a simple economy with no government and no imports or exports. In Chapter 9, we add the government to the economy. In Chapter 10 we introduce the *money market* and discuss the way the U.S. central bank (the Federal Reserve) controls the interest rate.

Chapter 11 introduces the aggregate supply (*AS*) curve. It also discusses the behavior of the Federal Reserve regarding its interest rate decision, which is approximated by a "Fed rule." The Fed rule is then added to the analysis of the goods market to derive the aggregate demand (*AD*) curve. The resulting model, the "*AS/AD*" model, determines the equilibrium values of the interest rate (*r*), aggregate output (income) (*Y*), and the price level (*P*). Chapter 12 uses the *AS/AD* model to analyze policy and cost effects. Finally, Chapter 13 discusses the supply of and demand for labor and the functioning of the labor market in the macroeconomy. This material is essential to understanding how modern, developed economies function.

# Aggregate Expenditure and Equilibrium Output

# 8

In the last several chapters we described a number of features of the U.S. economy, including real GDP, inflation, and unemployment, and we talked about how they are measured. Now we begin the analytical part of macroeconomics: How do the different parts of the economy interact to produce the time-profile of the U.S. economy that we described in the last few chapters?

We begin with the simplest case, focusing on households and firms, asking what happens to the economy as a whole when investment increases. If suddenly all the managers of firms in the economy decided to expand their plants, how would that affect households and aggregate output? Once we understand how households and firms interact at the aggregate level, we will introduce government in Chapter 9. In subsequent chapters, we will make our simple economic model both more realistic, and as a result more complex, but the basic intuitions of these early chapters will remain. As we work through our model of the economy, we will focus, at least initially, on understanding movements in real gross domestic product (GDP), one of the central measures of macroeconomic activity. Because we are interested in tracking real changes in the level of economic activity, we focus on real, rather than nominal, output. So, although we will typically use dollars to measure GDP, you should think about this as dollars corrected for price level changes.

We saw previously that GDP can be calculated in terms of either income or expenditures. We will use the variable $Y$ to refer to both **aggregate output** and **aggregate income**.

> In any given period, there is an exact equality between aggregate output (production) and aggregate income. You should be reminded of this fact whenever you encounter the combined term **aggregate output (income) ($Y$)**.

Aggregate output can also be considered the aggregate quantity supplied because it is the amount that firms are supplying (producing) during a period. In the discussions that follow, we use the term *aggregate output (income)* instead of *aggregate quantity supplied*, but keep in mind that the two are equivalent. Also remember that *aggregate output* means "real GDP." For ease of discussion we will sometimes refer to aggregate output (income) as simply "output" or "income."

From the outset, you must think in "real terms." For example, when we talk about output ($Y$), we mean real output, not nominal output. In the current chapter and the next, we will take as fixed the overall price level ($P$), so that nominal and real output are the same. Nevertheless, because eventually we will introduce the possibility of a changing price level, it is useful now to begin thinking of output ($Y$) as being in real terms.

**8.1 LEARNING OBJECTIVE**

Explain the principles of the Keynesian theory of consumption.

**aggregate output** The total quantity of goods and services produced (or supplied) in an economy in a given period.

**aggregate income** The total income received by all factors of production in a given period.

**aggregate output (income) (Y)** A combined term used to remind you of the exact equality between aggregate output and aggregate income.

**consumption function** The relationship between consumption and income.

# The Keynesian Theory of Consumption

In 2012, the average U.S. family spent about $1,700 on clothing. For high-income families earning more than $150,000, the amount spent on clothing was higher, at about $5,500. We all recognize that for consumption as a whole, as well as for consumption of most specific categories of goods and services, consumption rises with income. This relationship between consumption and income is central to Keynes's model of the economy. Although Keynes recognized that many factors, including wealth and interest rates, play a role in determining consumption levels in the economy, in his classic *The General Theory of Employment, Interest, and Money*, current income played the key role:

> The fundamental psychological law, upon which we are entitled to depend with great confidence both *a priori* from our knowledge of human nature and from the detailed facts of experience, is that men [and women, too] are disposed, as a rule and on average, to increase their consumption as their incomes increase, but not by as much as the increase in their income.[1]

Keynes is telling us two things in this quote. First, if you find your income going up, you will spend more than you did before. But Keynes is also saying something about how much more you will spend: He predicts—based on his looking at the data and his understanding of people—that the rise in consumption will be less than the full rise in income. This simple observation plays a large role in helping us understand the workings of the aggregate economy.

The relationship between consumption and income is called a **consumption function**. Figure 8.1 shows a hypothetical consumption function for an individual household. The curve is labeled $c(y)$, which is read "$c$ is a function of $y$," or "consumption is a function of income." Note that we have drawn the line with an upward slope, showing that consumption increases with income. To reflect Keynes's view that consumption increases less than one for one with income, we have drawn the consumption function with a slope of less than 1. The consumption function in Figure 8.1 is a straight line, telling us that an increase in income of $1 leads to the same increase in consumption regardless of the initial value of income. In practice, the consumption function may be curved, with the slope decreasing as income increases. This would tell us that the typical consumer spends less of the incremental income received as his or her income rises.

The consumption function in Figure 8.1 represents an individual household. In macroeconomics, however, we are interested in the behavior of the economy as a whole, the aggregate

▶ **FIGURE 8.1**

**A Consumption Function for a Household**

A consumption function for an individual household shows the level of consumption at each level of household income.

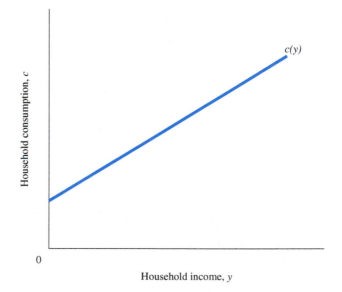

[1] John Maynard Keynes, *The General Theory of Employment, Interest, and Money* (1936), First Harbinger Ed. (New York: Harcourt Brace Jovanovich, 1964), p. 96.

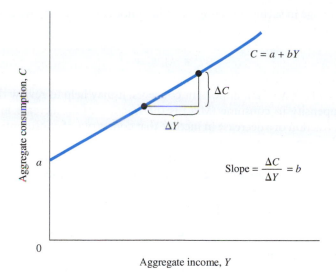

◀ **FIGURE 8.2    An Aggregate Consumption Function**
The aggregate consumption function shows the level of aggregate consumption at each level of aggregate income. The upward slope indicates that higher levels of income lead to higher levels of consumption spending.

consumption of all households in the economy in relation to aggregate income. Figure 8.2 shows this aggregate consumption function, again using a straight line, or constant slope, for simplicity. With a straight-line consumption curve, we can use the following equation to describe the curve:

$$C = a + bY$$

$Y$ is aggregate output (income), $C$ is aggregate consumption, and $a$ is the point at which the consumption function intersects the vertical axis—a constant. The letter $b$ is the slope of the line, in this case $\Delta C / \Delta Y$ [because consumption ($C$) is measured on the vertical axis and income ($Y$) is measured on the horizontal axis].[2] Every time income increases (say by $\Delta Y$), consumption increases by $b$ times $\Delta Y$. Thus, $\Delta C = b \times \Delta Y$ and $\Delta C/\Delta Y = b$. Suppose, for example, that the slope of the line in Figure 8.2 is 0.75 (that is, $b = .75$). An increase in income ($\Delta Y$) of $1,000 would then increase consumption by $b\Delta Y = 0.75 \times \$1,000$, or 750.

The **marginal propensity to consume (MPC)** is the fraction of a change in income that is consumed. In the consumption function here, $b$ is the MPC. An MPC of .75 means consumption changes by .75 of the change in income. The slope of the consumption function is the MPC. An MPC less than 1 tells us that individuals spend less than 100 percent of their additional income, just as Keynes suggested.

**marginal propensity to consume (MPC)**    That fraction of a change in income that is consumed, or spent.

marginal propensity to consume $\equiv$ slope of consumption function $\equiv \dfrac{\Delta C}{\Delta Y}$

**Aggregate saving (S)** in the economy, denoted $S$, is the difference between aggregate income and aggregate consumption:

**aggregate saving (S)**    The part of aggregate income that is not consumed.

$$S \equiv Y - C$$

The triple equal sign means that this equation is an **identity**, or something that is always true by definition. This equation simply says that income that is not consumed must be saved. If $0.75 of a $1.00 increase in income goes to consumption, $0.25 must go to saving. If income decreases by $1.00, consumption will decrease by $0.75 and saving will decrease by $0.25. The **marginal propensity to save (MPS)** is the fraction of a change in income that is saved: $\Delta S / \Delta Y$,

**identity**    Something that is always true by definition.

**marginal propensity to save (MPS)**    That fraction of a change in income that is saved.

---

[2] The Greek letter $\Delta$ (delta) means "change in." For example, $\Delta Y$ (read "delta Y") means the "change in income." If income ($Y$) in 2012 is $100 and income in 2013 is $110, then $\Delta Y$ for this period is $110 − $100 = $10. For a review of the concept of slope, see Appendix, Chapter 1.

where $\Delta S$ is the change in saving. Because everything not consumed is saved, the MPC and the MPS must add up to 1.

$$MPC + MPS \equiv 1$$

Because the MPC and the MPS are important concepts, it may help to review their definitions. The marginal propensity to consume (MPC) is the fraction of an increase in income that is consumed (or the fraction of a decrease in income that comes out of consumption).

The marginal propensity to save (MPS) is the fraction of an increase in income that is saved (or the fraction of a decrease in income that comes out of saving).

The numerical examples used in the rest of this chapter are based on the following consumption function:

$$C = \underbrace{100}_{a} + \underbrace{0.75\,Y}_{b}$$

This equation is simply an extension of the generic $C = a + bY$ consumption function we have been discussing, where $a$ is 100 and $b$ is 0.75. This function is graphed in Figure 8.3.

Because saving and consumption by definition add up to income, we can use the consumption curve to tell us about both consumption and saving. We do this in Figure 8.4. In this figure, we have drawn a 45-degree line from the origin. Everywhere along this line aggregate consumption is equal to aggregate income. Therefore, saving is zero. Where the consumption curve is *above* the 45-degree line, consumption exceeds income and saving is negative, that is, people borrow. Where the consumption function *crosses* the 45-degree line, consumption is equal to income and saving is zero. Where the consumption function is *below* the 45-degree line, consumption is less than income and saving is positive. Note that the slope of the saving function is $\Delta S/\Delta Y$, which is equal to the marginal propensity to save (MPS). The consumption function and the saving function are mirror images of each other. No information appears in one that

▶ **FIGURE 8.3   The Aggregate Consumption Function Derived from the Equation $C = 100 + 0.75Y$**
In this simple consumption function, consumption is 100 at an income of zero. As income rises, so does consumption. For every 100 increase in income, consumption rises by 75. The slope of the line is 0.75.

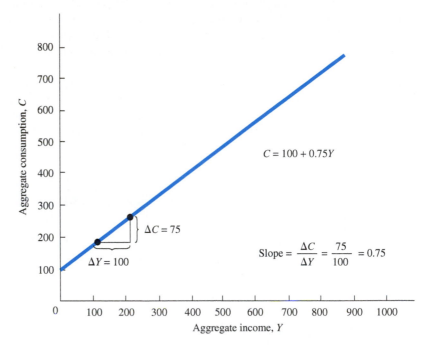

| Aggregate Income, Y | Aggregate Consumption, C |
|---|---|
| 0 | 100 |
| 80 | 160 |
| 100 | 175 |
| 200 | 250 |
| 400 | 400 |
| 600 | 550 |
| 800 | 700 |
| 1,000 | 850 |

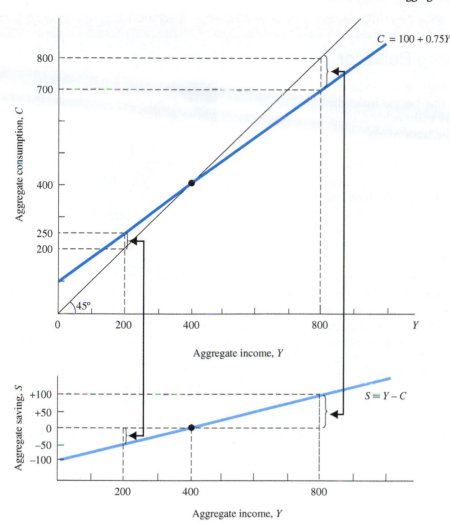

◀ **FIGURE 8.4**
**Deriving the Saving
Function from the
Consumption Function
in Figure 8.3**
Because $S \equiv Y - C$, it is easy
to derive the saving function
from the consumption function. A 45-degree line drawn
from the origin can be used
as a convenient tool to compare consumption and income
graphically. At $Y = 200$, consumption is 250. The 45-degree
line shows us that consumption
is larger than income by 50. Thus
$S \equiv Y - C = -50$. At $Y = 800$,
consumption is less than income
by 100. Thus $S = 100$ when
$Y = 800$.

| Y | − | C | = | S |
|---|---|---|---|---|
| Aggregate Income | | Aggregate Consumption | | Aggregate Saving |
| 0 | | 100 | | −100 |
| 80 | | 160 | | −80 |
| 100 | | 175 | | −75 |
| 200 | | 250 | | −50 |
| 400 | | 400 | | 0 |
| 600 | | 550 | | 50 |
| 800 | | 700 | | 100 |
| 1,000 | | 850 | | 150 |

does not appear in the other. These functions tell us how households in the aggregate will divide income between consumption spending and saving at every possible income level. In other words, they embody aggregate household behavior.

## Other Determinants of Consumption

The assumption that consumption depends only on income is obviously a simplification. In practice, the decisions of households on how much to consume in a given period are also affected by
their wealth, by the interest rate, and by their expectations of the future. Households with higher
wealth are likely to spend more, other things being equal, than households with less wealth, even
at the same income level. As we will see, these other factors shift the consumption function.

## ECONOMICS IN PRACTICE

### Behavioral Biases in Saving Behavior

This chapter has described how saving is related to income. Economists have generally assumed that people make their saving decisions rationally, just as they make other decisions about choices in consumption and the labor market. Saving decisions involve thinking about trade-offs between present and future consumption. Recent work in behavioral economics has highlighted the role of psychological biases in saving behavior and has demonstrated that seemingly small changes in the way saving programs are designed can result in big behavioral changes.

Many retirement plans are designed with an opt-in feature. That is, you need to take some action to enroll. Typically, when you begin a job, you need to check "yes" on the retirement plan enrollment form. Recent work in economics by James Choi of Yale University, Brigitte Madrian of Harvard and Dennis Shea, head of executive compensation at Aetna, suggests that simply changing the enrollment process from the opt-in structure just described to an opt-out system in which people are automatically enrolled unless they check the "no" box dramatically increases enrollment in retirement pension plans. In one study, the change from an opt-in to an opt-out system increased pension plan enrollment after 3 months of work from 65 percent to 98 percent of workers.

Behavioral economists have administered a number of surveys suggesting that people, on average, think they save too little of their income for retirement. Shlomo Benartzi, from the University of California, Los Angeles, and Richard Thaler, from the University of Chicago, devised a retirement program to try to increase saving rates. Under this plan, called Save More Tomorrow, employees are offered a program that allows them to precommit to save more whenever they get a pay raise. Behavioral economists argue that people find this option attractive because it is easier for them to

commit to making sacrifices tomorrow than it is for them to make those sacrifices today. (This is why many people resolve to diet some time in the future but continue to overeat today.) The Save More Tomorrow retirement plans have been put in place in a number of companies, including Vanguard, T. Rowe Price, and TIAA-CREF. Early results suggest dramatic increases in the saving rates of those enrolled, with saving rates quadrupling after 4 years and four pay raises.

#### THINKING PRACTICALLY

1. The Save More Tomorrow Plans encourage people to save more by committing themselves to future action. Can you think of examples in your own life of similar commitment devices you use?

---

The boom in the U.S. stock market in the last half of the 1990s and the boom in housing prices between 2003 and 2005, both of which increased household wealth substantially, led households to consume more than they otherwise would have in these periods. In 2009–2010, after a fall in housing prices and the stock market, consumption was less than it otherwise would have been.

For many households, interest rates also figure in to consumption and saving decisions. Lower interest rates reduce the cost of borrowing, so lower interest rates are likely to stimulate spending. (Conversely, higher interest rates increase the cost of borrowing and are likely to decrease spending.) Finally, as households think about what fraction of incremental income to consume versus save, their expectations about the future may also play a role. If households are optimistic and expect to do better in the future, they may spend more at present than if they think the future will be bleak.

Household expectations are also important regarding households' responses to changes in their income. If, for example, the government announces a tax cut, which increases after-tax income, households' responses to the tax cut will likely depend on whether the tax cut is expected to be temporary or permanent. If households expect that the tax cut will be in effect for only two years, their responses are likely to be smaller than if they expect the tax cut to be permanent.

We examine these issues in Chapter 15, where we take a closer look at household behavior regarding both consumption and labor supply. But for now, we will focus only on income, given that it is the most important determinant of consumption.

# Planned Investment (*I*) versus Actual Investment

**8.2 LEARNING** OBJECTIVE

Explain the difference between planned investment and actual investment.

The output of an economy consists not only of goods consumed by households, but investments made by firms. Some firms' investments are in the form of plants and equipment. These investments in many ways look like some consumption expenditures of households. In a given period, a firm might buy $500,000 of new machinery, which would be part of aggregate output for the period, as would the purchase of automobiles by households. In Chapter 6, you learned that firms' investments also include inventories. Understanding how firms invest in inventories is a little more complicated, but it is important for understanding the way the macroeconomy works.

A firm's inventory is the stock of goods that it has awaiting sale. For many reasons, most firms want to hold some inventory. It is hard to predict exactly when consumers will want to purchase a new refrigerator, and most customers are not patient. Sometimes it is cheaper to produce goods in larger volumes than current demand requires, which leads firms to want to have inventory. From a macroeconomic perspective, however, inventory differs from other capital investments in one important way: Although purchases by firms of machinery and equipment are *always* deliberate, *sometimes* inventories build up (or decline) without any deliberate plan by firms. For this reason, there can be a difference between **planned investment**, which consists of the investments firms *plan* to make, and **actual investment**, which consists of all of firms' investments, including their unplanned changes in inventories.

**planned investment (*I*)**   Those additions to capital stock and inventory that are planned by firms.

**actual investment**   The actual amount of investment that takes place; it includes items such as unplanned changes in inventories.

Why are inventories sometimes different from what was planned? Recall that firms hold planned inventories in anticipation of sales, recognizing that the exact timing of sales may be uncertain. If a firm overestimates how much it will sell in a period, it will end up with more in inventory than it planned to have. On other occasions, inventories may be lower than planned when sales are stronger than expected. We will use *I* to refer to planned investment, not necessarily actual investment. As we will see shortly, the economy is in equilibrium only when planned investment and actual investment are equal.

# Planned Investment and the Interest Rate (*r*)

**8.3 LEARNING** OBJECTIVE

Understand how planned investment is affected by the interest rate.

We have seen that there is an important difference between planned investment and actual investment, and this distinction will play a key role in the discussion of equilibrium in this chapter. But another important question is what determines planned investment in the first place? In practice planned investment depends on many factors, as you would expect, but here we focus on just one: the interest rate. Recall that investment includes a firm's purchase of new capital—new machines and plants. Whether a firm decides to invest in new capital depends on whether the expected profits from that machinery and those plants justify its costs. And one cost of an investment project is the interest cost. When a manufacturing firm builds a new plant, the contractor must be paid at the time the plant is built. The money needed to carry out such projects is generally borrowed and paid back over an extended period. The real cost of an investment project thus depends in part on the interest rate—the cost of borrowing. When the interest rate rises, it becomes more expensive to borrow and fewer projects are likely to be undertaken; increasing the interest rate, *ceteris paribus*, is likely to reduce the level of planned investment spending. When the interest rate falls, it becomes less costly to borrow and more investment projects are likely to be undertaken; reducing the interest rate, *ceteris paribus*, is likely to increase the level of planned investment spending.

The relationship between the interest rate and planned investment is illustrated by the downward-sloping demand curve in Figure 8.5. The higher the interest rate, the lower the level

**Planned Investment Schedule**

Planned investment spending is a negative function of the interest rate. An increase in the interest rate from 3 percent to 6 percent reduces planned investment from $I_0$ to $I_1$.

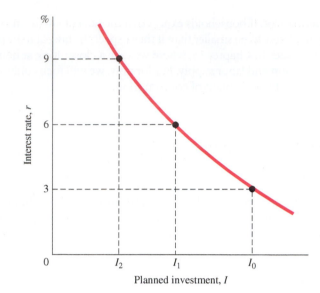

of planned investment. At an interest rate of 3 percent, planned investment is $I_0$. When the interest rate rises from 3 to 6 percent, planned investment falls from $I_0$ to $I_1$. As the interest rate falls, however, more projects become profitable, so more investment is undertaken. The curve in Figure 8.5 is sometimes called the "marginal efficiency of investment" curve.

## Other Determinants of Planned Investment

The assumption that planned investment depends only on the interest rate is obviously a simplification, just as is the assumption that consumption depends only on income. In practice, the decision of a firm on how much to invest depends on, among other things, its expectation of future sales. If a firm expects that its sales will increase in the future, it may begin to build up its capital stock—that is, to invest—now so that it will be able to produce more in the future to meet the increased level of sales. The optimism or pessimism of entrepreneurs about the future course of the economy can have an important effect on current planned investment. Keynes used the phrase *animal spirits* to describe the feelings of entrepreneurs, and he argued that these feelings affect investment decisions significantly.

We will come back to this issue in Chapter 15, where we will take a closer look at firm behavior (and household behavior), but until then to complete our simple model we will assume that planned investment depends only on the interest rate.

Explain how equilibrium output is determined.

**equilibrium**   Occurs when there is no tendency for change. In the macroeconomic goods market, equilibrium occurs when planned aggregate expenditure is equal to aggregate output.

# The Determination of Equilibrium Output (Income)

Thus far, we have described the behavior of firms and households. In this simple setting, how does the economy achieve equilibrium and what does that equilibrium look like?

A number of definitions of **equilibrium** are used in economics but all use the idea that at equilibrium, there is no tendency for change. In microeconomics, equilibrium is said to exist in a particular market (for example, the market for bananas) at the price for which the quantity demanded is equal to the quantity supplied. At this point, both suppliers and demanders are satisfied. The equilibrium price of a good is the price at which suppliers want to furnish the amount that demanders want to buy. In the macroeconomic goods market, we will use a similar definition of equilibrium focused on a match between what is planned and what actually happens.

To define equilibrium for the macroeconomy, we start with a new variable, **planned aggregate expenditure (AE)**. Planned aggregate expenditure is, by definition, consumption plus planned investment:

$$AE \equiv C + I$$

Note that $I$ is planned investment spending only. It does not include any unplanned increases or decreases in inventory. Note also that this is a definition. Aggregate expenditure is always equal to $C + I$, and we write it with the triple equal sign.

The economy is defined to be in equilibrium when aggregate output ($Y$) is equal to planned aggregate expenditure ($AE$).

$$\text{Equilibrium: } Y = AE$$

Because $AE$ is, by definition, $C + I$, equilibrium can also be written:

$$\text{Equilibrium: } Y = C + I$$

It will help in understanding the equilibrium concept to consider what happens if the economy is out of equilibrium. First, suppose aggregate output is greater than planned aggregate expenditure:

$$Y > C + I$$

aggregate output > planned aggregate expenditure

When output is greater than planned spending, there is unplanned inventory investment. Firms planned to sell more of their goods than they sold, and the difference shows up as an unplanned increase in inventories. Next, suppose planned aggregate expenditure is greater than aggregate output:

$$C + I > Y$$

planned aggregate expenditure > aggregate output

When planned spending exceeds output, firms have sold more than they planned to. Inventory investment is smaller than planned. Planned and actual investment are not equal. Only when output is exactly matched by planned spending will there be no unplanned inventory investment. If there is unplanned inventory investment, this will be a state of disequilibrium. The mechanism by which the economy returns to equilibrium will be discussed later. Equilibrium in the goods market is achieved only when aggregate output ($Y$) and planned aggregate expenditure ($C + I$) are equal, or when actual and planned investment are equal.

Table 8.1 derives a planned aggregate expenditure schedule and shows the point of equilibrium for our numerical example. $I$ is assumed to be fixed and equal to 25 for

**planned aggregate expenditure (AE)** The total amount the economy plans to spend in a given period. Equal to consumption plus planned investment: $AE \equiv C + I$

| TABLE 8.1 | Deriving the Planned Aggregate Expenditure Schedule and Finding Equilibrium.* | | | | |
|---|---|---|---|---|---|
| (1) Aggregate Output (Income) ($Y$) | (2) Aggregate Consumption ($C$) | (3) Planned Investment ($I$) | (4) Planned Aggregate Expenditure ($AE$) $C + I$ | (5) Unplanned Inventory Change $Y - (C + I)$ | (6) Equilibrium? ($Y = AE$?) |
| 100 | 175 | 25 | 200 | −100 | No |
| 200 | 250 | 25 | 275 | −75 | No |
| 400 | 400 | 25 | 425 | −25 | No |
| 500 | 475 | 25 | 500 | 0 | Yes |
| 600 | 550 | 25 | 575 | +25 | No |
| 800 | 700 | 25 | 725 | +75 | No |
| 1,000 | 850 | 25 | 875 | +125 | No |

*The figures in column 2 are based on the equation $C = 100 + 0.75Y$.

these calculations. Remember that $I$ depends on the interest rate, but the interest rate is fixed for purposes of this chapter. Remember also that all our calculations are based on $C = 100 + 0.75Y$. To determine planned aggregate expenditure, we add consumption spending ($C$) to planned investment spending ($I$) at every level of income. Glancing down columns 1 and 4, we see one and only one level at which aggregate output and planned aggregate expenditure are equal: $Y = 500$.

Figure 8.6 illustrates the same equilibrium graphically. Figure 8.6a adds planned investment, fixed at 25, to consumption at every level of income. Because planned investment is a constant, the planned aggregate expenditure function is simply the consumption function displaced vertically by that constant amount. Figure 8.6b shows the planned aggregate expenditure function with the 45-degree line. The 45-degree line represents all points on the graph where the variables on the horizontal and vertical axes are equal. Any point on the 45-degree line is a potential equilibrium point. The planned aggregate expenditure function crosses the 45-degree line at a single point, where $Y = 500$. (The point at which the two lines cross is sometimes called the *Keynesian cross*.) At that point, $Y = C + I$.

Now let us look at some other levels of aggregate output (income). First, consider $Y = 800$. Is this an equilibrium output? Clearly, it is not. At $Y = 800$, planned aggregate expenditure is 725 (see Table 8.1). This amount is less than aggregate output, which is 800. Because output is greater than planned spending, the difference ends up in inventory as unplanned inventory

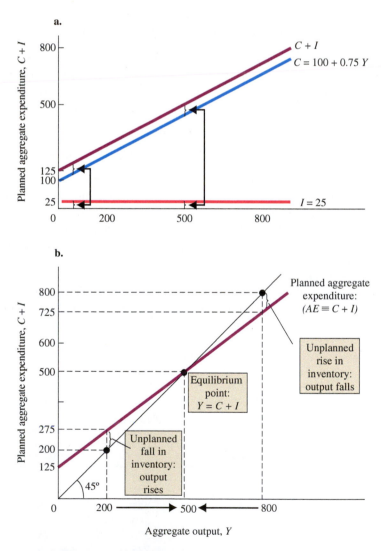

▲ **FIGURE 8.6** **Equilibrium Aggregate Output**
Equilibrium occurs when planned aggregate expenditure and aggregate output are equal. Planned aggregate expenditure is the sum of consumption spending and planned investment spending.

investment. In this case, unplanned inventory investment is 75. In the aggregate, firms have more inventory than desired. As a result, firms have an incentive to change their production plans going forward. In this sense, the economy will not be in equilibrium.

Next, consider $Y = 200$. Is this an equilibrium output? No. At $Y = 200$, planned aggregate expenditure is 275. Planned spending $(AE)$ is greater than output $(Y)$, and there is an unplanned fall in inventory investment of 75. Again, firms in the aggregate will experience a different result from what they expected.

At $Y = 200$ and $Y = 800$, planned investment and actual investment are unequal. There is unplanned investment, and the system is out of balance. Only at $Y = 500$, where planned aggregate expenditure and aggregate output are equal, will planned investment equal actual investment.

Finally, let us find the equilibrium level of output (income) algebraically. Recall that we know the following:

$$Y = C + I \qquad \text{(equilbrium)}$$
$$C = 100 + 0.75Y \quad \text{(consumption function)}$$
$$I = 25 \qquad \text{(planned investment)}$$

By substituting the second and third equations into the first, we get:

$$Y = \underbrace{100 + 0.75\,Y}_{C} + \underbrace{25.}_{I}$$

There is only one value of Y for which this statement is true, and we can find it by rearranging terms:

$$Y - 0.75Y = 100 + 25$$
$$0.25Y = 125$$
$$Y = \frac{125}{0.25} = 500$$

The equilibrium level of output is 500, as shown in Table 8.1 and Figure 8.6.

## The Saving/Investment Approach to Equilibrium

Because aggregate income must be saved or spent, by definition, $Y \equiv C + S$, which is an identity. The equilibrium condition is $Y = C + I$, but this is not an identity because it does not hold when we are out of equilibrium.[3] By substituting $C + S$ for Y in the equilibrium condition, we can write:

$$C + S = C + I$$

Because we can subtract $C$ from both sides of this equation, we are left with:

$$S = I$$

Thus, only when planned investment equals saving will there be equilibrium.

Figure 8.7 reproduces the saving schedule derived in Figure 8.4 and the horizontal investment function from Figure 8.6. Notice that $S = I$ at one and only one level of aggregate output, $Y = 500$. At $Y = 500$, $C = 475$ and $I = 25$. At this level of Y, saving equals 25 and so $S = I$ and we are at an equilibrium.

---

[3] It would be an identity if I included unplanned inventory accumulations—in other words, if I were actual investment instead of planned investment.

▶ **FIGURE 8.7 The S = I Approach to Equilibrium**
Aggregate output is equal to planned aggregate expenditure only when saving equals planned investment (S = I). Saving and planned investment are equal at Y = 500.

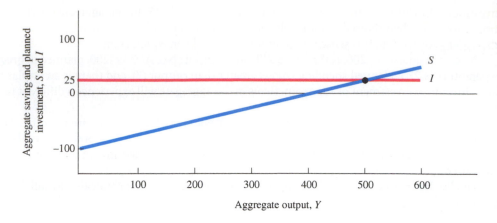

## Adjustment to Equilibrium

We have defined equilibrium and learned how to find it, but we have said nothing about how firms might react to *disequilibrium*. Let us consider the actions firms might take when planned aggregate expenditure exceeds aggregate output (income).

We already know the only way firms can sell more than they produce is by selling some inventory. This means that when planned aggregate expenditure exceeds aggregate output, unplanned inventory reductions have occurred. Firms have sold more than they planned. It seems reasonable to assume that firms will respond to unplanned inventory reductions by increasing output. If firms increase output, income must also increase. (Output and income are two ways of measuring the same thing.) As GM builds more cars, it hires more workers (or pays its existing workforce for working more hours), buys more steel, uses more electricity, and so on. These purchases by GM represent income for the producers of labor, steel, electricity, and so on. When firms try to keep their inventories stable by increasing production, this will generate more income in the economy as a whole. This will lead to more consumption. Remember, when income rises, so does consumption. The adjustment process will continue as long as output (income) is below planned aggregate expenditure. If firms react to unplanned inventory reductions by increasing output, an economy with planned spending greater than output will adjust to equilibrium, with Y higher than before.

If planned spending is less than output, there will be unplanned increases in inventories. In this case, firms will respond by reducing output. As output falls, income falls, consumption falls, and so on, until equilibrium is restored, with Y lower than before.

As Figure 8.6 shows, at any level of output above Y = 500, such as Y = 800, output will fall until it reaches equilibrium at Y = 500, and at any level of output below Y = 500, such as Y = 200, output will rise until it reaches equilibrium at Y = 500.[4]

**8.5 LEARNING** OBJECTIVE

Describe the multiplier process and use the multiplier equation to calculate changes in equilibrium.

## The Multiplier

We are now ready to answer the question posed at the beginning of this chapter: What happens to the level of real output if all of the managers in the economy suddenly decide to increase planned investment from, say, 25 to 50? It may surprise you to learn that the change in equilibrium output will be *greater* than the initial change in planned investment. In fact, output will change by a multiple of the change in planned investment.

---

[4] In discussing simple supply and demand equilibrium in Chapters 3 and 4, we saw that when quantity supplied exceeds quantity demanded, the price falls and the quantity supplied declines. Similarly, when quantity demanded exceeds quantity supplied, the price rises and the quantity supplied increases. In the analysis here, we are ignoring potential changes in prices or in the price level and focusing on changes in the level of real output (income). Later, after we have introduced money and the price level into the analysis, prices will be important. At this stage, however, only aggregate output (income) (Y) adjusts when aggregate expenditure exceeds aggregate output (with inventory falling) or when aggregate output exceeds aggregate expenditure (with inventory rising).

# ECONOMICS IN PRACTICE

## General Motors' Silverado

We have indicated in the text that a change in inventories is a component of firm investment. For an automobile firm, the size of its inventory of cars and trucks is large. For example, for General Motors the ratio of sales to inventory (also called the Inventory Turnover ratio) in normal times is between 9 and 10. Contrast this with Google, which had an Inventory Turnover ratio of 75! To run its business, Google needs little inventory. This should not surprise you because Google is a software company. In the case of cars, we have a physical product, produced in large volumes for cost efficiencies and distributed through a massive dealership network located all over the world. If Google gets a new customer, it can serve that client instantly. For GM, a large stock of inventories is needed to make sure the right car or truck is in the right place when customers call.

Given how important inventories are in the auto industry, it is an interesting place to look at what happens when we have unplanned inventories. As we know from the data we have looked at, the United States was hit by a large recession in late 2008. This recession hit the auto makers hard; indeed GM entered bankruptcy shortly thereafter. By 2011, many business people expected a recovery and the lead executives at the then- reorganized GM were among them. In anticipation of new business, GM increased its production of its most profitable pickup truck, the Silverado. As we have seen previously, however, 2011 did not bring a strong recovery. The consequence for GM? By mid-2011 there were more than 280,000 Silverados at dealerships throughout the country, an inventory level equivalent to 122 days of sales. The normal inventory levels for trucks are about 90 days of sales. In short, GM experienced a large unplanned increase in inventories.

What did GM do? It should not surprise you to learn that in the next Christmas period, plants producing the Silverado were shuttered for three weeks rather than the usual two, as GM cut its production levels. Unplanned inventories created disequilbrium to which the GM executives responded by production cutbacks.

### THINKING PRACTICALLY

1. Do you expect inventory turns for the average firm in the economy to increase or decrease as we enter a recession?

The **multiplier** is defined as the ratio of the change in the equilibrium level of output to a change in some exogenous variable. An **exogenous variable** is a variable that does not depend on the state of the economy—that is, a variable is exogenous if it does not change in response to changes in the economy. In this chapter, we treat planned investment as exogenous. This simplifies our analysis and provides a foundation for later discussions.

With planned investment exogenous, we can ask how much the equilibrium level of output changes when planned investment changes. Remember that we are not trying to explain *why* planned investment changes; we are simply asking how much the equilibrium level of output changes when (for whatever reason) planned investment changes. (Beginning in Chapter 11, we will no longer take planned investment as given and will explain how planned investment is determined.)

Consider a sustained increase in planned investment of 25—that is, suppose $I$ increases from 25 to 50 and stays at 50. If equilibrium existed at $I = 25$, an increase in planned investment of 25 will cause a disequilibrium, with planned aggregate expenditure greater than aggregate output by 25. Firms immediately see unplanned reductions in their inventories. As a result, firms begin to increase output.

Let us say the increase in planned investment comes from an anticipated increase in world travel that comes, for example, from a decision by a major world power to lift restrictions on its citizen's ability to travel. This increase in expected travel demand leads airlines to purchase more

**multiplier**  The ratio of the change in the equilibrium level of output to a change in some exogenous variable.

**exogenous variable**  A variable that is assumed not to depend on the state of the economy—that is, it does not change when the economy changes.

airplanes, car rental companies to increase purchases of automobiles, and bus companies to purchase more buses (all capital goods). The firms experiencing unplanned inventory declines will be automobile manufacturers, bus producers, and aircraft producers—GM, Ford, Boeing, and so on. In response to declining inventories of planes, buses, and cars, these firms will increase output.

Now suppose these firms raise output by the full 25 increase in planned investment. Does this restore equilibrium? No, it does not because when output goes up, people earn more income and a part of that income will be spent. This increases planned aggregate expenditure even further. In other words, an increase in $I$ also leads indirectly to an increase in $C$. To produce more airplanes, Boeing has to hire more workers or ask its existing employees to work more hours. It also must buy more engines from General Electric, more tires from Goodyear, and so on. Owners of these firms will earn more profits, produce more, hire more workers, and pay out more in wages and salaries. This added income does not vanish into thin air. It is paid to households that spend some of it and save the rest. The added production leads to added income, which leads to added consumption spending.

If planned investment ($I$) goes up by 25 initially *and is sustained at this higher level,* an increase of output of 25 will *not* restore equilibrium because it generates even more consumption spending ($C$). People buy more consumer goods. There are unplanned reductions of inventories of basic consumption items—washing machines, food, clothing, and so on—and this prompts other firms to increase output. The cycle starts all over again.

Output and income can rise significantly more than the initial increase in planned investment, but how much and how large is the multiplier? This is answered graphically in Figure 8.8. Assume that the economy is in equilibrium at point A, where equilibrium output is 500. The increase in $I$ of 25 shifts the $AE \equiv C + I$ curve up by 25 because $I$ is higher by 25 at every level of income. The new equilibrium occurs at point B, where the equilibrium level of output is 600. Like point A, point B is on the 45-degree line and is an equilibrium value. Output ($Y$) has increased by 100 (600–500), or four times the initial increase in planned investment of 25, between point A and point B. The multiplier in this example is 4. At point B, aggregate spending is also higher by 100. If 25 of this additional 100 is investment ($I$), as we know it is, the remaining 75 is added consumption ($C$). From point A to point B then, $\Delta Y = 100$, $\Delta I = 25$, and $\Delta C = 75$.

Why doesn't the multiplier process go on forever? The answer is that only a fraction of the increase in income is consumed in each round. Successive increases in income become smaller

▶ **FIGURE 8.8** **The Multiplier as Seen in the Planned Aggregate Expenditure Diagram**

At point A, the economy is in equilibrium at $Y = 500$. When $I$ increases by 25, planned aggregate expenditure is initially greater than aggregate output. As output rises in response, additional consumption is generated, pushing equilibrium output up by a multiple of the initial increase in $I$. The new equilibrium is found at point B, where $Y = 600$. Equilibrium output has increased by 100 (600 − 500), or *four times* the amount of the increase in planned investment.

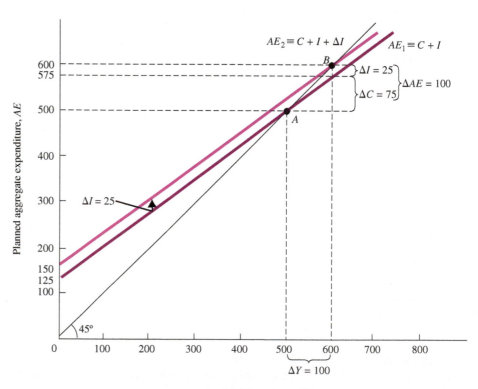

and smaller in each round of the multiplier process because of leakage as saving, until equilibrium is restored.

The size of the multiplier depends on the slope of the planned aggregate expenditure line. The steeper the slope of this line, the greater the change in output for a given change in investment. When planned investment is fixed, as in our example, the slope of the $AE \equiv C + I$ line is just the marginal propensity to consume ($\Delta C / \Delta Y$). The greater the MPC, the greater the multiplier. This should not be surprising. A large MPC means that consumption increases a great deal when income increases.

## The Multiplier Equation

Is there a way to determine the size of the multiplier without using graphic analysis? Yes, there is.

Assume that the market is in equilibrium at an income level of $Y = 500$. Now suppose planned investment (*I*)—thus, planned aggregate expenditure (*AE*)—increases and remains higher by 25. Planned aggregate expenditure is greater than output, there is an unplanned inventory reduction, and firms respond by increasing output (income) (*Y*). This leads to a second round of increases, and so on.

What will restore equilibrium? Look at Figure 8.7 and recall: Planned aggregate expenditure ($AE \equiv C + I$) is not equal to aggregate output (*Y*) unless $S = I$; the leakage of saving must exactly match the injection of planned investment spending for the economy to be in equilibrium. Recall also that we assumed that planned investment jumps to a new, higher level and stays there; it is a *sustained* increase of 25 in planned investment spending. As income rises, consumption rises and so does saving. Our $S = I$ approach to equilibrium leads us to conclude that equilibrium will be restored only when saving has increased by exactly the amount of the initial increase in *I*. Otherwise, *I* will continue to be greater than *S* and $C + I$ will continue to be greater than *Y*. (The $S = I$ approach to equilibrium leads to an interesting paradox in the macro-economy. See the *Economics in Practice*, "The Paradox of Thrift" on the next page.)

It is possible to figure how much *Y* must increase in response to the additional planned investment before equilibrium will be restored. *Y* will rise, pulling *S* up with it until the change in saving is exactly equal to the change in planned investment—that is, until *S* is again equal to *I* at its new higher level. Because added saving is a *fraction* of added income (the MPS), the increase in *income* required to restore equilibrium must be a *multiple* of the increase in planned investment.

Recall that the marginal propensity to save (MPS) is the fraction of a change in income that is saved. It is defined as the change in $S$ ($\Delta S$) over the change in income ($\Delta Y$):

$$MPS = \frac{\Delta S}{\Delta Y}$$

Because $\Delta S$ must be equal to $\Delta I$ for equilibrium to be restored, we can substitute $\Delta I$ for $\Delta S$ and solve:

$$MPS = \frac{\Delta I}{\Delta Y}$$

Therefore,

$$\Delta Y = \Delta I \times \frac{1}{MPS}$$

As you can see, the change in equilibrium income ($\Delta Y$) is equal to the initial change in planned investment ($\Delta I$) times $1/MPS$. The multiplier is $1/MPS$:

$$\text{multiplier} \equiv \frac{1}{MPS}$$

# ECONOMICS IN PRACTICE

## The Paradox of Thrift

An interesting paradox can arise when households attempt to increase their saving. What happens if households become concerned about the future and want to save more today to be prepared for hard times tomorrow? If households increase their planned saving, the saving schedule in the graph below shifts upward from $S_0$ to $S_1$. The plan to save more is a plan to consume less, and the resulting drop in spending leads to a drop in income. Income drops by a multiple of the initial shift in the saving schedule. Before the increase in saving, equilibrium exists at point A, where $S_0 = I$ and $Y = 500$. Increased saving shifts the equilibrium to point B, the point at which $S_1 = I$. New equilibrium output is 300—a decrease of 200 ($\Delta Y$) from the initial equilibrium.

By consuming less, households have actually *caused* the hard times about which they were apprehensive. Worse, the new equilibrium finds saving at the same level as it was before consumption dropped (25). In their attempt to save more, households have caused a contraction in output, and thus in income. They end up consuming less, but they have not saved any more.

It should be clear why saving at the new equilibrium is equal to saving at the old equilibrium. Equilibrium requires that saving equals planned investment, and because planned investment is unchanged, saving must remain unchanged for equilibrium to exist. This paradox shows that the interactions among sectors in the economy can be of crucial importance.

The paradox of thrift is "paradoxical" because it contradicts the widely held belief that "a penny saved is a penny earned." This may be true for an individual, but when society as a whole saves more, the result is a drop in income but no increased saving.

Does the paradox of thrift always hold? Recall our assumption that the interest rate is fixed. If the extra saving that the households want to do to ward off hard times leads to a fall in the interest rate, this will increase planned investment and thus shift up the $I$ schedule in the figure. The paradox might then be avoided. Planned investment could increase enough so that the new equilibrium occurs at a higher level of income (and saving).

### THINKING PRACTICALLY

1. Draw a consumption function corresponding to $S_0$ and $S_1$ and describe what is happening.

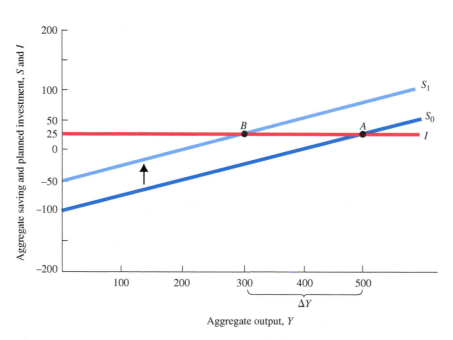

### The Paradox of Thrift

An increase in planned saving from $S_0$ to $S_1$ causes equilibrium output to decrease from 500 to 300. The decreased consumption that accompanies increased saving leads to a contraction of the economy and to a reduction of income. But at the new equilibrium, saving is the same as it was at the initial equilibrium. Increased efforts to save have caused a drop in income but no overall change in saving.

Because $MPS + MPC \equiv 1$, $MPS \equiv 1 - MPC$. It follows that the multiplier is also equal to

$$multiplier \equiv \frac{1}{1 - MPC}$$

In our example, the MPC is .75; so the MPS must equal $1 - 0.75$, or 0.25. Thus, the multiplier is 1 divided by .25, or 4. The change in the equilibrium level of Y is 4 × 25, or 100.[5] Also note that the same analysis holds when planned investment falls. If planned investment falls by a certain amount and is sustained at this lower level, output will fall by a multiple of the reduction in I. As the initial shock is felt and firms cut output, they lay people off. The result: Income, and subsequently consumption, falls.

## The Size of the Multiplier in the Real World

In considering the size of the multiplier, it is important to realize that the multiplier we derived in this chapter is based on a *very* simplified picture of the economy. First, we have assumed that planned investment is exogenous and does not respond to changes in the economy. Second, we have thus far ignored the role of government, financial markets, and the rest of the world in the macroeconomy. For these reasons, it would be a mistake to move on from this chapter thinking that national income can be increased by $100 billion simply by increasing planned investment spending by $25 billion. Nevertheless, even this simple model should give you some intuition as to why and how national income responds to increases in planned investment.

As we relax these assumptions in the following chapters, you will see that most of what we add to make our analysis more realistic has the effect of *reducing* the size of the multiplier. For example:

1. The Appendix to Chapter 9 shows that when tax payments depend on income (as they do in the real world), the size of the multiplier is reduced. As the economy expands, tax payments increase and act as a drag on the economy. The multiplier effect is smaller.
2. We will see in Chapter 11 that adding Fed behavior regarding the interest rate has the effect of reducing the size of the multiplier.
3. We will also see in Chapter 11 that adding the price level to the analysis reduces the size of the multiplier. We will see that part of an expansion of the economy is likely to take the form of an increase in the price level instead of an increase in real output. When this happens, the size of the multiplier is reduced.
4. The multiplier is also reduced when imports are introduced (in Chapter 19) because some domestic spending leaks into foreign markets.

These juicy tidbits give you something to look forward to as you proceed through the rest of this book. For now, however, it is enough to point out that in reality the size of the multiplier is probably about 2. This is much lower than the value of 4 that we used in this chapter but still tells us that an increase in planned investment has more of an effect than you might have expected before beginning this chapter!

## Looking Ahead

In this chapter, we took the first step toward understanding how the economy works. We assumed that consumption depends on income, that planned investment is fixed, and that there is equilibrium. We discussed how the economy might adjust back to equilibrium when it is out of equilibrium. We also discussed the effects on equilibrium output from a change in planned investment and derived the multiplier. In the next chapter, we retain these assumptions and add the government to the economy.

---

[5] The multiplier can also be derived algebraically, as the Appendix to this chapter demonstrates.

# SUMMARY

### 8.1 THE KEYNESIAN THEORY OF CONSUMPTION *p. 142*

1. Aggregate consumption is assumed to be a function of aggregate income.

2. The *marginal propensity to consume* (MPC) is the fraction of a change in income that is consumed, or spent. The *marginal propensity to save* (MPS) is the fraction of a change in income that is saved. Because all income must be saved or spent, $MPS + MPC \equiv 1$.

### 8.2 PLANNED INVESTMENT (*I*) VERSUS ACTUAL INVESTMENT *p. 147*

3. Planned investment may differ from actual investment because of unanticipated changes in inventories.

### 8.3 PLANNED INVESTMENT AND THE INTEREST RATE (*r*) *p. 147*

4. Planned investment depends on the interest rate, which is taken to be fixed for this chapter.

### 8.4 THE DETERMINATION OF EQUILIBRIUM OUTPUT (INCOME) *p. 148*

5. *Planned aggregate expenditure* (AE) equals consumption plus planned investment: $AE \equiv C + I$. *Equilibrium* in the goods market is achieved when planned aggregate expenditure equals aggregate output: $C + I = Y$. This holds if and only if planned investment and actual investment are equal.

6. Because aggregate income must be saved or spent, the equilibrium condition $Y = C + I$ can be rewritten as $C + S = C + I$, or $S = I$. Only when planned investment equals saving will there be equilibrium. This approach to equilibrium is the *saving/investment approach* to equilibrium.

7. When planned aggregate expenditure exceeds aggregate output (*income*), there is an unplanned fall in inventories. Firms will increase output. This increased output leads to increased income and even more consumption. This process will continue as long as output (income) is below planned aggregate expenditure. If firms react to unplanned inventory reductions by increasing output, an economy with planned spending greater than output will adjust to a new equilibrium, with Y higher than before.

### THE MULTIPLIER *p. 152*

8. Equilibrium output changes by a multiple of the change in planned investment or any other *exogenous variable*. The *multiplier* is equal to $1/MPS$.

9. When households increase their planned saving, income decreases and saving does not change. Saving does not increase because in equilibrium, saving must equal planned investment and planned investment is fixed. If planned investment also increased, this *paradox of thrift* could be averted and a new equilibrium could be achieved at a higher level of saving and income. This result depends on the existence of a channel through which additional household saving finances additional investment.

# REVIEW TERMS AND CONCEPTS

actual investment, *p. 147*

aggregate income, *p. 141*

aggregate output, *p. 141*

aggregate output (income) (Y), *p. 141*

aggregate saving (S), *p. 143*

consumption function, *p. 142*

equilibrium, *p. 148*

exogenous variable, *p. 153*

identity, *p. 143*

marginal propensity to consume (MPC), *p. 143*

marginal propensity to save (MPS), *p. 143*

multiplier, *p. 153*

planned aggregate expenditure (AE), *p. 149*

planned investment (I), *p. 147*

Equations: $S \equiv Y - C$, *p. 143*

$MPC \equiv$ slope of consumption

function $\equiv \dfrac{\Delta C}{\Delta Y}$, *p. 143*

$MPC + MPS \equiv 1$, *p. 144*

$AE \equiv C + I$, *p. 149*

Equilibrium condition: $Y = AE$ or $Y = C + I$, *p. 149*

Saving/investment approach to equilibrium: $S = I$, *p. 151*

Multiplier $\equiv \dfrac{1}{MPS} \equiv \dfrac{1}{1 - MPC}$, *p. 155*

# PROBLEMS

All problems are available on MyEconLab.

## 8.1 THE KEYNESIAN THEORY OF CONSUMPTION

LEARNING OBJECTIVE: Explain the principles of the Keynesian theory of consumption.

1.1 Briefly define the following terms and explain the relationship between MPC and MPS and the relationship between aggregate output and aggregate income.
   a. MPC
   b. MPS
   c. Aggregate output
   d. Aggregate income

1.2 Fill in the aggregate saving column in the following table. Use the data in the table to calculate the consumption function and the saving function, and plot these functions as well as the 45-degree line on a graph. What are the values for the MPC and the MPS?

| Aggregate Income, Y | Aggregate Consumption, C | Aggregate Saving, S |
|---|---|---|
| $ 0 | $200 | |
| 100 | 250 | |
| 200 | 300 | |
| 300 | 350 | |
| 400 | 400 | |
| 500 | 450 | |
| 600 | 500 | |

1.3 **[Related to the *Economics in Practice* on p. 146]** The *Economics in Practice* describes some of the difficulties that households have with regard to decisions involving trade-offs between the present and the future. Explain briefly how the problem of global warming and the problem of adequate household saving are similar. Describe ways in which the concept of opportunity cost can be used to frame these two problems. What barriers might prevent households or societies from achieving satisfactory outcomes?

1.4 Assume in a simple economy that the level of saving is −800 when aggregate output equals zero and that the marginal propensity to save is 0.25. Derive the saving function and the consumption function, and draw a graph showing these functions. At what level of aggregate output does the consumption curve cross the 45-degree line? Explain your answer and show this on the graph.

## 8.2 PLANNED INVESTMENT (I) VERSUS ACTUAL INVESTMENT

LEARNING OBJECTIVE: Explain the difference between planned investment and actual investment.

2.1 Explain the difference between actual investment and planned investment. When are actual investment and planned investment equal? When is actual investment greater than planned investment? When is actual investment less than planned investment?

2.2 Suppose that in the year 2015, Oceanaire, Inc. planned to produce 500,000 units of its lightweight scuba tanks. Of the 500,000 it planned to produce, a total of 50,000 units would be added to the inventory at its new plant in Arizona. Also assume that these units have been selling at a price of $250 each and that the price has been constant over time. Suppose further that this year the firm built a new plant for $20 million and acquired $5 million worth of equipment. It had no other investment projects, and to avoid complications, assume no depreciation.

   Now suppose that at the end of the year, Oceanaire had produced 500,000 units but had only sold 400,000 units and that inventories now contained 100,000 units more than they had at the beginning of the year. At $250 each, that means that the firm added $25,000,000 in new inventory.
   a. How much did Oceanaire actually invest this year?
   b. How much did it plan to invest?
   c. Would Oceanaire produce more or fewer units next year? Why?

## 8.3 PLANNED INVESTMENT AND THE INTEREST RATE (r)

LEARNING OBJECTIVE: Understand how planned investment is affected by the interest rate.

3.1 Explain whether you agree or disagree with the following statement: "All else equal, businesses will generally plan more investment projects when interest rates rise, because higher interest rates mean businesses will earn more on those investments."

## 8.4 THE DETERMINATION OF EQUILIBRIUM OUTPUT (INCOME)

LEARNING OBJECTIVE: Explain how equilibrium output is determined.

4.1 The following data are estimates for the small island nation of Kaboom

   Real GNP (Y........................ 800 million Kaboomian dollars
   Planned investment spending) ........................ 200 million Kaboomian dollars

   Kaboom is a simple economy with no government, no taxes, and no imports or exports. Kaboomers (citizens of Kaboom) are creatures of habit. They have a rule that everyone saves exactly 40 percent of income. Assume that planned investment is fixed and remains at 200 million Kaboomian dollars.

You are asked by the business editor of the *Explosive Times*, the local newspaper, to predict the economic events of the next few months. By using the data given, can you make a forecast? What is likely to happen to inventories? What is likely to happen to the level of real GDP? Is the economy at an equilibrium? When will things stop changing?

4.2 Go to www.commerce.gov. Click on "Bureau of Economic Analysis." Click next on "National" and then on the latest GDP release. Look through the report. Which of the components of aggregate expenditure appear to be growing or falling the fastest? What story can you tell about the current economic events from the data?

4.3 The following questions refer to this table:

| Aggregate Output/Income | Consumption | Planned Investment |
|---|---|---|
| 1,000 | 1,500 | 250 |
| 1,500 | 1,875 | 250 |
| 2,000 | 2,250 | 250 |
| 2,500 | 2,625 | 250 |
| 3,000 | 3,000 | 250 |
| 3,500 | 3,375 | 250 |
| 4,000 | 3,750 | 250 |
| 4,500 | 4,125 | 250 |

a. At each level of output, calculate saving. At each level of output, calculate unplanned investment (inventory change). What is likely to happen to aggregate output if the economy produces at each of the levels indicated? What is the equilibrium level of output?

b. Over each range of income (1,000 to 1,500, 1,500 to 2,000, and so on), calculate the marginal propensity to consume. Calculate the marginal propensity to save. What is the multiplier?

c. By assuming there is no change in the level of the *MPC* and the *MPS* and planned investment jumps by 125 and is sustained at that higher level, recompute the table. What is the new equilibrium level of *Y*? Is this consistent with what you compute using the multiplier?

4.4 This chapter argues that saving and spending behavior depend in part on wealth (accumulated savings and inheritance), but our simple model does not incorporate this effect. Consider the following model of a simple economy: $C = 50 + 0.8Y + 0.1W$

$$I = 200$$
$$W = 500$$
$$Y = C + I$$
$$S = Y - C$$

If you assume that wealth (*W*) and investment (*I*) remain constant (we are ignoring the fact that saving adds to the stock of wealth), what are the equilibrium levels of GDP (*Y*), consumption (*C*), and saving (*S*)? Now suppose that wealth increases by 100 percent to 1,000. Recalculate

the equilibrium levels of *Y*, *C*, and *S*. What impact does wealth accumulation have on GDP? Many were concerned with the large increase in stock values in the late 1990s. Does this present a problem for the economy? Explain.

4.5 You are given the following data concerning Freedonia, a legendary country:
(1) Consumption function: $C = 200 + 0.8Y$
(2) Investment function: $I = 100$
(3) $AE \equiv C + I$
(4) $AE = Y$

a. What is the marginal propensity to consume in Freedonia, and what is the marginal propensity to save?

b. Graph equations (3) and (4) and solve for equilibrium income.

c. Suppose equation (2) is changed to $(2') I = 110$. What is the new equilibrium level of income? By how much does the $10 increase in planned investment change equilibrium income? What is the value of the multiplier?

d. Calculate the saving function for Freedonia. Plot this saving function on a graph with equation (2). Explain why the equilibrium income in this graph must be the same as in part b.

## 8.5 THE MULTIPLIER

**LEARNING OBJECTIVE:** Describe the multiplier process and use the multiplier equation to calculate changes in equilibrium.

5.1 Explain the multiplier intuitively. Why is it that an increase in planned investment of $100 raises equilibrium output by more than $100? Why is the effect on equilibrium output finite? How do we know that the multiplier is 1/*MPS*?

5.2 **[Related to the *Economics in Practice* on p. 156]** If households decide to save more, saving in the aggregate may fall. Explain this in words.

5.3 Use the graph to answer the questions that follow.

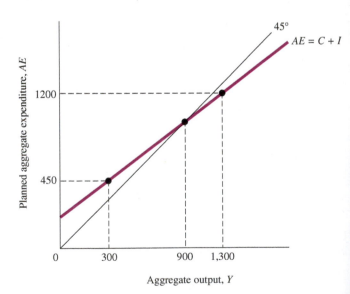

a. What is the value of the *MPC*?
b. What is the value of the *MPS*?
c. What is the value of the multiplier?
d. What is the amount of unplanned investment at aggregate output of 300, 900, and 1,300?

5.4 According to the Bureau of Economic Analysis, during the recession of 2008–2009, household saving as a fraction of disposable personal income increased from a low of just over 1 percent in the first quarter of 2008 to 5 percent in the second quarter of 2009. All else equal, what impact would this change in saving have on the *MPC*, *MPS*, and multiplier? How would this change affect equilibrium output when planned investment changes?

# CHAPTER 8 APPENDIX

## Deriving the Multiplier Algebraically

**LEARNING** OBJECTIVE
Show that the multiplier is 1 divided by 1 minus the MPC.

In addition to deriving the multiplier using the simple substitution we used in the chapter, we can also derive the formula for the multiplier by using simple algebra.

Recall that our consumption function is:

$$C = a + bY$$

where *b* is the marginal propensity to consume. In equilibrium:

$$Y = C + I$$

Now we solve these two equations for *Y* in terms of *I*. By substituting the first equation into the second, we get:

$$Y = \underbrace{a + bY}_{C} + I$$

This equation can be rearranged to yield:

$$Y - bY = a + I$$
$$Y(1 - b) = a + I$$

We can then solve for *Y* in terms of *I* by dividing through by $(I - b)$:

$$Y = (a + I)\left(\frac{1}{1 - b}\right)$$

Now look carefully at this expression and think about increasing *I* by some amount, $\Delta I$, with *a* held constant. If *I* increases by $\Delta I$, income will increase by

$$\Delta Y = \Delta I \times \frac{1}{1 - b}$$

Because $b \equiv MPC$, the expression becomes

$$\Delta Y = \Delta I \times \frac{1}{1 - MPC}$$

The multiplier is

$$\frac{1}{1 - MPC}$$

Finally, because $MPS + MPC \equiv 1$, *MPS* is equal to $1 - MPC$, making the alternative expression for the multiplier 1/*MPS*, just as we saw in this chapter.

MyEconLab Visit **www.myeconlab.com** to complete these exercises online and get instant feedback. Exercises that update with real-time data are marked with art ⬤.

# 9

# The Government and Fiscal Policy

There is considerable debate over what the government can and should do in managing the macroeconomy. At one end of the spectrum are the Keynesians and their intellectual descendants who believe that the macroeconomy is likely to fluctuate too much if left on its own and that the government should smooth out fluctuations in the business cycle. These ideas can be traced to Keynes's analysis in *The General Theory*, which suggests that governments can use their taxing and spending powers to increase aggregate expenditure (and thereby stimulate aggregate output) in recessions or depressions. At the other end of the spectrum are those who claim that government spending is incapable of stabilizing the economy, or worse, is destabilizing and harmful. In this chapter, we turn to this set of questions.

The government has a variety of powers—including regulating firms' entry into and exit from an industry, setting standards for product quality, setting minimum wage levels, and regulating the disclosure of information—but in macroeconomics, we focus on two policy instruments: fiscal policy and monetary policy. **Fiscal policy**, the focus of this chapter, refers to the government's spending and taxing behavior—in other words, its budget policy. (The word *fiscal* comes from the root *fisc*, which refers to the "treasury" of a government.) Fiscal policy is generally divided into three categories: (1) policies concerning government purchases of goods and services, (2) policies concerning taxes, and (3) policies concerning transfer payments (such as unemployment compensation, Social Security benefits, welfare payments, and veterans' benefits) to households. **Monetary policy**, which we consider in the next chapter, refers to the behavior of the nation's central bank, the Federal Reserve, with respect to the interest rate.

# Government in the Economy

**9.1 LEARNING OBJECTIVE**

Discuss the influence of fiscal policies on the economy.

Local, state, and federal governments have in some areas considerable control. In many cases, however, the *effect* of government decisions on the economy depends not only on the decision itself but also on the state of the economy. It is important to understand the limits of government control as well as its power. Taxes provide a good example. Tax rates are controlled by the government. By law, Congress has the authority to decide who and what should be taxed and at what rate. Tax *revenue*, on the other hand, is not subject to complete control by the government. Revenue from the personal income tax system depends on personal tax rates (which Congress sets) *and* on the income of the household sector (which depends on many factors not under direct government control, such as how much households decide to work). Revenue from the corporate profits tax depends on both corporate profits tax rates and the size of corporate profits. The government controls corporate tax rates but not the size of corporate profits.

**fiscal policy** The government's spending and taxing policies.

**monetary policy** The behavior of the Federal Reserve concerning interest rates.

Some government spending also depends on government decisions and on the state of the economy. In the United States, the unemployment insurance program pays benefits to unemployed people. When the economy goes into a recession, the number of unemployed workers increases and so does the level of government unemployment insurance payments. This occurs not because of a change in government decisions but because of the interaction between existing policies and the economy itself.

Because taxes and spending often go up or down in response to changes in the economy instead of as the result of deliberate decisions by policy makers, we will occasionally use **discretionary fiscal policy** to refer to changes in taxes or spending that are the result of deliberate changes in government policy.

**discretionary fiscal policy** Changes in taxes or spending that are the result of deliberate changes in government policy.

## Government Purchases ($G$), Net Taxes ($T$), and Disposable Income ($Y_d$)

We now add the government to the simple economy in Chapter 8. To keep things simple, we will combine two government activities—the collection of taxes and the payment of transfer payments—into a category we call **net taxes ($T$)**. Specifically, net taxes are equal to the tax payments made to the government by firms and households minus transfer payments made to households by the government. The other variable we will consider is government purchases of goods and services ($G$).

**net taxes ($T$)** Taxes paid by firms and households to the government minus transfer payments made to households by the government.

Our previous discussions of household consumption did not take taxes into account. We assumed that all the income generated in the economy was spent or saved by households. When we take into account the role of government, as Figure 9.1 does, we see that as income ($Y$) flows toward households, the government takes income from households in the form of net taxes ($T$). The income that ultimately gets to households is called **disposable, *or* after-tax, income ($Y_d$)**:

**disposable, *or* after-tax, income ($Y_d$)** Total income minus net taxes: $Y - T$.

$$\text{disposable income} \equiv \text{total income} - \text{net taxes}$$
$$Y_d \equiv Y - T$$

$Y_d$ excludes taxes paid by households and includes transfer payments made to households by the government. For now, we are assuming that $T$ does not depend on $Y$—that is, net taxes do not depend on income. This assumption is relaxed in Appendix B to this chapter. Taxes that do not depend on income are sometimes called *lump-sum taxes*.

As Figure 9.1 shows, the disposable income ($Y_d$) of households must end up as either consumption ($C$) or saving ($S$). Thus,

$$Y_d \equiv C + S$$

This equation is an identity—something that is always true.

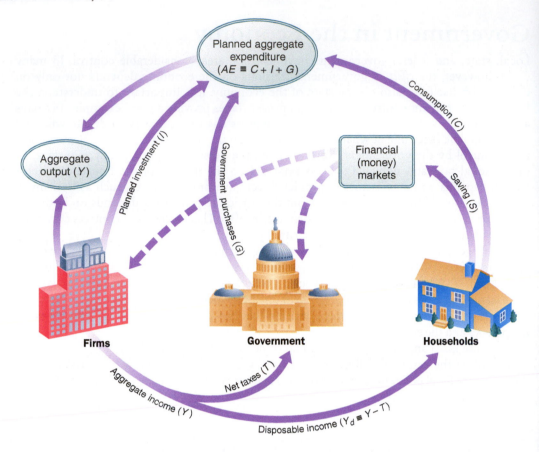

Because disposable income is aggregate income (*Y*) minus net taxes (*T*), we can write another identity:

$$Y - T \equiv C + S$$

By adding *T* to both sides:

$$Y \equiv C + S + T$$

This identity says that aggregate income gets cut into three pieces. Government takes a slice (net taxes, *T*), and then households divide the rest between consumption (*C*) and saving (*S*).

Because governments spend money on goods and services, we need to expand our definition of planned aggregate expenditure. Planned aggregate expenditure (*AE*) is the sum of consumption spending by households (*C*), planned investment by business firms (*I*), *and* government purchases of goods and services (*G*).

$$AE \equiv C + I + G$$

**budget deficit** The difference between what a government spends and what it collects in taxes in a given period: *G* − *T*.

A government's **budget deficit** is the difference between what it spends (*G*) and what it collects in taxes (*T*) in a given period:

$$\text{budget deficit} \equiv G - T$$

If *G* exceeds *T*, the government must borrow from the public to finance the deficit. It does so by selling Treasury bonds and bills (more on this later). In this case, a part of household saving (*S*) goes to the government. The dashed lines in Figure 9.1 mean that some household saving goes to firms to finance investment projects and some goes to the government to finance its deficit. If *G* is less than *T*, which means that the government is spending less than it is collecting in taxes, the government is running a *surplus*.

**Adding Taxes to the Consumption Function**    In Chapter 8, we assumed that aggregate consumption ($C$) depends on aggregate income ($Y$), and for the sake of illustration, we used a specific linear consumption function:

$$C = a + bY$$

where $b$ is the marginal propensity to consume. We need to modify this consumption function because we have added government to the economy. With taxes a part of the picture, it makes sense to assume that disposable income ($Y_d$), instead of before-tax income ($Y$), determines consumption behavior. If you earn a million dollars but have to pay $950,000 in taxes, you have no more disposable income than someone who earns only $50,000 but pays no taxes. What you have available for spending on current consumption is your disposable income, not your before-tax income.

To modify our aggregate consumption function to incorporate disposable income instead of before-tax income, instead of $C = a + bY$, we write

$$C = a + bY_d$$

or

$$C = a + b(Y - T)$$

Our consumption function now has consumption depending on disposable income instead of before-tax income.

**Planned Investment**    What about planned investment? The government can affect investment behavior through its tax treatment of depreciation and other tax policies. Also, planned investment depends on the interest rate, as discussed in the previous chapter. For purposes of this chapter, we continue to assume that the interest rate is fixed. We will ignore any tax effects on planned investment and thus continue to assume that it is fixed (because the interest rate is fixed).

## The Determination of Equilibrium Output (Income)

We know from Chapter 8 that equilibrium occurs where $Y = AE$—that is, where aggregate output equals planned aggregate expenditure. Remember that planned aggregate expenditure in an economy with a government is $AE \equiv C + I + G$, so equilibrium is

$$Y = C + I + G$$

The equilibrium analysis in Chapter 8 applies here also. If output ($Y$) exceeds planned aggregate expenditure ($C + I + G$), there will be an unplanned increase in inventories—actual investment will exceed planned investment. Conversely, if $C + I + G$ exceeds $Y$, there will be an unplanned decrease in inventories.

An example will illustrate the government's effect on the macroeconomy and the equilibrium condition. First, our consumption function, $C = 100 + 0.75Y$ before we introduced the government sector, now becomes

$$C = 100 + 0.75Y_d$$

or

$$C = 100 + 0.75(Y - T)$$

Second, we assume that $G$ is 100 and $T$ is 100.[1] In other words, the government is running a balanced budget, financing all of its spending with taxes. Third, we assume that planned investment ($I$) is 100.

---

[1] As we pointed out previously, the government does not have complete control over tax revenues and transfer payments. We ignore this problem here, however, and set $T$, tax revenues minus transfers, at a fixed amount. Things will become more realistic later in this chapter and in Appendix B.

| | (1) | (2) | (3) | (4) | (5) | (6) | (7) | (8) | (9) | (10) |
|---|---|---|---|---|---|---|---|---|---|---|
| | Output (Income) $Y$ | Net Taxes $T$ | Disposable Income $Y_d \equiv Y - T$ | Consumption Spending $C = 100 + 0.75 Y_d$ | Saving $S$ $Y_d - C$ | Planned Investment Spending $I$ | Government Purchases $G$ | Planned Aggregate Expenditure $C + I + G$ | Unplanned Inventory Change $Y - (C + I + G)$ | Adjustment to Disequilibrium |
| | 300 | 100 | 200 | 250 | −50 | 100 | 100 | 450 | −150 | Output ↑ |
| | 500 | 100 | 400 | 400 | 0 | 100 | 100 | 600 | −100 | Output ↑ |
| | 700 | 100 | 600 | 550 | 50 | 100 | 100 | 750 | −50 | Output ↑ |
| | 900 | 100 | 800 | 700 | 100 | 100 | 100 | 900 | 0 | Equilibrium |
| | 1,100 | 100 | 1,000 | 850 | 150 | 100 | 100 | 1,050 | +50 | Output ↓ |
| | 1,300 | 100 | 1,200 | 1,000 | 200 | 100 | 100 | 1,200 | +100 | Output ↓ |
| | 1,500 | 100 | 1,400 | 1,150 | 250 | 100 | 100 | 1,350 | +150 | Output ↓ |

**TABLE 9.1    Finding Equilibrium for $I = 100$, $G = 100$, and $T = 100$**

Table 9.1 calculates planned aggregate expenditure at several levels of disposable income. For example, at $Y = 500$, disposable income is $Y - T$, or 400. Therefore, $C = 100 + 0.75(400) = 400$. Assuming that $I$ is fixed at 100 and assuming that $G$ is fixed at 100, planned aggregate expenditure is 600 ($C + I + G = 400 + 100 + 100$). Because output ($Y$) is only 500, planned spending is greater than output by 100. As a result, there is an unplanned inventory decrease of 100, giving firms an incentive to raise output. Thus, output of 500 is below equilibrium.

If $Y = 1,300$, then $Y_d = 1,200$, $C = 1,000$, and planned aggregate expenditure is 1,200. Here planned spending is *less* than output, there will be an unplanned inventory increase of 100, and firms have an incentive to cut back output. Thus, output of 1,300 is above equilibrium. Only when output is 900 are output and planned aggregate expenditure equal, and only at $Y = 900$ does equilibrium exist.

In Figure 9.2, we derive the same equilibrium level of output graphically. First, the consumption function is drawn, taking into account net taxes of 100. The old function was $C = 100 + 0.75Y$. The new function is $C = 100 + 0.75(Y - T)$ or $C = 100 + 0.75(Y - 100)$, rewritten as $C = 100 + 0.75Y - 75$, or $C = 25 + 0.75Y$. For example, consumption at an income of zero is 25 ($C = 25 + 0.75Y = 25 + 0.75(0) = 25$). The marginal propensity to consume has not changed—we assume that it remains 0.75. Note that the consumption function in Figure 9.2 plots the points in columns 1 and 4 of Table 9.1.

Planned aggregate expenditure, recall, adds planned investment to consumption. Now in addition to 100 in investment, we have government purchases of 100. Because $I$ and $G$ are constant at 100 each at all levels of income, we add $I + G = 200$ to consumption at every level of income. The result is the new $AE$ curve. This curve is just a plot of the points in columns 1 and 8 of Table 9.1. The 45-degree line helps us find the equilibrium level of real output, which, we already know, is 900. If you examine any level of output above or below 900, you will find disequilibrium. At $Y = 500$, for example, people want to consume 400, which with planned investment of 100 and government purchases of 100, gives planned aggregate expenditure of 600. Output is, however, only 500. Inventories will fall below what was planned, and firms will have an incentive to increase output.

**The Saving/Investment Approach to Equilibrium** As in the last chapter, we can also examine equilibrium using the saving/investment approach. Look at the circular flow of income in Figure 9.1. The government takes out net taxes ($T$) from the flow of income—a leakage—and households save ($S$) some of their income—also a leakage from the flow of income. The planned spending injections are government purchases ($G$) and planned investment ($I$). If leakages ($S + T$) equal planned injections ($I + G$), there is equilibrium:

saving/investment approach to equilibrium: $S + T = I + G$

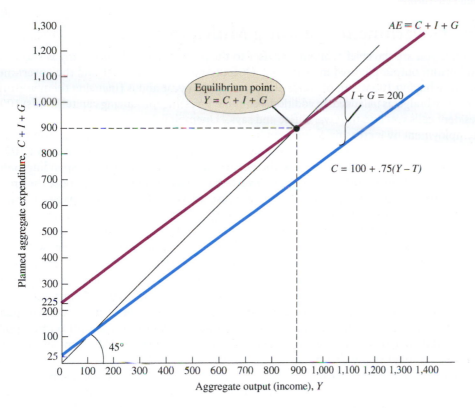

◀ **FIGURE 9.2**   **Finding Equilibrium Output/ Income Graphically**
Because *G* and *I* are both fixed at 100, the aggregate expenditure function is the new consumption function displaced upward by *I* + *G* = 200. Equilibrium occurs at *Y* = *C* + *I* + *G* = 900.

To derive this, we know that in equilibrium, aggregate output (income) (*Y*) equals planned aggregate expenditure (*AE*). By definition, *AE* equals *C* + *I* + *G*, and by definition, *Y* equals *C* + *S* + *T*. Therefore, at equilibrium

$$C + S + T = C + I + G$$

Subtracting *C* from both sides leaves:

$$S + T = I + G$$

Note that equilibrium does *not* require that *G* = *T* (a balanced government budget) or that *S* = *I*. It is only necessary that the sum of *S* and *T* equals the sum of *I* and *G*.

Column 5 of Table 9.1 calculates aggregate saving by subtracting consumption from disposal income at every level of disposable income ($S \equiv Y_d - C$). Because *I* and *G* are fixed, *I* + *G* equals 200 at every level of income. Using the table to add saving and taxes (*S* + *T*), we see that *S* + *T* equals 200 only at *Y* = 900. Thus, the equilibrium level of output (income) is 900, the same answer we arrived at through numerical and graphic analysis.

# Fiscal Policy at Work: Multiplier Effects

**9.2 LEARNING** OBJECTIVE

Describe the effects of three fiscal policy multipliers.

You can see from Figure 9.2 that if the government were able to change the levels of either *G* or *T*, it would be able to change the equilibrium level of output (income). At this point, we are assuming that the government controls *G* and *T*. In this section, we will review three multipliers:

- Government spending multiplier
- Tax multiplier
- Balanced-budget multiplier

# The Government Spending Multiplier

Suppose you are the chief economic adviser to the president and the economy is sitting at the equilibrium output pictured in Figure 9.2. Output and income are 900, and the government is currently buying 100 worth of goods and services each year and is financing them with 100 in taxes. The budget is balanced. In addition, firms are investing (producing capital goods) 100. The president calls you into the Oval Office and says, "Unemployment is too high. We need to lower unemployment by increasing output and income." After some research, you determine that an acceptable unemployment rate can be achieved only if aggregate output increases to 1,100.

You now need to determine how the government can use taxing and spending policy—fiscal policy—to increase the equilibrium level of national output by 200. Suppose the president has let it be known that taxes must remain at present levels—Congress just passed a major tax reform package—so adjusting $T$ is out of the question for several years. That leaves you with $G$. Your only option is to increase government spending while holding taxes constant.

To increase spending without raising taxes (which provides the government with revenue to spend), the government must borrow. When $G$ is bigger than $T$, the government runs a deficit and the difference between $G$ and $T$ must be borrowed. For the moment, we will ignore the possible effect of the deficit and focus only on the effect of a higher $G$ with $T$ constant.

Meanwhile, the president is awaiting your answer. How much of an increase in spending would be required to generate an increase of 200 in the equilibrium level of output, pushing it from 900 to 1,100 and reducing unemployment to the president's acceptable level? You might be tempted to say that because we need to increase income by 200 (1,100 − 900), we should increase government spending by the same amount. But what will happen if we raise $G$ by 200? The increased government spending will throw the economy out of equilibrium. Because $G$ is a component of aggregate spending, planned aggregate expenditure will increase by 200. Planned spending will be greater than output, inventories will be lower than planned, and firms will have an incentive to increase output. Suppose output rises by the desired 200. You might think, "We increased spending by 200 and output by 200, so equilibrium is restored."

There is more to the story than this. The moment output rises, the economy is generating more income. This was the desired effect: the creation of more employment. The newly employed workers are also consumers, and some of their income gets spent. With higher consumption spending, planned spending will be greater than output, inventories will be lower than planned, and firms will raise output (and thus raise income) again. This time firms are responding to the new consumption spending. Already, total income is over 1,100.

This story should sound familiar. It is the multiplier in action. Although this time it is government spending ($G$) that is changed rather than planned investment ($I$), the effect is the same as the multiplier effect we described in Chapter 8. An increase in government spending has the same impact on the equilibrium level of output and income as an increase in planned investment. A dollar of extra spending from either $G$ or $I$ is identical with respect to its impact on equilibrium output. The equation for the government spending multiplier is the same as the equation for the multiplier for a change in planned investment.

$$\text{government spending multiplier} \equiv \frac{1}{\text{MPS}} \equiv \frac{1}{1 - \text{MPC}}$$

We derive the government spending multiplier algebraically in Appendix A to this chapter.

**government spending multiplier** The ratio of the change in the equilibrium level of output to a change in government spending.

Formally, the **government spending multiplier** is defined as the ratio of the change in the equilibrium level of output to a change in government spending. This is the same definition we used in the previous chapter, but now the exogenous variable is government spending instead of planned investment.

Remember that we were thinking of increasing government spending ($G$) by 200. We can use the multiplier analysis to see what the new equilibrium level of $Y$ would be for an increase in $G$ of 200. The multiplier in our example is 4. (Because $b$—the MPC—is .75, the MPS must be 1 − 0.75 = 0.25; and 1/0.25 = 4.) Thus, $Y$ will increase by 800 (4 × 200). Because the initial level of $Y$ was 900, the new equilibrium level of $Y$ is 900 + 800 = 1,700 when $G$ is increased by 200.

## TABLE 9.2    Finding Equilibrium after a Government Spending Increase of 50*

| (1) | (2) | (3) | (4) | (5) | (6) | (7) | (8) | (9) | (10) |
|---|---|---|---|---|---|---|---|---|---|
| | | | | | Planned | | Planned | Unplanned | |
| Output | Net | Disposable | Consumption | | Investment | Government | Aggregate | Inventory | Adjustment |
| (Income) | Taxes | Income | Spending | Saving S | Spending | Purchases | Expenditure | Change | to Disequi- |
| $Y$ | $T$ | $Y_d \equiv Y - T$ | $C = 100 + .75Y_d$ | $Y_d - C$ | $I$ | $G$ | $C + I + G$ | $Y - (C + I + G)$ | librium |
| 300 | 100 | 200 | 250 | −50 | 100 | 150 | 500 | −200 | Output ↑ |
| 500 | 100 | 400 | 400 | 0 | 100 | 150 | 650 | −150 | Output ↑ |
| 700 | 100 | 600 | 550 | 50 | 100 | 150 | 800 | −100 | Output ↑ |
| 900 | 100 | 800 | 700 | 100 | 100 | 150 | 950 | −50 | Output ↑ |
| 1,100 | 100 | 1,000 | 850 | 150 | 100 | 150 | 1,100 | 0 | Equilibrium |
| 1,300 | 100 | 1,200 | 1,000 | 200 | 100 | 150 | 1,250 | +50 | Output ↓ |

*G has increased from 100 in Table 9.1 to 150 here.

The level of 1,700 is much larger than the level of 1,100 that we calculated as being necessary to lower unemployment to the desired level. Let us back up then. If we want Y to increase by 200 and if the multiplier is 4, we need G to increase by only 200 / 4 = 50. If G increases by 50, the equilibrium level of Y will change by 200 and the new value of Y will be 1,100 (900 + 200), as desired.

Looking at Table 9.2, we can check our answer to make sure it is an equilibrium. Look first at the old equilibrium of 900. When government purchases (G) were 100, aggregate output (income) was equal to planned aggregate expenditure (AE ≡ C + I + G) at Y = 900. Now G has increased to 150. At Y = 900, (C + I + G) is greater than Y, there is an unplanned fall in inventories, and output will rise, but by how much? The multiplier told us that equilibrium income would rise by four times the 50 change in G. Y should rise by 4 × 50 = 200, from 900 to 1,100, before equilibrium is restored. Let us check. If Y = 1,100, consumption is C = 100 + 0.75Y_d = 100 + 0.75(1,000) = 850. Because I equals 100 and G now equals 100 (the original level of G) + 50 (the additional G brought about by the fiscal policy change) = 150, C + I + G = 850 + 100 + 150 = 1,100. Y = AE, and the economy is in equilibrium.

The graphic solution to the president's problem is presented in Figure 9.3. An increase of 50 in G shifts the planned aggregate expenditure function up by 50. The new equilibrium income occurs where the new AE line (AE₂) crosses the 45-degree line, at Y = 1,100.

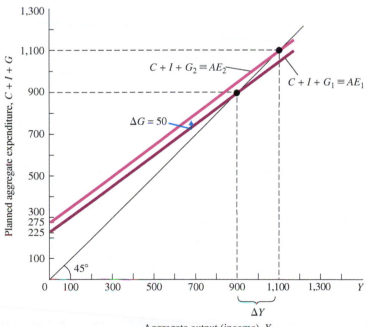

◀ **FIGURE 9.3    The Government Spending Multiplier**

Increasing government spending by 50 shifts the AE function up by 50. As Y rises in response, additional consumption is generated. Overall, the equilibrium level of Y increases by 200, from 900 to 1,100.

# The Tax Multiplier

Remember that fiscal policy includes policies concerning government spending *and* policies concerning taxation. To see what effect a change in tax policy has on the economy, imagine the following. You are still chief economic adviser to the president, but now you are instructed to devise a plan to reduce unemployment to an acceptable level *without* increasing the level of government spending. In your plan, instead of increasing government spending (*G*), you decide to cut taxes and maintain the current level of spending. A tax cut increases disposable income, which is likely to lead to added consumption spending. (Remember our general rule that increased income leads to increased consumption.) Would the decrease in taxes affect aggregate output (income) the same as an increase in *G*?

A decrease in taxes would certainly increase aggregate output. The government spends no less than it did before the tax cut, and households find that they have a larger after-tax (or disposable) income than they had before. This leads to an increase in consumption. Planned aggregate expenditure will increase, which will lead to inventories being lower than planned, which will lead to more workers being hired to increase output. With more workers employed, more income will be generated, causing a second-round increase in consumption, and so on. Thus, income will increase by a multiple of the decrease in taxes, but there is a "wrinkle." The multiplier for a change in taxes is *not the same* as the multiplier for a change in government spending. Why does the **tax multiplier**—the ratio of change in the equilibrium level of output to a change in taxes—differ from the spending multiplier? To answer that question, we need to compare the ways in which a tax cut and a spending increase work their way through the economy.

**tax multiplier** The ratio of change in the equilibrium level of output to a change in taxes.

Look at Figure 9.1. When the government increases spending, there is an immediate and direct impact on the economy's *total* spending. Because *G* is a component of planned aggregate expenditure, an increase in *G* leads to a dollar-for-dollar increase in planned aggregate expenditure. When taxes are cut, there is no direct impact on spending. Taxes enter the picture only because they have an effect on the household's disposable income, which influences household's consumption (which is part of total spending). As Figure 9.1 shows, the tax cut flows through households before affecting aggregate expenditure.

Let us assume that the government decides to cut taxes by $1. By how much would spending increase? We already know the answer. The marginal propensity to consume (*MPC*) tells us how much consumption spending changes when disposable income changes. In the example running through this chapter, the marginal propensity to consume out of disposable income is 0.75. This means that if households' after-tax incomes rise by $1.00, they will increase their consumption not by the full $1.00, but by only $0.75.[2]

In summary, when government spending increases by $1, planned aggregate expenditure increases initially by the full amount of the rise in *G*, or $1. When taxes are cut, however, the initial increase in planned aggregate expenditure is only the *MPC* times the change in taxes. Because the initial increase in planned aggregate expenditure is smaller for a tax cut than for a government spending increase, the final effect on the equilibrium level of income will also be smaller.

The size of the tax multiplier is calculated in the same way we derived the multiplier for an increase in investment and an increase in government purchases. The final change in the equilibrium level of output (income) (*Y*) is

$$\Delta Y = \text{(initial increase in aggregate expenditure)} \times \left( \frac{1}{MPS} \right)$$

Because the initial change in aggregate expenditure caused by a tax change of $\Delta T$ is $(-\Delta T \times MPC)$, we can solve for the tax multiplier by substitution:

$$\Delta Y = (-\Delta T \times MPC) \times \left( \frac{1}{MPS} \right) = -\Delta T \times \left( \frac{MPC}{MPS} \right)$$

---

[2] What happens to the other $0.25? Remember that whatever households do not consume is, by definition, saved. The other $0.25 thus gets allocated to saving.

Because a tax cut will cause an *increase* in consumption expenditures and output and a tax increase will cause a *reduction* in consumption expenditures and output, the tax multiplier is a negative multiplier:

$$\text{tax multiplier} \equiv -\left(\frac{MPC}{MPS}\right)$$

We derive the tax multiplier algebraically in Appendix A to this chapter.

If the *MPC* is .75, as in our example, the multiplier is $-0.75/0.25 = -3$. A tax cut of 100 will increase the equilibrium level of output by $-100 \times -3 = 300$. This is different from the effect of our government spending multiplier of 4. Under those same conditions, a 50 increase in *G* will increase the equilibrium level of output by 200 ($50 \times 4$). If we wanted to increase output by 200, we would need a tax cut of 200/3 or 66.67.

## The Balanced-Budget Multiplier

We have now discussed (1) changing government spending with no change in taxes and (2) changing taxes with no change in government spending. What if government spending and taxes are increased by the same amount? That is, what if the government decides to pay for its extra spending by increasing taxes by the same amount? The government's budget deficit would not change because the increase in expenditures would be matched by an increase in tax income.

You might think in this case that equal increases in government spending and taxes have no effect on equilibrium income. After all, the extra government spending equals the extra amount of tax revenues collected by the government. This is not so. Take, for example, a government spending increase of $40 billion. We know from the preceding analysis that an increase in *G* of 40, with taxes (*T*) held constant, should increase the equilibrium level of income by 40 × the government spending multiplier. The multiplier is 1/MPS or 1/0.25 = 4. The equilibrium level of income should rise by 160 (40 × 4).

Now suppose that instead of keeping tax revenues constant, we finance the 40 increase in government spending with an equal increase in taxes so as to maintain a balanced budget. What happens to aggregate spending as a result of the rise in *G* and the rise in *T*? There are two initial effects. First, government spending rises by 40. This effect is direct, immediate, and positive. Now the government also collects 40 more in taxes. The tax increase has a *negative* impact on overall spending in the economy, but it does not fully offset the increase in government spending.

The final impact of a tax increase on aggregate expenditure depends on how households respond to it. The only thing we know about household behavior so far is that households spend 75 percent of their added income and save 25 percent. We know that when disposable income falls, both consumption and saving are reduced. A tax *increase* of 40 reduces disposable income by 40, and that means consumption falls by 40 × MPC. Because MPC = 0.75, consumption falls by 30 (40 × 0.75). The net result in the beginning is that government spending rises by 40 and consumption spending falls by 30. Aggregate expenditure increases by 10 right after the simultaneous balanced-budget increases in *G* and *T*.

So a balanced-budget increase in *G* and *T* will raise output, but by how much? How large is this **balanced-budget multiplier?** The answer may surprise you:

$$\text{balanced-budget multiplier} \equiv 1$$

Let us combine what we know about the tax multiplier and the government spending multiplier to explain this. To find the final effect of a simultaneous increase in government spending and increase in net taxes, we need to add the multiplier effects of the two. The government spending multiplier is 1/MPS. The tax multiplier is −MPC/MPS. Their sum is $(1/MPS) + (-MPC/MPS) \equiv (1 - MPC)/MPS$. Because $MPC + MPS \equiv 1, 1 - MPC \equiv MPS$. This means that $(1 - MPC)/MPS \equiv MPS/MPS \equiv 1$. (We also derive the balanced-budget multiplier in Appendix A to this chapter.)

**balanced-budget multiplier**
The ratio of change in the equilibrium level of output to a change in government spending where the change in government spending is balanced by a change in taxes so as not to create any deficit. The balanced-budget multiplier is equal to 1: The change in *Y* resulting from the change in *G* and the equal change in *T* is exactly the same size as the initial change in *G* or *T*.

| TABLE 9.3 | Finding Equilibrium after a Balanced-Budget Increase in $G$ and $T$ of 200 Each* |
|---|---|

| (1) | (2) | (3) | (4) | (5) | (6) | (7) | (8) | (9) |
|---|---|---|---|---|---|---|---|---|
| Output (Income) $Y$ | Net Taxes $T$ | Disposable Income $Y_d = Y - T$ | Consumption Spending $C = 100 + 0.75Y_d$ | Planned Investment Spending $I$ | Government Purchases $G$ | Planned Aggregate Expenditure $C + I + G$ | Unplanned Inventory Change $Y - (C + I + G)$ | Adjustment to Disequilibrium |
| 500 | 300 | 200 | 250 | 100 | 300 | 650 | −150 | Output ↑ |
| 700 | 300 | 400 | 400 | 100 | 300 | 800 | −100 | Output ↑ |
| 900 | 300 | 600 | 550 | 100 | 300 | 950 | −50 | Output ↑ |
| 1,100 | 300 | 800 | 700 | 100 | 300 | 1,100 | 0 | Equilibrium |
| 1,300 | 300 | 1,000 | 850 | 100 | 300 | 1,250 | +50 | Output ↓ |
| 1,500 | 300 | 1,200 | 1,000 | 100 | 300 | 1,400 | +100 | Output ↓ |

*Both $G$ and $T$ have increased from 100 in Table 9.1 to 300 here.

Returning to our example, recall that by using the government spending multiplier, a 40 increase in $G$ would *raise* output at equilibrium by 160 (40 × the government spending multiplier of 4). By using the tax multiplier, we know that a tax hike of 40 will *reduce* the equilibrium level of output by 120 (40 × the tax multiplier, −3). The net effect is 160 minus 120, or 40. It should be clear then that the effect on equilibrium $Y$ is equal to the balanced increase in $G$ and $T$. In other words, the net increase in the equilibrium level of $Y$ resulting from the change in $G$ and the change in $T$ are exactly the size of the initial change in $G$ or $T$.

If the president wanted to raise $Y$ by 200 without increasing the deficit, a simultaneous increase in $G$ and $T$ of 200 would do it. To see why, look at the numbers in Table 9.3. In Table 9.1, we saw an equilibrium level of output at 900. With both $G$ and $T$ up by 200, the new equilibrium is 1,100—higher by 200. At no other level of $Y$ do we find $(C + I + G) = Y$. An increase in government spending has a direct initial effect on planned aggregate expenditure; a tax increase does not. The initial effect of the tax increase is that households cut consumption by the $MPC$ times the change in taxes. This change in consumption is less than the change in taxes because the $MPC$ is less than 1. The positive stimulus from the government spending increase is thus greater than the negative stimulus from the tax increase. The net effect is that the balanced-budget multiplier is 1.

Table 9.4 summarizes everything we have said about fiscal policy multipliers.

**A Warning**  Although we have added government, the story told about the multiplier is still incomplete and oversimplified. For example, we have been treating net taxes ($T$) as a lump-sum, fixed amount, whereas in practice, taxes depend on income. Appendix B to this chapter shows that the size of the multiplier is reduced when we make the more realistic assumption that taxes depend on income. We continue to add more realism and difficulty to our analysis in the chapters that follow.

| TABLE 9.4 | Summary of Fiscal Policy Multipliers |
|---|---|

| | Policy Stimulus | Multiplier | Final Impact on Equilibrium $Y$ |
|---|---|---|---|
| Government spending multiplier | Increase or decrease in the level of government purchases: $\Delta G$ | $\dfrac{1}{MPS}$ | $\Delta G \times \dfrac{1}{MPS}$ |
| Tax multiplier | Increase or decrease in the level of net taxes: $\Delta T$ | $\dfrac{-MPC}{MPS}$ | $\Delta T \times \dfrac{-MPC}{MPS}$ |
| Balanced-budget multiplier | Simultaneous balanced-budget increase or decrease in the level of government purchases and net taxes: $\Delta G = \Delta T$ | 1 | $\Delta G$ |

# The Federal Budget

The **federal budget** lists in detail all the things the government plans to spend money on and all the sources of government revenues for the coming year. It therefore describes the government's fiscal policy in granular detail. Of course, the budget is not simply an economic document but is the product of a complex interplay of social, political, and economic forces.

**9.3 LEARNING** OBJECTIVE

Compare and contrast the federal budgets of three U.S. government administrations.

**federal budget**    The budget of the federal government.

## The Budget in 2014

A highly aggregated version of the federal budget is shown in Table 9.5. In 2014, the government had total receipts of $3,300.8 billion, largely from personal income taxes ($1,374.2 billion) and contributions for social insurance ($1,149.4 billion). (Contributions for social insurance are employer and employee Social Security taxes.) Receipts from corporate income taxes accounted for $497.3 billion, or only 15.1 percent of total receipts. Not everyone is aware of the fact that corporate income taxes as a percentage of government receipts are quite small relative to personal income taxes and Social Security taxes.

The federal government also spent $3,883.1 billion in expenditures in 2014. Of this, $1,863.4 billion represented transfer payments to persons (Social Security benefits, military retirement benefits, and unemployment compensation).[3] Consumption ($965.2 billion) was the next-largest component, followed by grants-in-aid given to state and local governments by the federal government ($500.9 billion), and interest payments on the federal debt ($441.3 billion).

The difference between the federal government's receipts and its expenditures is the federal **surplus (+)** *or* **deficit (−)** , which is federal government saving. Table 9.5 shows that the federal government spent much more than it took in during 2014, resulting in a deficit of $582.3 billion.

**federal surplus (+)** *or* **(−)**
**deficit**    Federal government receipts minus expenditures.

**TABLE 9.5    Federal Government Receipts and Expenditures, 2014**

|  | Amount (Billions, $) | Percentage of Total (%) |
|---|---|---|
| Current receipts |  |  |
| Personal income taxes | 1,374.2 | 41.6 |
| Excise taxes and customs duties | 134.1 | 4.1 |
| Corporate income taxes | 497.3 | 15.1 |
| Taxes from the rest of the world | 18.9 | 0.6 |
| Contributions for social insurance | 1,149.4 | 34.8 |
| Interest receipts and rents and royalties | 78.1 | 2.4 |
| Current transfer receipts from business and persons | 68.5 | 2.1 |
| Current surplus of government enterprises | −19.7 | −0.6 |
| **Total** | 3,300.8 | 100.0 |
| Current expenditures |  |  |
| Consumption expenditures | 965.2 | 9.9 |
| Transfer payments to persons | 1,863.4 | 48.0 |
| Transfer payments to the rest of the world | 55.3 | 1.4 |
| Grants-in-aid to state and local governments | 500.9 | 12.9 |
| Interest payments | 441.3 | 11.4 |
| Subsidies | 56.9 | 1.5 |
| **Total** | 3,883.1 | 100.0 |
| **Net federal government saving–surplus ( + ) or deficit ( − )** |  |  |
| (Total current receipts – Total current expenditures) | −582.3 |  |

*Source*: Government Receipts and Expenditures First Quarter of 2015 , U.S. Bureau of Economic Analysis, March 27, 2015

MyEconLab Real-time data

---

[3] Remember that there is an important difference between transfer payments and government purchases of goods and services (consumption expenditures). Much of the government budget goes for things that an economist would classify as transfers (payments that are grants or gifts) instead of purchases of goods and services. Only the latter are included in our variable *G*. Transfers are counted as part of net taxes.

## Fiscal Policy since 1993: The Clinton, Bush, and Obama Administrations

Between 1993 and the current edition of this text, the United States has had three different presidents, two Democrats and a Republican. The fiscal policy implemented by each president reflects both the political philosophy of the administration and the differing economic conditions each faced. Figures 9.4, 9.5, and 9.6 trace the fiscal policies of the Clinton (1993–2000), Bush (2001–2008), and first and half of the second Obama administrations (2009–2014).

Figure 9.4 plots total federal personal income taxes as a percentage of total taxable income. This is a graph of the average personal income tax rate. As the figure shows, the average tax rate increased substantially during the Clinton administrations. Much of this increase was the result of a tax bill that was passed in 1993 during the first Clinton administration. The figure then shows the dramatic effects of the tax cuts during the first Bush administration. The large fall in the average tax rate in 2001 III was because of a tax rebate passed after the 9/11 terrorist attacks. Although the average tax rate went back up in 2001 IV, it then fell substantially as the Bush tax cuts began to be felt. The average tax rate remained low during the beginning of the first Obama administration. This was in part due to the large ($787 billion) stimulus bill that was passed in February 2009. The bill consisted of tax cuts and government spending increases, mostly for the 2009–2010 period enacted in response to the recession. In 2011–2012 the average tax rate was somewhat higher than it was in 2009–2010 because of the winding down of the stimulus bill. The average tax rate has continued to rise after 2010, reflecting various tax increases that were passed in this period. The overall tax policy of the federal government is thus clear from Figure 9.4. The average tax rate rose sharply under President Clinton, fell sharply under President Bush, and remained low initially under President Obama before beginning to rise.

Table 9.5 shows that the three most important spending variables of the federal government are consumption expenditures, transfer payments to persons, and grants-in-aid to state and local governments. Consumption expenditures, which are government expenditures on goods and services, are part of GDP. Transfer payments and grants-in-aid are not spending on current output (GDP), but just transfers from the federal government to people and state and local governments. Figure 9.5 plots two spending ratios. One is federal government consumption expenditures as a percentage of GDP, and the other is transfer payments to persons plus grants-in-aid to state and local governments as a percentage of GDP. The figure shows that consumption expenditures as a percentage of GDP generally fell during the Clinton administrations, generally rose during the Bush administrations, and remained high during the first Obama administration. The increase during the Bush administrations reflects primarily the spending on the Iraq war. The initial increase during the Obama administration reflects the effects of the stimulus bill

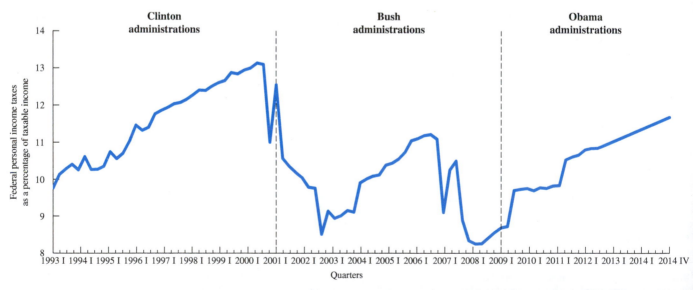

▲ **FIGURE 9.4** **Federal Personal Income Taxes as a Percentage of Taxable Income, 1993 I–2014 IV**

MyEconLab Real-time data

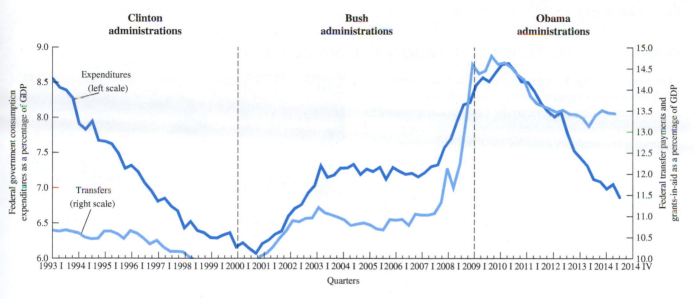

▲ **FIGURE 9.5** **Federal Government Consumption Expenditures as a Percentage of GDP and Federal Transfer Payments and Grants-in-Aid as a Percentage of GDP, 1993 I–2014 IV** MyEconLab Real-time data

and increased spending for the Afghanistan war. Expenditures as a fraction of GDP have been falling during the second Obama administration.

Figure 9.5 also shows that transfer payments as a percentage of GDP generally rose during the Bush administrations especially near the end, and remained high in the Obama administration. The percent was flat or slightly falling during the Clinton administrations. Some of the fall between 1996 and 2000 was because of President Clinton's welfare reform legislation. Some of the rise from 2001 on is as a result of increased Medicare payments. The high initial values in the Obama administration again reflect the effects of the stimulus bill and various extensions.

Figure 9.6 plots the federal government surplus (+) or deficit (−1) as a percentage of GDP. The figure shows that during the Clinton administrations the federal budget moved from

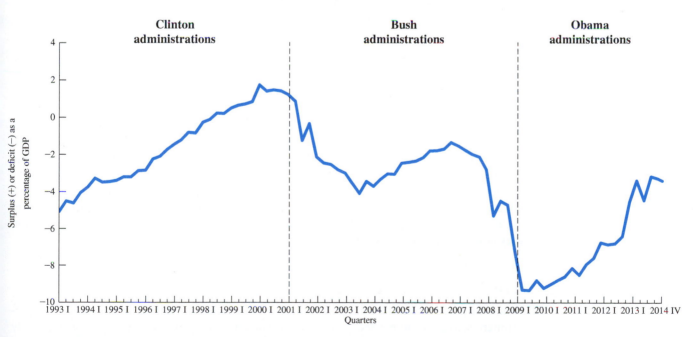

▲ **FIGURE 9.6** **The Federal Government Surplus (+) or Deficit (−) as a Percentage of GDP, 1993 I–2014 IV** MyEconLab Real-time data

## ECONOMICS IN PRACTICE

## Long-Term Projections of the Federal Government Debt

The Congressional Budget Office (CBO) is an administrative office of the Congress, given the task of providing independent, nonpartisan analysis to the Congress as it makes its budgetary decisions. It is staffed largely by economists.

Among the analyses done by the CBO is the state of the deficits and the national debt.[1] In 2014 the CBO estimated that the federal debt was 74 percent of GDP, the highest of any year since World War II. (The CBO definition of the debt is slightly different from that used in Figure 9.7, where the debt to GDP ratio is 64 percent in 2014.) In this report the CBO projected that with no change in the current laws in place, the debt as a percent of GDP will decrease over the next few years as the economy continues to recover. In the longer term, however, the CBO estimates that the debt will increase substantially, reaching more that 100 percent of GDP by 2039, largely because of the costs associated with the aging of the U.S. population. Of course, it is not expected by anyone—including the CBO—that laws and policies will

not respond to this problem for the next 20 years. But the analysis does suggest that some fairly major tax or spending changes will be needed in the future.

### THINKING PRACTICALLY

1. Why does the aging of the population increase the debt?

[1] CBO, "Long Term Budget Outlook," July 15, 2014.

substantial deficit to noticeable surplus. This, of course, should not be surprising because the average tax rate generally rose during this period and spending as a percentage of GDP generally fell. Figure 9.6 then shows that the surplus turned into a substantial deficit during the first Bush administration. This also should not be surprising since the average tax rate generally fell during this period and spending as a percentage of GDP generally rose. The deficit rose sharply in the beginning of the Obama administration—to 9.3 percent of GDP by the second quarter of 2009. Again, this is not a surprise. The average tax rate remained low and spending increased substantially. The deficit-to-GDP ratio has been improving during the second Obama administration, reflecting the increase in taxes in Figure 9.4 and the fall in spending in Figure 9.5. To summarize, Figures 9.4, 9.5, and 9.6 show clearly the large differences in the fiscal policies of the three administrations. Tax rates generally rose and spending as a percentage of GDP generally fell during the Clinton administrations, and the opposite generally happened during the Bush and first Obama administrations.

As you look at these differences, you should remember that the decisions that governments make about levels of spending and taxes reflect not only macroeconomic concerns but also microeconomic issues and political philosophy. President Clinton's welfare reform program resulted in a decrease in government transfer payments but was motivated in part by interest in improving market incentives. President Bush's early tax cuts were based less on macroeconomic concerns than on political philosophy, while the increased spending came from international relations. President Obama's fiscal policy, on the other hand, was motivated by macroeconomic concerns. The stimulus bill was designed to mitigate the effects of the recession that began in 2008. Whether tax and spending policies are motivated by macroeconomic concerns or not, they have macroeconomic consequences.

## The Federal Government Debt

**federal debt** The total amount owed by the federal government.

When the government runs a deficit, it must borrow to finance it. To borrow, the federal government sells government securities to the public. It issues pieces of paper promising to pay a certain amount, with interest, in the future. In return, it receives funds from the buyers of the paper and uses these funds to pay its bills. This borrowing increases the **federal debt**, the

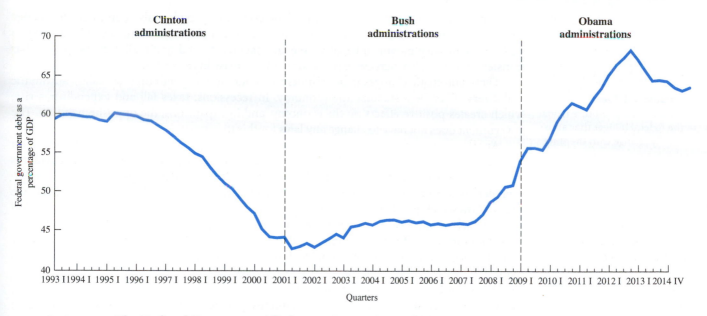

▲ **FIGURE 9.7** **The Federal Government Debt as a Percentage of GDP, 1993 I–2014 IV**

MyEconLab Real-time data

total amount owed by the federal government. The federal debt is the total of all accumulated deficits minus surpluses over time. Conversely, if the government runs a surplus, the federal debt falls.

Some of the securities that the government issues end up being held by the federal government at the Federal Reserve or in government trust funds, the largest of which is Social Security. The term **privately held federal debt** refers only to the *privately held* debt of the U.S. government.

The privately held federal government debt as a percentage of GDP is plotted in Figure 9.7 for the 1993 I–2014 IV period. The percentage fell during the second Clinton administration, when the budget was in surplus, and it mostly rose during the Bush administrations, when the budget was in deficit. The rise during the first Obama administration was dramatic. During the second Obama administration the debt to GDP ratio has leveled off.

**privately held federal debt** The privately held (non-government-owned) debt of the U.S. government.

# The Economy's Influence on the Government Budget

We have just seen that an administration's fiscal policy is sometimes affected by the state of the economy. The Obama administration, for example, increased government spending and lowered taxes in response to the recession of 2008–2009. It is also the case, however, that the economy affects the federal government budget even if there are no explicit fiscal policy changes. There are effects that the government has no direct control over. They can be lumped under the general heading of "automatic stabilizers and destabilizers."

**9.4 LEARNING OBJECTIVE**

Explain the influence of the economy on the federal government budget.

## Automatic Stabilizers and Destabilizers

Most of the tax revenues of the government result from applying a tax rate decided by the government to a base that reflects the underlying activity of the economy. The corporate profits tax, for example, comes from applying a rate (say 35 percent) to the profits earned by firms. Income taxes come from applying rates shown in tax tables to income earned by individuals. Tax revenues thus depend on the state of the economy even when the government does not change tax rates. When the economy goes into a recession, tax revenues will fall, even if rates remain constant, and when the economy picks up, so will tax revenues. As a result, deficits fall in expansions and rise in recessions, other things being equal.

Some items on the expenditure side of the government budget also automatically change as the economy changes. If the economy declines, unemployment increases, which leads to an increase in unemployment benefits. Welfare payments, food stamp allotments, and similar transfer payments also increase in recessions and decrease in expansions.

These automatic changes in government revenues and expenditures are called **automatic stabilizers**. They help stabilize the economy. In recessions, taxes fall and expenditures rise, which creates positive effects on the economy, and in expansions, the opposite happens. The government does not have to change any laws for this to happen.

Another reason that government spending is not completely controllable is that inflation often picks up in an expansion. We saw in Chapter 7 that some government transfer payments are tied to the rate of inflation (changes in the CPI); so these transfer payments increase as inflation increases. Some medical care transfer payments also increase as the prices of medical care rise, and these prices may be affected by the overall rate of inflation. To the extent that inflation is more likely to increase in an expansion than in a recession, inflation can be considered to be an **automatic destabilizer**. Government spending increases as inflation increases, which further fuels the expansion, which is destabilizing. If inflation decreases in a recession, there is an automatic decrease in government spending, which makes the recession worse.

We will see in later chapters that interest rates tend to rise in expansions and fall in recessions. When interest rates rise, government interest payments to households and firms increase (because households and firms hold much of the government debt), which is interest income to the households and firms. Government spending on interest payments thus tends to rise in expansions and fall in contractions, which, other things being equal, is destabilizing. We will see in later chapters, however, that interest rates also have negative effects on the economy, and these negative effects are generally larger than the positive effects from the increase in government interest payments. The net effect of an increase in interest rates on the economy is thus generally negative. But this is getting ahead of our story.

Since 1982 personal income tax brackets have been tied to the overall price level. Prior to this they were not, which led to what was called **fiscal drag**. If tax brackets are not tied to the price level, then as the price level rises and thus people's nominal incomes rise, people move into higher brackets; so the average tax rates that they pay increase. This is a "drag" on the economy, hence the name fiscal drag. In 1982, the United States instituted an alternative Minimum Tax (AMT), directed at higher income individuals who had a number of special tax deductions. These individuals were subject to an alternative calculation of their income taxes, which essentially eliminated some deductions and imposed a (lower) flat tax. In contrast to the standard tax tables, the income level at which the AMT would kick in remained constant over the subsequent 30 years until finally indexed to inflation in 2013. For this period, the AMT tax created fiscal drag. It is interesting to note that fiscal drag is actually an automatic stabilizer in that the number of people moving into higher tax brackets increases in expansions and falls in contractions. By indexing the tax brackets to the overall price level, the legislation in 1982 eliminated the fiscal drag caused by inflation from taxes other than the AMT. If incomes rise only because of inflation, there is no change in average tax rates because the brackets are changed each year. The inflation part of the automatic stabilizer has been eliminated.

## Full-Employment Budget

We have seen that the state of the economy has a big effect on the budget deficit. When the economy turns down, automatic stabilizers act to increase the deficit; the government may also take further actions intended to pull the economy out of a slump. Under these conditions, running a deficit may seem like a good idea. When the economy is thriving, however, deficits may be more problematic. In particular, if the government runs deficits in good times as well as bad, the overall debt is surely going to rise, which may be unsustainable in the long run. Instead of looking simply at the size of the surplus or deficit, economists have developed an alternative way to calibrate deficits. By examining what the budget would be like if the economy were producing at the full-employment level of output—the so-called **full-employment budget**—we can establish a benchmark for evaluating fiscal policy.

---

**automatic stabilizers**
Revenue and expenditure items in the federal budget that automatically change with the state of the economy in such a way as to stabilize GDP.

**automatic destabilizers**
Revenue and expenditure items in the federal budget that automatically change with the state of the economy in such a way as to destabilize GDP.

**fiscal drag** The negative effect on the economy that occurs when average tax rates increase because taxpayers have moved into higher income brackets during an expansion.

**full-employment budget**
What the federal budget would be if the economy were producing at the full-employment level of output.

The distinction between the actual and full-employment budget is important. Suppose the economy is in a slump and the deficit is $250 billion. Also suppose that if there were full employment, the deficit would fall to $75 billion. The $75 billion deficit that would remain even with full employment would be because of the structure of tax and spending programs instead of the state of the economy. This deficit—the deficit that remains at full employment—is sometimes called the **structural deficit**. The $175 billion ($250 billion − $75 billion) part of the deficit caused by the fact the economy is in a slump is known as the **cyclical deficit**. The existence of the cyclical deficit depends on where the economy is in the business cycle, and it ceases to exist when full employment is reached. By definition, the cyclical deficit of the full-employment budget is zero.

Table 9.5 shows that the federal government deficit in 2014 was $582.3 billion. How much of this was cyclical and how much was structural? The U.S. economy was still not quite at full employment in 2014, and so some of the deficit was cyclical.

**structural deficit** The deficit that remains at full employment.

**cyclical deficit** The deficit that occurs because of a downturn in the business cycle.

## Looking Ahead

We have now seen how households, firms, and the government interact in the goods market, how equilibrium output (income) is determined, and how the government uses fiscal policy to influence the economy. In the next chapter we analyze the money market and monetary policy—the government's other major tool for influencing the economy.

## — SUMMARY —

1. The government can affect the macroeconomy through two specific policy channels. *Fiscal policy* refers to the government's taxing and spending behavior. *Discretionary fiscal policy* refers to changes in taxes or spending that are the result of deliberate changes in government policy. *Monetary policy* refers to the behavior of the Federal Reserve concerning the interest rate.

### 9.1 GOVERNMENT IN THE ECONOMY *p. 163*

2. The government does not have complete control over tax revenues and certain expenditures, which are partially dictated by the state of the economy.

3. As a participant in the economy, the government makes purchases of goods and services (G), collects taxes, and makes transfer payments to households. *Net taxes* (T) is equal to the tax payments made to the government by firms and households minus transfer payments made to households by the government.

4. *Disposable*, or *after-tax*, income ($Y_d$) is equal to the amount of income received by households after taxes: $Y_d \equiv Y - T$. After-tax income determines households' consumption behavior.

5. The *budget deficit* is equal to the difference between what the government spends and what it collects in taxes: $G - T$. When G exceeds T, the government must borrow from the public to finance its deficit.

6. In an economy in which government is a participant, planned aggregate expenditure equals consumption spending by households (C) plus planned investment spending by firms (I) plus government spending on goods and services (G): $AE \equiv C + I + G$. Because the condition $Y = AE$ is necessary for the economy to be in equilibrium, it follows that $Y = C + I + G$ is the macroeconomic equilibrium condition. The economy is also in equilibrium when leakages out of the system equal injections into the system. This occurs when saving and net taxes (the leakages) equal planned investment and government purchases (the injections): $S + T = I + G$.

### 9.2 FISCAL POLICY AT WORK: MULTIPLIER EFFECTS *p. 167*

7. Fiscal policy has a multiplier effect on the economy. A change in government spending gives rise to a multiplier equal to $1/MPS$. A change in taxation brings about a multiplier equal to $-MPC/MPS$. A simultaneous equal increase or decrease in government spending and taxes has a multiplier effect of 1.

### 9.3 THE FEDERAL BUDGET *p. 173*

8. During the two Clinton administrations, the federal budget went from being in deficit to being in surplus. This was reversed during the two Bush administrations, driven by tax rate decreases and government spending increases. The deficit increased further during the beginning of the first Obama administration and then began to improve.

**MyEconLab** Visit **www.myeconlab.com** to complete these exercises online and get instant feedback. Exercises that update with real-time data are marked with art ⬮.

### 9.4 THE ECONOMY'S INFLUENCE ON THE GOVERNMENT BUDGET *p. 177*

9. *Automatic stabilizers* are revenue and expenditure items in the federal budget that automatically change with the state of the economy and that tend to stabilize GDP. For example, during expansions, the government automatically takes in more revenue because people are making more money that is taxed.

10. The *full-employment budget* is an economist's construction of what the federal budget would be if the economy were producing at a full-employment level of output. The *structural deficit* is the federal deficit that remains even at full employment. The *cyclical deficit* is that part of the total deficit caused by the economy operating at less than full employment.

---

## REVIEW TERMS AND CONCEPTS

automatic destabilizer, *p. 178*
automatic stabilizers, *p. 178*
balanced-budget multiplier, *p. 171*
budget deficit, *p. 164*
cyclical deficit, *p. 179*
discretionary fiscal policy, *p. 163*
disposable, *or after-tax, income* ($Y_d$), *p. 163*
federal budget, *p. 173*
federal debt, *p. 176*
federal surplus (+) *or deficit* (−), *p. 173*
fiscal drag, *p. 178*
fiscal policy, *p. 162*

full-employment budget, *p. 178*
government spending multiplier, *p. 168*
monetary policy, *p. 162*
net taxes ($T$), *p. 163*
privately held federal debt, *p. 177*
structural deficit, *p. 179*
tax multiplier, *p. 170*
Equations:
Disposable income: $Y_d \equiv Y - T$, *p. 163*
$AE \equiv C + I + G$, *p. 164*
Government budget deficit $\equiv G - T$, *p. 164*

Equilibrium in an economy with a government: $Y \equiv C + I + G$, *p. 165*

Saving/investment approach to equilibrium in an economy with a government: $S + T = I + G$, *p. 166*

Government spending multiplier
$$\equiv \frac{1}{MPS} \equiv \frac{1}{1 - MPC}, p. 168$$

Tax multiplier $\equiv -\left(\dfrac{MPC}{MPS}\right)$, *p. 171*

Balanced-budget multiplier $\equiv 1$, *p. 171*

---

## PROBLEMS

All problems are available on MyEconLab.

### 9.1 GOVERNMENT IN THE ECONOMY

**LEARNING OBJECTIVE:** Discuss the influence of fiscal policies on the economy.

**1.1** Define *saving* and *investment*. Data for the simple economy of Newt show that in 2015, saving exceeded investment and the government is running a balanced budget. What is likely to happen? What would happen if the government were running a deficit and saving were equal to investment?

**1.2** Expert economists in the economy of Bongo estimate the following:

|                                 | Billion Bongos |
|---------------------------------|:--------------:|
| Real output/income              | 1,200          |
| Government purchases            | 300            |
| Total net taxes                 | 300            |
| Investment spending (planned)   | 200            |

Assume that Bongoliers consume 80 percent of their disposable incomes and save 20 percent.
a. You are asked by the business editor of the *Bongo Tribune* to predict the events of the next few months. By using the data given, make a forecast. (Assume that investment is constant.)
b. If no changes were made, at what level of GDP (Y) would the economy of Bongo settle?

c. Some local conservatives blame Bongo's problems on the size of the government sector. They suggest cutting government purchases by 25 billion Bongos. What effect would such cuts have on the economy? (Be specific.)

**1.3** Assume that in 2015, the following prevails in the Republic of Nurd:

| | |
|---|---|
| $Y = \$200$ | $G = \$0$ |
| $C = \$160$ | $T = \$0$ |
| $S = \$40$ | |
| $I$ (planned) $= \$30$ | |

Assume that households consume 80 percent of their income, they save 20 percent of their income, $MPC = 0.8$, and $MPS = 0.2$. That is, $C = 0.8Y_d$ and $S = 0.2Y_d$.
a. Is the economy of Nurd in equilibrium? What is Nurd's equilibrium level of income? What is likely to happen in the coming months if the government takes no action?
b. If $200 is the "full-employment" level of Y, what fiscal policy might the government follow if its goal is full employment?
c. If the full-employment level of Y is $250, what fiscal policy might the government follow?
d. Suppose $Y = \$200$, $C = \$160$, $S = \$40$, and $I = \$40$. Is Nurd's economy in equilibrium?
e. Starting with the situation in part d, suppose the government starts spending $30 each year with no taxation and continues to spend $30 every period. If $I$ remains

---

constant, what will happen to the equilibrium level of Nurd's domestic product (Y)? What will the new levels of C and S be?

**f.** Starting with the situation in part d, suppose the government starts taxing the population $30 each year without spending anything and continues to tax at that rate every period. If I remains constant, what will happen to the equilibrium level of Nurd's domestic product (Y)? What will be the new levels of C and S? How does your answer to part f differ from your answer to part e? Why?

**1.4** Some economists claim World War II ended the Great Depression of the 1930s. The war effort was financed by borrowing massive sums of money from the public. Explain how a war could end a recession. Look at recent and back issues of the *Economic Report of the President* or the *Statistical Abstract of the United States*. How large was the federal government's debt as a percentage of GDP in 1946? How large is it today?

**1.5** Evaluate the following statement: For an economy to be in equilibrium, planned investment spending plus government purchases must equal saving plus net taxes.

**1.6** For the data in the following table, the consumption function is $C = 800 + 0.6(Y - T)$. Fill in the columns in the table and identify the equilibrium output.

| Output | Net Taxes | Disposable Income | Consumption Spending | Saving | Planned Investment Spending | Government Purchases | Planned Aggregate Expenditure | Unplanned Inventory Change |
|--------|-----------|-------------------|----------------------|--------|----------------------------|----------------------|-------------------------------|----------------------------|
| 2,100 | 100 | | | | 300 | 400 | | |
| 2,600 | 100 | | | | 300 | 400 | | |
| 3,100 | 100 | | | | 300 | 400 | | |
| 3,600 | 100 | | | | 300 | 400 | | |
| 4,100 | 100 | | | | 300 | 400 | | |
| 4,600 | 100 | | | | 300 | 400 | | |
| 5,100 | 100 | | | | 300 | 400 | | |

**1.7** For each of the following sets of data, determine if output will need to increase, decrease, or remain the same to move the economy to equilibrium:
  **a.** $Y = 1,000$; $C = 100 + 0.75(Y - T)$; $I = 200$; $G = 150$; $T = 100$
  **b.** $Y = 5,000$; $C = 200 + 0.9(Y - T)$; $I = 500$; $G = 400$; $T = 300$
  **c.** $Y = 2,000$; $C = 150 + 0.5(Y - T)$; $I = 150$; $G = 150$; $T = 50$
  **d.** $Y = 1,600$; $C = 300 + 0.6(Y - T)$; $I = 250$; $G = 150$; $T = 100$

## 9.2 FISCAL POLICY AT WORK: MULTIPLIER EFFECTS

LEARNING OBJECTIVE: Describe the effects of three fiscal policy multipliers.

**2.1** Use your answer to Problem 1.6 to calculate the *MPC*, *MPS*, government spending multiplier, and tax multiplier. Draw a graph showing the data for consumption spending, planned aggregate expenditures, and aggregate output. Be sure to identify the equilibrium point on your graph.

**2.2** Suppose that the government of Ansonia is experiencing a large budget deficit with fixed government expenditures of G = 250 and fixed taxes of T = 150. Assume that consumers of Ansonia behave as described in the following consumption function:

$$C = 300 + 0.8(Y - T)$$

Suppose further that investment spending is fixed at 200. Calculate the equilibrium level of GDP in Ansonia. Solve for equilibrium levels of Y, C, and S. Next, assume that the Republican Congress in Ansonia succeeds in reducing taxes by 30 to a new fixed level of 120. Recalculate the equilibrium level of GDP using the tax multiplier. Solve for equilibrium levels of Y, C, and S after the tax cut and check to ensure that the multiplier worked. What arguments are likely to be used in support of such a tax cut? What arguments might be used to oppose such a tax cut?

**2.3** A $1 increase in government spending will raise equilibrium income more than a $1 tax cut will, yet both have the same impact on the budget deficit. So if we care about the budget deficit, the best way to stimulate the economy is through increases in spending, not cuts in taxes. Comment.

**2.4** Answer the following:
  **a.** *MPS* = 0.1. What is the government spending multiplier?
  **b.** *MPC* = 0.6. What is the government spending multiplier?
  **c.** *MPS* = 0.25. What is the government spending multiplier?
  **d.** *MPC* = 0.5. What is the tax multiplier?
  **e.** *MPS* = 0.2. What is the tax multiplier?
  **f.** If the government spending multiplier is 8, what is the tax multiplier?
  **g.** If the tax multiplier is −5, what is the government spending multiplier?
  **h.** If government purchases and taxes are increased by $500 billion simultaneously, what will the effect be on equilibrium output (income)?

**2.5** What is the balanced-budget multiplier? Explain why the balanced-budget multiplier is equal to 1.

## 9.3 THE FEDERAL BUDGET

LEARNING OBJECTIVE: Compare and contrast the federal budgets of three U.S. government administrations.

**3.1** You are appointed secretary of the treasury of a recently independent country called Rugaria. The currency of Rugaria is the lav. The new nation began fiscal operations this year, and the budget situation is that the government will spend 10 million lavs and taxes will be 9 million lavs. The 1-million-lav difference will be borrowed from the public by selling 10-year government bonds paying 5 percent interest. The interest on the outstanding bonds must be added to spending each year, and we assume that additional taxes are raised to cover that interest. Assuming that the budget stays the same except for the interest on the debt for 10 years, what will be the accumulated debt? What will the size of the budget be after 10 years?

3.2 [Related to the *Economics in Practice* on p. 176] Federal government expenditures and receipts for the simple economy of the nation of Topanga are listed in the table in the next column. The government of Topanga would like to reduce the debt-to-GDP ratio, and the Finance Minister of Topanga has proposed the following: "The best way to reduce the debt-to-GDP ratio is to increase GDP, because with a larger GDP, the ratio will have to get smaller. I therefore propose that government expenditures be increased by 25 percent, personal income taxes be reduced by 25 percent, corporate income taxes be reduced by 25 percent, and contributions for social insurance be reduced by 25 percent. All of these moves will increase GDP by 10 percent by increasing consumer spending, business spending, and government spending by the exact amounts of the increased spending and reduced taxes." Assuming that GDP will, indeed, increase by 10 percent and the only changes to the data in the table are those proposed by the Finance Minister, answer the following questions:
   a. What is the current debt-to-GDP ratio?
   b. What is the amount of the current budget deficit or surplus?

   c. With the proposals made by the Finance Minister, what will be the amount of the new budget deficit or surplus and what will be the new debt-to-GDP ratio?
   d. Based on your answer to part (c), will the Finance Minister's proposals work to reduce the debt-to-GDP ratio? Explain.

| | |
|---|---|
| Debt | $20 million |
| GDP | $40 million |
| Government expenditures | $5 million |
| Government transfer payments | $5 million |
| Interest payment | $1 million |
| Personal income tax receipts | $6 million |
| Corporate income tax receipts | $1 million |
| Contributions for social insurance | $4 million |

## 9.4 THE ECONOMY'S INFLUENCE ON THE GOVERNMENT BUDGET

LEARNING OBJECTIVE: Explain the influence of the economy on the federal government budget.

4.1 Suppose all tax collections are fixed (instead of dependent on income) and all spending and transfer programs are fixed (in the sense that they do not depend on the state of the economy, as, for example, unemployment benefits now do). In this case, would there be any automatic stabilizers in the government budget? Would there be any distinction between the full-employment deficit and the actual budget deficit? Explain.

---

# CHAPTER 9 APPENDIX A

LEARNING OBJECTIVE

Show that the government spending multiplier is 1 divided by 1 minus the *MPC*.

## Deriving the Fiscal Policy Multipliers

### The Government Spending and Tax Multipliers

In the chapter, we noted that the government spending multiplier is $1/MPS$. (This is the same as the investment multiplier.) We can also derive the multiplier algebraically using our hypothetical consumption function:

$$C = a + b(Y - T)$$

where $b$ is the marginal propensity to consume. As you know, the equilibrium condition is

$$Y = C + I + G$$

By substituting for $C$, we get

$$Y = a + b(Y - T) + I + G$$
$$Y = a + bY - bT + I + G$$

This equation can be rearranged to yield

$$Y - bY = a + I + G - bT$$
$$Y(1 - b) = a + I + G - bT$$

Now solve for $Y$ by dividing through by $(1 - b)$:

$$Y = \frac{1}{(1 - b)}(a + I + G - bT)$$

We see from this last equation that if $G$ increases by 1 with the other determinants of $Y$ ($a$, $I$, and $T$) remaining constant, $Y$ increases by $1/(1 - b)$. The multiplier is, as before, simply $1/(1 - b)$, where $b$ is the marginal propensity to consume. Of course, $1 - b$ equals the marginal propensity to save, so the government spending multiplier is $1/MPS$.

We can also derive the tax multiplier. The last equation says that when $T$ increases by \$1, holding $a$, $I$, and $G$ constant, income decreases by $b/(1 - b)$ dollars. The tax multiplier is $-b/(1 - b)$, or $-MPC/(1 - MPC) = -MPC/MPS$. (Remember, the negative sign in the resulting tax multiplier shows that it is a *negative* multiplier.)

## The Balanced-Budget Multiplier

It is easy to show formally that the balanced-budget multiplier equals 1. When taxes and government spending are simultaneously increased by the same amount, there are two effects on planned aggregate expenditure: one positive and one negative. The initial impact of a balanced-budget increase in government spending and taxes on aggregate expenditure would be the *increase* in government purchases ($\Delta G$) minus the *decrease* in consumption ($\Delta C$) caused by the tax increase. The decrease in consumption brought about by the tax increase is equal to $\Delta C = \Delta T(MPC)$.

| | |
|---|---|
| initial increase in spending: | $\Delta G$ |
| $-$ initial decrease in spending: | $\Delta C = \Delta T(MPC)$ |
| $=$ net initial increase in spending | $\Delta G - \Delta T(MPC)$ |

In a balanced-budget increase, $\Delta G = \Delta T$; so in the above equation for the net initial increase in spending we can substitute $\Delta G$ for $\Delta T$.

$$\Delta G - \Delta G(MPC) = \Delta G(1 - MPC)$$

Because $MPS = (1 - MPC)$, the net initial increase in spending is:

$$\Delta G(MPS)$$

We can now apply the expenditure multiplier $\left(\dfrac{1}{MPS}\right)$ to this net initial increase in spending:

$$\Delta Y = \Delta G(MPS)\left(\frac{1}{MPS}\right) = \Delta G$$

Thus, the final total increase in the equilibrium level of $Y$ is just equal to the initial balanced increase in $G$ and $T$. That means the balanced-budget multiplier equals 1, so the final increase in real output is of the same magnitude as the initial change in spending.

# CHAPTER 9 APPENDIX B

## The Case in Which Tax Revenues Depend on Income

LEARNING OBJECTIVE

Explain why the multiplier falls when taxes depend on income.

In this chapter, we used the simplifying assumption that the government collects taxes in a lump sum. This made our discussion of the multiplier effects somewhat easier to follow. Now suppose that the government collects taxes not solely as a lump sum that is paid regardless of income but also partly in the form of a proportional levy against income. This is a more realistic assumption. Typically, tax collections either are based on income (as with the personal income tax) or follow the ups and downs in the economy (as with sales taxes). Instead of setting taxes equal to some fixed amount, let us say that tax revenues depend on income. If we call the amount of net taxes collected $T$, we can write $T = T_0 + tY$.

This equation contains two parts. First, we note that net taxes ($T$) will be equal to an amount $T_0$ if income ($Y$) is zero. Second, the tax rate ($t$) indicates how much net taxes change as income changes. Suppose $T_0$ is equal to $-200$ and $t$ is 1/3. The resulting tax function is $T = -200 + 1/3Y$, which is graphed in Figure 9B.1. Note that when income is zero, the government collects "negative net taxes," which simply means that it makes transfer payments of 200. As income rises, tax collections increase because every extra dollar of income generates $0.33 in extra revenues for the government.

How do we incorporate this new tax function into our discussion? All we do is replace the old value of $T$ (in the example in the chapter, $T$ was set equal to 100) with the new value, $-200 + 1/3Y$. Look first at the consumption equation. Consumption ($C$) still depends on disposable income, as it did before. Also, disposable income is still $Y - T$, or income minus taxes. Instead of disposable income equaling $Y - 100$, however, the new equation for disposable income is

$$Y_d = Y - T$$
$$Y_d = Y - (-200 + 1/3Y)$$
$$Y_d = Y + 200 - 1/3Y$$

Because consumption still depends on after-tax income, exactly as it did before, we have

$$C = 100 + 0.75Y_d$$
$$C = 100 + 0.75(Y + 200 - 1/3Y)$$

Nothing else needs to be changed. We solve for equilibrium income exactly as before, by setting planned aggregate expenditure equal to aggregate output. Recall that planned aggregate expenditure is $C + I + G$ and aggregate output is $Y$. If we assume, as before, that $I = 100$ and $G = 100$, the equilibrium is

$$Y = C + I + G$$
$$Y = \underbrace{100 + 0.75(Y + 200 - 1/3Y)}_{C} + \underbrace{100}_{I} + \underbrace{100}_{G}$$

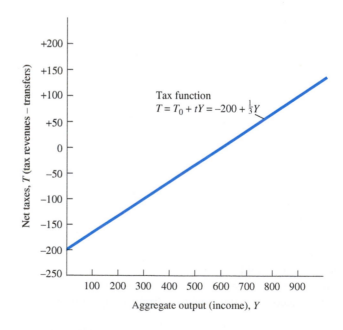

▶ **FIGURE 9B.1** **The Tax Function**

This graph shows net taxes (taxes minus transfer payments) as a function of aggregate income.

This equation may look difficult to solve, but it is not. It simplifies to

$$Y = 100 + 0.75Y + 150 - 25Y + 100 + 100$$
$$Y = 450 + 0.5Y$$
$$0.5Y = 450$$

This means that $Y = 450/0.5 = 900$, the new equilibrium level of income.

Consider the graphic analysis of this equation as shown in Figure 9B.2, where you should note that when we make taxes a function of income (instead of a lump-sum amount), the $AE$ function becomes *flatter* than it was before. Why? When tax collections do not depend on income, an increase in income of $1 means disposable income also increases by a dollar. Because taxes are a constant amount, adding more income does not raise the amount of taxes paid. Disposable income therefore changes dollar for dollar with any change in income.

When taxes depend on income, a $1 increase in income does not increase disposable income by a full dollar because some of the additional dollar goes to pay extra taxes. Under the modified tax function of Figure 9B.2, an extra dollar of income will increase disposable income by only $0.67 because $0.33 of the extra dollar goes to the government in the form of taxes.

No matter how taxes are calculated, the marginal propensity to consume out of disposable (or after-tax) income is the same—each extra dollar of disposable income will increase consumption spending by $0.75. However, a $1 change in before-tax income does not have the same effect on disposable income in each case. Suppose we were to increase income by $1. With the lump-sum tax function, disposable income would rise by $1.00, and consumption would increase by the $MPC$ times the change in $Y_d$, or $0.75. When taxes depend on income, disposable income would rise by only $0.67 from the $1.00 increase in income and consumption would rise by only the $MPC$ times the change in disposable income, or $0.75 \times 0.67 = $0.50.

If a $1.00 increase in income raises expenditure by $0.75 in one case and by only $0.50 in the other, the second aggregate expenditure function must be flatter than the first.

## The Government Spending and Tax Multipliers Algebraically

All this means that if taxes are a function of income, the three multipliers (investment, government spending, and tax) are less than they would be if taxes were a lump-sum amount. By using the same linear consumption function we used in Chapters 7 and 8, we can derive the multiplier:

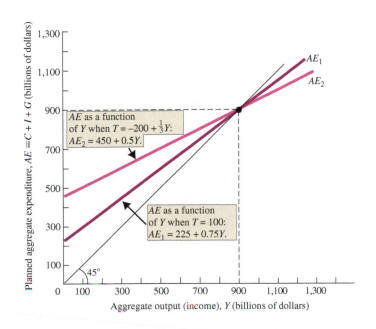

◀ **FIGURE 9B.2**
**Different Tax Systems**
When taxes are strictly lump-sum ($T = 100$) and do not depend on income, the aggregate expenditure function is steeper than when taxes depend on income.

$$C = a + b(Y - T)$$
$$C = a + b(Y - T_0 - tY)$$
$$C = a + bY - bT_0 - btY$$

We know that $Y = C + I + G$. Through substitution we get

$$Y = \underbrace{a + bY - bT_0 - btY}_{C} + I + G$$

Solving for $Y$:

$$Y = \frac{1}{1 - b + bt}(a + I + G - bT_0)$$

This means that a \$1 increase in $G$ or $I$ (holding $a$ and $T_0$ constant) will increase the equilibrium level of $Y$ by

$$\frac{1}{1 - b + bt}$$

If $b = MPC = 0.75$ and $t = 0.20$, the spending multiplier is 2.5. (Compare this to 4, which would be the value of the spending multiplier if taxes were a lump sum, that is, if $t = 0$.)

Holding $a$, $I$, and $G$ constant, a fixed or lump-sum tax cut (a cut in $T_0$) will increase the equilibrium level of income by

$$\frac{b}{1 - b + bt}$$

Thus, if $b = MPC = 0.75$ and $t = 0.20$, the tax multiplier is $-1.875$. (Compare this to $-3$, which would be the value of the tax multiplier if taxes were a lump sum.)

---

## APPENDIX SUMMARY

1. When taxes depend on income, a \$1 increase in income does not increase disposable income by a full dollar because some of the additional dollar must go to pay extra taxes. This means that if taxes are a function of income, the three multipliers (investment, government spending, and tax) are less than they would be if taxes were a lump-sum amount.

---

## APPENDIX PROBLEMS

All problems are available on MyEconLab.

### APPENDIX B: THE CASE IN WHICH TAX REVENUES DEPEND ON INCOME

LEARNING OBJECTIVE: Explain why the multiplier falls when taxes depend on income.

1A.1 Assume the following for the economy of a country:

  a. Consumption function: $C = 60 + 0.75Y_d$
  b. Investment: $I = 75$
  c. Government spending: $G = 45$
  d. Net taxes: $T = -25 + 0.2Y$
  e. Disposable income: $Y_d \equiv Y - T$
  f. Equilibrium: $Y = C + I + G$

Solve for equilibrium income. (Hint: Be very careful in doing the calculations. They are not difficult, but it is easy to make careless mistakes that produce wrong results.) How much does the government collect in net taxes when the economy is in equilibrium? What is the government's budget deficit or surplus?

# Money, the Federal Reserve, and the Interest Rate

# 10

In the last two chapters, we explored how consumers, firms, and the government interact in the goods market. In this chapter, we show how the money market works in the macroeconomy. We begin by defining money and describing its role in the U.S. economy. Microeconomics has little to say about money. Microeconomic theories and models are concerned primarily with *real* quantities (apples, oranges, hours of labor) and *relative* prices (the price of apples relative to the price of oranges or the price of labor relative to the prices of other goods). By contrast, as we will now see, money is an important part of the macroeconomy.

# An Overview of Money

You often hear people say things like, "He makes a lot of money" (in other words, "He has a high income") or "She's worth a lot of money" (meaning "She is very wealthy"). It is true that your employer uses money to pay you your income, and your wealth may be accumulated in the form of money. However, "money" is defined differently in macroeconomics.

## What Is Money?

Most people take the ability to obtain and use money for granted. When the whole monetary system works well, as it generally does in the United States, the basic mechanics of the system are virtually invisible. People take for granted that they can walk into any store, restaurant, boutique, or gas station and buy whatever they want as long as they have enough green pieces of paper or a debit card with a large enough balance in their checking account.

The idea that you can buy things with money is so natural and obvious that it seems absurd to mention it, but stop and ask yourself: "How is it that a store owner is willing to part with a steak and a loaf of bread that I can eat in exchange for access to some pieces of paper that are intrinsically worthless?" Why, on the other hand, are there times and places where it takes a shopping cart full of money to purchase a dozen eggs? The answers to these questions lie in what money is—a means of payment, a store of value, and a unit of account.

**barter** The direct exchange of goods and services for other goods and services.

### A Means of Payment, or Medium of Exchange

Money is vital to the working of a market economy. Imagine what life would be like without it. The alternative to a monetary economy is **barter**, people exchanging goods and services for other goods and services directly instead of exchanging via the medium of money.

How does a barter system work? Suppose you want bacon, eggs, and orange juice for breakfast. Instead of going to the store and buying these things with money, you would have to find someone who has the items and is willing to trade them. You would also have to have something the bacon seller, the orange juice purveyor, and the egg vendor want. Having pencils to trade will do you no good if the bacon, orange juice, and egg sellers do not want pencils.

A barter system requires a *double coincidence of wants* for trade to take place. That is, to effect a trade, you have to find someone who has what you want and that person must also want what you have. Where the range of goods traded is small, as it is in relatively unsophisticated economies, it is not difficult to find someone to trade with and barter is often used. In a complex society with many goods, barter exchanges involve an intolerable amount of effort. Imagine trying to find people who offer for sale all the things you buy in a typical trip to the supermarket and who are willing to accept goods that you have to offer in exchange for their goods.

**medium of exchange, or means of payment** What sellers generally accept and buyers generally use to pay for goods and services.

Some agreed-to **medium of exchange (*or* means of payment)** neatly eliminates the double-coincidence-of-wants problem. Under a monetary system, money is exchanged for goods or services when people buy things; goods or services are exchanged for money when people sell things. No one ever has to trade goods for other goods directly. Money is a lubricant in the functioning of a market economy.

**store of value** An asset that can be used to transport purchasing power from one time period to another.

### A Store of Value

Economists have identified other roles for money aside from its primary function as a medium of exchange. Money also serves as a **store of value**—an asset that can be used to transport purchasing power from one time period to another. If you raise chickens and at the end of the month sell them for more than you want to spend and consume immediately, you may keep some of your earnings in the form of money until the time you want to spend it.

There are many other stores of value besides money. You could have decided to hold your "surplus" earnings by buying such things as antique paintings, or diamonds, which you could sell later when you want to spend your earnings. Money has several advantages over these other stores of value. First, it comes in convenient denominations and is easily portable. Debit cards and phones that provide access to the money in your checking account make money even more convenient. You do not have to worry about making change for a Renoir painting to buy a gallon

## ECONOMICS IN PRACTICE

### Don't Kill the Birds!

In most countries commodity monies were abandoned many years ago. At one point, sea shells and other artifacts from nature were commonly used. One of the more interesting examples of a commodity money is described by David Houston, an ethno-ornithologist.[1]

In the nineteenth century, elaborate rolls of red feathers harvested from the Scarlet Honeyeater bird were used as currency between the island of Santa Cruz and nearby Pacific Islands. Feathers were made into rolls of more than 10 meters in length and were never worn, displayed, or used. Their sole role was to serve as currency in a complex valuation system. Houston tells us that more than 20,000 of these birds were killed each year to create this "money," adding considerably to bird mortality. Running the printing presses is much easier.

Today, one of the few remaining uses of commodity monies is the use of dolphin teeth in the Solomon Islands. Apparently there is even a problem with counterfeiting as people try to pass off fruit bat teeth as dolphin teeth![2]

**THINKING PRACTICALLY**

1. Why do red feather rolls and dolphin teeth make good commodity monies, whereas coconut shells would not?

[1]*David Houston, "The Impact of the Red Feather Currency on the Population of the Scarlet Honeyeater on Santa Cruz," in Sonia Tidemann and Andrew Gosler, eds., Ethno-Ornithology: Birds, Indigenous Peoples, Culture and Society (London, Earthscan Publishers, 2010), pp. 55–66.*

[2]*The Wall Street Journal, excerpted from "Shrinking Dollar Meets Its Match in Dolphin Teeth" by Yaroslav Trofimov. Copyright 2008 by Dow Jones & Company, Inc. Reproduced with permission of Dow Jones & Company, Inc. via Copyright Clearance Center.*

---

of gasoline. Second, because money is also a means of payment, it is easily exchanged for goods at all times. These two factors compose the **liquidity property of money**. Money is easily spent, flowing out of your hands like liquid.

The main disadvantage of money as a store of value is that the value of money falls when the prices of goods and services rise. If the price of potato chips rises from $1 per bag to $2 per bag, the value of a dollar bill in terms of potato chips falls from one bag to half a bag. When this happens, it may be better to use potato chips (or antiques or real estate) as a store of value. Indeed, there have been times of rising prices when people hoard goods rather than storing money to support their future needs.

**A Unit of Account**   Money also serves as a **unit of account**—a consistent way of quoting prices. All prices are quoted in monetary units. A textbook is quoted as costing $90, not 150 bananas or 5 pizzas. Obviously, a standard unit of account is extremely useful when quoting prices. This function of money may have escaped your notice—what else would people quote prices in except money?

**liquidity property of money** The property of money that makes it a good medium of exchange as well as a store of value: It is portable and readily accepted and thus easily exchanged for goods.

**unit of account**   A standard unit that provides a consistent way of quoting prices.

## Commodity and Fiat Monies

Introductory economics textbooks are full of stories about the various items that have been used as money by various cultures—candy bars, cigarettes (in World War II prisoner-of-war camps), huge wheels of carved stone (on the island of Yap in the South Pacific, beads (among North American Indians), cattle (in southern Africa), and small green scraps of

**commodity monies** Items used as money that also have intrinsic value in some other use.

**fiat, or token, money** Items designated as money that are intrinsically worthless.

**legal tender** Money that a government has required to be accepted in settlement of debts.

**currency debasement** The decrease in the value of money that occurs when its supply is increased rapidly.

paper (in contemporary North America). The *Economics in Practice* box on the preceding page describes the use of bird feathers as money. These various kinds of money are generally divided into two groups, commodity monies and fiat money.

**Commodity monies** are those items used as money that also have an intrinsic value in some other use. For example, prisoners of war made purchases with cigarettes, quoted prices in terms of cigarettes, and held their wealth in the form of accumulated cigarettes. Of course, cigarettes could also be smoked—they had an alternative use apart from serving as money. In fact, one of the problems with commodity monies, like cigarettes, is that their value may change when demand for them as items of use falls. If no one in prison smoked, the value of the cigarettes would likely fall, perhaps even to zero. Gold represents another form of commodity money. For hundreds of years gold could be used directly to buy things, but it also had other uses, ranging from jewelry to dental fillings.

By contrast, money in the United States today is mostly fiat money. **Fiat money**, sometimes called **token money**, is money that is intrinsically worthless. The actual value of a 1-, 10-, or 50-dollar bill is basically zero; what other uses are there for a small piece of paper with some green ink on it?

Why would anyone accept worthless scraps of paper as money instead of something that has some value, such as gold, cigarettes, or cattle? If your answer is "because the paper money is backed by gold or silver," you are wrong. There was a time when dollar bills were convertible directly into gold. The government backed each dollar bill in circulation by holding a certain amount of gold in its vaults. If the price of gold were $35 per ounce, for example, the government agreed to sell 1 ounce of gold for 35 dollar bills. However, dollar bills are no longer backed by any commodity—gold, silver, or anything else. They are exchangeable only for dimes, nickels, pennies, other dollars, and so on. The good news here is that the value of this money does not depend on the value of money in another use, as in the case of cigarettes. The harder question is why it has any value at all!

The public accepts paper money as a means of payment and a store of value because the government has taken steps to ensure that its money is accepted. The government declares its paper money to be **legal tender**. That is, the government declares that its money must be accepted in settlement of debts. It does this by fiat (hence *fiat money*). It passes laws defining certain pieces of paper printed in certain inks on certain plates to be legal tender, and that is that. Printed on every Federal Reserve note in the United States is "This note is legal tender for all debts, public and private." Often the government can get a start on gaining acceptance for its paper money by requiring that it be used to pay taxes.

Aside from declaring its currency legal tender, the government usually does one other thing to ensure that paper money will be accepted: It promises the public that it will not print paper money so fast that it loses its value. Expanding the supply of currency so rapidly that it loses much of its value has been a problem throughout history and is known as **currency debasement**. Debasement of the currency has been a special problem of governments that lack the strength to take the politically unpopular step of raising taxes. Printing money to be used on government expenditures of goods and services can serve as a substitute for tax increases, and weak governments have often relied on the printing press to finance their expenditures. An interesting example is Zimbabwe. In 2007, faced with a need to improve the public water system, Zimbabwe's president, Robert Mugabe, said, "Where money for projects cannot be found, we will print it" (reported in the *Washington Post*, July 29, 2007). In later chapters we will see the way in which this strategy for funding public projects can lead to serious inflation.

## Measuring the Supply of Money in the United States

We now turn to the various kinds of money in the United States. Recall that money is used to buy things (a means of payment), to hold wealth (a store of value), and to quote prices (a unit of account). Unfortunately, these characteristics apply to a broad range of assets in the U.S. economy in addition to dollar bills. As we will see, it is not at all clear where we should draw the line and say, "Up to this is money, beyond this is something else."

To solve the problem of multiple monies, economists have given different names to different measures of money. The two most common measures of money are transactions money, also called M1, and broad money, also called M2.

**M1: Transactions Money**   What should be counted as money? Coins and dollar bills, as well as higher denominations of currency, must be counted as money—they fit all the requirements. What about checking accounts? Checks, too, can be used to buy things and can serve as a store of value. Debit cards provide even easier access to funds in checking accounts, as do smartphones linked to checking accounts. In fact, bankers call checking accounts *demand deposits* because depositors have the right to cash in (demand) their entire checking account balance at any time. That makes your checking account balance virtually equivalent to bills in your wallet, and it should be included as part of the amount of money you hold, as we have done thus far in our discussion.

If we take the value of all currency (including coins) held outside of bank vaults and add to it the value of all demand deposits, traveler's checks, and other checkable deposits, we have defined **M1, *or* transactions money**. As its name suggests, this is the money that can be directly used for transactions—to buy things.

**M1, *or* transactions money**   Money that can be directly used for transactions.

$$M1 \equiv \text{currency held outside banks} + \text{demand deposits} + \text{traveler's checks} + \text{other checkable deposits}$$

M1 at the end of February 2015 was \$2,988.2 billion. M1 is a stock measure—it is measured at a point in time. It is the total amount of coins and currency outside of banks and the total dollar amount in checking accounts.

**M2: Broad Money**   Although M1 is the most widely used measure of the money supply, there are other measures as well. Although many savings accounts cannot be used for transactions directly, it is easy to convert them into cash or to transfer funds from them into a checking account. What about money market accounts (which allow only a few checks per month but pay market-determined interest rates) and money market mutual funds (which sell shares and use the proceeds to purchase short-term securities)? These can be used to write checks and make purchases, although only over a certain amount.

If we add **near monies**, close substitutes for transactions money, to M1, we get **M2**, called **broad money** because it includes not-quite-money monies such as savings accounts, money market accounts, and other near monies.

**near monies**   Close substitutes for transactions money, such as savings accounts and money market accounts.

**M2, *or* broad money**   M1 plus savings accounts, money market accounts, and other near monies.

$$M2 \equiv M1 + \text{Savings accounts} + \text{Money market accounts} + \text{Other near monies}$$

M2 at the end of February 2015 was \$11,820.3 billion, considerably larger than the total M1 of \$2,988.2 billion. The main advantage of looking at M2 instead of M1 is that M2 is sometimes more stable. For instance, when banks introduced new forms of interest-bearing checking accounts in the early 1980s, M1 shot up as people switched their funds from savings accounts to checking accounts. However, M2 remained fairly constant because the fall in savings account deposits and the rise in checking account balances were both part of M2, canceling each other out.

**Beyond M2**   Because a wide variety of financial instruments bear some resemblance to money, some economists have advocated including almost all of them as part of the money supply. For example, credit cards are used extensively in exchange. Everyone who has a credit card has a credit limit—you can charge only a certain amount on your card before you have to pay it off. One of the very broad definitions of money includes the amount of available credit on credit cards (your charge limit minus what you have charged but not paid) as part of the money supply.

There are no rules for deciding what is and is not money. However, *for our purposes, "money" will always refer to transactions money, or M1.* For simplicity, we will say that M1 is the sum of two *general* categories: currency in circulation and deposits. Keep in mind, however, that M1 has *four* specific components: currency held outside banks, demand deposits, traveler's checks, and other checkable deposits.

# How Banks Create Money

So far we have described the general way that money works and the way the supply of money is measured in the United States, but how much money is available at a given time? Who supplies it, and how does it get supplied? We are now ready to analyze these questions in detail. In particular, we want to explore a process that many find mysterious: the way banks *create money*.

## A Historical Perspective: Goldsmiths

To begin to see how banks create money, consider the origins of the modern banking system. In the fifteenth and sixteenth centuries, citizens of many lands used gold as money, particularly for large transactions. Because gold is both inconvenient to carry around and susceptible to theft, people began to place their gold with goldsmiths for safekeeping. On receiving the gold, a goldsmith would issue a receipt to the depositor, charging him a small fee for looking after his gold. After a time, these receipts themselves, rather than the gold that they represented, began to be traded for goods. The receipts became a form of paper money, making it unnecessary to go to the goldsmith to withdraw gold for a transaction. The receipts of the de Medici's, who were both art patrons and goldsmith-bankers in Italy in the Renaissance period, were reputedly accepted in wide areas of Europe as currency.

At this point, all the receipts issued by goldsmiths were backed 100 percent by gold. If a goldsmith had 100 ounces of gold in his safe, he would issue receipts for 100 ounces of gold, and no more. Goldsmiths functioned as warehouses where people stored gold for safekeeping. The goldsmiths found, however, that people did not come often to withdraw gold. Why should they, when paper receipts that could easily be converted to gold were "as good as gold"? (In fact, receipts were better than gold—more portable, safer from theft, and so on.) As a result, goldsmiths had a large stock of gold continuously on hand.

Because they had what amounted to "extra" gold sitting around, goldsmiths gradually realized that they could lend out some of this gold without any fear of running out of gold. Why would they do this? Because instead of just keeping their gold idly in their vaults, they could earn interest on loans. Something subtle, but dramatic, happened at this point. The goldsmiths changed from mere depositories for gold into banklike institutions that had the power to create money. This transformation occurred as soon as goldsmiths began making loans. Without adding any more real gold to the system, the goldsmiths increased the amount of money in circulation by creating additional claims to gold—that is, receipts that entitled the bearer to receive a certain number of ounces of gold on demand.[1] Thus, there were more claims than there were ounces of gold.

A detailed example may help to clarify what might look at first to you like a sleight of hand. Suppose you go to a goldsmith who is functioning only as a depository, or warehouse, and ask for a loan to buy a plot of land that costs 20 ounces of gold. Also suppose that the goldsmith has 100 ounces of gold on deposit in his safe and receipts for exactly 100 ounces of gold out to the various people who deposited the gold. If the goldsmith decides he is tired of being a mere goldsmith and wants to become a real bank, he will loan you some gold. You don't want the gold itself, of course; rather, you want a slip of paper that represents 20 ounces of gold. The goldsmith in essence "creates" money for you by giving you a receipt for 20 ounces of gold (even though his entire supply of gold already belongs to various other people).[2] When he does, there will be receipts for 120 ounces of gold in circulation instead of the 100 ounces worth of receipts before your loan and the supply of money will have increased.

People think the creation of money is mysterious. Far from it! The creation of money is simply an accounting procedure, among the most mundane of human endeavors. You may suspect the whole process is fundamentally unsound or somehow dubious. After all, the banking system began when someone issued claims for gold that already belonged to someone else. Here you may be on slightly firmer ground.

---

[1] Remember, these receipts circulated as money, and people used them to make transactions without feeling the need to cash them in—that is, to exchange them for gold itself.

[2] In return for lending you the receipt for 20 ounces of gold, the goldsmith expects to get an IOU promising to repay the amount (in gold itself or with a receipt from another goldsmith) with interest after a certain period of time.

## ECONOMICS IN PRACTICE

## A Run on the Bank: George Bailey, Mary Poppins, Wyatt Earp

Frank Capra's 1946 classic film, *It's a Wonderful Life*, stars Jimmy Stewart as George Bailey, the-salt-of-the- earth head of a small town building and loan bank. At one point late in the movie, as a result of some devilry by a competitor, the sound-ness of Bailey's bank comes to be questioned. The result? A classic run on the bank, shown in the movie by a mob trying to get their deposits back at the bank window. Stewart's explana-tion to his depositors could be straight out of an economics textbook. "I don't have your money here," he tells them. "Your money is being used to build your neighbor's new house. "Just like the goldsmiths of yore, George Bailey's banks lent out their deposits, creating money. Bailey's defense against the bank run was easier in a time when people knew their bankers. "What we need now," Bailey assured us with Jimmy Stewart's earnest acting, "is faith in each other." In today's market, faith in the government is the more typical defense against a bank run.

Another cinematic look at bank runs, by the way, comes in *Mary Poppins* when Tommy, one of Poppins' two young charges, loudly insists in the middle of the bank where his father works that he wants his tuppence back and the bank won't give it to him. The result? Another bank run, British style!

Finally, there is Wyatt Earp, in this case a true story. Earp in 1909, near the end of his colorful life, was hired by a bank in Los Angeles. Rumors were out that the bank had loaned more money than it had gold in its vaults. Depositors, we assume not understanding that this is common, were storming the bank to get their money out. Earp was hired to calm things down. His response was different from George Bailey's. He took empty money sacks from the bank, hired a wagon and driver, drove to a nearby iron works, and filled the sacks with iron slugs about the size of $20 gold pieces. He drove back to the bank, where police were holding back the mob. He announced that he had about a million dollars in the wagon and began unloading the bars into the bank. He told the police to tell the crowd that "any gent who thinks he can find a better bank to put his money

Wyatt Earp and some of his buddies were members of the Dodge City Peace Commission in 1883. From left to right (top row): William H. Harris, Luke Short, William Bat Masterson, (bottom row): Charles E. Bassett, Wyatt Earp, Frank McLain, Jerry Hausman

into to go and find it. But he'd better be damned careful he don't get hit over the head and robbed while he's doing it." As the bars were being loaded into the bank, the crowd dispersed.

### THINKING PRACTICALLY

1. How do Earp's remarks illustrate the advantages of paper money over gold?

Casey Tefertiller, *Wyatt Earp: The Life Behind the Legend*, John Wiley & Sons, Inc., 1997.

Goldsmiths-turned-bankers did face certain problems. Once they started making loans, their receipts outstanding (claims on gold) were greater than the amount of gold they had in their vaults at any given moment. If the owners of the 120 ounces worth of gold receipts all presented their receipts and demanded their gold at the same time, the goldsmith would be in trouble. With only 100 ounces of gold on hand, people could not get their gold at once.

In normal times, people would be happy to hold receipts instead of real gold, and this problem would never arise. If, however, people began to worry about the goldsmith's financial safety, they might begin to have doubts about whether their receipts really were as good as gold. Knowing there were more receipts outstanding than there were ounces of gold in the goldsmith's vault, they might start to demand gold for receipts.

This situation leads to a paradox. It makes perfect sense for people to hold paper receipts (instead of gold) if they know they can always get gold for their paper. In normal times, gold-smiths could feel perfectly safe in loaning out more gold than they actually had in their posses-sion. But once people start to doubt the safety of the goldsmith, they are foolish not to demand their gold back from the vault.

**run on a bank** Occurs when many of those who have claims on a bank (deposits) present them at the same time.

A run on a goldsmith (or in our day, a **run on a bank**) occurs when many people present their claims at the same time. These runs tend to feed on themselves. If I see you going to the goldsmith to withdraw your gold, I may become nervous and decide to withdraw my gold as well. It is the *fear* of a run that usually causes the run. Runs on a bank can be triggered by a variety of causes: rumors that an institution may have made loans to borrowers who cannot repay, wars, failures of other institutions that have borrowed money from the bank, and so on. As you will see later in this chapter, today's bankers differ from goldsmiths—today's banks are subject to a "required reserve ratio." Goldsmiths had no legal reserve requirements, although the amount they loaned out was subject to the restriction imposed on them by their fear of running out of gold. The *Economics in Practice* box on page 193 describes several fictional bank runs, along with a description of Wyatt Earp's role in preventing a real bank run!

## The Modern Banking System

To understand how the modern banking system works, you need to be familiar with some basic principles of accounting. Once you are comfortable with the way banks keep their books, you will see that the process is not so dissimilar to the world of the goldsmith.

**A Brief Review of Accounting** Central to accounting practices is the statement that "the books always balance." In practice, this means that if we take a snapshot of a firm—any firm, including a bank—at a particular moment in time, then by definition:

$$\text{Assets} - \text{Liabilities} \equiv \text{Net Worth}$$
$$\text{or}$$
$$\text{Assets} \equiv \text{Liabilities} + \text{Net Worth}$$

*Assets* are things a firm owns that are worth something. For a bank, these assets include the bank building, its furniture, its holdings of government securities, cash in its vaults, bonds, stocks, and so on. Most important among a bank's assets, for our purposes at least, are the loans it has made. A borrower gives the bank an *IOU*, a promise to repay a certain sum of money on or by a certain date. This promise is an asset of the bank because it is worth something. The bank could (and sometimes does) sell the IOU to another bank for cash.

**Federal Reserve Bank (the Fed)** The central bank of the United States.

Other bank assets include cash on hand (sometimes called *vault cash*) and deposits with the U.S. central bank—the **Federal Reserve Bank (the Fed)**. As we will see later in this chapter, federal banking regulations require that banks keep a certain portion of their deposits on hand as vault cash or on deposit with the Fed.

A firm's *liabilities* are its debts—what it owes. A bank's liabilities are the promises to pay, or IOUs, that it has issued. A bank's most important liabilities are its deposits. *Deposits* are debts owed to the depositors because when you deposit money in your account, you are in essence making a loan to the bank.

The basic rule of accounting says that if we add up a firm's assets and then subtract the total amount it owes to all those who have lent it funds, the difference is the firm's net worth. *Net worth* represents the value of the firm to its stockholders or owners. How much would you pay for a firm that owns $200,000 worth of diamonds and had borrowed $150,000 from a bank to pay for them? The firm is worth $50,000—the difference between what it owns and what it owes. If the price of diamonds were to fall, bringing their value down to only $150,000, the firm would be worth nothing.

We can keep track of a bank's financial position using a simplified balance sheet called a T-account. By convention, the bank's assets are listed on the left side of the T-account and its liabilities and net worth are on the right side. By definition, the balance sheet always balances, so that the sum of the items on the left side of the T-account is equal to the sum of the items on the right side.

**reserves** The deposits that a bank has at the Federal Reserve bank plus its vault cash on hand.

The T-account in Figure 10.1 shows a bank having $110 million in *assets*, of which $20 million are **reserves**, the deposits the bank has made at the Fed, and its cash on hand (coins and currency). Reserves are an asset to the bank because it can go to the Fed and get cash for them,

| Assets | | Liabilities | |
|---|---|---|---|
| Reserves | 20 | 100 | Deposits |
| Loans | 90 | 10 | Net worth |
| Total | 110 | 110 | Total |

◀ **FIGURE 10.1**

**T-Account for a Typical Bank (millions of dollars)**
The balance sheet of a bank must always balance, so that the sum of assets (reserves and loans) equals the sum of liabilities (deposits) and net worth.

the same way you can go to the bank and get cash for the amount in your savings account. Our bank's other asset is its loans, worth $90 million.

Why do banks hold reserves/deposits at the Fed? There are many reasons, but perhaps the most important is the legal requirement that they hold a certain percentage of their deposit liabilities as reserves. The percentage of its deposits that a bank must keep as reserves is known as the **required reserve ratio**. If the reserve ratio is 20 percent, a bank with deposits of $100 million must hold $20 million as reserves, either as cash or as deposits at the Fed. To simplify, we will assume that banks hold all of their reserves in the form of deposits at the Fed.

On the liabilities side of the T-account, the bank has deposits of $100 million, which it owes to its depositors. This means that the bank has a net worth of $10 million to its owners ($110 million in assets − $100 million in liabilities = $10 million net worth). The net worth of the bank is what "balances" the balance sheet. Remember that when some item on a bank's balance sheet changes, there must be at least one other change somewhere else to maintain balance. If a bank's reserves increase by $1, one of the following must also be true: (1) Its other assets (for example, loans) decrease by $1, (2) its liabilities (deposits) increase by $1, or (3) its net worth increases by $1. Various fractional combinations of these are also possible.

**required reserve ratio**   The percentage of its total deposits that a bank must keep as cash or reserves at the Federal Reserve.

## The Creation of Money

Like the goldsmiths, today's bankers can earn income by lending money out at a higher interest rate than they pay depositors for use of their money. In modern times, the chances of a run on a bank are fairly small, and even if there is a run, the central bank protects the private banks in various ways. Therefore, banks if they choose to can make loans up to the reserve requirement restriction. A bank's required amount of reserves is equal to the required reserve ratio times the total deposits in the bank. If a bank has deposits of $100 and the required ratio is 20 percent, the required amount of reserves is $20. The difference between a bank's actual reserves and its required reserves is its **excess reserves**:

**excess reserves**   The difference between a bank's actual reserves and its required reserves.

$$\text{excess reserves} \equiv \text{actual reserves} - \text{required reserves}$$

When a bank's excess reserves are zero, it can no longer make loans. Why is this? When a bank makes a loan, it creates a demand deposit for the borrower. That demand deposit, in turn, requires reserves to back it up, just like the other deposits in the bank. With excess reserves at zero, and no new cash coming in, the bank has no way to reserve against the new deposit.

An example will help to show the connection between loans and excess reserves more generally. Assume that there is only one private bank in the country, the required reserve ratio is 20 percent, and the bank starts off with nothing, as shown in panel 1 of Figure 10.2. Now suppose dollar bills are in circulation and someone deposits 100 of them in the bank. The bank deposits the $100 with the central bank, so it now has $100 in reserves, as shown in panel 2. The bank now has assets (reserves) of $100 and liabilities (deposits) of $100. If the required reserve ratio is 20 percent, the bank has excess reserves of $80.

How much can the bank lend and still meet the reserve requirement? For the moment, let us assume that anyone who gets a loan keeps the entire proceeds in the bank or pays them to

| Panel 1 | | Panel 2 | | Panel 3 | |
|---|---|---|---|---|---|
| Assets | Liabilities | Assets | Liabilities | Assets | Liabilities |
| Reserves 0 | 0 Deposits | Reserves 100 | 100 Deposits | Reserves 100<br>Loans 400 | 500 Deposits |

▲ **FIGURE 10.2   Balance Sheets of a Bank in a Single-Bank Economy**
In panel 2, there is an initial deposit of $100. In panel 3, the bank has made loans of $400.

someone else who does. Nothing is withdrawn as cash. In this case, the bank can lend $400 and still meet the reserve requirement. Panel 3 shows the balance sheet of the bank after completing the maximum amount of loans it is allowed with a 20 percent reserve ratio. With $80 of excess reserves, the bank can have up to $400 of additional deposits. The $100 original deposit, now in reserves, plus $400 in loans (which are made as deposits) equals $500 in deposits. With $500 in deposits and a required reserve ratio of 20 percent, the bank must have reserves of $100 (20 percent of $500)—and it does. The bank can lend no more than $400 because that is all its $100 of reserves will support, given its initial deposit. Another way to see this is to recognize that the bank originally had $80 in excess reserves. That $80 would support $400 in new deposits (loans) because 20% of $400 equals the $80 excess reserve figure. The $400 in loans uses up all of the excess reserves. When a bank has no excess reserves and thus can make no more loans, it is said to be *loaned up*.

Remember, the money supply (M1) equals cash in circulation plus deposits. Before the initial deposit, the money supply was $100 ($100 cash and no deposits). After the deposit and the loans, the money supply is $500 (no cash outside bank vaults and $500 in deposits). It is clear then that when loans are converted into deposits, the supply of money will increase.

The bank whose T-accounts are presented in Figure 10.2 is allowed to make loans of $400 based on the assumption that loans that are made *stay in the bank* in the form of deposits. Now suppose you borrow from the bank to buy a personal computer and you write a check to the computer store. If the store also deposits its money in the bank, your check merely results in a reduction in your account balance and an increase to the store's account balance within the bank. No cash has left the bank. As long as the system is closed in this way—remember that so far we have assumed that there is only one bank—the bank knows that it will never be called on to release any of its $100 in reserves. It can expand its loans up to the point where its total deposits are $500.

Of course, there are many banks in the country, a situation that is depicted in Figure 10.3. As long as the banking system as a whole is closed, it is still possible for an initial deposit of $100 to result in an expansion of the money supply to $500, but more steps are involved when there is more than one bank.

To see why, assume that Mary makes an initial deposit of $100 in Bank 1 and the bank deposits the entire $100 with the Fed (panel 1 of Figure 10.3). All loans that a bank makes are withdrawn from the bank as the individual borrowers write checks to pay for merchandise. After Mary's deposit, Bank 1 can make a loan of up to $80 to Bill because it needs to keep only $20 of its $100 deposit as reserves. (We are assuming a 20 percent required reserve ratio.) In other words, Bank 1 has $80 in excess reserves.

Bank 1's balance sheet at the moment of the loan to Bill appears in panel 2 of Figure 10.3. Bank 1 now has loans of $80. It has credited Bill's account with the $80, so its total deposits are $180 ($80 in loans plus $100 in reserves). Bill then writes a check for $80 for a set of shock absorbers for his car. Bill wrote his check to Sam's Car Shop, and Sam deposits Bill's check in Bank 2. When the check clears, Bank 1 transfers $80 in reserves to Bank 2. Bank 1's balance sheet now looks like the top of panel 3. Its assets include reserves of $20 and loans of $80; its liabilities are $100 in deposits. Both sides of the T-account balance: The bank's reserves are 20 percent of its deposits, as required by law, and it is fully loaned up.

| | Panel 1 | | Panel 2 | | Panel 3 | |
|---|---|---|---|---|---|---|
| | Assets | Liabilities | Assets | Liabilities | Assets | Liabilities |
| **Bank 1** | Reserves 100 | 100 Deposits | Reserves 100<br>Loans 80 | 180 Deposits | Reserves 20<br>Loans 80 | 100 Deposits |
| **Bank 2** | Reserves 80 | 80 Deposits | Reserves 80<br>Loans 64 | 144 Deposits | Reserves 16<br>Loans 64 | 80 Deposits |
| **Bank 3** | Reserves 64 | 64 Deposits | Reserves 64<br>Loans 51.20 | 115.20 Deposits | Reserves 12.80<br>Loans 51.20 | 64 Deposits |

| Summary: | Loans | Deposits |
|---|---|---|
| Bank 1 | 80 | 100 |
| Bank 2 | 64 | 80 |
| Bank 3 | 51.20 | 64 |
| Bank 4 | 40.96 | 51.20 |
| ⋮ | ⋮ | ⋮ |
| Total | 400.00 | 500.00 |

▲ **FIGURE 10.3  The Creation of Money When There Are Many Banks**
In panel 1, there is an initial deposit of $100 in Bank 1. In panel 2, Bank 1 makes a loan of $80 by creating a deposit of $80. A check for $80 by the borrower is then written on Bank 1 (panel 3) and deposited in Bank 2 (panel 1). The process continues with Bank 2 making loans and so on. In the end, loans of $400 have been made and the total level of deposits is $500.

Now look at bank 2. Because Bank 1 has transferred $80 in reserves to Bank 2, Bank 2 now has $80 in deposits and $80 in reserves (panel 1, Bank 2). Its reserve requirement is also 20 percent, so it has excess reserves of $64 on which it can make loans.

Now assume that Bank 2 loans the $64 to Kate to pay for a textbook and Kate writes a check for $64 payable to the Manhattan College Bookstore. The final position of Bank 2, after it honors Kate's $64 check by transferring $64 in reserves to the bookstore's bank, is reserves of $16, loans of $64, and deposits of $80 (panel 3, Bank 2).

The Manhattan College Bookstore deposits Kate's check in its account with Bank 3. Bank 3 now has excess reserves because it has added $64 to its reserves. With a reserve ratio of 20 percent, Bank 3 can loan out $51.20 (80 percent of $64, leaving 20 percent in required reserves to back the $64 deposit).

As the process is repeated over and over, the total amount of deposits created is $500, the sum of the deposits in each of the banks. Because the banking system can be looked on as one big bank, the outcome here for many banks is the same as the outcome in Figure 10.2 for one bank.[3]

## The Money Multiplier

In practice, the banking system is not completely closed—there is some leakage out of the system, as people send money abroad or even hide it under their mattresses! Still, the point here is that an increase in bank reserves can lead to a greater than one-for-one increase in the money supply. Economists call the relationship between the final change in deposits and the change in reserves that caused this change the money multiplier. Stated somewhat differently, the **money multiplier** is the multiple by which deposits can increase for every dollar increase in reserves. Do not confuse the money multiplier with the spending multipliers we discussed in the last two chapters. They are not the same thing.

**money multiplier**  The multiple by which deposits can increase for every dollar increase in reserves; equal to 1 divided by the required reserve ratio.

---

[3] If banks create money when they make loans, does repaying a loan "destroy" money? The answer is yes.

In the example we just examined, reserves increased by $100 when the $100 in cash was deposited in a bank and the amount of deposits increased by $500 ($100 from the initial deposit, $400 from the loans made by the various banks from their excess reserves). The money multiplier in this case is $500/$100 = 5. Mathematically, the money multiplier can be defined as follows:[4]

$$\text{money multiplier} \equiv \frac{1}{\text{required reserve ratio}}$$

In the United States, the required reserve ratio varies depending on the size of the bank and the type of deposit. For large banks and for checking deposits, the ratio is currently 10 percent, which makes the potential money multiplier 1/.10 = 10. This means that an increase in reserves of $1 could cause an increase in deposits of $10 if there were no leakage out of the system.

It is important to remember that the money multiplier is derived under the assumption that banks hold no excess reserves. For example, when Bank 1 gets the deposit of $100, it loans out the maximum that it can, namely $100 times 1 minus the reserve requirement ratio. If instead Bank 1 held the $100 as excess reserves, the increase in the money supply would just be the initial $100 in deposits (brought in, say, from outside the banking system). We return to the question of excess reserves later in this chapter.

**10.3 LEARNING** OBJECTIVE

Describe the functions and structure of the Federal Reserve System.

# The Federal Reserve System

We have seen how the private banking system can create money by making loans. However, private banks are not free to create money at will. We have already seen the way that their ability to create money is governed by the reserve requirements set by the Fed. We will now examine the structure and function of the Fed.

Founded in 1913 by an act of Congress (to which major reforms were added in the 1930s), the Fed is the central bank of the United States. The Fed is a complicated institution with many responsibilities, including the regulation and supervision of about 6,000 commercial banks. The organization of the Federal Reserve System is presented in Figure 10.4.

The *Board of Governors* is the most important group within the Federal Reserve System. The board consists of seven members, each appointed for 14 years by the president of the United States. The *chair* of the Fed, who is appointed by the president and whose term runs for 4 years, usually dominates the entire Federal Reserve System and is sometimes said to be the second most powerful person in the United States. The Fed is an independent agency in that it does not take orders from the president or from Congress. The United States is divided into 12 Federal Reserve districts, each with its own Federal Reserve bank. These districts are indicated on the map in Figure 10.4. The district banks are like branch offices of the Fed in that they carry out the rules, regulations, and functions of the central system in their districts and report to the Board of Governors on local economic conditions.

U.S. monetary policy is formally set by the **Federal Open Market Committee (FOMC)** The FOMC consists of the seven members of the Fed's Board of Governors; the president of the New York Federal Reserve Bank; and on a rotating basis, four of the presidents of the 11 other district banks. The FOMC sets goals concerning interest rates, and it directs the **Open Market Desk** in the New York Federal Reserve Bank to buy and/or sell government securities. (We discuss the specifics of open market operations later in this chapter.)

**Federal Open Market Committee (FOMC)** A group composed of the seven members of the Fed's Board of Governors, the president of the New York Federal Reserve Bank, and 4 of the other 11 district bank presidents on a rotating basis; it sets goals concerning the money supply and interest rates and directs the operation of the Open Market Desk in New York.

**Open Market Desk** The office in the New York Federal Reserve Bank from which government securities are bought and sold by the Fed.

---

[4] To show this mathematically, let *rr* denote the reserve requirement ratio, like 0.20. Say someone deposits 100 in Bank 1 in Figure 10.3. Bank 1 can create $100(1 - rr)$ in loans, which are then deposits in Bank 2. Bank 2 can create $100(1 - rr)(1 - rr)$ in loans, which are then deposits in Bank 3, and so on. The sum of the deposits is thus $100[1 + (1 - rr) + (1 - rr)^2 + (1 - rr)^3 + \ldots]$. The sum of the infinite series in brackets is $1/rr$, which is the money multiplier.

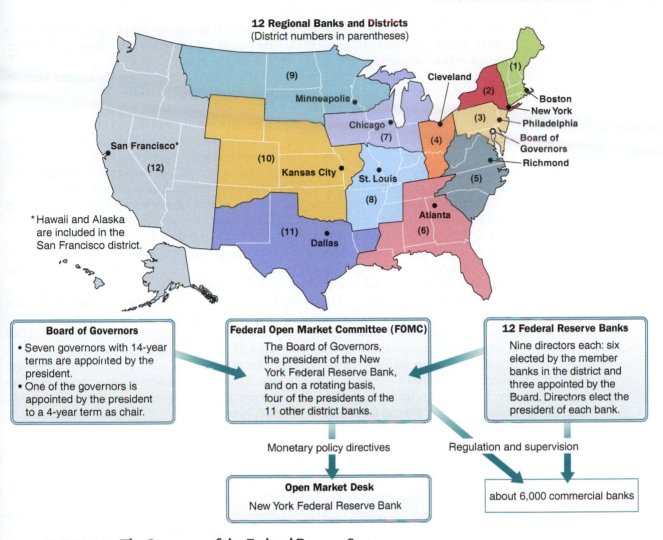

▲ **FIGURE 10.4   The Structure of the Federal Reserve System**

# Functions of the Federal Reserve

The Fed is the central bank of the United States. Central banks are sometimes known as "bankers' banks" because only banks (and occasionally foreign governments) can have accounts in them. As a private citizen, you cannot go to the nearest branch of the Fed and open a checking account or apply to borrow money.

As we will see shortly, the Fed is responsible for monetary policy in the United States, but it also performs several important administrative functions for banks. These functions include clearing interbank payments, regulating the banking system, and assisting banks in a difficult financial position. The Fed is also responsible for managing exchange rates and the nation's foreign exchange reserves.[5] In addition, it is often involved in intercountry negotiations on international economic issues.

Clearing interbank payments works as follows. Suppose you write a $100 check drawn on your bank, the First Bank of Fresno (FBF), to pay for tulip bulbs from Crockett Importers of Miami, Florida. How does your money get from your bank in Fresno to Crockett's bank in Florida? The Fed does it. Both FBF and Banco de Miami have accounts at the Fed. When Crockett Importers receives your check and deposits it at Banco de Miami, the bank submits the check to the Fed, asking it to collect the funds from FBF. The Fed presents the check to FBF and is instructed to debit FBF's account for the $100 and to credit the account of Banco de Miami.

---

[5] *Foreign exchange reserves* are holdings of the currencies of other countries—for example, Japanese yen—by the U.S. government. We discuss exchange rates and foreign exchange markets at length in Chapter 19.

Accounts at the Fed count as reserves, so FBF loses $100 in reserves, and Banco de Miami gains $100 in reserves. The two banks effectively have traded ownerships of their deposits at the Fed. The *total* volume of reserves has not changed, nor has the money supply.

This way of clearing interbank payments allows banks to shift money around virtually instantaneously. All they need to do is wire the Fed and request a transfer, and the funds move from one computer account to another.

Besides facilitating the transfer of funds among banks, the Fed is responsible for many of the regulations governing banking practices and standards. For example, the Fed has the authority to control mergers among banks, and it is responsible for examining banks to ensure that they are financially sound and that they conform to a host of government accounting regulations. As we saw previously, the Fed also sets reserve requirements for all financial institutions.

**lender of last resort** One of the functions of the Fed: It provides funds to troubled banks that cannot find any other sources of funds.

An important responsibility of the Fed is to act as the **lender of last resort** for the banking system. As our discussion of goldsmiths suggested, banks are subject to the possibility of runs on their deposits. In the United States, most deposits of less than $250,000 are insured by the Federal Deposit Insurance Corporation (FDIC), a U.S. government agency that was established in 1933 during the Great Depression. Deposit insurance makes panics less likely but the Fed stands ready to provide funds to a troubled bank that cannot find any other sources of funds.

The Fed is the ideal lender of last resort for two reasons. As a nonprofit institution whose function is to serve the overall welfare of the public, the Fed has an interest in preventing catastrophic banking panics such as those that occurred in the late 1920s and the 1930s. The Fed also has an essentially unlimited supply of funds with which to help banks facing the possibility of runs since as we shall see, it can create reserves at will. These administrative and regulatory functions of the Fed are important, but its central function is to help manage the macroeconomy by setting the interest rate. To see how this process works we need to add to our analysis a discussion of the demand for money, to which we now turn.

**10.4 LEARNING** OBJECTIVE

Describe the determinants of money demand.

# The Demand for Money

Think about the financial assets of a household. Some of those assets are held in what we have called in this chapter M1 money, cash and checking accounts offering little or no interest but great convenience in use. One can access these accounts by withdrawing money, but also by using a debit card or smartphone connected to a checking account. Other assets likely held by a household include interest-bearing savings accounts and securities which are less convenient to use, but do earn interest. In this section we consider how households think about dividing their assets between these two broad categories. What determines how much money people choose to hold?

As we have seen, one of the major functions of money is as a means of exchange, to facilitate transactions. We have already discussed the transactions use of money. Convenience in transactions is an obvious motive for people to hold some money, rather than keep all their assets in a harder-to-use savings account. In this section we consider what determines *how much* money people choose to hold. We will assume in this discussion that money as we are defining it earns no interest. It can take the form of either cash or deposits in non-interest-bearing checking accounts. Note that if debit cards or cell phones are used to pay for items in stores, deposits in checking accounts are needed to back this up. So "money" is being used for these kinds of payments.

Consider a simple example of how the decision to hold money versus an interest-bearing instrument might work. We will also assume for simplicity that there is only one other form other than money in which financial assets can be held, namely in a "savings account," which earns interest. Say at the end of the month the firm you work for deposits $5,000 in your checking account. If you leave the deposits in your checking account, you earn no interest. If you move some or all to your savings account, you earn interest on the amount moved. How much should you move? The gain from moving is the interest you earn on the amount moved. The constraint is that you may need the deposits in your checking account to support your transactions, via checks, debit card, or smartphone. The deposits in your checking account support your transactions. The more of your assets you move to your savings account, the more often you will have to move deposits back to your checking account as it is drawn down by your transactions.

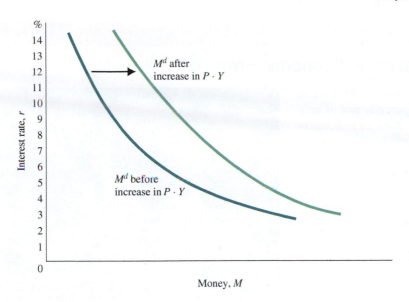

◀ **FIGURE 10.5**  **The Demand for Money**
The quantity of money demanded (Md) depends negatively on the interest rate because the opportunity cost of holding money decreases as the interest rate falls. An increase in transactions ($P * Y$) shifts the money demand curve to the right.

We thus have a typical economic trade-off here. You gain interest by moving checking account deposits to your savings account, but the more you move, the more often you will have to move some back, which is costly in time. How much should you move? Here is where the interest rate plays a key role. The higher the interest rate, the more costly it is to keep deposits in your checking account. If the interest rate is close to zero, as it has been for a number of years, you earn very little by moving deposits to your savings account, so there is little reason to do so. There is a time cost of moving deposits back and forth, and there is no reason to bear this cost if you are earning practically nothing on your savings account. On the other hand, if the interest rate rises, the opportunity cost of keeping deposits in your checking account rises, and you should move some of the deposits to your savings account. The higher the interest rate, the more deposits you should keep on average in your savings account, other things being equal. Or, put another way, the higher the interest rate, the less on average you should hold in the form of money in your checking account. The amount of money you should hold thus depends negatively on the interest rate. Again, this is because a high interest rate means the opportunity cost of holding money is high because of the interest lost by not moving deposits to your savings account. You trade off convenience against an interest rate.

The amount of money you want to hold obviously also depends on the size of your transactions. The more you spend in a given period, the more deposits on average you will want to have in your checking account, other things being equal. If you hold very little in your checking account relative to the size of your transactions, the more time you will need to spend moving deposits from your savings account to your checking account, which is costly.

To summarize then, the demand for money depends positively on the size of total transactions in a period and negatively on the interest rate. In what follows we will use nominal income $P * Y$ as the measure of transactions. Figure 10.5 shows the demand for money schedule. The schedule slopes down because, as just discussed, the demand for money rises as the interest rate falls. The figure also shows that the demand for money curve shifts to the right as $P * Y$ increases because of the increase in transactions. The relationship between money demand and the interest rate will be an important part of our story of monetary policy and the Fed.

# Interest Rates and Security Prices

**10.5 LEARNING** OBJECTIVE

Define interest and discuss the relationship between interest rates and security prices.

Before we discuss how the Fed controls the interest rate, we need to briefly digress and consider the relationship between interest rates and security prices.

In our discussion thus far we have described the way in which households choose between holding money and holding their assets in interest-bearing securities or accounts. Interest-bearing

# ECONOMICS IN PRACTICE

## Professor Serebryakov Makes an Economic Error

In Chekhov's play *Uncle Vanya*, Alexander Vladimirovitch Serebryakov, a retired professor, but apparently not of economics, calls his household together to make an announcement. He has retired to his country estate, but he does not like living there. Unfortunately, the estate does not derive enough income to allow him to live in town. To his gathered household, he thus proposes the following:

> Omitting details, I will put it before you in rough outline. Our estate yields on an average not more than two per cent, on its capital value. I propose to sell it. If we invest the money in suitable securities, we should get from four to five per cent, and I think we might even have a few thousand roubles to spare for buying a small villa in Finland.

This idea was not well received by the household, especially by Uncle Vanya, who lost it for a while and tried to kill Professor Serebryakov, but no one pointed out that this was bad economics. As discussed in the text, if you buy a bond and interest rates rise, the price of your bond falls. What Professor Serebryakov does not realize is that what he is calling the capital value of the estate, on which he is earning 2 percent, is not the value for which he could sell the estate if the interest rate on "suitable" securities is 5 percent. If an investor in Russia can earn 5 percent on these securities, why would he or she buy an estate earning only 2 percent? The price of the estate would have to fall until the return to the investor was 5 percent. To make matters worse, it may have been that the estate was a riskier investment than the securities, and if this were so,

a return higher than 5 percent would have been required on the estate purchase to compensate the investor for the extra risk. This would, of course, lower the price of the estate even more. In short, this is not a scheme by which the professor could earn more money than what the estate is currently yielding. Perhaps had Uncle Vanya taken an introductory economics course and known this, he would have been less agitated.

### THINKING PRACTICALLY

1. What would happen to the value of the estate if the interest rate on the securities that Professor Serebryakov is talking about fell?

securities are issued by firms and the government seeking to borrow money. Short-term securities are usually called "bills," and long-term securities are usually called "bonds." Both types of securities work in similar ways. To induce lenders to buy these securities and provide funds, borrowers promise no only to return the funds borrowed at some later date but also to pay interest. For our discussion we will look at a 10-year U.S. Treasury security, a government bond.

Bonds are issued with a face value, typically in denominations of $1,000. They also come with a maturity date, which is the date the borrower agrees to pay the lender the face value of the bond. A bond also specifies a fixed dollar payment that will be paid to the bondholder each year. This payment is known as a coupon. Say that on January 2, 2015, the U.S. Treasury issued a 10-year bond that had a face value of $1,000 and paid a coupon of $20 per year. The bond was sold on this date in the bond market. The price at which the bond sold would be whatever price the market determined it to be. Say that the market-determined price was in fact $1,000. (The Treasury when issuing bonds tries to choose the coupon to be such that the price that the bond initially sells for is roughly equal to its face value.) The lender would give the Treasury a check for $1,000, and every January for the next 10 years the Treasury would send the lender a check for $20. Then on January 2, 2025, the Treasury would send the lender a check for the face value of the bond—$1,000—plus the last coupon payment—$20—and that would square all accounts.

In this example the interest rate that the lender receives each year on his or her $1,000 investment is 2 percent. In return for the $1,000 payment the lender receives $20 each year, or 2 percent of the market price of the bond.

Suppose that just before the government put its bond on the market, many other, identical-looking bonds were offered to lenders with coupons of $30, face values of $1,000, and maturity of 10 years. And suppose that these bonds were selling for $1,000. Could the Treasury still sell its bond? The answer is yes, but at a lower price. What would that price be? The other securities are offering lenders 3 percent interest, so the Treasury will have to do the same. With a coupon value fixed at $20, the only way to raise the interest rate to the required 3 percent is to lower the price of the bond. The market price of the bond will be less than $1,000.

A key relationship that we can see from this example and that we will use later in this chapter is that market-determined prices of existing bonds and interest rates are inversely related. When the Treasury (or a firm) issues a bond, the face value, coupon, and maturity are set. This means that the market price of the bond will change as market interest rates change. When interest rates rise, prices of existing bonds fall. We will use the inverse relationship between interest rates and bond prices as we explore monetary policy post 2008 near the end of the next section. We turn now to put money supply and money demand together to look at how monetary policy works through the Fed.

# How the Federal Reserve Controls the Interest Rate

**10.6 LEARNING OBJECTIVE**
Understand how the Fed can change the interest rate.

## Tools Prior to 2008

Traditionally the Fed had three tools available to it to control the interest rate via changing the money supply: open market operations, changing the reserve requirement ratio, and changing the discount rate that banks pay to the Fed to borrow reserves.

Consider again Figure 10.2. We see in this figure that if commercial bank reserves increase by $100 with a reserve requirement ratio of 20 percent, bank loans can increase by $400, with the money supply increasing by $500 ($400 in loans plus the initial $100 in reserves). This calculation assumes that no excess reserves are held. So one way the Fed can increase the money supply is by simply increasing reserves. How does the Fed do this? Its principal tool is to buy U.S. Treasury securities from the banks, which the banks hold. These securities do not count as reserves when held by the banks. If the Fed buys $100 in securities from a bank, it credits the bank with $100 in reserves. The bank's reserves have gone up by $100, so it can make loans of $400, thus increasing the money supply by $500. (We are assuming a single-bank economy, but the analysis goes through with many banks, as in Figure 10.3.) Conversely, if the Fed sells $100 in securities, the bank's reserves go down by $100 (the securities are paid for by the bank by a debit to the bank's reserves), and loans must be decreased by $400, thus decreasing the money supply by $500. This buying and selling of government securities by the Fed is called **open market operations**. Prior to 2008, when essentially no excess reserves were held by banks, it was the main way in which the Fed changed the money supply.

**open market operations** The purchase and sale by the Fed of government securities in the open market.

Deposits in Figure 10.2 can also be increased if the reserve requirement ratio is lowered. We have already seen this in our discussion of the creation of money. If the reserve requirement ratio were 10 percent rather than 20 percent, loans of $900 could be made, thus increasing the money supply (deposits) to $1,000. Conversely, if the reserve requirement ratio were increased, loans would have to fall and thus the money supply (deposits) would fall. In the period before 2008, when banks rarely held excess reserves, changing the reserve requirement ratio was another tool the Fed could use to change the money supply, although it used this tool infrequently.

Banks also have the option to borrow reserves from the Fed, which they did now and again prior to 2008. Borrowed reserves are counted as reserves that can back loans, so when there is an increase in borrowed reserves, there is an increase in the money supply as banks increase their loans. Banks pay interest on the borrowed reserves, called the **discount rate**, and so a third way the Fed can increase the money supply is to lower the discount rate, inducing banks to borrow more and thus expand loans. Conversely, the Fed can raise the discount rate, inducing banks to pay back some of their borrowed reserves and thus contract loans. This third tool to change the money supply, changing the discount rate, was also infrequently used.

**discount rate** The interest rate that banks pay to the Fed to borrow from it.

How do these tools give the Fed the ability to control the interest rate? We have just seen that when no excess reserves are held, the Fed can change the money supply through one of the three tools, the main tool being open market operations. The Fed can thus set the value of the money supply, the quantity of money, at whatever it wants. Assuming that the money market clears, which it does in practice, we can combine the demand for money schedule in Figure 10.5 with the money supply that the Fed chooses to determine the equilibrium value of the interest rate. This is done in Figure 10.6. Given the quantity of money that the Fed chooses to supply, the interest rate can simply be read off the money demand schedule. A value of $M_0$ leads to an interest rate of $r_0$ in the figure. Figure 10.6 also shows that if the Fed increases the money supply, from $M_0$ to $M_1$, the interest rate falls from $r_0$ to $r_1$. So any change in the money supply that the Fed might make leads to a change in the interest rate, with the magnitude of the interest rate change depending on the shape of the money demand function.

Prior to 2008 the preceding discussion would be the end of the story. Banks essentially held no excess reserves, and the Fed engaged in open market operations to change the money supply and the interest rate. This channel for monetary policy changed in 2008, as the Fed responded to the financial crisis.

## Expanded Fed Activities Beginning in 2008

In March 2008, faced with many large financial institutions simultaneously in serious financial trouble, the Fed began to broaden its role in the banking system. No longer would it be simply a lender of last resort to banks, but it would become an active participant in the private banking system. How did this change come about?

Beginning in about 2003, the U.S. economy experienced rapidly rising housing prices, in what some called a "housing bubble." Financial institutions began issuing mortgages with less oversight, in some cases to households with poor credit ratings (so-called sub prime borrowers). Some households bought homes they could not afford based on their incomes, expecting to eventually "cash in" on the rising housing prices. Regulation, by the Fed or other federal or state agencies, was lax, and many financial firms took very large risks. When housing prices began to fall in late 2005, the stage was set for a financial crisis. Financial institutions, even large ones, began to experience very large losses, as home owners began defaulting on their loans, setting off a chain reaction that many people thought threatened the economic system.

The Fed responded to these events in a number of ways. In March 2008 it participated in an attempted bailout of Bear Stearns, a large financial institution, by guaranteeing $30 billion of Bear Stearns' liabilities to JPMorgan. On September 7, 2008, it participated in a government takeover of the Federal National Mortgage Association (Fannie Mae) and the Federal Home Loan Mortgage Corporation (Freddie Mac), which at that time owned or guaranteed about half of the $12 trillion mortgage market in the United States. On September 17, 2008, the Fed loaned $85 billion to the

▶ **FIGURE 10.6** **The Equilibrium Interest Rate**
Given a value of the money supply that the Fed chooses, the equilibrium interest rate can be read off of the money demand schedule. If the Fed increases the money supply from $M_0$ to $M_1$, the interest rate falls from $r_0$ to $r_1$.

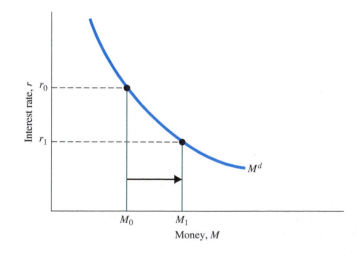

American International Group (AIG) insurance company to help it avoid bankruptcy. In mid-September, the Fed urged Congress to pass a $700 billion bailout bill, which was signed into law on October 3.

In the process of bailing out Fannie Mae and Freddie Mac, in September 2008 the Fed began buying securities of these two associations, called "federal agency debt securities." More remarkable, however, is that in January 2009 the Fed began buying mortgage-backed securities, securities that the private sector was reluctant to hold because of their perceived riskiness, and long-term government bonds. By September 2012 the Fed was buying mortgage-backed securities and long-term government bonds to the tune of $85 billion per month. This practice ended in November 2014. Most of these purchases ended up as an increase in excess reserves of commercial banks, as we will see in the next section.

As is not surprising, there has been much political discussion of whether the Fed should have regulated financial institutions more in 2003–2005 and whether its subsequent active role in the system was warranted. Whatever one's views, it is certainly the case that the Fed has taken a much more active role in financial markets since 2008.

## The Federal Reserve Balance Sheet

The expanded Fed activities we have just described can be seen clearly by examining the way in which the Fed's balance sheet changed during the period after 2008.

Although the Fed is a special bank, it is similar to an ordinary commercial bank in that it has a balance sheet that records its asset and liability position at any moment of time. The balance sheet for April 9, 2015, is presented in Table 10.1.

On April 9, 2015, the Fed had $4,528 billion in assets, of which $11 billion was gold, $2,460 billion was U.S. Treasury securities, $37 billion was federal agency debt securities, $1,732 billion was mortgage-backed securities, and $288 billion was other.

Gold is trivial. *Do not think that this gold has anything to do with money in circulation*. Most of the gold was acquired during the 1930s, when it was purchased from the U.S. Treasury Department. Since 1934, the dollar has not been backed by (is not convertible into) gold. You cannot take a dollar bill to the Fed to receive gold for it; all you can get for your old dollar bill is a new dollar bill.[6] Although it is unrelated to the money supply, the Fed's gold counts as an asset on its balance sheet because it is something of value the Fed owns.

U.S. Treasury securities are the traditional assets held by the Fed. These are obligations of the federal government that the Fed has purchased over the years. As we discussed previously, when banks hold no excess reserves the buying and selling of Treasury securities (open market operations) is the way the Fed affects the money supply and the interest rate. Before the change in Fed behavior in 2008, almost all of its assets were in the form of U.S. Treasury securities. For

**TABLE 10.1**   Assets and Liabilities of the Federal Reserve System, April 9, 2015 (Billions of Dollars)

| Assets | | | Liabilities |
|---|---|---|---|
| Gold | $   11 | $1,363 | Currency in circulation |
| U.S. Treasury securities | 2,460 | 2,793 | Reserve balances (about 110 required) |
| Federal agency debt securities | 37 | 62 | U.S. Treasury deposits |
| Mortgage-backed securities | 1,732 | 310 | All other liabilities and net worth |
| All other assets | 288 | $4,528 | Total |
| Total | $4,528 | | |

*Source:* Federal Reserve Statistical Release, Factors affecting Reserve Balances, Board of Governors of the Federal Reserve System.

MyEconLab Real-time data

---

[6] The fact that the Fed is not obliged to provide gold for currency means it can never go bankrupt. When the currency was backed by gold, it would have been possible for the Fed to run out of gold if too many of its depositors came to it at the same time and asked to exchange their deposits for gold. If depositors come to the Fed to withdraw their deposits today, all they can get is dollar bills. The dollar was convertible into gold internationally until August 15, 1971.

example, in the ninth edition of this text, the balance sheet presented was for October 24, 2007, where total Fed assets were $885 billion, of which $780 billion were U.S. Treasury securities.

The new assets of the Fed (since 2008) are federal agency debt securities and mortgage-backed securities. (These were both zero in the October 24, 2007 balance sheet.) U.S. Treasury securities, federal agency debt securities, and mortgage-backed securities now total $4.229 trillion. The Fed's intervention in these markets has been huge. Of the Fed's liabilities, $1,363 billion is currency in circulation, $2,793 billion is reserve balances, $62 billion is U.S. Treasury deposits, and $310 billion is other. The Fed acts as a bank for the U.S. government, and so U.S. Treasury deposits are held by the U.S. government at the Fed. When the government needs to pay for something like a new aircraft carrier, it may write a check to the supplier of the ship drawn on its "checking account" at the Fed. Similarly, when the government receives revenues from tax collections, fines, or sales of government assets, it may deposit these funds at the Fed.

Currency in circulation accounts for about 30 percnt of the Fed's liabilities. The dollar bill that you use to buy a pack of gum is clearly an asset from your point of view. Because every financial asset is by definition a liability of some other agent in the economy, whose liability is the dollar bill? The dollar bill is a liability—an IOU—of the Fed. It is, of course, a strange IOU because it can only be redeemed for another IOU of the same type. It is nonetheless classified as a liability of the Fed.

Reserve balances account for about 62 percent of the Fed's liabilities. These are the reserves that commercial banks hold at the Fed. Remember that commercial banks are required to keep a certain fraction of their deposits at the Fed. These deposits are assets of the commercial banks and liabilities of the Fed. What is remarkable about the $2,793 billion in reserve balances at the Fed is that only about $110 billion are required reserves. The rest—more than $2,600 billion—are excess reserves, reserves that the commercial banks could lend to the private sector if they wanted to. The existence of these excess reserves complicates our story of the Fed's operations.

## Tools After 2008

After 2008 we see that we are no longer in a world of zero excess reserves. Indeed, excess reserves on April 9, 2015, were more than $2.6 trillion, which is considerably above zero! What does this do to the Fed's ability to change the money supply and the interest rate?

Since the end of 2008 the short-term interest rate has been low, close to but not quite zero. However, by the spring of 2015 the financial markets expected that the Fed would begin raising the interest rate by at least the fall of 2015. How can the Fed do this? Not through the traditional tools of open market operations, reserve requirement ratio, and discount rate. Consider open market operations. Prior to 2008 the Fed would sell government securities, which would decrease reserves, contract bank loans, drive down the money supply, and thus increase the interest rate. Now, however, if the Fed sold government securities, the securities would mostly be bought by the banks with their excess reserves. Bank reserves would decrease, but with ample excess reserves remaining no contraction in bank loans is needed. Look at Table 10.1. If the Fed sold $1 trillion in U.S. Treasury securities, there would be a fall in U.S. Treasury securities of $1 trillion and a fall in Reserve balances of $1 trillion. Both Fed assets and liabilities would be lower by $1 trillion, but there would be no change in the interest rate! Banks would now have $1 trillion less in reserves, but still have more than $1.6 trillion in excess reserves. Just swapping Treasury securities for reserves does not change the interest rate. For the same reason, changing the reserve requirement ratio is also useless: the banks are already well over the requirement.

When the time comes that the Fed wants to raise the interest rate, the tool that it will probably use is to increase the rate it pays to banks on their reserves. Beginning in the post-2008 period, the Fed began paying a small interest rate on the bank reserves it holds. Indeed, this may help to explain why banks are holding these reserves rather than lending them out. The interest rate that the Fed pays on reserves is about the same as the interest rate on short-term U.S. Treasury securities (small, but not zero). (The following analysis is somewhat speculative because as of the time of this writing, September 2015, the Fed had not yet tried to increase the interest rate.) Suppose the Fed decided to raise the rate it pays banks on their reserves by 0.50 percentage points. What effect does this have on the short-term U.S. Treasury securities market? With some simplification, the story is roughly as follows. Banks hold both reserves and Treasury securities. Before the Fed increases the rate paid on bank reserves, the interest rate on reserves and short-term Treasury securities is roughly the same. After the Fed's move, the interest rate on reserves is 0.50 points higher. This higher rate induces banks to try to sell their now unattractive securities to the Fed. If the Fed won't buy, the price of the securities will fall because supply has increased and demand is unchanged. As we saw in the previous section, when the price of a security falls, the interest rate rises, so with security prices falling, the interest rate on the securities rises. The new equilibrium will be where the interest rate on the securities is also 0.50 points higher. The interest rate on short-term Treasury securities can thus be changed by the Fed simply increasing the rate it pays on bank reserves. This requires no change in the Fed's balance sheet.

Finally, we should add that when the Fed changes the short-term interest rate, this also changes longer-term interest rates. This is briefly explained in the appendix to this chapter. The appendix also discusses some of the key interest rates in the U.S. economy. Although in the text we are primarily focusing on one interest rate, denoted $r$, in practice there are many.

## Looking Ahead

This has been a long chapter, but for future analysis we really only need one point, namely that the Fed has the ability to control the short-term interest rate. Before 2008 it did this primarily through open market operations, and in the future (2015 or later) it will probably do this by changing the rate it pays banks on their reserves with the Fed.

---

## — S U M M A R Y —

### 10.1 AN OVERVIEW OF MONEY  *p. 188*

1. Money has three distinguishing characteristics: (1) a *means of payment*, or *medium of exchange*; (2) *a store of value*; and (3) *a unit of account*. The alternative to using money is *barter*, in which goods are exchanged directly for other goods. Barter is costly and inefficient in an economy with many different kinds of goods.

2. *Commodity monies* are items that are used as money and that have an intrinsic value in some other use—for example, gold and cigarettes. *Fiat monies* are intrinsically worthless apart from their use as money. To ensure the acceptance of fiat monies, governments use their power to declare money *legal tender* and promise the public they will not debase the currency by expanding its supply rapidly.

3. There are various definitions of money. Currency plus demand deposits plus traveler's checks plus other checkable deposits compose M1, or *transactions money*—money that can be used directly to buy things. The addition of savings accounts and money market accounts (*near monies*) to M1 gives M2, or *broad money*.

### 10.2 HOW BANKS CREATE MONEY  *p. 192*

4. The *required reserve ratio* is the percentage of a bank's deposits that must be kept as *reserves* at the nation's central bank, the *Federal Reserve*.

5. Banks create money by making loans. When a bank makes a loan to a customer, it creates a deposit in that customer's account. This deposit becomes part of the money supply. Banks can create money only when they have *excess reserves*—reserves in excess of the amount set by the required reserve ratio.

6. The *money multiplier* is the multiple by which the total supply of money can increase for every dollar increase in reserves. The money multiplier is equal to 1/required reserve ratio.

### 10.3 THE FEDERAL RESERVE SYSTEM  *p. 198*

7. The Fed's most important function is controlling the short-term interest rate. The Fed also performs several other functions: It clears interbank payments, is responsible for many of the regulations governing banking practices and standards, and acts as a *lender of last resort* for troubled banks that cannot find any other sources of funds. The Fed also acts as the bank for the U.S. government.

### 10.4 THE DEMAND FOR MONEY  *p. 200*

8. The demand for money depends negatively on the interest rate. The higher the interest rate, the higher the opportunity cost (more interest forgone) from holding money and the less money people will want to hold. An increase in the interest rate reduces the quantity demanded for money, and the money demand curve slopes downward.

---

**MyEconLab** Visit **www.myeconlab.com** to complete these exercises online and get instant feedback. Exercises that update with real-time data are marked with art ⬤.

9. The demand for money depends positively on nominal income. Aggregate nominal income is $P \cdot Y$, where $P$ is the aggregate price level and $Y$ is aggregate real income. An increase in either $P$ or $Y$ increases the demand for money.

## 10.5 INTEREST RATES AND SECURITY PRICES   *p. 201*

10. Interest rates and security prices are inversely related. If market interest rates rise, prices of existing bonds fall.

## 10.6 HOW THE FEDERAL RESERVE CONTROLS THE INTEREST RATE   *p. 203*

11. Prior to 2008 the Fed had three tools to control the money supply: (1) changing the required reserve ratio, (2) changing the *discount rate* (the interest rate member banks pay when they borrow from the Fed), and (3) engaging in *open market operations* (the buying and selling of already-existing government securities). To increase the money supply, the Fed could create additional reserves by lowering the discount rate or by buying government securities, or the Fed could increase the number of deposits that can be created from a given quantity of reserves by lowering the required reserve ratio. To decrease the money supply, the Fed could reduce reserves by raising the discount rate or by selling government securities or it could raise the required reserve ratio.

12. In the post-2008 period large quantities of excess reserves have been held by banks. The Fed is now paying interest on these reserves. When the Fed wants to raise interest rates in the future it will likely do so by increasing the interest rate it pays on bank reserves.

## ——— REVIEW TERMS AND CONCEPTS ———

barter, *p. 188*

commodity monies, *p. 190*

currency debasement, *p. 190*

discount rate, *p. 203*

excess reserves, *p. 195*

Federal Open Market Committee (FOMC), *p. 198*

Federal Reserve Bank (the Fed), *p. 194*

fiat, *or* token, money, *p. 190*

legal tender, *p. 190*

lender of last resort, *p. 200*

liquidity property of money, *p. 189*

M1, *or* transactions money, *p. 191*

M2, *or* broad money, *p. 191*

medium of exchange, *or* means of payment, *p. 188*

money multiplier, *p. 197*

near monies, *p. 191*

Open Market Desk, *p. 198*

open market operations, *p. 203*

required reserve ratio, *p. 195*

reserves, *p. 194*

run on a bank, *p. 194*

store of value, *p. 188*

unit of account, *p. 189*

Equations:

M1 ≡ currency held outside banks + demand deposits + traveler's checks + other checkable deposits, *p. 191*

M2 ≡ M1 + savings accounts + money market accounts + other near monies, *p. 191*

Assets ≡ Liabilities + Net Worth, *p. 194*

Excess reserves ≡ actual reserves − required reserves, *p. 195*

$$\text{Money multiplier} \equiv \frac{1}{\text{required reserve ratio}}, \textit{p. 198}$$

## ——— PROBLEMS ———

All problems are available on MyEconLab.

## 10.1  AN OVERVIEW OF MONEY

LEARNING OBJECTIVE:  Define money and discuss its functions.

1.1 **[Related to the *Economics in Practice* on p. 189]** It is well known that cigarettes served as money for prisoners of war in World War II. Do an Internet search using the key word cigarettes and write a description of how this came to be and how it worked.

1.2 As king of Medivalia, you are constantly strapped for funds to pay your army. Your chief economic wizard suggests the following plan: "When you collect your tax payments from your subjects, insist on being paid in gold coins. Take those gold coins, melt them down, and remint them with an extra 10 percent of brass thrown in. You will then have 10 percent more money than you started with." What do you think of the plan? Will it work?

1.3 Why is M2 sometimes a more stable measure of money than M1? Explain in your own words using the definitions of M1 and M2.

1.4 After suffering two years of staggering hyperinflation, the African nation of Zimbabwe officially abandoned its currency, the Zimbabwean dollar, in April 2009 and made the U.S. dollar its official currency. Why would anyone in Zimbabwe be willing to accept U.S. dollars in exchange for goods and services?

1.5 Although the official currency of the United States is the U.S. dollar, some towns and cities actually issue their own money. In these communities, consumers are able to buy local currency at a discounted rate using U.S. dollars (for example, a consumer may spend 95 U.S. cents to buy one local dollar, thereby receiving a 5 percent discount), and then can spend the local currency at stores that have agreed to accept it. The idea is to help local consumers save money and at the same time give local businesses a boost. These local currencies are being issued in communities as diverse as small towns in North Carolina and Massachusetts to cities as large as Detroit, Michigan. Do these local currencies qualify as money based on the description of what money is in the chapter?

1.6 Suppose on your 21st birthday, your eccentric grandmother invites you to her house, takes you into her library, removes a black velvet painting of Elvis Presley from the wall, opens a hidden safe where she removes 50 crisp $100 bills, and hands them to you as a present, claiming you are her favorite grandchild. After thanking your grandmother profusely (and helping her rehang the picture of Elvis), you proceed to your bank and deposit half of your gift in your checking account and half in your savings account. How will these transactions affect M1 and M2? How will these transactions change M1 and M2 in the short run? What about the long run?"

## 10.2 HOW BANKS CREATE MONEY

**LEARNING OBJECTIVE:** Explain how banks create money.

2.1 For each of the following, determine whether it is an asset or a liability on the accounting books of a bank. Explain why in each case.
   – Cash in the vault
   – Demand deposits
   – Savings deposits
   – Reserves
   – Loans
   – Deposits at the Federal Reserve

2.2 The U.S. money supply (M1) at the beginning of 2015 was $2,683.3 billion broken down as follows: $1165.7 billion in currency, $3.5 billion in traveler's checks, and $1,514.1 billion in checking deposits. Suppose the Fed decided to decrease the money supply by increasing the reserve requirement from 10 percent to 12 percent. Assuming all banks were initially loaned up (had no excess reserves) and currency held outside of banks did not change, how large a change in the money supply would have resulted from the change in the reserve requirement?

2.3 Do you agree or disagree with each of the following statements? Explain your answers.
   **a.** When the Treasury of the United States issues bonds and sells them to the public to finance the deficit, the money supply remains unchanged because every dollar of money taken in by the Treasury goes right back into circulation through government spending. This is not true when the Fed sells bonds to the public.

   **b.** The money multiplier depends on the marginal propensity to save.

*2.4 When the Fed adds new reserves to the system, some of these new reserves find their way out of the country into foreign banks or foreign investment funds. In addition, some portion of the new reserves ends up in people's pockets and under their mattresses instead of in bank vaults. These "leakages" reduce the money multiplier and sometimes make it difficult for the Fed to control the money supply precisely. Explain why this is true.

2.5 You are given this account for a bank:

| Assets | | Liabilities | |
|---|---|---|---|
| Reserves | $1,200 | $8,000 | Deposits |
| Loans | 6,800 | | |

The required reserve ratio is 10 percent.
   **a.** How much is the bank required to hold as reserves given its deposits of $8,000?
   **b.** How much are its excess reserves?
   **c.** By how much can the bank increase its loans?
   **d.** Suppose a depositor comes to the bank and withdraws $500 in cash. Show the bank's new balance sheet, assuming the bank obtains the cash by drawing down its reserves. Does the bank now hold excess reserves? Is it meeting the required reserve ratio? If not, what can it do?

2.6 Suppose Ginger deposits $12,000 in cash into her checking account at the Bank of Skidoo. The Bank of Skidoo has no excess reserves and is subject to a 4 percent required reserve ratio.
   **a.** Show this transaction in a T-account for the Bank of Skidoo.
   **b.** Assume the Bank of Skidoo makes the maximum loan possible from Ginger's deposit to Thurston and show this transaction in a new T-account.
   **c.** Thurston decides to use the money he borrowed to purchase a sail boat. He writes a check for the entire loan amount to Gilligan's Seagoing Vessels, which deposits the check in its bank, the Paradise Bank of Kona, Hawaii. When the check clears, the Skidoo Bank transfers the funds to the Paradise Bank. Show these transactions in a new T-account for the Skidoo Bank and in a T-account for the Paradise Bank.
   **d.** What is the maximum amount of deposits that can be created from Ginger's initial deposit?
   **e.** What is the maximum amount of loans that can be created from Ginger's initial deposit?

## 10.3 THE FEDERAL RESERVE SYSTEM

**LEARNING OBJECTIVE:** Define the functions and structure of the Federal Reserve System.

3.1 The United States is divided into 12 Federal Reserve districts, each with a District Bank. These Districts and the locations for the District Bank in each region are shown in Figure 10.4. Do some research to find out why the districts are divided as they are, why the District Banks are located in the 12 cities shown in Figure 10.4, and why so many districts are located in the Eastern portion of the United States.

## 10.4   THE DEMAND FOR MONEY

LEARNING OBJECTIVE: Describe the determinants of money demand.

4.1   What if, at a low level of interest rates, the money demand curve became nearly horizontal, as in the following graph. That is, with interest rates so low, the public would not find it attractive to hold bonds; thus, money demand would be very high. Many argue that this was the position of the U.S. economy in 2003. If the Fed decided to expand the money supply in the graph, what would be the impact on interest rates?

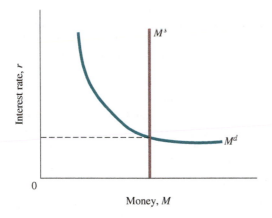

4.2   Explain why there is a negative relationship between the amount of money you should hold and the interest rate.

## 10.5   INTEREST RATES AND SECURITY PRICES

LEARNING OBJECTIVE: Define interest and discuss the relationship between interest rates and security prices.

5.1   [**Related to the *Economics in Practice* on p. 202**]
The *Economics in Practice* states that the capital value of Professor Serebryakov's estate is not the value for which he could sell the estate if the interest rate on "suitable" securities is higher than the average yield from the estate. What would happen to:
a.  the value of the estate if the interest rate on "suitable" securities rose?
b.  the value of the estate if investment in the estate was suddenly viewed as being less risky than investment in the securities?
c.  the yield on the securities if the securities were suddenly viewed as being more risky than was previously thought?

5.2   The United States entered a deep recession at the end of 2007. The Fed under Ben Bernanke used aggressive monetary policy to prevent the recession from becoming another Great Depression. The Fed Funds target rate was 5.25 percent in the fall of 2007; by mid-2008, it stood at 2 percent; and in January 2009, it went to a range of 0 – 0.25 percent, where it still stood through mid-2015. Lower interest rates reduce the cost of borrowing and encourage firms to borrow and invest. They also have an effect on the value of the bonds (private and government) outstanding in the economy. Explain briefly but clearly why the value of bonds changes when interest rates change. Go to federalreserve.gov, click on "Economic Research & Data," and click on "Flow of Funds." Look at the most recent release and find balance sheet table B.100. How big is the value of Credit Market Instruments held by households?

5.3   Normally, people from the United States and from around the world think of highly rated corporate or government bonds as a safe place to put their savings relative to common stocks. Because the stock market had performed so poorly during the recession and because many foreigners turned to the United States as a safe place to invest, bond sales boomed.

If you were a holder of high-grade fixed-rate bonds that you purchased a few years earlier when rates were much higher, you found yourself with big capital gains. That is, as rates went lower, the value of previously issued bonds increased.
a.  Suppose you bought a $10,000 ten-year fixed-rate bond issued by the U.S. Treasury in July 2007 that paid 5% interest. In July 2010, new seven-year fixed-rate bonds were being sold by the Treasury that paid 2.43%. Explain clearly what was likely to have happened to the value of your bond which still has seven years to run paying 5%.
b.  Why would bond prices rise if people feared a recession was coming?

## 10.6   HOW THE FEDERAL RESERVE CONTROLS THE INTEREST RATE

LEARNING OBJECTIVE: Understand how the Fed can change the interest rate.

6.1   In the Republic of Doppelganger, the currency is the ditto. During 2015, the Treasury of Doppelganger sold bonds to finance the Doppelganger budget deficit. In all, the Treasury sold 80,000 ten-year bonds with a face value of 1,000 dittos each. The total deficit was 80 million dittos. The Doppelganger Central Bank reserve requirement was 16 percent and in the same year, the bank bought 10 million dittos' worth of outstanding bonds on the open market. All of the Doppelganger debt is held by either the private sector (the public) or the central bank.
a.  What is the combined effect of the Treasury sale and the central bank purchase on the total Doppelganger debt outstanding? On the debt held by the private sector?
b.  What is the effect of the Treasury sale on the money supply in Doppelganger?

**c.** Assuming no leakage of reserves out of the banking system, what is the effect of the central bank purchase of bonds on the money supply?

6.2 In 2000, the federal debt was being paid down because the federal budget was in surplus. Recall that surplus means that tax collections (T) exceed government spending (G). The surplus (T − G) was used to buy back government bonds from the public, reducing the federal debt. As we discussed in this chapter, the main method by which the Fed increases the money supply is to buy government bonds by using open market operations. What is the impact on the money supply of using the fiscal surplus to buy back bonds? In terms of their impacts on the money supply, what is the difference between Fed open market purchases of bonds and Treasury purchases of bonds using tax revenues?

6.3 If the head of the Central Bank of Brazil wanted to decrease the supply of money in Brazil in 2015, which of the following would do it? Explain your answer.
Increase the required reserve ratio
Decrease the required reserve ratio
Increase the discount rate
Decrease the discount rate
Buy government securities in the open market
Sell government securities in the open market

6.4 Suppose in the Republic of Sasquatch that the regulation of banking rested with the Sasquatchian Congress, including the determination of the reserve ratio. The Central Bank of Sasquatch is charged with regulating the money supply by using open market operations. In September 2015, the money supply was estimated to be 84 million yetis. At the same time, bank reserves were 12.6 million yetis and the reserve requirement was 15 percent. The banking industry, being "loaned up," lobbied the Congress to cut the reserve ratio. The Congress yielded and cut required reserves to 12 percent. What is the potential impact on the money supply? Suppose the central bank decided that the money supply should not be increased. What countermeasures could it take to prevent the Congress from expanding the money supply?

6.5 What are the three traditional tools the Fed can use to control the interest rate via changing the money supply? Briefly describe how the Fed can use each of these tools to either increase or decrease the money supply.

# CHAPTER 10 APPENDIX

## The Various Interest Rates in the U.S. Economy

**LEARNING OBJECTIVE**

Explain the relationship between a 2-year interest rate and a 1-year interest rate.

Although there are many different interest rates in the economy, they tend to move up or down with one another. Here we discuss some of their differences. We first look at the relationship between interest rates on securities with different maturities, or terms. We then briefly discuss some of the main interest rates in the U.S. economy.

### The Term Structure of Interest Rates

The term structure of interest rates is the relationship among the interest rates offered on securities of different maturities. The key here is understanding issues such as these: How are these different rates related? Does a 2-year security (an IOU that promises to repay principal, plus interest, after 2 years) pay a lower annual rate than a 1-year security (an IOU to be repaid, with interest, after 1 year)? What happens to the rate of interest offered on 1-year securities if the rate of interest on 2-year securities increases?

Assume that you want to invest some money for 2 years and at the end of the 2 years you want it back. Assume that you want to buy government securities. For this analysis, we restrict your choices to two: (1) You can buy a 2-year security today and hold it for 2 years, at which time you cash it in (we will assume that the interest rate on the 2-year security is 3 percent per year), or (2) you can buy a 1-year security today. At the end of 1 year, you must cash this security in; you can then buy another 1-year security. At the end of the second year, you will cash in the second security. Assume that the interest rate on the first 1-year security is 2 percent.

Which would you prefer? Currently, you do not have enough data to answer this question. To consider choice (2) sensibly, you need to know the interest rate on the 1-year security that you intend to buy in the second year. This rate will not be known until the second year. All you know now is the rate on the 2-year security and the rate on the current 1-year security.

To decide what to do, you must form an expectation of the rate on the 1-year security a year from now. If you expect the 1-year rate (2 percent) to remain the same in the second year, you should buy the 2-year security. You would earn 3 percent per year on the 2-year security but only 2 percent per year on the two 1-year securities. If you expect the 1-year rate to rise to 5 percent a year from now, you should make the second choice. You would earn 2 percent in the first year, and you expect to earn 5 percent in the second year. The expected rate of return over the 2 years is about 3.5 percent, which is better than the 3 percent you can get on the 2-year security. If you expect the 1-year rate a year from now to be 4 percent, it does not matter much which of the two choices you make. The rate of return over the 2-year period will be roughly 3 percent for both choices.

We now alter the focus of our discussion to get to the topic we are really interested in—how the 2-year rate is determined. Assume that the 1-year rate has been set by the Fed and it is 2 percent. Also assume that people expect the 1-year rate a year from now to be 4 percent. What is the 2-year rate? According to a theory called the *expectations theory of the term structure of interest rates*, the 2-year rate is equal to the average of the current 1-year rate and the 1-year rate expected a year from now. In this example, the 2-year rate would be 3 percent (the average of 2 percent and 4 percent).

If the 2-year rate were lower than the average of the two 1-year rates, people would not be indifferent as to which security they held. They would want to hold only the short-term 1-year securities. To find a buyer for a 2-year security, the seller would be forced to increase the interest rate it offers on the 2-year security until it is equal to the average of the current 1-year rate and the expected 1-year rate for next year. The interest rate on the 2-year security will continue to rise until people are once again indifferent between one 2-year security and two 1-year securities.

Let us now return to Fed behavior. We know that the Fed can affect the short-term interest rate, but does it also affect long-term interest rates? The answer is "somewhat." Because the 2-year rate is an average of the current 1-year rate and the expected 1-year rate a year from now, the Fed influences the 2-year rate to the extent that it influences the current 1-year rate. The same holds for 3-year rates and beyond. The current short-term rate is a means by which the Fed can influence longer-term rates.

In addition, Fed behavior may directly affect people's expectations of the future short-term rates, which will then affect long-term rates. If the chair of the Fed testifies before Congress that raising short-term interest rates is under consideration, people's expectations of higher future short-term interest rates are likely to increase. These expectations will then be reflected in current long-term interest rates.

## Types of Interest Rates

The following are some widely followed interest rates in the United States.

**Three-Month Treasury Bill Rate**   Government securities that mature in less than a year are called *Treasury bills*, or sometimes *T-bills*. The interest rate on 3-month Treasury bills is probably the most widely followed short-term interest rate.

**Government Bond Rate**   Government securities with terms of 1 year or more are called *government bonds*. There are 1-year bonds, 2-year bonds, and so on, up to 30-year bonds. Bonds of different terms have different interest rates. The relationship among the interest rates on the various maturities is the term structure of interest rates that we discussed in the first part of this Appendix.

**Federal Funds Rate**   Banks borrow not only from the Fed but also from each other. If one bank has excess reserves, it can lend some of those reserves to other banks through the federal funds market. The interest rate in this market is called the *federal funds rate*—the rate banks are charged to borrow reserves from other banks.

The federal funds market is really a desk in New York City. From all over the country, banks with excess reserves to lend and banks in need of reserves call the desk and negotiate a rate of interest. Account balances with the Fed are changed for the period of the loan without any physical movement of money.

This borrowing and lending, which takes place near the close of each working day, is generally for 1 day ("overnight"), so the federal funds rate is a 1-day rate. It is the rate on which the Fed has the most effect through its open market operations.

**Commercial Paper Rate** Firms have several alternatives for raising funds. They can sell stocks, issue bonds, or borrow from a bank. Large firms can also borrow directly from the public by issuing "commercial paper," which is essentially short-term corporate IOUs that offer a designated rate of interest. The interest rate offered on commercial paper depends on the financial condition of the firm and the maturity date of the IOU.

**Prime Rate** Banks charge different interest rates to different customers depending on how risky the banks perceive the customers to be. You would expect to pay a higher interest rate for a car loan than General Motors would pay for a $1 million loan to finance investment. Also, you would pay more interest for an unsecured loan, a "personal" loan, than for one that was secured by some asset, such as a house or car, to be used as collateral.

The prime rate is a benchmark that banks often use in quoting interest rates to their customers. A very low-risk corporation might be able to borrow at (or even below) the prime rate. A less well-known firm might be quoted a rate of "prime plus three-fourths," which means that if the prime rate is, say, 5 percent, the firm would have to pay interest of 5.75 percent. The prime rate depends on the cost of funds to the bank; it moves up and down with changes in the economy.

**AAA Corporate Bond Rate** Corporations finance much of their investment by selling bonds to the public. Corporate bonds are classified by various bond dealers according to their risk. Bonds issued by General Motors are in less risk of default than bonds issued by a new risky biotech research firm. Bonds differ from commercial paper in one important way: Bonds have a longer maturity.

Bonds are graded in much the same way students are. The highest grade is AAA, the next highest AA, and so on. The interest rate on bonds rated AAA is the triple A corporate bond rate, the rate that the least risky firms pay on the bonds that they issue.

--- **APPENDIX PROBLEMS** ---

All problems are available on MyEconLab.

### APPENDIX 10: THE VARIOUS INTEREST RATES IN THE U.S. ECONOMY

**LEARNING OBJECTIVE:** Explain the relationship between a 2-year interest rate and a 1-year interest rate.

1A.1 The following table gives three key U.S. interest rates in 1980 and again in 1993:

| | 1980 (%) | 1993 (%) |
|---|---|---|
| Three-month U.S. government bills | 11.39 | 3.00 |
| Long-term U.S. government bonds | 11.27 | 6.59 |
| Prime rate | 15.26 | 6.00 |

Provide an explanation for the extreme differences that you see. Specifically, comment on (1) the fact that rates in 1980 were much higher than in 1993 and (2) the fact that the long-term rate was higher than the short-term rate in 1993 but lower in 1980.

# 11

# The Determination of Aggregate Output, the Price Level, and the Interest Rate

In the last three chapters we have been exploring the key elements of the macroeconomy one element at a time. In Chapters 8 and 9 we looked at how the output level in the economy is determined, keeping the interest rate and the price level fixed. In Chapter 10 we turned our attention to the interest rate, holding output and the price level fixed. We are now ready to bring together these key pieces of the economy—output, the price level, and the interest rate.

This chapter and the next one will give you the ability to think about the key issues policy makers face in trying to manage the economy. We will see how the output level is determined. We will see what forces push the overall price level up, creating inflation, in an economy. By the time you finish these two chapters, we hope you will be much better able to understand what lies behind many of the current policy debates in the United States.

As we complete the story in this chapter, we will focus on the behavior of two key players in the macroeconomy: firms, who make price and output decisions, and the Federal Reserve (the Fed), which controls the interest rate. We begin with the price and output decisions of firms, which will be summarized in an aggregate supply curve.

# The Aggregate Supply (AS) Curve

**Aggregate supply** is the total supply of goods and services in an economy. The **aggregate supply (AS) curve** shows the relationship between the aggregate quantity of output supplied by all the firms in an economy and the overall price level. To understand the aggregate supply curve, we need to understand something about the behavior of the individual firms that make up the economy.

Consider a situation in which all prices, including the price of labor (wages), simultaneously doubled. What would we expect to see happen to the level of output produced by the firms in this economy? Likely nothing. With all prices doubling, all costs double as well. In effect a firm is in exactly the same position it was in before the doubling. If wages and prices are both rising, firms get more for their products and pay proportionately more for workers. The AS curve in this case would be vertical. Product prices would increase, but firms would not increase output because it would not be profitable to do so. Indeed, as we will see later in this chapter, many economists think this describes reasonably well the long-run relationship between the aggregate price level and aggregate output, arguing that given enough time, price adjustments across all inputs and outputs will fall into line. We will have more to say about this long-run situation a bit later in the chapter.

Suppose, on the other hand, that wages and prices do not move at the same time. What do we expect the firms in our macroeconomy to do? If wages respond more slowly to a demand change than do product prices, firms will increase output as product prices rise and the profitability of output increases. Here the AS curve will have an upward slope, rather than being vertical. Many economists believe that in the short run wages do respond more slowly than prices, particularly at some points in the business cycle, and that the short-run AS curve in fact slopes up.

Before looking further at the shape of the AS curve, it is worth pointing out that the AS curve is *not* the sum of individual supply curves. First, we note that imperfectly competitive firms, who make up a substantial part of the economy, do not have individual supply curves. Firms choose both output and price at the same time. To derive an individual supply curve, we need to imagine calling out a price to a firm and having the firm tell us how much output it will supply at that price. We cannot do this if firms are also setting prices. What this means is that you should not think of the AS curve as being the sum of individual supply curves. If individual supply curves do not exist, we certainly can't add them together!

So if the AS curve is *not* the sum of individual supply curves, what is it? The AS curve shows what happens to the aggregate price level and aggregate output as aggregate demand rises and falls. The AS curve traces out aggregate output and aggregate price level points corresponding to different levels of aggregate demand. Although it is called an aggregate *supply* curve, it is really misnamed. It is better thought of as a "price/output response" curve—a curve that traces out the price decisions and output decisions of all firms in the economy under different levels of aggregate demand.

## Aggregate Supply in the Short Run

The AS curve (or price-output response curve) shows how changes in aggregate demand affect the price level and output in an economy. When aggregate demand in an economy increases, how much, if at all, does the price level increase? How much does output increase? Most economists believe that, at least for a period of time, an increase in aggregate demand will result in an increase in *both* the price level and output. Many economists also believe that how much a demand increase affects the price level versus output depends on the strength of the economy at the time the demand increase occurred. Figure 11.1 shows a curve reflecting these ideas. At low levels of aggregate output—for example, when the economy is in a recession—the aggregate supply curve is fairly flat and while at high levels of output—for example, when the economy is experiencing a boom—it is vertical or nearly vertical.

**Why an Upward Slope**  In our discussion so far, we noted that if all prices—including wages—move simultaneously, the AS curve will be vertical. So a key question in whether the short run AS curve slopes up or is vertical is whether wages are "sticky," moving more slowly

**11.1 LEARNING** OBJECTIVE

Define the aggregate supply curve and discuss shifts in the short-run AS curve.

**aggregate supply**  The total supply of all goods and services in an economy.

**aggregate supply (AS) curve**  A graph that shows the relationship between the aggregate quantity of output supplied by all firms in an economy and the overall price level.

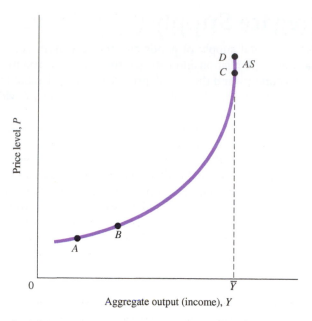

**▲ FIGURE 11.1** **The Short-Run Aggregate Supply Curve**
In the short run, the aggregate supply curve (the price/output response curve) has a positive slope. At low levels of aggregate output, the curve is fairly flat. As the economy approaches capacity, the curve becomes nearly vertical. At capacity, $\overline{Y}$, the curve is vertical.

than other prices. With sticky wages, demand increases occur without proportional wage increases and so firms' marginal cost curves do not shift proportionally. Here increases in prices make output increases more attractive. The empirical evidence suggests that wages do in fact lag prices, that they are slower to change. We discuss in Chapter 13 various reasons that have been advanced for why wages might be sticky in the short run. One key issue debated in macroeconomics is just how sticky wages might be, and how long it takes in practice for wages to adjust.

We should add a word of caution at this point. It may be that some of a firm's input costs are rising even in the short run after the aggregate demand increase has taken place because some of a firm's inputs may be purchased from other firms who are raising prices. For example, one input to a Dell computer is a chip produced by Intel or AMD. The fact that some of a firm's input costs rise along with a shift in the demand for its product complicates the picture because it means that at the same time there is an outward shift in a firm's demand curve, there is some upward shift in its marginal cost curve. In deriving an upward-sloping AS curve, we are in effect assuming that these kinds of input costs are small relative to wage costs. So the story is that wages are a large fraction of total costs and that wage changes lag behind price changes. This gives us an upward-sloping short-run AS curve.

**Why the Particular Shape?** Notice the AS curve in Figure 11.1 begins with a flat section and ends with a more-or-less vertical section. Why might the AS curve have this shape? It should not surprise you that the shape of the AS curve reflects economists' views on when in an economy we might expect wages to be most and least sticky.

Consider the vertical portion first. At some level the overall economy is using all its capital and all the labor that wants to work at the market wage. The economy is running full tilt. At this level ($\overline{Y}$), increased demand for output can be met only by increased prices and similarly for increased demand for labor. Neither wages nor prices are likely to be sticky at this level of economic activity.

What about the flat portion of the curve? Here we are at levels of output that are low relative to historical levels. Many firms are likely to have excess capacity in terms of their plant and equipment and their workforce. With excess capacity, firms may be able to increase output from A to B without a proportionate cost increase. Small price increases may thus be associated with relatively large output responses. We may also observe relatively sticky wages upward at this point on the AS curve if firms have held any excess workers in the downturn as a way to preserve worker morale or for other reasons.

# Shifts of the Short-Run Aggregate Supply Curve

The AS curve shows how the overall price level and output move with a change in aggregate demand, and we have seen that the answer to whether the price level or output is more affected depends on how the economy is doing at the time of the change. Now we can think about how other features of the economy might affect, or *shift*, the position of the AS curve.

What does a rightward shift of the AS curve mean? A rightward shift says that society can get a larger aggregate output at a given price level. What might cause such a shift? Clearly, if a society had an increase in labor or capital, the AS curve would shift to the right because the capacity of the economy would increase. Also, broad-based technical changes that increased productivity would shift the AS curve to the right by lowering marginal costs of production in the economy. With lower marginal costs, firms in the economy are willing to produce more for a given price level. Recall that the vertical part of the short-run AS curve represents the economy's maximum (capacity) output. This maximum output is determined by the economy's existing resources, like the size of its labor force, capital stock, and the current state of technology. The labor force grows naturally with an increase in the working-age population, but it can also increase for other reasons. Since the 1960s, for example, the percentage of women in the labor force has grown sharply. This increase in the supply of women workers has shifted the AS curve to the right. Immigration can also shift the AS curve. We discuss economic growth in more detail in Chapter 16.

We have focused on labor and capital as factors of production, but for a modern economy, energy is also an important input. New discoveries of oil or problems in the production of energy can also shift the AS curve through effects on the marginal cost of production in many parts of the economy.

Figures 11.2(a) and (b) show the effects of shifts in the short-run AS curve coming from changes in wage rates or energy prices. This type of shift is sometimes called a **cost shock or supply shock**. Oil has historically had quite volatile prices and has often been thought to contribute to shifts in the AS curve that, as we will shortly see, contribute to economy-wide fluctuations.

**cost shock, or supply shock**   A change in costs that shifts the short-run aggregate supply (AS) curve.

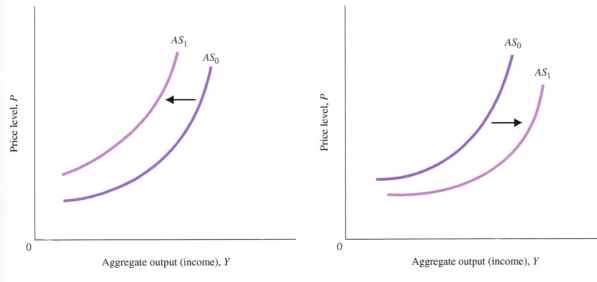

**a. A decrease in aggregate supply**

A leftward shift of the AS curve from $AS_0$ to $AS_1$ could be caused by an increase in costs—for example, an increase in wage rates or energy prices.

**b. An increase in aggregate supply**

A rightward shift of the AS curve from $AS_0$ to $AS_1$ could be caused by a decrease in costs—for example, a decrease in wage rates or energy prices or advances in technology.

▲ **FIGURE 11.2   Shifts of the Short-Run Aggregate Supply Curve**

**11.2 LEARNING OBJECTIVE**

Derive the aggregate demand curve and explain why the *AD* curve is downward sloping.

# The Aggregate Demand (*AD*) Curve

The *AS* curve in Figure 11.1 shows us all possible combinations of aggregate output and the price level consistent with firms' output and price decisions. But where on the curve will an economy be? To answer this question we need to consider the demand side of the economy. In this section we will derive an aggregate demand (*AD*) curve. This curve is derived from the model of the goods market in Chapters 8 and 9 and from the behavior of the Fed. We begin with the goods market.

## Planned Aggregate Expenditure and the Interest Rate

We can use the fact that planned investment depends on the interest rate to consider how planned aggregate expenditure (*AE*) depends on the interest rate. Recall that planned aggregate expenditure is the sum of consumption, planned investment, and government purchases. That is,

$$AE \equiv C + I + G$$

We know that there are many possible levels of *I*, each corresponding to a different interest rate. When the interest rate rises, planned investment falls. Therefore, a rise in the interest rate (*r*) will lead to a fall in total planned spending (*C* + *I* + *G*) as well.[1]

Figure 11.3 shows what happens to planned aggregate expenditure and output when the interest rate rises from 3 percent to 6 percent. At the higher interest rate, planned investment is lower; planned aggregate expenditure thus shifts *downward*. Recall from Chapters 8 and 9 that a fall in any component of aggregate spending has an even larger (or "multiplier") effect on output. When the interest rate rises, planned investment (and thus planned aggregate expenditure) falls and equilibrium output (income) falls by even more than the fall in planned investment. In Figure 11.3, equilibrium output falls from $Y_0$ to $Y_1$ when the interest rate rises from 3 percent to 6 percent.

We can summarize the effects of a change in the interest rate on the equilibrium level of output in the goods market. The effects of a change in the interest rate include:

- A high interest rate (*r*) discourages planned investment (*I*).
- Planned investment is a part of planned aggregate expenditure (*AE*).

▶ **FIGURE 11.3** **The Effect of an Interest Rate Increase on Planned Aggregate Expenditure and Equilibrium Output**
An increase in the interest rate from 3 percent to 6 percent lowers planned aggregate expenditure and thus reduces equilibrium output from $Y_0$ to $Y_1$.

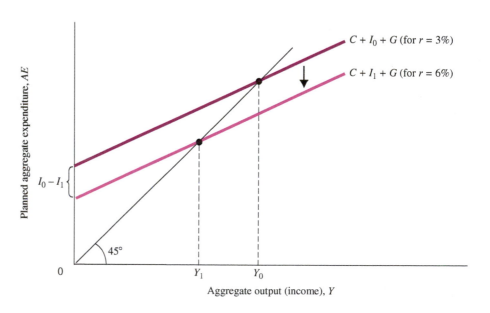

---

[1] When we look in detail in Chapter 16 at the behavior of households in the macroeconomy, we will see that consumption spending (*C*) is also stimulated by lower interest rates and discouraged by higher interest rates.

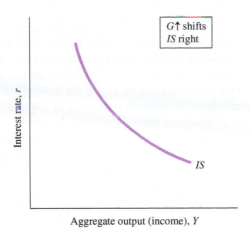

In the goods market, there is a negative relationship between output and the interest rate because planned investment depends negatively on the interest rate. Any point on the _IS_ curve is an equilibrium in the goods market for the given interest rate.

■ Thus, when the interest rate rises, planned aggregate expenditure (_AE_) at every level of income falls.

■ Finally, a decrease in planned aggregate expenditure lowers equilibrium output (income) (_Y_) by a multiple of the initial decrease in planned investment.

Using a convenient shorthand:

$$r\uparrow \;\longrightarrow\; I\downarrow \;\rightarrow\; AE\downarrow \;\rightarrow\; Y\downarrow$$
$$r\downarrow \;\rightarrow\; I\uparrow \;\rightarrow\; AE\uparrow \;\rightarrow\; Y\uparrow$$

This relationship between output and the interest rate is summarized in Figure 11.4. This curve is called the **_IS_ curve**. Any point on the _IS_ curve is an equilibrium in the goods market for the particular interest rate. Equilibrium means that planned investment equals saving, hence the _IS_ notation. It is noted in the box in the figure that an increase in government spending (_G_) shifts the _IS_ curve to the right. _With the interest rate fixed_, an increase in _G_ increases _AE_ and thus _Y_ in equilibrium. Just to be clear, this shift is shown in Figure 11.5. If for a given interest rate, an increase in _G_ increases output from $Y_1$ to $Y_2$, this is a shift of the _IS_ curve from $IS_1$ to $IS_2$.

**_IS_ curve**    Relationship between aggregate output and the interest rate in the goods market.

## The Behavior of the Fed

The _IS_ curve shows the relationship between the interest rate and output. When the interest rate is high, planned investment is low, so output is low. When the interest rate is low, planned investment is high, so output is high. But where on the curve is the actual economy? To answer this question we need to know the value of the interest rate. We know from Chapter 10 how the Fed controls the interest rate. This was the main point of Chapter 10. We will now consider

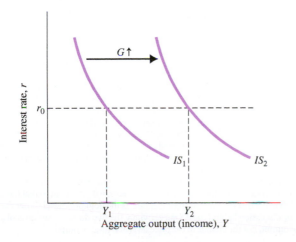

An increase in government spending (_G_) with the interest rate fixed increases output (_Y_), which is a shift of the _IS_ curve to the right.

*why* the Fed might want to change the interest rate. Every six weeks, the Federal Open Market Committee (FOMC) meets. This committee is headed by the chair of the Fed, currently Janet Yellen. The FOMC decides on the value of the interest rate (the exact rate it sets is called the "federal funds" rate). After the meeting, it instructs the Open Market Desk at the New York Federal Reserve Bank to buy or sell government securities until the desired interest rate value is reached.

The FOMC usually announces the interest rate value at 2:15 P.M. eastern time on the day it meets. This is a key time for financial markets around the world. At 2:14 P.M., thousands of people are staring at their computer screens waiting from word on high. If the announcement is a surprise, it can have large and immediate effects on bond and stock markets.

How does the Fed decide on what interest rate value to choose? The Fed's main goals are high levels of output and employment and a low rate of inflation. From the Fed's point of view, the best situation is a fully employed economy with a low inflation rate. The worst situation is stagflation—high unemployment and high inflation. In fact, the Humphrey-Hawkins Full Employment Act of 1978 mandated the Fed to aim for full employment and price stability, and when the bill was sunsetted in 2000, the expectation was that the Fed would continue to aim for full employment and price stability. In virtually all current announcements concerning the interest rate, the Fed makes reference to these two goals.

The Fed examines data on the current state of the economy, particularly output and inflation, and also considers the likely future course of the economy. In this setting, the Fed faces some hard choices. It knows—as we do from the *IS* curve in Figure 11.4—that increasing the interest rate will result in lower output, while reducing the interest rate will result in higher output. So one factor the Fed uses to choose the interest rate value is whether it believes output to be too low, too high, or about right. But we know that the Fed also cares about inflation. If the Fed finds inflation higher than it wishes, it will raise the interest rate, other things being equal, and vice versa if it finds inflation lower than it wishes.

The discussion so far has focused on output and inflation as the two main inputs into the Fed's interest rate decision. But the Fed is not just a mechanical calculator. The Fed chair brings to the FOMC meeting his or her own considerable expertise about the working of the economy. Janet Yellen, as you likely know, is a distinguished researcher, with experience both in academics and in running the San Francisco Fed. Most of the other members of the FOMC have long experience in business and economics. The Vice-Chair, Stanley Fisher, was an MIT professor and more recently the head of the Bank of Israel. As the Fed thinks about its interest rate setting, it considers factors other than current output and inflation. Levels of consumer confidence, possible fragility of the domestic banking sector, and possible financial problems abroad, say a potential euro crisis, may play a role in its interest rate decision. For our purposes we will label all these factors (all factors except output and inflation) as "Z" factors. These factors lie outside our model, and they are likely to vary from period to period in ways that are hard to predict.

**Fed rule** Equation that shows how the Fed's interest rate decision depends on the state of the economy.

If we put all of this together, we can describe the interest rate behavior of the Fed by using a simple linear equation, which we will call the **Fed rule**:

$$r = \alpha Y + \beta P + \gamma Z$$

Describing the Fed rule via an equation will allow us to incorporate Fed behavior formally into the *AS/AD* model we are building.[2] It is, of course, only an approximation as to how the Fed actually behaves.

---

[2] The Fed rule used here differs somewhat from that advocated for teaching purposes by David Romer, "Keynesian Macroeconomics without the LM Curve," *Journal of Economic Perspectives*, 14, Spring 2000, 149–169. First, the left-hand side variable is the nominal interest rate (*r*) rather than the real interest rate advocated by Romer. The Fed does in fact set the nominal rate at each FOMC meeting, so the use of the nominal rate is more realistic and easier to understand for students. Second, the price level, not the rate of inflation, is used in the rule. The *AS/AD* model is a static model. Introducing inflation brings in dynamics, which complicates the analysis. *P* is used here instead of the change in *P*. The insights still hold, and the story is much simpler. Third, the nominal interest rate is used in the (real) goods market in the determination of planned investment. Again, this is an approximation to avoid dynamics, and the insights still hold.

The research of one of the authors (Fair) actually supports the use of the nominal rate in the goods market. The results suggest that people (both consumers and investors) respond more to nominal rates than to real rates. Also, the left-hand side variable in Fair's price equation in his U.S. macroeconometric model is the (log) price level rather than the rate of inflation. This equation is consistent with the discussion behind the *AS* curve, where the two decision variables of a firm are taken to be the firm's price level and level of output, not the change in the price level and level of output.

# ECONOMICS IN PRACTICE

## The Federal Reserve Bank gets a New Chair, Janet Yellen

On January 6, 2014, Janet Yellen began her term as the Chair of the Board of Governors of the Federal Reserve System. Yellen is the first woman to serve in this post and the first Democrat since Paul Volcker ended his term in 1979.

Yellen came to the Chair position from a mix of academic and public sector experience. She holds a BA from Brown, a PhD from Yale, and has held positions at Harvard University and the University of California, Berkeley, for much of her career. While in academics, Yellen wrote on a wide range of topics, both in microeconomics and in macroeconomics. At Harvard, Yellen wrote an important paper in the field of industrial organization on bundling with Jim Adams from Michigan, pursuing pricing questions like: Why is it that MacDonald's prices a bundle that includes soda, fries, and a burger, rather than just selling them separately? But most of Yellen's work is in the area of macroeconomics, particularly on the puzzle of unemployment, a puzzle we explore in this text. What keeps wages from falling in times of unemployment? Why do we not see labor markets clearing in the way we see other markets clearing? These questions still form the basis on which much macro research is pursued.

Before being appointed as Chair of the Fed, Yellen served as its Vice Chair. She was also President of the San Francisco Fed and a member of the Council of Economic Advisors.

### THINKING PRACTICALLY

1. The Fed Chair is sometimes said to be the second most powerful person in the United States after the President. Why might this be so?

---

What does this equation tell us? We will assume that the three coefficients, $\alpha$, $\beta$, and $\gamma$, are positive. When output is high, all else equal, the Fed favors a higher interest rate then it would in a low-output economy. Likewise, when the price level is high, all else equal, the Fed favors a higher interest rate then it would when price stability is not a problem. High interest rates will thus be associated with high output and price levels. Positive coefficients tell us that the Fed "leans against the wind." That is, when output and/or the price level are high, the Fed sets a high interest rate to try to rein the economy in. Note that we are using the price level, $P$, as the variable in the rule. In practice, the Fed cares about inflation, which is the change in $P$, rather than the level of $P$, and we are approximating this by using just the level of $P$.

$Z$ in the rule stands for all the factors that affect the Fed's interest rate decision except for $Y$ and $P$. Since we have taken $\gamma$ to be positive, the factors in $Z$ are defined to be such that a high value of a factor makes the Fed inclined to have a high interest-rate value, other things being equal. Strong consumer confidence, for example, might be a $Z$ factor, reinforcing the Fed's belief that the economy is doing well on the output side. In 2015, it is clear that concerns about the economy in Europe and China had an influence on Fed interest rate setting behavior; this would be included as a $Z$ factor.

We are now ready to add the Fed rule to our model. Figure 11.6 adds the Fed rule to the $IS$ curve from Figure 11.4. The line depicting the Fed rule in the graph shows the relationship between the Fed's choice of the interest rate and aggregate output, holding the price level and the $Z$ factors constant. The slope is positive because the coefficient $\alpha$ in the Fed rule is positive: When output is high, the interest rate that the Fed sets is high, other things being equal. The intersection of the $IS$ curve and the Fed rule determines the equilibrium values of output and the interest rate. At this point there is equilibrium in the goods market *and* the value of the interest rate is what the Fed rule calls for.

Figure 11.6 shows the equilibrium values of output and the interest rate for given values of government spending ($G$), the price level ($P$), and all factors in $Z$. Suppose the government decides to increase its spending. How do the equilibrium values of the interest rate and output change? Remember that an increase in government spending shifts the $IS$ curve to the right. This will in Figure 11.6 increase the equilibrium values of both the interest rate and output. Now what happens

▶ **FIGURE 11.6**
**Equilibrium Values of the Interest Rate and Output**
In the Fed rule, the Fed raises the interest rate as output increases, other things being equal. Along the *IS* curve, output falls as the interest rate increases because planned investment depends negatively on the interest rate. The intersection of the two curves gives the equilibrium values of output and the interest rate for given values of government spending (*G*), the price level (*P*), and the factors in *Z*.

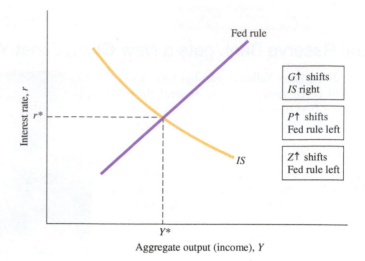

if instead of a change in government spending, we have an increase in the price level, say from an economy wide cost shock? Remember that the price level is in the Fed rule–the Fed cares about price stability. The Fed would thus respond to an increase in the price level by raising the interest rate. This means that in Figure 11.6 an increase in the price level shifts the Fed rule to the left—for a given value of output, the interest rate is higher for a higher value of the price level. Finally, if any of the "Z" factors we described increase, like an increase in consumer confidence, this leads the Fed to increase the interest rate, which also shifts the Fed rule to the left in Figure 11.6.

## Deriving the *AD* Curve

We can now derive the *AD* curve. The *AD* curve (and the *AS* curve) is a relationship between the overall price level (*P*) and aggregate output (income) (*Y*). We know from Figure 11.6 that an increase in *P* shifts the Fed rule to the left (and has no effect on the *IS* curve). When the Fed rule shifts to the left along an unchanged *IS* curve, the new equilibrium is at a higher interest rate and a lower level of output. Be sure you understand why output is lower when *P* is higher. When *P* increases, the Fed, according to the rule, responds by raising the interest rate, other things being equal. The higher interest rate has a negative effect on planned investment and thus on *AE* and thus on *Y*. This is the relationship reflected in the *IS* curve. Conversely, a decrease in *P* shifts the Fed rule to the right, resulting in a new equilibrium with a lower interest rate and higher level of output. There is thus a negative relationship between *P* and *Y* in the goods market with the Fed rule, and this is the *AD* curve. The *AD* curve is presented in Figure 11.7.

It is noted in Figure 11.7 that an increase in government spending (*G*) shifts the *AD* curve to the right. We can see this from Figure 11.6. When *G* increases, the *IS* curve shifts to the right since *AE* and thus *Y* are larger for a given value of the interest rate. (Remember that *AE* = *C* + *I* + *G*.)

▶ **FIGURE 11.7  The Aggregate Demand (*AD*) Curve**

The *AD* curve is derived from Figure 11.6. Each point on the *AD* curve is an equilibrium point in Figure 11.6 for a given value of *P*. When *P* increases, the Fed raises the interest rate (the Fed rule in Figure 11.6 shifts to the left), which has a negative effect on planned investment and thus on *Y*. The *AD* curve reflects this negative relationship between *P* and *Y*.

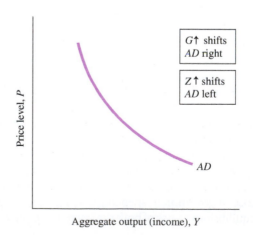

# ECONOMICS IN PRACTICE

## How Does the Fed Look at Inflation?

As we indicated in the text, price stability is one of the main goals of the Fed's monetary policy. But you may recall from Chapters 6 and 7, there are different measures of the aggregate price level: the consumer price index, the producer price index, the GDP deflator. What does the Fed consider the most important?

In practice, the Fed pays most attention to a price index called the Core PCE, or Core Personal Consumption Expenditures. Personal consumption expenditures are all the goods and services consumed by households. Core PCE eliminates from this list most food and energy goods. Why should the Fed leave out food and energy? After all, for most households these are large consumption items. Shouldn't the Fed care about price increases in these categories?

The answer lies in the term *core*. In thinking about its policies, the Fed is interested in gauging whether the economy as a whole is overheated, that is, near the point of full capacity. Energy and food prices might well increase, even dramatically, but not necessarily because the economy is near capacity. They may increase because of a bad shock on the cost side. Bad weather can cause a food price spike even if the economy is far from capacity. A war in the Middle East can lead to a large increase in oil prices, again even if the economy is far from full employment. Because these two categories of expenditures are so volatile, the Fed relies more heavily on the Core PCE as it decides whether the economy is facing the spectre of inflation.

Some economists have criticized the Fed's use of the Core PCE price index because it includes import prices. Personal consumption expenditures, including nonenergy and nonfood expenditures, include purchases of goods and

services from abroad (imports). Import prices are for the most part set by producers in other countries, and Fed policy has little effect on these producers. What the Fed should care about, the argument goes, are the prices set by U.S. producers, prices that are affected by the state of the U.S. economy, which the Fed can influence. The GDP deflator does not include import prices; it is a price index of domestically produced goods and services. It is thus an alternative for the Fed to use, although it does include domestically produced food and energy items.

### THINKING PRACTICALLY

1. How do you think Fed policy might change if it included energy and food prices in its measure of the price level?

The new equilibrium for the G increase has a higher interest rate and a higher level of output. The higher level of output means that the AD curve shifts to the right when G increases.

It is also noted in Figure 11.7 that an increase in Z shifts the AD curve to the left. Remember that an increase in Z means that the Fed is raising the interest rate, other things being equal: The coefficient γ is positive. We can see why the AD curve shifts to the left when Z increases from Figure 11.6. When Z increases, the Fed rule shifts to the left in Figure 11.6, which results in a higher interest rate and a lower level of output. The lower level of output means that the AD curve shifts to the left when Z increases.

It is important to realize that the AD curve is *not* a market demand curve, and it is *not* the sum of all market demand curves in the economy. To understand why, recall the logic behind a simple downward-sloping household demand curve. A demand curve shows the quantity of output demanded (by an individual household or in a single market) at every possible price, *ceteris paribus*. In drawing a simple demand curve, we are assuming that *other prices* and *income* are fixed. From these assumptions, it follows that one reason the quantity demanded of a particular good falls when its price rises is that other prices do *not* rise. The good in question therefore becomes more expensive relative to other goods, and households respond by substituting other goods for the good whose price increased. In addition, if income does not rise when the price of a good does, real income falls. This may also lead to a lower quantity demanded of the good whose price has risen.

Things are different when the *overall price level* rises. When the overall price level rises, many prices rise together. For this reason, we cannot use the *ceteris paribus* assumption to draw the AD

▶ **FIGURE 11.8**
**Equilibrium Output and the Price Level**
Aggregate output and the aggregate price level are determined by the intersection of the *AS* and *AD* curves. These two curves embed within them decisions of households, firms, and the government.

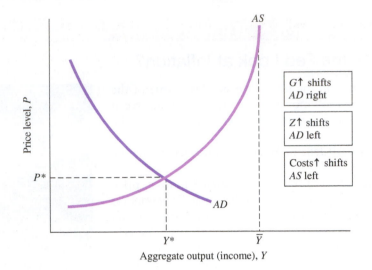

curve. The logic that explains why a simple demand curve slopes downward fails to explain why the *AD* curve also has a negative slope. Aggregate demand falls when the price level increases because the higher price level leads the Fed to raise the interest rate, which decreases planned investment and thus aggregate output. *It is the higher interest rate that causes aggregate output to fall.*

**11.3 LEARNING OBJECTIVE**

Explain why the intersection of the *AD* and *AS* curves is an equilibrium point.

## The Final Equilibrium

Figure 11.8 combines the *AS* curve from Figure 11.1 and the *AD* curve from Figure 11.7. Consider for a moment what these two curves have embedded in them. Every point on the *AS* curve is one in which firms make output and price decisions to maximize their profits. Every point on the *AD* curve reflects equilibrium in the goods market with the Fed behaving according to the Fed rule. The intersection of these two curves is the final equilibrium. The equilibrium values of aggregate output ($Y$) and the price level ($P$) are determined. Behind the scenes, equilibrium values of the interest rate ($r$), consumption ($C$), and planned investment ($I$) are determined.

The variables that are exogenous to the *AS/AD* model (i.e., not explained by the model) are government spending ($G$), the factors in $Z$, and exogenous costs, like oil prices, that shift the *AS* curve. Net taxes ($T$), which have not been discussed in this chapter but are discussed in Chapter 9, are also exogenous. (Net taxes are part of the expanded model of the goods market in Chapter 9.) It is noted in Figure 11.8 that an increase in $G$ shifts the *AD* curve to the right and that an increase in $Z$ shifts the *AD* curve to the left. These shifts have already been discussed. The figure also notes that an increase in costs shifts the *AS* curve to the left. These costs are best thought of as costs like oil prices.

The rest of this chapter discusses the *AD* and *AS* curves in a little more detail, and then Chapter 12 uses the *AS/AD* framework to analyze monetary and fiscal policy effects and other macroeconomic issues. Chapter 12 shows the power of the *AS/AD* model to analyze many interesting and important questions in macroeconomics.

**11.4 LEARNING OBJECTIVE**

Give two additional reasons why the *AD* curve may slope down.

## Other Reasons for a Downward-Sloping *AD* Curve

The *AD* curve slopes down in the preceding analysis because the Fed raises the interest rate when $P$ increases and because planned investment depends negatively on the interest rate. It is also the case in practice that consumption depends negatively on the interest rate, so planned investment depending on the interest rate is not the only link between the interest rate and planned aggregate expenditure. We noted briefly in Chapter 8 that consumption depends on the interest rate, and we will discuss this in more detail in Chapter 15. The main point here is that planned investment does not bear the full burden of linking changes in the interest rate to changes in planned aggregate expenditure and thus the downward-sloping *AD* curve.

There is also a real wealth effect on consumption that contributes to a downward-sloping *AD* curve. We noted in Chapter 8 and will discuss in detail in Chapter 15 that consumption depends on wealth. Other things being equal, the more wealth households have, the more they consume. Wealth includes holdings of money, shares of stock, bonds, and housing, among other things. If household wealth decreases, the result will be less consumption now and in the future. The price level has an effect on some kinds of wealth. Suppose you are holding $1,000 in a checking account or in a money market fund and the price level rises by 10 percent. Your holding is now worth 10 percent less because the prices of the goods that you could buy with your $1,000 have all increased by 10 percent. The purchasing power (or "real value") of your holding has decreased by 10 percent. An increase in the price level may also lower the real value of stocks and housing, although whether it does depends on what happens to stock prices and housing prices when the overall price level rises. If stock prices and housing prices rise by the same percentage as the overall price level, the real value of stocks and housing will remain unchanged. If an increase in the price level does lower the real value of wealth, this is another reason for the downward slope of the *AD* curve. If real wealth falls, this leads to a decrease in consumption, which leads to a decrease in planned aggregate expenditure. So if real wealth falls when there is an increase in the price level, there is a negative relationship between the price level and output through this **real wealth effect**.

> **real wealth effect**  The change in consumption brought about by a change in real wealth that results from a change in the price level.

# The Long-Run *AS* Curve

**11.5 LEARNING OBJECTIVE**

Discuss the shape of the long-run aggregate supply curve and explain long-run market adjustment to potential GDP.

We derived the short-run *AS* curve under the assumption that wages were sticky. This does not mean, however, that stickiness persists forever. Over time, wages adjust to higher prices. When workers negotiate with firms over their wages, they take into account what prices have been doing in the recent past. If wages fully adjust to prices in the long run, then the long-run *AS* curve will be vertical. We can see why in Figure 11.9. Initially, the economy is in equilibrium at a price level of $P_0$ and aggregate output of $Y_0$ (the point $A$ at which $AD_0$ and $AS_0$ intersect). Now imagine a shift of the *AD* curve from $AD_0$ to $AD_1$. In response to this shift, both the price level and aggregate output rise in the short run, to $P_1$ and $Y_1$, respectively (the point $B$ at which $AD_1$ and $AS_0$ intersect). The movement along the upward-sloping $AS_0$ curve as $Y$ increases from $Y_0$ to $Y_1$ assumes that wages lag prices. At point $B$ real wages (nominal wages divided by prices) are lower then they are at point $A$.

Now, as wages increase, the short-run *AS* curve shifts to the left. If wages fully adjust, the *AS* curve will over time have shifted from $AS_0$ to $AS_1$ in Figure 11.9, and output will be back to $Y_0$ (the point $C$ at which $AD_1$ and $AS_1$ intersect). So when wages fully adjust to prices, the long-run *AS* curve is vertical. At point $C$ real wages are back to where they were at point $A$. The price level is, of course, higher.

By looking at Figure 11.9, you can begin to see why arguments about the shape of the *AS* curve are so important in policy debates. If the long-run *AS* curve is vertical as we have drawn it, factors that shift the *AD* curve to the right—such as increasing government spending—simply end up increasing the price level. If the short-run *AS* curve also is quite steep, even in the short run most of the effect of any shift in the *AD* curve will be felt in an increase in the price level rather than an increase in aggregate output. If the *AS* curve, on the other hand, is flat, *AD* shifts can have a large effect on aggregate output, at least in the short run. We discuss these effects of policy in more detail in the next chapter.

## Potential GDP

Recall that even the short-run *AS* curve becomes vertical at some particular level of output. The vertical portion of the short-run *AS* curve exists because there are physical limits to the amount that an economy can produce in any given time period. At the physical limit, all

▶ **FIGURE 11.9  The Long-Run Aggregate Supply Curve**

When the *AD* curve shifts from $AD_0$ to $AD_1$, the equilibrium price level initially rises from $P_0$ to $P_1$ and output rises from $Y_0$ to $Y_1$. Wages respond in the longer run, shifting the *AS* curve from $AS_0$ to $AS_1$. If wages fully adjust, output will be back to $Y_0$. $Y_0$ is sometimes called *potential GDP*.

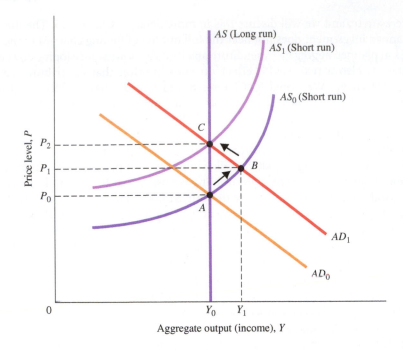

plants are operating around the clock, many workers are on overtime, and there is no cyclical unemployment.

Note that the vertical portions of the short-run *AS* curves in Figure 11.9 are to the right of $Y_0$. If the vertical portions of the short-run *AS* curves represent "capacity," what is the nature of $Y_0$, the level of output corresponding to the long-run *AS* curve? $Y_0$ represents the level of aggregate output that can be *sustained* in the long run without inflation. It is sometimes called **potential output *or* potential GDP.** Output can be pushed above $Y_0$ under a variety of circumstances, but when it is, there is upward pressure on wages. (Remember that real wages are lower at point *B* than at point *A* in Figure 11.9.) As the economy approaches short-run capacity, wage rates tend to rise as firms try to attract more people into the labor force and to induce more workers to work overtime. Rising wages shift the short-run *AS* curve to the left (in Figure 11.9 from $AS_0$ to $AS_1$) and drive output back to $Y_0$.

**potential output, *or* potential GDP**   The level of aggregate output that can be sustained in the long run without inflation.

### Short-Run Equilibrium Below Potential Output

Thus far, we have argued that if the short-run *AS* and *AD* curves intersect to the right of $Y_0$ in Figure 11.9, wages will rise, causing the short-run *AS* curve to shift to the left and pushing aggregate output back down to $Y_0$. Although different economists have different opinions on how to determine whether an economy is operating at or above potential output, there is general agreement that there is a maximum level of output (below the vertical portion of the short-run *AS* curve) that can be sustained without inflation.

What about short-run equilibria that occur to the *left* of $Y_0$? If the short-run *AS* and *AD* curves intersect at a level of output below potential output, what will happen? Here again economists disagree. Those who believe the *AS* curve is vertical in the long run believe that when short-run equilibria exist below $Y_0$, output will tend to rise—just as output tends to fall when short-run equilibria exist above $Y_0$. The argument is that when the economy is operating below full employment with excess capacity and high unemployment, wages are likely to *fall*. A decline in wages shifts the *AS* curve to the *right*, causing the price level to fall and the level of aggregate output to rise back to $Y_0$. This automatic adjustment works only if wages fall quickly when excess capacity and unemployment exist. We will discuss wage adjustment during periods of unemployment in detail in Chapter 13.

# ECONOMICS IN PRACTICE

## The Simple "Keynesian" Aggregate Supply Curve

There is a great deal of disagreement concerning the shape of the AS curve. One view of the aggregate supply curve, the simple "Keynesian" view, holds that at any given moment, the economy has a clearly defined capacity, or maximum, output. This maximum output, denoted by $Y_F$, is defined by the existing labor force, the current capital stock, and the existing state of technology. If planned aggregate expenditure increases when the economy is producing *below* this maximum capacity, this view holds, inventories will be lower than planned, and firms will increase output, but the price level will not change. Firms are operating with underutilized plants (excess capacity), and there is cyclical unemployment. Expansion does not exert any upward pressure on prices. However, if planned aggregate expenditure increases when the economy is producing near or at its maximum ($Y_F$), inventories will be lower than planned, but firms cannot increase their output. The result will be an increase in the price level, or inflation.

This view is illustrated in the figure. In the top half of the diagram, aggregate output (income) (Y) and planned aggregate expenditure ($C + I + G \equiv AE$) are initially in equilibrium at $AE_1$, $Y_1$, and price level $P_1$. Now suppose an increase in government spending increases planned aggregate expenditure. If such an increase shifts the AE curve from $AE_1$ to $AE_2$ and the corresponding aggregate demand curve from $AD_1$ to $AD_2$, the equilibrium level of output will rise from $Y_1$ to $Y_F$. (Remember, an expansionary policy shifts the AD curve to the right.) Because we were initially producing below capacity output ($Y_1$ is lower than $Y_F$), the price level will be unaffected, remaining at $P_1$.

Now consider what would happen if AE increased even further. Suppose planned aggregate expenditure shifted from $AE_2$ to $AE_3$, with a corresponding shift of $AD_2$ to $AD_3$. If the economy were producing below capacity output, the equilibrium level of output would rise to $Y_3$. However, the output of the economy cannot exceed the maximum output of $Y_F$. As inventories fall below what was planned, firms encounter a fully employed labor market and fully utilized plants. Therefore, they cannot increase their output. The result is that the aggregate supply curve becomes vertical at $Y_F$, and the price level is driven up to $P_3$.

The difference between planned aggregate expenditure and aggregate output at full capacity is sometimes referred to as an *inflationary gap*. You can see the inflationary gap in the

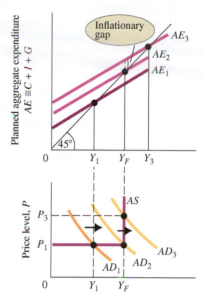

With planned aggregate expenditure of $AE_1$ and aggregate demand of $AD_1$, equilibrium output is $Y_1$. A shift of planned aggregate expenditure to $AE_2$, corresponding to a shift of the AD curve to $AD_2$, causes output to rise but the price level to remain at $P_1$. If planned aggregate expenditure and aggregate demand exceed $Y_F$, however, there is an inflationary gap and the price level rises to $P_3$.

top half of the figure. At $Y_F$ (capacity output), planned aggregate expenditure (shown by $AE_3$) is greater than $Y_F$. The price level rises to $P_3$ until the aggregate quantity supplied and the aggregate quantity demanded are equal.

Despite the fact that the kinked aggregate supply curve provides some insights, most economists find it unrealistic. It does not seem likely that the whole economy suddenly runs into a capacity "wall" at a specific level of output. As output expands, some firms and industries will hit capacity before others.

### THINKING PRACTICALLY

1. Why is the distance between $AE_3$ and $AE_2$ called an *inflationary gap*?

# SUMMARY

## 11.1 THE AGGREGATE SUPPLY (AS) CURVE p. 215

1. *Aggregate supply* is the total supply of goods and services in an economy. The *aggregate supply (AS) curve* shows the relationship between the aggregate quantity of output supplied by all the firms in the economy and the overall price level. The *AS* curve is *not* a market supply curve, and it is *not* the simple sum of individual supply curves. For this reason, it is helpful to think of the *AS* curve as a "price/output response" curve—that is, a curve that traces out the price and output decisions of all firms in the economy under a given set of circumstances.

2. The shape of the short-run *AS* curve is a source of much controversy in macroeconomics. Many economists believe that at low levels of aggregate output, the *AS* curve is fairly flat and that at high levels of aggregate output, the *AS* curve is vertical or nearly vertical.

3. Anything that affects an individual firm's marginal cost curve can shift the *AS* curve. The two main factors are wage rates and energy prices.

## 11.2 THE AGGREGATE DEMAND (AD) CURVE p. 218

4. The *IS* curve summarizes the relationship between the interest rate and equilibrium output in the goods market. Government spending (*G*) shifts the *IS* curve.

5. Fed behavior is described by an interest rate rule, the *Fed rule*. The Fed's choice of the interest rate value depends on the state of the economy, approximated in the rule by output (*Y*), the price level (*P*), and other factors (*Z*). The Fed uses

open market operations to achieve the interest rate value that it wants.

6. Each point on the *AD* curve is, for a given value of *P*, an equilibrium in the goods market with the Fed rule. Increases in *G* shift the *AD* curve to the right, and increases in *Z* shift the *AD* curve to the left.

## 11.3 THE FINAL EQUILIBRIUM p. 224

7. The final equilibrium is the point of intersection of the *AS* and *AD* curves. Determined at this point are equilibrium values of output, the price level, the interest rate, consumption, planned investment, the demand for money, and the supply of money. Exogenous variables (variables not explained by the model) are government spending, the factors in *Z*, net taxes (used in the next chapter), and cost shocks.

## 11.4 OTHER REASONS FOR A DOWNWARD-SLOPING AD CURVE p. 224

8. Consumption as well as planned investment depends on the interest rate, and this is another reason for a downward-sloping *AD* curve. Another reason is that consumption also depends on real wealth.

## 11.5 THE LONG-RUN AS CURVE p. 225

9. The long-run *AS* curve is vertical if wages adjust completely to prices in the long run.

# REVIEW TERMS AND CONCEPTS

aggregate supply, *p. 215*
aggregate supply (AS) curve, *p. 215*
cost shock, or supply shock, *p. 217*

Fed rule, *p. 220*
IS curve, *p. 219*
potential output, or potential GDP, *p. 226*

real wealth effect, *p. 225*
Equations: $AE \equiv C + I + G$, *p. 218*
$r = \alpha Y + \beta P + \gamma Z$, *p. 220*

# PROBLEMS

All problems are available on MyEconLab.

## 11.1 THE AGGREGATE SUPPLY (AS) CURVE

LEARNING OBJECTIVE: Define the aggregate supply curve and discuss shifts in the short-run *AS* curve.

1.1 Illustrate each of the following situations with a graph showing short-run aggregate supply:
   a. A decrease in the size of the labor force
   b. An increase in available capital
   c. An increase in productivity as a result of a technological change
   d. A decrease in the price of oil

## 11.2 THE AGGREGATE DEMAND (AD) CURVE

LEARNING OBJECTIVE: Derive the aggregate demand curve and explain why the *AD* curve is downward sloping.

2.1 On November 9, 2011, the European Central Bank acted to decrease the short-term interest rate in Europe by one-fourth of a percentage point, to 1.25 percent, and additional cuts were made over the next three years, to a low rate of 0.05 percent by September 2014. The rate cuts were made because European countries were growing very slowly or were in recession. What

MyEconLab Visit www.myeconlab.com to complete these exercises online and get instant feedback. Exercises that update with real-time data are marked with art 🎨.

effect did the bank hope the action would have on the economy? Be specific. What was the hoped-for result on C, I, and Y?

2.2 Some economists argue that the "animal spirits" of investors are so important in determining the level of investment in the economy that interest rates do not matter at all. Suppose that this were true, that investment in no way depends on interest rates.

a. How would Figure 11.4 be different?

b. What would happen to the level of planned aggregate expenditure if the interest rate changed?

2.3 Describe the Fed's tendency to "lean against the wind." Do the Fed's policies tend to stabilize or destabilize the economy?

2.4 Illustrate each of the following situations with a graph showing the *IS* curve and the Fed rule, and explain what happens to the equilibrium values of the interest rate and output:

a. A decrease in G with the money supply held constant by the Fed

b. A decrease in G with the Fed changing $M^s$ by enough to keep interest rates constant

c. A decrease in P with no change in government spending

d. An increase in Z with no change in government spending

e. An increase in P and a decrease in G

2.5 The *AD* curve slopes downward because when the price level is lower, people can afford to buy more and aggregate demand rises. When prices rise, people can afford to buy less and aggregate demand falls. Is this a good explanation of the shape of the *AD* curve? Why or why not?

2.6 In the first few chapters of this book, we introduced the notion of supply and demand. One of the first things we did was to derive the relationship between the price of a product and the quantity demanded per time period by an individual household. Now we have derived what is called the *aggregate* demand curve. The two look the same and both seem to have a negative slope, but the logic is completely different. Tell one story that explains the negative slope of a simple demand curve and another story that explains the more complex *AD* curve.

2.7 [**Related to the *Economics in Practice* on p. 221**] In a June 17, 2015, press conference, Fed Chair Janet Yellen indicated the possibility of the Fed raising interest rates by the end of the year. On this date, the federal funds rate target set by the Fed was 0.00 − 0.25 percent, where it had been since January 2009. What has happened to the Fed's target for the federal funds rate since June 2015? Using the Fed rule, explain the Fed's decision to either change or not change the interest rate.

2.8 [**Related to the *Economics in Practice* on p. 223**] The Federal Reserve Bank of St. Louis publishes PCE price index data on its Website at: https://research .stlouisfed.org/fred2/categories/9. Go to this Web site and look at the 1-, 5-, and 10-year graphs for both

"Personal Consumption Expenditures: Chain-type Price Index" and "Personal Consumption Expenditures Excluding Food and Energy (Chain-Type Price Index)". Using the data represented in the graphs for these two PCE indexes, explain whether you believe the Fed obtains a more accurate representation of inflation and the state of the economy by concentration on the PCE index which excludes food and energy pricing.

## 11.3 THE FINAL EQUILIBRIUM

**LEARNING OBJECTIVE:** Explain why the intersection of the *AD* and *AS* curves is an equilibrium point.

3.1 Illustrate each of the following situations with a graph showing *AS* and *AD* curves, and explain what happens to the equilibrium values of the price level and aggregate output:

a. A decrease in G with the money supply held constant by the Fed

b. A decrease in the price of oil with no change in government spending

c. An increase in Z with no change in government spending

d. An increase in the price of oil and a decrease in G

## 11.4 OTHER REASONS FOR A DOWNWARD-SLOPING *AD* CURVE

**LEARNING OBJECTIVE:** Give two additional reasons why the *AD* curve may slope down.

4.1 In the tiny island nation of Bongo, the nation's wealth is broken down as follows: 50 percent is cash in checking and savings accounts, 25 percent is housing, and 25 percent is stock holdings. Last year, Bongo experienced an inflation rate of 25 percent, and housing prices and stock prices each increased by 10 percent. Explain what happened to real wealth in Bongo last year, and how this change in real wealth helps explain the downward slope of the aggregate demand curve.

## 11.5 THE LONG-RUN *AS* CURVE

**LEARNING OBJECTIVE:** Discuss the shape of the long-run aggregate supply curve and explain long-run market adjustment to potential GDP.

5.1 The economy of Mayberry is currently in equilibrium at point A on the graph. Prince Barney of Mayberry has decided that he wants the economy to grow and has ordered the Royal Central Bank of Mayberry to print more currency so banks can expand their loans to stimulate growth. Explain what will most likely happen to the economy of Mayberry as a result of Prince Barney's actions and show the result on the graph.

**MyEconLab** Visit **www.myeconlab.com** to complete these exercises online and get instant feedback. Exercises that update with real-time data are marked with art 🔴 .

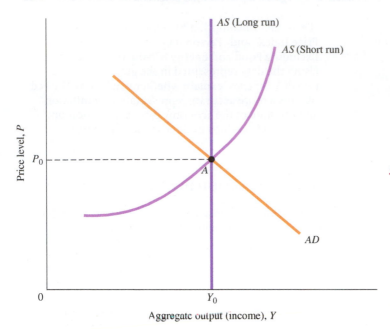

By using aggregate supply and demand curves and other useful graphs, illustrate the following:

a. Those pushing the Fed to act were right, and prices start to rise more rapidly in 2000. The Fed acts belatedly to slow money growth (contract the money supply), driving up interest rates and pushing the economy back to potential GDP.

b. The worldwide glut gets worse, and the result is a falling price level (deflation) in the United States despite expanding aggregate demand.

5.4 Using *AS* and *AD* curves to illustrate, describe the effects of the following events on the price level and on equilibrium GDP in the *long run* assuming that input prices fully adjust to output prices after some lag:

a. An increase occurs in the money supply above potential GDP

b. GDP is above potential GDP, and a decrease in government spending and in the money supply occurs

c. Starting with the economy at potential GDP, a war in the Middle East pushes up energy prices temporarily. The Fed expands the money supply to accommodate the inflation.

5.2 Two separate capacity constraints are discussed in this chapter: (1) the actual physical capacity of existing plants and equipment, shown as the vertical portion of the short-run *AS* curve, and (2) potential GDP, leading to a vertical long-run *AS* curve. Explain the difference between the two. Which is greater, full-capacity GDP or potential GDP? Why?

5.3 During 1999 and 2000, a debate raged over whether the United States was at or above potential GDP. Some economists feared the economy was operating at a level of output above potential GDP and inflationary pressures were building. They urged the Fed to tighten monetary policy and increase interest rates to slow the economy. Others argued that a worldwide glut of cheap products was causing input prices to be lower, keeping prices from rising.

5.5 [**Related to the *Economics in Practice* on p. 227**] The *Economics in Practice* describes the simple Keynesian *AS* curve as one in which there is a maximum level of output given the constraints of a fixed capital stock and a fixed supply of labor. The presumption is that increases in demand when firms are operating below capacity will result in output increases and no input price or output price changes but that at levels of output above full capacity, firms have no choice but to raise prices if demand increases. In reality, however, the short-run *AS* curve isn't flat and then vertical. Rather, it becomes steeper as we move from left to right on the diagram. Explain why. What circumstances might lead to an equilibrium at a very flat portion of the *AS* curve? At a very steep portion?

# Policy Effects and Cost Shocks in the AS/AD Model

# 12

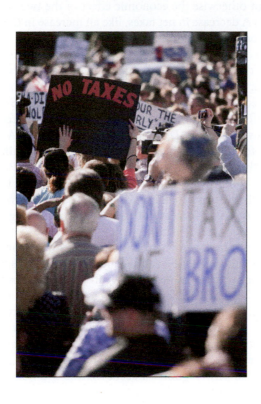

Throughout the two Obama administrations, Republicans and Democrats argued vehemently about the overall government budget. What should be done to raise or lower taxes? What about government spending? Some of this debate was ideological, as U.S. political leaders differed in questions like how big the government should be. Other debate focused on more economic issues: Was the economy firmly on a growth path or still vulnerable to unemployment problems? Whatever the motivations for particular policies, decisions made in the political process about taxes and spending have important macroeconomic consequences. The *AS/AD* model developed in the last chapter is a key tool in allowing us to explore these consequences.

# Fiscal Policy Effects

In Chapter 11, we discussed government spending on goods and services (*G*) as our fiscal policy variable. But the government also collects taxes and spends money on transfer payments, and these too are an important part of the fiscal policy story. In fact, recently in the United States most of the political debate has centered on the question of the right tax level. We turn now to look at government spending and taxes using the lenses of the *AS/AD* model.

We will continue in this chapter to use *T* to denote net taxes, that is, taxes minus transfer payments. A decrease in *T* has the same qualitative effect as an increase in *G*. With lower taxes, households have more disposable income and that causes an increase in their consumption. We know from Chapter 9 that the tax multiplier is smaller in absolute value than is the government spending multiplier, but otherwise the economic effect of the two is similar. (You might want to review this material.) A decrease in net taxes, like an increase in *G*, shifts the *AD* curve to the right (just not as much because of the smaller multiplier).

What happens to the economy when government spending increases or net taxes decrease, thus shifting the *AD* curve shifts right? Key to the answer to this question is knowing where on the *AS* curve the economy is when this fiscal stimulus is applied. In Figure 12.1, the economy is assumed to be on the nearly flat portion of the *AS* curve (point A) when we use fiscal policy to shift the *AD* curve. Here the economy is not producing close to capacity. As the figure shows, a shift of the *AD* curve in this region of the *AS* curve results in a small price increase relative to the output increase. The increase in equilibrium *Y* (from $Y_0$ to $Y_1$) is much greater than the increase in equilibrium *P* (from $P_0$ to $P_1$). Here an expansionary fiscal policy works well, increasing output with little increase in the price level. When the economy is on the nearly flat portion of the *AS* curve, firms are producing well below capacity, and they will respond to an increase in demand by increasing output much more than they increase prices.

Figure 12.2 shows what happens when stimulus occurs when the economy is operating on the steep part of the *AS* curve (point B), at a high level relative to its resources. In this case, an expansionary fiscal policy results in a small change in equilibrium output (from $Y_0$ to $Y_1$) and a large change in the equilibrium price level (from $P_0$ to $P_1$). Here, an expansionary fiscal policy does not work well. The output multiplier is close to zero. Output is initially close to capacity, and attempts to increase it further mostly lead to a higher price level.

Make sure you understand what is happening behind the scenes in Figure 12.2 when we are on the steep part of the *AS* curve. The increase in government spending, *G*, increases the demand for firms' goods. Because firms are near capacity, raising output

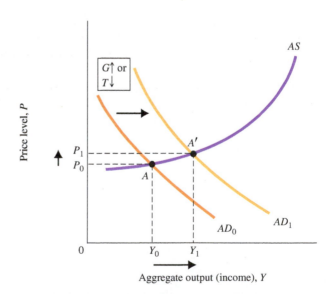

▲ **FIGURE 12.1    A Shift of the *AD* Curve When the Economy Is on the Nearly Flat Part of the *AS* Curve**

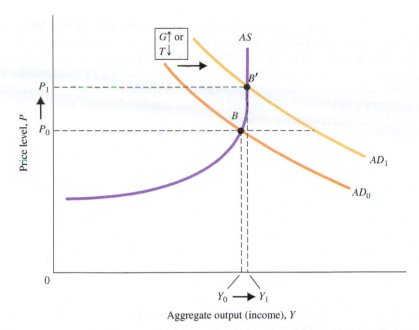

▲ **FIGURE 12.2    A Shift of the *AD* Curve When the Economy Is Operating at or Near Capacity**

is difficult and firms respond by mostly raising their prices. The rise in the overall price level (*P*) induces action by the Fed because the price level is in the Fed rule. Thus, when *P* rises, the Fed increases the interest rate (*r*). The higher interest rate lowers planned investment. If total output cannot be increased very much because the economy is near capacity, the interest rate must rise enough to decrease planned investment enough to offset the increase in government spending in the new equilibrium. In this case there is almost complete crowding out of planned investment. Government spending has displaced private investment.

What is behind the scenes if there is a decrease in net taxes (*T*) in Figure 12.2 on the steep part of the *AS* curve? In this case, consumption demand for firms' goods increases (because after tax income has increased). Firms again mostly raise their prices, so *P* increases, and so the Fed raises the interest rate, which lowers planned investment. If total output is little changed, the interest rate must rise such that the decrease in planned investment is roughly equal to the increase in consumption in the new equilibrium. In this case, consumption rather than government spending crowds out planned investment. Consumption is higher even though output is little changed because after-tax income is higher because of the decrease in *T* (disposable income, *Y*–*T*, is higher).

Note that in Figure 12.1, where the economy is on the flat part of the *AS* curve, there is very little crowding out of planned investment. Output expands to meet the increased demand. Because the price level increases very little, the Fed does not raise the interest rate much, and so there is little change in planned investment.

# Fiscal Policy Effects in the Long Run

We can now turn to look at the long-run effects of fiscal policy. Most economists believe that in the long run wages adjust to some extent to match rising prices. Eventually, as prices rise, we would expect workers to demand and get higher wages. If wages adjust fully, then the long-run *AS* curve is vertical. In this case it is easy to see that fiscal policy will have no effect on output. If the government increases *G* or decreases *T*, thus shifting up the *AD* curve, the full effect is felt on the price level. Here, the long-run response to fiscal policy looks very much like that on the steep part of the short-run *AS* curve.

So we see that the key question, much debated in macroeconomics, is how fast wages adjust to changes in prices. If wages adjust to prices in a matter of a few months, the AS curve quickly becomes vertical and output benefits from fiscal policy will be short-lived. If wages are slower to adjust, the AS curve might retain some upward slope for a long period and one would be more confident about the usefulness of fiscal policy. Although most economists believe that wages are slow to adjust in the short run and therefore that fiscal policy has potential effects in the short run, there is less consensus about the shape of the long-run AS curve. In an interesting way, economists' views about how effective fiscal policy can be—whether the government can *ever* spend itself out of a low output state—is summarized in whether they believe the long-run AS curve is vertical or upward sloping.

Another source of disagreement among macroeconomists centers on whether equilibria below potential output, $\overline{Y}$ in Figure 11.8 in Chapter 11, are self-correcting (that is, without government intervention). If equilibria below potential output are self-correcting, the economy will spend little time on the horizontal part of the AS curve. Recall that those who believe in a vertical long-run AS curve believe that slack in the economy will put downward pressure on wages, causing the short-run AS curve to shift to the right and pushing aggregate output back toward potential output. Other economists argue that wages do *not* fall much during slack periods and that the economy can get "stuck" at an equilibrium below potential output in the flat region of the AS curve. In this case, monetary and fiscal policy would be necessary to restore full employment. We will return to this debate in Chapter 13.

The "new classical" economics, which we will discuss in Chapter 17, assumes that prices and wages are fully flexible and adjust quickly to changing conditions. New classical economists believe, for example, that wage rate changes do not lag behind price changes. The new classical view is consistent with the existence of a vertical AS curve, even in the short run. At the other end of the spectrum is what is sometimes called the simple "Keynesian" view of aggregate supply. Those who hold this view believe there is a kink in the AS curve at capacity output, as we discussed in the *Economics in Practice*, "The Simple 'Keynesian' Aggregate Supply Curve," in Chapter 11. As we have seen, these differences in perceptions of the way the markets act have large effects on the advice economists give to the government.

**12.2 LEARNING** OBJECTIVE

Use the *AS/AD* model to analyze the short-run and long-run effects of monetary policy.

# Monetary Policy Effects

Monetary policy is controlled by the Fed, which we are assuming behaves according to the Fed rule described in Chapter 11. The interest rate value that the Fed chooses (r) depends on output (Y), the price level (P), and other factors (Z). The Fed achieves the interest rate value that it wants though open market operations. But how effective is the Fed in moving the economy as it follows its rule? There are several features of the AS/AD model that we need to consider regarding the effectiveness of the Fed, which we turn to now.

## The Fed's Response to the Z Factors

We noted in Chapter 11 that the Fed is not just a calculator, responding in a mechanical way to Y and P. The Fed is affected by things outside of our model. Looking at reports of consumer sentiment, the Fed may decide that the economy is more fragile than one might have thought looking at only output and the price level. Or perhaps the Fed is worried about something unfavorable in the international arena. If one of these "Z" factors, as we have called them, changes, the Fed may decide to set the interest rate above or below what the values of Y and P alone call for in the rule.

Because Z is outside of the AS/AD model (that is, exogenous to the model), we can ask what changes in Z do to the model. We have in fact already seen the answer to this question in Figure 11.7 in Chapter 11. An increase in Z, like an increase in consumer confidence, may prompt the Fed to increase the interest rate, thus shifting the AD curve to the left. Remember that an increase in Z induces the Fed to set the interest rate higher than what Y and P alone would call for. Similarly, a decrease in Z like a worry about the economy of China or Europe leads to an easing of monetary policy, shifting the AD curve to the right by encouraging more planned investment.

In the previous section, we used the fact that G and T shift the AD curve to analyze the effectiveness of fiscal policy in different situations (flat, normal, or steep part of the AS curve). This same analysis pertains to Z. Changes to the interest rate set by the Fed in response to changes in Z also have differential effects depending on where we are on the *AS* curve.

## Shape of the *AD* Curve When the Fed Cares More About the Price Level than Output

In the equation representing the Fed rule, we used a weight of $\alpha$ for output and a weight of $\beta$ for the price level. The relative size of these two coefficients can be thought of as a measure of how much the Fed cares about output versus the price level.[1] If $\alpha$ is small relative to $\beta$, this means that the Fed has a strong preference for stable prices relative to output. In this case, when the Fed sees a price increase, it responds with a large increase in the interest rate, thus driving down planned investment and thus output. In this case, the *AD* curve is relatively flat, as depicted in Figure 12.3. The Fed is willing to accept large changes in Y to keep P stable. We will return to Figure 12.3 when we discuss cost shocks.

The issue of how much weight the Fed puts on the price level relative to output is related to the issue of inflation targeting, which is discussed at the end of this chapter. If a monetary authority is engaged in inflation targeting, then it behaves as if inflation is the only variable in its interest rate rule.

## What Happens When There Is a Zero Interest Rate Bound?

Since 2008 short-term interest rates in the United States have been close to zero. For all practical purposes, an interest rate cannot be negative. We don't charge people when they save money or pay them to borrow money. The fact that the interest rate is bounded by zero has implications for the shape of the *AD* curve, which we will now explain.

Let us begin with the Fed rule. Suppose the conditions of the economy in terms of output, the price level, and the Z factors are such that the Fed wants a *negative* interest rate. In this case, the best that the Fed can do is to choose zero for the value of r, which again it has mostly done since 2008 (at the time of this writing). This is called a **zero interest rate bound**. If Y or P or Z begin to increase, there is some point at which the rule will call for a positive value for r (the interest rate), at which time the Fed will move from zero to the positive value. The fact that the interest rate has remained at roughly zero for many years in the United States suggests that levels of Y, P, and Z may well have called for a negative interest rate for many years. In this case the values of Y, P, and Z are far below what they would have to be to induce the Fed to move the to a positive interest rate in the Fed rule. We will call this situation a **binding situation**.

**zero interest rate bound** The interest rate cannot go below zero.

**binding situation** State of the economy in which the Fed rule calls for a negative interest rate.

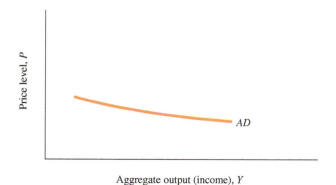

**FIGURE 12.3** The Shape of the *AD* Curve When the Fed Has a Strong Preference for Price Stability Relative to Output

---

[1] Remember that the Fed actually cares about inflation, the change in P, rather than the level of P itself. We are using P as an approximation. Also, the Fed cares about output because of its effect on employment.

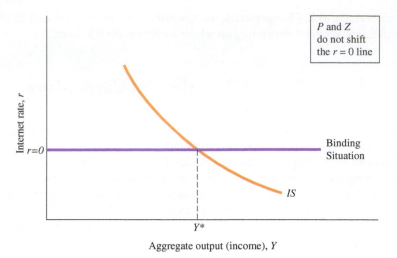

▲ **FIGURE 12.4** **Equilibrium in the Goods Market When the Interest Rate Is Zero.** In a binding situation changes in *P* and *Z* do not shift the *r* = 0 line.

What does Figure 11.6 in Chapter 11 look like in a binding situation? This is shown in Figure 12.4. In this situation the interest rate is always zero, and so equilibrium is just where the *IS* curve crosses zero. In this binding situation, changes in *P* and *Z* do not shift anything (as they did in Figure 11.6) because the interest rate is always zero. In a binding situation the *AD* curve is vertical, as shown in Figure 12.5. It is easy to see why. In the normal case, an increase in *P* leads the Fed through the rule to increase the interest rate, which lowers planned investment and thus output. A decrease in *P* leads to the opposite. In the binding case, the interest rate does not change when *P* changes (it is always zero), and so planned investment and thus output do not change. For the *AD* curve to have a slope, the interest rate must change when the price level changes, which does not happen in the binding situation. Note also that changes in *Z* do not shift the *AD* curve in a binding situation (unlike the case in Figure 11.7 in Chapter 11). Again, the interest rate is always zero; it does not change when *Z* changes in a binding situation.

You should note that changes in government spending (*G*) and net taxes (*T*) still shift the *AD* curve even if it is vertical. In fact, because there is no crowding out of planned investment or consumption when *G* increases or *T* decreases because the interest rate does not increase, the shift is even greater. With a vertical *AD* curve, fiscal policy can be used to increase output, but monetary policy cannot. You might ask, what if the economy is on

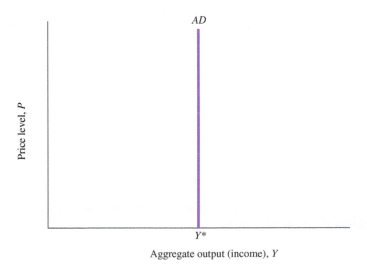

▲ **FIGURE 12.5** **The *AD* Curve in a Binding Situation. In a binding situation the interest rate is always zero.**

the nearly vertical part of the *AS* curve and a vertical *AD* curve is shifted to the right of the vertical part? Alas, there would be no intersection any more. Here the model would break down, but fortunately this is not a realistic case. If the economy is on the nearly vertical part of the *AS* curve, output and possibly the price level would be high, and it is unlikely the Fed would want a negative interest rate in this case. The *AD* curve would thus not be vertical.

# Shocks to the System

## Cost Shocks

Suppose we have a sudden and severe cold spell that kills off a large fraction of the feeder-fish stock in the world. Or suppose that war breaks out in the Middle East and oil supplies from the region are cut off. How do events like these affect aggregate output and the price level in an economy? When things like this happen, what is the Fed likely to do? The *AS/AD* model can help guide us through to answers to these questions.

These examples are cost shocks, which were introduced in Chapter 11. We chose the examples carefully. In both cases the shock occurred in products that are used as inputs into a wide variety of other products. So a disaster in the fish or oil markets is likely to increase all at once the costs of many firms. The *AS* curve shifts to the left as firms who experience these new costs raise their prices to cover their new higher costs.

Figure 12.6 shows what happens to the economy when the *AS* curve shifts to the left. This leads to **stagflation**, which is the simultaneous increase in unemployment and inflation. Stagflation is illustrated in Figure 12.6 where equilibrium output falls from $Y_0$ to $Y_1$ (and unemployment rises), and simultaneously the equilibrium price level rises from $P_0$ to $P_1$ (an increase in inflation). The reason output falls is that the increase in $P$ leads the Fed to raise the interest rate, which lowers planned investment and thus output. Remember that the Fed rule is a "leaning against the wind" rule, and when the price level rises the Fed leans against the wind by raising the interest rate.

**stagflation**   The simultaneous increase in unemployment and inflation.

We have seen in the previous two sections that when analyzing the effects of changing *G*, *T*, and *Z*, the shape of the *AS* curve matters. When analyzing the effects of cost shocks, on the other hand, it is the shape of the *AD* curve that matters. Consider, for example, the case where the *AD* curve is fairly flat, as in Figure 12.3. This is the case where the Fed puts a large weight on price stability relative to output because they are less concerned about the costs of unemployment. In this case, a leftward shift of the *AS* curve results in a large decrease in output relative to the increase in the price level. Behind the scenes the Fed is raising the interest rate a lot, lowering planned investment and thus output a lot, to offset much of the price effect of the cost shock. The price level rises less and output falls more than it would if the *AD* curve were shaped more like the one in Figure 12.6.

An interesting case is when the *AD* curve is vertical, as in Figure 12.5. Remember that this is the case of a binding situation with a zero interest rate. When the *AD* curve is vertical and the *AS* curve shifts to the left, there is no change in output. The only change is a higher price level. In a binding situation the increase in $P$ does not change $r$ ($r$ is still zero), so planned investment

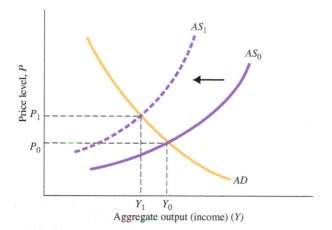

▲ **FIGURE 12.6   A Positive Cost Shock**

## ECONOMICS IN PRACTICE

### A Bad Monsoon Season Fuels Indian Inflation

In 2012, the Indian monsoons came with less rain than normal. For the rice crop, this was a large and adverse shock. Rice is grown in water-laden paddies, and domestic production fell dramatically with the weather shock. The result for India, which is a large consumer of rice, was a substantial increase in the price of rice. Nearby countries also growing rice, like Thailand, were not able to make up for India's production deficiencies, and rice prices rose throughout much of Southeast Asia.

For a country like the United States, a rise in rice prices would likely have little effect on overall prices. There are many substitutes for rice in the United States and rice plays a small role in the average household budget. The same is not true for India, which is both poorer (meaning that food in general is a larger part of the budget) and much more dependent on rice. For India, the weather shock on rice threatened to increase the overall inflation rate, which at 10 percent was already high by U.S. standards, and the Indian government struggled to try to manage this (supply) shock.

#### THINKING PRACTICALLY

1. What two features of the Indian economy meant that an increase in rice prices was likely to spread through the economy and influence the overall inflation rate?

is unaffected, and thus output is unaffected. Remember that this story holds only as long as the situation remains binding. At some point if there are large leftward shifts in the *AS* curve, *P* will be high enough that the binding situation no longer holds. When this happens, Figure 12.5 is not relevant, and we are back to Figure 12.6.

**cost-push, *or* supply-side, inflation** Inflation caused by an increase in costs.

When the price level rises because the *AS* curve shifts to the left, this is called **cost-push, *or* supply-side, inflation**. As we have seen, this is accompanied by lower output. There is thus higher inflation and lower output, or *stagflation*.

### Demand-Side Shocks

We know from the previous two sections that an expansionary fiscal policy (an increase in *G* or a decrease in *T*) and an expansionary monetary policy (a decrease in *Z*) shifts the *AD* curve to the right and results in a higher price level. This is an increase in the price level caused by an increase in demand and is called **demand-pull inflation**. Contrary to cost-push inflation, demand-pull inflation corresponds to higher output rather than lower output.

**demand-pull inflation** Inflation that is initiated by an increase in aggregate demand.

There are other sources of demand shifts, exogenous to the model, that are interesting to consider. These we can put under the general heading of demand-side shocks. As mentioned in Chapter 5, in the 1930s when macroeconomics was just beginning, John Maynard Keynes introduced the idea of "animal spirits" of investors. Keynes' animal spirits were his way of describing a kind of optimism or pessimism about the economy which could bolster or hinder the economy. Animal spirits, although maybe important to the economy, are not explained by our model. Within the present context, an improvement in animal spirits—for example, a rise in consumer confidence—can be thought of as a "demand-side shock."

What happens when, say, there is a positive demand-side shock? The *AD* curve shifts to the right. This will lead to some increase in output and some increase in the price level, how much of each depends on where the economy is on the *AS* curve. There is nothing new to our story about aggregate demand increases except that instead of being triggered by a fiscal or monetary policy change, the demand increase is triggered by something outside of the model. Any price increase that results from a demand-side shock is also considered demand-pull inflation.

# Expectations

Animal spirits can be considered expectations of the future. Expectations in general likely have important effects on the economy, but they are hard to predict or to quantify. However formed, firms' expectations of future prices may affect their current price decisions. If a firm expects that its competitors will raise their prices, it may raise its own price in anticipation of this. An increase in future price expectations may thus shift the AS curve to the left and thus act like a cost shock. How might this work?

Consider a firm that manufactures toasters in an imperfectly competitive market. The toaster maker must decide what price to charge retail stores for its toaster. If it overestimates price and charges much more than other toaster manufacturers are charging, it will lose many customers. If it underestimates price and charges much less than other toaster makers are charging, it will gain customers but at a considerable loss in revenue per sale. The firm's *optimum price*—the price that maximizes the firm's profits—is presumably not too far from the average of its competitors' prices. If it does not know its competitors' projected prices before it sets its own price, as is often the case, it must base its price on what it expects its competitors' prices to be.

Suppose inflation has been running at about 10 percent per year. Our firm probably expects its competitors will raise their prices about 10 percent this year, so it is likely to raise the price of its own toaster by about 10 percent. This response is how expectations can get "built into the system." If every firm expects every other firm to raise prices by 10 percent, every firm will raise prices by about 10 percent. Every firm ends up with the price increase it expected.

The fact that expectations can affect the price level is vexing. Expectations can lead to an inertia that makes it difficult to stop an inflationary spiral. If prices have been rising and if people's expectations are *adaptive*—that is, if they form their expectations on the basis of past pricing behavior—firms may continue raising prices even if demand is slowing or contracting. In terms of the AS/AD diagram, an increase in inflationary expectations that causes firms to increase their prices shifts the AS curve to the left. Remember that the AS curve represents the price/output responses of firms. If firms increase their prices because of a change in inflationary expectations, the result is a leftward shift of the AS curve.

Given the importance of expectations in inflation, the central banks of many countries survey consumers about their expectations. In Great Britain, for example, a February 2013 survey by the Bank of England found that consumers expected inflation of 3.2 percent for the period 2013–2014. A similar survey by the Bank of India found consumer expectations of inflation in this period to be in the 10 percent range. One of the aims of central banks is to try to keep these expectations low.

# Monetary Policy since 1970

**12.4 LEARNING** OBJECTIVE

Discuss monetary policy since 1970.

At the end of Chapter 9, we compared the fiscal policies of the Clinton, Bush, and Obama administrations. In this section, we will review what monetary policy has been like since 1970. Remember by monetary policy we mean the interest rate behavior of the Fed. How has the Fed changed the interest rate in response to economic conditions?

Figure 12.7 plots three variables that can be used to describe Fed behavior. The interest rate is the 3-month Treasury bill rate, which moves closely with the interest rate that the Fed actually controls, which is the federal funds rate. For simplicity, we will take the 3-month Treasury bill rate to be the rate that the Fed controls and we will just call it "the interest rate." Inflation is the percentage change in the GDP deflator over the previous four quarters. This variable is also plotted in Figure 5.6 on p. 100. Output is the percentage deviation of real GDP from its trend. (Real GDP itself is plotted in Figure 5.4 on p. 99.) It is easier to see fluctuations in real GDP by looking at percentage deviations from its trend.

Recall from Chapter 5 that we have called five periods since 1970 "recessionary periods" and two periods "high inflation periods." These periods are highlighted in Figure 12.7. The recessionary and high inflation periods have considerable overlap in the last half of the 1970s and early 1980s. After 1981, there are no more high inflation periods and three more recessionary periods. There is thus some stagflation in the early part of the period but not in the later part.

We know from earlier in this chapter that stagflation is bad news for policy makers. No matter what the Fed does, it will result in a worsening of either output or inflation. Should the Fed raise the interest rate to lessen inflation at a cost of making the output situation (and therefore unemployment) worse, or should it lower the interest rate to help output growth (which will lower unemployment) at a cost of making inflation worse? What did the Fed actually do? You can see from Figure 12.7 that the Fed generally raised the interest rate when inflation was high—even when output was low and unemployment was high. So, the Fed seems to have worried more in this period about inflation than unemployment. The interest rate was very high in the 1979–1983 period even though output was low. Had the Fed not had such high interest rates in this period, the recession would likely have been less severe, but inflation would have been even worse. Paul Volcker, Fed chair at that time, was both hailed as an inflation-fighting hero and pilloried for what was labeled the "Volcker recession."

After inflation got back down to about 4 percent in 1983, the Fed began lowering the interest rate, which helped to increase output. The Fed increased the interest rate in 1988 as inflation began to pick up a little and output was strong. The Fed acted aggressively in lowering the interest rate during the 1990–1991 recession and again in the 2001 recession. The Treasury bill rate got below 1 percent in 2003. The Fed then reversed course, and the interest rate rose to nearly 5 percent in 2006. The Fed then reversed course again near the end of 2007 and began lowering the interest rate in an effort to fight a recession that it expected was coming. The recession did come, and the Fed lowered the interest rate to near zero beginning in 2008 IV. The interest rate has remained at essentially zero since then. This is the zero interest rate bound discussed previously in this chapter. The period 2008 IV–2014 IV is a "binding situation" period.

Fed behavior in the period since 1970 is thus fairly easy to summarize. The Fed generally had high interest rates in the 1970s and early 1980s as it fought inflation. Since 1983,

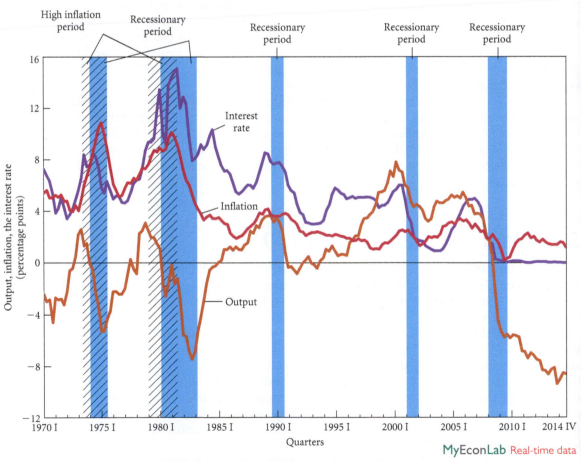

▲ **FIGURE 12.7** **Output, Inflation, and the Interest Rate 1970 I–2014 IV**
The Fed generally had high interest rates in the two inflationary periods and low interest rates from the mid-1980s on. It aggressively lowered interest rates in the 1990 III–1991 I, 2001 I–2001 III, and 2008 I–2009 II recessions. Output is the percentage deviation of real GDP from its trend. Inflation is the four-quarter average of the percentage change in the GDP deflator. The interest rate is the 3-month Treasury bill rate.

inflation has been low by historical standards, and the Fed focused between 1983 and 2008 on trying to smooth fluctuations in output. Since the end of 2008, there has been a zero interest rate bound.

# Inflation Targeting

Some monetary authorities in the world engage in what is called **inflation targeting**. If a monetary authority behaves this way, it announces a *target* value of the inflation rate, usually for a horizon of a year or more, and then it chooses its interest rate values with the aim of keeping the actual inflation rate within some specified band around the target value. For example, the target value might be 2 percent with a band of 1 to 3 percent. Then the monetary authority would try to keep the actual inflation rate between 1 and 3 percent. With a horizon of a year or more, the monetary authority would not expect to keep the inflation rate between 1 and 3 percent each month because there are a number of temporary factors that move the inflation rate around each month (such as weather) over which the monetary authority has no control. But over a year or more, the expectation would be that the inflation rate would be between 1 and 3 percent. India, which had continuing struggles with inflation in recent years, has set an inflation target of 6 percent for 2015-2016, falling to 4 percent by 2017–2018.

**inflation targeting**   When a monetary authority chooses its interest rate values with the aim of keeping the inflation rate within some specified band over some specified horizon.

There has been much debate about whether inflation targeting is a good idea. It can lower fluctuations in inflation, but possibly at a cost of larger fluctuations in output.

When Ben Bernanke was appointed chair of the Fed in 2006, some wondered whether the Fed would move in the direction of inflation targeting. Bernanke had argued in the past in favor of inflation targeting. There is, however, no evidence that the Fed did this during Bernanke's tenure as the Fed chair. You can see in Figure 12.7 that the Fed began lowering the interest rate in 2007 in anticipation of a recession, which doesn't look like inflation targeting.

# Looking Ahead

We have so far said little about employment, unemployment, and the functioning of the labor market in the macroeconomy except to note the central role of sticky wages in the construction of the *AS* curve. The next chapter will link everything we have done so far to this third major market arena—the labor market—and to the problem of unemployment.

─────────────────── **SUMMARY** ───────────────────

### 12.1 FISCAL POLICY EFFECTS  *p. 232*

1. Increases in government spending (*G*) and decreases in net taxes (*T*) shift the *AD* curve to the right and increase output and the price level. How much each increases depends on where the economy is on the *AS* curve before the change.

2. If the *AS* curve is vertical in the long run, then changes in *G* and *T* have no effect on output in the long run.

### 12.2 MONETARY POLICY EFFECTS  *p. 234*

3. Monetary policy is determined by the Fed rule, which includes output, the price level, and the factors in Z. Changes in Z shift the *AD* curve.

4. The *AD* curve is flatter the more the Fed weights price stability relative to output stability.

5. A binding situation is a state of the economy in which the Fed rule calls for a negative interest rate. In this case the best the Fed can do is have a zero interest rate.

6. The *AD* curve is vertical in a binding situation.

### 12.3 SHOCKS TO THE SYSTEM  *p. 237*

7. Positive cost shocks shift the *AS* curve to the left, creating *cost-push inflation*.

8. Positive demand-side shocks shift the *AD* curve to the right, creating *demand-pull inflation*.

### 12.4 MONETARY POLICY SINCE 1970 *p. 239*

9. The Fed generally had high interest rates in the 1970s and early 1980s as it fought inflation. Since 1983, inflation has been low by historical standards, and the Fed focused between 1983 and 2008 on trying to smooth fluctuations in output. Since the end of 2008, there has been a zero interest rate bound.

10. Inflation targeting is the case where the monetary authority weights only inflation. It chooses its interest rate value with the aim of keeping the inflation rate within some specified band over some specified horizon.

---

## REVIEW TERMS AND CONCEPTS

binding situation, *p. 235*

cost-push, *or* supply-side inflation, *p. 238*

demand-pull inflation, *p. 238*

inflation targeting, *p. 241*

stagflation, *p. 238*

zero interest rate bound, *p. 235*

---

## PROBLEMS

All problems are available on MyEconLab.

### 12.1 FISCAL POLICY EFFECTS

**LEARNING OBJECTIVE:** Use the *AS/AD* model to analyze the short-run and long-run effects of fiscal policy.

1.1 During the third quarter of 1997, Japanese GDP was falling at a rate of over 11 percent. Many blamed the big increase in Japan's taxes in the spring of 1997, which was designed to balance the budget. Explain how an increase in taxes with the economy growing slowly could precipitate a recession. Do not skip steps in your answer. If you were head of the Japanese central bank, how would you respond? What impact would your policy have on the level of investment?

1.2 By using aggregate supply and aggregate demand curves to illustrate your points, discuss the impacts of the following events on the price level and on equilibrium GDP (*Y*) in the *short run*:
   **a.** A tax cut holding government purchases constant with the economy operating well below full capacity
   **b.** An increase in consumer confidence and business optimism with the economy operating at near full capacity

### 12.2 MONETARY POLICY EFFECTS

**LEARNING OBJECTIVE:** Use the *AS/AD* model to analyze the short-run and long-run effects of monetary policy.

2.1 For each of the following scenarios, tell a story and predict the effects on the equilibrium level of aggregate output (*Y*) and the interest rate (*r*):
   **a.** During 2009, the Federal Reserve was easing monetary policy in an attempt to boost the economy. That same year, Congress passed the American Recovery and Reinvestment Act which cut taxes and expanded existing tax credits for working families and businesses.
   **b.** On January 1, 2013, the Social Security portion of the payroll tax rose from 4.2 percent to 6.2 percent and the top marginal tax rate increased to 39.6 percent from 35 percent. Assume that the Fed holds $M^s$ fixed.

   **c.** In 2014, the government raised taxes. At the same time, the Fed was pursuing an expansionary monetary policy.
   **d.** In January 2015, consumer confidence in the United States rose to its highest level since 2007, reflected by a rise in consumption. Assume that the Fed holds the money supply constant.
   **e.** The Fed attempts to increase the money supply to stimulate the economy, but plants are operating at 65 percent of their capacities and businesses are pessimistic about the future.

2.2 Paranoia, the largest country in central Antarctica, receives word of an imminent penguin attack. The news causes expectations about the future to be shaken. As a consequence, there is a sharp decline in investment spending plans.
   **a.** Explain in detail the effects of such an event on the economy of Paranoia, assuming no response on the part of the central bank or the Treasury ($M^s$, *T*, and *G* all remain constant.) Make sure you discuss the adjustments in the goods market and the money market.
   **b.** To counter the fall in investment, the King of Paranoia calls for a proposal to increase government spending. To finance the program, the Chancellor of the Exchequer has proposed three alternative options:
   (1) Finance the expenditures with an equal increase in taxes
   (2) Keep tax revenues constant and borrow the money from the public by issuing new government bonds
   (3) Keep taxes constant and finance expenditures by printing new money
   Consider the three financing options and rank them from most expansionary to least expansionary. Explain your ranking.

2.3 By late summer 2010, the target federal funds rate was between zero and 0.25 percent. At the same time, "animal spirits" were dormant and there was excess capacity in most industries. That is, businesses were in no mood to build new plant and equipment because many were not using their already existing capital. Interest rates were at or near zero, and yet investment demand remained quite low. The unemployment rate was 9.6 percent in

---

August 2010. These conditions suggest that monetary policy is likely to be a more effective tool to promote expansion than fiscal policy. Do you agree or disagree? Explain your answer.

2.4 Describe what will happen to the interest rate and aggregate output with the implementation of the following policy mixes:

a. Expansionary fiscal policy and expansionary monetary policy

b. Expansionary fiscal policy and contractionary monetary policy

c. Contractionary fiscal policy and expansionary monetary policy

d. Contractionary fiscal policy and contractionary monetary policy

2.5 Contractionary policies are designed to slow the economy and reduce inflation by decreasing aggregate demand and aggregate output. Explain why contractionary fiscal policy and contractionary monetary policy have opposite effects on the interest rate despite having the same goal of decreasing aggregate demand and aggregate output. Illustrate your answer with graphs of the money market.

2.6 Explain the effect, if any, that each of the following occurrences should have on the aggregate demand curve.

a. The Fed raises the discount rate.

b. The price level increases.

c. The federal government decreases federal income tax rates in an effort to stimulate the economy.

d. Optimistic firms increase investment spending.

e. The inflation rate rises by 6 percent.

f. The federal government decreases purchases in an effort to reduce the federal deficit.

2.7 In Japan during the first half of 2000, the Bank of Japan kept interest rates at a near zero level in an attempt to stimulate demand. In addition, the government passed a substantial increase in government expenditure and cut taxes. Slowly, Japanese GDP began to grow with absolutely no sign of an increase in the price level. Illustrate the position of the Japanese economy with aggregate supply and aggregate demand curves. Where on the short-run *AS* curve was Japan in 2000?

2.8 By using aggregate supply and aggregate demand curves to illustrate your points, discuss the impacts of the following events on the price level and on equilibrium GDP (*Y*) in the *short run*:

a. An increase in the money supply with the economy operating at near full capacity

b. A decrease in taxes and an increase in government spending supported by a cooperative Fed acting to keep output from rising

2.9 In country A, all wage contracts are indexed to inflation. That is, each month wages are adjusted to reflect increases in the cost of living as reflected in changes in the price level. In country B, there are no cost-of-living adjustments to wages, but the workforce is completely unionized. Unions negotiate 3-year contracts. In which country is an expansionary monetary policy likely to have a larger effect

on aggregate output? Explain your answer using aggregate supply and aggregate demand curves.

## 12.3 SHOCKS TO THE SYSTEM

**LEARNING OBJECTIVE:** Explain how economic shocks affect the *AS/AD* model.

3.1 From May 2014 to March 2015, the price of oil dropped sharply on world markets. What impact would you expect there to be on the aggregate price level and on real GDP? Illustrate your answer with aggregate demand and aggregate supply curves. What would you expect to be the effect on interest rates if the Fed held the money supply constant? Tell a complete story.

3.2 From the following graph, identify the initial equilibrium, the short-run equilibrium, and the long-run equilibrium based on the scenarios below. Explain your answers and identify what happened to the price level and aggregate output.

Scenario 1. The economy is initially in long-run equilibrium at point A, and a cost shock causes cost-push inflation. The government reacts by implementing an expansionary fiscal policy.

Scenario 2. The economy is initially in long-run equilibrium at point A, and an increase in government purchases causes demand-pull inflation. In the long run, wages respond to the inflation.

Scenario 3. The economy is initially in long-run equilibrium at point C, and the federal government implements an increase in corporate taxes and personal income taxes. In the long run, firms and workers adjust to the new price level and costs adjust accordingly.

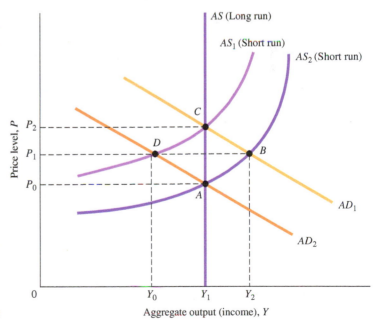

Scenario 4. The economy is initially in long-run equilibrium at point C, and energy prices decrease significantly. The government reacts by implementing a contractionary fiscal policy.

3.3 Evaluate the following statement: In the short run, if an economy experiences inflation of 10 percent, the cause of the inflation is unimportant. Whatever the cause, the only important issue the government needs to be concerned with is the 10 percent increase in the price level.

3.4 [**Related to the** *Economics in Practice* **on p. 238**] Use aggregate supply and aggregate demand curves to illustrate the effect the mild monsoon season had on the rice crop in India. Explain what affect this had on the levels of aggregate output and inflation in India.

## 12.4 MONETARY POLICY SINCE 1970

**LEARNING OBJECTIVE:** Discuss monetary policy since 1970.

4.1 During 2001, the U.S. economy slipped into a recession. For the next several years, the Fed and Congress used monetary and fiscal policies in an attempt to stimulate the economy. Obtain data on interest rates (such as the prime rate or the federal funds rate). Do you see evidence of the Fed's action? When did the Fed begin its expansionary policy? Obtain data on total federal expenditures, tax receipts, and the deficit. (Try www.commerce.gov). When did fiscal policy become "expansionary"? Which policy seems to have suffered more from policy lags?

# The Labor Market in the Macroeconomy

# 13

In Chapter 7 we described some features of the U.S. labor market and explained how the unemployment rate is measured. In Chapter 11 we considered the labor market briefly in our discussion of the aggregate supply curve. We learned that the labor market is key to understanding how and when government policy can be useful. Sticky wages in the labor market cause the *AS* curve to be upward sloping and create room for government spending and tax policy to increase aggregate output. If wages are completely flexible and rise every time the price level rises by the same percentage, the *AS* curve will be vertical and government attempts to stimulate the economy will only lead to price increases.

Understanding how wages are set is thus key to macroeconomics. It is also one of the most disputed parts of the field. We begin our discussion with a review of the classical view, which holds that wages always adjust to clear the labor market, that is, to equate the supply of and demand for labor. We then consider what might be wrong with the classical set of assumptions, why the labor market may not always clear, and why unemployment may exist. Finally, we discuss the relationship between inflation and unemployment. As we go through the analysis, it is important to recall why unemployment is one of the three primary concerns of macroeconomics. Go back and reread "The Costs of Unemployment" in Chapter 7 (pp. 127–129). Unemployment imposes heavy costs on society.

**13.1 LEARNING OBJECTIVE**
Define fundamental concepts of the labor market.

# The Labor Market: Basic Concepts

On the first Friday of every month, the Labor Department releases the results of a household survey that provides an estimate of the number of people with a job, the employed (*E*), as well as the number of people who are looking for work but cannot find a job, the unemployed (*U*). The labor force (*LF*) is the number of employed plus unemployed:

$$LF = E + U$$

**unemployment rate**   The number of people unemployed as a percentage of the labor force.

The **unemployment rate** is the number of people unemployed as a percentage of the labor force:

$$\text{unemployment rate} = \frac{U}{LF}$$

To repeat, to be unemployed, a person must be out of a job and actively looking for work. When a person stops looking for work, he or she is considered *out of the labor force* and is no longer counted as unemployed.

It is important to realize that even if the economy is running at or near full capacity, the unemployment rate will never be zero. The economy is dynamic. Students graduate from schools and training programs; some businesses make profits and grow, whereas others suffer losses and go out of business; people move in and out of the labor force and change careers. It takes time for people to find the right job and for employers to match the right worker with the jobs they have. This **frictional** and **structural unemployment** is inevitable and in many ways desirable.

**frictional unemployment**   The portion of unemployment that is due to the normal working of the labor market; used to denote short-run job/skill matching problems.

**structural unemployment**   The portion of unemployment that is due to changes in the structure of the economy that result in a significant loss of jobs in certain industries.

**cyclical unemployment**   The increase in unemployment that occurs during recessions and depressions.

In this chapter, we are primarily concerned with **cyclical unemployment**, the increase in unemployment that occurs during recessions and depressions. When the economy contracts, the number of people unemployed and the unemployment rate rise. The United States has experienced several periods of high unemployment. During the Great Depression, the unemployment rate remained high for nearly a decade. In December 1982, more than 12 million people were unemployed, putting the unemployment rate at 10.8 percent. In the recession of 2008–2009, the unemployment rate rose to more than 10 percent.

In one sense, the reason employment falls when the economy experiences a downturn is obvious. When firms cut back on production, they need fewer workers, so people get laid off. Employment tends to fall when aggregate output falls and to rise when aggregate output rises. *Nevertheless, a decline in the demand for labor does not necessarily mean that unemployment will rise.* If markets work as we described in Chapters 3 and 4, a decline in the demand for labor will initially create an excess supply of labor. As a result, the wage rate should fall until the quantity of labor supplied again equals the quantity of labor demanded, restoring equilibrium in the labor market. Although the equilibrium quantity of labor is lower, at the new wage rate everyone who wants a job will have one.

If the quantity of labor demanded and the quantity of labor supplied are brought into equilibrium by rising and falling wage rates, there should be no persistent unemployment above the frictional and structural amount. Labor markets should behave just like output markets described by supply and demand curves. This was the view held by the classical economists who preceded Keynes, and it is still the view of a number of economists. Other economists believe that the labor market is different from other markets and that wage rates adjust only slowly to decreases in the demand for labor. If true, economies can suffer bouts of involuntary unemployment.

**13.2 LEARNING OBJECTIVE**
Explain the classical view of the labor market.

# The Classical View of the Labor Market

The classical view of the labor market is illustrated in Figure 13.1. Classical economists assumed that the wage rate adjusts to equate the quantity demanded with the quantity supplied, thereby implying that unemployment does not exist. If we see people out of work, it just means that they are not interested in working at the going market wage for someone with their skills. To see how wage adjustment might take place, we can use the supply and demand curves in Figure 13.1. Curve $D_0$ is the **labor demand curve**. Each point on $D_0$ represents the amount of labor firms want to employ at each given wage rate. Each firm's decision about how much labor to demand is part of its overall profit-maximizing decision. A firm makes a profit by selling output to

**labor demand curve**   A graph that illustrates the amount of labor that firms want to employ at each given wage rate.

households. It will hire workers if the value of its output is sufficient to justify the wage that is being paid. Thus, the amount of labor that a firm hires depends on the value of output that workers produce.

Figure 13.1 also shows a **labor supply curve**, labeled S. Each point on the labor supply curve represents the amount of labor households want to supply at each given wage rate. Each household's decision concerning how much labor to supply is part of the overall consumer choice problem of a household. Each household member looks at the market wage rate, the prices of outputs, and the value of leisure time (including the value of staying at home and working in the yard or raising children) and chooses the amount of labor to supply (if any). A household member not in the labor force has decided that his or her time is more valuable in nonmarket activities.

In Figure 13.1 the labor market is initially in equilibrium at $W_0$ and $L_0$. Now consider what classical economists think would happen if there is a decrease in the demand for labor. The demand for labor curve shifts in from $D_0$ to $D_1$. The new demand curve intersects the labor supply curve at $L_1$ and $W_1$. There is a new equilibrium at a lower wage rate, in which fewer people are employed. Note that the fall in the demand for labor has not caused any unemployment. There are fewer people working, but all people interested in working at the wage $W_1$ are in fact employed.

The classical economists saw the workings of the labor market—the behavior of labor supply and labor demand—as optimal from the standpoint of both individual households and firms and from the standpoint of society. If households want more output than is currently being produced, output demand will increase, output prices will rise, the demand for labor will increase, the wage rate will rise, and more workers will be drawn into the labor force. (Some of those who preferred not to be a part of the labor force at the lower wage rate will be lured into the labor force at the higher wage rate.) At equilibrium, prices and wages reflect a trade-off between the value households place on outputs and the value of time spent in leisure and non-market work. At equilibrium, the people who are not working have *chosen* not to work at that market wage. There is always *full employment* in this sense. The classical economists believed that the market would achieve the optimal result if left to its own devices, and there is nothing the government can do to make things better.

## The Classical Labor Market and the Aggregate Supply Curve

How does the classical view of the labor market relate to the theory of the vertical AS curve we covered in Chapter 11? The classical idea that wages adjust to clear the labor market is consistent with the view that wages respond quickly to price changes. In the absence of sticky wages, the

**labor supply curve** A graph that illustrates the amount of labor that households want to supply at each given wage rate.

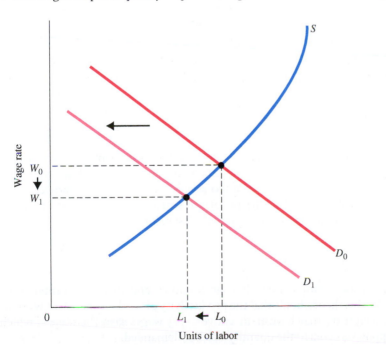

◀ **FIGURE 13.1** **The Classical Labor Market** Classical economists believe that the labor market always clears. If the demand for labor shifts from $D_0$ to $D_1$, the equilibrium wage will fall from $W_0$ to $W_1$. Anyone who wants a job at $W_1$ will have one.

AS curve will be vertical. In this case, monetary and fiscal policy will have no effect on real output. Indeed, in this view, there is no unemployment problem to be solved!

## The Unemployment Rate and the Classical View

If, as the classical economists assumed, the labor market works well, how can we account for the fact that the unemployment rate at times seems high? There seem to be times when millions of people who want jobs at prevailing wage rates cannot find them. How can we reconcile this situation with the classical assumption about the labor market?

Some economists answer by arguing that the unemployment rate is not a good measure of whether the labor market is working well. We know the economy is dynamic and at any given time some industries are expanding and some are contracting. Consider, for example, a carpenter who is laid off because of a contraction in the construction industry. He had probably developed specific skills related to the construction industry—skills not necessarily useful for jobs in other industries. If he were earning $40,000 per year as a carpenter, he may be able to earn only $30,000 per year in another industry. Will this carpenter take a job at $30,000? There are at least two reasons he may not. First, he may believe that the slump in the construction industry is temporary and that he will soon get his job back. Second, he may mistakenly believe that he can earn more than $30,000 in another industry and will continue to look for a better job.

If our carpenter decides to continue looking for a job paying more than $30,000 per year, he will be considered unemployed because he is actively looking for work. This does not necessarily mean that the labor market is not working properly. The carpenter has *chosen* not to work for a wage of $30,000 per year, but if his value to any firm outside the construction industry is no more than $30,000 per year, we would not expect him to find a job paying more than $30,000. In this case, a positive unemployment rate as measured by the government does not necessarily indicate that the labor market is working poorly. It just tells us that people are slow to adjust their expectations about what they can earn in the labor market.

If the degree to which industries are changing in the economy fluctuates over time, there will be more people like our carpenter at some times than at others. This variation will cause the measured unemployment rate to fluctuate. Some economists argue that the measured unemployment rate may sometimes *seem* high even though the labor market is working well. The quantity of labor supplied at the current wage is equal to the quantity demanded at the current wage. The fact that there are people willing to work at a wage higher than the current wage does not mean that the labor market is not working. Whenever there is an upward-sloping supply curve in a market (as is usually the case in the labor market), the quantity supplied at a price higher than the equilibrium price is always greater than the quantity supplied at the equilibrium price.

Economists who view unemployment this way do not see it as a major problem. Yet the haunting images of the bread lines in the 1930s are still with us, and many find it difficult to believe everything was optimal when more than 12 million people were counted as unemployed in 2012. There are other views of unemployment, as we will now see.

Discuss four reasons for the existence of unemployment.

# Explaining the Existence of Unemployment

We noted previously and in Chapter 7 that some unemployment is frictional or structural. The rest we categorized as cyclical—unemployement that moves up and down with the business cycle. This categorization is, however, a little too simple. Economists have argued that there may be unemployment that is higher than frictional plus structural and yet does not fluctuate much with the business cycle. We turn to these arguments first before considering cyclical unemployment.

**efficiency wage theory** An explanation for unemployment that holds that the productivity of workers increases with the wage rate. If this is so, firms may have an incentive to pay wages above the market-clearing rate.

## Efficiency Wage Theory

One argument for unemployment beyond frictional and structural centers on the **efficiency wage theory**. This theory holds that the productivity of workers increases with the wage rate. If this is true, then firms may have an incentive to pay wages *above* the wage at which the quantity of labor supplied is equal to the quantity of labor demanded.

The key argument of the efficiency wage theory is that by offering workers a wage in excess of the market wage, the productivity of those workers is increased. Some economists have likened the payment of this higher wage to a gift-exchange: Firms pay a wage in excess of the market wage, and in return, workers work harder or more productively than they otherwise would. Empirical studies of labor markets have identified several potential benefits that firms might receive from paying workers more than the market-clearing wage. Among them are lower turnover, improved morale, and reduced "shirking" of work.

Under these circumstances, there will be people who want to work at the wage paid by firms and cannot find employment. Indeed, for the efficiency wage theory to operate, it must be the case that the wage offered by firms is above the market wage. It is the gap between the two that motivates workers who do have jobs to outdo themselves.

# Imperfect Information

Thus far we have been assuming that firms know exactly what wage rates they need to set to clear the labor market. They may not choose to set their wages at this level, but at least they know what the market-clearing wage is. In practice, however, firms may not have enough information at their disposal to know what the market-clearing wage is. In this case, firms are said to have imperfect information. If firms have imperfect or incomplete information, they may simply set wages wrong—wages that do not clear the labor market.

If a firm sets its wages too high, more workers will want to work for that firm than the firm wants to employ, resulting in some potential workers being turned away. The result is, of course, unemployment. One objection to this explanation is that it accounts for the existence of unemployment only in the very short run. As soon as a firm sees that it has made a mistake, why would it not immediately correct its mistake and adjust its wages to the correct market-clearing level? Why would unemployment persist?

If the economy were simple, it should take no more than a few months for firms to correct their mistakes, but the economy is complex. Although firms may be aware of their past mistakes and may try to correct them, new events are happening all the time. Because constant change—including a constantly changing equilibrium wage level—is characteristic of the economy, firms may find it hard to adjust wages to the market-clearing level. The labor market is not like the stock market or the market for wheat, where prices are determined in organized exchanges every day. Instead, thousands of firms are setting wages and millions of workers are responding to these wages. It may take considerable time for the market-clearing wages to be determined after they have been disturbed from an equilibrium position.

# Minimum Wage Laws

**Minimum wage laws** set a floor for wage rates—a minimum hourly rate for any kind of labor. In 2015, the federal minimum wage was $7.25 per hour. If the market-clearing wage for some groups of workers is below this amount, this group will be unemployed.

Out-of-school teenagers, who have relatively little job experience, are most likely to be hurt by minimum wage laws. If some teenagers can produce only $6.90 worth of output per hour, no firm would be willing to hire them at a wage of $7.25. To do so would incur a loss of $0.35 per hour. In an unregulated market, these teenagers would be able to find work at the market-clearing wage of $6.90 per hour. If the minimum wage laws prevent the wage from falling below $7.25, these workers will not be able to find jobs and they will be unemployed. Others who may be hurt include people with very low skills and some recent immigrants.

To the extent that minimum wage legislation prevents wages from falling, causing unemployment, it does not provide a challenge to the classical view, but rather an explanation for what happens when the government prevents that market model from working. In the United States the federal minimum wages has not changed in a number of years and most economists view its effect on unemployment at present to be small.

Like the theories of the efficiency wage and imperfect information, the existence of government rules on how low wages can fall tell us little about the causes of cyclical unemployment. We turn to this now.

**minimum wage laws**  Laws that set a floor for wage rates—that is, a minimum hourly rate for any kind of labor.

# Explaining the Existence of Cyclical Unemployment

The classical model of wage setting, even in a world of imperfect information and efficiency wages, does not lead us to predict cyclical unemployment. Explaining cyclical unemployment requires us to look to other theories. Key to these theories is explaining why wages might have trouble adjusting downward when economic activity causes firms to seek fewer workers. If wages are sticky in a downward direction, the frictional and structural unemployment that we see in a normal economy will grow in a downturn, and we will experience cyclical unemployment.

## Sticky Wages

**sticky wages** The downward rigidity of wages as an explanation for the existence of unemployment.

Unemployment (above and beyond normal frictional and structural unemployment) occurs because wages are **sticky** on the downward side. We described this briefly in our building of the $AS$ curve. This situation is illustrated in Figure 13.2, where the equilibrium wage gets stuck at $W_0$ (the original wage) and does not fall to $W^*$ when demand decreases from $D_0$ to $D_1$. The result is unemployment of the amount $L_0 - L_1$, where $L_0$ is the quantity of labor that households want to supply at wage rate $W_0$ and $L_1$ is the amount of labor that firms want to hire at wage rate $W_0$. $L_0 - L_1$ is the number of workers who would like to work at $W_0$ but cannot find jobs.

The sticky wage explanation of unemployment, however, begs the question: *Why* are wages sticky, if they are, and *why* do wages not fall to clear the labor market during periods of high unemployment? Many answers have been proposed, but as yet no one answer has been agreed on. This lack of consensus is one reason macroeconomics has been in a state of flux for so long. The existence of unemployment continues to be a puzzle. Although we will discuss the major theories that economists have proposed to explain why wages may not clear the labor market, we can offer no conclusions. The question is still open.

**social, or implicit, contracts**
Unspoken agreements between workers and firms that firms will not cut wages.

**Social, or Implicit, Contracts** One explanation for downwardly sticky wages is that firms enter into **social, or implicit, contracts** with workers not to cut wages. It seems that extreme events—deep recession, deregulation, or threat of bankruptcy—are necessary for firms to cut wages. Wage cuts did occur in the Great Depression, in the airline industry following deregulation of the industry in the 1980s, and recently when some U.S. manufacturing firms found themselves in danger of bankruptcy from stiff foreign competition. Even then, wage cuts were typically imposed only on new workers, not existing workers, as in the auto industry in 2008–2009. Broad-based wage cuts are exceptions to the general rule. For reasons that may be more sociological than economic, cutting wages seems close to being a taboo. In one study, Truman

▶ **FIGURE 13.2 Sticky Wages**
If wages "stick" at $W_0$ instead of falling to the new equilibrium wage of $W^*$ following a shift of demand from $D_0$ to $D_1$, the result will be unemployment equal to $L_0 - L_1$.

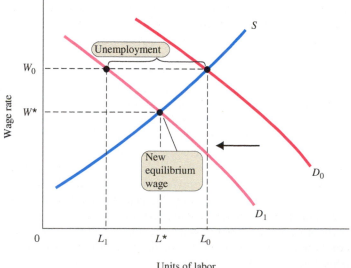

## ECONOMICS IN PRACTICE

### The Longer You Are Unemployed, the Harder It Is to Get a Job

Almost everyone has been or will be unemployed for a period of time during his or her work career. After graduation, it may take you a while to find a new job. If your firm closes, you may not find something right away. But in some cases, for some people, unemployment lasts a long time. What are the consequences of long-term unemployment?

Simply comparing job market results for people who are unemployed for a long time versus those with no or short spells of unemployment clearly does not tell us the answer. In most cases, people with long spells of unemployment do not look exactly like those with only short spells, and at least some of the differences across those groups may be hard to observe. The authors of a recent paper conducted an interesting experiment to try to figure out what long-term unemployment does to one's eventual job prospects.

Kory Kroft, Fabian Lange, and Matthew Notowidigdo sent out fictitious job resumes to real job postings in 100 U.S. cities.[1] More than 12,000 resumes were sent in response to 3,000 job postings. Fictitious job applicants were randomly assigned unemployment durations of 1 to 36 months. The researchers then tracked "call backs" to these resumes. The result? Call backs decreased dramatically as a response to unemployment duration. This effect was especially strong in cities that had strong job markets. The researchers suggested

that employers were likely inferring low worker quality based on long duration of unemployment.

#### THINKING PRACTICALLY

1. What does this result tell us about how easy it is for firms to see worker quality?

[1] Kory Kroft, Fabian Lange, Matthew Notowidigdo, "Duration Dependence and Labor Market Conditions: Theory and Evidence From a Field Experiment." *Quarterly Journal of Economics*, October 2013.

---

Bewley of Yale University surveyed hundreds of managers about why they did not reduce wage rates in downturns. The most common response was that wage cuts hurt worker morale and thus negatively affect worker productivity. Breaking the taboo and cutting wages may be costly in this sense. Firms seem to prefer laying off existing workers to lowering their wages.

A related argument, the **relative-wage explanation of unemployment**, holds that workers are concerned about their wages *relative* to the wages of other workers in other firms and industries and may be unwilling to accept wage cuts unless they know that other workers are receiving similar cuts. Because it is difficult to reassure any one group of workers that all other workers are in the same situation, workers may resist any cut in their wages. There may be an implicit understanding between firms and workers that firms will not do anything that would make their workers worse off relative to workers in other firms.

**relative-wage explanation of unemployment** An explanation for sticky wages (and therefore unemployment): If workers are concerned about their wages relative to the wages of other workers in other firms and industries, they may be unwilling to accept a wage cut unless they know that all other workers are receiving similar cuts.

**Explicit Contracts** Many workers—in particular unionized workers—sign 1- to 3-year employment contracts with firms. These contracts stipulate the workers' wages for each year of the contract. Wages set in this way do not fluctuate with economic conditions, either upward or downward. If the economy slows down and firms demand fewer workers, the wage will not fall. Instead, some workers will be laid off.

Although **explicit contracts** can explain why some wages are sticky, a deeper question must also be considered. Workers and firms surely know at the time a contract is signed that unforeseen events may cause the wages set by the contract to be too high or too low. Why do firms and workers bind themselves in this way? One explanation is that negotiating wages is costly. Negotiations between unions and firms can take a considerable amount of time—time that could be spent producing output—and it would be very costly to negotiate wages weekly or monthly. Contracts are a way of bearing these costs at no more than 1-, 2-, or 3-year intervals. There is a trade-off between the costs of locking workers and firms into contracts for long periods of time

**explicit contracts** Employment contracts that stipulate workers' wages, usually for a period of 1 to 3 years.

and the costs of wage negotiations. The length of contracts that minimizes negotiation costs seems to be (from what we observe in practice) between 1 and 3 years.

Some multiyear contracts adjust for unforeseen events by **cost-of-living adjustments (COLAs)** written into the contract. COLAs tie wages to changes in the cost of living: The greater the rate of inflation, the more wages are raised. COLAs thus protect workers from unexpected inflation, although many COLAs adjust wages by a smaller percentage than the percentage increase in prices. Regarding deflation, few contracts allow for wage cuts in the face of deflation.

### An Open Question

As we have seen, there are many explanations for why we might see unemployment. Some of these explanations focus on why we might see levels of unemployment higher than frictional plus structural. Other explanations focus on the reasons for cyclical unemployment. The theories we have just set forth are not necessarily mutually exclusive, and there may be elements of truth in all of them. The aggregate labor market is complicated, and there are no simple answers to why there is unemployment. Much current work in macroeconomics is concerned directly or indirectly with this question, and it is an exciting area of study. Which argument or arguments will win out in the end is an open question.

**13.5 LEARNING OBJECTIVE**

Analyze the short-run relationship between unemployment and inflation.

# The Short-Run Relationship Between the Unemployment Rate and Inflation

In chapter 11 we described the Fed as concerned about both output and the price level. In practice, the Fed typically describes its interests as being unemployment on the one hand and inflation on the other. For example, Janet Yellen, the Fed chair, gave a speech at the San Francisco Fed on March 27, 2015, in which she said, "Our goal in adjusting the federal funds rate over time will be to achieve and sustain economic conditions close to maximum employment with inflation averaging 2 percent." We are now in a position to connect the Fed interest in output with the unemployment rate and to explore the connection between unemployment and prices.

We begin by looking at the relation between aggregate output (income) ($Y$) and the unemployment rate ($U$). For an economy to increase aggregate output, firms must hire more labor to produce that output. Thus, more output implies greater employment. An increase in employment means more people working (fewer people unemployed) and a lower unemployment rate. An increase in $Y$ corresponds to a *decrease* in $U$. Thus, $U$ and $Y$ are *negatively* related: When $Y$ rises, the unemployment rate falls, and when $Y$ falls, the unemployment rate rises, all else equal.

What about the relationship between aggregate output and the overall price level? The $AS$ curve, reproduced in Figure 13.3, shows the relationship between $Y$ and the overall price level ($P$). The relationship is a positive one: When $P$ increases, $Y$ increases, and when $P$ decreases, $Y$ decreases.

▶ **FIGURE 13.3** **The Aggregate Supply Curve**
The *AS* curve shows a positive relationship between the price level (*P*) and aggregate output (income) (*Y*).

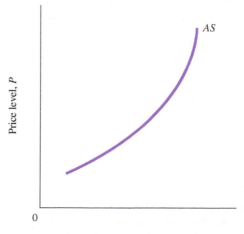

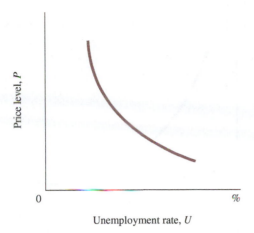

◀ **FIGURE 13.4**  **The Relationship Between the Price Level and the Unemployment Rate**
This curve shows a negative relationship between the price level (*P*) and the unemployment rate (*U*). As the unemployment rate declines in response to the economy's moving closer and closer to capacity output, the price level rises more and more.

As you will recall from the last chapter, the shape of the *AS* curve is determined by the behavior of firms in reacting to an increase in demand. If aggregate demand shifts to the right and the economy is operating on the nearly flat part of the *AS* curve—far from capacity—output will increase, but the price level will not change much. However, if the economy is operating on the steep part of the *AS* curve—close to capacity—an increase in demand will drive up the price level, but output will be constrained by capacity and will not increase much.

Now let us put the two pieces together and think about what will happen following an event that leads to an increase in aggregate demand. First, firms experience an unanticipated decline in inventories. They respond by increasing output (*Y*) and hiring workers—the unemployment rate falls. If the economy is not close to capacity, there will be little increase in the price level. If, however, aggregate demand continues to grow, the ability of the economy to increase output will eventually reach its limit. As aggregate demand shifts farther and farther to the right along the *AS* curve, the price level increases more and more and output begins to reach its limit. At the point at which the *AS* curve becomes vertical, output cannot rise any farther. If output cannot grow, the unemployment rate cannot be pushed any lower. There is a negative relationship between the unemployment rate and the price level. As the unemployment rate declines in response to the economy's moving closer and closer to capacity output, the overall price level rises more and more, as shown in Figure 13.4.

The *AS* curve in Figure 13.3 shows the relationship between the price level and aggregate output and thus implicitly between the price level and the unemployment rate, which is depicted in Figure 13.4. In policy formulation and discussions, however, economists have focused less on the relationship between the price level and the unemployment rate than on the relationship between the **inflation rate**—the percentage change in the price level—and the unemployment rate. Note that the price level and the percentage change in the price level are not the same. The curve describing the relationship between the inflation rate and the unemployment rate, which is shown in Figure 13.5, is called the **Phillips Curve**, after British economist A. W. Phillips, who first examined it using data for the United Kingdom. Fortunately, the analysis behind the *AS* curve (and thus the analysis behind the curve in Figure 13.4) will enable us to see both why the Phillips Curve initially looked so appealing as an explanation of the relationship between inflation and the unemployment rate and how more recent history has changed our views of the interpretation of the Phillips Curve.

**inflation rate**  The percentage change in the price level.

**Phillips Curve**  A curve showing the relationship between the inflation rate and the unemployment rate.

## The Phillips Curve: A Historical Perspective

In the 1950s and 1960s, there was a remarkably smooth relationship between the unemployment rate and the rate of inflation, as Figure 13.6 shows for the 1960s. As you can see, the data points fit fairly closely around a downward-sloping curve; in general, the higher the unemployment rate is, the lower the rate of inflation. The Phillips Curve in Figure 13.5 shows a trade-off between inflation and unemployment. The curve says that to lower the inflation rate, we must accept a higher unemployment rate, and to lower the unemployment rate, we must accept a higher rate of inflation.

Textbooks written in the 1960s and early 1970s relied on the Phillips Curve as the main explanation of inflation. Things seemed simple—inflation appeared to respond in a fairly predictable

▶ **FIGURE 13.5** **The Phillips Curve**
The Phillips Curve shows the relationship between the inflation rate and the unemployment rate.

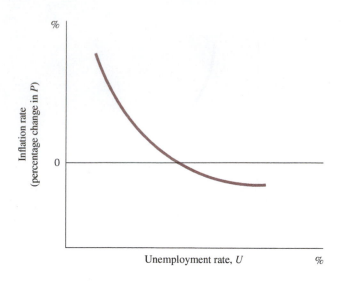

▶ **FIGURE 13.6**
**Unemployment and Inflation, 1960–1969**
During the 1960s, there seemed to be an obvious trade-off between inflation and unemployment. Policy debates during the period revolved around this apparent trade-off.

*Source:* U.S Bureau of Labor Statistics.

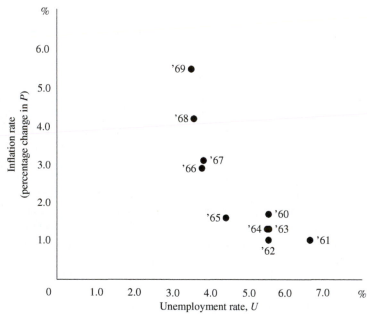

way to changes in the unemployment rate. Policy discussions in the 1960s often revolved around the Phillips Curve. The role of the policy maker, it was thought, was to choose a point on the curve. Conservatives usually argued for choosing a point with a low rate of inflation and were willing to accept a higher unemployment rate in exchange for this. Liberals usually argued for accepting more inflation to keep unemployment at a low level.

Life did not turn out to be quite so simple. The Phillips Curve broke down in the 1970s and 1980s. This change can be seen in Figure 13.7, which graphs the unemployment rate and inflation rate for the period from 1970 to 2014. The points in Figure 13.7 show no particular relationship between inflation and the unemployment rate.

## Aggregate Supply and Aggregate Demand Analysis and the Phillips Curve

How can we explain the stability of the Phillips Curve in the 1950s and 1960s and the lack of stability after that? To answer, we need to return to *AS/AD* analysis.

If the *AD* curve shifts from year to year but the *AS* curve does not, the values of *P* and *Y* each year will lie along the *AS* curve [Figure 13.8(a)]. The shifting *AD* curve creates a set of *AS/AD* intersections that trace out the *AS* curve. (Try doing this yourself on a graph of the *AS* and *AD* curves.) The plot of the relationship between *P* and *Y* will be upward sloping in this case. Correspondingly,

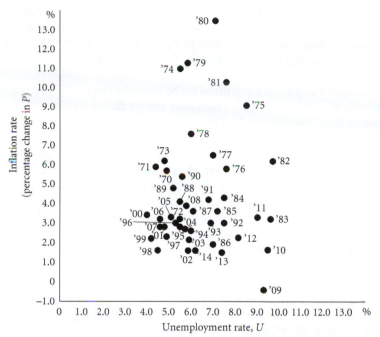

◀ **FIGURE 13.7**

**Unemployment and Inflation, 1970–2014**

From the 1970s on, it became clear that the relationship between unemployment and inflation was anything but simple.

*Source:* U.S Bureau of Labor Statistics.

MyEconLab Real-time data

the plot of the relationship between the unemployment rate (which decreases with increased output) and the rate of inflation will be a curve that slopes downward. In other words, if the new equilibrium data reflect a stable *AS* curve and a shifting *AD* curve, we would expect to see a negative relationship between the unemployment rate and the inflation rate, just as we see in Figure 13.6 for the 1960s.

However, the relationship between the unemployment rate and the inflation rate will look different if the *AS* curve shifts from year to year, perhaps from a change in oil prices, but the *AD* curve does not move. A leftward shift of the *AS* curve with the *AD* curve stable will cause an *increase* in the price level (*P*) and a *decrease* in aggregate output (*Y*) [Figure 13.8(b)]. When the *AS* curve shifts to the left, the economy experiences both inflation *and* an increase in the unemployment rate (because decreased output means increased unemployment). In other words, if the *AS* curve is shifting from year to year, we would expect to see a positive relationship between the unemployment rate and the inflation rate.

If both the *AS* and the *AD* curves are shifting simultaneously, however, there is no systematic relationship between *P* and *Y* [Figure 13.8(c)] and thus no systematic relationship between

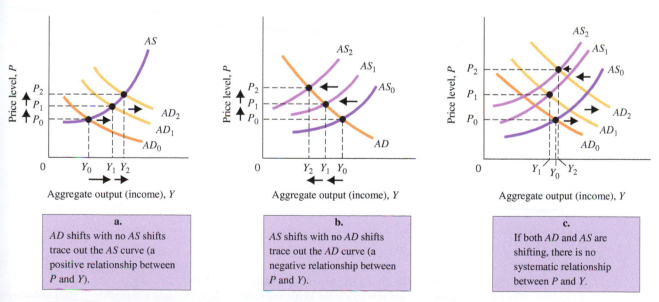

| a. | b. | c. |
|---|---|---|
| *AD* shifts with no *AS* shifts trace out the *AS* curve (a positive relationship between *P* and *Y*). | *AS* shifts with no *AD* shifts trace out the *AD* curve (a negative relationship between *P* and *Y*). | If both *AD* and *AS* are shifting, there is no systematic relationship between *P* and *Y*. |

▲ **FIGURE 13.8**  **Changes in the Price Level and Aggregate Output Depend on Shifts in Both Aggregate Demand and Aggregate Supply**

the unemployment rate and the inflation rate. One explanation for the change in the Phillips Curve between the 1960s and later periods is that both the *AS* and the *AD* curves appear to be shifting in the later periods—both shifts from the supply side and shifts from the demand side. This can be seen by examining a key cost variable: the price of imports.

**The Role of Import Prices**   We discussed in the previous chapter that one of the main factors that causes the *AS* curve to shift are changes in energy prices, particularly the price of oil. Because the United States imports much of its oil, the price index of U.S. imports is highly correlated with the (world) price of oil. As a result, a change in the U.S. import price index, which we will call "the price of imports," shifts the *AS* curve. The price of imports is plotted in Figure 13.9 for the 1960 I–2014 IV period. As you can see, the price of imports changed very little between 1960 and 1970. There were no large shifts in the *AS* curve in the 1960s due to changes in the price of imports. There were also no other large changes in input prices in the 1960s, so overall the *AS* curve shifted very little during the decade. The main variation in the 1960s was in aggregate demand, so the shifting *AD* curve traced out points along the *AS* curve.

Figure 13.9 also shows that the price of imports increased considerably in the 1970s. This rise led to large shifts in the *AS* curve during the decade, but the *AD* curve was also shifting throughout the 1970s. With both curves shifting, the data points for *P* and *Y* were scattered all over the graph and the observed relationship between *P* and *Y* was not at all systematic.

This story about import prices and the *AS* and *AD* curves in the 1960s and 1970s carries over to the Phillips Curve. The Phillips Curve was stable in the 1960s because the primary source of variation in the economy was demand, not costs. In the 1970s, both demand *and* costs were varying so no obvious relationship between the unemployment rate and the inflation rate was apparent. To some extent, what is remarkable about the Phillips Curve is not that it was not smooth after the 1960s, but that it ever was smooth.

## Expectations and the Phillips Curve

Another reason the Phillips Curve is not stable concerns expectations. We saw in Chapter 12 that if a firm expects other firms to raise their prices, the firm may raise the price of its own product. If all firms are behaving this way, prices will rise because they are expected to rise. In this sense, expectations are self-fulfilling. Similarly, if inflation is expected to be high in the future, negotiated wages are likely to be higher than if inflation is expected to be low. Wage inflation is thus affected by expectations of future price inflation. Because wages are input costs, prices rise as firms respond to the higher wage costs. Price expectations that affect wage contracts eventually affect prices themselves.

If the rate of inflation depends on expectations, the Phillips Curve will shift as expectations change. For example, if inflationary expectations increase, the result will be an increase in the rate of inflation even though the unemployment rate may not have changed. In this case, the

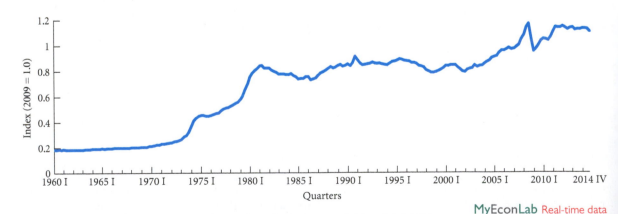

MyEconLab Real-time data

▲ **FIGURE 13.9**   **The Price of Imports, 1960 I–2014 IV**
The price of imports changed very little in the 1960s and early 1970s. It increased substantially in 1974 and again in 1979–1980. Between 1981 and 2002, the price of imports changed very little. It generally rose between 2003 and 2008, fell somewhat in late 2008 and early 2009, rose slightly in 2011 and then remained flat.

Phillips Curve will shift to the right. If inflationary expectations decrease, the Phillips Curve will shift to the left—there will be less inflation at any given level of the unemployment rate.

It so happened that inflationary expectations were quite stable in the 1950s and 1960s. The inflation rate was moderate during most of this period, and people expected it to remain moderate. With inflationary expectations not changing very much, there were no major shifts of the Phillips Curve, a situation that helps explain its stability during the period.

Near the end of the 1960s, inflationary expectations began to increase, primarily in response to the actual increase in inflation that was occurring because of the tight economy caused by the Vietnam War. Inflationary expectations increased even further in the 1970s as a result of large oil price increases. These changing expectations led to shifts of the Phillips Curve and are another reason the curve was not stable during the 1970s.

## Inflation and Aggregate Demand

It is important to realize that the fact that the Phillips Curve broke down during the 1970s does not mean that aggregate demand has no effect on inflation. It simply means that inflation is affected by more than just aggregate demand. If, say, inflation is also affected by cost variables like the price of imports, there will be no stable relationship between just inflation and aggregate demand unless the cost variables are not changing. Similarly, if the unemployment rate is taken to be a measure of aggregate demand, where inflation depends on both the unemployment rate and cost variables, there will be no stable Phillips Curve unless the cost variables are not changing. Therefore, the unemployment rate can have an important effect on inflation even though this will not be evident from a plot of inflation against the unemployment rate—that is, from the Phillips Curve.

## The Long-Run Aggregate Supply Curve, Potential Output, and the Natural Rate of Unemployment

**13.6 LEARNING** OBJECTIVE

Discuss the long-run relationship between unemployment and output.

Thus far we have been discussing the relationship between inflation and unemployment, looking at the short-run $AS$ and $AD$ curves. We turn now to look at the long run, focusing on the connection between output and unemployment.

Recall from Chapter 11 that many economists believe that in the long run, the $AS$ curve is vertical. We have illustrated this case in Figure 13.10. Assume that the initial equilibrium is at the intersection of $AD_0$ and the long-run aggregate supply curve. Now consider a shift of the aggregate demand curve from $AD_0$ to $AD_1$. If wages are sticky and lag prices, in the short run, aggregate output will rise from $Y_0$ to $Y_1$. (This is a movement along the short-run $AS$ curve $AS_0$.) In the longer run, wages catch up. For example, next year's labor contracts may make up for the fact that wage increases did not keep up with the cost of living this year. If wages catch up in the longer run, the $AS$ curve will shift from $AS_0$ to $AS_1$ and drive aggregate output back to $Y_0$. If wages ultimately rise by exactly the same percentage as output prices, firms will produce the same level of output as they did before the increase in aggregate demand.

In Chapter 11, we said that $Y_0$ is sometimes called *potential output*. Aggregate output can be pushed above $Y_0$ in the short run. When aggregate output exceeds $Y_0$, however, there is upward pressure on input prices and costs. The unemployment rate is already quite low, firms are beginning to encounter the limits of their plant capacities, and so on. At levels of aggregate output above $Y_0$, costs will rise, the $AS$ curve will shift to the left, and the price level will rise. Thus, potential output is the level of aggregate output that can be sustained in the long run without inflation.

This story is directly related to the Phillips Curve. Those who believe that the $AS$ curve is vertical in the long run at potential output also believe that the Phillips Curve is vertical in the long run at some natural rate of unemployment. Changes in aggregate demand—including increases in government spending—increase prices, but do not change employment. Recall from Chapter 7 that the **natural rate of unemployment** refers to unemployment that occurs as a normal part of the functioning of the economy. It is sometimes taken as the sum of frictional unemployment and structural unemployment. The logic behind the vertical Phillips Curve is that whenever the

**natural rate of unemployment**
The unemployment that occurs as a normal part of the functioning of the economy. Sometimes taken as the sum of frictional unemployment and structural unemployment.

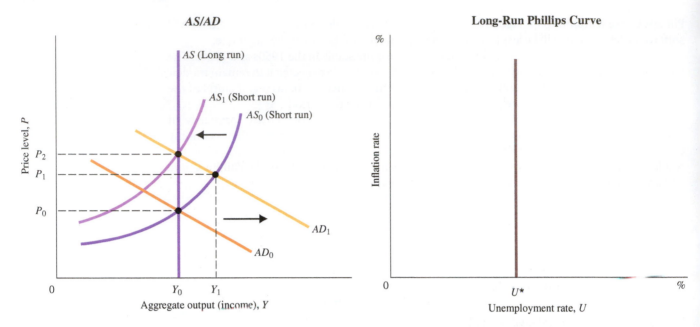

▲ **FIGURE 13.10** **The Long-Run Phillips Curve: The Natural Rate of Unemployment**
If the *AS* curve is vertical in the long run, so is the Phillips Curve. In the long run, the Phillips Curve corresponds to the natural rate of unemployment—that is, the unemployment rate that is consistent with the notion of a fixed long-run output at potential output. $U^*$ is the natural rate of unemployment.

unemployment rate is pushed below the natural rate, wages begin to rise, thus pushing up costs. This leads to a *lower* level of output, which pushes the unemployment rate back up to the natural rate. At the natural rate, the economy can be considered to be at full employment.

## The Nonaccelerating Inflation Rate of Unemployment (NAIRU)

In Figure 13.10, the long-run vertical Phillips Curve is a graph with the inflation rate on the vertical axis and the unemployment rate on the horizontal axis. The natural rate of unemployment is $U^*$. In the long run, with a long-run vertical Phillips Curve, the actual unemployment rate moves to $U^*$ because of the natural workings of the economy.

Another graph of interest is Figure 13.11, which plots the *change in* the inflation rate on the vertical axis and the unemployment rate on the horizontal axis. Many economists believe that the relationship between the change in the inflation rate and the unemployment rate is as depicted by the *PP* curve in the figure. The value of the unemployment rate where the *PP* curve crosses zero is called the *nonaccelerating inflation rate of unemployment* (**NAIRU**). If the actual unemployment rate is below the NAIRU, the change in the inflation rate will be positive. As depicted in the figure, at $U_1$, the change in the inflation rate is 1. Conversely, if the actual unemployment rate is above the NAIRU, the change in the inflation rate is negative: At $U_2$, the change is −1.

Consider what happens if the unemployment rate decreases from the NAIRU to $U_1$ and stays at $U_1$ for many periods. Assume also that the inflation rate at the NAIRU is 2 percent. Then in the first period the inflation rate will increase from 2 percent to 3 percent. The inflation rate does not, however, just stay at the higher 3 percent value. In the next period, the inflation rate will increase from 3 percent to 4 percent and so on. The price level will be accelerating—that is, the change in the inflation rate will be positive—when the actual unemployment rate is below the NAIRU. Conversely, the price level will be decelerating—that is, the change in the inflation rate will be negative—when the actual unemployment rate is above the NAIRU.[1]

**NAIRU** The nonaccelerating inflation rate of unemployment.

---

[1] The NAIRU is actually misnamed. It is the *price level* that is accelerating or decelerating, not the inflation rate, when the actual unemployment rate differs from the NAIRU. The inflation rate is not accelerating or decelerating, but simply changing by the same amount each period. The namers of the NAIRU forgot their physics.

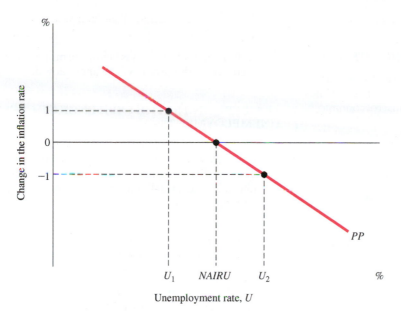

**▲ FIGURE 13.11   The NAIRU Diagram**
At an unemployment rate below the NAIRU, the price level is accelerating (positive changes in the inflation rate); at an unemployment rate above the NAIRU, the price level is decelerating (negative changes in the inflation rate). Only when the unemployment rate is equal to the NAIRU is the price level changing at a constant rate (no change in the inflation rate).

The PP curve in Figure 13.11 is like the AS curve in Figure 13.3—the same factors that shift the AS curve, such as cost shocks, can also shift the PP curve. Figure 11.2 on p. 217 summarizes the various factors that can cause the AS curve to shift, and these are also relevant for the PP curve. A favorable shift for the PP curve is to the left because the PP curve crosses zero at a lower unemployment rate, indicating that the NAIRU is lower. Some have argued that one possible recent source of favorable shifts is increased foreign competition, which may have kept wage costs and other input costs down.

Before about 1995, proponents of the NAIRU theory argued that the value of the NAIRU in the United States was around 6 percent. By the end of 1995, the unemployment rate declined to 5.6 percent, and by 2000, the unemployment rate was down to 3.8 percent. If the NAIRU had been 6 percent, one should have seen a continuing increase in the inflation rate beginning about 1995. In fact, the 1995 to 2000 period saw slightly declining inflation. Not only did inflation not continually increase, it did not even increase once to a new, higher value and then stay there. As the unemployment rate declined during this period, proponents of the NAIRU lowered their estimates of it, more or less in line with the actual fall in the unemployment rate. This recalibration can be justified by arguing that there have been continuing favorable shifts of the PP curve, such as possible increased foreign competition. Critics, however, have argued that this procedure is close to making the NAIRU theory vacuous. Can the theory really be tested if the estimate of the NAIRU is changed whenever it is not consistent with the data? How trustworthy is the appeal to favorable shifts?

Macroeconomists are currently debating whether equations estimated under the NAIRU theory are good approximations. More time is needed before any definitive answers can be given.

## Looking Ahead

This chapter concludes our basic analysis of how the macroeconomy works. In the preceding six chapters, we have examined how households and firms behave in the three market arenas—the goods market, the money market, and the labor market. We have seen how aggregate output (income), the interest rate, and the price level are determined in the economy, and we have examined the relationship between two of the most important macroeconomic variables, the inflation rate and the unemployment rate. In Chapter 14, we use everything we have learned up to this point to examine a number of important policy issues.

# SUMMARY

## 13.1 THE LABOR MARKET: BASIC CONCEPTS *p. 246*

1. Because the economy is dynamic, *frictional* and *structural unemployment* are inevitable and in some ways desirable. Times of *cyclical unemployment* are of concern to macroeconomic policy makers.

2. In general, employment tends to fall when aggregate output falls and rise when aggregate output rises.

## 13.2 THE CLASSICAL VIEW OF THE LABOR MARKET *p. 246*

3. Classical economists believe that the interaction of supply and demand in the labor market brings about equilibrium and that unemployment (beyond the frictional and structural amounts) does not exist.

4. The classical view of the labor market is consistent with the theory of a vertical aggregate supply curve.

5. Some economists argue that the unemployment rate is not an accurate indicator of whether the labor market is working properly. Unemployed people who are considered part of the labor force may be offered jobs but may be unwilling to take those jobs at the offered salaries. Some of the unemployed may have chosen not to work, but this result does not mean that the labor market has malfunctioned.

## 13.3 EXPLAINING THE EXISTENCE OF UNEMPLOYMENT *p. 248*

6. Efficiency wage theory holds that the productivity of workers increases with the wage rate. If this is true, firms may have an incentive to pay wages above the wage at which the quantity of labor supplied is equal to the quantity of labor demanded. At all wages above the equilibrium, there will be an excess supply of labor and therefore unemployment.

7. If firms are operating with incomplete or imperfect information, they may not know what the market-clearing wage is. As a result, they may set their wages incorrectly and bring about unemployment. Because the economy is so complex, it may take considerable time for firms to correct these mistakes.

8. Minimum wage laws, which set a floor for wage rates, are one factor contributing to unemployment of teenagers and very low-skilled workers. If the market-clearing wage for some groups of workers is below the minimum wage, some members of this group will be unemployed.

## 13.4 EXPLAINING THE EXISTENCE OF CYCLICAL UNEMPLOYMENT *p. 250*

9. If wages are sticky downward, cyclical unemployment may result. Downwardly *sticky wages* may be brought about by *social (implicit)* or *explicit contracts* not to cut wages. If the equilibrium wage rate falls but wages are prevented from falling also, the result will be unemployment.

## 13.5 THE SHORT-RUN RELATIONSHIP BETWEEN THE UNEMPLOYMENT RATE AND INFLATION *p. 252*

10. There is a negative relationship between the unemployment rate ($U$) and aggregate output (income) ($Y$): When $Y$ rises, $U$ falls. When $Y$ falls, $U$ rises.

11. The relationship between the unemployment rate and the price level is negative: As the unemployment rate declines and the economy moves closer to capacity, the price level rises more and more.

12. The *Phillips Curve* represents the relationship between the *inflation rate* and the *unemployment rate*. During the 1950s and 1960s, this relationship was stable and there seemed to be a predictable trade-off between inflation and unemployment. As a result of import price increases (which led to shifts in aggregate supply), the relationship between the inflation rate and the unemployment rate was erratic in the 1970s. Inflation depends on more than just the unemployment rate.

## 13.6 THE LONG-RUN AGGREGATE SUPPLY CURVE, POTENTIAL OUTPUT, AND THE NATURAL RATE OF UNEMPLOYMENT *p. 257*

13. Those who believe that the *AS* curve is vertical in the long run also believe that the Phillips Curve is vertical in the long run at the *natural rate of unemployment*. The natural rate is generally the sum of the frictional and structural rates. If the Phillips Curve is vertical in the long run, then there is a limit to how low government policy can push the unemployment rate without setting off inflation.

14. The *NAIRU* theory says that the price level will accelerate when the unemployment rate is below the NAIRU and decelerate when the unemployment rate is above the NAIRU.

# REVIEW TERMS AND CONCEPTS

cost-of-living adjustments (COLAs), *p. 252*

cyclical unemployment, *p. 246*

efficiency wage theory, *p. 248*

explicit contracts, *p. 251*

frictional unemployment, *p. 246*

inflation rate, *p. 253*

labor demand curve, *p. 246*

labor supply curve, *p. 247*

minimum wage laws, *p. 249*

MyEconLab Visit **www.myeconlab.com** to complete these exercises online and get instant feedback. Exercises that update with real-time data are marked with art ⊕.

NAIRU, *p. 258*

natural rate of unemployment, *p. 257*

Phillips Curve, *p. 253*

relative-wage explanation
of unemployment, *p. 251*

social, *or implicit*, contracts, *p. 250*

sticky wages, *p. 250*

structural unemployment, *p. 246*

unemployment rate, *p. 246*

---

# PROBLEMS

All problems are available on MyEconLab.

## 13.1 THE LABOR MARKET: BASIC CONCEPTS

LEARNING OBJECTIVE: Define fundamental concepts of the labor market.

1.1 The following policies have at times been advocated for coping with unemployment. Briefly explain how each might work and explain which type or types of unemployment (frictional, structural, or cyclical) each policy is designed to alter.
   a. A computer list of job openings and a service that matches employees with job vacancies (sometimes called an "economic dating service")
   b. Lower minimum wage for teenagers
   c. Retraining programs for workers who need to learn new skills to find employment
   d. Public employment for people without jobs
   e. Improved information about available jobs and current wage rates
   f. The president's going on nationwide TV and attempting to convince firms and workers that the inflation rate next year will be low

1.2 How will the following affect labor force participation rates, labor supply, and unemployment?
   a. In an attempt to get a handle on increasing Social Security shortfalls, Congress and the president decide to raise the Social Security tax on individuals and to cut Social Security payments to retirees.
   b. A national maternity leave program is enacted, requiring employers to provide 18 weeks of paid maternity leave for both parents of a newborn child.
   c. The U.S. government increases restrictions on immigration into the United States.
   d. The government enacts policy making it easier for more people to collect welfare benefits.
   e. The government eliminates investment tax credits and therefore no longer subsidizes the purchase of new capital by firms.

## 13.2 THE CLASSICAL VIEW OF THE LABOR MARKET

LEARNING OBJECTIVE: Explain the classical view of the labor market.

2.1 Using a supply and demand graph for the labor market, explain the classical view that the economy will remain at full employment, even with a decrease in the demand for labor. How will this labor market graph change in the absence of sticky wages?

## 13.3 EXPLAINING THE EXISTENCE OF UNEMPLOYMENT

LEARNING OBJECTIVE: Discuss four reasons for the existence of unemployment.

3.1 In 2015, the country of Sorbet was suffering from a period of high unemployment. The new president, Gelato, appointed Sherrie Sherbert as his chief economist. Ms. Sherbert and her staff estimated these supply and demand curves for labor from data obtained from the secretary of labor, Jerry Benjamin:

$$Q_D = 175 - 4W$$
$$Q_S = 16W - 30$$

where Q is the quantity of labor supplied/demanded in millions of workers and W is the wage rate in scoops, the currency of Sorbet.
   a. Currently, the law in Sorbet says that no worker shall be paid less than 12 scoops per hour. Estimate the quantity of labor supplied, the number of unemployed, and the unemployment rate.
   b. President Gelato, over the objection of Secretary Benjamin, has recommended to Congress that the law be changed to allow the wage rate to be determined in the market. If such a law was passed and the market adjusted quickly, what would happen to total employment, the size of the labor force, and the unemployment rate? Show the results graphically.
   c. Will the Sorbet labor market adjust quickly to such a change in the law? Why or why not?

3.2 The unemployment rate stood at 9.6 percent late in 2010. Despite the fact that the economy had been growing out of the recession for over a year (real GDP was up 3 percent by Q2 2010), there was only modest job growth during 2010. Although a fiscal stimulus package provided some help, labor was "stuck in the mud." Which of the following factors contributed to the problem and which ones were important?
   a. Employment and unemployment are always lagging indicators because it is difficult to hire and fire in a downturn.
   b. Productivity has grown considerably this decade; people are working hard and being paid less—in short, firms are "mean and lean."

c. Construction employment, which is a traditional engine of growth in recoveries, has gone nowhere largely because of the fact that we dramatically overbuilt.

d. We have minimum wage laws in the United States.

e. Wages are sticky on the downward side, preventing the labor market from clearing.

f. The Census Bureau hired and then fired thousands of workers, throwing all the numbers off.

Choose two of these statements and write a short essay. Use data to support your claims.

## 13.4 EXPLAINING THE EXISTENCE OF CYCLICAL UNEMPLOYMENT

**LEARNING OBJECTIVE:** Discuss the reasons for the existence of cyclical unemployment.

4.1 Economists and politicians have long debated the extent to which unemployment benefits affect the duration of unemployment. The table below represents unemployment and unemployment benefit data for five high-income countries. The unemployment rate and the duration of unemployment benefits for each of these countries are shown for 2007, prior to the recession of 2008–2009, for 2010, the first full year following the end of the recession, and for June 2013, 4 years after the end of the recession. As the data shows, three of these countries extended the duration of unemployment benefits as a result of the recession and two of those countries have since reduced the extended duration. The data for 2007, 2010, and 2013 show a positive relationship between the duration of unemployment benefits and the unemployment rate. Discuss whether you believe the length of time in which a person can receive unemployment benefits directly affects the unemployment rate, and whether your answer applies to 2007, 2010, and 2013. Look up the unemployment rates in each of the five countries. Discuss whether a positive relationship still exists between the duration of unemployment benefits and the unemployment rate, and whether you believe the extension of unemployment benefits in three of those countries played a role in their current unemployment rates.

| Country | 2007 Unemployment Rate | Unemployment Benefits Duration, 2007 | 2010 Unemployment Rate | Unemployment Benefits Duration, 2010 | June 2013 Unemployment Rate | Unemployment Benefits Duration, 2013 |
|---|---|---|---|---|---|---|
| Canada | 6.4% | 50 weeks | 7.1% | 50 weeks | 6.2% | 45 weeks |
| France | 8.7% | 52 weeks | 9.4% | 104 weeks | 10.7% | 104 weeks |
| Great Britain | 5.3% | 26 weeks | 7.9% | 26 weeks | 7.8% | 26 weeks |
| Japan | 3.9% | 13 weeks | 4.7% | 21 weeks | 3.4% | 13 weeks |
| United States | 4.6% | 26 weeks | 9.6% | 99 weeks | 7.6% | 73 weeks |

4.2 [**Related to the *Economics in Practice* on p. 251**] The *Economics in Practice* states that job applicants who have been unemployed for a long period of time have a more difficult time getting job interviews than do those applicants who have been unemployed for a shorter time period. Go to www.bls.gov and do a search for "Table A-12: Unemployed persons by duration of unemployment." Look at the seasonally adjusted data for the current month and for the same month in the previous year. What happened to the "number of unemployed" and the "percent distribution" over that year for those who were unemployed 15 to 26 weeks and for those who were unemployed 27 weeks and over? Does this data seem to support the findings in the *Economics in Practice*? Explain.

4.3 In which if the following situations will you be best off, and in which will you be worst off, in terms of your real wage? Explain your answer.

a. You are offered a 5 percent wage increase and the inflation rate for the year turns out to be 7 percent.

b. You are offered a 1 percent wage increase and the inflation rate for the year turns out to be −2 percent.

c. You are offered a 12 percent wage increase and the inflation rate for the year turns out to be 16 percent.

d. You are offered a 6 percent wage increase and the inflation rate for the year turns out to be 6 percent.

e. You are offered a 7 percent wage increase and the inflation rate for the year turns out to be 3 percent.

4.4 How might social, or implicit, contracts result in sticky wages? Use a labor market graph to show the effect of social contracts on wages and on unemployment if the economy enters a recession.

## 13.5 THE SHORT-RUN RELATIONSHIP BETWEEN THE UNEMPLOYMENT RATE AND INFLATION

**LEARNING OBJECTIVE:** Analyze the short-run relationship between unemployment and inflation.

5.1 In June 2015, the U.S. unemployment rate dropped to 5.3 percent, its lowest level in more than 7 years. At the same time, inflation remained at a very low level by historical standards. Can you offer an explanation for what seems to be an improved trade-off between inflation and unemployment? What factors might improve the trade-off? What factors might make it worse?

5.2 Obtain monthly data on the unemployment rate and the inflation rate for the last 2 years. (This data can be found at www.bls.gov or in a recent issue of the *Survey of Current*

*Business* or in the *Monthly Labor Review* or *Employment and Earnings,* all published by the government and available in many college libraries.)

a.  What trends do you observe? Can you explain what you see using aggregate supply and aggregate demand curves?

b.  Plot the 24 monthly rates on a graph with the unemployment rate measured on the x-axis and the inflation rate on the y-axis. Is there evidence of a trade-off between these two variables? Provide an explanation.

5.3  Suppose the inflation–unemployment relationship depicted by the Phillips Curve was stable. Do you think the U.S. trade-off and the Japanese trade-off would be identical? If not, what kinds of factors might make the trade-offs dissimilar?

## 13.6  THE LONG-RUN AGGREGATE SUPPLY CURVE, POTENTIAL OUTPUT, AND THE NATURAL RATE OF UNEMPLOYMENT

**LEARNING OBJECTIVE:** Discuss the long-run relationship between unemployment and output.

6.1  Obtain data on "average hourly earnings of production workers" and the unemployment rate for your state or area over a recent 2-year period. Has unemployment increased or decreased? What has happened to wages? Does the pattern of unemployment help explain the movement of wages? Provide an explanation.

# 14

# Financial Crises, Stabilization, and Deficits

We have seen in the last several chapters the way in which the government can use fiscal and monetary policies to affect the economy. And, yet, if you look back at Figure 5.5 on page 100 you can see that the unemployment rate still fluctuates widely. What accounts for these large fluctuations? Why can't policy makers do a better job of controlling the economy? This chapter covers a number of topics, but they are all concerned at least indirectly with trying to help answer this question.

In the next section we will consider the stock market and the housing market. Both of these markets have important effects on the economy through a household wealth effect. When stock prices or housing prices rise, household wealth rises, and households respond to this by consuming more. Economic models do a reasonably good job of estimating the effects of a wealth change on consumption. But they do a poor job of predicting the stock price and housing price changes that create that wealth change in the first place. Stock prices and housing prices are asset prices, and changes in these prices are, for the most part, unpredictable. Neither policy makers nor anyone else in the economy have the ability to predict how the stock and housing markets will behave in the future. This is then the first problem that policy makers face. If stock and housing prices are unpredictable, the best that policy makers can do is to try to react quickly to these changes once they occur. In this section we will also describe the way in which large unpredictable changes in these asset prices can lead to "financial crises" and what policy makers can and cannot do about them.

A second problem policy makers confront in stabilizing the economy is getting the timing right, which we cover in the second section of this chapter. We will see that there is a danger of overreacting to changes in the economy—making the fluctuations in the economy even worse than they otherwise would be. The third section of this chapter discusses government deficit issues. We learned at the end of Chapter 9 that it is important to distinguish between cyclical deficits and structural deficits. One expects that the government will run a deficit in a recession since tax revenue is down because of the sluggish economy and spending may be up as the government tries to stimulate the economy. If at full employment the government is *still* running a deficit, this part of the deficit is described as a structural deficit.

In 2015 many countries, including the United States, faced serious structural deficit problems. Many countries in the European Union struggled to meet the structural deficit targets set by the European Commission. We discuss various problems that may arise if a government runs large deficits year after year, including the possibility of a financial crisis. We will also look at some of the historical ways that have been used to control deficits in the United States.

# The Stock Market, the Housing Market, and Financial Crises

Introductory macroeconomic textbooks written before 1990 could largely ignore the stock and housing markets. The effects of these markets on the macroeconomy were small enough to be put aside in introductory discussions. In the 1990s this changed. The boom in the U.S. economy in the late 1990s and the subsequent recession owed a good deal to the rise and later fall in the stock market in that period. Similarly, in the period after 2000, the rise and later fall in housing prices contributed to cycles in the real economy. Now even introductory macroeconomics courses must spend some time looking at these two markets. We first turn to some background material on the stock market.

## Stocks and Bonds

It will be useful to begin by briefly discussing the three main ways in which firms borrow or raise money to finance their investments. How do firms use financial markets in practice?

When a firm wants to make a large purchase to build a new factory or buy machines, it often cannot pay for the purchase out of its own funds. In this case, it must "finance" the investment. One way to do this is to borrow from a bank. The bank loans the money to the firm, the firm uses the money to buy the factory or machine, and the firm pays back the loan (with interest) to the bank over time.

Another possible way for a firm to borrow money is for the firm to issue a bond. If you buy a bond from a firm, you are making a loan to the firm. Bonds were discussed in Chapter 10 in our discussion of U.S. Treasury securities. We noted in that chapter that a bond is a promise to pay a fixed coupon periodically during the term of the bond and then to repay the full amount of the bond at the end of its term. Bonds issued by firms are called corporate bonds and are part of a firm's debt.

A third way for a firm to finance an investment is for it to issue additional shares of **stock**. Just as with bonds, typically only corporations have the ability to issue stock. When a firm issues new shares of stock, it does not add to its debt. Instead, it brings in additional owners of the firm, owners who agree to supply it with funds. Such owners are treated differently than bondholders, who are owed the amount they have loaned.

A *share of common stock* is a certificate that represents the ownership of a share of a business, almost always a corporation. In some cases, firms pay a portion of their annual profits directly to their shareholders in the form of a *dividend*. For example, General Electric is a large, well-established diversified firm with its headquarters in Fairfield, Connecticut. GE has more than 10 billion shares outstanding and generates just over $15 billion in profits each year. GE shares are owned by many endowment and pension funds as well as by individuals. Major shareholders in 2015 included Vanguard and Blackrock. In 2015, GE paid just over one half of its $1.50 a share earnings out in dividends. The remainder was retained for firm investments. Stockholders who own stocks that increase in value earn what are called **capital gains**. **Realized capital gains** (or losses) are increases (or decreases) in the value of assets, including stocks, that households receive when they actually sell those assets. The government considers realized capital gains net of losses to be income, although their treatment under the tax code has been complex and subject to change every few years. The total return that an owner of a share of stock receives is the sum of the dividends received and the capital gain or loss.

**stock** A certificate that certifies ownership of a certain portion of a firm.

**capital gain** An increase in the value of an asset.

**realized capital gain** The gain that occurs when the owner of an asset actually sells it for more than he or she paid for it.

## Determining the Price of a Stock

What determines the price of a stock? If a share of stock is selling for $25, why is someone willing to pay that much for it? As we have noted, when you buy a share of stock, you own part of the firm. If a firm is making profits, it may be paying dividends to its shareholders. If it is not paying dividends but is making profits, people may expect that it will pay dividends in the future. Microsoft, for example, only began paying dividends in 2003 as it entered a more mature phase of its business. Apple began paying dividends in 2012. Dividends are important in thinking about stocks because dividends are the form in which shareholders receive income from the firm. So one thing that is likely to affect the price of a stock is what people expect its future dividends will be. The larger the expected future dividends, the higher the current stock price, other things being equal.

Another important consideration in thinking about the price of a stock is when the dividends are expected to begin to be paid. A $2-per-share dividend stream that is expected to start 4 years from now is worth less than a $2-per-share dividend that starts next year. In other words, the farther into the future the dividend is expected to be paid, the more it will be "discounted." The amount by which expected future dividends are discounted depends on the interest rate. The higher the interest rate, the more expected future dividends will be discounted. If the interest rate is 10 percent, I can invest $100 today and receive $110 a year from now. I am thus willing to pay $100 today to someone who will pay me $110 in a year. If instead, the interest rate were only 5 percent, I would be willing to pay $104.76 today to receive $110 a year from now because the alternative of $104.76 today at a 5 percent interest rate also yields $110.00 at the end of the year. I am thus willing to pay more for the promise of $110 a year from now when the interest rate is lower. In other words, I "discount" the $110 less when the interest rate is lower.

When investors buy a bond, that bond comes with a fixed coupon. When investors buy a stock, they can look at the current and past dividends, but there is no guarantee that future dividends will be the same. Dividends are voted each year by the board of a company, and in difficult times a board may decide to reduce or even eliminate dividends. So dividend payments come with a risk and that risk affects the stock price. People prefer certain outcomes to uncertain ones for the same expected values. For example, I prefer a certain $50 over a bet in which there is a 50 percent chance I will get $100 and a 50 percent chance I will get nothing, even though the expected value of the two deals are equal. The same reasoning holds for future dividends. If, say, I expect dividends for both firms A and B to be $2 per share next year but firm B has a much wider range of possibilities (is riskier), I will prefer firm A. Put another way, I will "discount" firm B's expected future dividends more than firm A's because the outcome for firm B is more uncertain.

We can thus say that the price of a stock should equal the discounted value of its expected future dividends, where the discount factors depend on the interest rate and risk. If for some reason (say, a positive surprise news announcement from the firm) we expect a firm to increase its future dividends, this should lead to an increase in the price of the stock. If there is a surprise fall in the interest rate, this decrease should also lead to a stock price increase. Finally, if the perceived risk of a firm falls, this perception should increase the firm's stock price.

Some stock analysts talk about the possibility of stock market "bubbles." Given the preceding discussion, what might a bubble be? Assume that given your expectations about the future dividends of a firm and given the discount rate, you value the firm's stock at $20 per share. Is there any case in which you would pay more than $20 for a share? We noted previously that the total return to an owner of a share of stock includes any capital gains that come from selling the stock. If the stock is currently selling for $25, which is above your value of $20, but you think that the stock will rise to $30 in the next few months, you might buy it now in anticipation of selling it later for a higher price and reap these capital gains. If others have similar views, the price of the stock may be driven up.

In this case, what counts is not the discounted value of expected future dividends, but rather your view of what others will pay for the stock in the future. You will recall we suggested that stock prices cannot be predicted. Sometimes stocks rise and give their owners capital gains, while other times they fall and there are capital losses. One way to define a bubble is a time in which everyone expects that everyone else expects that stock prices in general will be driven up. This expectation of general price appreciation itself fuels the market as people come to expect capital gains as part of the return on their investments. When a firm's stock price has risen rapidly, it is difficult to know whether the reason is that people have increased their expectations of the firm's future dividends or that there is a bubble. Because people's expectations of future dividends are not directly observed, it is hard to test alternative theories.

## The Stock Market Since 1948

Most investors are interested in following the fortunes of individual firms. Macroeconomists, tracking the connection between stocks and overall levels of economic activity, need instead a measure of the stock market in general. There are several indices available. If you follow

▲ **FIGURE 14.1**  **The S&P 500 Stock Price Index, 1948 I–2014 IV**

the stock market at all, you know that much attention is paid to two stock price indices: the **Dow Jones Industrial Average** and the **NASDAQ Composite**. From a macroeconomic perspective, however, these two indices cover too small a sample of firms. One would like an index that includes firms whose total market value is close to the market value of all firms in the economy. For this purpose a much better measure is the **Standard and Poor's 500 stock price index**, called the **S&P 500**. This index includes most of the larger companies in the economy by market value.

The S&P 500 index is plotted in Figure 14.1 for 1948 I–2014 IV. What perhaps stands out most in this plot is the huge increase in the index between 1995 and 2000. Between December 31, 1994, and March 31, 2000, the S&P 500 index rose 226 percent, an annual rate of increase of 25 percent. This is by far the largest stock market boom in U.S. history, completely dominating the boom of the 1920s. Remember that we are talking about the S&P 500 index, which includes most of the firms in the U.S. economy by market value. We are not talking about just a few dot-com companies. The entire stock market went up 25 percent per year for 5 years! This boom added roughly $14 trillion to household wealth, about $2.5 trillion per year.[1]

What caused this boom? You can see from Figure 12.7 in Chapter 12 that interest rates did not change much in the last half of the 1990s, so the boom cannot be explained by any large fall in interest rates. Perhaps profits rose substantially during this period, and this growth led to a large increase in expected future dividends? We know from the preceding discussion that if expected future dividends increase, stock prices should increase. Figure 14.2 plots for 1948 I–2014 IV the ratio of after-tax profits to GDP. It is clear from the figure that nothing unusual happened to profits in the last half of the 1990s. The share of after-tax profits in GDP rose from the middle of 1995 to the middle of 1997, but then generally fell after that through 2000. Thus, there does not appear to be any surge of profits that would have led people to expect much higher future dividends.

It could be that the perceived riskiness of stocks fell in the last half of the 1990s. This change would have led to smaller discount rates for stocks and thus, other things being equal, to higher stock prices. Although this possibility cannot be completely ruled out, there is no strong independent evidence that perceived riskiness fell.

The stock market boom is thus a puzzle, and many people speculate that it was simply a bubble. For some reason, stock prices started rising rapidly in 1995 and people expected that other people expected that prices would continue to rise. This led stock prices to rise further, thus fulfilling the expectations, which led to expectations of further increases, and so on. Bubble believers note that once stock prices started falling in 2000, they fell a great deal. It is not the case that stock prices just leveled out in 2000; they fell rapidly. People of the bubble view argue that this was simply the bubble bursting.

**Dow Jones Industrial Average**  An index based on the stock prices of 30 actively traded large companies. The oldest and most widely followed index of stock market performance.

**NASDAQ Composite**  An index based on the stock prices of more than 5,000 companies traded on the NASDAQ Stock Market. The NASDAQ market takes its name from the National Association of Securities Dealers Automated Quotation System.

**Standard and Poor's 500 (S&P 500)**  An index based on the stock prices of 500 of the largest firms by market value.

---

[1] It is worth noting that S&P changes the firms that are in its index as firms either prosper or fade. This selection tells us that the index will overestimate actual stock market gains as a result of survivor bias.

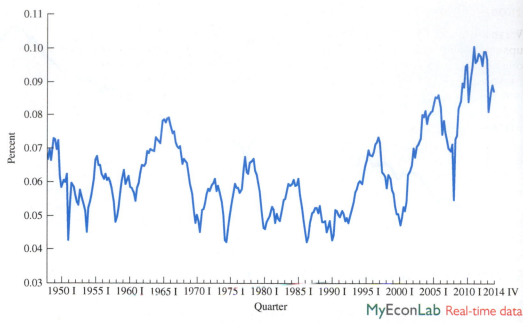

▲ **FIGURE 14.2** **Ratio of After-Tax Profits to GDP, 1948 I–2014 IV**

The first problem then for the stability of the macroeconomy is the large and seemingly unpredictable swings in the stock market. As we will see, these swings induce behavior changes by households and firms that affect the real economy. Before we explore this link, however, we turn to a second volatile series: housing prices.

## Housing Prices Since 1952

Figure 14.3 plots the relative price of housing for 1952 I–2014 IV. The plotted figure is the ratio of an index of housing prices to the GDP deflator. When this ratio is rising, it means that housing prices are rising faster than the overall price level, and vice versa when the ratio is falling.

The plot in Figure 14.3 is remarkable. Housing prices grew roughly in line with the overall price level until about 2000. The increase between 2000 and 2006 was then huge, followed by an equivalent fall between 2006 and 2009. Between 2000 I and 2006 I the value of housing wealth increased by about $13 trillion, roughly $500 billion per quarter. Between 2006 II and 2009 I the fall in the value of housing wealth was about $7 trillion, more than $600 billion per quarter. Once again, it is hard to find a cogent reason for this based on the use value of housing. Rental prices, for example, did not rise and fall in this way.

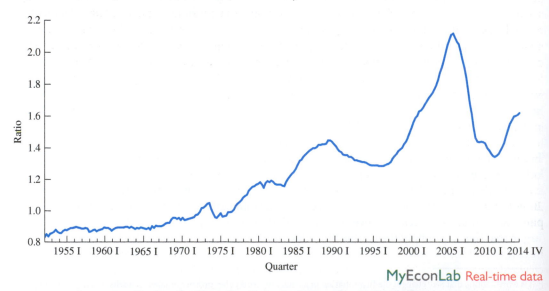

▲ **FIGURE 14.3** **Ratio of a Housing Price Index to the GDP Deflator, 1952 I–2014 IV**

# Household Wealth Effects on the Economy

We see that both the stock market and the housing market have periods of large unpredictable ups and downs. How are these swings felt in the real economy? We mentioned in Chapter 8 that one of the factors that affects consumption expenditures is wealth. Other things being equal, the more wealth a family has, the more it spends. Much of the fluctuation in household wealth in the recent past is because of fluctuations in stock prices and housing prices. When housing and stock values rise, households feel richer and they spend more. As a rough rule of thumb, a $1.00 change in the value of wealth (either stocks or housing) leads to about a $0.03 to $0.04 change in consumer spending per year. With unpredictable wealth changes, we end up with unpredictable consumption changes and thus unpredictable changes in GDP.

An increase in stock prices may also increase investment. If a firm is considering an investment project, one way in which it can finance the project is to issue additional shares of stock. The higher the price of the firm's stock, the more money it can get per additional share. A firm is thus likely to undertake more investment projects the higher its stock price. The cost of an investment project in terms of shares of stock is smaller the higher the price of the stock. This is the way a stock market boom may increase investment and a stock market contraction may decrease investment. Stock price changes affect a firm's cost of capital.

# Financial Crises and the 2008 Bailout

It is clear that the stock market boom in the last half of the 1990s contributed to the strong economy in that period and that the contraction in the stock market after that contributed to the 2000–2001 recession. It is also clear that the boom in housing prices in the 2000–2005 period contributed to the expansion that followed the 2000–2001 recession and that the collapse of housing prices between 2006 and 2009 contributed to the 2008–2009 recession. This is just the household wealth effect at work combined in the case of stock prices with an effect on the investment spending of firms.

The recession of 2008–2009 was also characterized by some observers as a period of financial crisis. Although there is no precise definition of a financial crisis, most financial writers identify financial crises as periods in which the financial institutions that facilitate the movement of capital across households and firms cease to work smoothly. In a financial crisis, macroeconomic problems caused by the wealth effect of a falling stock market or housing market are accentuated.

Many people consider the large fall in housing prices that began at the end of 2006 to have led to the financial crisis of 2008–2009. We discussed briefly in Chapter 10 some of the reasons for this fall in housing prices. Lax government regulations led to excessive risk taking during the housing boom, with many people taking out mortgages that could only be sustained if housing prices kept rising. People bought houses expecting capital gains from those houses once they sold. The problem was exacerbated by low "teaser-rate" mortgage loans in which people paid very low interest rates for the first few years of home ownership. Once housing prices started to fall, the possibility of capital gains from a house sale lessened and it became clear that many households would not be able to afford their homes once teaser rates expired. With no prospect of a profitable house sale and higher mortgage interest rates, many people defaulted on those mortgages and the value of many mortgage-backed securities dropped sharply. Many large financial institutions were involved in the mortgage market, and they began to experience financial trouble. With the exception of Lehman Brothers, which went bankrupt, most of the large financial institutions were bailed out by the federal government—a $700 billion bailout bill that was passed in October 2008. These institutions included Goldman Sachs, Citigroup, Morgan Stanley, J.P. Morgan Chase, and A.I.G. The government provided capital to these firms to ease their financial difficulties. The Federal Reserve also participated in the bailout, buying huge amounts of mortgage-backed securities. We saw in Chapter 10 that in mid-April 2015, the Fed held about $1,732 billion in mortgage-backed securities, many of which it purchased in 2008 and 2009. Many other countries had similar issues with their own financial institutions, in part because many of them had purchased U.S. mortgage-backed securities as an investment.

What would have happened had the U.S. government not bailed out the large financial institutions? This is a matter of debate among economists and politicians. But some effects are clear. Absent intervention, the negative wealth effect would have been larger. Some of the financial institutions would have gone bankrupt, which would have wiped out their bondholders.

# ECONOMICS IN PRACTICE

## Predicting Recessions

How good are economists at predicting recessions? The answer is: not always that good. The 2008–2009 recession is a good example. A study by the Federal Reserve Bank of New York (FRBNY)[1] documents the failure of both policy makers and private economists to forecast the recession. The forecast errors were quite large. The unemployment rate rose from 4.8 percent in 2007 to 6.9 percent in 2008 and then to 10.0 percent in 2009. In late 2007 the FRBNY predicted that the unemployment rate would be 4.6 percent in 2008, an error of 2.3 points. Private forecasters were not much better, predicting a rate of 4.9 percent.[2] But even worse, in April 2008 the FRBNY forecast that the unemployment rate would be 5.6 percent in 2009, an error of 4.4 points. Private forecasters were essentially the same, predicting a rate of 5.5 percent. Even in November 2008 the FRBNY was forecasting an unemployment rate of only 8.1 percent for 2009. Private forecasters were forecasting only 7.7 percent. It wasn't until early 2009 that the severity of the recession was being predicted.

The fact that recessions can be hard to forecast means that the recognition lag discussed in the text can be long. It may take time for policy makers to realize how the economy is doing if their forecasts are no good. This being said, the Fed reacted faster to the 2008–2009 recession than might have been expected given the lag in predicting the severity of the recession. Figure 12.7 in Chapter 12 shows the quarterly path of the 3-month Treasury bill rate, which the Fed essentially controls. It is hard to see the exact numbers from the figure, but the bill rate fell from 4.7 percent in the second quarter of 2007 to 4.3 percent in the third, 3.4 percent in the fourth, 2.0 percent in the first quarter of 2008, 1.6 percent in the second, 1.5 percent in the third, and then roughly zero in the fourth quarter of 2008 and beyond. The Fed thus began to move in a fairly aggressive way near the end of 2007, even though the unemployment rate was not yet predicted to rise very much. And the Fed moved aggressively in 2008, reaching essentially zero by the end, again even though the severity of the recession was not yet forecast by the end of 2008.

The Fed was thus ahead of the curve regarding the 2008–2009 recession. One possibility is that the Fed governors were more pessimistic about the economy that the forecasts were and reacted accordingly. They may have thought there was more downside risk than upside risk in the forecasts

at the time. On the other hand, the forecasts were predicting increases in the unemployment rate, not just as large as turned out to be the case, and it could be that the Fed was simply responding to these predicted increases. When it then reached the zero lower bound at the end of 2008, it could go no further. At any rate, the Fed's timing looks pretty good in this period, especially given the forecast errors.

Why was the 2008–2009 recession so poorly predicted? A characteristic of the recession is that much of it was driven by the fall in housing and stock prices. This led to a negative wealth effect, which exacerbated the recession. The problem with predicting this recession was that it is difficult to predict changes in asset prices like housing prices and stock prices. Changes in these prices are essentially unpredictable. So if much of the recession was driven by unpredictable changes in asset prices, the recession itself will be unpredictable, which it was.

### THINKING PRACTICALLY

1. Why might it have been hard to predict the boom in the U.S. economy in the last half of the 1990s?

[1] Simon Potter, "The Failure to Forecast the Great Recession," *Liberty Street Economics*, Federal Reserve Bank of New York, November 25, 2011.
[2] The private forecasters used here are those responding to the Blue Chip Survey.

Many of these bonds are held by the household sector, so household wealth would have fallen from the loss in the value of the bonds. The fall in overall stock prices would also likely have been larger, thus contributing to the negative wealth effect. The government bailout thus reduced the fall in wealth that took place during this period. Some people also argue that lending to businesses would have been lower had there been no bailout. This would have forced businesses to cut investment, thereby contributing to the contraction in aggregate demand. It is not clear how important this effect is since, as seen in Chapter 10, much of the Fed's purchase of mortgage-backed securities ended up as excess reserves in banks, not as increased loans.

It is important to distinguish between the stimulus measures the government took to fight the 2008–2009 recession, which were tax cuts and spending increases, and the bailout activity, which was direct help to financial institutions to keep them from failing. Putting aside the stimulus measures, was the bailout a good idea? On the positive side, it lessened the negative wealth effect and possibly led to more loans to businesses. Also, much of the lending to the financial institutions has or will be repaid; so the final total cost will be less than $700 billion. On the negative side, there were political and social costs. Most of the people who benefited from the bailout were wealthy—certainly wealthier than average. The bond holders of financial institutions tend to come from the top end of the income distribution. Many people noted that expenditures bailing out the financial institutions that made bad loans dwarfed expenditures to help home owners who took out those bad loans. Also, the jobs in the financial institutions that were saved were mostly jobs of high-income earners. People who will pay for the bailout in the long run are the U.S. taxpayers, who are on average less wealthy than those who benefited from the bailout. The bailout thus likely had, or at least was perceived by many to have had, bad income distribution consequences, which put a strain on the body politic.

We have seen how difficult it is to predict changes in asset prices like stock and housing prices, and we have also seen how much impact these changes can have on the real economy. But many have noted that while the government may not be able to predict asset bubbles, it does influence those fluctuations through other policies. In the case of housing, at least some of the fuel driving the bubble was likely lax credit standards, credit standards controlled in part by government agencies. Recent asset bubbles also may have reflected risk taking by financial institutions, risk behavior that is also under the control of government agencies. The substantial macroeconomic costs of the most recent recession stimulated numerous calls for regulatory reform in the financial market. In 2010 a financial regulation bill, known as the *Dodd-Frank bill*, was passed to try to tighten up financial regulations in the hope of preventing a recurrence of the 2008–2009 financial crisis.

# Time Lags Regarding Monetary and Fiscal Policy

We have so far seen that the unpredictability of asset-price changes is difficult for policy makers to deal with. At best, policy makers can only react to these changes. The goal of **stabilization policy** is to smooth out fluctuation in GDP as much as possible. Consider the two possible time paths for aggregate output (income) (Y) shown in Figure 14.4. Path A (the dark blue line) represents GDP absent stabilization policies by the government; Path B (the light blue line) shows the smoother path that stabilization policy aims to produce. Stabilization policy is also concerned with the stability of prices. Here the goal is not to prevent the overall price level from rising at all, but instead to achieve an inflation rate that is as close as possible to a target rate of about 2 percent given the government's other goals of high and stable levels of output and employment.

**14.2 LEARNING OBJECTIVE**

Explain the purpose of stabilization policies and differentiate between three types of time lags.

**stabilization policy** Describes both monetary and fiscal policy, the goals of which are to smooth out fluctuations in output and employment and to keep prices as stable as possible.

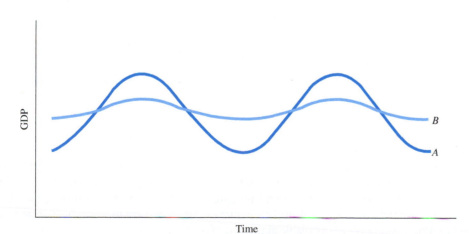

◀ **FIGURE 14.4** Two Possible Time Paths for GDP
Path *A* is less stable—it varies more over time—than path *B*. Other things being equal, society prefers path *B* to path *A*.

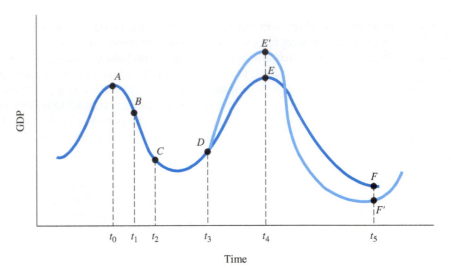

▲ **FIGURE 14.5** **Possible Stabilization Timing Problems**
Attempts to stabilize the economy can prove destabilizing because of time lags. An expansionary policy that should have begun to take effect at point A does not actually begin to have an impact until point D, when the economy is already on an upswing. Hence, the policy pushes the economy to points E' and F' (instead of points E and F). Income varies more widely than it would have if no policy had been implemented.

**time lags** Delays in the economy's response to stabilization policies.

Stabilization goals are not easy to achieve, particularly in the light of various kinds of **time lags**, or delays in the response of the economy to stabilization policies. Economists generally recognize three kinds of time lags: recognition lags, implementation lags, and response lags.

Figure 14.5 shows timing problems a government may face when trying to stabilize the economy. Suppose the economy reaches a peak and begins to slide into recession at point A (at time $t_0$). Given the need to collect and process economic data, policy makers do not observe the decline in GDP until it has sunk to point B (at time $t_1$). By the time they have begun to stimulate the economy (point C, time $t_2$), the recession is well advanced and the economy has almost bottomed out. When the policies finally begin to take effect (point D, time $t_3$), the economy is already on its road to recovery. The policies push the economy to point E'—a much greater fluctuation than point E, which is where the economy would have been without the stabilization policy. Sometime after point D, policy makers may begin to realize that the economy is expanding too quickly. By the time they have implemented contractionary policies and the policies have made their effects felt, the economy is starting to weaken. The contractionary policies therefore end up pushing GDP to point F' instead of point F.

Because of the various time lags, the expansionary policies that should have been instituted at time $t_0$ do not begin to have an effect until time $t_3$, when they are no longer needed. The light blue line in Figure 14.5 shows how the economy behaves as a result of the "stabilization" policies. The dark blue line shows the time path of GDP if the economy had been allowed to run its course and no stabilization policies had been attempted. In this case, stabilization policy makes income more erratic, not less—the policy results in a peak income of E' as opposed to E and a trough income of F' instead of F.

Critics of stabilization policy argue that the situation in Figure 14.5 is typical of the interaction between the government and the rest of the economy. This claim is not necessarily true. We need to know more about the nature of the various kinds of lags before deciding whether stabilization policy is good or bad.

## Recognition Lags

It takes time for policy makers to recognize a boom or a slump. Many important data—those from the national income and product accounts, for example—are available only quarterly. It usually takes several weeks to compile and prepare even the preliminary estimates for these figures. If the economy goes into a slump on January 1, the recession may not be detected until the data for the first quarter are available at the end of April.

Moreover, the early national income and product accounts data are only preliminary, based on an incomplete compilation of the various data sources. These estimates can, and often do, change as better data become available. (For example, when the Bureau of Economic Analysis first announced the results for the fourth quarter of 2012, it indicated that the economy had negative growth, –0.1%. This announcement was at the end of January 2013. At the end of February the growth rate was revised to plus 0.1%. Then at the end of March it was further revised to plus 0.4%.) This situation makes the interpretation of the initial estimates difficult, and **recognition lags** result.

Recognition lag also kicks in on the upside of the cycle as the economy recovers from slow growth in response to government policy. When has the government done enough to stimulate the economy and when will further efforts lead to over stimulation? Janet Yellen, current chair of the Fed, spoke of exactly this concern as she contemplated changing the Fed's easy monetary policy in the spring of 2015 in a speech in San Francisco. "We need to keep in mind the well-established fact that the full effects of monetary policy are felt only after long lags. This means that policymakers cannot wait until they have achieved their objectives to begin adjusting policy. I would not consider it prudent to postpone the onset of normalization until we have reached, or are on the verge of reaching, our inflation objective. Doing so would create too great a risk of significantly overshooting *both* our objectives of maximum sustainable employment and 2 percent inflation, potentially undermining economic growth and employment if the FOMC is subsequently forced to tighten policy markedly or abruptly."

> **recognition lag** The time it takes for policy makers to recognize the existence of a boom or a slump.

## Implementation Lags

The problems that lags pose for stabilization policy do not end once economists and policy makers recognize that the economy is in a boom or a slump. Even if everyone knows that the economy needs to be stimulated or reined in, it takes time to put the desired policy into effect, especially for actions that involve fiscal policy. **Implementation lags** result.

Each year Congress decides on the federal government's budget for the coming year. The tax laws and spending programs embodied in this budget are hard to change once they are in place. If it becomes clear that the economy is entering a recession and is in need of a fiscal stimulus during the middle of the year, there is a limited amount that can be done. Until Congress authorizes more spending or a cut in taxes, changes in fiscal policy are not possible.[2]

Monetary policy is less subject to the kinds of restrictions that slow down changes in fiscal policy. As we saw in Chapter 10, the Fed's current tool for changing the interest rate is to change the rate it pays on bank reserves. This change can be made very quickly, and there is in effect no implementation lag once the decision has been made to make the change.

> **implementation lag** The time it takes to put the desired policy into effect once economists and policy makers recognize that the economy is in a boom or a slump.

## Response Lags

Even after a macroeconomic problem has been recognized and the appropriate corrective policies have been implemented, there are **response lags**—The time that it takes for the economy to adjust to the new conditions after a new policy is implemented; lags that occur because of the operation of the economy itself. Even after the government has formulated a policy and put it into place, the economy takes time to adjust to the new conditions. Although monetary policy can be adjusted and implemented more quickly than fiscal policy, it takes longer to make its effect felt on the economy because of response lags. What is most important is the total lag between the time a problem first occurs and the time the corrective policies are felt.

> **response lag** The time that it takes for the economy to adjust to the new conditions after a new policy is implemented; the lag that occurs because of the operation of the economy itself.

### Response Lags for Fiscal Policy
One way to think about the response lag in fiscal policy is through the government spending multiplier. This multiplier measures the change in GDP caused by a given change in government spending or net taxes. It takes time for the multiplier to reach its full value. The result is a lag between the time a fiscal policy action is initiated and the time the full change in GDP is realized.

The reason for the response lag in fiscal policy—the delay in the multiplier process—is simple. During the first few months after an increase in government spending or a tax cut, there

---

[2] Do not forget, however, about the existence of automatic stabilizers (Chapter 9). Many programs contain built-in countercyclical features that expand spending or cut tax collections automatically (without the need for congressional or executive action) during a recession.

is not enough time for the firms or individuals who benefit directly from the extra government spending or the tax cut to increase their own spending. Neither individuals nor firms revise their spending plans instantaneously. Until they can make those revisions, the increase in government spending does not stimulate extra private spending.

Changes in government purchases are a component of aggregate expenditure. When $G$ rises, aggregate expenditure increases directly; when $G$ falls, aggregate expenditure decreases directly. When personal taxes are changed, however, an additional step intervenes, giving rise to another lag. Suppose a tax cut has lowered personal income taxes across the board. Each household must decide what portion of its tax cut to spend and what portion to save. This decision is the extra step. Before the tax cut gets translated into extra spending, households must take the step of increasing their spending, which usually takes some time.

With a business tax cut, there is a further complication. Firms must decide what to do with their added after-tax profits. If they pay out their added profits to households as dividends, the result is the same as with a personal tax cut. Households must decide whether to spend or to save the extra funds. Firms may also retain their added profits and use them for investment, but investment is a component of aggregate expenditure that requires planning and time.

In practice, it takes about a year for a change in taxes or in government spending to have its full effect on the economy. This response lag means that if we increase spending to counteract a recession today, the full effects will not be felt for 12 months. By that time, the state of the economy might be different.

**Response Lags for Monetary Policy** Monetary policy works by changing interest rates—assuming that interest rates are not at the zero lower bound—which then change planned investment. Interest rates can also affect consumption spending, as we discuss further in Chapter 15. For now, it is enough to know that lower interest rates usually stimulate consumption spending and that higher interest rates decrease consumption spending.

The response of consumption and investment to interest rate changes takes time. Even if interest rates were to rise by 5 percent overnight, firms would not immediately decrease their investment purchases. Firms generally make their investment plans several years in advance. If General Motors (GM) wants to respond to an increase in interest rates by investing less, it will take time—perhaps up to a year—for the firm to come up with plans to scrap some of its investment projects. The response lags for monetary policy are even longer than response lags for fiscal policy. When government spending changes, there is a direct change in the sales of firms, which would sell more as a result of an increase in government purchases. When interest rates change, however, the sales of firms do not change until households change their consumption spending and/or firms change their investment spending. It takes time for households and firms to respond to interest rate changes. In this sense, interest rate changes are like tax-rate changes. The resulting change in firms' sales must wait for households and firms to change their purchases of goods.

## Summary

Stabilization is thus not easily achieved even if there are no surprise asset-price changes. It takes time for policy makers to recognize the existence of a problem, more time for them to implement a solution, and yet more time for firms and households to respond to the stabilization policies taken. Monetary policy can be adjusted more quickly and easily than taxes or government spending, making it a useful instrument in stabilizing the economy. However, because the economy's response to monetary changes is probably slower than its response to changes in fiscal policy, tax and spending changes may also play a useful role in macroeconomic management.

**14.3 LEARNING OBJECTIVE**

Discuss the effects of government deficits and deficit targeting.

# Government Deficit Issues

If a government is trying to stimulate the economy through tax cuts or spending increases, this, other things being equal, will increase the government deficit. One thus expects deficits in recessions—cyclical deficits. These deficits are temporary and do not impose any long-run problems, especially if modest surpluses are run when there is full employment. If, however, at full employment the deficit—the structural deficit—is still large, this can have negative long-run consequences.

Figure 9.6 in Chapter 9 shows that the U.S. government deficit as a percentage of GDP rose rapidly beginning in 2008. In 2009 the deficit as a percentage of GDP was about 9 percent. This is huge, but most of it was cyclical because of the sharp recession. Earlier, in 2005–2007, there was roughly full employment, and during this period the deficit was about 2 percent of GDP, which we can think of as a structural deficit given that it occurred in a full employment period. By the end of 2014, with the economy close to but not quite at full employment, the deficit was at 3 percent of GDP. At that point, the deficit had both structural and (small) cyclical elements.

The large deficits beginning in 2008 led to a large rise in the ratio of the federal government debt to GDP. Figure 9.7 in Chapter 9 shows that the ratio peaked at the end of 2012, where it was 68.4 percent. (This is up from about 46 percent in 2007). By the end of 2014, the ratio had fallen to 63.6 percent. Deficits and debts are always hot political issues. Should anything be done to lower the deficit or not? If action is needed, should we raise taxes or lower spending? Sometimes there are threats to shut down the government. A significant change in policy was made at the end of 2012. The Bush tax cuts, which had been in effect for 12 years, were not extended for high-income tax payers. These many debates about the deficit in fact led to a change in policy at the end of 2012. In addition, the payroll tax cut, which had been in effect for 2 years, was not extended. You can see from Figure 9.7 that the debt/GDP ratio has roughly flattened out since 2012, due in part to these changes.

One concern about a rising debt-to-GDP ratio for a country is that at some point investors may begin to perceive that the bonds the country is selling to finance its deficits are now more risky. This will increase the interest rate that the country must pay on its bonds, which will add further to the deficit as interest payments rise. This may in turn force the country to drastically cut spending or increase taxes, which may have large negative effects on the economy.

## Deficit Targeting

Debates about deficits have been around for a long time. In the 1980s the U.S. government was spending much more than it was receiving in taxes. In response to the large deficits, in 1986 the U.S. Congress passed and President Reagan signed the **Gramm-Rudman-Hollings Act** (named for its three congressional sponsors), referred to as GRH. It is interesting to look back on this in the context of the current deficit problem. GRH set a target for reducing the federal deficit by a set amount each year. As Figure 14.6 shows, the deficit was to decline by $36 billion per year between 1987 and 1991, with a deficit of zero slated for fiscal year 1991. What was interesting about the GRH legislation was that the targets were not merely guidelines. If Congress, through its decisions about taxes and spending programs, produced a budget with a deficit larger than the targeted amount, GRH called for automatic spending cuts. The cuts were divided proportionately among most federal spending programs so that a program that made up 5 percent of total spending was to endure a cut equal to 5 percent of the total spending cut.[3]

In 1986, the U.S. Supreme Court declared part of the GRH bill unconstitutional. In effect, the Court said that Congress would have to approve the "automatic" spending cuts before they could take place. The law was changed in 1986 to meet the Supreme Court ruling and again in 1987, when new targets were established. The new targets had the deficit reaching zero in 1993

**Gramm-Rudman-Hollings Act**
Passed by the U.S. Congress and signed by President Reagan in 1986, this law set out to reduce the federal deficit by $36 billion per year, with a deficit of zero slated for 1991.

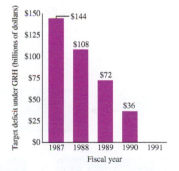

◄ **FIGURE 14.6** **Deficit Reduction Targets under Gramm-Rudman-Hollings**
The GRH legislation, passed in 1986, set out to lower the federal deficit by $36 billion per year. If the plan had worked, a zero deficit would have been achieved by 1991.

---

[3] Programs such as Social Security were exempt from cuts or were treated differently. Interest payments on the federal debt were also immune from cuts.

instead of 1991. The targets were revised again in 1991, when the year to achieve a zero deficit was changed from 1993 to 1996. In practice, these targets never came close to being achieved. As time wore on, even the revised targets became completely unrealistic, and by the end of the 1980s, the GRH legislation was not taken seriously.

Although the GRH legislation is history, it is useful to consider the stabilization consequences of deficit targeting. What if deficit targeting is taken seriously? Is this good policy? The answer is probably not. We will now show how deficit targeting can make the economy more unstable.

In a world with no deficit targeting, the Congress and the president make decisions each year about how much to spend and how much to tax. The federal government deficit is a result of these decisions and the state of the economy. However, with deficit targeting, the size of the deficit is set in advance. Taxes and government spending must be adjusted to produce the required deficit. In this situation, the deficit is no longer a consequence of the tax and spending decisions. Instead, taxes and spending become a consequence of the deficit decision.

What difference does it make whether Congress chooses a target deficit and adjusts government spending and taxes to achieve that target or decides how much to spend and tax and lets the deficit adjust itself? The difference may be substantial. Consider a leftward shift of the *AD* curve caused by some negative demand shock. A negative demand shock is something that causes a negative shift in consumption or investment schedules or that leads to a decrease in U.S. exports.

We know that a leftward shift of the *AD* curve lowers aggregate output (income), which causes the government deficit to increase. In a world without deficit targeting, the increase in the deficit during contractions provides an **automatic stabilizer** for the economy. (Review Chapter 9 if this point is hazy.) The contraction-induced decrease in tax revenues and increase in transfer payments tend to reduce the fall in after-tax income and consumer spending because of the negative demand shock. Thus, the decrease in aggregate output (income) caused by the negative demand shock is lessened somewhat by the growth of the deficit [Figure 14.7(a)].

In a world with deficit targeting, the deficit is not allowed to rise. Some combination of tax increases and government spending cuts would be needed to offset what would have otherwise been an increase in the deficit. We know that increases in taxes or cuts in spending are contractionary in themselves. The contraction in the economy will therefore be larger than it would have been without deficit targeting because the initial effect of the negative demand shock is worsened by the rise in taxes or the cut in government spending required to keep the deficit from rising. As Figure 14.7(b) shows, deficit targeting acts as an **automatic destabilizer**.

**automatic stabilizers**
Revenue and expenditure items in the federal budget that automatically change with the economy in such a way as to stabilize GDP.

**automatic destabilizers**
Revenue and expenditure items in the federal budget that automatically change with the economy in such a way as to destabilize GDP.

▶ **FIGURE 14.7** **Deficit Targeting as an Automatic Destabilizer**
Deficit targeting changes the way the economy responds to negative demand shocks because it does not allow the deficit to increase. The result is a smaller deficit but a larger decline in income than would have otherwise occurred.

**a. Without Deficit Targeting**

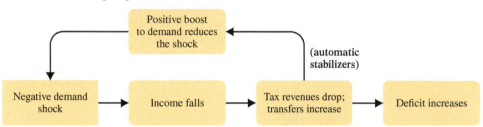

**b. With Deficit Targeting**

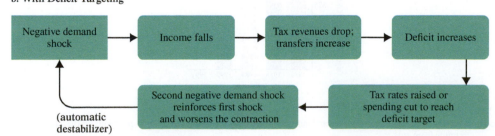

It requires taxes to be raised and government spending to be cut during a contraction. This reinforces, rather than counteracts, the shock that started the contraction.

Deficit targeting thus has undesirable macroeconomic consequences. It requires cuts in spending or increases in taxes at times when the economy is already experiencing problems. This drawback does not mean, of course, that a government should ignore structural deficit problems. But locking in spending cuts or tax increases during periods of negative demand shocks is not a good way to manage the economy. Moving forward, policy makers around the globe will have to devise other methods to control growing structural deficits.

# SUMMARY

## 14.1 THE STOCK MARKET, THE HOUSING MARKET, AND FINANCIAL CRISES *p. 265*

1. A firm can finance an investment project by borrowing from banks, by issuing *bonds*, or by issuing new shares of its stock. People who own shares of *stock* own a fraction of the firm.

2. The price of a stock should equal the discounted value of its expected future dividends, where the discount factors depend on the interest rate and risk.

3. A bubble exists when the price of a stock exceeds the discounted value of its expected future dividends. In this case what matters is what people expect that other people expect about how much the stock can be sold for in the future.

4. The largest stock market boom in U.S. history occurred between 1995 and 2000, when the S&P 500 index rose by 25 percent per year. The boom added $14 trillion to household wealth.

5. Why there was a stock market boom in 1995–2000 appears to be a puzzle. There was nothing unusual about earnings that would predict such a boom. Many people believe that the boom was merely a bubble.

6. Housing prices rose rapidly between 2000 and 2006 and fell rapidly between 2006 and 2009. Many consider that the fall in housing prices beginning in 2006 led to the recession and financial crisis of 2008–2009.

7. Changes in stock prices and housing prices change household wealth, which affects consumption and thus the real economy. Changes in stock and housing prices are largely unpredictable, which makes many fluctuations in the economy unpredictable.

## 14.2 TIME LAGS REGARDING MONETARY AND FISCAL POLICY *p. 271*

8. *Stabilization policy* describes both fiscal and monetary policies, the goals of which are to smooth out fluctuations in output and employment and to keep prices as stable as possible. Stabilization goals are not necessarily easy to achieve because of the existence of certain *time lags*, or delays in the response of the economy to macroeconomic policies.

9. A *recognition lag* is the time it takes for policy makers to recognize the existence of a boom or a slump. An *implementation lag* is the time it takes to put the desired policy into effect once economists and policy makers recognize that the economy is in a boom or a slump. A *response lag* is the time it takes for the economy to adjust to the new conditions after a new policy is implemented—in other words, a lag that occurs because of the operation of the economy itself. In general, monetary policy can be implemented more rapidly than fiscal policy but fiscal policy generally has a shorter response lag than monetary policy.

## 14.3 GOVERNMENT DEFICIT ISSUES *p. 274*

10. The U.S. debt-to-GDP ratio has flattened out since 2012, due in part to policy changes that were made at the end of 2012.

11. In 1986 Congress passed and President Reagan signed the *Gramm-Rudman-Hollings Act (GRH)*, which set deficit targets for each year. The aim was to reduce the large structural deficit that existed.

12. Deficit-targeting measures that call for automatic spending cuts to eliminate or reduce the deficit, like the GRH legislation, may have the effect of destabilizing the economy.

# REVIEW TERMS AND CONCEPTS

automatic destabilizers, *p. 276*
automatic stabilizers, *p. 276*
capital gain, *p. 265*
Dow Jones Industrial Average, *p. 267*
Gramm-Rudman-Hollings Act, *p. 275*

implementation lag, *p. 273*
NASDAQ Composite, *p. 267*
realized capital gain, *p. 265*
recognition lag, *p. 273*
response lag, *p. 273*

stabilization policy, *p. 271*
Standard and Poor's 500 (S&P 500), *p. 267*
stock, *p. 265*
time lags, *p. 272*

**MyEconLab** Visit **www.myeconlab.com** to complete these exercises online and get instant feedback. Exercises that update with real-time data are marked with art 🔴.

# PROBLEMS

All problems are available on MyEconLab.

## 14.1 THE STOCK MARKET, THE HOUSING MARKET, AND FINANCIAL CRISES

LEARNING OBJECTIVE: Discuss the effects of historical fluctuations in stock and housing prices on the economy.

1.1 In July 2009, the S&P 500 index was at 1,000.
   a. What is the S&P 500 index?
   b. Where is the S&P today?
   c. If you had invested $10,000 in July 2009 and your investments had increased in value by the same percentage as the S&P 500 index had increased, how much would you have today?
   d. Assume that the total stock market holdings of the household sector were about $20 trillion and that the entire stock market went up/down by the same percentage as the S&P. Evidence suggests that the "wealth effect" of stock market holdings on consumer spending is about 4 percent of wealth annually. How much additional or reduced spending would you expect to see as a result of the stock market moves since July 2009? Assuming a multiplier of 2 and a GDP of $18,000 billion, how much additional/less GDP would you predict for next year if all of this was true?

1.2 During 1997, stock markets in Asia collapsed. Hong Kong's was down nearly 30 percent, Thailand's was down 62 percent, and Malaysia's was down 60 percent. Japan and Korea experienced big drops as well. What impacts would these events have on the economies of the countries themselves? Explain your answer. In what ways would you have expected these events to influence the U.S. economy? How might the spending of Asians on American goods be affected? What about Americans who have invested in these countries?

## 14.2 TIME LAGS REGARDING MONETARY AND FISCAL POLICY

LEARNING OBJECTIVE: Explain the purpose of stabilization policies and differentiate between three types of time lags.

2.1 Some states are required to balance their budgets. Is this measure stabilizing or destabilizing? Suppose all states were committed to a balanced-budget philosophy and the economy moved into a recession. What effects would this philosophy have on the size of the federal deficit?

2.2 Explain why stabilization policy may be difficult to carry out. How is it possible that stabilization policies can actually be destabilizing?

2.3 [Related to the *Economics in Practice* on p. 270] The *Economics in Practice* states that since recessions can be hard to forecast, the recognition lag can be long, as was the case with the recession of 2008–2009. Assuming that the recognition lag with regards to this recession was the same for both federal government and Federal Reserve policy makers, explain which type of policy, fiscal or monetary, should have been the quickest to take effect in the economy and with which of these policies should the economy have most rapidly adjusted to the newly implemented conditions.

## 14.3 GOVERNMENT DEFICIT ISSUES

LEARNING OBJECTIVE: Discuss the effects of government deficits and deficit targeting

3.1 Explain why the government deficit rises as the economy contracts and why the government deficit falls when the economy expands.

3.2 You are given the following information about the economy in 2015 (all in billions of dollars):

| | |
|---|---|
| Consumption function: | $C = 100 + (.8 \times Y_d)$ |
| Taxes: | $T = -150 + (.25 \times Y)$ |
| Investment function: | $I = 60$ |
| Disposable income: | $Y_d = Y - T$ |
| Government spending: | $G = 80$ |
| Equilibrium: | $Y = C + I + G$ |

*Hint:* Deficit is $D = G - T = G - [-150 + (.25 \times Y)]$.

   a. Find equilibrium income. Show that the government budget deficit (the difference between government spending and tax revenues) is $5 billion.
   b. Congress passes the Foghorn-Leghorn (F-L) amendment, which requires that the deficit be zero this year. If the budget adopted by Congress has a deficit that is larger than zero, the deficit target must be met by cutting spending. Suppose spending is cut by $5 billion (to $75 billion). What is the new value for equilibrium GDP? What is the new deficit? Explain carefully why the deficit is not zero.
   c. Suppose the F-L amendment was not in effect and planned investment falls to $I = 55$. What is the new value of GDP? What is the new government budget deficit? What happens to GDP if the F-L amendment is in effect and spending is cut to reach the deficit target? (*Hint:* Spending must be cut by $21.666 billion to balance the budget.)

3.3 Since the year 2000, several countries have defaulted on their sovereign bonds. Do some research to find information on three countries that have defaulted since 2000. For each of the three countries you have researched, explain when the default occurred, how much debt was involved in the default, what interest rates each government had to pay on its bonds immediately following the default, and what interest rates the government is now paying on its bonds. How do these interest rates compare to the interest rates being paid on current U.S. government bonds?

3.4 Suppose the government decides to decrease spending and increase taxes in an attempt to decrease its deficit.

Is it possible for the Fed to ease the macroeconomic effects of the spending and tax changes? Explain.

**3.5** If the government implements a spending and tax policy in which it promises to neither increase nor decrease spending and taxes, is it still possible for the budget deficit to increase or decrease? Explain.

**3.6** In January 2015, the Congressional Budget Office (CBO) issued a report estimating that the federal budget deficit for 2015 was expected to fall slightly to $468 billion, or 2.6 percent of GDP. Working under the assumption that current laws affecting the budget will not change (i.e., no revisions in planned tax changes or fiscal stimulus spending), the CBO also estimated that the deficit as a percentage of GDP would hold steady at 2.6 percent through 2018 but rise thereafter, with a projected deficit of 4.0 percent of GDP in 2025. Go to www.cbo.gov and look up the current and estimated deficit-to-GDP ratios. Were the CBO's estimates accurate, and have its projections changed? Explain whether any policy changes enacted since January 2015 might have been responsible for changes in the CBO's projections.

# 15

# Household and Firm Behavior in the Macroeconomy: A Further Look*

In Chapters 8 through 14, we considered the interactions of households, firms, and the government in the goods, money, and labor markets. In these chapters, we assumed that household consumption (C) depends only on income and that firms' planned investment (I) depends only on the interest rate. In this chapter, we present a more realistic picture of the influences on households' consumption and labor supply decisions and on firms' investment and employment decisions. We use the insights developed here to then analyze a richer set of macroeconomic issues.

---

*This chapter is somewhat more advanced, but it contains a lot of interesting information!

# Households: Consumption and Labor Supply Decisions

**15.1 LEARNING OBJECTIVE**

Describe factors that affect household consumption and labor supply decisions.

For most of our analysis so far, we have been assuming that consumption depends simply on income. Although this is a useful starting point, and income is in fact the most important determinant of consumption, it is not the only thing that determines household consumption decisions. We need to consider other theories of consumption to build a more realistic description of household behavior.

## The Life-Cycle Theory of Consumption

Most people make consumption decisions based not only on current income but also on what they expect to earn later in life. Many of you, as young college students, are consuming more than you currently earn as you anticipate future earnings, whereas a number of your instructors are consuming less than they currently earn as they save for retirement without labor earnings. The model of consumption that is based on the idea that people track lifetime income when they make consumption decisions is called the **life-cycle theory of consumption.**

**life-cycle theory of consumption** A theory of household consumption: Households make lifetime consumption decisions based on their expectations of lifetime income.

The lifetime income and consumption pattern of a representative individual is shown in Figure 15.1. As you can see, this person has a low income during the first part of her life, high income in the middle, and low income again in retirement. Her income in retirement is not zero because she has income from sources other than her own labor—Social Security payments, interest and dividends, and so on.

The consumption path as drawn in Figure 15.1 is constant over the person's life. This is an extreme assumption, but it illustrates the point that the path of consumption over a lifetime is likely to be more stable than the path of income. We consume an amount greater than our incomes during our early working careers. We do so by borrowing against future income by taking out a car loan, a mortgage to buy a house, or a loan to pay for college. This debt is repaid when our incomes have risen and we can afford to use some of our income to pay off past borrowing without substantially lowering our consumption. The reverse is true for our retirement years. Here, too, our incomes are low. Because we consume less than we earn during our prime working years, we can save up a "nest egg" that allows us to maintain an acceptable standard of living during retirement.

Fluctuations in wealth are also an important component of the life-cycle story. Many young households borrow in anticipation of higher income in the future. Some households actually have *negative wealth*—the value of their assets is less than the debts they owe. A household in its prime working years saves to pay off debts and to build up assets for its later years, when income typically

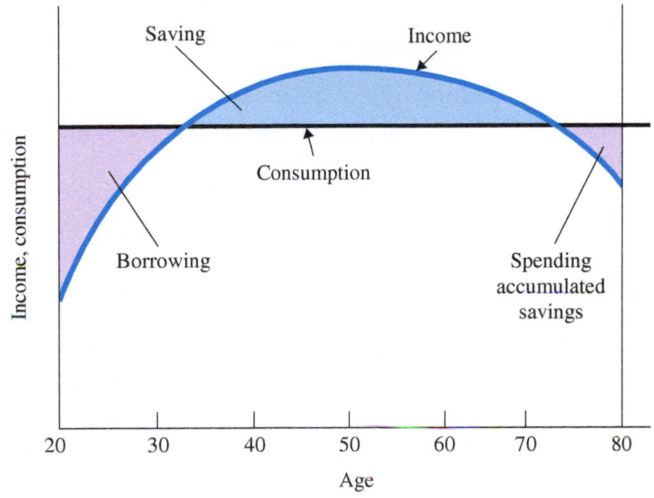


▲ **FIGURE 15.1 Life-Cycle Theory of Consumption**
In their early working years, people consume more than they earn. This is also true in the retirement years. In between, people save (consume less than they earn) to pay off debts from borrowing and to accumulate savings for retirement.

goes down. Households whose assets are greater than the debts they owe have *positive wealth*. With its wage earners retired, a household consumes its accumulated wealth. Generally speaking, wealth starts out negative, turns positive, and then approaches zero near the end of life. Wealth, therefore, is intimately linked to the cumulative saving and dissaving behavior of households.

The key difference between the Keynesian theory of consumption and the life-cycle theory is that the life-cycle theory suggests that consumption and saving decisions are likely to be based not only on current income but also on expectations of future income. The consumption behavior of households immediately following World War II clearly supports the life-cycle story. Just after the war ended, income fell as wage earners moved out of war-related work. However, consumption spending did not fall commensurately, as Keynesian theory would predict. People expected to find jobs in other sectors eventually, and they did not adjust their consumption spending to the temporarily lower incomes they were earning in the meantime.

**permanent income** The average level of a person's expected future income stream.

The term **permanent income** is sometimes used to refer to the average level of a person's expected future income stream. If you expect your income will be high in the future (even though it may not be high now), your permanent income is said to be high. With this concept, we can sum up the life-cycle theory by saying that current consumption decisions are likely to be based on permanent income instead of current income.[1] This means that policy changes such as tax-rate changes are likely to have more of an effect on household behavior if they are expected to be permanent instead of temporary.

One-time tax rebates such as we saw in the United States in 2001 and 2008 provide an interesting test of the permanent income hypothesis. In both cases, the tax rebate was a one-time stimulus. In 2008, for example, the tax rebate was $300 to $600 for individual tax payers eligible for the rebate. How much would we expect this rebate to influence consumption? The simple Keynesian model that we introduced previously in this text would just apply the marginal propensity to consume to the $600. If the marginal propensity to consume is 0.8, we would expect the $600 to generate $480 in incremental spending per rebate. The permanent income hypothesis instead looks at the $600 in the context of an individual's permanent income. As a fraction of one's lifetime income, $600 is a modest number, and we would thus expect individuals to increase their spending only modestly in response to the rebate. Research on the 2001 tax rebate by Matthew Shapiro and Joel Slemrod, based on surveys of consumers, suggested that most people planned to use their rebates to lower debt, rather than increase spending. This is consistent with the life-cycle model.

Although the life-cycle model enriches our understanding of the consumption behavior of households, the analysis is still missing something. What is missing is the other main decision of households: the labor supply decision.

## The Labor Supply Decision

The size of the labor force in an economy is of obvious importance. A growing labor force is one of the ways in which national income/output can be expanded, and the larger the percentage of people who work, the higher the potential output per capita.

So far we have said little about what determines the size of the labor force. Of course, demographics are a key element; the number of children born in 2014 will go a long way toward determining the potential number of 20-year-old workers in 2034. In addition, immigration, both legal and illegal, plays a role.

Behavior also plays a role. Households make decisions about whether to work and how much to work. These decisions are closely tied to consumption decisions because for most households, the bulk of their spending is financed out of wages and salaries. Households make consumption and labor supply decisions simultaneously. Consumption cannot be considered separately from labor supply because it is precisely by selling your labor that you earn income to pay for your consumption.

---

[1] The pioneering work on this topic was done by Milton Friedman, *A Theory of the Consumption Function* (Princeton, NJ: Princeton University Press, 1957). In the mid-1960s, Franco Modigliani did closely related work that included the formulation of the life-cycle theory.

As we discussed in Chapter 3, the alternative to supplying your labor in exchange for a wage or a salary is leisure or other nonmarket activities. Nonmarket activities include raising a child, going to school, keeping a house, or—in a developing economy—working as a subsistence farmer. What determines the quantity of labor supplied by a household? Among the list of factors are the wage rate, prices, wealth, and nonlabor income.

**The Wage Rate**    A changing wage rate can affect labor supply, but whether the effect is positive or negative is ambiguous. An increase in the wage rate affects a household in two ways. First, work becomes more attractive relative to leisure and other nonmarket activities. Because every hour spent in leisure now requires giving up a higher wage, the opportunity cost of leisure is higher. As a result, you would expect that a higher wage would lead to a larger quantity of labor supplied—a larger workforce. This is called the *substitution effect of a wage rate increase*.

On the other hand, household members who work are clearly better off after a wage rate increase. By working the same number of hours as they did before, they will earn more income. If we assume that leisure is a normal good, people with higher income will spend some of it on leisure by working less. This is the *income effect of a wage rate increase*.

When wage rates rise, the substitution effect suggests that people will work more, whereas the income effect suggests that they will work less. The ultimate effect depends on which separate effect is more powerful. The data suggest that the substitution effect seems to win in most cases. That is, higher wage rates usually lead to a larger labor supply and lower wage rates usually lead to a lower labor supply.

**Prices**    Prices also play a major role in the consumption/labor supply decision. In our discussions of the possible effects of an increase in the wage rate, we have been assuming that the prices of goods and services do not rise at the same time. If the wage rate and all other prices rise simultaneously, the story is different. To make things clear, we need to distinguish between the nominal wage rate and the real wage rate.

The **nominal wage rate** is the wage rate in current dollars. When we adjust the nominal wage rate for changes in the price level, we obtain the **real wage rate**. The real wage rate measures the amount that wages can buy in terms of goods and services. Workers do not care about their nominal wage—they care about the purchasing power of this wage—the real wage.

> **nominal wage rate**    The wage rate in current dollars.

> **real wage rate**    The amount the nominal wage rate can buy in terms of goods and services.

Suppose skilled workers in Indianapolis were paid a wage rate of $20 per hour in 2014. Now suppose their wage rate rose to $22 in 2015, a 10 percent increase. If the prices of goods and services were the same in 2015 as they were in 2014, the real wage rate would have increased by 10 percent. An hour of work in 2015 ($22) buys 10 percent more than an hour of work in 2014 ($20). What if the prices of all goods and services also increased by 10 percent between 2014 and 2015? The purchasing power of an hour's wages has not changed. The real wage rate has not increased at all. In 2015, $22 bought the same quantity of goods and services that $20 bought in 2014.

To measure the real wage rate, we adjust the nominal wage rate with a price index. As we saw in Chapter 7, there are several such indexes that we might use, including the consumer price index and the GDP price deflator.[2]

We can now apply what we have learned from the life-cycle theory to our wage/price story. Recall that the life-cycle theory says that people look ahead in making their decisions. Translated to real wage rates, this idea says that households look at expected future real wage rates as well as the current real wage rate in making their current consumption and labor supply decisions. Consider, for example, medical students who expect that their real wage rate will be higher in the future. This expectation obviously has an effect on current decisions about things like how much to buy and whether to take a part-time job.

**Wealth and Nonlabor Income**    Life-cycle theory implies that wealth fluctuates over the life cycle. Households accumulate wealth during their working years to pay off debts accumulated when they were young and to support themselves in retirement. This role of wealth is

---

[2] To calculate the real wage rate, we divide the nominal wage rate by the price index. Suppose the wage rate rose from $10 per hour in 1998 to $18 per hour in 2010 and the price level rose 50 percent during the same period. Using 1998 as the base year, the price index would be 1.00 in 1998 and 1.50 in 2010. The real wage rate is $W/P$, where $W$ is the nominal wage rate and $P$ is the price level. Using 1998 as the base year, the real wage rate is $10 in 1998 ($10.00/1.00) and $12 in 2010 ($18.00/1.50).

clear, but the existence of wealth poses another question. Consider two households that are at the same stage in their life cycle and have similar expectations about future wage rates, prices, and so on. They expect to live the same length of time, and both plan to leave the same amount to their children. They differ only in their wealth. Because of a past inheritance, household 1 has more wealth than household 2. Which household is likely to have a higher consumption path for the rest of its life? Household 1 is because it has more wealth to spread out over the rest of its life. Holding everything else constant (including the stage in the life cycle), the more wealth a household has, the more it will consume both now and in the future.

Now consider a household that has a sudden unexpected increase in wealth, perhaps an inheritance from a distant relative. How will the household's consumption pattern be affected? Few spend the entire inheritance all at once. Most households will increase consumption both now and in the future, spending the inheritance over the course of the rest of their lives.

**nonlabor, or nonwage, income** Any income received from sources other than working—inheritances, interest, dividends, transfer payments, and so on.

An increase in wealth can also be looked on as an increase in nonlabor income. **Nonlabor, *or* nonwage, income** is income received from sources other than working—inheritances, interest, dividends, and transfer payments, such as welfare payments and Social Security payments. As with wealth, an unexpected increase in nonlabor income will have a positive effect on a household's consumption.

What about the effect of an increase in wealth or nonlabor income on labor supply? We already know that an increase in income results in an increase in the consumption of normal goods, including leisure. Therefore, an unexpected increase in wealth or nonlabor income results in an increase in consumption and an increase in leisure. With leisure increasing, labor supply must fall. So an unexpected increase in wealth or nonlabor income leads to a *decrease* in labor supply. This point should be obvious. If you suddenly win a million dollars in the state lottery or make a killing in the stock market, you will probably work less in the future than you otherwise would have.

## Interest Rate Effects on Consumption

Recall from the last few chapters that the interest rate affects a firm's investment decision. A higher interest rate leads to a lower level of planned investment and vice versa. This was a key link between the money market and the goods market, and it was the channel through which monetary policy had an impact on planned aggregate expenditure.

We can now expand on this link: The interest rate also affects household behavior. Consider the effect of a fall in the interest rate on consumption. A fall in the interest rate lowers the reward to saving. If the interest rate falls from 10 percent to 5 percent, you earn 5¢ instead of 10¢ per year on every dollar saved. This means that the opportunity cost of spending a dollar today (instead of saving it and consuming it plus the interest income a year from now) has fallen. You will substitute toward current consumption and away from future consumption when the interest rate falls: You consume more today and save less. A rise in the interest rate leads you to consume less today and save more. This effect is called the *substitution effect*.

There is also an *income effect* of an interest rate change on consumption. If a household has positive wealth and is earning interest on that wealth, a fall in the interest rate leads to a fall in interest income. This is a decrease in its nonlabor income, which, as we just saw, has a negative effect on consumption. For households with positive wealth, the income effect works in the opposite direction from the substitution effect. On the other hand, if a household is a debtor and is paying interest on its debt, a fall in the interest rate will lead to a fall in interest payments. The household is better off in this case and will consume more. In this case, the income and substitution effects work in the same direction. The total household sector in the United States has positive wealth, and so in the aggregate, the income and substitution effects work in the opposite direction.

## Government Effects on Consumption and Labor Supply: Taxes and Transfers

The government influences household behavior mainly through income tax rates and transfer payments. When the government raises income tax rates, after-tax real wages decrease, lowering consumption. When the government lowers income tax rates, after-tax real wages increase, raising consumption. A change in income tax rates also affects labor supply. If the substitution

| TABLE 15.1 | The Effects of Government on Household Consumption and Labor Supply | | | |
|---|---|---|---|---|
| | Income Tax Rates | | Transfer Payments | |
| | Increase | Decrease | Increase | Decrease |
| Effect on consumption | Negative | Positive | Positive | Negative |
| Effect on labor supply | Negative* | Positive* | Negative | Positive |

* If the substitution effect dominates.

*Note:* The effects are larger if they are expected to be permanent instead of temporary.

effect dominates, as we are generally assuming, an increase in income tax rates, which lowers after-tax wages, will lower labor supply. A decrease in income tax rates will increase labor supply. There is much debate about the size of these effects. If the labor elasticity is very high, raising rates could substantially reduce economic activity and even lead to a reduction in aggregate tax revenue. A recent review article, however, suggests that labor supply is relatively inelastic to changes in the marginal tax rate, indicating that increasing tax rates somewhat would likely increase total tax revenues.[3]

*Transfer payments* are payments such as Social Security benefits, veterans' benefits, and welfare benefits. An increase in transfer payments is an increase in nonlabor income, which we have seen has a positive effect on consumption and a negative effect on labor supply. Increases in transfer payments thus increase consumption and decrease labor supply, whereas decreases in transfer payments decrease consumption and increase labor supply. Table 15.1 summarizes these results.

# A Possible Employment Constraint on Households

Our discussion of the labor supply decision has so far proceeded as if households were free to choose how much to work each period. If a member of a household wants to work an additional 5 hours a week at the current wage rate, we have assumed that the person *can* work 5 hours more—that work is available. If someone who has not been working decides to work at the current wage rate, we have assumed that the person *can find a job.*

There are times when these assumptions do not hold and individuals are constrained in the hours they can work. A household constrained from working as much as it would like at the current wage rate faces a different decision from the decision facing a household that can work as much as it wants. The work decision of the former household is, in effect, forced on it. The household works as much as it can—a certain number of hours per week or perhaps none at all—but this amount is less than the household would choose to work at the current wage rate if it could find more work. The amount that a household would like to work at the current wage rate if it could find the work is called its **unconstrained supply of labor.** The amount that the household actually works in a given period at current wage rates is called its **constrained supply of labor.**

A household's constrained supply of labor is not a variable over which it has any control. The amount of labor the household supplies is imposed on it from the outside by the workings of the economy. Under these conditions, we do not expect changes in tax rates, for example, to influence labor supply behavior in the way we see in unconstrained markets. However, the household's consumption *is* under its control. We know that the less a household works—that is, the smaller the household's constrained supply of labor is—the lower will be its consumption. Constraints on the supply of labor are an important determinant of consumption.

**unconstrained supply of labor** The amount a household would like to work within a given period at the current wage rate if it could find the work.

**constrained supply of labor** The amount a household actually works in a given period at the current wage rate.

**Keynesian Theory Revisited** Recall the Keynesian theory that current income determines current consumption. We now know the consumption decision is made jointly with the labor supply decision and the two depend on the real wage rate. It is incorrect to think that consumption depends only on income, at least when there is full employment. However, if there is unemployment, and labor supply is constrained on the upside, Keynes is closer to being correct because the

[3] Emmanuel Saez, Joel Slemrod and Seth Giertz," The elasticity of taxable income with respect to marginal tax rates: A critical review," *Journal of Economic Literature*, March 2012 3-50.

level of income (at least workers' income) depends exclusively on the employment decisions made by firms and not on household decisions. In this case, it is income that affects consumption, not the wage rate. For this reason Keynesian theory is considered to pertain to periods of unemployment. It was, of course, precisely during such a period that the theory was developed.

## A Summary of Household Behavior

This completes our discussion of household behavior in the macroeconomy. Household consumption depends on more than current income. Households determine consumption and labor supply simultaneously, and they look ahead in making their decisions.

The following factors affect household consumption and labor supply decisions:

- Current and expected future real wage rates
- Initial value of wealth
- Current and expected future nonlabor income
- Interest rates
- Current and expected future tax rates and transfer payments

If households are constrained in their labor supply decisions, income is directly determined by firms' hiring decisions. In this case, the Keynesian focus on consumption as a function of income alone has more power.

## The Household Sector Since 1970

To better understand household behavior, we will examine how some of the aggregate household variables have changed over time. We will discuss the period 1970 I–2014 IV. (Remember, Roman numerals refer to quarters, that is, 1970 I means the first quarter of 1970.) Within this span, there have been five recessionary periods: 1974 I–1975 I, 1980 II–1982 IV, 1990 III–1991 I, 2001 I–2001 III, and 2008 I–2009 II. How did the household variables behave during each period?

**Consumption**   Data on the total consumption of the household sector are in the national income accounts. As we saw in Table 6.2 in Chapter 6, personal consumption expenditures accounted for 68.5 percent of GDP in 2014. The three basic categories of consumption expenditures are services, nondurable goods, and durable goods.

Figure 15.2 plots the data for consumption expenditures on services and nondurable goods combined and for consumption expenditures on durable goods. The variables are in real terms. You can see that expenditures on services and nondurable goods are "smoother" over time

MyEconLab Real-time data

▶ **FIGURE 15.2**
**Consumption Expenditures, 1970 I–2014 IV**
Over time, expenditures on services and nondurable goods are "smoother" than expenditures on durable goods.

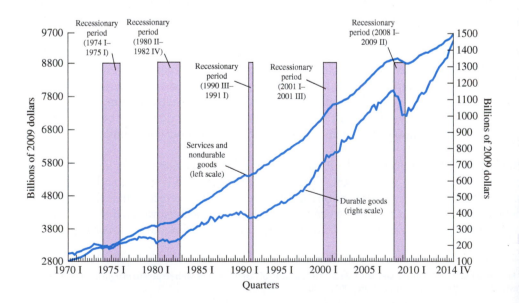

# ECONOMICS IN PRACTICE

## Measuring Housing Price Changes

We have suggested in the text that the rapid rise in housing prices in the period from 2000 to 2006 and the subsequent rapid fall of those prices after 2006 may have played a role in the 2008–2009 recession. There has been a good deal of work in economics tracing the links between what has been called the housing bubble and that recession, particularly on the bursting of the bubble on bank stability.

But how do we measure housing price changes? After all, houses are all different. Measuring price changes in houses is much harder than measuring price changes in oil, or even price changes in milk or cans of tuna fish. One possibility is to look at changes in the *average* price of a house in a city over time. However, if in year 1 mostly modest split-levels change hands, while in year 2 most of the houses sold are McMansions, then changes in the average price will not do a very good job of capturing housing price inflation. An alternative is to try to standardize the house type, say looking at the change in the average price of a four-bedroom house in an area over time. This is better, but still leaves one with a lot of heterogeneity. In fact, one of the authors of this text, Karl Case, working with Robert Shiller, a behavioral finance economist, developed an index (aptly named the Case-Shiller index) that neatly solves the problem that houses are all different. The Case-Shiller index looks only at houses that have sold multiple times and asks the question: How much does an identical house sell for now versus that same house in the past? The index, developed first in Boston, is now computed for a number of large housing areas. In fact, the index itself

is commonly reported on the financial pages and shows housing price changes for 10-city and 20-city bundles.

So what does the Case-Shiller index tell us about the present? From 1996 to 2006, the Case-Shiller index increased by 125 percent, only to fall by 38 percent from 2006 to 2011. But 2012 and early 2013 looked much better, with an annual increase of 7.3 percent in the 10-city index and 8.1 percent for the 20-city index as of April 2013.

### THINKING PRACTICALLY

1. Who, other than macroeconomists, might be interested in the Case-Schiller index?

than expenditures on durable goods. For example, the decrease in expenditures on services and nondurable goods was much smaller during the five recessionary periods than the decrease in expenditures on durable goods.

Why do expenditures on durables fluctuate more than expenditures on services and nondurables? When times are bad, people can postpone the purchase of durable goods, which they do. It follows that expenditures on these goods change the most. When times are tough, you do not *have* to have a new car or a new smartphone; you can make do with your old Chevy or iPhone until things get better. When your income falls, it is not as easy to postpone the service costs of day care or health care. Nondurables fall into an intermediate category, with some items (such as new clothes) easier to postpone than others (such as food).

**Housing Investment**   Another important expenditure of the household sector is housing investment (purchases of new housing), plotted in Figure 15.3. Housing investment is the most easily postponable of all household expenditures, and it has large fluctuations. The fluctuations are remarkable between 2003 and 2010. Housing investment rose rapidly between 2003 and 2005 and then came crashing down. As discussed in Chapter 14, much of this was driven by a huge increase and then decrease in housing prices.

**Labor Supply**   As we noted in Chapters 7 and 13, a person is considered a part of the labor force when he or she is working or has been actively looking for work in the past few weeks. The ratio of the labor force to the total working-age population—those 16 and over—is the *labor force participation rate.*

▶ **FIGURE 15.3**
**Housing Investment of the Household Sector, 1970 I–2014 IV**

Housing investment fell during the five recessionary periods since 1970. Like expenditures for durable goods, expenditures for housing investment are postponable.

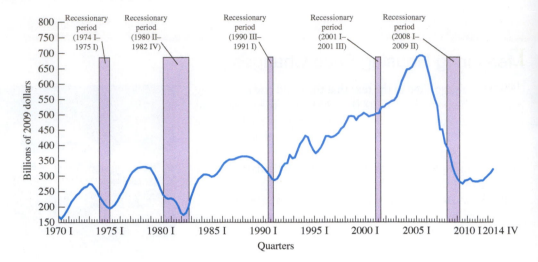

It is informative to divide the labor force into three categories: males 25 to 54, females 25 to 54, and all others 16 and over. Ages 25 to 54 are sometimes called "prime" ages, presuming that a person is in the prime of working life during these ages. The participation rates for these three groups are plotted in Figure 15.4.

As the figure shows, most men of prime age are in the labor force, although the participation rate has fallen since 1970—from 0.961 in 1970 I to 0.882 in 2014 IV. (A rate of 0.882 means that 88.2 percent of prime-age men were in the labor force.) The participation rate for prime-age women, on the other hand, rose dramatically between 1970 and 1990—from 0.501 in 1970 I to 0.741 in 1990 I. Although economic factors account for some of this increase, a change in social attitudes and preferences probably explains much of the increase. Since 1990, the participation rate for prime-age women has changed very little. In 2014 IV, it was 0.739, still considerably below the 0.882 rate for prime-age men.

Figure 15.4 also shows the participation rate for all individuals 16 and over except prime-age men and women. This rate has some cyclical features—it tends to fall in recessions and to rise or fall less during expansions. These features reveal the operation of the *discouraged-worker effect*, discussed in Chapter 7. During recessions, some people get discouraged about ever finding a job. They stop looking and are then not considered a part of the labor force. During expansions, people become encouraged again. Once they begin looking for jobs, they are again considered a part of the labor force. Because prime-age women and men are likely to be fairly attached to the labor force, the discouraged-worker effect for them is quite small.

▶ **FIGURE 15.4**  **Labor Force Participation Rates for Men 25 to 54, Women 25 to 54, and All Others 16 and Over, 1970 I–2014 IV**

Since 1970, the labor force participation rate for prime-age men has been decreasing slightly. The rate for prime-age women has been increasing dramatically. The rate for all others 16 and over has been declining since 1979 and shows a tendency to fall during recessions (the discouraged-worker effect).

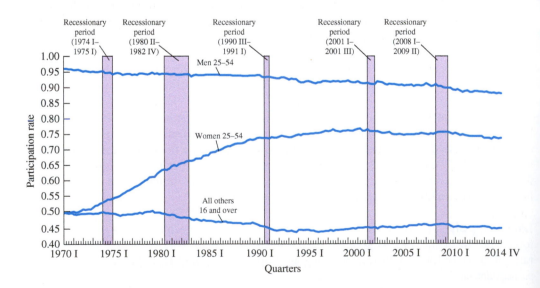

# Firms: Investment and Employment Decisions

Describe factors that affect the investment and employment decisions of firms.

Having taken a closer look at the behavior of households in the macroeconomy, we now look more closely at the behavior of firms—the other major decision-making unit in the economy. In discussing firm behavior previously, we assumed that planned investment depends only on the interest rate. However, there are several other determinants of planned investment. We now discuss them and the factors that affect firms' employment decisions. Once again, microeconomic theory can help us gain some insight into the working of the macroeconomy.

In a market economy, firms determine which goods and services are available to consumers today and which will be available in the future, how many workers are needed for what kinds of jobs, and how much investment will be undertaken. Stated in macroeconomic terms, the decisions of firms, taken together, determine output, labor demand, and investment.

## Expectations and Animal Spirits

Time is a key factor in investment decisions. Capital has a life that typically extends over many years. A developer who decides to build an office tower is making an investment that will be around (barring earthquakes, floods, or tornadoes) for several decades. In deciding where to build a plant, a manufacturing firm is committing a large amount of resources to purchase capital that will presumably yield services over a long time. Furthermore, the decision to build a plant or to purchase large equipment must often be made years before the actual project is completed. Whereas the acquisition of a small business computer may take only a few days, the planning process for downtown developments in large U.S. cities has been known to take decades.

For these reasons, investment decisions require looking into the future and forming expectations about it. In forming their expectations, firms consider numerous factors. At a minimum, they gather information about the demand for their specific products, about what their competitors are planning, and about the macroeconomy's overall health. A firm is not likely to increase its production capacity if it does not expect to sell more of its product in the future. Hilton will not put up a new hotel if it does not expect to fill the rooms at a profitable rate. Ford will not build a new plant if it expects the economy to enter a long recession.

Forecasting the future is fraught with dangers. Many events cannot be foreseen. Investments are therefore always made with imperfect knowledge. Keynes pointed this out in 1936:

> The outstanding fact is the extreme precariousness of the basis of knowledge on which our estimates of prospective yield have to be made. Our knowledge of the factors which will govern the yield of an investment some years hence is usually very slight and often negligible. If we speak frankly, we have to admit that our basis of knowledge for estimating the yield ten years hence of a railway, a copper mine, a textile factory, the goodwill of a patent medicine, an Atlantic liner, a building in the City of London amounts to little and sometimes nothing.

Keynes concludes from this line of thought that much investment activity depends on psychology and on what he calls the **animal spirits of entrepreneurs**:

**animal spirits of entrepreneurs**
A term coined by Keynes to describe investors' feelings.

> Our decisions . . . can only be taken as a result of animal spirits. In estimating the prospects of investment, we must have regard, therefore, to nerves and hysteria and even the digestions and reactions to the weather of those upon whose spontaneous activity it largely depends.[4]

Because expectations about the future are, as Keynes points out, subject to great uncertainty, they may change often. Thus, animal spirits help to make investment a volatile component of gross domestic product (GDP).

---

[4] John Maynard Keynes, *The General Theory of Employment, Interest, and Money (1936)*, First Harbinger Ed. (New York: Harcourt Brace Jovanovich, 1964), pp. 149, 152.

**The Accelerator Effect**   Keynes' reference to animal spirits suggest that expectations play a role in determining the level of planned investment spending. At any interest rate, the level of investment is likely to be higher if businesses are optimistic and lower if they are pessimistic. A key question is then what determines expectations? One possibility is that expectations are optimistic when aggregate output ($Y$) is rising and pessimistic when aggregate output is falling. At any given level of the interest rate, expectations may be more optimistic and planned investment higher when output is growing rapidly than when it is growing slowly or falling. It is easy to see why this might be so. When firms expect future prospects to be good, they may plan now to add productive capacity, and one indicator of future prospects is the current growth rate.

If this is the case, the result will be what is called an **accelerator effect**. If aggregate output (income) ($Y$) is rising, investment will increase even though the level of $Y$ may be low. Higher investment spending leads to an added increase in output, further "accelerating" the growth of aggregate output. If $Y$ is falling, expectations are dampened and investment spending will be cut even though the level of $Y$ may be high, accelerating the decline.

**accelerator effect**   The tendency for investment to increase when aggregate output increases and to decrease when aggregate output decreases, accelerating the growth or decline of output.

## Excess Labor and Excess Capital Effects

In our simple model of the macroeconomy, to produce more output the firms in the economy need to hire more labor and capital. In practice, firms appear at times to hold what we will call **excess labor** and/or **excess capital**. A firm holds excess labor (or capital) if it can reduce the amount of labor it employs (or capital it holds) and still produce the same amount of output. The possibility that large numbers of firms may at times be holding excess labor or capital complicates our story of the investment-output relationship.

**excess labor, excess capital**   Labor and capital that are not needed to produce the firm's current level of output.

Why might a firm want to employ more workers or have more capital on hand than it needs? Both labor and capital are costly—a firm has to pay wages to its workers, and it forgoes interest on funds tied up in machinery or buildings. Why would a firm want to incur costs that do not yield revenue?

To see why, suppose a firm suffers a sudden and large decrease in sales, but it expects the lower sales level to last only a few months, after which it believes sales will pick up again. In this case, the firm is likely to lower production in response to the sales change to avoid too large an increase in its stock of inventories. This decrease in production means that the firm could get rid of some workers and some machines because it needs less labor and less capital to produce the now-lower level of output.

However, things are not that simple. Decreasing its workforce and capital stock quickly can be costly for a firm. Abrupt cuts in the workforce hurt worker morale and may increase personnel administration costs, and abrupt reductions in capital stock may be disadvantageous because of the difficulty of selling used machines. These types of costs are sometimes called **adjustment costs** because they are the costs of adjusting to the new level of output. There are also adjustment costs to increasing output. For example, it is usually costly to recruit and train new workers.

**adjustment costs**   The costs that a firm incurs when it changes its production level—for example, the administration costs of laying off employees or the training costs of hiring new workers.

Adjustment costs may be large enough that a firm chooses not to decrease its workforce and capital stock when production falls. The firm may at times choose to have more labor and capital on hand than it needs to produce its current amount of output simply because getting rid of them is more costly than keeping them and the firm expects it will need the workers in the near future. In practice, excess labor takes the form of workers not working at their normal level of activity (more coffee breaks and more idle time, for instance). Some of this excess labor may receive new training so that productivity will be higher when production picks up again.

The existence of excess labor and capital at any given moment is likely to affect future employment and investment decisions. Suppose a firm already has excess labor and capital as a result of a fall in its sales and production. When production picks up again, the firm will not need to hire as many new workers or acquire as much new capital as it would otherwise. The more excess capital a firm already has, the less likely it is to invest in new capital in the future. The more excess labor it has, the less likely it is to hire new workers in the future. As you can see, predicting what happens as an economy recovers is made more complicated if in a down period many firms hold excess inputs.

# Inventory Investment

We now turn to a brief discussion of the inventory investment decision. **Inventory investment** is the change in the stock of inventories. Although inventory investment is another way in which a firm adds to its capital stock, the inventory investment decision is quite different from the plant-and-equipment investment decision.

**inventory investment** The change in the stock of inventories.

**The Role of Inventories** Recall the distinction between a firm's sales and its output. If a firm can hold goods in inventory, which is usually the case unless the good is perishable or unless the firm produces services, then within a given period, it can sell a quantity of goods that differs from the quantity of goods it produces during that period. When a firm sells more than it produces, its stock of inventories decreases; when it sells less than it produces, its stock of inventories increases.

$$\text{Stock of inventories (end of period)} = \text{Stock of inventories (beginning of period)} + \text{Production} - \text{Sales}$$

If a firm starts a period with 100 umbrellas in inventory, produces 15 umbrellas during the period, and sells 10 umbrellas in this same interval, it will have 105 umbrellas $(100 + 15 - 10)$ in inventory at the end of the period. A change in the stock of inventories is actually investment because inventories are counted as part of a firm's capital stock. In our example, inventory investment during the period is a positive number, 5 umbrellas $(105 - 100)$. When the number of goods produced is less than the number of goods sold, such as 5 produced and 10 sold, inventory investment is negative.

**The Optimal Inventory Policy** We can now consider firms' inventory decisions. Firms are concerned with what they are going to sell and produce in the future as well as what they are selling and producing currently. At each point in time, a firm has some idea of how much it is going to sell in the current period and in future periods. Given these expectations and its knowledge of how much of its good it already has in stock, a firm must decide how much to produce in the current period. Inventories are costly to a firm because they take up space and they tie up funds that could be earning interest. However, if a firm's stock of inventories gets too low, the firm may have difficulty meeting the demand for its product, especially if demand increases unexpectedly. The firm may lose sales. The point between too low and too high a stock of inventory is called the **desired, *or* optimal, level of inventories**. This is the level at which the extra cost (in lost sales) from decreasing inventories by a small amount is just equal to the extra gain (in interest revenue and decreased storage costs).

**desired, *or* optimal, level of inventories** The level of inventory at which the extra cost (in lost sales) from lowering inventories by a small amount is just equal to the extra gain (in interest revenue and decreased storage costs).

A firm that had no costs other than inventory costs would always aim to produce in a period exactly the volume of goods necessary to make its stock of inventories at the end of the period equal to the desired stock. If the stock of inventory fell lower than desired, the firm would produce more than it expected to sell to bring the stock up. If the stock of inventory grew above the desired level, the firm would produce less than it expected to sell to reduce the stock.

There are other costs to running a firm besides inventory costs. In particular, large and abrupt changes in production can be costly because it is often disruptive to change a production process geared to a certain rate of output. If production is to be increased, there may be adjustment costs for hiring more labor and increasing the capital stock. If production is to be decreased, there may be adjustment costs in laying off workers and decreasing the capital stock.

Because holding inventories and changing production levels are both costly, firms face a trade-off between them. Because of adjustment costs, a firm is likely to smooth its production path relative to its sales path. This means that a firm is likely to have its production fluctuate less than its sales, with changes in inventories to absorb the difference each period. However, because there are incentives not to stray too far from the optimal level of inventories, fluctuations in production are not eliminated completely. Production is still likely to fluctuate, just not as much as sales fluctuate.

Two other points need to be made here. First, if a firm's stock of inventories is unusually or unexpectedly high, as a result of unexpected shortfalls in sales, the firm is likely to produce less in the future than it otherwise would have to decrease its high stock of inventories. In this way, unexpected inventories also influence current production levels. An unexpectedly high stock of inventories will have a negative effect on production in the future, and an unexpectedly low stock will have a positive effect on production in the future. We have seen that lower than expected past sales will influence optimal production as firms seek to reduce unplanned inventories. Future sales expectations also have an effect on inventory policy and on production. If a firm expects its sales to be high in the future, it will adjust its planned production path accordingly, recognizing that a higher level of sales also requires a higher level of inventories to support those sales. Because production is likely to depend on expectations of the future, animal spirits may play a role. If firms become more optimistic about the future, they are likely to produce more now as they build up inventories in anticipation of increased future sales. Keynes's view that animal spirits affect investment is also likely to pertain to output.

## A Summary of Firm Behavior

The following factors affect firms' investment and employment decisions:

- Firms' expectations of future output
- Wage rate and cost of capital (The interest rate is an important component of the cost of capital.)
- Amount of excess labor and excess capital on hand

The most important points to remember about the relationship among production, sales, and inventory investment are

- Inventory investment—that is, the change in the stock of inventories—equals production minus sales.
- An unexpected increase in the stock of inventories has a negative effect on future production.
- Current production depends on expected future sales.

## The Firm Sector Since 1970

To close our discussion of firm behavior, we now examine some aggregate investment and employment variables for the period 1970 I–2014 IV. We will see the way in which our expanded model of firm behavior helps us to understand patterns in those data.

**Plant-and-Equipment Investment**   Plant-and-equipment investment by the firm sector is plotted in Figure 15.5. Investment fared poorly in the five recessionary periods after 1970. This observation is consistent with the observation that investment depends in part on output. An examination of the plot of real GDP in Figure 5.4 in Chapter 5 and the plot of investment in Figure 15.5 shows that investment generally does poorly when GDP does poorly and that investment generally does well when GDP does well.

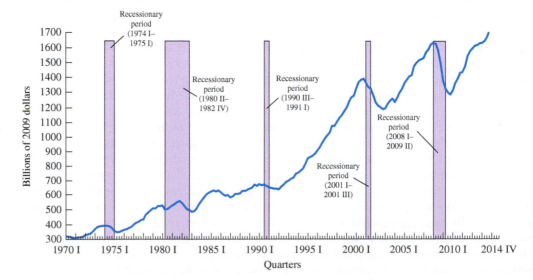

**MyEconLab** Real-time data

▶ **FIGURE 15.5  Plant and Equipment Investment of the Firm Sector, 1970 I–2014 IV**
Overall, plant and equipment investment declined in the five recessionary periods since 1970.

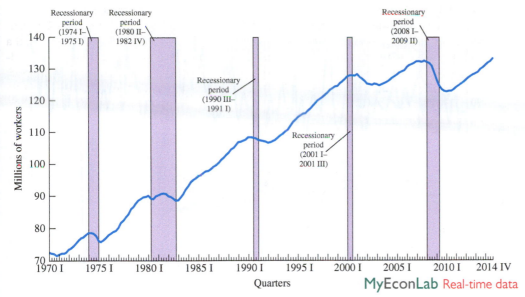

**Employment in the Firm Sector, 1970 I–2014 IV**
Growth in employment was generally negative in the five recessions the U.S. economy has experienced since 1970.

Figure 15.5 also shows that investment fluctuates greatly. This is not surprising. The animal spirits of entrepreneurs are likely to be volatile, and if animal spirits affect investment, it follows that investment too will be volatile.

Despite the volatility of plant-and-equipment investment, however, it is still true that housing investment fluctuates more than plant-and-equipment investment (as you can see by comparing Figures 15.3 and 15.5). Plant and equipment investment is not the most volatile component of GDP.

**Employment**  Employment in the firm sector is plotted in Figure 15.6, which shows that employment fell in all five recessionary periods. This is consistent with the theory that employment depends in part on output. Otherwise, employment has grown over time in response to the growing economy. Employment in the firm sector rose from 72.5 million in 1970 I to 132.4 million in 2007 IV (before the recession of 2008–2009). During the 2008–2009 recession, employment fell by 9.5 million—from 132.4 million in 2007 IV to 122.9 million in 2009 IV. You can see that employment has recovered fairly slowly since 2009.

**Inventory Investment**  Recall that *inventory investment* is the difference between the level of output and the level of sales. Recall also that some inventory investment is usually unplanned. This occurs when the actual level of sales is different from the expected level of sales.

Inventory investment of the firm sector is plotted in Figure 15.7. Also plotted in this figure is the ratio of the stock of inventories to the level of sales—the *inventory-to-sales ratio*. The figure shows that inventory investment is volatile—more volatile than housing investment and plant and equipment investment. Some of this volatility is undoubtedly as a result of the unplanned component of inventory investment, which is likely to fluctuate greatly from one period to the next.

When the inventory-to-sales ratio is high, the actual stock of inventories is likely to be larger than the desired stock. In such a case, firms have overestimated demand and produced too much relative to sales and they are likely to want to produce less in the future to draw down their stock. You can find several examples of this trend in Figure 15.7—the clearest occurred during the 1974–1975 period. At the end of 1974, the stock of inventories was high relative to sales, an indication that firms probably had undesired inventories at the end of 1974. In 1975, firms worked off these undesired inventories by producing less than they sold. Thus, inventory investment was low in 1975. The year 1975 is clearly a year in which output would have been higher had the stock of inventories at the beginning of the year not been so high. There were large declines in inventory investment in the recessions of 2001 and 2008–2009.

▶ **FIGURE 15.7**

**Inventory Investment of the Firm Sector and the Inventory-to-Sales Ratio, 1970 I–2014 IV**

The inventory-to-sales ratio is the ratio of the firm sector's stock of inventories to the level of sales. Inventory investment is volatile.

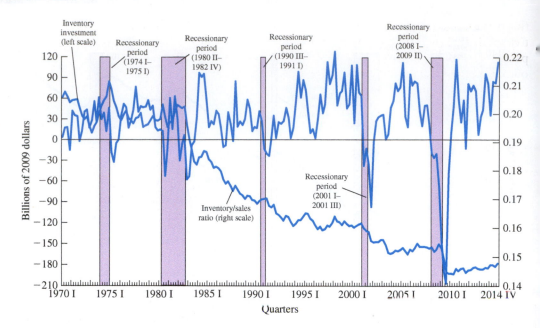

On average, the inventory-to-sales ratio has been declining over time, evidence that firms are becoming more efficient in their management of inventory stocks. Firms are becoming more efficient in the sense of being able (other things equal) to hold smaller and smaller stocks of inventories relative to sales.

**15.3 LEARNING OBJECTIVE**

Explain why productivity is procyclical.

**productivity, or labor productivity** Output per worker hour.

# Productivity and the Business Cycle

We can now use what we have just learned about firm behavior to analyze movements in productivity. **Productivity**, sometimes called **labor productivity**, is defined as output per worker hour. If output is $Y$ and the number of hours worked in the economy is $H$, productivity is $Y/H$. Simply stated, productivity measures how much output an average worker produces per hour.

Productivity fluctuates over the business cycle, tending to rise during expansions and fall during contractions. See Figure 7.2 in Chapter 7 for a plot of productivity for 1952 I–2014 IV. You can see from this figure that productivity fluctuates up and down around a positive trend. The fact that firms at times hold excess labor explains why productivity fluctuates in the same direction as output.

Figure 15.8 shows the pattern of employment and output over time for a hypothetical economy. Employment does not fluctuate as much as output over the business cycle. It is precisely

▶ **FIGURE 15.8**

**Employment and Output over the Business Cycle**

In general, employment does not fluctuate as much as output over the business cycle. As a result, measured productivity (the output-to-labor ratio) tends to rise during expansionary periods and decline during contractionary periods.

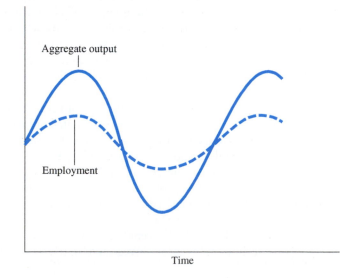

this pattern that leads to higher productivity during periods of high output and lower productivity during periods of low output. During expansions in the economy, output rises by a larger percentage than employment and the ratio of output to workers rises. During downswings, output falls faster than employment and the ratio of output to workers falls.

The existence of excess labor when the economy is in a slump means that productivity as measured by the ratio $Y/H$ tends to fall at such times. Does this trend mean that labor is in some sense "less productive" during recessions than before? Not really: It means only that firms choose to employ more labor than would be profit-maximizing. For this reason, some workers are in effect idle some of the time even though they are considered employed. They are not less productive in the sense of having less potential to produce output; they are merely not working part of the time that they are *counted* as working.

# The Short-Run Relationship Between Output and Unemployment

**15.4 LEARNING** OBJECTIVE
Describe the short-run relationship between output and unemployment.

We can also use what we have learned about household and firm behavior to analyze the relationship between output and unemployment. When we discussed the connections between the $AS/AD$ diagram and the Phillips Curve in Chapter 14, we mentioned that output ($Y$) and the unemployment rate ($U$) are inversely related. When output rises, the unemployment rate falls, and when output falls, the unemployment rate rises. At one time, it was believed that the short-run relationship between the two variables was fairly stable. **Okun's Law** (after U.S. economist Arthur Okun, who first studied the relationship) stated that in the short run the unemployment rate decreased about 1 percentage point for every 3 percent increase in real GDP. As with the Phillips Curve, Okun's Law has not turned out to be a "law." The economy is far too complex for there to be such a simple and stable relationship between two macroeconomic variables.

Although the short-run relationship between output and the unemployment rate is not the simple relationship Okun believed, it is true that a 1 percent increase in output tends to correspond to a less than 1 percentage point decrease in the unemployment rate in the short run. In other words, there are a number of "slippages" between changes in output and changes in the unemployment rate.

The first slippage is between the change in output and the change in the number of jobs in the economy. When output increases by 1 percent, the number of jobs does not tend to rise by 1 percent in the short run. There are two reasons for this. First, a firm is likely to meet some of the increase in output by increasing the number of hours worked per job. Instead of having the labor force work 40 hours per week, the firm may pay overtime and have the labor force work 42 hours per week. Second, if a firm is holding excess labor at the time of the output increase, at least part of the increase in output can come from putting the excess labor back to work. For both reasons, the number of jobs is likely to rise by a smaller percentage than the increase in output.

The second slippage is between the change in the number of *jobs* and the change in the *number of people employed*. If you have two jobs, you are counted twice in the job data but only once in the persons-employed data. Because some people have two jobs, there are more jobs than there are people employed. When the number of jobs increases, some of the new jobs are filled by people who already have one job (instead of by people who are unemployed). This means that the increase in the number of people employed is less than the increase in the number of jobs. This is a slippage between output and the unemployment rate because the unemployment rate is calculated from data on the number of people employed, not the number of jobs.

The third slippage concerns the response of the labor force to an increase in output. Let $E$ denote the number of people employed, let $L$ denote the number of people in the labor force, and let $u$ denote the unemployment rate. In these terms, the unemployment rate is

**Okun's Law**  The theory, put forth by Arthur Okun, that in the short run the unemployment rate decreases about 1 percentage point for every 3 percent increase in real GDP. Later research and data have shown that the relationship between output and unemployment is not as stable as Okun's "Law" predicts.

$$u = 1 - E/L$$

The unemployment rate is 1 minus the employment rate, $E/L$.

When we discussed how the unemployment rate is measured in Chapter 7, we introduced the **discouraged-worker effect**. A discouraged worker is one who would like a job but has stopped

**discouraged-worker effect** The decline in the measured unemployment rate that results when people who want to work but cannot find work grow discouraged and stop looking, dropping out of the ranks of the unemployed and the labor force.

looking because the prospects seem so bleak. When output increases, job prospects begin to look better and some people who had stopped looking for work begin looking again. When they do, they are once again counted as part of the labor force. The labor force increases when output increases because discouraged workers are moving back into the labor force. This is another reason the unemployment rate does not fall as much as might be expected when output increases.

These three slippages show that the link from changes in output to changes in the unemployment rate is complicated. All three combine to make the change in the unemployment rate less than the percentage change in output in the short run. They also show that the relationship between changes in output and changes in the unemployment rate is not likely to be stable. The size of the first slippage, for example, depends on how much excess labor is being held at the time of the output increase, and the size of the third slippage depends on what else is affecting the labor force (such as changes in real wage rates) at the time of the output increase. The relationship between output and unemployment depends on the state of the economy at the time of the output change.

**15.5 LEARNING** OBJECTIVE

Identify factors that affect multiplier size.

# The Size of the Multiplier

We can finally bring together the material in this chapter and in previous chapters to consider the size of the multiplier. We mentioned in Chapter 8 that much of the analysis we would do after deriving the simple multiplier would have the effect of decreasing the size of the multiplier. We can now summarize why.

1. There are *automatic stabilizers*. We saw in the Appendix to Chapter 9 that if taxes are not a fixed amount but instead depend on income (which is surely the case in practice), the size of the multiplier is decreased. When the economy expands and income increases, the amount of taxes collected increases. The rise in taxes acts to offset some of the expansion (thus, a smaller multiplier). When the economy contracts and income decreases, the amount of taxes collected decreases. This decrease in taxes helps to lessen the contraction. Some transfer payments also respond to the state of the economy and act as automatic stabilizers, lowering the value of the multiplier. Unemployment benefits are the best example of transfer payments that increase during contractions and decrease during expansions.

2. There is the *interest rate*. We saw in Chapter 11 that in normal times the Fed increases the interest rate as output increases, which decreases planned investment. The increase in output from a government spending increase is thus smaller than if the interest rate did not rise because of the crowding out of planned investment. As we saw previously in this chapter, increases in the interest rate also have a negative effect on consumption. Consumption is also crowded out in the same way that planned investment is, and this effect lowers the value of the multiplier even further.

3. There is the response of the *price level*. We also saw in Chapter 11 that some of the effect of an expansionary policy is to increase the price level. The multiplier is smaller because of this price response. The multiplier is particularly small when the economy is on the steep part of the AS curve, where most of the effect of an expansionary policy is to increase prices.

4. There are *excess capital* and *excess labor*. When firms are holding excess labor and capital, part of any output increase can come from putting the excess labor and capital back to work instead of increasing employment and investment. This lowers the value of the multiplier because (1) investment increases less than it would have if there were no excess capital and (2) consumption increases less than it would have if employment (and thus household income) had increased more.

5. There are *inventories*. Part of any initial increase in sales can come from drawing down inventories instead of increasing output. To the extent that firms draw down their inventories in the short run, the value of the multiplier is lower because output does not respond as quickly to demand changes.

6. There are people's *expectations* about the future. People look ahead, and they respond less to temporary changes than to permanent changes. The multiplier effects for policy changes perceived to be temporary are smaller than those for policy changes perceived to be permanent.

**The Size of the Multiplier in Practice** In practice, the multiplier probably has a value of around 2.0. Its size also depends on how long ago the spending increase began. For example, in the first quarter of an increase in government spending, the multiplier is only about 1.1. If government spending rises by $1 billion, GDP will increase by about $1.1 billion during the first quarter. In the second quarter, the multiplier will rise to about 1.6. The multiplier then will rise to its peak of about 2.0 in the fourth quarter.

One of the main points to remember here is that if the government is contemplating a monetary or fiscal policy change, the response of the economy to the change is not likely to be large and quick. It takes time for the full effects to be felt, and in the final analysis, the effects are much smaller than the simple multiplier we discussed in Chapter 8 would lead one to believe.

A good way to review much of the material since Chapter 8 is to make sure you clearly understand how the value of the multiplier is affected by each of the additions to the simple model in Chapter 8. We have come a long way since then, and this review may help you to put all the pieces together.

———— **S U M M A R Y** ————

### 15.1 HOUSEHOLDS: CONSUMPTION AND LABOR SUPPLY DECISIONS *p. 281*

1. The *life-cycle theory of consumption* says that households make lifetime consumption decisions based on their expectations of lifetime income. Generally, households consume an amount less than their incomes during their prime working years and an amount greater than their incomes during their early working years and after they have retired.

2. Households make consumption and labor supply decisions simultaneously. Consumption cannot be considered separately from labor supply because it is precisely by selling your labor that you earn the income that makes consumption possible.

3. There is a trade-off between the goods and services that wage income will buy and leisure or other nonmarket activities. The wage rate is the key variable that determines how a household responds to this trade-off.

4. Changes in the wage rate have both an income effect and a substitution effect. The evidence suggests that the substitution effect seems to dominate for most people, which means that the aggregate labor supply responds positively to an increase in the wage rate.

5. Consumption increases when the wage rate increases.

6. The *nominal wage rate* is the wage rate in current dollars. The *real wage rate* is the amount the nominal wage can buy in terms of goods and services. Households look at expected future real wage rates as well as the current real wage rate in making their consumption and labor supply decisions.

7. Holding all else constant (including the stage in the life cycle), the more wealth a household has, the more it will consume both now and in the future.

8. An unexpected increase in *nonlabor income* (any income received from sources other than working, such as inheritances, interest, and dividends) will have a positive effect on a household's consumption and will lead to a decrease in labor supply.

9. The interest rate also affects consumption, although the direction of the total effect depends on the relative sizes of the income and substitution effects. There is some evidence that the income effect is larger now than it used to be, making monetary policy less effective than it used to be.

10. The government influences household behavior mainly through income tax rates and transfer payments. If the substitution effect dominates, an increase in tax rates lowers after-tax income, decreases consumption, and decreases the labor supply; a decrease in tax rates raises after-tax income, increases consumption, and increases labor supply. Increases in transfer payments increase consumption and decrease labor supply; decreases in transfer payments decrease consumption and increase labor supply.

11. During times of unemployment, households' labor supply may be constrained. Households may want to work a certain number of hours at current wage rates but may not be allowed to do so by firms. In this case, the level of income (at least workers' income) depends exclusively on the employment decisions made by firms. Households consume less if they are constrained from working.

### 15.2 FIRMS: INVESTMENT AND EMPLOYMENT DECISIONS *p. 289*

12. Expectations affect investment and employment decisions. Keynes used the term *animal spirits of entrepreneurs* to refer to investors' feelings.

13. At any level of the interest rate, expectations are likely to be more optimistic and planned investment is likely to be higher when output is growing rapidly than when it is growing slowly or falling. The result is an *accelerator effect* that can cause the economy to expand more rapidly during an expansion and contract more quickly during a recession.

14. *Excess labor and capital* are labor and capital not needed to produce a firm's current level of output. Holding excess labor and capital may be more efficient than laying off workers or selling used equipment. The more excess capital a firm has, the less likely it is to invest in new capital in the future. The more excess labor it has, the less likely it is to hire new workers in the future.

15. Holding inventories is costly to a firm because they take up space and they tie up funds that could be earning interest. Not holding inventories can cause a firm to lose sales if demand increases. The *desired*, or *optimal, level of inventories* is the level at which the extra cost (in lost sales) from lowering inventories by a small amount is equal to the extra gain (in interest revenue and decreased storage costs).

16. An unexpected increase in inventories has a negative effect on future production, and an unexpected decrease in inventories has a positive effect on future production.

17. The level of a firm's planned production path depends on the level of its expected future sales path. If a firm's expectations of its future sales path decrease, the firm is likely to decrease the level of its planned production path, including its actual production in the current period.

### 15.3 PRODUCTIVITY AND THE BUSINESS CYCLE *p. 294*

18. *Productivity*, or *labor productivity*, is output per worker hour—the amount of output produced by an average worker in 1 hour. Productivity fluctuates over the business cycle, tending to rise during expansions and fall during contractions. That workers are less productive during contractions does not mean that they have less potential to produce output;

it means that excess labor exists and that workers are not working at their capacity.

### 15.4 THE SHORT-RUN RELATIONSHIP BETWEEN OUTPUT AND UNEMPLOYMENT *p. 295*

19. There is a negative relationship between output and unemployment: When output ($Y$) rises, the unemployment rate ($U$) falls, and when output falls, the unemployment rate rises. *Okun's Law* states that in the short run the unemployment rate decreases about 1 percentage point for every 3 percent increase in GDP. Okun's Law is not a "law"—the economy is too complex for there to be a stable relationship between two macroeconomic variables. In general, the relationship between output and unemployment depends on the state of the economy at the time of the output change.

### 15.5 THE SIZE OF THE MULTIPLIER *p. 296*

20. There are several reasons why the actual value of the multiplier is smaller than the size that would be expected from the simple multiplier model: (1) Automatic stabilizers help to offset contractions or limit expansions. (2) When government spending increases, the increased interest rate crowds out planned investment and consumption spending. (3) Expansionary policies increase the price level. (4) Firms sometimes hold excess capital and excess labor. (5) Firms may meet increased demand by drawing down inventories instead of increasing output. (6) Households and firms change their behavior less when they expect changes to be temporary instead of permanent.

21. In practice, the size of the multiplier at its peak is about 2.

## REVIEW TERMS AND CONCEPTS

accelerator effect, *p. 290*

adjustment costs, *p. 290*

animal spirits of entrepreneurs, *p. 289*

constrained supply of labor, *p. 285*

desired, *or* optimal, level of inventories, *p. 291*

discouraged-worker effect, *p. 295*

excess labor, excess capital, *p. 290*

inventory investment, *p. 291*

life-cycle theory of consumption, *p. 281*

nominal wage rate, *p. 283*

nonlabor, *or* nonwage, income, *p. 284*

Okun's Law, *p. 295*

permanent income, *p. 282*

productivity, *or* labor productivity, *p. 294*

real wage rate, *p. 283*

unconstrained supply of labor, *p. 285*

## PROBLEMS

All problems are available on MyEconLab.

### 15.1 HOUSEHOLDS: CONSUMPTION AND LABOR SUPPLY DECISIONS

LEARNING OBJECTIVE:  Describe factors that affect household consumption and labor supply decisions.

1.1 During 2015, the Federal Reserve Bank discussed the probability of raising interest rates by the end of the year, the first time in over 7 years they will have raised rates.

a. What direct effects do higher interest rates have on household and firm behavior?

b. One of the consequences of higher interest rates is that the value of existing bonds (both corporate bonds and government bonds) will fall. Explain why higher interest rates would decrease the value of existing fixed-rate bonds held by the public.

c. Some economists argue that the wealth effect of higher interest rates on consumption is as important as the direct effect of higher interest rates on investment. Explain what economists mean by "wealth effects on consumption" and illustrate with AS/AD curves.

**1.2** On January 1, 2014, the top federal income tax bracket in the United States went from 35 percent to 39.6 percent. Many republicans claimed that lowering the rewards for working (the net after-tax wage rate) would lead to less work effort and a lower labor supply. Proponents of the tax increase replied that this claim was baseless because it "ignored the income effect of the tax increase (net wage decrease)." Explain what these critics meant.

**1.3** Graph the following two consumption functions:

$$(1)\ C = 500 + 0.8\,Y$$
$$(2)\ C = 0.8\,Y$$

  **a.** For each function, calculate and graph the average propensity to consume (*APC*) when income is $200, $500, and $1,000.

  **b.** For each function, what happens to the *APC* as income rises?

  **c.** For each function, what is the relationship between the *APC* and the marginal propensity to consume?

  **d.** Under the first consumption function, a family with income of $75,000 consumes a smaller proportion of its income than a family with income of $30,000; yet if we take a dollar of income away from the rich family and give it to the poor family, total consumption by the two families does not change. Explain how this is possible.

**1.4** [**Related to the *Economics in Practice* on p. 287**] From March 2007 to May 2009, the price of houses decreased dramatically in many parts of the country.

  **a.** What impact would you expect decreases and increases in home values to have on the consumption behavior of home owners? Explain.

  **b.** In what ways might events in the housing market have influenced the rest of the economy through their effects on consumption spending? Be specific.

\*1.5 Lydia Lopokova is 40 years old. She has assets (wealth) of $80,000 and has no debts or liabilities. She knows that she will work for 30 more years and will live 10 years after that, when she will earn nothing. Her salary each year for the rest of her working career is $35,000. (There are no taxes.) She wants to distribute her consumption over the rest of her life in such a way that she consumes the same amount each year. She cannot consume in total more than her current wealth plus the sum of her income for the next 30 years. Assume that the rate of interest is zero and that Lopokova decides not to leave any inheritance to her children.

  **a.** How much will Lydia consume this year and next year? How did you arrive at your answer?

  **b.** Plot on a graph Lydia's income, consumption, and wealth from the time she is 40 until she is 80 years old. What is the relationship between the annual increase in her wealth and her annual saving (income minus consumption)? In what year does Lydia's wealth start to decline? Why? How much wealth does she have when she dies?

  **c.** Suppose Lydia receives a tax rebate of $1,000 per year, so her income is $36,000 per year for the rest of her working career. By how much does her consumption increase this year and next year?

  **d.** Now suppose Lydia receives a 1-year-only tax refund of $1,000—her income this year is $36,000; but in all succeeding years, her income is $35,000. What happens to her consumption this year? in succeeding years?

**1.6** Explain why a household's consumption and labor supply decisions are interdependent. What impact does this interdependence have on the way in which consumption and income are related?

## 15.2 FIRMS: INVESTMENT AND EMPLOYMENT DECISIONS

LEARNING OBJECTIVE: Describe factors that affect the investment and employment decisions of firms.

**2.1** Why do expectations play such an important role in investment demand? How, if at all, does this explain why investment is so volatile?

**2.2** How can a firm maintain a smooth production schedule even when sales are fluctuating? What are the benefits of a smooth production schedule? What are the costs?

**2.3** George Jetson has recently been promoted to inventory control manager at Spacely Sprockets, and he must decide on the optimal level of sprockets to keep in inventory. How should Jetson decide on the optimal level of inventory? How would a change in interest rates affect the optimal level of inventory? What costs and benefits will Spacely Sprockets experience by holding inventory?

**2.4** Futurama Medical is a high-tech medical equipment manufacturer that uses custom-designed machinery and a highly skilled, well-trained labor force in its production factory. Gonzo Garments is a mid-level clothing manufacturer that uses mass-produced machinery and readily available labor in its production factory. Which of these two firms would you expect to have more significant adjustment costs? Which firm would be more likely to hold excess labor? excess capital? Explain your answers.

## 15.3 PRODUCTIVITY AND THE BUSINESS CYCLE

LEARNING OBJECTIVE: Explain why productivity is procyclical.

**3.1** Between December 2012 and December 2013, real GDP in the United States increased by 3.18 percent, whereas nonfarm payroll jobs increased by only 1.77 percent. How is it possible for output to increase without a proportional increase in the number of workers?

\* Note: Problems marked with an asterisk are more challenging.

## 15.4 THE SHORT-RUN RELATIONSHIP BETWEEN OUTPUT AND UNEMPLOYMENT

**LEARNING OBJECTIVE:** Describe the short-run relationship between output and unemployment.

4.1 The Bureau of Labor Statistics reported that in June 2010, the unemployment rate in the United States was 9.4 percent. In June 2015, the BLS reported an unemployment rate of 5.3 percent.
   a. According to Okun's Law, by how much would GDP need to increase for the unemployment rate to decrease from the June 2010 rate to the rate of June 2015?
   b. In June 2010, the annual GDP growth rate in the United States was 2.4 percent. At this rate of growth, how long does Okun's Law predict it would take for the economy to reach the unemployment rate of June 2015? Based on the unemployment rates and annual GDP growth rate listed above, how accurate was the prediction?

4.2 In the short run, the percentage increase in output tends to correspond to a smaller percentage decrease in the unemployment rate as a result of "slippages." Explain the three slippages between changes in output and changes in the unemployment rate.

## 15.5 THE SIZE OF THE MULTIPLIER

**LEARNING OBJECTIVE:** Identify factors that affect multiplier size.

5.1 Explain the effect that each of the following situations will have on the size of the multiplier.
   a. Firms have excess inventories as the economy begins to recover from a recession.
   b. Expansionary policy causes the price level to increase.
   c. People expect a $500 tax rebate to be a one-time occurrence.
   d. The government decreases spending, and the Fed does not change the money supply.
   e. The economy expands, and income taxes are progressive.
   f. The government extends unemployment benefits as a response to a lingering recession.

# Long-Run Growth

# 16

Think about how many hours your great-grandparents had to work to pay for basic necessities like food and clothing. Now think about how many hours you will have to work for the same things. You will likely spend many fewer hours. Today, people on average earn more in real terms per hour than did people of previous generations. This is true in almost all economies, but certainly in all developed economies. In almost all economies the amount of output produced per worker has risen over time. Why? Why are we able to produce more per hour than prior generations did? This is the subject matter of this chapter. We explore the long-run growth process.

We briefly introduced long-run growth in Chapter 7. We distinguished between **output growth**, which is the growth rate of output of the entire economy, and **per-capita output growth**, which is the growth rate of output per person in the economy. Another important measure is the growth rate of output per worker, called **labor productivity growth**. Output per capita is a measure of the standard of living in a country. It is not the same as output per worker because not everyone in the population works. Output per capita can fall even when output per worker is increasing if the fraction of the population that is working is falling (as it might be in a country with an increasing number of children per working-age adult). Output per capita is a useful measure because it tells us how much output each person would receive if total output were evenly divided across the entire population. Output per worker is a useful measure because it tells us how much output each worker on average is producing and how that is changing over time.

We begin this chapter with a brief history of economic growth since the Industrial Revolution. We then discuss the sources of growth—answering the question why output per worker has risen over time. We then turn to look more narrowly at the U.S. growth picture. We conclude with a discussion of growth and the environment, returning to the world perspective.

**output growth** The growth rate of the output of the entire economy.

**per-capita output growth** The growth rate of output per person in the economy.

**labor productivity growth** The growth rate of output per worker.

# The Growth Process: From Agriculture to Industry

Before the Industrial Revolution in Great Britain, every society in the world was agrarian. Towns and cities existed here and there, but almost everyone lived in rural areas. People spent most of their time producing food and other basic subsistence goods. Then beginning in England around 1750, technical change and capital accumulation increased productivity significantly in two important industries: agriculture and textiles. New and more efficient methods of farming were developed. New inventions and new machinery in spinning and weaving meant that more could be produced with fewer resources. Higher productivity made it possible to feed and clothe the population and have time left to spend working on other projects and new "products," as the British moved from being largely an agrarian society to industrial production. Peasants and workers in eighteenth-century England who in the past would have continued in subsistence farming could make a better living as urban workers. Growth brought with it new products, more output, and wider choice.

The changes described here as Britain experienced productivity growth can be represented graphically. In Chapter 2, we defined a society's *production possibility frontier (ppf)*, which shows all possible combinations of output that can be produced given present technology. Economic growth expands those limits and shifts society's production possibilities frontier out to the right, as Figure 16.1 shows.

The transition from agriculture to industry has been more recent in developing countries in Asia. One of the hallmarks of current growth in China and Vietnam, for example, has been the focus on manufacturing exports as a growth strategy. A visitor to Vietnam cannot help but be struck by the pace of industrialization.

Economic growth continues today in the developed world. Just as a shovel makes it possible to dig a bigger hole, new microwave towers bring cell phone service to places that had been out of range. Capital continues to bring productivity growth albeit in different form. Scientists work on finding a cure for Alzheimer's disease using tools they couldn't have dreamed of a decade ago. Tools available on the Web make it possible for a single law clerk in a busy law office to check hundreds of documents for the opinions of potential expert witnesses in a court case in an hour, a task that took a dozen law clerks weeks to perform just a few years ago. In each case, we have become more proficient at producing what we want and need and we have freed up resources to produce new things that we want and need.

Although the nature of economic growth has changed over time, its basic building blocks are the same. Growth comes from a bigger workforce and more productive workers. Higher productivity comes from tools (capital), a better-educated and more highly-skilled workforce (human capital), and increasingly from innovation and technical change (new techniques of production) and newly developed products and services.

▶ **FIGURE 16.1**

**Economic Growth Shifts Society's Production Possibility Frontier Up and to the Right**

The production possibility frontier shows all the combinations of output that can be produced if all society's scarce resources are fully and efficiently employed. Economic growth expands society's production possibilities, shifting the *ppf* up and to the right.

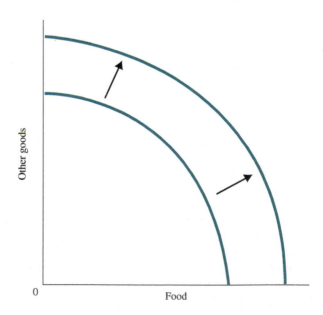

MyEconLab Real-time data

| TABLE 16.1   Growth of Real GDP: 1996–2013 | |
| --- | --- |
| Country | Average Growth Rates per Year, Percentage Points, 1996–2013 |
| United States | 2.4 |
| Japan | 0.8 |
| Germany | 1.3 |
| France | 1.6 |
| United Kingdom | 2.1 |
| China | 9.6 |
| India | 6.8 |
| Sub-Saharan Africa | 5.6 |

*Source: Economic Report of the President, 2015,* Table B-4

Table 16.1 provides estimates of the growth of gross domestic product (GDP) for a number of developed and developing countries for the 18 years 1996–2013. One fact that should strike you as you look at these numbers is the high rates of growth of China and India relative to those of the developed countries. Some economists argue that when poorer, less developed countries begin to develop, they typically have higher growth rates as they **catch-up** with the more developed countries. This idea is called *convergence theory* because it suggests that gaps in national incomes tend to close over time. Indeed, more than 50 years ago, the economic historian Alexander Gerschenkron coined the term *the advantages of backwardness* as a description of the phenomenon by which less developed countries could leap ahead by borrowing technology from more developed countries. This idea seems to fit the current experiences of China and India, as shown in the table. In the last few years, growth rates in China have slowed a bit, which some have argued reflects the progress China has already made in catching up to the technological frontier. You might also note that growth rates in sub-Saharan Africa are more modest than those in Asia, although still higher than those for the developed countries. We turn now to look at the sources of economic growth as we try to explain these patterns.

**catch-up** The theory stating that the growth rates of less developed countries will exceed the growth rates of developed countries, allowing the less developed countries to catch up.

# Sources of Economic Growth

It will be useful to begin with a simple case where the quality of labor, *L,* and the quality of capital, *K,* do not change over time. A worker is a worker is a worker, and a machine is a machine is a machine. Output, *Y,* is produced in a production process using *L* and *K.* In most situations it seems reasonable to assume that as labor and capital increase, so will output. The exact relationship between these inputs and output can be described with an **aggregate production function**, which is a mathematical relationship stating that total GDP (output) (*Y*) depends on the total amount of labor used (*L*) and the total amount of capital (*K*) used. (Land is another possible input in the production process, but we are assuming that land is fixed.) The numbers that are used in tables 16.2 and 16.4, which follow, are based on the simple hypothetical production function $Y = 3 \times K^{1/3} L^{2/3}$. This production function tells us that both capital and labor are needed for production (if either is equal to zero, so is output) and increases in either result in more output. Using this construct we can now explore exactly how an economy achieves higher output levels over time as it experiences changes in labor and capital.

**16.2 LEARNING OBJECTIVE**

Describe the sources of economic growth.

**aggregate production function** A mathematical relationship stating that total GDP (output) depends on the total amount of labor used and the total amount of capital used.

## Increase in Labor Supply

In most situations, it seems logical that if we increase the number of workers in a society, output will increase. Indeed, we see this in the production function we are working with here. A key question is how much does that added labor hour add to output? Both economic theory and practice tell us that in the absence of increases in the capital stock, as labor increases, less and less output will be added by each new worker. This effect is called *diminishing returns.* It has been discussed for well more than a hundred years, beginning with early economists like Thomas Malthus and David Ricardo who began thinking about the effects of population growth.

# ECONOMICS IN PRACTICE

## Government Strategy for Growth

Figure 16.1 shows how a country's production possibility frontier shifts out with technology. Another characteristic of a country that you might want to think about is how far an individual country is from the technological frontier of the rest of the world and how distance from that frontier might influence growth strategies pursued by a country.

One of the puzzles in the growth area has been the fact that government strategies for growth seem to succeed in one place and then fail dismally in another. Work by Acemoglu, Aghion, and Zilibotti suggests that one key to successful government policies is how far a country is from the world frontier.[1]

Suppose a country is behind relative to the world at large. A government's job here is helping its industries to catch up. What policies work for this? Acemoglu et al. suggest that industrial policy like that used by Japan and South Korea may be helpful for this case. Here the government knows what the right technology is and just has to help its firms find the world frontier. As firms develop, however, and approach the world technological frontier, things change. Now growth comes through innovation, by finding out new ways to do things that are the best in the world. How does the government help in this task? Here, markets with sharp incentives and some encouragement of risk taking likely will be more useful. For this, policies to support entrepreneurship and improve the workings of venture capital will likely work better. Acemoglu and his colleagues argue that governments often shift too late

from policies supporting adoption of other countries' ideas to support of their own innovative efforts.

### THINKING PRACTICALLY

1. In recent years China has begun to strengthen its laws on patents. How does this fit in with the research described here?

[1] Daron Acemoglu, Philippe Aghion, and Fabrizio Zilibotti, "Distance to Frontier, Selection, and Economic Growth," *Journal of the European Economic Association*, March 2006, 37–74.

Malthus and Ricardo focused on agricultural output for which the central form of capital was land. With land in limited supply, the economists reckoned that new farm laborers would be forced to work the land more intensively. As labor supply grew, output would increase, but at a declining rate. Increases in the labor supply would reduce labor productivity, or output per worker.

In developed economies, labor works not so much with land as with other forms of capital—machines, computers, and the like. But diminishing returns occur in this setting as well. Table 16.2 provides an arithmetic example of diminishing returns using the aggregate production function discussed previously. Notice in the table the relationship between the level of output and the level of labor. With capital fixed at 100, as labor increases from 100 to eventually 130, total output increases, but at a diminishing rate. In the last column, we see that labor productivity falls. Simply increasing the amount of labor with no other changes in the economy decreases labor productivity because of diminishing returns. Although we have used a hypothetical production function here, empirical work suggests this form with its diminishing returns is typical of production more generally.

| TABLE 16.2 | Economic Growth from an Increase in Labor: More Output But Diminishing Returns and Lower Labor Productivity | | | | |
|---|---|---|---|---|---|
| Period | Quantity of Labor $L$ | Quantity of Capital $K$ | Total Output $Y$ | Labor Productivity $Y/L$ | Marginal Return to Labor $\Delta Y/\Delta L$ |
| 1 | 100 | 100 | 300 | 3.0 | — |
| 2 | 110 | 100 | 320 | 2.9 | 2.0 |
| 3 | 120 | 100 | 339 | 2.8 | 1.9 |
| 4 | 130 | 100 | 357 | 2.7 | 1.8 |

**TABLE 16.3  Employment, Labor Force, and Population Growth, 1960–2014**

| | Civilian Noninstitutional Population 16 and Older (Millions) | Civilian Labor Force | | Employment (Millions) |
|---|---|---|---|---|
| | | Number (Millions) | Percentage of Population | |
| 1960 | 117.3 | 69.6 | 59.3 | 65.8 |
| 1970 | 137.1 | 82.8 | 60.4 | 78.7 |
| 1980 | 167.7 | 106.9 | 63.7 | 99.3 |
| 1990 | 189.2 | 125.8 | 66.5 | 118.8 |
| 2000 | 212.6 | 142.6 | 67.1 | 136.9 |
| 2010 | 237.8 | 153.9 | 64.7 | 139.1 |
| 2014 | 247.9 | 155.9 | 62.9 | 146.3 |
| Total percentage change, 1960–2014 | +113.4% | +124.0% | | +122.3% |
| Percentage change at an annual rate | +1.4% | +1.5% | | +1.5% |

Source: *Economic Report of the President, 2015*, Table B-11.

The U.S. population and labor force have grown over time. Table 16.3. shows the growth of the population, labor force, and employment between 1960 and 2014. In this period, the population 16 and older grew at an annual rate of 1.4 percent, the labor force grew at an annual rate of 1.5 percent, and employment grew at an annual rate of 1.5 percent. We will come back to this table later in the chapter. We would expect that this increase in labor would, by itself, end up increasing overall output levels in the United States.

## Increase in Physical Capital

It is easy to see how physical capital contributes to output. Two people digging a garden with one shovel will be able to do more if a second shovel is added. How much more? We saw that there are diminishing returns to labor as more and more labor is added to a fixed amount of capital. There are likewise diminishing returns to capital as more and more capital is added to a fixed supply of labor. The extra output from the garden that can be produced when a second shovel is added is likely to be smaller than the extra output that was produced when the first shovel was added. If a third shovel were added, even less extra output would likely be produced (if any).

Table 16.4 shows how an increase in capital without a corresponding increase in labor increases output. It uses the same aggregate production function employed in Table 16.2. Observe two things about these numbers. First, additional capital increases labor productivity—it rises from 3.0 to 3.3 as capital is added. Second, there are diminishing returns to capital. Increasing capital by 10 first increases output by 10—from 300 to 310. However, the second increase of 10 yields only an output increase of 9, and the third increase of 10 yields only an output increase of 8 or 0.8 per unit of capital. The last column in the table shows the decline in output per capital as capital is increased.

Table 16.4 shows what happens to output as capital increases with a hypothetical production function. Table 16.5 uses actual U.S. data to show the growth of capital equipment and capital structures between 1960 and 2013. (The increase in the capital stock is the difference

**TABLE 16.4  Economic Growth from an Increase in Capital: More Output, Diminishing Returns to Added Capital, Higher Labor Productivity**

| Period | Quantity of Labor $L$ | Quantity of Capital $K$ | Total Output $Y$ | Labor Productivity $Y/L$ | Output per Capital $Y/K$ | Marginal Return to Capital $\Delta Y/\Delta K$ |
|---|---|---|---|---|---|---|
| 1 | 100 | 100 | 300 | 3.0 | 3.0 | — |
| 2 | 100 | 110 | 310 | 3.1 | 2.8 | 1.0 |
| 3 | 100 | 120 | 319 | 3.2 | 2.7 | 0.9 |
| 4 | 100 | 130 | 327 | 3.3 | 2.5 | 0.8 |

| TABLE 16.5 | Fixed Private Nonresidential Net Capital Stock, 1960–2013 (Billions of 2009 Dollars) | |
| --- | --- | --- |
| | Equipment | Structures |
| 1960 | 706.1 | 3,451.3 |
| 1970 | 1,202.0 | 4,769.3 |
| 1980 | 1,994.0 | 6,294.8 |
| 1990 | 2,629.0 | 8,336.5 |
| 2000 | 4,039.4 | 9,808.9 |
| 2010 | 5,208.2 | 10,967.0 |
| 2013 | 5,605.8 | 11,151.8 |
| Total percentage change, 1960–2013 | +693.9% | +223.1% |
| Percentage change at an annual rate | +4.0% | +2.2% |

Source: U.S. Department of Commerce, Bureau of Economic Analysis., Fixed Asset Tables

between gross investment and depreciation. Remember that some capital becomes obsolete and some wears out each year.) Between 1960 and 2013 the stock of equipment grew at an annual rate of 4.0 percent and the stock of structures grew at an annual rate of 2.2 percent.

Notice the growth rates of capital in Table 16.5 (4.0 percent and 2.2 percent) are larger than the growth rate of labor in Table 16.3 (1.5 percent). Capital has grown relative to labor in the United States. As a result, each U.S. worker has more capital to work with now than he or she had a hundred years ago. We see in Table 16.4 that adding more capital relative to labor increases labor productivity. We thus have one answer so far as to why labor productivity has grown over time in the United States—the amount of capital per worker has grown. You are able to produce more output per hour than your grandparents did because you have more capital to work with. In almost all economies, capital has been growing faster than labor, which is an important source of labor productivity growth in these economies.

The importance of capital in a country's economic growth naturally leads one to ask the question of what determines a country's stock of capital. In the modern open economy, new capital can come from the saving of a country's residents or from the investments of foreigners. **Foreign direct investment** is any investment in enterprises made in a country by residents outside that country. Foreign direct investment has been quite influential in providing needed capital for growth in much of Southeast Asia. In Vietnam, for example, rapid growth has been led by foreign direct investment. More recently, we have seen signs of Chinese foreign direct investment in parts of Africa and in other parts of Asia.

**foreign direct investment (FDI)** Investment in enterprises made in a country by residents outside that country.

Recent work in economics has focused on the role that institutions play in creating a capital-friendly environment that encourages home savings and foreign investment. In a series of papers, LaPorta, Lopez de Silanes, Shleifer, and Vishny argue that countries with English common-law origins (as opposed to French) provide the strongest protection for shareholders, less corrupt governments, and better court systems. In turn, these financial and legal institutions promote growth by encouraging capital investment. Countries with poor institutions, corruption, and inadequate protection for lenders and investors struggle to attract capital. The World Bank calls countries with weak institutions *fragile countries*.

Many of the World Bank's fragile countries are in sub-Saharan Africa. Many observers believe that the relative stagnation of some of the sub-Saharan African nations comes in part from their relatively weak institutions. High costs of doing business, including corruption and investment risks associated with conflict, have made countries such as Zimbabwe less attractive to domestic and foreign capital. Ethnic and linguistic fractionalization have also played a role.

## Increase in the Quality of the Labor Supply (Human Capital)

So far we have looked at what happens when an economy gets more units of identical workers. But as we well know, in most societies, populations have grown more educated and healthier over time. The quality of labor has changed, as well as its quantity, and this too leads to long-run growth.

When the quality of labor increases, this is referred to as an increase in human capital. If a worker's human capital has increased, he or she can produce more output working with the same amount of physical capital. Labor input in efficiency terms has increased.

Human capital can be produced in many ways. Individuals can invest in themselves by going to college or by completing vocational training programs. Firms can invest in human capital through on-the-job training. The government invests in human capital with programs that improve health and that provide schooling and job training. In many developing economies, we have seen high returns from educating women who had previously been largely unschooled.

In the developing countries of sub-Saharan Africa, health is a major issue because of the high incidence of HIV and other diseases. Programs to improve the health of the population increase the quality of the labor force, which increases output.

In the United States, considerable resources have been put into education over the decades. Table 16.6 shows that the level of educational attainment in the United States has risen significantly since 1940. The percentage of the population with at least 4 years of college rose from 4.6 percent in 1940 to 32.0 percent in 2014. In 1940 less than one person in four had completed high school; in 2014, 88.1 percent had. This is a substantial increase in human capital. We thus have our second answer as to why labor productivity has increased in the United States—the quality of labor has increased through more education. Policy makers in many developed economies are concerned about their ability to continue to generate growth through human capital improvements.

## Increase in the Quality of Capital (Embodied Technical Change)

Just as workers have changed in the last one hundred years, so have machines. A present-day word processor is quite different from the manual typewriter of the mid-twentieth century. An increase in the quality of a machine will increase output in the production process for the same amount of labor used. How does an increase in the quality of capital come about? It comes about in what we will call **embodied technical change**. Some technical innovation takes place, such as a faster computer chip, which is then incorporated into machines. Usually the technical innovations are incorporated into new machines, with older machines simply discarded when they become obsolete. In this case the quality of the total capital stock increases over time as more efficient new machines replace less efficient old ones. In some cases, however, innovations are incorporated into old machines. Commercial airplanes last for many decades, and many innovations that affect airplanes are incorporated into existing ones. But in general, one thinks of embodied technical change as showing up in new machines rather than existing ones.

An increase in the quality of capital increases labor productivity (more output for the same amount of labor). We thus have our third answer as to why labor productivity has increased over time—the quality of capital has increased because of embodied technical change.

**embodied technical change** Technical change that results in an improvement in the quality of capital.

| TABLE 16.6 | Years of School Completed by People Older Than 25 Years, 1940–2014 | | |
|---|---|---|---|
| | Percentage with Less than 5 Years of School | Percentage with 4 Years of High School or More | Percentage with 4 Years of College or More |
| 1940 | 13.7 | 24.5 | 4.6 |
| 1950 | 11.1 | 34.3 | 6.2 |
| 1960 | 8.3 | 41.1 | 7.7 |
| 1970 | 5.5 | 52.3 | 10.7 |
| 1980 | 3.6 | 66.5 | 16.2 |
| 1990 | NA | 77.6 | 21.3 |
| 2000 | NA | 84.1 | 25.6 |
| 2010 | NA | 87.1 | 29.9 |
| 2014 | NA | 88.1 | 32.0 |

NA = not available

*Source: Statistical Abstract of the United States, 1990,* Table 215, and 2012, Table 229, and Bureau of the Census, 2014, Table 2, Educational Attainment.

## ECONOMICS IN PRACTICE

### German Jewish Émigrés Contribute to U.S. Growth

Sometimes terrible events in history can be used by social scientists to test theories in ways not as easily done in normal times. The emigration of Jewish scientists from Germany in the late 1930s and early 1940s is an example.

By the time World War II began, more than 133,000 Jewish émigrés found their way to the United States. Among them were several thousand academics, including many scientists. Petra Moser, Alessandra Voena, and Fabian Waldinger in a recent paper decided to see if they could find any effect of this move on the well-being of the United States.[1]

Among the émigrés were a number of chemists. Moser et al. using a series of directories, identified all of the chemists who relocated to the United States in this period along with their fields within chemistry. The chemists brought with them their considerable human capital. From the point of view of this chapter, the United States experienced an unexpected shift in the human capital of its population. Moser and her colleagues then compared the rate of patenting in the United States in the period before the emigration with the one right after, looking specifically at the fields within chemistry in which the new émigrés worked. Their results? The work indicates that these new U.S. citizens may have increased patent rates in their fields by more than 30 percent!

### THINKING PRACTICALLY

1. Show on a production possibility frontier the effects of the new German emigration.

[1] Petra Moser, Alessandra Voena, and Fabian Waldinger, "German-Jewish émigrés and U.S. Invention," *American Economic Review*, October, 2014, 3222-55.

---

We will come back to embodied technical change, but to finish the train of thought we turn next to disembodied technical change.

## Disembodied Technical Change

In some situations we can achieve higher levels of output over time even if the quantity and quality of labor and capital don't change. How might we do this? Perhaps we learn how to better organize the plant floor or manage the labor force. In recent years operational improvements like lean manufacturing and vendor inventory management systems have increased the ability of many manufacturing firms to get more output from a fixed amount and quality of labor and capital. Even improvements in information and accounting systems or incentive systems can lead to improved output levels. A type of technical change that is not specifically embedded in either labor or capital but works instead to allow us to get more out of both is called **disembodied technical change**.

**disembodied technical change** Technical change that results in a change in the production process.

Recent experiences in the Chinese economy provide an interesting example of what might be considered disembodied technical change broadly defined. Working at the IMF, Zuliu Hu and Mohsin Khan have pointed to the large role of productivity gains in the 20 years following the market reforms in China. In the period after the reforms, productivity growth rates tripled, averaging almost 4 percent a year. Hu and Khan argue that the productivity gains came principally from the unleashing of profit incentives that came with opening business to the private sector. Better incentives produced better use of labor and capital.

Positive disembodied technical changes is our fourth answer as to why labor productivity has increased. People have figured out how to run production processes and how to manage firms more efficiently.

# More on Technical Change

We have seen that both embodied and disembodied technical change increase labor productivity. It is not always easy to decide whether a particular technical innovation is embodied or disembodied, and in many discussions this distinction is not made. In the rest of this section we will talk in general about technical innovations. The main point to keep in mind is that technical change, regardless of how it is categorized, increases labor productivity.

The Industrial Revolution was in part sparked by new technological developments. New techniques of spinning and weaving—the invention of the machines known as the mule and the spinning jenny, for example—were critical. The high-tech boom that swept the United States in the early 1980s was driven by the rapid development and dissemination of semiconductor technology. The high-tech boom in the 1990s was driven by the rise of the Internet and the technology associated with it. In India in the 1960s, new high-yielding seeds helped to create a "green revolution" in agriculture.

Technical change generally takes place in two stages. First, there is an advance in knowledge, or an **invention**. However, knowledge by itself does nothing unless it is used. When new knowledge is used to produce a new product or to produce an existing product more efficiently, there is **innovation**.

Given the centrality of innovation to growth, it is interesting to look at what has been happening to research in the United States over time. A commonly used measure of inputs into research is the fraction of GDP spent. In 2011, the United States spent 2.7 percent of it GDP on research and design (R&D), down slightly from a high of 2.9 percent in the early 1960s. Over time the balance of research funding has shifted away from government toward industry. Because industry research tends to be more applied, some observers are concerned that the United States will lose some of its edge in technology unless more funding is provided. In 2007, the National Academies of Science argued as follows:

> Although many people assume that the United States will always be a world leader in science and technology, this may not continue to be the case inasmuch as great minds and ideas exist throughout the world. We fear the abruptness with which a lead in science and technology can be lost—and the difficulty of recovering a lead once lost, if indeed it can be recovered at all.[1]

**invention** An advance in knowledge.

**innovation** The use of new knowledge to produce a new product or to produce an existing product more efficiently.

As we suggested previously, the theory of convergence suggests that newly developing countries can leap forward by exploiting the technology of the developed countries. Indeed, all countries benefit when a better way of doing things is discovered. Innovation and the diffusion of that innovation push the production possibility frontier outward. But there is at least some evidence that a country that leads in a discovery retains some advantage in exploiting it, at least for some time.

What evidence do we have that the United States might be losing its edge? Looking at R&D as a share of GDP, the United States ranked seventh among Organisation for Co-operation and Development (OECD) countries in 2006. If we look at patenting data, the evidence is more encouraging: For patents simultaneously sought in the United States, Japan, and the European Union (EU), known as triadic patents, U.S. inventors are the leading source, having taken the lead from the EU in 1989. On the output side, then, the United States appears still to be quite strong in the area of research.

# U.S. Labor Productivity: 1952 I–2014 IV

Now that we have considered the various answers as to why U.S. labor productivity has increased over time, we can return to the data and see what the actual growth has been. In Figure 7.2 in Chapter 7, we presented a plot of U.S. labor productivity for the 1952 I–2014 IV period. This figure is repeated in Figure 16.2. Remember that the line segments are drawn to

---

[1] National Academies, "Rising Above the Gathering Storm: Energizing the Employing America for a Brighter Future," National Academies Press, 2007.

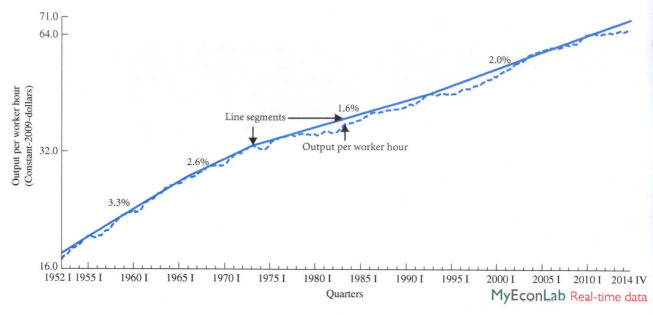

▲ **FIGURE 16.2** **Output per Worker Hour (Productivity), 1952 I–2014 IV**

smooth out the short-run fluctuations in productivity. We saw in the last chapter that given how productivity is measured, it moves with the business cycle because firms tend to hold excess labor in recessions. We are not interested in business cycles in this chapter, and the line segments are a way of ignoring business cycle effects.

There was much talk in the late 1970s and early 1980s about the U.S. "productivity problem." Some economics textbooks published in the early 1980s had entire chapters discussing the decline in productivity that seemed to be taking place during the late 1970s. In January 1981, the Congressional Budget Office published a report, *The Productivity Problem: Alternatives for Action.*

It is clear from Figure 16.2 that there was a slowdown in productivity growth in the 1970s. The growth rate went from 3.3 percent in the 1950s and first half of the 1960s to 2.6 percent in the last half of the 1960s and early 1970s and then to 1.6 percent from the early 1970s to the 1990s. Many explanations were offered at the time for the productivity slowdown of the late 1970s and early 1980s. Some economists pointed to the low rate of saving in the United States compared with other parts of the world. Others blamed increased environmental and government regulation of U.S. business. Still others argued that the country was not spending as much on R&D as it should have been. Finally, some suggested that high energy costs in the 1970s led to investment designed to save energy instead of to enhance labor productivity.

Many of these factors turned around in the 1980s and 1990s and yet, as you can see from Figure 16.2, productivity growth rose to 2.0 percent in the 1990s and through 2014. The interesting question as we move into the second decade of the twenty-first century is whether the continued growth of the Internet and wireless devices will return productivity growth to the values observed in the 1950s and 1960s or whether the period of the 1950s and 1960s was simply an unusually good period for productivity growth and the United States will continue to have productivity growth of around 2 percent. The *Economics in Practice* box on page 308 discusses this issue.

**16.3 LEARNING OBJECTIVE**

Discuss environmental issues associated with economic growth.

# Growth and the Environment and Issues of Sustainability

In 2000, the United Nations (UN) unanimously adopted the Millennium Development Goals, a set of quantifiable, time-based targets for developing countries to meet. Included in these targets, as you might expect, were measures of education, mortality, and income growth. But the UN

| TABLE 16.7 | Environmental Scores in the World Bank Country Policy and Institutional Assessment 2005 Scores (min = 1, max = 6) |
|---|---|
| Albania | 3 |
| Angola | 2.5 |
| Bhutan | 4.5 |
| Cambodia | 2.5 |
| Cameroon | 4 |
| Gambia | 3 |
| Haiti | 2.5 |
| Madagascar | 4 |
| Mozambique | 3 |
| Papua New Guinea | 1.5 |
| Sierra Leone | 2.5 |
| Sudan | 2.5 |
| Tajikistan | 2.5 |
| Uganda | 4 |
| Vietnam | 3.5 |
| Zimbabwe | 2.5 |

*Source:* International Bank for Reconstruction and Development / The World Bank: World Development Indicators Database 2005.

resolution also included a set of environmental criteria. Specific criteria have been developed around clean air, clean water, and conservation management. Table 16.7 provides the 2005 ranking of a series of developing countries on the UN index.

The inclusion of environmental considerations in the development goals speaks to the importance of environmental infrastructure in the long-run growth prospects of a country. Environmental considerations also address some concerns that in the process of growth, environmental degradation will occur. Evidence on global warming has increased some of the international concerns about growth and the environment. The connections between the environment and growth are complex and remain debated among economists.

The classic work on growth and the environment was done in the mid-1990s by Gene Grossman and Alan Krueger.[2] It is well known that as countries develop, they typically generate air and water pollutants. China's recent rapid growth provides a strong example of this fact. Grossman and Krueger found, however, that as growth progresses and countries become richer, pollution tends to fall. The relationship between growth, as measured in per-capita income, and pollution is an inverted *U*. Figure 16.3 shows Grossman and Krueger's evidence on one measure of air pollution.

How do we explain the inverted *U*? Clean water and clean air are what economists call *normal goods*. That is, as people get richer, they want to consume more of these goods. You have

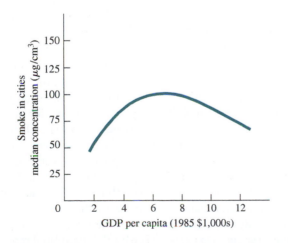

◀ **FIGURE 16.3  The Relationship Between Per-Capita GDP and Urban Air Pollution**
One measure of air pollution is smoke in cities. The relationship between smoke concentration and per-capita GDP is an inverted *U*: As countries grow wealthier, smoke increases and then declines.

*Source:* Gene Grossman and Alan Krueger, *QJE*, May 1995.

---

[2] Gene Grossman and Alan Krueger, "Economic Growth and the Environment," *Quarterly Journal of Economics*, May 1995.

already seen in the Keynesian model that aggregate consumption increases with income. As it happens, microeconomics finds that this relationship is true for most individual types of goods as well. Demand for clean water and clean air turns out to increase with income levels. As countries develop, their populace increasingly demands improvements on these fronts. We have seen an increasing number of public projects about the environment in China, for example. So although increased industrialization with growth initially degrades the environment, in the long run environmental quality typically improves.

Grossman and Krueger found this inverted U in a number of countries. Economic historians remind us that in the heyday of industrialization, northern England suffered from serious air pollution. Some of you may recall the description of air pollution in nineteenth-century English novels such as Elizabeth Gaskell's *North and South*.

If environmental pollution eventually declines as growth brings rising per-capita incomes, why should we be worried? First, as Grossman and Krueger point out, the inverted U represents historical experience, but it is not inevitable. In particular, if public opinion moves governments and the economy at large toward technologies that reduce pollution, this requires an empowered populace and a responsive government. Here too we see the importance of institutions in growth. A second issue arises in cases in which high levels of current emissions produce irreversible outcomes. Some would argue that by the time nations such as China and Vietnam develop enough to reduce their emissions, it will be too late. Many believe that global warming is such an example.

Another important problem that has made itself known recently comes from pollution sources that move across country boundaries. Carbon emissions associated with global warming are one such by-product of increased industrialization. Other air pollution problems move across national borders as well. In the heyday of industrialization by the Soviet Union, prevailing winds blew much of the Soviet-produced pollution to Finland. Choices that countries make about levels of growth and levels of environmental control affect the well-being of other countries' populations. Nor is it easy for countries at different levels of GDP per capita to agree on common standards of environmental control. As we suggested previously, demand for clean air increases with income, when needs for food and shelter are better met. It should surprise no one who has studied economics that there are debates between developing countries and developed countries about optimal levels of environmental control. These debates are further complicated when we recognize the gains that consumers in developed economies reap from economic activity in the developing world. Much of the increased carbon emitted by Chinese businesses, for example, is associated with goods that are transported and traded to Europe and the United States. These consumers thus share the benefits of this air pollution through the cheaper goods they consume.

Much of Southeast Asia has fueled its growth through export-led manufacturing. For countries that have based their growth on resource extraction, there is another set of potential sustainability issues. Many of the African nations are in this category. Nigeria relies heavily on oil; South Africa and the Congo are large producers of diamonds and other gems. Extraction methods, of course, may carry environmental problems. Many people also question whether growth based on extraction is economically sustainable: What happens when the oil or minerals run out? The answer is quite complicated and depends in some measure on how the profits from the extraction process are used. Because extraction can be accomplished without a well-educated labor force, whereas other forms of development are more dependent on a skilled-labor base, public investment in infrastructure is especially important. To the extent that countries use the revenues from extraction to invest in infrastructure such as roads and schools and to increase the education and health of their populace, the basis for growth can be shifted over time. With weak institutions, these proceeds may be expropriated by corrupt governments or invested outside the country, and long-run sustainable growth will not result.

The question of whether the natural resource base imposes strong natural limits on growth has been debated since the time of Malthus. Malthus as early as the 18th century worried that population growth in England would outstrip the ability of the land to provide. In that period, technology provided an answer, facilitating output growth.

In 1972, the Club of Rome, a group of "concerned citizens," contracted with a group at MIT to do a study titled *The Limits to Growth*.[3] The book-length final report presented the results

---

[3] Donella H. Meadows et al., *The Limits to Growth* (Washington, D.C.: Potomac Associates, 1972).

of computer simulations that assumed present growth rates of population, food, industrial output, and resource exhaustion. According to these data, sometime after the year 2000 the limits will be reached and the entire world economy will come crashing down:

> Collapse occurs because of nonrenewable resource depletion. The industrial capital stock grows to a level that requires an enormous input of resources. In the very process of that growth, it depletes a large fraction of the resource reserves available. As resource prices rise and mines are depleted, more and more capital must be used for obtaining resources, leaving less to be invested for future growth. Finally, investment cannot keep up with depreciation and the industrial base collapses, taking with it the service and agricultural systems, which have become dependent on industrial inputs (such as fertilizers, pesticides, hospital laboratories, computers, and especially energy for mechanization).... Population finally decreases when the death rate is driven upward by the lack of food and health services.[4]

This argument is similar to one offered almost 200 years ago by Thomas Malthus, mentioned previously in this chapter.

In the early 1970s, many thought that the Club of Rome's predictions had come true. It seemed the world was starting to run up against the limits of world energy supplies. In the years since, new reserves have been found and new sources of energy, including large reserves of gas and oil produced by fracking, have been discovered and developed. At present, issues of global warming and biodiversity are causing many people to question the process of growth. How should one trade off the obvious gains from growth in terms of the lives of those in the poorer nations against environmental goals? Recognizing the existence of these trade-offs and trying to design policies to deal with them is one of the key tasks of policy makers.

---

[4] Meadows et al., pp. 131–132.

---

# SUMMARY

1. In almost all countries output per worker, *labor productivity*, has been growing over time.

## 16.1 THE GROWTH PROCESS: FROM AGRICULTURE TO INDUSTRY  *p. 302*

2. All societies face limits imposed by the resources and technologies available to them. Economic growth expands these limits and shifts society's production possibilities frontier up and to the right.

3. There is considerable variation across the globe in growth rates. Some countries—particularly in Southeast Asia—appear to be catching up.

4. The process by which some less developed, poorer countries experience high growth and begin to catch up to more developed areas is known as convergence.

## 16.2 SOURCES OF ECONOMIC GROWTH  *p. 303*

5. An *aggregate production function* embodies the relationship between inputs—the labor force and the stock of capital—and total national output.

6. A number of factors contribute to economic growth: (1) an increase in the labor supply, (2) an increase in physical capital—plant and equipment, (3) an increase in the quality of the labor supply—human capital, (4) an increase in the quality of physical capital—embodied technical change, and (5) disembodied technical change—for example, an increase in managerial skills.

7. The growth rate of labor productivity in the United States has decreased from about 3.3 percent in the 1950s and 1960s to about 2.0 percent in the 1990s and 2000s. It was only about 1.6 percent in the 1970s.

## 16.3 GROWTH AND THE ENVIRONMENT AND ISSUES OF SUSTAINABILITY  *p. 310*

8. As countries begin to develop and industrialize, environmental problems are common. As development progresses further, however, most countries experience improvements in their environmental quality.

9. The limits placed on a country's growth by its natural resources have been debated for several hundred years. Growth strategies based on extraction of resources may pose special challenges to a country's growth.

**MyEconLab** Visit **www.myeconlab.com** to complete these exercises online and get instant feedback. Exercises that update with real-time data are marked with art 🔴.

## REVIEW TERMS AND CONCEPTS

aggregate production function, *p. 303*

catch-up, *p. 303*

disembodied technical change, *p. 308*

embodied technical change, *p. 307*

foreign direct investment (FDI), *p. 306*

innovation, *p. 309*

invention, *p. 309*

labor productivity growth, *p. 301*

output growth, *p. 301*

per-capita output growth, *p. 301*

## PROBLEMS

All problems are available on MyEconLab.

### 16.1 THE GROWTH PROCESS: FROM AGRICULTURE TO INDUSTRY

**LEARNING OBJECTIVE:** Summarize the history and process of economic growth.

**1.1** Go to a recent issue of *The Economist* magazine. In the back of each issue is a section called "economic indicators." That section lists the most recent growth data for a substantial number of countries. Which countries around the world are growing most rapidly according to the most recent data? Which countries around the world are growing more slowly? Flip through the stories in *The Economist* to see if there is any explanation for the pattern that you observe. Write a brief essay on current general economic conditions around the world.

**1.2** The data in the following table represents real GDP from 2011–2014 for five countries.

 **a.** Calculate the growth rate in real GDP for all five countries from 2011–2012. Which country experienced the highest rate of economic growth from 2011–2012?

 **b.** Calculate the growth rate in real GDP for all five countries from 2012–2013. Which country experienced the highest rate of economic growth from 2012–2013?

 **c.** Calculate the growth rate in real GDP for all five countries from 2013–2014. Which country experienced the highest rate of economic growth from 2013–2014?

 **d.** Calculate the average annual growth rate in real GDP for all five countries from 2011–2014. Which country experienced the highest average annual rate of economic growth from 2011–2014?

| Country | 2011 | 2012 | 2013 | 2014 |
|---|---|---|---|---|
| United States | 15,204.00 | 15,556.86 | 15,902.12 | 16,271.05 |
| El Salvador | 21.89 | 22.30 | 22.68 | 23.18 |
| Republic of South Africa | 378.11 | 387.44 | 394.76 | 408.58 |
| Cambodia | 11.98 | 12.86 | 13.82 | 14.83 |
| Russia | 1,589.91 | 1,644.53 | 1,666.22 | 1,670.38 |

All values are in billions of 2010 U.S. dollars.
*Source:* United States Department of Agriculture.

**1.3** The data in the following table represents real GDP per capita in 1974 and 2014 for five countries. Fill in the table by calculating the annual growth rate in real GDP per capita from 1974 to 2014. Is the data in the completed table consistent with convergence theory? Explain.

| Country | Real GDP per Capita in 1974 | Real GDP per Capita in 2014 | Annual Growth in Real GDP per Capita 1974–2014 |
|---|---|---|---|
| United States | 25,602 | 51,056 | |
| El Salvador | 2,884 | 3,785 | |
| Republic of South Africa | 6,214 | 8,446 | |
| Cambodia | 157 | 959 | |
| Russia | 7,192 | 11,724 | |

All values are in 2010 U.S. dollars.
*Source:* United States Department of Agriculture.

**1.4** Use the data in the following table to explain what happened with respect to economic growth and the standard of living in each of the three countries.

| Country | Real GDP 2015 | Real GDP 2014 | Population 2015 | Population 2014 |
|---|---|---|---|---|
| Astoria | 12,400 | 10,850 | 1,800 | 1,575 |
| Tiberius | 4,275 | 3,820 | 575 | 450 |
| Zorba | 60,500 | 64,100 | 13,800 | 15,250 |

### 16.2 SOURCES OF ECONOMIC GROWTH

**LEARNING OBJECTIVE:** Describe the sources of economic growth.

**2.1** One way that less developed countries catch up with the growth of the more developed countries is by adopting the technology of the developed countries. On average, however, developed countries are capital-rich and labor-short relative to the developing nations. Think of the kinds of technology that a typical developing country with a short supply of capital and a large marginally employed labor force would find when "shopping" for technology in a more developed country. As a hint, the Japanese have developed the field of robotics such as assembly line machines. Such machines are designed to replace expensive workers with capital (robots) to lower the overall cost of production. In what ways does it help a developing country to transfer and use a new technology in its country? What are the costs?

**2.2** Tables 1, 2, and 3 that follow present some data on three hypothetical economies. Complete the tables by figuring the measured productivity of labor and the rate of output growth. What do the data tell you about the causes of economic growth? (*Hint:* How fast are *L* and *K* growing?)

## TABLE 1

| PERIOD | L | K | Y | Y/L | GROWTH RATE OF OUTPUT |
|--------|------|-------|-------|-----|-----------------------|
| 1 | 1,120 | 3,205 | 4,650 | | |
| 2 | 1,135 | 3,500 | 4,795 | | |
| 3 | 1,152 | 3,798 | 4,945 | | |
| 4 | 1,170 | 4,045 | 5,100 | | |

## TABLE 2

| PERIOD | L | K | Y | Y/L | GROWTH RATE OF OUTPUT |
|--------|------|-------|-------|-----|-----------------------|
| 1 | 1,120 | 3,205 | 4,650 | | |
| 2 | 1,175 | 3,246 | 4,775 | | |
| 3 | 1,255 | 3,288 | 4,904 | | |
| 4 | 1,344 | 3,315 | 5,036 | | |

## TABLE 3

| PERIOD | L | K | Y | Y/L | GROWTH RATE OF OUTPUT |
|--------|------|-------|-------|-----|-----------------------|
| 1 | 1,120 | 3,205 | 4,650 | | |
| 2 | 1,135 | 3,246 | 4,840 | | |
| 3 | 1,152 | 3,288 | 5,038 | | |
| 4 | 1,170 | 3,315 | 5,244 | | |

2.3 In the fall of 2005, the president's tax reform commission issued a final report. The commission called for a general cut in marginal tax rates; lower tax rates on dividends, capital gains, and interest income; and, more importantly, the expensing of investment in capital equipment. These provisions were argued to be "pro-growth." In what ways would you expect each of these proposals to be favorable to economic growth?

2.4 [Related to the *Economics in Practice* on p. 304] In a March 2013 press release, the World Bank announced its support to assist Indonesia in accelerating its economic growth through the Research and Innovation in Science and Technology Project (RISET). This project is designed to boost research and innovation in Indonesia and assist the country in evolving into a knowledge-based economy. According to Stefan G. Koeberle, World Bank Country Director for Indonesia, "Improving human resources and national capabilities in science and technology is a key pillar in Indonesia's masterplan to accelerate and expand its economy. Shifting from a resource-based economy to a knowledge-based economy will bring Indonesia up the value chain in a wide range of sectors, with the help of homegrown innovation and a vast pool of human resources." The press release states that a large part of the RISET program will involve assistance in raising the academic credentials of Indonesian researchers involved with science and engineering, and it is hoped that the program will eventually lead to increased investment in R&D, where as a percentage of GDP, Indonesia's R&D investment falls significantly below many of its Asian neighbors. Using the information presented in this chapter, explain how increasing research and innovation and raising the academic credentials of researchers can assist in increasing long-run economic growth in Indonesia.

*Source:* "World Bank Supports Move to Accelerate Indonesia's Economic Growth through Science, Technology, and Innovation," www.worldbank.org, March 29, 2013. Used by permission.

2.5 Education is an area in which it has been hard to create productivity gains that reduce costs. Collect data on the tuition rates of your own college in the last 20 years and compare that increase to the overall rate of inflation using the consumer price index. What do you observe? Can you suggest some productivity-enhancing measures?

2.6 Economists generally agree that high budget deficits today will reduce the growth rate of the economy in the future. Why? Do the reasons for the high budget deficit matter? In other words, does it matter whether the deficit is caused by lower taxes, increased defense spending, more job-training programs, and so on?

2.7 Why can growth lead to a more unequal distribution of income? By assuming this is true, how is it possible for the poor to benefit from economic growth?

2.8 According to the Bureau of Labor Statistics, during the first quarter of 2015 nonfarm business productivity in the United States fell 3.1 percent and manufacturing productivity fell 1.0 percent compared to the first quarter of 2014. During this same time, real GDP in the United States increased by 2.9 percent. Explain how productivity can decrease when real GDP is increasing.

2.9 How do each of the following relate to the rates of productivity and growth in an economy?
   a. Spending on research and development
   b. Government regulation
   c. Changes in human capital
   d. Output per worker hour
   e. Embodied technical change
   f. Disembodied technical change

2.10 [Related to the *Economics in Practice* on p. 308] One source of long-run economic growth is an increase in the quality of labor, or human capital, of which education plays a major role. Go to www.bls.gov and look up the current unemployment rate. Compare this to the current unemployment rates for those without a high school diploma, those with only a high school diploma, and those with a bachelor's degree or higher. What does this data suggest about education requirements for jobs in the United States? Then go to www.census.gov and look at the current population survey historical table A-2. Find the percentage of the total population 25 years and older who have completed four years of high school or more and the percentage who have completed four years of college or more. Compare this data with the unemployment data. What does this information suggest about future productivity and growth for the U.S. economy?

## 16.3 GROWTH AND THE ENVIRONMENT AND ISSUES OF SUSTAINABILITY

**LEARNING OBJECTIVE:** Discuss environmental issues associated with economic growth.

3.1 From 2005 through 2014, Mexico's per-capita real GDP increased from $8,966 to $9,938 as measured in 2010 U.S. dollars, yet despite this increase in the standard of living, environmental issues such as air and water pollution continue to be major concerns for the country. In 2012, the U.S. Environmental Protection Agency, with support from the Mexican government, implemented its Border 2020 program in a continued effort to address environmental and public health issues in the U.S.-Mexico border region. You can find information about this program at: http://www2.epa.gov/border2020. Among the goals of the program are to reduce air pollution and improve access to clean and safe water on both sides of the U.S.-Mexico border. Explain how the attainment of the goals of the Border 2020 program could align with the inverted-*U* relationship described by Gene Grossman and Alan Krueger.

# Alternative Views in Macroeconomics

# 17

Throughout this book, we have noted that there are many disagreements and questions in macroeconomics. For example, economists disagree on whether the aggregate supply curve is vertical, either in the short run or in the long run. Some economists even doubt that the aggregate supply curve is a useful macroeconomic concept. There are different views on whether cyclical employment exists and, if it does, what causes it. Economists disagree about whether monetary and fiscal policies are effective at stabilizing the economy, and they support different views on the primary determinants of consumption and investment spending.

We discussed some of these disagreements in previous chapters, but only briefly. In this chapter, we discuss in more detail a number of alternative views of how the macroeconomy works.

**17.1 LEARNING** OBJECTIVE

Summarize Keynesian economics.

# Keynesian Economics

John Maynard Keynes's *General Theory of Employment, Interest, and Money*, published in 1936, remains one of the most important works in economics. Although a great deal of the material in the previous 9 chapters is drawn from modern research that postdates Keynes, much of the material is built around a framework constructed by Keynes.

What exactly is *Keynesian economics*? In one sense, it is the foundation of all of macroeconomics. Keynes was the first to emphasize aggregate demand and links between the money market and the goods market. Keynes also emphasized the possible problem of sticky wages. In recent years, the term *Keynesian* has been used more narrowly. Keynes believed in an activist federal government. He believed that the government had a role to play in fighting inflation and unemployment, and he believed that monetary and fiscal policies should be used to manage the macroeconomy. This is why *Keynesian* is sometimes used to refer to economists who advocate active government intervention in the macroeconomy.

During the 1970s and 1980s, it became clear that managing the macroeconomy was more easily accomplished on paper than in practice. The inflation problems of the 1970s and early 1980s and the seriousness of the recessions of 1974–1975 and 1980–1982 led many economists to challenge the idea of active government intervention in the economy. Some of the challenges were simple attacks on the bureaucracy's ability to act in a timely manner. Others were theoretical assaults that claimed to show that monetary and fiscal policies had no or little effect on the economy.

We begin with an old debate—that between Keynesians and monetarists.

**17.2 LEARNING** OBJECTIVE

Explain the quantity theory of money.

**velocity of money**   The number of times a dollar bill changes hands, on average, during a year; the ratio of nominal *GDP* to the stock of money.

# Monetarism

## The Velocity of Money

A key variable in monetarism is the **velocity of money**. Think of velocity as the number of times a dollar bill changes hands, on average, during a year. Suppose on January 1 you buy a new ballpoint pen with a $5 bill. The owner of the stationery store does not spend your $5 right away. She may hold it until, say, May 1, when she uses it to buy a dozen doughnuts. The doughnut store owner does not spend the $5 he receives until July 1, when he uses it (along with other cash) to buy 100 gallons of oil. The oil distributor uses the bill to buy an engagement ring for his fiancée on September 1, but the $5 bill is not used again in the remaining 3 months of the year. Because this $5 bill has changed hands four times during the year, its velocity of circulation is 4. A velocity of 4 means that the $5 bill stays with each owner for an average of 3 months, or one quarter of a year.

In practice, we use gross domestic product (GDP), instead of the total value of all transactions in the economy, to measure velocity[1] because GDP data are more readily available. The income velocity of money (V) is the ratio of nominal GDP to the stock of money (M):

$$V \equiv \frac{GDP}{M}$$

If $12 trillion worth of final goods and services is produced in a year and if the money stock is $1 trillion, then the velocity of money is $12 trillion ÷ $1 trillion, or 12.0.

We can expand this definition slightly by noting that nominal income (GDP) is equal to real output (income) (Y) times the overall price level (P):

$$GDP \equiv P \times Y$$

---

[1] Recall that GDP does not include transactions in intermediate goods (for example, flour sold to a baker to be made into bread) or in existing assets (for example, the sale of a used car). If these transactions are made using money, however, they do influence the number of times money changes hands during the course of a year. GDP is an imperfect measure of transactions to use in calculating the velocity of money.

Through substitution:

$$V \equiv \frac{P \times Y}{M}$$

or

$$M \times V \equiv P \times Y$$

At this point, it is worth pausing to ask whether our definition has provided us with any insights into the workings of the economy. The answer is no. Because we defined V as the ratio of GDP to the money supply, the statement $M \times V \equiv P \times Y$ is an identity—it is true by definition. It contains no more useful information than the statement "A bachelor is an unmarried man." The definition does not, for example, say anything about what will happen to $P \times Y$ when M changes. The final value of $P \times Y$ depends on what happens to V. If V falls when M increases, the product $M \times V$ could stay the same, in which case the change in M would have had no effect on nominal income. To give monetarism some economic content, a simple version of monetarism known as the **quantity theory of money** is used.

## The Quantity Theory of Money

The key assumption of the quantity theory of money is that the velocity of money is constant (or virtually constant) over time. If we let V denote the constant value of V, the equation for the quantity theory can be written as follows:

$$M \times \overline{V} = P \times Y$$

Note that the double equal sign has replaced the triple equal sign because the equation is no longer an identity. The equation is true if velocity is constant (and equal to V) but not otherwise. If the equation is true, it provides an easy way to explain nominal GDP. Given M, which can be considered a policy variable set by the Federal Reserve (Fed), nominal GDP is just $M \times \overline{V}$. In this case, the effects of monetary policy are clear. Changes in M cause equal percentage changes in nominal GDP. For example, if the money supply doubles, nominal GDP also doubles. If the money supply remains unchanged, nominal GDP remains unchanged.

The key is whether the velocity of money is really constant. Early economists believed that the velocity of money was determined largely by institutional considerations, such as how often people are paid and how the banking system clears transactions between banks. Because these factors change gradually, early economists believed velocity was essentially constant.

When there is equilibrium in the money market, then the quantity of money supplied is equal to the quantity of money demanded. That could mean that M in the quantity-theory equation equals both the quantity of money supplied and the quantity of money demanded. If the quantity-theory equation is looked on as a demand-for-money equation, it says that the demand for money depends on nominal income (GDP, or $P \times Y$), but *not* on the interest rate. If the interest rate changes and nominal income does not, the equation says that the quantity of money demanded will not change. This is contrary to the theory of the demand for money in Chapter 10, which had the demand for money depending on both income and the interest rate.

**Testing the Quantity Theory of Money**   One way to test the validity of the quantity theory of money is to look at the demand for money using recent data on the U.S. economy. The key is this: Does money demand depend on the interest rate? Most empirical work says yes. When demand-for-money equations are estimated (or "fit to the data"), the interest rate usually turns out to be a significant factor. The demand for money does not appear to depend only on nominal income.

Another way of testing the quantity theory is to plot velocity over time and see how it behaves. Figure 17.1 plots the velocity of money for the 1960 I–2014 IV period. The data

**quantity theory of money**
The theory based on the identity $M \times V \equiv P \times Y$ and the assumption that the velocity of money (V) is constant (or virtually constant).

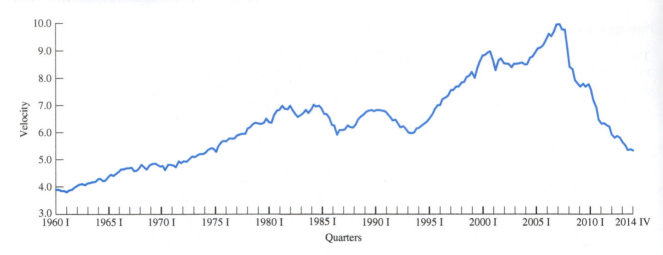

▲ **FIGURE 17.1** **The Velocity of Money, 1960 I–2014 IV** MyEconLab Real-time data

Velocity has not been constant over the period from 1960 to 2014. This was a long-term positive trend, which has now reversed.

show that velocity is far from constant. There was a positive trend until 2007, but also large fluctuations around this trend. For example, velocity rose from 6.4 in 1980 III to 7.0 in 1981 III, fell to 6.6 in 1983 I, rose to 7.0 in 1984 III, and fell to 5.9 in 1986 IV. Changes of a few tenths of a point may seem small, but they are actually large. For example, the money supply in 1986 IV was about $800 billion. If velocity changes by 0.3 with a money supply of this amount and if the money supply is unchanged, we have a change in nominal GDP ($P \times Y$) of $240 billion ($0.3 \times $800$ billion), which is about 5 percent of the level of GDP in 1986. The change in velocity in since 2008 has been remarkable. Velocity fell from 9.8 in 2008 I to 5.3 in 2014 IV!

The debate over monetarist theories is more subtle than our discussion so far indicates. First, there are many definitions of the money supply. M1 is the money supply variable used for the graph in Figure 17.1, but there may be some other measure of the money supply that would lead to a smoother plot. For example, many people shifted their funds from checking account deposits to money market accounts when the latter became available in the late 1970s. Because GDP did not change as a result of this shift while M1 decreased, velocity—the ratio of GDP to M1—must have gone up. Suppose instead we measured the supply of money by M2 (which includes both checking accounts and money market accounts). In this case, the decrease in checking deposits would be exactly offset by the rise in money market account deposits and M2 would not change. With no change in GDP and no change in M2, the velocity of money would not change. Whether or not velocity is constant may depend partly on how we measure the money supply.

Second, there may be a time lag between a change in the money supply and its effects on nominal GDP. Suppose we experience a 10 percent increase in the money supply today, but it takes 1 year for nominal GDP to increase by 10 percent. If we measured the ratio of today's money supply to today's GDP, it would seem that velocity had fallen by 10 percent. However, if we measured today's money supply against GDP 1 year from now, when the increase in the supply of money had its full effect on income, velocity would have been constant.

The debate over the quantity theory of money is primarily empirical. It is a debate that can be resolved by looking at facts about the real world and seeing whether they are in accord with the predictions of theory. Is there a measure of the money supply and a choice of the time lag between a change in the money supply and its effects on nominal GDP such that $V$ is in effect constant? If so, the monetarist theory is a useful approach to understanding how the macroeconomy works and how changes in the money supply will cause a proportionate increase in nominal GDP. If not, some other theory is likely to be more appropriate. (We discuss the testing of alternative theories at the end of this chapter.)

# The Keynesian/Monetarist Debate

The debate between Keynesians and monetarists was perhaps the central controversy in macroeconomics in the 1960s. The leading spokesman for monetarism was Milton Friedman from the University of Chicago. Most monetarists, including Friedman, blamed much of the instability in the economy on the Federal Reserve, arguing that the high inflation that the United States encountered from time to time could have been avoided if only the Fed had not expanded the money supply so rapidly. Monetarists were skeptical of the Fed's ability to "manage" the economy—to expand the money supply during bad times and contract it during good times. A common argument against such management is the one discussed in Chapter 14: Time lags may make attempts to stimulate and contract the economy counterproductive.

Friedman advocated instead a policy of steady and slow money growth—specifically, that the money supply should grow at a rate equal to the average growth of real output (income) ($Y$). That is, the Fed should pursue a constant policy that accommodates real growth but not inflation.

Many Keynesians, on the other hand, advocated the application of coordinated monetary and fiscal policy tools to reduce instability in the economy—to fight inflation and unemployment. However, not all Keynesians advocated an activist federal government. Some rejected the strict monetarist position that changes in money affect only the price level in favor of the view that both monetary and fiscal policies make a difference. *At the same time,* though, they believed that the best possible policy for the government to pursue was basically noninterventionist.

Most economists now agree, after the experience of the 1970s, that neither monetary nor a fiscal tools are finely calibrated. The notion that monetary and fiscal expansions and contractions can "fine-tune" the economy is gone forever. Still, many believe that the experiences of the 1970s also show that stabilization policies can help prevent even bigger economic disasters. Had the government not cut taxes and expanded the money supply in 1975 and in 1982, they argue, the recessions of those years might have been significantly worse. The same people would also argue that had the government not resisted the inflations of 1974–1975 and 1979–1981 with tight monetary policies, the inflations probably would have become much worse.

The debate between Keynesians and monetarists subsided with the advent of what we will call "new classical macroeconomics." Before turning to this, however, it will be useful to consider a minor but interesting footnote in macroeconomic history: supply-side economics.

# Supply-Side Economics

**17.3 LEARNING OBJECTIVE**

Explain the fundamentals of supply-side economics.

From our discussion of equilibrium in the goods market, beginning with the simple multiplier in Chapter 8 and continuing through Chapter 12, we have focused primarily on *demand*. Supply increases and decreases in response to changes in aggregate expenditure (which is closely linked to aggregate demand). Fiscal policy works by influencing aggregate expenditure through tax policy and government spending. Monetary policy works by influencing investment and consumption spending through increases and decreases in the interest rate. The theories we have been discussing are "demand-oriented." *Supply-side economics,* as the name suggests, focuses on the supply side.

The argument of the supply-siders about the economy in the late 1970s and early 1980s was simple. The real problem, they said, was not demand, but high rates of taxation and heavy regulation that reduced the incentive to work, to save, and to invest. What was needed was not a demand stimulus, but better incentives to stimulate *supply*.

If we cut taxes so people take home more of their paychecks, the argument continued, they will work harder and save more. If businesses get to keep more of their profits and can get away from government regulations, they will invest more. This added labor supply and investment, or capital supply, will lead to an expansion of the supply of goods and services, which will reduce inflation and unemployment at the same time.

At their most extreme, supply-siders argued that the incentive effects of supply-side policies were likely to be so great that a major cut in tax rates would actually *increase* tax revenues.

Even though *tax rates* would be lower, more people would be working and earning income and firms would earn more profits, so that the increases in the *tax bases* (profits, sales, and income) would then outweigh the decreases in rates, resulting in increased government revenues.

## The Laffer Curve

Figure 17.2 presents a key diagram of supply-side economics. The tax rate is measured on the vertical axis, and tax revenue is measured on the horizontal axis. The assumption behind this curve is that there is some tax rate beyond which the supply response is large enough to lead to a decrease in tax revenue for further increases in the tax rate. There is obviously some tax rate between zero and 100 percent at which tax revenue is at a maximum. At a tax rate of zero, work effort is high but there is no tax revenue. At a tax rate of 100, the labor supply is presumably zero because people are not allowed to keep any of their income. Somewhere between zero and 100 is the maximum-revenue rate.

The big debate in the 1980s was whether tax rates in the United States put the country on the upper or lower part of the curve in Figure 17.2. The supply-side school claimed that the United States was around *A* and that taxes should be cut. Others argued that the United States was nearer *B* and that tax cuts would lead to lower tax revenue.

**Laffer curve** With the tax rate measured on the vertical axis and tax revenue measured on the horizontal axis, the Laffer curve shows that there is some tax rate beyond which the supply response is large enough to lead to a decrease in tax revenue for further increases in the tax rate.

The diagram in Figure 17.2 is the **Laffer curve**, named after economist Arthur Laffer, who, legend has it, first drew it on the back of a napkin at a cocktail party. The Laffer curve had some influence on the passage of the Economic Recovery Tax Act of 1981, the tax package put forward by the Reagan administration that brought with it substantial cuts in both personal and business taxes. Individual income tax rates were cut by as much as 25 percent over 3 years. Corporate taxes were cut sharply in a way designed to stimulate capital investment. The new law allowed firms to depreciate their capital at a rapid rate for tax purposes, and the bigger deductions led to taxes that were significantly lower than before.

## Evaluating Supply-Side Economics

Supporters of supply-side economics claim that Reagan's tax policies were successful in stimulating the economy. They point to the fact that almost immediately after the tax cuts of 1981 were put into place, the economy expanded and the recession of 1980–1982 came to an end. In addition, inflation rates fell sharply from the high rates of 1980 and 1981. Except for 1 year, federal receipts continued to rise throughout the 1980s despite the cut in tax rates.

Critics of supply-side policies do not dispute these facts, but offer an alternative explanation of how the economy recovered. The Reagan tax cuts were enacted just as the U.S. economy was in the middle of its deepest recession since the Great Depression. The unemployment rate stood at 10.7 percent in the fourth quarter of 1982. It was the recession, critics argue, that was responsible for the reduction in inflation—not the supply-side policies. Also among the criticisms of supply-side economics is that it is unlikely a tax cut would substantially increase the supply of labor. In addition, in theory, a tax cut could even lead to a *reduction* in labor supply. Recall our

▶ **FIGURE 17.2** **The Laffer Curve**
The Laffer curve shows that the amount of revenue the government collects is a function of the tax rate. It shows that when tax rates are high, an increase in the tax rate could cause tax revenues to fall. Similarly, under the same circumstances, a cut in the tax rate could generate enough additional economic activity to cause revenues to rise.

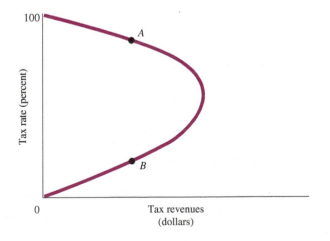

discussion of income and substitution effects in Chapter 15. Although it is true that a higher after-tax wage rate provides a higher reward for each hour of work and thus more incentive to work, a tax cut also means that households receive a higher income for a given number of hours of work. Because they can earn the same amount of money working fewer hours, households might choose to work *less*. They might spend some of their added income on leisure. Research done during the 1980s suggests that tax cuts seem to increase the supply of labor somewhat but that the increases are very modest.

What about the recovery from the recession? Why did real output begin to grow rapidly in late 1982, precisely when the supply-side tax cuts were taking effect? Two reasons have been suggested. First, the supply-side tax cuts had large *demand*-side effects that stimulated the economy. Second, the Fed pumped up the money supply and drove interest rates down at the same time the tax cuts were being put into effect. The money supply expanded about 20 percent between 1981 and 1983, and interest rates fell. In the third quarter of 1981, the average 3-month U.S. Treasury bill paid 15 percent interest. By the first quarter of 1983, the rate had dropped to 8.1 percent.

Certainly, traditional theory suggests that a huge tax cut will lead to an increase in disposable income and, in turn, an increase in consumption spending (a component of aggregate expenditure). In addition, although an increase in planned investment (brought about by a lower interest rate) leads to added productive capacity and added supply in the long run, it also increases expenditures on capital goods (new plant and equipment investment) in the short run.

Whether the recovery from the 1981–1982 recession was the result of supply-side expansion or supply-side policies that had demand-side effects, one thing is clear: The extreme promises of the supply-siders did not materialize. President Reagan argued that because of the effect depicted in the Laffer curve, the government could maintain expenditures (and even increase defense expenditures sharply), cut tax rates, *and* balance the budget. This was not the case. Government revenues fell sharply from levels that would have been realized without the tax cuts. After 1982, the federal government ran huge deficits, with about $2 trillion added to the national debt between 1983 and 1992.

# New Classical Macroeconomics

**17.4 LEARNING** OBJECTIVE

Discuss the real business cycle theory and new Keynesian economics.

The challenge to Keynesian and related theories has come from a school sometimes referred to as the new classical macroeconomics.[2] Like monetarism and Keynesianism, this term is vague. No two new classical macroeconomists think exactly alike, and no single model completely represents this school. The following discussion, however, conveys the flavor of the new classical views.

## The Development of New Classical Macroeconomics

In previous chapters we emphasized the importance of households' and firms' expectations about the future. A firm's decision to build a new plant depends on its expectations of future sales. The amount of saving a household undertakes today depends on its expectations about future interest rates, wages, and prices.

Keynes himself recognized that expectations (in the form of "animal spirits") play a big part in economic behavior. But how are these expectations formed? Many of the current debates in macroeconomics turn on this question.

Traditional models assume that expectations are formed in naive ways. A common assumption, for example, is that people form their expectations of future inflation by assuming present inflation will continue. If they turn out to be wrong, they adjust their expectations by some fraction of the difference between their original forecast and the actual inflation rate. Suppose you expect 4 percent inflation next year. When next year comes, the inflation rate turns out to

---

[2] The term *new classical* is used because many of the assumptions and conclusions of this group of economists resemble those of the classical economists—that is, those who wrote before Keynes.

be only 2 percent, so you have made an error of 2 percentage points. You might then predict an inflation rate for the following year of 3 percent, halfway between your earlier expectation (4 percent) and actual inflation last year (2 percent).

The problem with this somewhat mechanical treatment of expectations is that it is not consistent with the assumptions that we make in microeconomics of individual maximizing behavior. This "naïve" characterization of expectations implies that people systematically overlook information that would allow them to make better forecasts, even though there are costs to being wrong. Consumers and firms who maximize should form their expectations in a smarter way, or so the argument goes. Instead of naively assuming the future will be like the past or the present, they should actively seek to forecast the future. Operationalizing this idea of more informed expectations is at the heart of new macroeconomics.

## Rational Expectations

**rational-expectations hypothesis** The hypothesis that people know the "true model" of the economy and that they use this model to form their expectations of the future.

One of the earliest theories which assumes a more sophisticated model of expectations formation is the **rational-expectations hypothesis**.

The debate among macroeconomists about expectations is made well if we think about inflation. In many contexts, as in setting up a loan contract, decision makers need to forecast inflation. What do we assume when we say decision makers form those forecasts using rational expectations? Rational-expectations theorists assume that people know the "true model" that generates inflation—they know how inflation is determined in the economy—and they use this model to forecast future inflation rates. What do we do about the fact that many events that affect the inflation rate are not predictable—they are random? Even if decision makers did know the model of the full economy, they would sometimes make mistakes, mistakes generated by these random shocks. The best one can achieve is that on average the model is correct, equally underestimating and overestimating inflation as random events occur. This is the working model used in rational expectations theory.

Assuming that decision makers know the full model of the economy before they make their forecasts is thought by many other macroeconomists to be unrealistic. A slightly less ambitious definition of rational expectations is to assume decision makers use "all available information" in forming their expectations. This definition is satisfied when decision makers have the true full model, but is less clear on what "all available information" means short of having the full model.

A key debate among macroeconomists around the issue of expectations is the cost of decision making. If forming the correct expectations, gathering relevant data, is costly, then assuming people use a rule of thumb to project future inflation or economic growth is more reasonable. If relevant information can be obtained at no cost, people are not behaving rationally when they fail to use all available information given that there are usually costs to making a wrong forecast. The *Economics in Practice* box on page 325 provides some survey data relevant to this issue.

**Rational Expectations and Market Clearing** The assumption of rational expectations has important implications for what we think should be the role of the government in the macroeconomy. If firms have rational expectations and if they set prices and wages on this basis, on average, prices and wages will be set at levels that ensure equilibrium in the goods and labor markets. When a firm has rational expectations, it knows the demand curve for its output and the supply curve of labor that it faces, except when random shocks disrupt those curves. Therefore, on average, the firm will set the market-clearing prices and wages. The firm knows the true model, and it will not set wages different from those it expects will attract the number of workers it wants. If all firms behave this way, wages will be set in such a way that the total amount of labor supplied will, on average, be equal to the total amount of labor that firms demand. In other words, on average, there will be full employment.

In Chapter 13, we argued that there might be disequilibrium in the labor market (in the form of either unemployment or excess demand for workers) because firms may make mistakes in their wage-setting behavior as a result of expectation errors. If, on average, firms do not make errors, on average, there will be equilibrium. When expectations are rational, disequilibrium

## ECONOMICS IN PRACTICE

### How Are Expectations Formed?

A current debate among macroeconomists and policy makers is how people form expectations about the future state of the economy. Of particular interest is the formation of inflationary expectations. One possible way that inflation can be transmitted in an economy is if individuals expect there to be inflation and then, because of these expectations, demand higher wages, leading in turn to increases in inflation. In 2010, a number of economists began to worry about the possibility of inflationary expectations heating up in the United States in the next few years because of the large federal government deficit.

How, in fact, are expectations formed? Are expectations rational, as some macroeconomists believe, reflecting an accurate understanding of how the economy works? Or are they formed in simpler, more mechanical ways?[1] A research paper by Ronnie Driver and Richard Windram from the Bank of England sheds some light on this issue. Since 1999, the Bank of England has done a survey four times a year of 2,000 British consumers about their views of future inflation and future interest rates. The surveys suggest that consumers tend to expect future inflation to be what they perceive past inflation to have been. Also, there are some differences between what consumers perceive past inflation to have been and the actual estimates of past inflation made by the government. In other words, consumers are more influenced by their own experiences than by actual government numbers and their expectations of the future are based on their past experiences. Consumers mostly expect the future to look the way they perceive the past to have looked. Two factors that appear to be important in influencing consumer perceptions of inflation are gas prices and the attention

the media pays to price increases. All this suggests that, at least for the British consumers surveyed, the formation of inflationary expectations is a less sophisticated process than some economic theorists suggest. This research also suggests that to the extent that gas prices increase and media attention to inflation increases, inflationary expectations will increase.

#### THINKING PRACTICALLY

1. Why do you think that consumers are so sensitive to gas prices in forming their expectations?

[1] "Public Attitude Towards Inflation and Interest Rates," Quarterly Bulletin, Bank of England, Q2, 2007.

exists only temporarily as a result of random, unpredictable shocks—obviously an important conclusion. If true, it means that disequilibrium in any market is only temporary because firms, on average, set market-clearing wages and prices.

The assumption that expectations are rational radically changes the way we view the economy. We go from a world in which unemployment can exist for substantial periods and the multiplier can operate to a world in which (on average) all markets clear and there is full employment. In this world, there is no need for government stabilization policies. Unemployment is not a problem that governments need to worry about; if it exists at all, it is because of unpredictable shocks that, on average, amount to zero. There is no more reason for the government to try to change the outcome in the labor market than there is for it to change the outcome in the banana market. On average, prices and wages are set at market-clearing levels.

**The Lucas Supply Function**    One critique of the rational expectations model is that it seems to demand a good deal of household and firm decision makers. Another new classical approach to expectation setting that starts by recognizing difficulties in information gathering is from Robert E. Lucas of the University of Chicago.

Lucas begins by assuming that people and firms are specialists in production but generalists in consumption. If someone you know is a manual laborer, the chances are that she sells only one thing—labor. If she is a lawyer, she sells only legal services. In contrast, people buy a large bundle of goods—ranging from gasoline to ice cream and pretzels—on a regular basis.

The same is true for firms. Most companies tend to concentrate on producing a small range of products, but they typically buy a larger range of inputs—raw materials, labor, energy, and capital. According to Lucas, this divergence between buying and selling creates an asymmetry. People know more about the prices of the things they sell than they do about the prices of the things they buy.

As firms make decisions, they care about both their own output prices and the general price level. With respect to their own output, firms quickly learn when their prices increase. But firms are slower to learn about the general price level in the economy. At the beginning of each period, a firm has some expectation of the average price level of goods in general for that period. If the actual price level turns out to be different, there is a price surprise. Suppose the average price level is higher than expected. Because the firm learns about the actual price level slowly, some time goes by before it realizes that all prices have gone up. The firm perceives—incorrectly, it turns out—that its own price has risen relative to other prices, and this perception leads it to produce more output.

A similar argument holds for workers. When there is a positive price surprise, workers at first believe that their "price"—their wage rate—has increased relative to other prices. Workers believe that their real wage rate has risen. We know from theory that an increase in the real wage is likely to encourage workers to work more hours.[3] The real wage has not actually risen, but it takes workers a while to figure this out. In the meantime, they supply more hours of work than they would have. This increase means that the economy produces more output when prices are unexpectedly higher than when prices are at their expected level.

This simple model of expectation formation leads to what has been called the **Lucas supply function**, which yields, as we shall see, a surprising policy conclusion. The function is deceptively simple. It says that real output ($Y$) depends on (is a function of) the difference between the actual price level ($P$) and the expected price level ($P^e$):

$$Y = f(P - P^e)$$

The actual price level minus the expected price level ($P - P^e$) is the **price surprise**.

In short, the Lucas supply function tells us that unexpected increases in the price level can fool workers and firms into thinking that relative prices have changed, causing them to alter the amount of labor or goods they choose to supply.

### Policy Implications of the Lucas Supply Function

The Lucas supply function in combination with the assumption that expectations are rational implies that *anticipated* policy changes have no effect on real output. It is only policy surprises that have an effect, and that effect is temporary.

Consider a change in monetary policy. In general, the change will have some effect on the average price level. If the policy change is announced to the public, people will know the effect on the price level because they have rational expectations (and know the way changes in monetary policy affect the price level). This means that the change in monetary policy affects the actual price level and the expected price level in the same way. The new price level minus the new expected price level is zero—no price surprise. In such a case, there will be no change in real output because the Lucas supply function states that real output can change from its fixed level only if there is a price surprise.

The general conclusion is that *any* announced policy change—in fiscal policy or any other policy—has no effect on real output because the policy change affects both actual and expected price levels in the same way. If people have rational expectations, known policy changes can produce no price surprises—and no increases in real output. The only way any change in government policy can affect real output is if it is kept in the dark so it is not generally known. Government policy can affect real output only if it surprises people; otherwise, it cannot. Rational-expectations theory combined with the Lucas supply function proposes a very small role for government policy in the economy.

**Lucas supply function** The supply function embodies the idea that output ($Y$) depends on the difference between the actual price level and the expected price level.

**price surprise** Actual price level minus expected price level.

---

[3] This is true if we assume that the substitution effect dominates the income effect (see Chapter 15).

# Real Business Cycle Theory and New Keynesian Economics

Research that followed Lucas's work was concerned with whether the existence of business cycles can be explained under the assumptions of complete price and wage flexibility (market clearing) and rational expectations. This work is called **real business cycle theory**. As we discussed in Chapter 11, if prices and wages are completely flexible, then the AS curve is vertical, even in the short run. If the AS curve is vertical, then events or phenomena that shift the AD curve (such as changes in government spending, and taxes) have no effect on real output. Real output does fluctuate over time, so the puzzle is how the fluctuations can be explained if they are not the result of policy changes or other shocks that shift the AD curve. Solving this puzzle is one of the main missions of real business cycle theory.

It is clear that if shifts of the AD curve cannot account for real output fluctuations (because the AS curve is vertical), then shifts of the AS curve must be responsible. However, the task is to come up with convincing explanations as to what causes these shifts and why they persist over a number of periods. The problem is particularly difficult when it comes to the labor market. If prices and wages are completely flexible, then there is never any unemployment aside from frictional unemployment. For example, because the measured U.S. unemployment rate was 4.0 percent in 2000 and 9.3 percent in 2009, the puzzle is to explain why so many more people chose not to work in 2009 than in 2000.

Early real business cycle theorists emphasized shocks to the production technology. Suppose there is a negative shock in a given year that causes the marginal product of labor to decline. This leads to a fall in the real wage, which leads to a decrease in the quantity of labor supplied. People work less because the negative technology shock has led to a lower return from working. The opposite happens when there is a positive shock: The marginal product of labor rises, the real wage rises, and people choose to work more. This research was not as successful as some had hoped because it required what seemed to be unrealistically large shocks to explain the observed movements in labor supply over time.

What has come to be called **new Keynesian economics** retains the assumption of rational expectations, but drops the assumption of completely flexible prices and wages. Prices and wages are assumed to be sticky. The existence of menu costs is often cited as a justification of the assumption of sticky prices. It may be costly for firms to change prices, which prevents firms from having completely flexible prices. Sticky wages are discussed in Chapter 13, and some of the arguments given there as to why wages might be sticky may be relevant to new Keynesian models. A main issue regarding these models is that any justification has to be consistent with all agents in the model having rational expectations.

Current research in new Keynesian economics broadly defined is vast. There are many models, often called dynamic stochastic general equilibrium (DSGE) models. The properties of these models vary, but most have the feature—because of the assumption of sticky prices and wages—that monetary policy can affect real output. The government generally has some role to play in these models.

**real business cycle theory** An attempt to explain business cycle fluctuations under the assumptions of complete price and wage flexibility and rational expectations. It emphasizes shocks to technology and other shocks.

**new Keynesian economics** A field in which models are developed under the assumptions of rational expectations and sticky prices and wages.

# Evaluating the Rational Expectations Assumption

Almost all models in new classical macroeconomics—Lucas's model, real business cycle models, new Keynesian models—assume rational expectations. A key question concerning how realistic these models are is thus how realistic the assumption of rational expectations is. If this assumption approximates the way expectations are actually formed, then it calls into question any theory that relies at least in part on expectation errors for the existence of disequilibrium. The arguments in favor of the rational expectations assumption sound persuasive from the perspective of microeconomic theory. When expectations are not rational, there are likely to be unexploited profit opportunities, and most economists believe such opportunities are rare and short-lived.

The argument *against* rational expectations is that it requires households and firms to know too much. This argument says that it is unrealistic to think that these basic decision-making units know as much as they need to know to form rational expectations. People must know the true model (or at least a good approximation of the true model) to form rational expectations, and this knowledge is a lot to expect. Even if firms and households are capable of learning the true model, it may be costly to take the time and gather the relevant information to learn it. The gain from learning the true model (or a good approximation of it) may not be worth the cost. In this sense, there may not be unexploited profit opportunities around. Gathering information and learning economic models may be too costly to bother with, given the expected gain from improving forecasts.

Although the assumption that expectations are rational seems consistent with the satisfaction-maximizing and profit-maximizing postulates of microeconomics, the rational expectations assumption is more extreme and demanding because it requires more information on the part of households and firms. Consider a firm engaged in maximizing profits. In some way or other, it forms expectations of the relevant future variables, and given these expectations, it figures out the best thing to do from the point of view of maximizing profits. Given a set of expectations, the problem of maximizing profits may not be too hard. What may be hard is forming accurate expectations in the first place. This requires firms to know much more about the overall economy than they are likely to, so the assumption that their expectations are rational is not necessarily realistic. Firms, like the rest of us—so the argument goes—grope around in a world that is difficult to understand, trying to do their best but not always understanding enough to avoid mistakes.

In the final analysis, the issue is empirical. Does the assumption of rational expectations stand up well against empirical tests? This question is difficult to answer. Much work is currently being done to answer it. There are no conclusive results yet, although the results discussed in the *Economics in Practice* on p. 325 are not supportive of the rational expectations assumption.

**17.5 LEARNING** OBJECTIVE

Discuss why it is difficult to test alternative macroeconomic theories.

# Testing Alternative Macroeconomic Models

You may wonder why there is so much disagreement in macroeconomics. Why can't macroeconomists test their models against one another and see which performs best?

One problem is that macroeconomic models differ in ways that are hard to standardize. If one model takes the price level to be given, or not explained within the model, and another one does not, the model with the given price level may do better in, for instance, predicting output—not because it is a better model but simply because the errors in predicting prices have not been allowed to affect the predictions of output. The model that takes prices as given has a head start, so to speak.

Another problem arises in the testing of the rational expectations assumption. Remember, if people have rational expectations, they are using the true model to form their expectations. Therefore, to test this assumption, we need the true model. There is no way to be sure that whatever model is taken to be the true model is in fact the true one. Any test of the rational expectations hypothesis is therefore a *joint* test: (1) that expectations are formed rationally and (2) that the model being used is the true one. If the test rejects the hypothesis, it may be that the model is wrong rather than that the expectations are not rational.

Another problem for macroeconomists is the small amount of data available. Most empirical work uses data beginning about 1950, which in 2014 was about 65 years' (260 quarters) worth of data. Although this may seem like a lot of data, it is not. Macroeconomic data are fairly "smooth," which means that a typical variable does not vary much from quarter to quarter or from year to year. For example, the number of business cycles within this 65-year period is small, about eight. Testing various macroeconomic hypotheses on the basis of eight business cycle observations is not easy, and any conclusions must be interpreted with caution.

To give an example of the problem of a small number of observations, consider trying to test the hypothesis that import prices affect domestic prices. Import prices changed very little in the 1950s and 1960s. Therefore, it would have been difficult at the end of the 1960s to estimate the effect of import prices on domestic prices. The variation in import prices was not great enough to show any effects. We cannot demonstrate that changes in import prices help explain changes in domestic prices if import prices do not change. The situation was different by the end of the 1970s because by then, import prices had varied considerably. By the end of the 1970s, there were good estimates of the import price effect, but not before. This kind of problem is encountered again and again in empirical macroeconomics. In many cases, there are not enough observations for much to be said and hence there is considerable room for disagreement.

We said in Chapter 1 that it is difficult in economics to perform controlled experiments. Economists, are for the most part, at the mercy of the historical data. If we were able to perform experiments, we could probably learn more about the economy in a shorter time. Alas, we must wait. In time, the current range of disagreements in macroeconomics should be considerably narrowed.

# SUMMARY

## 17.1 KEYNESIAN ECONOMICS *p. 318*

1. In a broad sense, Keynesian economics is the foundation of modern macroeconomics. In a narrower sense, *Keynesian* refers to economists who advocate active government intervention in the economy.

## 17.2 MONETARISM *p. 318*

2. The monetarist analysis of the economy places a great deal of emphasis on the *velocity of money*, which is defined as the number of times a dollar bill changes hands, on average, during the course of a year. The velocity of money is the ratio of nominal GDP to the stock of money, or $V \equiv GDP/M \equiv (P \times Y)/M$. Alternately, $M \times V \equiv P \times Y$.

3. The *quantity theory of money* assumes that velocity is constant (or virtually constant). This implies that changes in the supply of money will lead to equal percentage changes in nominal GDP. The quantity theory of money equation is $M \times \overline{V} = P \times Y$. The equation says that demand for money does not depend on the interest rate.

4. Most monetarists blame most of the instability in the economy on the federal government and are skeptical of the government's ability to manage the macroeconomy. They argue that the money supply should grow at a rate equal to the average growth of real output (income) (Y)—the Fed should expand the money supply to accommodate real growth but not inflation.

## 17.3 SUPPLY-SIDE ECONOMICS *p. 321*

5. *Supply-side economics* focuses on incentives to stimulate supply. Supply-side economists believe that if we lower taxes, workers will work harder and save more and firms will invest more and produce more. At their most extreme, supply-siders argue that incentive effects are likely to be so great that a major cut in taxes will actually increase tax revenues.

6. The *Laffer curve* shows the relationship between tax rates and tax revenues. Supply-side economists use it to argue that it is possible to generate higher revenues by cutting tax rates. This does not appear to have been the case during the Reagan administration, however, where lower tax rates decreased tax revenues significantly and contributed to the large increase in the federal debt during the 1980s.

## 17.4 NEW CLASSICAL MACROECONOMICS *p. 323*

7. *New classical macroeconomics* uses the assumption of rational expectations. The *rational expectations hypothesis* assumes that people know the "true model" that generates economic variables. For example, rational expectations assumes that people know how inflation is determined in the economy and use this model to forecast future inflation rates.

8. The *Lucas supply function* assumes that real output (Y) depends on the actual price level minus the expected price level, or the *price surprise*. This function combined with the assumption that expectations are rational implies that anticipated policy changes have no effect on real output.

9. *Real business cycle theory* is an attempt to explain business cycle fluctuations under the assumptions of complete price and wage flexibility and rational expectations. It emphasizes shocks to technology and other shocks.

10. *New Keynesian economics* relaxes the assumption of complete price and wage flexibility. There is usually a role for government policy in these models.

## 17.5 TESTING ALTERNATIVE MACROECONOMIC MODELS *p. 328*

11. Economists disagree about which macroeconomic model is best for several reasons: (1) Macroeconomic models differ in ways that are hard to standardize; (2) when testing the rational-expectations assumption, we are never sure that whatever model is taken to be the true model is the true one; and (3) the amount of data available is fairly small.

## REVIEW TERMS AND CONCEPTS

Laffer curve, *p. 322*
Lucas supply function, *p. 326*
new Keynesian economics, *p. 327*
price surprise, *p. 326*

quantity theory of money, *p. 319*
rational expectations hypothesis, *p. 324*
real business cycle theory, *p. 327*
velocity of money, *p. 318*

Equations:
$$V \equiv \frac{GDP}{M}, p.\ 318$$
$$M \times V \equiv P \times Y, p.\ 319$$
$$M \times \overline{V} = P \times Y, p.\ 319$$

## PROBLEMS

All problems are available on MyEconLab.

### 17.1 KEYNESIAN ECONOMICS

LEARNING OBJECTIVE: Summarize Keynesian economics.

1.1 Use aggregate supply and aggregate demand curves to show the predictions of Keynesian economic theory of the likely effects of a major tax cut when the economy is not operating at capacity and the Fed accommodates by increasing the money supply. Explain what happens to the level of real GDP and to the price level.

### 17.2 MONETARISM

LEARNING OBJECTIVE: Explain the quantity theory of money.

2.1 The table gives estimates of the rate of the M2 money supply growth and the rate of real GDP growth for five countries in 2014:

| | Rate of Growth in Money Supply (M2) | Rate of Growth of Real Gdp |
|---|---|---|
| Australia | +7.4 percent | +2.5 percent |
| United Kingdom | −2.5 percent | +2.6 percent |
| Argentina | +29.8 percent | +0.5 percent |
| Japan | +3.0 percent | −0.1 percent |
| United States | +5.2 percent | +2.4 percent |

  a. If you were a monetarist, what would you predict about the rate of inflation across the five countries?
  b. If you were a Keynesian and assuming activist central banks, how might you interpret the same data?

2.2 You are a monetarist given the following information: The money supply is $1 million. The velocity of money is 4. What is nominal income? real income? What happens to nominal income if the money supply is doubled? What happens to real income?

2.3 The following is data from 2015 for the tiny island nation of Coco Loco: money supply = $800 million; price level = 3.2; velocity of money = 3. Use the quantity theory of money to answer the following questions.
  a. What is the value of real output (income) in 2015?
  b. What is the value of nominal GDP in 2015?
  c. If real output doubled, by how much would the money supply need to change?

  d. If velocity is constant and Coco Loco was experiencing a recession in 2015, what impact would an easy money policy have on nominal GDP?
  e. If the annual GDP growth rate is 12 percent in Coco Loco, by how much will the money supply need to change in 2016?

2.4 In the nation of Lower Vicuna, the velocity of money is fairly constant, and in the nation of Upper Vicuna, the velocity of money fluctuates greatly. For which nation would the quantity theory of money better explain changes in nominal GDP? Explain.

### 17.3 SUPPLY-SIDE ECONOMICS

LEARNING OBJECTIVE: Explain the fundamentals of supply-side economics.

3.1 In 2000, a well-known economist was heard to say, "The problem with supply-side economics is that when you cut taxes, they have both supply and demand side effects and you cannot separate the effects." Explain this comment. Be specific and use the 1997 tax cuts or the Reagan tax cuts of 1981 as an example.

3.2 When Bill Clinton took office in January 1993, he faced two major economic problems: a large federal budget deficit and high unemployment resulting from a slow recovery from the recession of 1990 to 1991. In his first State of the Union message, the president called for spending cuts and substantial tax increases to reduce the deficit. Most of these proposed spending cuts were in the defense budget. The following day Alan Greenspan, chair of the Federal Reserve Board of Governors, signaled his support for the president's plan. Many elements of the president's original plan were later incorporated into the deficit reduction bill passed in 1993.
  a. Some said at the time that without the Fed's support, the Clinton plan would be a disaster. Explain this argument.
  b. Supply-side economists and monetarists were worried about the plan and the support it received from the Fed. What specific problems might a monetarist and a supply-side economist worry about?
  c. Suppose you were hired by the Federal Reserve Bank of St. Louis to report on the events of 1995 and 1996. What

specific evidence would you look for to see whether the Clinton plan was effective or whether the critics were right to be skeptical?

3.3 During the 1980 presidential campaign, Ronald Reagan promised to cut taxes, increase expenditures on national defense, and balance the budget. During the New Hampshire primary of 1980, George Bush called this policy "voodoo economics." The two men were arguing about the relative merits of supply-side economics. Explain their disagreement.

3.4 In a hypothetical economy, there is a simple proportional tax on wages imposed at a rate $t$. There are plenty of jobs around, so if people enter the labor force, they can find work. We define total government receipts from the tax as

$$T = t \times W \times L$$

where $t$ = the tax rate, $W$ = the gross wage rate, and $L$ = the total supply of labor. The net wage rate is

$$W_n = (1 - t)W$$

The elasticity of labor supply is defined as

$$\frac{\text{Percentage of change in } L}{\text{Percentage of change in } W_n} = \frac{\Delta L/\Delta L}{\Delta W_n/W_n}$$

Suppose $t$ was cut from 0.25 to 0.20. For such a cut to *increase* total government receipts from the tax, how elastic must the supply of labor be? (Assume a constant gross wage.) What does your answer imply about the supply-side assertion that a cut in taxes can increase tax revenues?

## 17.4 NEW CLASSICAL MACROECONOMICS

LEARNING OBJECTIVE: Discuss the real business cycle theory and new Keynesian economics.

4.1 [Related to the *Economics in Practice* on p. 325] Suppose you are thinking about where to live after you finish your degree. You discover that an apartment building near your new job has identical units—one is for rent and the other for sale as a condominium. Given your salary, both are affordable and you like them. Would you buy or rent? How would you go about deciding? Would your expectations play a role? Be specific. Where do you think those expectations come from? In what ways could expectations change things in the housing market as a whole?

4.2 A cornerstone of new classical economics is the notion that expectations are "rational." What do you think will happen to the prices of single-family homes in your community over the next several years? On what do you base your expectations? Is your thinking consistent with the notion of rational expectations? Explain.

4.3 In an economy with reasonably flexible prices and wages, full employment is almost always maintained. Explain why that statement is true.

4.4 The economy of Borealis is represented by the following Lucas supply function: $Y = 750 + 50(P - P^e)$. The current

price level in Borealis is 1.45, and the expected price level is 1.70.
a. What will be the new level of real output if inflation expectations are correct?
b. What will be the new level of real output if inflation expectations are wrong and the actual price level rises to 1.80?
c. What will be the new level of real output if the actual price level does not change?
d. What is the value of the "price surprise" in parts a, b, and c?

4.5 If households and firms have rational expectations, is it possible for the unemployment rate to exceed the natural rate of unemployment? Explain.

4.6 Assume people and firms have rational expectations. Explain how each of the following events will affect aggregate output and the price level.
a. The Fed announces it will increase the required reserve ratio.
b. Congress unexpectedly passes a bill that will immediately decrease taxes.
c. The Fed announces it will increase the supply of money.
d. Without notice, OPEC increases oil production by 40 percent.
e. The government passes a previously unannounced disaster relief spending bill, authorizing an immediate $400 billion increase in funding.

## 17.5 TESTING ALTERNATIVE MACROECONOMIC MODELS

LEARNING OBJECTIVE: Discuss why it is difficult to test alternative macroeconomic theories.

5.1 The following data is for the small, recently independent island nation of Hibiscus:

Tax rate: 10% flat tax on all citizens since its independence in 2010

Labor supply: 200 workers in 2010, and has grown by 3 percent each successive year

Inflation rate: Has fluctuated between 2 percent and 3 percent annually since 2010

Unemployment rate: A constant 4.5 percent each year since 2010

Exchange rate: Since 2010 has fluctuated by more than 20 percent, both up and down, relative to the rates of major currencies

Interest rate: Has risen from 2.5 percent to 3.5 percent since 2010

Explain why macroeconomists would find it difficult to test the following hypotheses for Hibiscus:
a. Tax rates affect the supply of labor
b. The inflation rate affects the unemployment rate
c. The exchange rate affects the interest rate

*Note: Problems marked with an asterisk are more challenging.

# 18

# International Trade, Comparative Advantage, and Protectionism

Over the last 44 years, international transactions have become increasingly important to the U.S. economy. In 1970, imports represented only about 5.2 percent of U.S. gross domestic product (GDP). The share in 2014 was 16.5 percent. The increased trade we observe in the United States is mirrored throughout the world. From 1980 to 2014, world trade in real terms has grown more than sixfold. This trend has been especially rapid in the newly

industrialized Asian economies, but many developing countries such as Malaysia and Vietnam have also been increasing their openness to trade.

The "internationalization" or "globalization" of the U.S. economy has occurred in the private and public sectors, in input and output markets, and in firms and households. Once uncommon, foreign products are now everywhere, from the utensils we eat with to the cars we drive. Nor is it easy to tell where products are made. The iPhone, which most people think of as an iconic U.S. product, is assembled in China from parts produced in four other countries: Korea, Germany, Japan, and the United States. Honda, which most people think of as a Japanese company, started producing Japanese motorcycles in Ohio in 1977 with 64 employees in Marysville. The company now employs many thousand workers, who assemble Honda automobiles in eleven manufacturing plants in Ohio, Georgia, and North Carolina.

In addition to the fact that goods and services (outputs) flow easily across borders, so too do inputs: capital and labor. Certainly, it is easy to buy financial assets abroad. Millions of Americans own shares in foreign stocks or have invested in bonds issued by foreign countries. At the same time, millions of foreigners have put money into the U.S. stock and bond markets.

Outsourcing is also changing the nature of the global labor market. It is now simple and common for a customer service call to a software company from a user of its product in Bend, Oregon, to be routed to Bangalore, India, where a young, ambitious Indian man or woman provides assistance to a customer over the Internet. The Internet has in essence made it possible for some types of labor to flow smoothly across international borders.

To get you more acquainted with the international economy, this chapter discusses the economics of international trade. First, we describe the trends in imports and exports to the United States. Next, we explore the basic logic of trade. Why should the United States or any other country engage in international trade? Finally, we address the controversial issue of protectionism. Should a country provide certain industries with protection in the form of import quotas or tariffs, which are taxes imposed on imports? Should a country help a domestic industry compete in international markets by providing subsidies?

# Trade Surpluses and Deficits

Until the 1970s, the United States generally exported more than it imported. When a country exports more than it imports, it runs a **trade surplus**. When a country imports more than it exports, it runs a **trade deficit**. In the mid-1970s the United States began to run trade deficits. In 2009 the trade deficit was 5.6 percent of GDP. Since then it has fallen somewhat—to 3.1 percent in 2014.

The large U.S. trade deficits have sparked political controversy. Less expensive foreign goods—among them steel, textiles, and automobiles—create competition for locally produced substitute goods, and many believe that domestic jobs are lost as a result. In recent times, the outsourcing of software development to India has caused complaints from white-collar workers again reflecting a concern about employment displacement.

The natural reaction to trade-related job dislocation is to call for protection of U.S. industries. Many people want the president and Congress to impose taxes and import restrictions that would make foreign goods less available and more expensive, protecting U.S. jobs. This argument is not new. For hundreds of years, industries have petitioned their governments for protection and societies have debated the pros and cons of free and open trade. For the last century and a half, the principal argument against protection has been the theory of comparative advantage, first discussed in Chapter 2.

# The Economic Basis for Trade: Comparative Advantage

Perhaps the best-known debate on the issue of free trade took place in the British Parliament during the early years of the nineteenth century. At that time, the landed gentry—the landowners—controlled Parliament. For a number of years, imports and exports of grain had been subject to a set of tariffs, subsidies, and restrictions collectively called the **Corn Laws**. Designed to discourage imports of grain and to encourage exports, the Corn Laws' purpose was to keep the price of food high. The landlords' incomes, of course, depended on the prices they got for what their land produced. The Corn Laws clearly worked to the advantage of those in power.

With the Industrial Revolution, a class of wealthy industrial capitalists emerged. The industrial sector had to pay workers at least enough to live on, and a living wage depended greatly on the price of food. Tariffs on grain imports and export subsidies that kept grain and food prices high increased the wages that capitalists had to pay, cutting into their profits. The political battle raged for years. However, as time went by, the power of the landowners in the House of Lords was significantly reduced. When the conflict ended in 1848, the Corn Laws were repealed.

On the side of repeal was David Ricardo, a businessman, economist, member of Parliament, and one of the fathers of modern economics. Ricardo's principal work, *Principles of Political Economy and Taxation*, was published in 1817, two years before he entered Parliament. Ricardo's **theory of comparative advantage**, which he used to argue against the Corn Laws, claimed that trade enables countries to specialize in producing the products they produce best. According to the theory specialization and free trade will benefit all trading partners (real wages will rise), even those that may be absolutely less efficient producers. This basic argument remains at the heart of free-trade debates even today, as policy makers argue about the effects of tariffs on agricultural development in sub-Saharan Africa and the gains and losses from outsourcing software development to India.

## Absolute Advantage versus Comparative Advantage

A country enjoys an **absolute advantage** over another country in the production of a good if it uses fewer resources to produce that good than the other country does. Suppose country A and country B produce wheat, but A's climate is more suited to wheat and its labor is more productive. Country

**18.1 LEARNING** OBJECTIVE

How are trade surpluses and trade deficits defined?

**trade surplus** The situation when a country exports more than it imports.

**trade deficit** The situation when a country imports more than it exports.

**18.2 LEARNING** OBJECTIVE

Explain how international trade emerges from the theory of comparative advantage and what determines the terms of trade.

**Corn Laws** The tariffs, subsidies, and restrictions enacted by the British Parliament in the early nineteenth century to discourage imports and encourage exports of grain.

**theory of comparative advantage** Ricardo's theory that specialization and free trade will benefit all trading partners (real wages will rise), even those that may be absolutely less efficient producers.

**absolute advantage** The advantage in the production of a good enjoyed by one country over another when it uses fewer resources to produce that good than the other country does.

**comparative advantage** The advantage in the production of a good enjoyed by one country over another when that good can be produced at a lower opportunity cost (in terms of other goods that must be foregone) than it could be in the other country.

A will produce more wheat per acre than country B and use less labor in growing it and bringing it to market. Country A enjoys an absolute advantage over country B in the production of wheat.

A country enjoys a **comparative advantage** in the production of a good if that good can be produced at a lower opportunity cost (in terms of other goods that must be foregone). Suppose countries C and D both produce wheat and corn and C enjoys an absolute advantage in the production of both—that is, C's climate is better than D's and fewer of C's resources are needed to produce a given quantity of both wheat and corn. Now C and D must each choose between planting land with either wheat or corn. To produce more wheat, either country must transfer land from corn production; to produce more corn, either country must transfer land from wheat production. The cost of wheat in each country can be measured in foregone bushels of corn, and the cost of corn can be measured in foregone bushels of wheat.

Suppose that in country C, a bushel of wheat has an opportunity cost of 2 bushels of corn. That is, to produce an additional bushel of wheat, C must give up 2 bushels of corn. At the same time, producing a bushel of wheat in country D requires the sacrifice of only 1 bushel of corn. Even though C has an *absolute* advantage in the production of both products, D enjoys a *comparative* advantage in the production of wheat because the *opportunity cost* of producing wheat is lower in D. Under these circumstances, Ricardo claims, both countries will benefit from specialization in the good for which they have a comparative advantage and then trading with each other. We turn now to a discussion of that claim.

**Gains from Mutual Absolute Advantage**  To illustrate Ricardo's logic in more detail, suppose Australia and New Zealand each have a fixed amount of land and do not trade with the rest of the world. There are only two goods—wheat to produce bread and cotton to produce clothing. The conclusions we get from working with this two-country/two-good world can be easily generalized to many countries and many goods.

To proceed, we have to make some assumptions about the preferences of the people living in New Zealand and the people living in Australia. We will assume the populations of both countries use both cotton and wheat, and preferences for food and clothing are such that before trade both countries consume equal amounts of wheat and cotton.

Finally, we assume that each country has only 100 acres of land for planting and that land yields are as given in Table 18.1. New Zealand can produce 3 times the wheat that Australia can on 1 acre of land, and Australia can produce 3 times the cotton that New Zealand can in the same space. New Zealand has an absolute advantage in the production of wheat, and Australia has an absolute advantage in the production of cotton. In cases like this, we say the two countries have *mutual absolute advantage*.

If there is no trade and each country divides its land to obtain equal units of cotton and wheat production, each country produces 150 bushels of wheat and 150 bales of cotton. New Zealand puts 75 acres into cotton but only 25 acres into wheat, while Australia does the reverse (Table 18.2).

We can organize the same information in graphic form as production possibility frontiers for each country. In Figure 18.1, which presents the positions of the two countries before trade, each country is constrained by its own resources and productivity. If Australia put all its land into cotton, it would produce 600 bales of cotton (100 acres × 6 bales/acre) and no wheat; if it

| TABLE 18.1 | Yield per Acre of Wheat and Cotton | |
|---|---|---|
| | New Zealand | Australia |
| Wheat | 6 bushels | 2 bushels |
| Cotton | 2 bales | 6 bales |

| TABLE 18.2 | Total Production of Wheat and Cotton Assuming No Trade, Mutual Absolute Advantage, and 100 Available Acres | |
|---|---|---|
| | New Zealand | Australia |
| Wheat | 25 acres × 6 bushels/acre = 150 bushels | 75 acres × 2 bushels/acre = 150 bushels |
| Cotton | 75 acres × 2 bales/acre = 150 bales | 25 acres × 6 bales/acre = 150 bales |

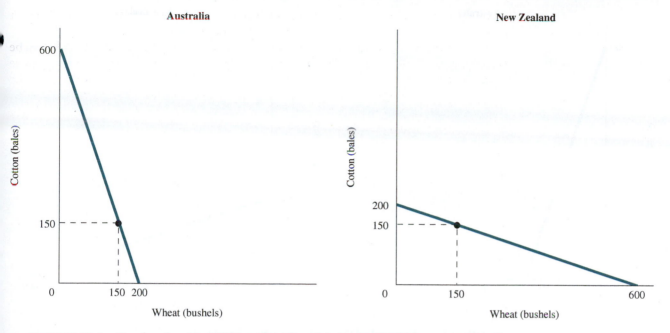

▲ **FIGURE 18.1** **Production Possibility Frontiers for Australia and New Zealand Before Trade**
Without trade, countries are constrained by their own resources and productivity.

put all its land into wheat, it would produce 200 bushels of wheat (100 acres × 2 bushels/acre) and no cotton. The opposite is true for New Zealand. Recall from Chapter 2 that a country's production possibility frontier represents all combinations of goods that can be produced, given the country's resources and state of technology. Each country must pick a point along its own production possibility curve. We can see that both countries have the option of producing and consuming 150 units of each good, marked on the two figures.

When both countries have an absolute advantage in the production of one product, it is easy to see that specialization and trade will benefit both. Australia should produce cotton, and New Zealand should produce wheat. Transferring all land to wheat production in New Zealand yields 600 bushels, while transferring all land to cotton production in Australia yields 600 bales. Because both countries want to consume both goods, they will then need to trade. Suppose the countries agree to trade 300 bushels of wheat for 300 bales of cotton. Prior to specialization, each country consumed 150 units of each good. Now each country has 300 units of each good. Specialization has allowed the countries to double their consumption of both goods! Final production and trade figures are provided in Table 18.3 and Figure 18.2. Trade enables both countries to move beyond their previous resource and productivity constraints.

The advantages of specialization and trade seem obvious when one country is technologically superior at producing one product and another country is technologically superior at producing another product. However, let us turn to the case in which one country has an absolute advantage in the production of *both* goods.

**TABLE 18.3** **Production and Consumption of Wheat and Cotton After Specialization**

| | Production | | | Consumption | |
|---|---|---|---|---|---|
| | New Zealand | Australia | | New Zealand | Australia |
| Wheat | 100 acres × 6 bushels/acre 600 bushels | 0 acres  0 | Wheat | 300 bushels | 300 bushels |
| Cotton | 0 acres  0 | 100 acres × 6 bales/acre 600 bales | Cotton | 300 bales | 300 bales |

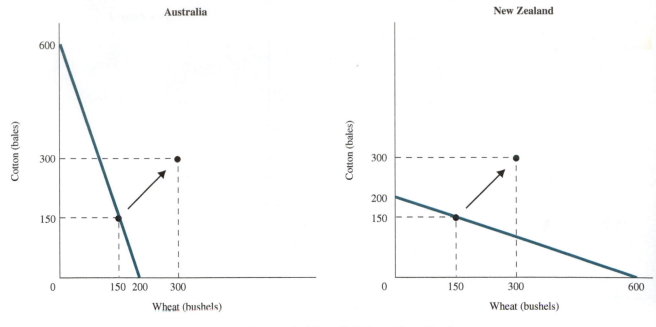

▲ **FIGURE 18.2** **Expanded Possibilities After Trade**

Trade enables both countries to consume beyond their own domestic resource constraints—beyond their individual production possibility frontiers.

**Gains from Comparative Advantage** Table 18.4 changes the land yield figures for New Zealand and Australia. Now New Zealand has a considerable absolute advantage in the production of both cotton and wheat, with 1 acre of land yielding 6 times as much wheat and twice as much cotton as 1 acre in Australia. Ricardo would argue that *specialization and trade are still mutually beneficial.*

Again, we assume preferences imply consumption of equal units of cotton and wheat in both countries. With no trade, New Zealand would divide its 100 available acres evenly, or 50/50, between the two crops. The result would be 300 bales of cotton and 300 bushels of wheat. Australia would divide its land 75/25. Table 18.5 shows that final production in Australia would be 75 bales of cotton and 75 bushels of wheat. (Remember, we are assuming that in each country, people consume equal amounts of cotton and wheat.) Again, before any trade takes place, each country is constrained by its own domestic production possibility curve.

Imagine we are at a meeting of trade representatives of both countries. As a special adviser, David Ricardo is asked to demonstrate that trade can benefit both countries. He divides his demonstration into three stages, which you can follow in Table 18.6. For Ricardo to be correct about the gains from specialization, it must be true that moving resources around in the two

| TABLE 18.4 | Yield per Acre of Wheat and Cotton | |
|---|---|---|
| | New Zealand | Australia |
| Wheat | 6 bushels | 1 bushel |
| Cotton | 6 bales | 3 bales |

| TABLE 18.5 | Total Production of Wheat and Cotton Assuming No Trade and 100 Available Acres | |
|---|---|---|
| | New Zealand | Australia |
| Wheat | 50 acres × 6 bushels/acre<br>300 bushels | 75 acres × 1 bushel/acre<br>75 bushels |
| Cotton | 50 acres × 6 bales/acre<br>300 bales | 25 acres × 3 bales/acre<br>75 bales |

| TABLE 18.6 | Realizing a Gain from Trade when One Country Has a Double Absolute Advantage | | | | | |
|---|---|---|---|---|---|---|

| | STAGE 1 | | | STAGE 2 | |
|---|---|---|---|---|---|
| | New Zealand | Australia | | New Zealand | Australia |
| Wheat | 50 acres × 6 bushels/acre 300 bushels | 0 acres 0 | Wheat | 75 acres × 6 bushels/acre 450 bushels | 0 acres 0 |
| Cotton | 50 acres × 6 bales/acre 300 bales | 100 acres × 3 bales/acre 300 bales | Cotton | 25 acres × 6 bales/acre 150 bales | 100 acres × 3 bales/acre 300 bales |

| | STAGE 3 | |
|---|---|---|
| | New Zealand | Australia |
| Wheat | 100 bushels (trade) →  350 bushels (after trade) | 100 bushels |
| Cotton | 200 bales (trade) ←  350 bales (after trade) | 100 bales |

countries generates more than the 375 bushels of wheat and bales of cotton that we had before specialization. To see how this is managed, we move in stages.

In Stage 1, let Australia move all its land into cotton production, where it is least disadvantaged. Australia would then produce 300 bales of cotton, as we see in Stage 1 of Table 18.6. Now the question is whether Ricardo can help us use New Zealand's land to add at least 75 bales of cotton to the total while producing more than the original 375 bushels of wheat. In Stage 2, Ricardo tells New Zealand to use 25 acres to produce cotton and 75 acres for wheat production. With that allocation of land, New Zealand produces 450 bushels of wheat (far more than the total produced in the nonspecialization case by both countries) and 150 bales of cotton, leaving us with 450 bales of cotton as well. Specialization has increased the world production of both wheat and cotton by 75 units! With trade, which we show in Stage 3 for the case in which both countries prefer equal consumption of the two goods, both countries can be better off than they were earlier.

**Why Does Ricardo's Plan Work?**  To understand why Ricardo's scheme works, let us return to the definition of comparative advantage.

The real cost, which is an opportunity cost, of producing cotton is the wheat that must be sacrificed to produce it. *When we think of cost this way, it is less costly to produce cotton in Australia than to produce it in New Zealand, even though an acre of land produces more cotton in New Zealand.* Consider the "cost" of 3 bales of cotton in the two countries. In terms of opportunity cost, 3 bales of cotton in New Zealand cost 3 bushels of wheat; in Australia, 3 bales of cotton cost only 1 bushel of wheat. Because 3 bales are produced by 1 acre of Australian land, to get 3 bales, an Australian must transfer 1 acre of land from wheat to cotton production. Because an acre of land produces a bushel of wheat, losing 1 acre to cotton implies the loss of 1 bushel of wheat. *Australia has a comparative advantage in cotton production* because its opportunity cost, in terms of wheat, is lower than New Zealand's. This is illustrated in Figure 18.3.

Conversely, New Zealand has a comparative advantage in wheat production. A unit of wheat in New Zealand costs 1 unit of cotton, whereas a unit of wheat in Australia costs 3 units of cotton. When countries specialize in producing goods in which they have a comparative advantage, they maximize their combined output and allocate their resources more efficiently.

▶ **FIGURE 18.3**
**Comparative Advantage Means Lower Opportunity Cost**
The real cost of cotton is the wheat sacrificed to obtain it. The cost of 3 bales of cotton in New Zealand is 3 bushels of wheat (a half-acre of land must be transferred from wheat to cotton—refer to Table 18.4). However, the cost of 3 bales of cotton in Australia is only 1 bushel of wheat. Australia has a comparative advantage over New Zealand in cotton production, and New Zealand has a comparative advantage over Australia in wheat production.

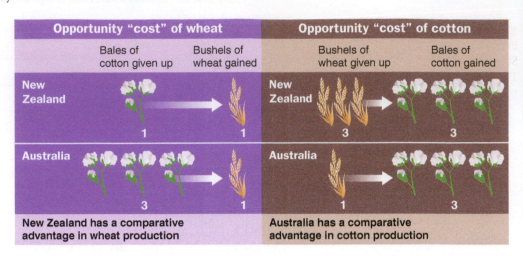

**terms of trade** The ratio at which a country can trade domestic products for imported products.

## Terms of Trade

We see that specialization and trade increases the size of the pie to be shared between the two countries. Our next question is how that bigger pie is to be divided up between the two countries. In stage three above we have offered one possibility for this division, which benefitted both parties. But this is only one of many possible ways to divide the pie. What would we expect to see happen in practice?

The ratio at which a country can trade domestic products for imported products is the **terms of trade**. The terms of trade determine how the gains from trade are distributed among trading partners. In the case just considered, the agreed-to terms of trade were 1 bushel of wheat for 2 bales of cotton. Such terms of trade benefit New Zealand, which can get 2 bales of cotton for each bushel of wheat. If it were to transfer its own land from wheat to cotton, it would get only 1 bale of cotton. The same terms of trade benefit Australia, which can get 1 bushel of wheat for 2 bales of cotton. A direct transfer of its own land would force it to give up 3 bales of cotton for 1 bushel of wheat.

If the terms of trade changed to 3 bales of cotton for every bushel of wheat, only New Zealand would benefit. At those terms of trade, *all* the gains from trade would flow to New Zealand. Such terms do not benefit Australia at all because the opportunity cost of producing wheat domestically is *exactly the same* as the trade cost: A bushel of wheat costs 3 bales of cotton. If the terms of trade went the other way—1 bale of cotton for each bushel of wheat—only Australia would benefit. New Zealand gains nothing because it can already substitute cotton for wheat at that ratio. To get a bushel of wheat domestically, however, Australia must give up 3 bales of cotton, and one-for-one terms of trade would make wheat much less costly for Australia.

Both parties must have something to gain for trade to take place. In this case, you can see that both Australia and New Zealand will gain when the terms of trade are set between 1:1 and 3:1, cotton to wheat.

## Exchange Rates

The examples used thus far have shown that trade can result in gains to both parties. When trade is free—unimpeded by government-instituted barriers—patterns of trade and trade flows result from the independent decisions of thousands of importers and exporters and millions of private households and firms.

Private households decide whether to buy Toyotas or Chevrolets, and private firms decide whether to buy machine tools made in the United States or machine tools made in Taiwan, raw steel produced in Germany or raw steel produced in Pittsburgh.

But how does this trade actually come about? In international markets, as in domestic markets, barter is rarely used. Instead trade happens with money. But in the international marketplace, there are a number of different types of currency or money. Before a citizen of one country can buy a product made in another country or sold by someone in another country, a currency swap must take place. Someone who buys a Toyota built in Japan from a dealer in Boston pays in dollars, but the Japanese workers who made the car receive their salaries in yen. Somewhere between the buyer of the car and the producer, a currency exchange must be made. The regional distributor probably takes payment in dollars and converts them into yen before remitting the proceeds to Japan.

To buy a foreign-produced good, a consumer, or an intermediary, has to buy foreign currency. The price of a Toyota in dollars depends on the price of the car stated in yen and the dollar price of yen. You probably know the ins and outs of currency exchange very well if you have ever traveled in another country.

In April 2015, the British pound was worth $1.52. Now suppose you are in London having dinner. On the menu is a nice bottle of wine for 15 pounds. How can you figure out whether you want to buy it? You know what dollars will buy in the United States, so you have to convert the price into dollars. Each pound will cost you $1.52, so 15 pounds will cost you $1.52 × 15 = $22.80.

The attractiveness of foreign goods to U.S. buyers and of U.S. goods to foreign buyers depends in part on the **exchange rate**, the ratio at which two currencies are traded. In May 2008, the British pound was worth $1.97, and that same bottle of wine would have cost $29.55. In the last decade it has become more attractive for American tourists to visit Great Britain ( and the rest of Europe as well) because the dollar is strong relative to other currencies.

> **exchange rate**   The ratio at which two currencies are traded. The price of one currency in terms of another.

So how are these exchange rates determined? Why is the dollar stronger now than it was ten years ago? Exchange rate determination is complicated, but we can say a few things. First, for any pair of countries, there is a range of exchange rates that can lead automatically to both countries' realizing the gains from specialization and comparative advantage. Second, within that range, the exchange rate will determine which country gains the most from trade. In short, exchange rates determine the terms of trade.

**Trade and Exchange Rates in a Two-Country/Two-Good World**   Consider first a simple two-country/two-good model. Suppose both the United States and Brazil produce only two goods—raw timber and rolled steel. Table 18.7 gives the current prices of both goods as domestic buyers see them. In Brazil, timber is priced at 3 reals (R) per foot and steel is priced at 4 R per meter. In the United States, timber costs $1 per foot and steel costs $2 per meter.

Suppose U.S. and Brazilian buyers have the option of buying at home or importing to meet their needs. The options they choose will depend on the exchange rate. For the time being, we will ignore transportation costs between countries and assume that Brazilian and U.S. products are of equal quality.

Let us start with the assumption that the exchange rate is $1 = 1 R. From the standpoint of U.S. buyers, neither Brazilian steel nor Brazilian timber is competitive at this exchange rate. A dollar buys a foot of timber in the United States, but if converted into a real, it will buy only one-third of a foot. The price of Brazilian timber to an American is $3 because it will take $3 to buy the necessary 3 R. Similarly, $2 buys a meter of rolled steel in the United States, but the same $2 buys only half a meter of Brazilian steel. The price of Brazilian steel to an American is $4, twice the price of domestically produced steel.

At this exchange rate, however, Brazilians find that U.S.-produced steel and timber are less expensive than steel and timber produced in Brazil. Timber at home—Brazil—costs 3 R, but 3 R buys $3, which buys 3 times as much timber in the United States. Similarly, steel costs 4 R at home, but 4 R buys $4, which buys twice as much U.S.-made steel. At an exchange rate of $1 = 1 R, Brazil will import steel and timber and the United States will import nothing.

However, now suppose the exchange rate is 1 R = $0.25. This means that 1 dollar buys 4 R. At this exchange rate, the Brazilians buy timber and steel at home and the Americans import

| TABLE 18.7 | Domestic Prices of Timber (per Foot) and Rolled Steel (per Meter) in the United States and Brazil | |
| --- | --- | --- |
| | **United States** | **Brazil** |
| Timber | $1 | 3 Reals |
| Rolled steel | $2 | 4 Reals |

both goods. At this exchange rate, Americans must pay a dollar for a foot of U.S. timber, but the same amount of timber can be had in Brazil for the equivalent of $0.75. (Because 1 R costs $0.25, 3 R can be purchased for $0.75.) Similarly, steel that costs $2 per meter in the United States costs an American half as much in Brazil because $2 buys 8 R, which buys 2 meters of Brazilian steel. At the same time, Brazilians are not interested in importing because both goods are cheaper when purchased from a Brazilian producer. In this case, the United States imports both goods and Brazil imports nothing.

So far we can see that at exchange rates of $1 = 1 R and $1 = 4 R, we get trade flowing in only one direction. Let us now try an exchange rate of $1 = 2 R, or $1 R = 0.50. First, Brazilians will buy timber in the United States. Brazilian timber costs 3 R per foot, but 3 R buys $1.50, which is enough to buy 1.5 feet of U.S. timber. Buyers in the United States will find Brazilian timber too expensive, but Brazil will import timber from the United States. At this same exchange rate, however, both Brazilian and U.S. buyers will be indifferent between Brazilian and U.S. steel. To U.S. buyers, domestically produced steel costs $2. Because $2 buys 4 R, a meter of imported Brazilian steel also costs $2. Brazilian buyers also find that steel costs 4 R, whether domestically produced or imported. Thus, there is likely to be no trade in steel.

What happens if the exchange rate changes so that $1 buys 2.1 R? Although U.S. timber is still cheaper to both Brazilians and Americans, Brazilian steel begins to look good to U.S. buyers. Steel produced in the United States costs $2 per meter, but $2 buys 4.2 R, which buys more than a meter of steel in Brazil. When $1 buys more than 2 R, trade begins to flow in both directions: Brazil will import timber, and the United States will import steel.

If you examine Table 18.8 carefully, you will see that trade flows in both directions as long as the exchange rate settles between $1 = 2 R and $1 = 3 R. Stated the other way around, trade will flow in both directions if the price of a real is between $0.33 and $0.50.

**Exchange Rates and Comparative Advantage**    If the foreign exchange market drives the exchange rate to anywhere between 2 and 3 R per dollar, the countries will automatically adjust and comparative advantage will be realized. At these exchange rates, U.S. buyers begin buying all their steel in Brazil. The U.S. steel industry finds itself in trouble. Plants close, and U.S. workers begin to lobby for tariff protection against Brazilian steel. At the same time, the U.S. timber industry does well, fueled by strong export demand from Brazil. The timber-producing sector expands. Resources, including capital and labor, are attracted into timber production.

The opposite occurs in Brazil. The Brazilian timber industry suffers losses as export demand dries up and Brazilians turn to cheaper U.S. imports. In Brazil, lumber companies turn to the government and ask for protection from cheap U.S. timber. However, steel producers in Brazil are happy. They are not only supplying 100 percent of the domestically demanded steel but also selling to U.S. buyers. The steel industry expands, and the timber industry contracts. Resources, including labor, flow into steel.

With this expansion-and-contraction scenario in mind, let us look again at our original definition of comparative advantage. If we assume that prices reflect resource use and resources can be transferred from sector to sector, we can calculate the opportunity cost of steel/timber in both countries. In the United States, the production of a meter of rolled steel consumes twice the resources that the production of a foot of timber consumes. Assuming that resources can be transferred, the opportunity cost of a meter of steel is 2 feet of timber (Table 18.7). In Brazil,

| TABLE 18.8 | Trade Flows Determined by Exchange Rates | |
|---|---|---|
| **Exchange Rate** | **Price of Real** | **Result** |
| $1 = 1 R | $ 1.00 | Brazil imports timber and steel. |
| $1 = 2 R | .50 | Brazil imports timber. |
| $1 = 2.1 R | .48 | Brazil imports timber; United States imports steel. |
| $1 = 2.9 R | .34 | Brazil imports timber; United States imports steel. |
| $1 = 3 R | .33 | United States imports steel. |
| $1 = 4 R | .25 | United States imports timber and steel. |

a meter of steel uses resources costing 4 R, while a unit of timber costs 3 R. To produce a meter of steel means the sacrifice of only four-thirds (or one and one-third) feet of timber. Because the opportunity cost of a meter of steel (in terms of timber) is lower in Brazil, we say that Brazil has a comparative advantage in steel production.

Conversely, consider the opportunity cost of timber in the two countries. Increasing timber production in the United States requires the sacrifice of half a meter of steel for every foot of timber—producing a meter of steel uses $2 worth of resources, while producing a foot of timber requires only $1 worth of resources. Nevertheless, each foot of timber production in Brazil requires the sacrifice of three-fourths of a meter of steel. Because the opportunity cost of timber is lower in the United States, the United States has a comparative advantage in the production of timber. If exchange rates end up in the right ranges, the free market will drive each country to shift resources into those sectors in which it enjoys a comparative advantage. Only in a country with a comparative advantage will those products be competitive in world markets.

# The Sources of Comparative Advantage

Specialization and trade can benefit all trading partners, even those that may be inefficient producers in an absolute sense. If markets are competitive and if foreign exchange markets are linked to goods-and-services exchange, countries will specialize in producing products in which they have a comparative advantage.

So far, we have said nothing about the sources of comparative advantage. What determines whether a country has a comparative advantage in heavy manufacturing or in agriculture? What explains the actual trade flows observed around the world? Various theories and empirical work on international trade have provided some answers. Most economists look to **factor endowments**—the quantity and quality of labor, land, and natural resources of a country—as the principal sources of comparative advantage. Factor endowments seem to explain a significant portion of actual world trade patterns.

**factor endowments** The quantity and quality of labor, land, and natural resources of a country.

## The Heckscher-Ohlin Theorem

Eli Heckscher and Bertil Ohlin, two Swedish economists who wrote in the first half of the twentieth century, expanded and elaborated on Ricardo's theory of comparative advantage. The **Heckscher-Ohlin theorem** ties the theory of comparative advantage to factor endowments. It assumes that products can be produced using differing proportions of inputs and that inputs are mobile between sectors in each economy, but that factors are not mobile *between* economies. According to this theorem, a country has a comparative advantage in the production of a product if that country is relatively well endowed with inputs used intensively in the production of that product.

This idea is simple. A country with a great deal of good fertile land is likely to have a comparative advantage in agriculture. A country with a large amount of accumulated capital is likely to have a comparative advantage in heavy manufacturing. A country well-endowed with human capital is likely to have a comparative advantage in highly technical goods.

**Heckscher-Ohlin theorem** A theory that explains the existence of a country's comparative advantage by its factor endowments: A country has a comparative advantage in the production of a product if that country is relatively well endowed with inputs used intensively in the production of that product.

## Other Explanations for Observed Trade Flows

Comparative advantage is not the only reason countries trade. It does not explain why many countries import and export the same kinds of goods. The United States, for example, exports Velveeta cheese and imports blue cheese.

Just as industries within a country differentiate their products to capture a domestic market, they also differentiate their products to please the wide variety of tastes that exists worldwide. The Japanese automobile industry, for example, began producing small, fuel-efficient cars long before U.S. automobile makers did. In doing so, the Japanese auto industry developed expertise in creating products that attracted a devoted following and considerable brand loyalty. BMWs, made mostly in Germany, and Lexus, made mostly in Japan, also have their champions in many countries. Just as product differentiation is a natural response to diverse preferences within an economy, it is also a natural response to diverse preferences across economies. Paul Krugman did some of the earliest work in this area, sometimes called *new trade theory*.

New trade theory also relies on the idea of comparative advantage. If the Japanese developed skills and knowledge that gave them an edge in the production of fuel-efficient cars, that knowledge can be thought of as a very specific kind of capital that is not currently available to other producers. Toyota in producing the Lexus, invested in a form of intangible capital called *goodwill*. That goodwill, which may come from establishing a reputation for performance and quality over the years, is one source of the comparative advantage that keeps Lexus selling on the international market. Some economists distinguish between gains from *acquired comparative advantages* and gains from *natural comparative advantages*.

## 18.4 LEARNING OBJECTIVE

Analyze the economic effects of trade barriers.

# Trade Barriers: Tariffs, Export Subsidies, and Quotas

We have seen the capacity for specialization and trade to increases the size of the economic pie for nations. Nevertheless, most countries impose some barriers to trade principally on the grounds of protecting domestic jobs.

Trade barriers—also called *obstacles to trade*—take many forms. The three most common are tariffs, export subsidies, and quotas. All are forms of **protection** shielding some sector of the economy from foreign competition.

**protection**   The practice of shielding a sector of the economy from foreign competition.

A **tariff** is a tax on imports. The average tariff on imports into the United States is less than 5 percent. Certain protected items have much higher tariffs. For example, the United States levies tariffs of 30 percent and more on solar panels imported from China.

**tariff**   A tax on imports.

**export subsidies**   Government payments made to domestic firms to encourage exports.

**Export subsidies**—government payments made to domestic firms to encourage exports—can also act as a barrier to trade. One of the provisions of the Corn Laws that stimulated Ricardo's musings was an export subsidy automatically paid to farmers by the British government when the price of grain fell below a specified level. The subsidy served to keep domestic prices high, but it flooded the world market with cheap subsidized grain. Foreign farmers who were not subsidized were driven out of the international marketplace by the artificially low prices.

Farm subsidies remain a part of the international trade landscape today. Many countries continue to appease their farmers by heavily subsidizing exports of agricultural products. The political power of the farm lobby in many countries has had an important effect on recent international trade negotiations aimed at reducing trade barriers. The prevalence of farm subsidies in the developed world has become a major rallying point for less developed countries as they strive to compete in the global marketplace. Many African nations, in particular, have a comparative advantage in agricultural land. In producing agricultural goods for export to the world marketplace, however, they must compete with food produced on heavily subsidized farms in Europe and the United States. Countries such as France have particularly high farm subsidies, which, it argues, helps preserve the rural heritage of France. One side effect of these subsidies, however, is to make it more difficult for some of the poorer nations in the world to compete. Some have argued that if developed nations eliminated their farm subsidies, this would have a much larger effect on the economies of some African nations than is currently achieved by charitable aid programs.

**dumping**   A firm's or an industry's sale of products on the world market at prices below its own cost of production.

Closely related to subsidies is **dumping**. Dumping occurs when a firm or industry sells its products on the world market at prices lower than its cost of production. Charges of dumping are often brought by a domestic producer that believes itself to be subject to unfair competition. In the United States, claims of dumping are brought before the International Trade Commission. In 2007, for example, a small manufacturer of thermal paper charged China and Germany with dumping. In 2006, the European Union charged China with dumping shoes. In 2009, China brought a dumping charge against U.S. chicken producers. Determining whether dumping has actually occurred can be difficult. Domestic producers argue that foreign firms will dump their product in the United States, drive out U.S. competitors, and then raise prices, thus harming consumers. Foreign exporters, on the other hand, claim that their prices are low simply because

# ECONOMICS IN PRACTICE

## Globalization Improves Firm Productivity

In the text we described the way in which free trade allows countries to make the most of what they do well. Recent work in the trade area has also described the way in which free trade improves the productivity of firms within a country.[1]

Within a country we typically see firms of varying productivity. If firms were in fact all producing exactly the same product, we would expect higher-cost firms to be driven out of business. In fact, firms are often producing products that are close substitutes, but not identical. Matchbox cars are like Hot Wheels cars but not identical. Under these conditions, industries will have firms with a range of productivity levels because some people will pay a little more for the particular product a firm supplies.

What happens when trade opens up? Now competition grows. Firms with good products and low costs can expand to serve markets elsewhere. They grow and often improve their cost through scale economies while doing so. Less productive firms find themselves facing tough competition from both foreign producers and from their domestic counterparts who now look even more productive than before. Melitz and other economists have found that when we look at the distribution of firm productivity after big trade changes (like the free trade agreement between the United States and Canada in 1989) we see a big drop-off in the less productive firms.

Trade not only exploits comparative advantage of countries, but it improves the efficiency of firms more generally.

### THINKING PRACTICALLY

1. What do you expect to see happen to average prices after trade opens up?

[1] Marc Melitz at Harvard did much of the early work in this area. For a review see Marc Melitz and Daniel Trefler, "Gains from Trade when Firms Matter," *Journal of Economic Perspectives*, Spring 2012, 90–117. See also Andrew B. Bernard, Jonathan Eaton, J. Bradford Jensen and Samuel Kortum, "Plants and Productivity in International Trade," *American Economic Review*, Winter 2003, 1268–90.

---

their costs are low and that no dumping has occurred. Figuring out the costs for German thermal paper or Chinese shoes is not easy. In the case of the Chinese shoe claim, for example, the Chinese government pointed out that shoes are a labor-intensive product and that given China's low wages, it should not be a surprise that it is able to produce shoes cheaply. In other words, the Chinese claim that shoes are an example of the theory of comparative advantage at work rather than predatory dumping.

A **quota** is a limit on the quantity of imports. Quotas can be mandatory or "voluntary," and they may be legislated or negotiated with foreign governments. The best-known voluntary quota, or "voluntary restraint," was negotiated with the Japanese government in 1981. Japan agreed to reduce its automobile exports to the United States by 7.7 percent, from the 1980 level of 1.82 million units to 1.68 million units. Many quotas limit trade around the world today. Perhaps the best-known recent case is the textile quota imposed in August 2005 by the European Union (EU) on imports of textiles from China. Because China had exceeded quotas that had been agreed to earlier in the year, the EU blocked the entry of Chinese-produced textiles into Europe; as a result, more than 100 million garments piled up in European ports. In the *Economics in Practice* box on the next page we look at the effects of lifting quotas.

**quota**  A limit on the quantity of imports.

## U.S. Trade Policies, GATT, and the WTO

The United States has been a high-tariff nation, with average tariffs higher than 50 percent, for much of its history. The highest were in effect during the Great Depression following the **Smoot-Hawley tariff**, which pushed the average tariff rate to 60 percent in 1930. The Smoot-Hawley tariff set off an international trade war when U.S. trading partners retaliated with tariffs

**Smoot-Hawley tariff**  The U.S. tariff law of the 1930s, which set the highest tariffs in U.S. history (60 percent). It set off an international trade war and caused the decline in trade that is often considered one of the causes of the worldwide depression of the 1930s.

## ECONOMICS IN PRACTICE

### What Happens When We Lift a Quota?

Prior to 2005, textiles and clothing from China and much of the emerging world, heading for the United States, Canada, and the European Union, were subject to quotas. In an interesting new paper, Peter Schott from Yale and Amit Khandelwal and Shang-Jin Wei from Columbia University, investigated what happened once the quota was lifted.[1]

It should come as no surprise that lifting the quota increased the textiles and clothing exported to all three areas. A more interesting question is what happened to the composition of the firms doing the exporting after quotas were lifted. Did the same firms just send more goods, for example?

When an exporting country faces a quota on its products, someone has to decide which firms get the privilege of sending their goods abroad. Typically, governments make this decision. In some cases, governments auction off the rights to export, seeking to maximize public revenue; here we might expect that more efficient firms would be the most likely exporters because they could bid the most due to their cost advantage in selling the goods. In other cases, governments may give export rights to friends and family.

In this case, Schott et al. did not know how China had allocated the export rights or what objective it had in mind. But the results they found were instructive. After quotas were lifted in 2005, exports did increase dramatically. Moreover, most of the exports were produced not by the older firms which had dominated the quota-laden era, but by new entrants! Without quotas, firms need to be efficient to export and most of the older firms now subject to the new competition rapidly lost market share. The evidence of this paper tells

us that however China was allocating its licenses, it was not to the most efficient firms.

#### THINKING PRACTICALLY

1. If in fact the Chinese government was allocating the rights to export under a quota to the most productive firms, what would you expect to see happen once the quota is lifted?

[1] Amit Khandelwal, Peter Schott, Shang-Jin Wei, "Trade Liberalization and Embedded Institutional Reform: Evidence from Chinese Exporters," *American Economic Review*, forthcoming, 2013.

---

**General Agreement on Tariffs and Trade (GATT)**   An international agreement signed by the United States and 22 other countries in 1947 to promote the liberalization of foreign trade.

**World Trade Organization (WTO)**   A negotiating forum dealing with rules of trade across nations.

of their own. Many economists say the decline in trade that followed was one of the causes of the worldwide depression of the 1930s.[1]

In 1947, the United States, with 22 other nations, agreed to reduce barriers to trade. It also established an organization to promote liberalization of foreign trade. The **General Agreement on Tariffs and Trade (GATT)** proved to be successful in helping reduce tariff levels and encourage trade. In 1986, GATT sponsored a round of world trade talks known as the Uruguay Round that were focused on reducing trade barriers further. After much debate, the Uruguay Round was signed by the U.S. Congress in 1993 and became a model for multilateral trade agreements.

In 1995, the **World Trade Organization (WTO)** was established as a negotiating forum to deal with the rules of trade established under GATT and other agreements. It remains the key institution focused on facilitating freer trade across nations and negotiating trade disputes. The WTO consists of 153 member nations and serves as a negotiating forum for countries as they work through complexities of trade under the Uruguay Round and other agreements. At this time, the WTO is the central institution for promoting and facilitating free trade. In 2015, the WTO heard international tariff and subsidy disputes ranging from disputes between China and Indonesia on flat rolled steel, to China and the EU on poultry, to Indonesia versus the United States on paper.

---

[1] See especially Charles Kindleberger, *The World in Depression 1929–1939* (London: Allen Lane, 1973).

Although the WTO was founded to promote free trade, its member countries clearly have different incentives as they confront trade cases. In recent years, differences between developed and developing countries have come to the fore. In 2001, at a WTO meeting in Doha, Qatar, the WTO launched a new initiative, the **Doha Development Agenda**, to deal with some of the issues that intersect the areas of trade and development. In 2007, the Doha Development Agenda continued to struggle over the issue of agriculture and farm subsidies that were described in this chapter. The less-developed countries, with sub-Saharan Africa taking the lead, seek to eliminate all farm subsidies currently paid by the United States and the EU. The EU has, for its part, tried to push the less-developed countries toward better environmental policies as part of a broader free trade package. In 2015 the Doha Round talks were continuing but little progress on the central agricultural disagreements across the developed and developing worlds had been made.

The movement in the United States has been away from tariffs and quotas and toward freer trade. The Reciprocal Trade Agreements Act of 1934 authorized the president to negotiate trade agreements on behalf of the United States. As part of trade negotiations, the president can confer *most-favored-nation status* on individual trading partners. Imports from countries with most-favored-nation status are taxed at the lowest negotiated tariff rates. In addition, in recent years, several successful rounds of tariff-reduction negotiations have reduced trade barriers to their lowest levels ever. In late 2015, the U.S. Congress heavily debated the passage of the Trans Pacific Partnership, a new trade pact designed to lower tariffs among the United States and eleven Pacific rim countries.

Despite this general trend toward freer trade, most U.S. presidents in the last 50 years have made exceptions to protect one economic sector or another. Eisenhower and Kennedy restricted imports of Japanese textiles; Johnson restricted meat imports to protect Texas beef producers; Nixon restricted steel imports; Reagan restricted automobiles from Japan. In early 2002, President George W. Bush imposed a 30 percent tariff on steel imported from the EU. In 2003, the WTO ruled that these tariffs were unfair and allowed the EU to slap retaliatory tariffs on U.S. products. Shortly thereafter, the steel tariffs were rolled back, at least on EU steel. At present, the United States has high tariffs on sugar-based ethanol, an energy source competitive with corn-based ethanol, on solar panels and on tires imported from China.

## Economic Integration

**Economic integration** occurs when two or more nations join to form a free-trade zone. In 1991, the European Community (EC, or the Common Market) began forming the largest free-trade zone in the world. The economic integration process began that December, when the 12 original members (the United Kingdom, Belgium, France, Germany, Italy, the Netherlands, Luxembourg, Denmark, Greece, Ireland, Spain, and Portugal) signed the Maastricht Treaty. The treaty called for the end of border controls, a common currency, an end to all tariffs, and the coordination of monetary and political affairs. The **European Union (EU)**, as the EC is now called, has 28 members (for a list, see the Summary, p. 352). On January 1, 1993, all tariffs and trade barriers were dropped among the member countries. Border checkpoints were closed in early 1995. Citizens can now travel among member countries without passports.

The United States is not a part of the EU. However, in 1988, the United States (under President Reagan) and Canada (under Prime Minister Mulroney) signed the **U.S.-Canadian Free Trade Agreement**, which removed all barriers to trade, including tariffs and quotas, between the two countries by 1998.

During the last days of the George H. W. Bush administration in 1992, the United States, Mexico, and Canada signed the **North American Free Trade Agreement (NAFTA)**, with the three countries agreeing to establish all of North America as a free-trade zone. The agreement eliminated all tariffs over a 10- to 15-year period and removed restrictions on most investments. During the presidential campaign of 1992, NAFTA was hotly debated. Both Bill Clinton and George Bush supported the agreement. Industrial labor unions that might be affected by increased imports from Mexico (such as those in the automobile industry) opposed the agreement, while industries whose exports to Mexico might increase as a result of the agreement—for example, the machine tool industry—supported it. Another concern was that Mexican companies were not subject to the same environmental regulations as U.S. firms, so U.S. firms might move to Mexico for this reason.

NAFTA was ratified by the U.S. Congress in late 1993 and went into effect on the first day of 1994. The U.S. Department of Commerce estimated that as a result of NAFTA, trade between the United States and Mexico increased by nearly $16 billion in 1994. In addition, exports from the United States to Mexico outpaced imports from Mexico during 1994. In 1995, however, the

**Doha Development Agenda** An initiative of the World Trade Organization focused on issues of trade and development.

**economic integration** Occurs when two or more nations join to form a free-trade zone.

**European Union (EU)** The European trading bloc composed of 28 countries (of the 28 countries in the EU, 17 have the same currency—the euro).

**U.S.-Canadian Free Trade Agreement** An agreement in which the United States and Canada agreed to eliminate all barriers to trade between the two countries by 1998.

**North American Free Trade Agreement (NAFTA)** An agreement signed by the United States, Mexico, and Canada in which the three countries agreed to establish all North America as a free-trade zone.

agreement fell under the shadow of a dramatic collapse of the value of the peso. U.S. exports to Mexico dropped sharply, and the United States shifted from a trade surplus to a large trade deficit with Mexico. Aside from a handful of tariffs, however, all of NAFTA's commitments were fully implemented by 2003, and an 8-year report signed by all three countries declared the pact a success. The report concludes, "Eight years of expanded trade, increased employment and investment, and enhanced opportunity for the citizens of all three countries have demonstrated that NAFTA works and will continue to work." From 1993–2011 trade among NAFTA countries more than tripled from $288 billion to $1 trillion.

**18.5 LEARNING** OBJECTIVE

Evaluate the arguments over free trade and protectionism.

# Free Trade or Protection?

One of the great economic debates of all time revolves around the free-trade-versus-protection controversy. We briefly summarize the arguments in favor of each.

## The Case for Free Trade

In one sense, the theory of comparative advantage *is* the case for free trade. Trade has potential benefits for all nations. A good is not imported unless its net price to buyers is below the net price of the domestically produced alternative. When the Brazilians in our example found U.S. timber less expensive than their own, they bought it, yet they continued to pay the same price for homemade steel. Americans bought less expensive Brazilian steel, but they continued to buy domestic timber at the same lower price. Under these conditions, *both Americans and Brazilians ended up paying less and consuming more.*

At the same time, resources (including labor) move out of steel production and into timber production in the United States. In Brazil, resources (including labor) move out of timber production and into steel production. The resources in both countries are used more efficiently. Tariffs, export subsidies, and quotas, which interfere with the free movement of goods and services around the world, reduce or eliminate the gains of comparative advantage.

We can use supply and demand curves to illustrate this. Suppose Figure 18.4 shows domestic supply and demand for textiles. In the absence of trade, the market clears at a price of $4.20. At equilibrium, 450 million yards of textiles are produced and consumed.

Assume now that textiles are available at a world price of $2. This is the price in dollars that Americans must pay for textiles from foreign sources. If we assume that an unlimited quantity of textiles is available at $2 and there is no difference in quality between domestic and foreign textiles, no domestic producer will be able to charge more than $2. In the absence of trade barriers, the world price sets the price in the United States. As the price in the United States falls from $4.20 to $2.00, the quantity demanded by consumers increases from 450 million yards to 700 million yards, but the quantity supplied by domestic producers drops from 450 million yards to 200 million yards. The difference, 500 million yards, is the quantity of textiles imported.

The argument for free trade is that each country should specialize in producing the goods and services in which it enjoys a comparative advantage. If foreign producers can produce textiles at a much lower price than domestic producers, they have a comparative advantage. As the world price of textiles falls to $2, domestic (U.S.) quantity supplied drops and resources are transferred to other sectors. These other sectors, which may be export industries or domestic industries, are not shown in Figure 18.4a. It is clear that the allocation of resources is more efficient at a price of $2. Why should the United States use domestic resources to produce what foreign producers can produce at a lower cost? U.S. resources should move into the production of the things it produces best.

Now consider what happens to the domestic price of textiles when a trade barrier is imposed. Figure 18.4b shows the effect of a set tariff of $1 per yard imposed on imported textiles. The tariff raises the domestic price of textiles to $2 + $1 = $3. The result is that some of the gains from trade are lost. First, consumers are forced to pay a higher price for the same good. The quantity of textiles demanded drops from 700 million yards under free trade to 600 million yards because some consumers are not willing to pay the higher price. Notice in Figure 18.4b the triangle labeled ABC. This is the deadweight loss or excess burden resulting from the tariff.

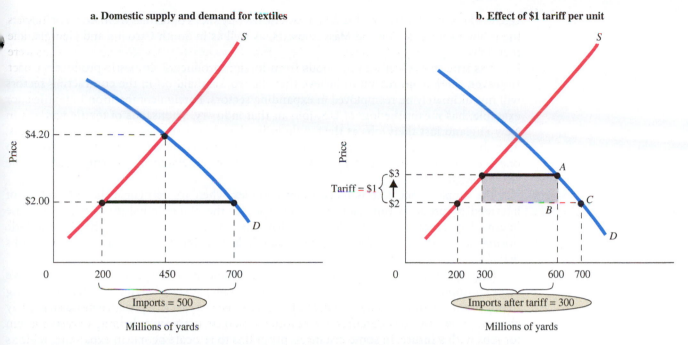

▲ **FIGURE 18.4   The Gains from Trade and Losses from the Imposition of a Tariff**
A tariff of $1 increases the market price facing consumers from $2 per yard to $3 per yard. The government collects revenues equal to the gray shaded area in **b**. The loss of efficiency has two components. First, consumers must pay a higher price for goods that could be produced at lower cost. Second, marginal producers are drawn into textiles and away from other goods, resulting in inefficient domestic production. The triangle labeled ABC in **b** is the deadweight loss or excess burden resulting from the tariff.

Absent the tariff, these 100 added units of textiles would have generated benefits in excess of the $2 that each one cost.

At the same time, the higher price of textiles draws some marginal domestic producers who could not make a profit at $2 into textile production. (Recall that domestic producers do not pay a tariff.) As the price rises to $3, the quantity supplied by domestic producers rises from 200 million yards to 300 million yards. The result is a decrease in imports from 500 million yards to 300 million yards.

Finally, the imposition of the tariff means that the government collects revenue equal to the shaded area in Figure 18.4b. This shaded area is equal to the tariff rate per unit ($1) times the number of units imported after the tariff is in place (300 million yards). Thus, receipts from the tariff are $300 million.

What is the final result of the tariff? Domestic producers receiving revenues of only $2 per unit before the tariff was imposed now receive a higher price and earn higher profits. However, these higher profits are achieved at a loss of efficiency. Trade barriers prevent a nation from reaping the benefits of specialization, push it to adopt relatively inefficient production techniques, and force consumers to pay higher prices for protected products than they would otherwise pay.

## The Case for Protection

A case can also be made in favor of tariffs and quotas. Over the course of U.S. history, protectionist arguments have been made so many times by so many industries before so many congressional committees that it seems all pleas for protection share the same themes. We describe the most frequently heard pleas next.

**Protection Saves Jobs**   The main argument for protection is that foreign competition costs Americans their jobs. When Americans buy imported Toyotas, U.S.-produced cars go unsold. Layoffs in the domestic auto industry follow. When Americans buy Chinese textiles,

U.S. workers may lose their jobs. When Americans buy shoes or textiles from Korea or Taiwan, the millworkers in Maine and Massachusetts, as well as in South Carolina and Georgia, lose their jobs.

It is true that when we buy goods from foreign producers, domestic producers suffer. However, there is no reason to believe that the workers laid off in the contracting sectors will not ultimately be reemployed in expanding sectors. Foreign competition in textiles, for example, has meant the loss of U.S. jobs in that industry. Thousands of textile workers in New England lost their jobs as the textile mills closed over the last 40 years. Nevertheless, with the expansion of high-tech industries, the unemployment rate in Massachusetts fell to one of the lowest in the country in the mid-1980s, and New Hampshire, Vermont, and Maine also boomed.

The employment case is made more complex when we recognize that protection of intermediate products can result in higher costs for the domestic industries who use those intermediate products, thus making those firms less competitive. Protecting the U.S. domestic tire industry raises the costs of the domestic auto industry, potentially costing the economy jobs in that sector.

Employment problems coming from open trade can be handled in several ways. We can ban imports and give up the gains from free trade, acknowledging that we are willing to pay premium prices to save domestic jobs in industries that can produce more efficiently abroad, or we can aid the victims of free trade in a constructive way, helping to retrain them for jobs with a future. In some instances, programs to relocate people in expanding regions may be in order. Some programs deal directly with the transition without forgoing the gains from trade.

### Some Countries Engage in Unfair Trade Practices

Attempts by U.S. firms to monopolize an industry are illegal under the Sherman and Clayton acts. If a strong company decides to drive the competition out of the market by setting prices below cost, it would be aggressively prosecuted by the Antitrust Division of the Justice Department. However, the argument goes, if we will not allow a U.S. firm to engage in predatory pricing or monopolize an industry or a market, can we stand by and let a German firm or a Japanese firm do so in the name of free trade? This is a legitimate argument and one that has gained significant favor in recent years. How should we respond when a large international company or a country behaves strategically against a domestic firm or industry? Free trade may be the best solution when everybody plays by the rules, but sometimes we have to fight back. The WTO is the vehicle currently used to negotiate disputes of this sort.

### Cheap Foreign Labor Makes Competition Unfair

Let us say that a particular country gained its "comparative advantage" in textiles by paying its workers low wages. How can U.S. textile companies compete with companies that pay wages that are less than a quarter of what U.S. companies pay? Questions like this are often asked by those concerned with competition from China and India.

First, remember that wages in a competitive economy reflect productivity: a high ratio of output to units of labor. Workers in the United States earn higher wages because they are more productive. The United States has more capital per worker; that is, the average worker works with better machinery and equipment and its workers are better trained. Second, trade flows not according to *absolute* advantage, but according to *comparative* advantage: All countries benefit, even if one country is more efficient at producing everything.

### Protection Safeguards National Security

Beyond saving jobs, certain sectors of the economy may appeal for protection for other reasons. The steel industry has argued for years with some success that it is vital to national defense. In the event of a war, the United States would not want to depend on foreign countries for a product as vital as steel. Even if we acknowledge another country's comparative advantage, we may want to protect our own resources.

Virtually no industry has ever asked for protection without invoking the national defense argument. Testimony that was once given on behalf of the scissors and shears industry argued that "in the event of a national emergency and imports cutoff, the United States would be

# ECONOMICS IN PRACTICE

## A Petition

Although most economists argue in favor of free trade, it is important to recognize that some groups are likely to lose from freer trade. Arguments by the losing groups against trade have been around for hundreds of years. In the following article, you will find an essay by a French satirist of the nineteenth century, Frederic Bastiat, complaining about the unfair competition that the sun provides to candle makers. You see that the author proposes a quota, as opposed to a tariff, on the sun.

From the Manufacturers of Candles, Tapers, Lanterns, Sticks, Street Lamps, Snuffers, and Extinguishers, and from Producers of Tallow, Oil, Resin, Alcohol, and Generally of Everything Connected with Lighting.

To the Honourable Members of the Chamber of Deputies.

Gentlemen:

You are on the right track. You reject abstract theories and [have] little regard for abundance and low prices. You concern yourselves mainly with the fate of the producer. You wish to free him from foreign competition, that is, to reserve the *domestic market* for *domestic industry*.

We come to offer you a wonderful opportunity for your—what shall we call it? Your theory? No, nothing is more deceptive than theory. Your doctrine? Your system? Your principle? But you dislike doctrines, you have a horror of systems, as for principles, you deny that there are any in political economy; therefore we shall call it your practice —your practice without theory and without principle.

We are suffering from the ruinous competition of a rival who apparently works under conditions so far superior to our own for the production of light that he is *flooding* the *domestic market* with it at an incredibly low price; for the moment he appears, our sales cease, all the consumers turn to him, and a branch of French industry whose ramifications are innumerable is all at once reduced to complete stagnation. This rival, which is none other than the sun, is waging war on us so

Screening out the sun would increase the demand for candles. Should candlemakers be protected from unfair competition?

mercilessly we suspect he is being stirred up against us by perfidious Albion (excellent diplomacy nowadays!), particularly because he has for that haughty island a respect that he does not show for us. [A reference to Britain's reputation as a foggy island.]

We ask you to be so good as to pass a law requiring the closing of all windows, dormers, skylights, inside and outside shutters, curtains, casements, bull's-eyes, deadlights, and blinds—in short, all openings, holes, chinks, and fissures through which the light of the sun is wont to enter houses, to the detriment of the fair industries with which, we are proud to say, we have endowed the country, a country that cannot, without betraying ingratitude, abandon us today to so unequal a combat.

### THINKING PRACTICALLY

1. Using supply-and-demand curves, show the effect of screening out the sun on the price of candles.

*Source:* An Open Letter to the French Parliament by Frederic Bastiat (1801–1850), originally published in 1845.

without a source of scissors and shears, basic tools for many industries and trades essential to our national defense." The question lies not in the merit of the argument, but in just how seriously it can be taken if *every* industry uses it.

**Protection Discourages Dependency**   Closely related to the national defense argument is the claim that countries, particularly small or developing countries, may come to rely too heavily on one or more trading partners for many items. If a small country comes to rely on a major power for food or energy or some important raw material in which the large nation has a comparative advantage, it may be difficult for the smaller nation to remain politically neutral.

Some critics of free trade argue that larger countries, such as the United States, Russia, and China have consciously engaged in trade with smaller countries to create these kinds of dependencies.

Therefore, should small, independent countries consciously avoid trading relationships that might lead to political dependence? This objective may involve developing domestic industries in areas where a country has a comparative disadvantage. To do so would mean protecting that industry from international competition.

**Environmental Concerns**    In recent years, concern about the environment has led some people to question advantages of free trade. Some environmental groups, for example, argue that the WTO's free trade policies may harm the environment. The central argument is that poor countries will become havens for polluting industries that will operate their steel and auto factories with few environmental controls. The absence of environmental controls gives firms in these countries, it is argued, a phantom advantage.

These issues are quite complex, and there is much dispute among economists about the interaction between free trade and the environment. One relatively recent study of sulphur dioxide, for example, found that in the long run, free trade reduces pollution, largely by increasing the income of countries; richer countries typically choose policies to improve the environment.[2] Thus, although free trade and increased development initially may cause pollution levels to rise, in the long run, prosperity is a benefit to the environment. Many also argue that there are complex trade-offs to be made between pollution control and problems such as malnutrition and health for poor countries. The United States and Europe both traded off faster economic growth and income against cleaner air and water at earlier times in their development. Some argue that it is unfair for the developed countries to impose their preferences on other countries facing more difficult trade-offs.

Nevertheless, the concern with global climate change has stimulated new thinking in this area. A study by the Tyndall Centre for Climate Change Research in Britain found that in 2004, 23 percent of the greenhouse gas emissions produced by China were created in the production of exports. In other words, these emissions come not as a result of goods that China's population is enjoying as its income rises, but as a consequence of the consumption of the United States and Europe, where most of these goods are going. In a world in which the effects of carbon emissions are global and all countries are not willing to sign binding global agreements to control emissions, trade with China may be a way for developed nations to avoid their commitments to pollution reduction. Some have argued that penalties could be imposed on high-polluting products produced in countries that have not signed international climate control treaties as a way to ensure that the prices of goods imported this way reflect the harm that those products cause the environment.[3] Implementing these policies is, however, likely to be complex, and some have argued that it is a mistake to bundle trade and environmental issues. As with other areas covered in this book, there is still disagreement among economists as to the right answer.

**Protection Safeguards Infant Industries**    Young industries in a given country may have a difficult time competing with established industries in other countries. In a dynamic world, a protected **infant industry** might mature into a strong industry worldwide because of an acquired, but real, comparative advantage. If such an industry is undercut and driven out of world markets at the beginning of its life, that comparative advantage might never develop.

Yet efforts to protect infant industries can backfire. In July 1991, the U.S. government imposed a 62.67 percent tariff on imports of active-matrix liquid crystal display screens (also referred to as "flat-panel displays" used primarily for laptop computers) from Japan. The Commerce Department and the International Trade Commission agreed that Japanese producers were selling their screens in the U.S. market at a price below cost and that this dumping

**infant industry**   A young industry that may need temporary protection from competition from the established industries of other countries to develop an acquired comparative advantage.

---

[2] Werner Antweiler, Brian Copeland, and M. Scott Taylor, "Is Free Trade Good for the Environment?" *American Economic Review,* September, 2001.
[3] Judith Chevalier, "A Carbon Cap That Starts in Washington," *New York Times,* December 16, 2007.

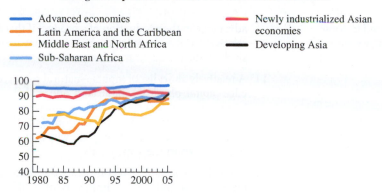

Changes in Openness to Trade over Time across the World

*Source:* International Monetary Fund, *2007 World Economic Outlook.*
Trade openness is measured as 100 minus the average effective tariff rate in the region.

▲ **FIGURE 18.5**   **Trade Openness across the World (Index is 100 minus the average effective tariff rate in the region.)**
The case for free trade has been made across the world as increasing numbers of countries have joined the world marketplace. This Figure traces the path of tariffs across the world from 1980 to 2005. The lines show an index of trade openness, calculated as 100 minus the tariff rate. (So higher numbers mean lower tariffs.) We see rapid reductions in the last 25 years across the world, most notably in countries in the emerging and developing markets.

threatened the survival of domestic laptop screen producers. The tariff was meant to protect the infant U.S. industry until it could compete head-on with the Japanese.

Unfortunately for U.S. producers of laptop computers and for consumers who purchase them, the tariff had an unintended (although predictable) effect on the industry. Because U.S. laptop screens were generally recognized to be of lower quality than their Japanese counterparts, imposition of the tariff left U.S. computer manufacturers with three options: (1) They could use the screens available from U.S. producers and watch sales of their final product decline in the face of *higher-quality* competition from abroad, (2) they could pay the tariff for the higher-quality screens and watch sales of their final product decline in the face of *lower-priced* competition from abroad, or (3) they could do what was most profitable for them to do—move their production facilities abroad to avoid the tariff completely. The last option is what Apple and IBM did. In the end, not only were the laptop industry and its consumers hurt by the imposition of the tariff (due to higher costs of production and to higher laptop computer prices), but the U.S. screen industry was hurt as well (due to its loss of buyers for its product) by a policy specifically designed to help it.

# An Economic Consensus

Critical to our study of international economics is the debate between free traders and protectionists. On one side is the theory of comparative advantage, formalized by David Ricardo in the early part of the nineteenth century. According to this view, all countries benefit from specialization and trade. The gains from trade are real, and they can be large; free international trade raises real incomes and improves the standard of living.

On the other side are the protectionists, who point to the loss of jobs and argue for the protection of workers from foreign competition. Although foreign competition can cause job loss in specific sectors, it is unlikely to cause net job loss in an economy and workers will, over time, be absorbed into expanding sectors. Foreign trade and full employment can be pursued simultaneously. Although economists disagree about many things, the vast majority of them favor free trade.

**18.6 LEARNING** OBJECTIVE

Outline how international trade fits into the structure of the economy.

# SUMMARY

1. All economies, regardless of their size, depend to some extent on other economies and are affected by events outside their borders.

## 18.1 TRADE SURPLUSES AND DEFICITS   *p. 333*

2. Until the 1970s, the United States generally exported more than it imported—it ran a *trade surplus*. In the mid-1970s, the United States began to import more merchandise than it exported—a *trade deficit*.

## 18.2 THE ECONOMIC BASIS FOR TRADE: COMPARATIVE ADVANTAGE   *p. 333*

3. The *theory of comparative advantage*, dating to David Ricardo in the nineteenth century, holds that specialization and free trade will benefit all trading partners, even those that may be absolutely less efficient producers.

4. A country enjoys an *absolute advantage* over another country in the production of a product if it uses fewer resources to produce that product than the other country does. A country has a *comparative advantage* in the production of a product if that product can be produced at a lower opportunity cost in terms of other goods foregone.

5. Trade enables countries to move beyond their previous resource and productivity constraints. When countries specialize in producing those goods in which they have a comparative advantage, they maximize their combined output and allocate their resources more efficiently.

6. When trade is free, patterns of trade and trade flows result from the independent decisions of thousands of importers and exporters and millions of private households and firms.

7. The relative attractiveness of foreign goods to U.S. buyers and of U.S. goods to foreign buyers depends in part on *exchange rates*, the ratios at which two currencies are traded for each other.

8. For any pair of countries, there is a range of exchange rates that will lead automatically to both countries realizing the gains from specialization and comparative advantage. Within that range, the exchange rate will determine which country gains the most from trade. This leads us to conclude that exchange rates determine the terms of trade.

9. If exchange rates end up in the right range (that is, in a range that facilitates the flow of goods between nations), the free market will drive each country to shift resources into those sectors in which it enjoys a comparative advantage. Only those products in which a country has a comparative advantage will be competitive in world markets.

## 18.3 THE SOURCES OF COMPARATIVE ADVANTAGE   *p. 341*

10. The *Heckscher-Ohlin theorem* looks to relative *factor endowments* to explain comparative advantage and trade flows. According to the theorem, a country has a comparative advantage in the production of a product if that country is relatively well endowed with the inputs that are used intensively in the production of that product.

11. A relatively short list of inputs—natural resources, knowledge capital, physical capital, land, and skilled and unskilled labor—explains a surprisingly large portion of world trade patterns. However, the simple version of the theory of comparative advantage cannot explain why many countries import and export the same goods.

12. Some theories argue that comparative advantage can be acquired. Just as industries within a country differentiate their products to capture a domestic market, they also differentiate their products to please the wide variety of tastes that exists worldwide. This theory is consistent with the theory of comparative advantage.

## 18.4 TRADE BARRIERS: TARIFFS, EXPORT SUBSIDIES, AND QUOTAS   *p. 342*

13. Trade barriers take many forms. The three most common are *tariffs, export subsidies*, and *quotas*. All are forms of *protection* through which some sector of the economy is shielded from foreign competition.

14. Although the United States has historically been a high-tariff nation, the general movement is now away from tariffs and quotas. The *General Agreement on Tariffs and Trade (GATT)*, signed by the United States and 22 other countries in 1947, continues in effect today; its purpose is to reduce barriers to world trade and keep them down. Also important are the *U.S.-Canadian Free Trade Agreement*, signed in 1988, and the *North American Free Trade Agreement*, signed by the United States, Mexico, and Canada in the last days of the George H. W. Bush administration in 1992, taking effect in 1994.

15. The World Trade Organization (WTO) was set up by GATT to act as a negotiating forum for trade disputes across countries.

16. The *European Union (EU)* is a free-trade bloc composed of 28 nations: Austria, Belgium, Bulgaria, Croatia, Cyprus, the Czech Republic, Denmark, Estonia, Finland, France, Germany, Greece, Hungary, Ireland, Italy, Latvia, Lithuania, Luxembourg, Malta, the Netherlands, Poland, Portugal, Romania, Slovakia, Slovenia, Spain, Sweden, and the United Kingdom. Many economists believe that the advantages of free trade within the bloc, a reunited Germany, and the ability to work well as a bloc will make the EU the most powerful player in the international marketplace in the coming decades.

## 18.5 FREE TRADE OR PROTECTION?   *p. 346*

17. In one sense, the theory of comparative advantage is the case for free trade. Trade barriers prevent a nation from reaping the benefits of specialization, push it to adopt relatively inefficient production techniques, and force consumers to pay higher prices for protected products than they would otherwise pay.

**18.** The case for protection rests on a number of propositions, one of which is that foreign competition results in a loss of domestic jobs, but there is no reason to believe that the workers laid off in the contracting sectors will not be ultimately reemployed in other expanding sectors. This adjustment process is far from costless, however.

**19.** Other arguments for protection hold that cheap foreign labor makes competition unfair; that some countries engage in unfair trade practices; that free trade might harm the environment; and that protection safeguards the national security, discourages dependency, and shields *infant industries*. Despite these arguments, most economists favor free trade.

# REVIEW TERMS AND CONCEPTS

absolute advantage, *p. 333*

comparative advantage, *p. 334*

Corn Laws, *p. 333*

Doha Development Agenda, *p. 345*

dumping, *p. 342*

economic integration, *p. 345*

European Union (EU), *p. 345*

exchange rate, *p. 339*

export subsidies, *p. 342*

factor endowments, *p. 341*

General Agreement on Tariffs and Trade (GATT), *p. 344*

Heckscher-Ohlin theorem, *p. 341*

infant industry, *p. 350*

North American Free Trade Agreement (NAFTA), *p. 345*

protection, *p. 342*

quota, *p. 343*

Smoot-Hawley tariff, *p. 343*

tariff, *p. 342*

terms of trade, *p. 338*

theory of comparative advantage, *p. 333*

trade deficit, *p. 333*

trade surplus, *p. 333*

U.S.-Canadian Free Trade Agreement, *p. 345*

World Trade Organization (WTO), *p. 344*

# PROBLEMS

All problems are available on MyEconLab.

## 18.1 TRADE SURPLUSES AND DEFICITS

LEARNING OBJECTIVE: How are trade surpluses and trade deficits defined?

**1.1** In terms of value of imports and exports, the top five trading partners for the United States are Canada, China, Mexico, Japan, and Germany. Go to www.bea.gov and search for "U.S. Trade in Goods and Services by Selected Countries and Areas." Find the total value of exports, imports, and the balance of trade with each of these countries for the most recent year. For which of these countries is the United States running a trade surplus? trade deficit? Do an Internet search and find some of the main goods and services the United States imports from and exports to these five countries. Are you surprised by any of the goods or services that you found? Why or why not?

## 18.2 THE ECONOMIC BASIS FOR TRADE: COMPARATIVE ADVANTAGE

LEARNING OBJECTIVE: Explain how international trade emerges from the theory of comparative advantage and what determines the terms of trade.

**2.1** Suppose Latvia and Estonia each produce only two goods, tractors and bobsleds. Both are produced using labor alone. Assuming both countries are at full employment, you are given the following information:

| | |
|---|---|
| Latvia: | 12 units of labor required to produce 1 tractor |
| | 4 units of labor required to produce 1 bobsled |
| | Total labor force: 900,000 units |
| Estonia: | 16 units of labor required to produce 1 tractor |
| | 8 units of labor required to produce 1 bobsled |
| | Total labor force: 600,000 units |

**a.** Draw the production possibility frontiers for each country in the absence of trade.

**b.** If transportation costs are ignored and trade is allowed, will Latvia and Estonia engage in trade? Explain.

**c.** If a trade agreement is negotiated, at what rate (number of tractors per bobsled) would they agree to exchange?

**2.2** The United States and Brazil each produce only cheese and wine. Domestic prices are given in the following table:

| | | Brazil | United States |
|---|---|---|---|
| Cheese | Per pound | 4 BRL | $ 6 |
| Wine | Per bottle | 7 BRL | $ 9 |

On April 1, the London exchange listed an exchange rate of $1 = 1BRL.

**a.** Which country has an absolute advantage in the production of cheese? wine?

**b.** Which country has a comparative advantage in the production of cheese? wine?

**c.** If the United States and Brazil were the only two countries engaging in trade, what adjustments would you predict assuming exchange rates are freely determined by the laws of supply and demand?

**2.3** The following table gives recent figures for yield per acre in Illinois and Kansas:

|          | Wheat | Soybeans |
|----------|-------|----------|
| Illinois | 48    | 39       |
| Kansas   | 40    | 24       |

*Source:* U.S. Department of Agriculture, *Crop Production.*

a. If we assume that farmers in Illinois and Kansas use the same amount of labor, capital, and fertilizer, which state has an absolute advantage in wheat production? soybean production?

b. If we transfer land out of wheat into soybeans, how many bushels of wheat do we give up in Illinois per additional bushel of soybeans produced? in Kansas?

c. Which state has a comparative advantage in wheat production? in soybean production?

d. The following table gives the distribution of land planted for each state in millions of acres in the same year.

|          | Total Acres Under Till | Wheat          | Soybeans       |
|----------|------------------------|----------------|----------------|
| Illinois | 22.9                   | 1.9 (8.3%)     | 9.1 (39.7%)    |
| Kansas   | 20.7                   | 11.8 (57.0%)   | 1.9 (9.2%)     |

Are these data consistent with your answer to part c? Explain.

**2.4** Great Britain and the United States produce cheddar cheese and blue cheese. Current domestic prices per pound for each type of cheese are given in the following table:

|                | Great Britain | United States |
|----------------|---------------|---------------|
| Cheddar cheese | £3            | $6            |
| Blue cheese    | £6            | $9            |

Suppose the exchange rate is £1 = $1.

a. If the price ratios within each country reflect resource use, which country has a comparative advantage in the production of cheddar cheese? blue cheese?

b. Assume that there are no other trading partners and that the only motive for holding foreign currency is to buy foreign goods. Will the current exchange rate lead to trade flows in both directions between the two countries? Explain.

c. What adjustments might you expect in the exchange rate? Be specific.

d. What would you predict about trade flows between Great Britain and the United States after the exchange rate has adjusted?

**2.5** The nation of Pixley has an absolute advantage in everything it produces compared to the nation of Hooterville. Could these two nations still benefit by trading with each other? Explain.

**2.6** Evaluate the following statement: If lower exchange rates increase a nation's exports, the government should do everything in its power to ensure that the exchange rate for its currency is as low as possible.

## 18.3 THE SOURCES OF COMPARATIVE ADVANTAGE

**LEARNING OBJECTIVE:** Describe the sources of comparative advantage.

**3.1** The following table shows imports and exports of goods during 2013 for the United States:

|                                   | Exports | Imports |
|-----------------------------------|---------|---------|
| Total                             | 1,592.0 | 2,294.6 |
| Civilian aircraft                 | 53.7    | 14.1    |
| Apparel, household goods—textile  | 6.9     | 93.7    |
| Crude oil                         | 4.9     | 272.8   |
| Vehicles, parts, and engines      | 152.6   | 308.8   |
| Foods, feeds, and beverages       | 136.2   | 115.1   |

All figures are rounded to the nearest billion dollars.
*Source:* www.census.gov.

What, if anything, can you conclude about the comparative advantage that the United States has relative to its trading partners in the production of goods? What stories can you tell about the wide disparities in apparel and aircraft?

**3.2** You can think of the United States as a set of 50 separate economies with no trade barriers. In such an open environment, each state specializes in the products that it produces best.

a. What product or products does your state specialize in?

b. Can you identify the source of the comparative advantage that lies behind the production of one or more of these products (for example, a natural resource, plentiful cheap labor, or a skilled labor force)?

c. Do you think that the theory of comparative advantage and the Heckscher-Ohlin theorem help to explain why your state specializes the way that it does? Explain your answer.

**3.3** Some empirical trade economists have noted that for many products, countries are both importers and exporters. For example, the United States both imports and exports shirts. How do you explain this?

## 18.4 TRADE BARRIERS: TARIFFS, EXPORT SUBSIDIES, AND QUOTAS

**LEARNING OBJECTIVE:** Analyze the economic effects of trade barriers.

**4.1** [**Related to the *Economics in Practice* on p. 343**] As is stated in the text, NAFTA was ratified by the U.S. Congress in 1993 and went into effect on January 1, 1994, and aside from a few tariffs, all of NAFTA's commitments were fully implemented by 2003. Go to http://www.usa.gov and do a search for "NAFTA: A Decade of Success" to find a document from the Office of the United States Trade Representative which details the benefits of this free-trade agreement between the United States, Canada, and Mexico.

Describe what happened to the following in the NAFTA countries by 2003, when NAFTA's commitments were fully implemented: economic growth, exports, total trade volume, and productivity. Now conduct a Web search to find any disadvantages of NAFTA and see how they relate to the arguments for protectionism in the text. Explain whether you believe any of these disadvantages outweigh the benefits you described regarding economic growth, exports, trade volume, and productivity.

4.2 The following graph represents the domestic supply and demand for coal.

   **a.** In the absence of trade, what is the equilibrium price and equilibrium quantity?

   **b.** The government opens the market to free trade, and Indonesia enters the market, pricing coal at $40 per ton. What will happen to the domestic price of coal? What will be the new domestic quantity supplied and domestic quantity demanded? How much coal will be imported from Indonesia?

   **c.** After numerous complaints from domestic coal producers, the government imposes a $10 per ton tariff on all imported coal. What will happen to the domestic price of coal? What will be the new domestic quantity supplied and domestic quantity demanded? How much coal will now be imported from Indonesia?

   **d.** How much revenue will the government receive from the $10 per ton tariff?

   **e.** Who ultimately ends up paying the $10 per ton tariff? Why?

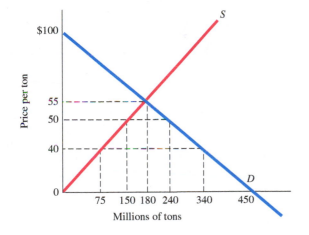

4.3 Refer to the previous problem. Assume the market is opened to trade and Indonesia still enters the market by pricing coal at $40 per ton. But as a response to complaints from domestic coal producers, instead of imposing a $10 per ton tariff, the government imposes an import quota of 90 million tons on Indonesian coal. How will the results of the quota differ from the results of the tariff?

4.4 [**Related to the *Economics in Practice* on p. 344**] In 2015, the United States and Cuba re-established diplomatic relations, reopening embassies in each other's capitals for the first time since 1961. Since the early 1960s, the United States has had an embargo in place on Cuba, virtually eliminating all trade between the two countries. With diplomatic relations restored, the Cuban government is seeking an end to this embargo and is urging the U.S. government to resume trade between the two countries. Suppose the United States decided to lift the embargo on exports to Cuba while maintaining the embargo on Cuban imports. Explain whether this one-sided change would benefit neither country, just one country, or both countries?

## 18.5 FREE TRADE OR PROTECTION?

**LEARNING OBJECTIVE:** Evaluate the arguments over free trade and protectionism.

5.1 [**Related to the *Economics in Practice* on p. 349**] When a president presents a trade agreement for ratification to Congress, many domestic industries fight the ratification. In 2005, the United States was negotiating the Central America-Dominican Republic Free Trade Agreement (CAFTA-DR). Write a brief essay on the U.S. political opposition to CAFTA-DR in 2004 and 2005. What industries in the United States opposed the trade agreement? Is it fair to compare the arguments of these industries to the arguments posed by the candle makers?

# 19 Open-Economy Macroeconomics: The Balance of Payments and Exchange Rates

The growth of international trade has made the economies of the world increasingly interdependent. U.S. imports now account for about 17 percent of U.S. gross domestic product (GDP), and billions of dollars flow through the international capital market each day. In the previous chapter we explored the gains that come to countries from trade, as they exploit comparative advantage and gain access to new goods. But the ubiquity of this trade also means that economic problems in one part of the world can often be felt by their trading partners elsewhere. In this chapter we explore the ways in which the openness of the economy affects macroeconomic policy making.

From a macroeconomic point of view, the main difference between an international transaction and a domestic transaction concerns currency exchange. When people in countries with different currencies buy from and sell to each other, an exchange of currencies must also take place. Brazilian coffee exporters cannot spend U.S. dollars in Brazil; they need Brazilian reals. A U.S. wheat exporter cannot use Brazilian reals to buy a tractor from a U.S. company or to pay the rent on warehouse facilities. Somehow international exchange must be managed in a way that allows both partners in the transaction to wind up with their own currency.

The amount of trade between two countries depends on the **exchange rate**—the price of one country's currency in terms of the other country's currency. If the Japanese yen were expensive (making the dollar cheap), both Japanese and Americans would buy from U.S. producers. If the yen were cheap (making the U.S. dollar expensive), both Japanese and Americans would buy from Japanese producers. Within a certain range of exchange rates, trade flows in both directions, each country specializes in producing the goods in which it enjoys a comparative advantage, and trade is mutually beneficial.

Because exchange rates are a factor in determining the flow of international trade, the way they are determined is important. A discussion of the various exchange rate systems that have been in place since 1900 is provided in the appendix to this chapter. Since 1900, the world monetary system has been changed several times by international agreements and events. In the early part of the twentieth century, nearly all currencies were backed by gold. Their values were fixed in terms of a specific number of ounces of gold, which determined their values in international trading—exchange rates.

In 1944, with the international monetary system in chaos as the end of World War II drew near, a large group of experts unofficially representing 44 countries met in Bretton Woods, New Hampshire, and drew up a number of agreements. One of those agreements established a system of essentially fixed exchange rates under which each country agreed to intervene by buying and selling currencies in the foreign exchange market when necessary to maintain the agreed-to value of its currency.

In 1971, most countries, including the United States, began to allow exchange rates to be flexible, determined essentially by supply and demand. Although there are considerable intricacies in the way flexible exchange rates operate, the logic is straightforward. If British goods are popular with U.S. consumers, there will be a large demand for British pounds by the U.S. customers for those goods. If the British don't like U.S. goods, few will demand U.S. dollars to buy those goods. Without government intervention in the marketplace, the price of British pounds in dollars would rise in this situation as those who want to exchange dollars for pounds (those who "demand" pounds) exceed those who want to exchange pounds for dollars (those who "supply" pounds). The exchange rate market thus reflects the markets for real goods in the various economies. We will look more carefully at this connection later in this chapter.

We begin our discussion of open-economy macroeconomics by looking at the *balance of payments*—the record of a nation's transactions with the rest of the world. We then go on to consider how our model of the macroeconomy changes when we allow for the international exchange of goods, services, and capital.

**exchange rate** The price of one country's currency in terms of another country's currency; the ratio at which two currencies are traded for each other.

# The Balance of Payments

All foreign currencies—euros, Swiss francs, Japanese yen, Brazilian reals, and so forth—can be grouped together as "foreign exchange." **Foreign exchange** is simply all currencies other than the domestic currency of a given country (in the case of the United States, the U.S. dollar). U.S. demand for foreign exchange arises because its citizens want to buy things whose prices are quoted in other currencies, such as Australian jewelry, vacations in Mexico, and bonds or stocks issued by Sony Corporation of Japan. Whenever U.S. citizens make these purchases, foreign currencies must first be purchased. Typically this happens indirectly without most customers thinking about it at all.

Where does the *supply* of foreign exchange come from? The answer is simple: The United States (actually U.S. citizens or firms) earns foreign exchange when it sells products, services, or assets to another country. Some of these foreign exchange transactions are transparent to the consumer. When Mexican tourists visit Disney World, they turn their pesos into dollars and make purchases. Other transactions are less transparent. Saudi Arabian purchases of stock in General Motors and Colombian purchases of real estate in Miami also increase the U.S. supply of foreign exchange although the currency exchange is often done by a middleman.

The record of a country's transactions in goods, services, and assets with the rest of the world is its **balance of payments.** The balance of payments is also the record of a country's sources (supply) and uses (demand) of foreign exchange.[1]

**19.1 LEARNING** OBJECTIVE

Explain how the balance of payments is calculated.

**foreign exchange** All currencies other than the domestic currency of a given country.

**balance of payments** The record of a country's transactions in goods, services, and assets with the rest of the world; also the record of a country's sources (supply) and uses (demand) of foreign exchange.

## The Current Account

The balance of payments is divided into two major accounts, the *current account* and the *capital account*. These are shown in Table 19.1, which provides data on the U.S. balance of payments for 2014. We begin with the current account.

The first two items in the current account are exports and imports of goods. Among the biggest exports of the United States are commercial aircraft, chemicals, and agricultural products. U.S. exports *earn* foreign exchange for the United States and are a credit (+) item on the current account. U.S. imports *use up* foreign exchange and are a debit (−) item. In 2014 the United States exported $1,635.1 billion in goods and imported $2,370.9 billion, thus using up more foreign exchange than it earned regarding trade in goods.

---

[1] Bear in mind the distinction between the balance of payments and a balance sheet. A *balance sheet* for a firm or a country measures that entity's stock of assets and liabilities at a moment in time. The *balance of payments*, by contrast, measures *flows*, usually over a period of a month, a quarter, or a year. Despite its name, the balance of payments is *not* a balance sheet.

Next in the current account is trade in services. Like most other countries, the United States buys services from and sells services to other countries. For example, a U.S. firm shipping wheat to England might purchase insurance from a British insurance company. A Dutch flower grower may fly flowers to the United States aboard a U.S. airliner. In the first case, the United States is importing services and therefore using up foreign exchange; in the second case, it is selling services to foreigners and earning foreign exchange. In 2014 the United States exported $709.4 billion in services and imported $478.3 billion, thus earning more foreign exchange than it used up regarding trade in services.

**balance of trade** A country's exports of goods and services minus its imports of goods and services.

The difference between a country's exports of goods and services and its imports of goods and services is its **balance of trade**. When exports of goods and services are less than imports of goods and services, a country has a **trade deficit**. Table 19.1 shows that the U.S. trade deficit in 2014 was fairly large at $504.7 billion.

**trade deficit** Occurs when a country's exports of goods and services are less than its imports of goods and services.

Next in Table 19.1 comes investment income. U.S. citizens hold foreign assets (stocks, bonds, and real assets such as buildings and factories). Dividends, interest, rent, and profits paid to U.S. asset holders are a source of foreign exchange. Conversely, when foreigners earn dividends, interest, and profits on assets held in the United States, foreign exchange is used up. In 2014 the United States earned $819.7 in investment income and paid out $601.8 billion.

Last in the current account comes transfer payments. Transfer payments from the United States to foreigners are another use of foreign exchange. Some of these transfer payments are from private U.S. citizens, and some are from the U.S. government. You may send a check to a relief agency in Africa. Many immigrants in the United States send remittances to their countries of origin to help support extended families. Conversely, foreigners make transfer payments to the United States, which earns income for the United States. In 2014 the United States received $127.1 billion in transfer payments from abroad and sent $250.9 billion abroad.

**balance on current account** The sum of income from exports of goods and services and income from investments and transfers minus payments for imports of goods and services and payments for investments and transfers.

Line (10) in Table 19.1 shows the balance on current account. This is the balance of trade plus investment and transfer income and minus investment and transfer payments. Put another way, the **balance on current account** is the sum of income from exports of goods and services and income from investments and transfers minus payments for imports of goods and services and payments for investments and transfers. The balance on current account shows how much a nation has spent on foreign goods, services, investment income payments, and transfers relative to how much it has earned from other countries. When the balance is negative, which it was for the United States in 2014, a nation has spent more on foreign goods and

MyEconLab Real-time data

**TABLE 19.1   U.S. Balance of Payments, 2014**

| Current Account | Billions of dollars |
|---|---|
| (1)  Goods exports | 1,635.1 |
| (2)  Goods imports | −2,370.9 |
| (3)  Exports of services | 709.4 |
| (4)  Imports of services | −478.3 |
| (5)  Balance of trade: $(1) - (2) + (3) - (4)$ | −504.7 |
| (6)  Investment income | 819.7 |
| (7)  Investment payments | −601.8 |
| (8)  Transfer income | 127.1 |
| (9)  Transfer payments | −250.9 |
| (10) Balance on current account: $(5) + (6) - (7) + (8) - (9)$ | −410.6 |

| Capital Account | |
|---|---|
| (11) Change in net U.S. liabilities | 88.1 |
| (12) Net receipts from financial derivatives | 53.5 |
| (13) Statisical discrepancy | 269.0 |
| (14) Balance of payments: $(10) + (11) + (12) + (13)$ | 0.0 |

Item (11) is the change in foreign assets in the United States minus the change in U.S. assets abroad. In 2014 this number was positive, which means that there was an increase in net U.S. liabilities.
*Source:* Bureau of Economic Analysis, March 19, 2015.

services (plus investment income and transfers paid) than it has earned through the sales of its goods and services to the rest of the world (plus investment income and transfers received).

# The Capital Account

For each transaction recorded in the current account, there is an offsetting transaction recorded in the capital account. Consider, for example, the $410.6 billion current account deficit that the United States ran in 2014. This deficit must be paid for, and how it is paid shows up in the capital account. The first line under the capital account in Table 19.1 shows that net U.S. liabilities (to the rest of the world) increased by $88.1 billion. So the United States borrowed from the rest of the world (on net) $88.1 billion to partly finance the $410.6 billion deficit. The next line shows an increase in net U.S. receipts from financial derivatives of $53.5 billion, which also partly financed the deficit. If there were no measurement errors, the entire deficit would be financed by these two items. There are, in fact, measurement errors, where the total error is called the *statistical discrepancy*. In 2014 the statistical discrepancy was $269.0 billion. This is, of course, a large error. But the main point to take away from this analysis is that aside from measurement errors, a current account deficit must be financed by changes in a country's net liabilities to the rest of the world and its net financial-derivative receipts. The balance of payments—line (14) in Table 19.1—is always zero.

An example may help in seeing the link between the current and capital accounts. Say a U.S. citizen buys a beer in a store on Caye Caulker, Belize, for $1.75 using U.S. currency, which is accepted in Belize along with the local currency. This is an import of the United States, so the U.S. current-account deficit has increased by $1.75. What happens on the capital account? The Belize store owner now has the $1.75, which is an asset for him (i.e., for Belize) and a liability for the United States. Net U.S. liabilities to the rest of the world have thus increased by $1.75—line (11) in Table 19.1.

There are many international financial transactions that do not lead to a change in net U.S. liabilities in the capital account. If the Chinese central bank buys a U.S. government bond with yuan, its U.S. assets have increased (the bond), but so has its foreign liabilities (the yuan). In the United States there is an increase in foreign liabilities (the bond), but also an increase in foreign assets (the yuan). The *net* position of each country has not changed. The only way the net position of a country can change is through a positive or negative value of its current account. If in the Belize example the U.S. citizen had simply exchanged $1.75 U.S. for $3.50 Belize (the exchange rate between the Belize dollar and the U.S. dollar is 2 to 1), this would not have led to a change in net U.S. liabilities. This is just a swap of assets with no change in the current account.

The balance of payments pertains to flows. In Table 19.1 these are flows for the year 2014. Regarding stocks, we know that stocks and flows are related. For example, the net wealth of a country vis-à-vis the rest of the world at the end of a given year is equal to its net wealth at the end of the previous year plus its current-account balance during the year. In 2014 the net wealth of the United States vis-à-vis the rest of the world decreased by $410.6 billion—its current account deficit for 2014. It is important to realize that the *only* way a country's net wealth position can change is if its current account balance is nonzero. Simply switching one form of asset for another does not change a country's net wealth position. A country's net wealth position is simply the sum of all its past current account balances.

Prior to the mid-1970s, the United States had generally run current account surpluses, and thus its net wealth position was positive. It was a creditor nation. This began to turn around in the mid-1970s, and by the mid-1980s, the United States was running large current account deficits. Sometime during this period, the United States changed from having a positive net wealth position vis-à-vis the rest of the world to having a negative position. In other words, the United States changed from a creditor nation to a debtor nation. The current account deficits have persisted, and the United States is now the largest debtor nation in the world. At the end of 2014 foreign assets in the United States totaled $31.6 trillion and U.S. assets abroad totaled $24.7 trillion.[2] The U.S. net wealth position was thus -$6.9 trillion. This large negative position reflects the fact that the United States has spent much more since the 1970s on foreign goods and services (plus investment income and transfers paid) than it earned through the sales of its goods and services to the rest of the world (plus investment income and transfers received).

---

[2] Bureau of Economic Analysis, March 31, 2015.

# ECONOMICS IN PRACTICE

## Who Are the Debtor Nations?

The International Monetary Fund (IMF) was created in 1944 as part of the Bretton Woods conference described in the appendix to this chapter. Its principal purpose is to promote the stability of the international monetary system. As part of its mandate, the IMF collects data on trade and finances across the world. Christine Lagarde has run the IMF since 2011.

One of the measures that the IMF uses to assess the financial condition of various nations is the NIIP, a country's net international investment position. NIIP is the difference between a country's external financial assets and its external financial liabilities. Based on these data, we typically describe nations as net creditors or net debtors. So who are the big creditor and debtor nations looked at this way?[1]

The top six debtor nations in 2013 were (the numbers are in billions of U.S. dollars):

United States 5,383
Spain 1,385
Brazil 755
Australia 743
Italy 680
Mexico 494

The top six creditor nations were

Japan 3,086
China 1,972
Germany 1,145
Switzerland 839
Saudi Arabia 763
Hong Kong 758

The United States is by far the largest debtor nation. It has been running current account deficits since the 1970s. Europe is a mixed bag. Spain and Italy are large debtor nations, and Germany and Switzerland are large creditor nations. By far the two largest creditor nations are Japan and China. Saudi Arabia is a large creditor nation because it has been running large current account surpluses for years from its oil exports.

### THINKING PRACTICALLY

1. What are potential long-run costs of being a large debtor nation?

[1] The data come from "IMF Multi Country Report" July 29, 2014.

---

**19.2 LEARNING** OBJECTIVE

Discuss how equilibrium output is determined in an open economy, and describe the trade feedback effect and the price feedback effect.

# Equilibrium Output (Income) in an Open Economy

Everything we have said so far has been descriptive. Now we turn to analysis. How are all these trade and capital flows determined? What impacts do they have on the economies of the countries involved? To simplify our discussion, we will assume that exchange rates are fixed. We will relax this assumption later.

## The International Sector and Planned Aggregate Expenditure

The first change we will have to make to take into account the openness of the economy is in the calculation of the multiplier, one of the backbones of economic policy analysis. Our earlier calculations of the multiplier defined aggregate expenditure (*AE*) as consisting of the consumption of households (*C*), the planned investment of firms (*I*), and the spending of the government (*G*).

With an open economy, we must now include in aggregate expenditures the goods and services a country exports to the rest of the world, *EX*, and we will also have to make an adjustment for what it imports, *IM*. Clearly *EX* should be included as part of total output and income.

A U.S. razor sold to a buyer in Mexico is as much a part of U.S. production as a similar razor sold in Pittsburgh. Exports simply represent demand for domestic products not by domestic households and firms and the government, but by the rest of the world.

What about imports? Imports are *not a part of domestic output (Y)* because they are produced outside the home country. But, when we calculate households' total consumption spending, firms' total investment spending, and total government spending, imports are included. Therefore, to calculate domestic output correctly, we must subtract the parts of consumption, investment, and government spending that constitute imports. The definition of planned aggregate expenditure becomes:

Planned aggregate expenditure in an open economy:

$$AE \equiv C + I + G + EX - IM$$

The last two terms ($EX - IM$) together are the country's **net exports of goods and services.**

### Determining the Level of Imports

What determines the level of imports and exports in a country? Clearly the level of imports is a function of income ($Y$). When U.S. income increases, U.S. citizens buy more of everything, including, Japanese cars and Korean smartphones. When income rises, imports tend to go up. Algebraically,

$$IM = mY$$

where $Y$ is income and $m$ is some positive number. ($m$ is assumed to be less than 1; otherwise, a \$1 increase in income generates an increase in imports of more than \$1, which is unrealistic.) Recall from Chapter 8 that the marginal propensity to consume (MPC) measures the change in consumption that results from a \$1 change in income. Similarly, the **marginal propensity to import**, abbreviated as MPM or $m$, is the change in imports caused by a \$1 change in income. If $m = 0.2$, or 20 percent, and income is \$1,000, then imports, $IM$, are equal to $0.2 \times \$1,000 = \$200$. If income rises by \$100 to \$1,100, the change in imports will equal $m \times$ (the change in income) $= 0.2 \times \$100 = \$20$.

For now we will assume that exports ($EX$) are given (that is, they are not affected, even indirectly, by the state of the domestic economy.) This assumption is relaxed later in this chapter.

### Solving for Equilibrium

Given the assumption about how imports are determined, we can solve for equilibrium income. This procedure is illustrated in Figure 19.1. Starting from the consumption function (blue line) in Figure 19.1(a), we gradually build up the components of planned aggregate expenditure (red line). Assuming for simplicity that planned investment, government purchases, and exports are all constant and do not depend on income, we move easily from the blue line to the red line by adding the fixed amounts of $I$, $G$, and $EX$ to consumption at every level of income. In this example, we take $I + G + EX$ to equal 80.

$C + I + G + EX$, however, includes spending on imports, which are not part of domestic production. To get spending on domestically produced goods, we must subtract the amount that is imported at each level of income. In Figure 19.1(b), we assume $m = 0.25$, so that 25 percent of total income is spent on goods and services produced in foreign countries. For example, at $Y = 200$, $IM = 0.25 Y$, or 50. Similarly, at $Y = 400$, $IM = 0.25 Y$, or 100. Figure 19.1(b) shows the planned *domestic* aggregate expenditure curve that nets out imports from expenditures.

Equilibrium is reached when planned domestic aggregate expenditure equals domestic aggregate output (income). This is true at only one level of aggregate output, $Y^* = 200$, in Figure 19.1(b). If $Y$ were below $Y^*$, planned expenditure would exceed output, inventories would be lower than planned, and output would rise. At levels above $Y^*$, output would exceed planned expenditure, inventories would be larger than planned, and output would fall.

### The Open-Economy Multiplier

All of this has implications for the size of the multiplier. Recall the multiplier, introduced in Chapter 8, and consider a sustained rise in government purchases ($G$). Initially, the increase in $G$ will cause planned aggregate expenditure to be greater than

**net exports of goods and services ($EX - IM$)**    The difference between a country's total exports and total imports.

**marginal propensity to import (MPM)**    The change in imports caused by a \$1 change in income.

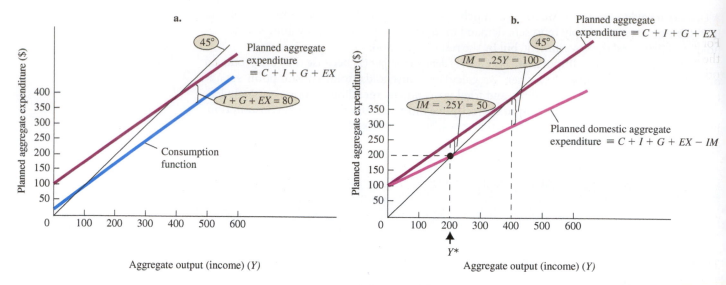

▲ **FIGURE 19.1** **Determining Equilibrium Output in an Open Economy**

In **a.**, planned investment spending (*I*), government spending (*G*), and total exports (*EX*) are added to consumption (*C*) to arrive at planned aggregate expenditure. However, *C* + *I* + *G* + *EX* includes spending on imports. In **b.**, the amount imported at every level of income is subtracted from planned aggregate expenditure. Equilibrium output occurs at *Y*\* = 200, the point at which planned domestic aggregate expenditure crosses the 45-degree line.

aggregate output. Domestic firms will find their inventories to be lower than planned and thus will increase their output, but added output means more income. More workers are hired, and profits are higher. Some of the added income is saved, and some is spent. The added consumption spending leads to a second round of inventories being lower than planned and raising output. Equilibrium output rises by a multiple of the initial increase in government purchases. This is the multiplier effect.

In Chapters 8 and 9, we showed that the simple multiplier equals 1/(1 − *MPC*), or (1/*MPS*). That is, a sustained increase in government purchases equal to Δ*G* will lead to an increase in aggregate output (income) of Δ*G* [1/(1 − *MPC*)]. If the *MPC* were 0.75 and government purchases rose by $10 billion, equilibrium income would rise by 4 × $10 billion, or $40 billion. The multiplier is [1/(1 − 0.75)] = [1/0.25] = 4.0.

In an open economy, some of the increase in income brought about by the increase in *G* is spent on imports instead of domestically produced goods and services. The part of income spent on imports does not increase domestic income (*Y*) because imports are produced by foreigners. To compute the multiplier, we need to know how much of the increased income is used to increase domestic consumption. (We are assuming all imports are consumption goods. In practice, some imports are investment goods and some are goods purchased by the government.) In other words, we need to know the marginal propensity to consume *domestically produced* goods. Domestic consumption is *C* − *IM*. So the marginal propensity to consume domestic goods is the marginal propensity to consume all goods (the *MPC*) minus the marginal propensity to import (the *MPM*). The marginal propensity to consume domestic goods is (*MPC* − *MPM*). Consequently,

$$\text{open-economy multipler} = \frac{1}{1 - (MPC - MPM)}$$

If the *MPC* is 0.75 and the *MPM* is 0.25, then the multiplier is 1/0.5, or 2.0. This multiplier is smaller than the multiplier in which imports are not taken into account, which is 1/0.25, or 4.0. The effect of a sustained increase in government spending (or investment) on income—that is, the multiplier—is smaller in an open economy than in a closed economy. The reason: When government spending (or investment) increases and income and consumption rise, some of the extra consumption spending that results is on foreign products and not on domestically produced goods and services. In an open economy the impact of government spending on the domestic economy is less than it otherwise would be. At the same time, one country's government spending increases affects other countries. Fiscal policy in one country can affect the macroeconomy is its trading partners.

# Imports and Exports and the Trade Feedback Effect

For simplicity, we have so far assumed that the level of imports depends only on income and that the level of exports is fixed. In reality, the amount of spending on imports also depends on factors other than income and exports are not fixed. We will now consider the more realistic picture.

**The Determinants of Imports**   The same factors that affect households' consumption behavior and firms' investment behavior are likely to affect the demand for imports because some imported goods are consumption goods and some are investment goods. For example, anything that increases consumption spending is likely to increase the demand for imports. We saw in Chapters 8 and 11 that factors such as the after-tax real wage, after-tax nonlabor income, and interest rates affect consumption spending; thus, they should also affect spending on imports. Similarly, anything that increases investment spending is likely to increase the demand for imports. A decrease in interest rates, for example, should encourage spending on both domestically produced goods and foreign-produced goods.

There is one additional consideration in determining spending on imports: the *relative prices* of domestically produced and foreign-produced goods. If the prices of foreign goods fall relative to the prices of domestic goods, people will consume more foreign goods relative to domestic goods. When Japanese cars are inexpensive relative to U.S. cars, consumption of Japanese cars should be high and vice versa.

**The Determinants of Exports**   We now relax our assumption that exports are fixed. The foreign demand for U.S. exports is identical to the foreign countries' imports from the United States. Germany imports goods, some of which are U.S.-produced. France, Spain, and so on do the same. Total expenditure on imports in Germany is a function of the factors we just discussed except that the variables are German variables instead of U.S. variables. This is true for all other countries as well. The demand for U.S. exports depends on economic activity in the rest of the world—rest-of-the-world real wages, wealth, nonlabor income, interest rates, and so forth—as well as on the prices of U.S. goods relative to the prices of rest-of-the-world goods. When foreign output increases, U.S. exports tend to increase. In this way economic growth in the rest of the world stimulates the economy in the United States. U.S. exports also tend to increase when U.S. prices fall relative to foreign goods prices. With an open economy, countries are interdependent. U.S. exports also tend to increase when U.S. prices fall relative to foreign prices.

**The Trade Feedback Effect**   We can now combine what we know about the demand for imports and the demand for exports to discuss the **trade feedback effect**. Suppose the United States finds its exports increasing, perhaps because the world suddenly decides it prefers U.S. computers to other computers. Rising exports will lead to an increase in U.S. output (income), which leads to an increase in U.S. imports. Here is where the trade feedback begins. Because U.S. imports are somebody else's exports, the extra import demand from the United States raises the exports of the rest of the world. When other countries' exports to the United States go up, their output and incomes also rise, in turn leading to an increase in the demand for imports from the rest of the world. Some of the extra imports demanded by the rest of the world come from the United States, so U.S. exports increase. The increase in U.S. exports stimulates U.S. economic activity even more, triggering a further increase in the U.S. demand for imports and so on. An increase in U.S. imports increases other countries' exports, which stimulates those countries' economies and increases their imports, which increases U.S. exports, and so on. This is the trade feedback effect. In other words, an increase in U.S. economic activity leads to a worldwide increase in economic activity, which then "feeds back" to the United States.

> **trade feedback effect**   The tendency for an increase in the economic activity of one country to lead to a worldwide increase in economic activity, which then feeds back to that country.

# Import and Export Prices and the Price Feedback Effect

We have talked about the price of imports, but we have not yet discussed the factors that influence import prices. The consideration of import prices is complicated because more than one currency is involved. When we talk about "the price of imports," do we mean the price in dollars, in yen, or in euros? Because the exports of one country are the imports of another, the same question holds for the price of exports. When Mexico exports auto parts to the United States, Mexican manufacturers are interested in the price of auto parts in terms of pesos because pesos are what they use for transactions in Mexico. U.S. consumers are interested in the price of auto parts in dollars because dollars are what they use for transactions in the United States. The link between the two prices is the dollar/peso exchange rate.

Suppose Mexico is experiencing inflation and the price of radiators in pesos rises from 1,000 pesos to 1,200 pesos per radiator. If the dollar/peso exchange rate remains unchanged at, say, $0.10 per peso, Mexico's export price for radiators in terms of dollars will also rise, from $100 to $120 per radiator. Because Mexico's exports to the United States are, by definition, U.S. imports from Mexico, an increase in the dollar prices of Mexican exports to the United States means an increase in the prices of U.S. imports from Mexico. Therefore, when Mexico's export prices rise with no change in the dollar/peso exchange rate, U.S. import prices rise. Export prices of other countries affect U.S. import prices.

A country's export prices tend to move fairly closely with the general price level in that country. If Mexico is experiencing a general increase in prices, this change likely will be reflected in price increases of all domestically produced goods, both exportable and nonexportable. The general rate of inflation abroad is likely to affect U.S. import prices. If the inflation rate abroad is high, U.S. import prices are likely to rise.

### The Price Feedback Effect

We have just seen that when a country experiences an increase in domestic prices, the prices of its exports will increase. It is also true that when the prices of a country's *imports* increase, the prices of domestic goods may increase in response. There are at least two ways this effect can occur.

First, an increase in the prices of imported inputs will increase the costs of firms which use these imports as inputs, causing a country's aggregate supply curve to shift to the left. Recall from Chapter 12 that a leftward shift in the aggregate supply curve resulting from a cost increase causes aggregate output to fall and prices to rise (stagflation).

Second, if import prices rise relative to domestic prices, households will tend to substitute domestically produced goods and services for imports. This is equivalent to a rightward shift of the aggregate demand curve. If the domestic economy is operating on the upward-sloping part of the aggregate supply curve, the overall domestic price level will rise in response to an increase in aggregate demand. Perfectly competitive firms will see market-determined prices rise, and imperfectly competitive firms will experience an increase in the demand for their products. Studies have shown, for example, that the price of automobiles produced in the United States moves closely with the price of imported cars.

Still, this is not the end of the story. Suppose a country—say, Mexico—experiences an increase in its domestic price level. This will increase the price of its exports to Canada (and to all other countries). The increase in the price of Canadian imports from Mexico will lead to an increase in domestic prices in Canada. Canada also exports to Mexico. The increase in Canadian prices causes an increase in the price of Canadian exports to Mexico, which then further increases the Mexican price level.

This is called the **price feedback effect**, in the sense that inflation is "exportable." An increase in the price level in one country can drive up prices in other countries, which in turn further increases the price level in the first country. Through export and import prices, a domestic price increase can "feed back" on itself.

It is important to realize that the discussion so far has been based on the assumption of fixed exchange rates. Life is more complicated under flexible exchange rates, to which we now turn.

**price feedback effect** The process by which a domestic price increase in one country can "feed back" on itself through export and import prices. An increase in the price level in one country can drive up prices in other countries. This in turn further increases the price level in the first country.

**floating,** *or* **market-determined, exchange rates** Exchange rates that are determined by the unregulated forces of supply and demand.

# The Open Economy with Flexible Exchange Rates

To a large extent, the fixed exchange rates set by the Bretton Woods agreements served as international monetary arrangements until 1971. Then in 1971, the United States and most other countries decided to abandon the fixed exchange rate system in favor of **floating,** *or* **market-determined, exchange rates**. Although governments still intervene to ensure that exchange rate movements are "orderly," exchange rates today are largely determined by the unregulated forces of supply and demand.

Understanding how an economy interacts with the rest of the world when exchange rates are not fixed is not as simple as when we assume fixed exchange rates. Exchange rates determine the price of imported goods relative to domestic goods and can have significant effects on the level of imports and exports. Consider a 20 percent drop in the value of the dollar against the British pound. Dollars buy fewer pounds, and pounds buy more dollars. Both British residents, who now get more dollars for pounds, and U.S. residents, who get fewer pounds for dollars, find that U.S. goods and services are more attractive. Exchange rate movements have important impacts on imports, exports, and the movement of capital between countries.

# The Market for Foreign Exchange

What determines exchange rates under a floating rate system? To explore this question, we assume that there are just two countries, the United States and Great Britain. It is easier to understand a world with only two countries, and most of the points we will make can be generalized to a world with many trading partners.

### The Supply of and Demand for Pounds
Governments, private citizens, banks, and corporations exchange pounds for dollars and dollars for pounds every day. In our two-country case, those who *demand* pounds are holders of dollars seeking to exchange them for pounds to buy British goods, travel to Britain, or invest in British stocks and bonds. Those who *supply* pounds are holders of pounds seeking to exchange them for dollars to buy U.S. goods, visit or invest in the United States. The supply of dollars on the foreign exchange market is the number of dollars that holders seek to exchange for pounds in a given time period. The demand for and supply of dollars on foreign exchange markets determine *exchange* rates.

In addition to buyers and sellers who exchange money to engage in transactions, some people and institutions hold currency balances for speculative reasons. If you think that the U.S. dollar is going to decline in value relative to the pound, you may want to hold some of your wealth in the form of pounds. Table 19.2 summarizes some of the major categories of private foreign exchange demanders and suppliers in the two-country case of the United States and Great Britain.

We can use a variant of supply and demand analysis to help us understand the exchange rate in currency markets. Figure 19.2 shows the demand curve for pounds in the foreign exchange market. On the vertical axis is the price of pounds, expressed in dollars per pound, and on the horizontal axis is the quantity of pounds. Thus, as we move down the vertical axis, the pound depreciates relative to the dollar—it takes fewer dollars to buy a pound. Suppose we start at a point at which it costs $2 to buy 1 pound and the price of a British good is 1 pound.

| TABLE 19.2    Some Buyers and Sellers in International Exchange Markets: United States and Great Britain |
| --- |

**The Demand for Pounds (Supply of Dollars)**

1. Firms, households, or governments that import British goods into the United States or want to buy British-made goods and services
2. U.S. citizens traveling in Great Britain
3. Holders of dollars who want to buy British stocks, bonds, or other financial instruments
4. U.S. companies that want to invest in Great Britain
5. Speculators who anticipate a decline in the value of the dollar relative to the pound

**The Supply of Pounds (Demand for Dollars)**

1. Firms, households, or governments that import U.S. goods into Great Britain or want to buy U.S.-made goods and services
2. British citizens traveling in the United States
3. Holders of pounds who want to buy stocks, bonds, or other financial instruments in the United States
4. British companies that want to invest in the United States
5. Speculators who anticipate a rise in the value of the dollar relative to the pound

▶ **FIGURE 19.2   The Demand for Pounds in the Foreign Exchange Market**

When the price of pounds falls, British-made goods and services appear less expensive to U.S. buyers. If British prices are constant, U.S. buyers will buy more British goods and services and the quantity of pounds demanded will rise.

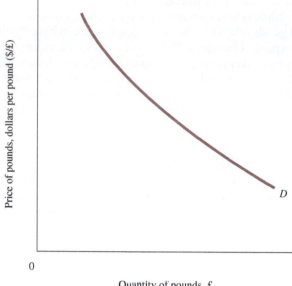

To buy that good at the existing exchange rate would cost an American $2. Let us suppose at that exchange rate 100 units of the good are demanded, giving rise to a demand for 100 pounds in the currency market. Now let the pound depreciate, so that it costs only $1 to buy a pound. It seems likely that the British good will look more attractive to Americans. With a fixed price in pounds for the good in question, Americans can buy that 1 pound good for only $1 rather than the original $2. Whereas people originally wanted 100 units of the good, with a dollar price much reduced they will likely want more than 100 units. To facilitate that transaction will thus require more than 100 pounds. The demand-for-pounds curve in the foreign exchange market thus has a negative slope.

What about the supply of pounds? Pounds are supplied by the British who want to buy U.S. goods. Figure 19.3 shows a supply curve for pounds in the foreign exchange market. As we move up the vertical axis, the dollar becomes cheaper; each pound translates into more dollars, making the price of U.S.-produced goods and services lower to the British. The British buy more U.S.-made goods when the price of pounds is high (the value of the dollar is low). If the demand for U.S. imports is elastic then that increase in British demand for U.S. goods and services increases the quantity of pounds supplied. The curve representing the supply of pounds in the foreign exchange market has a positive slope.

The key to understanding the supply and demand curves represented here is to recognize that the price on the vertical axis is the price of one currency relative to a second. As we go down

▶ **FIGURE 19.3   The Supply of Pounds in the Foreign Exchange Market**

When the price of pounds rises, the British can obtain more dollars for each pound. This means that U.S.-made goods and services appear less expensive to British buyers. Thus, the quantity of pounds supplied is likely to rise with the exchange rate.

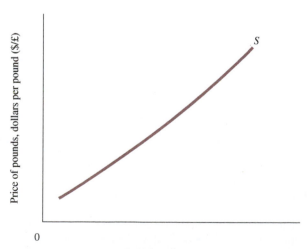

the vertical axis in this case, the pound becomes less expensive relative to the dollar, or equivalently, the dollar becomes more expensive relative to the pound. Moving down the vertical axis to the origin, the low relative price of the pound induces demand for pounds by Americans to buy British goods. At the same time, however, British buyers are less interested in the now expensive American goods, and fewer pounds are supplied.

**The Equilibrium Exchange Rate**    When exchange rates are allowed to float, they are determined the same way other prices are determined: The equilibrium exchange rate occurs at the point at which the quantity demanded of a foreign currency equals the quantity of that currency supplied. This is illustrated in Figure 19.4. An excess demand for pounds (quantity demanded in excess of quantity supplied) will cause the price of pounds to rise—the pound will **appreciate** relative to the dollar. An excess supply of pounds will cause the price of pounds to fall—the pound will **depreciate** relative to the dollar.[3]

**appreciation of a currency**
The rise in value of one currency relative to another.

**depreciation of a currency**
The fall in value of one currency relative to another.

# Factors That Affect Exchange Rates

We now know enough to discuss the factors likely to influence exchange rates. Anything that changes the behavior of the people in Table 19.2 can cause demand and supply curves to shift and the exchange rate to adjust accordingly.

**Purchasing Power Parity: The Law of One Price**    If the costs of transporting goods between two countries are small, we would expect the price of the same good in both countries to be roughly the same. The price of basketballs should be roughly the same in Canada and the United States, for example.

It is not hard to see why. If the price of basketballs is cheaper in Canada, it will benefit someone to buy balls in Canada at a low price and sell them in the United States at a higher price. This decreases the supply of basketballs in Canada and pushes up the price and increases the supply

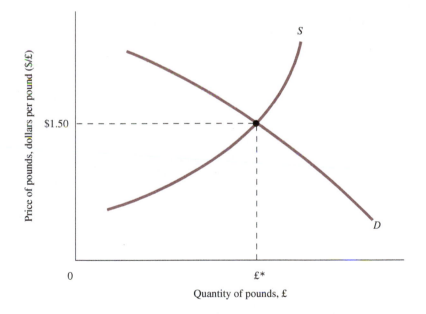

◀ **FIGURE 19.4    The Equilibrium Exchange Rate**
When exchange rates are allowed to float, they are determined by the forces of supply and demand. An excess demand for pounds will cause the pound to appreciate against the dollar. An excess supply of pounds will lead to a depreciating pound.

---

[3] Although Figure 19.3 shows the supply-of-pounds curve in the foreign exchange market with a positive slope, under certain circumstances the curve may bend back. Suppose the price of a pound rises from $1.50 to $2.00. Consider a British importer who buys 10 Chevrolets each month at $15,000 each, including transportation costs. When a pound exchanges for $1.50, he will supply 100,000 pounds per month to the foreign exchange market—100,000 pounds brings $150,000, enough to buy 10 cars. Now suppose the cheaper dollar causes him to buy 12 cars. Twelve cars will cost a total of $180,000; but at $2 = 1 pound, he will spend only 90,000 pounds per month. The supply of pounds on the market falls when the price of pounds rises. The reason for this seeming paradox is simple. The number of pounds a British importer needs to buy U.S. goods depends on both the quantity of goods he buys and the price of those goods in pounds. If demand for imports is inelastic so that the percentage decrease in price resulting from the depreciated currency is greater than the percentage increase in the quantity of imports demanded, importers will spend fewer pounds and the quantity of pounds supplied in the foreign exchange market will fall. The supply of pounds will slope upward as long as the demand for U.S. imports is elastic.

**law of one price** If the costs of transportation are small, the price of the same good in different countries should be roughly the same.

of balls in the United States, and pushes down the price. This process should continue as long as the price differential, and therefore the profit opportunity, persists. For a good with trivial transportation costs, we would expect this **law of one price** to hold. The price of a good should be the same regardless of where we buy it.

If the law of one price held for all goods and if each country consumed the same market basket of goods, the exchange rate between the two currencies would be determined simply by the relative price levels in the two countries. If the price of a basketball were $10 in the United States and $12 in Canada, the U.S.–Canada exchange rate would have to be $1 U.S. per $1.20 Canadian. If the rate were instead one-to-one, it would be worth it for people to buy the balls in the United States and sell them in Canada. This would increase the demand for U.S. dollars in Canada, thereby driving up their price in terms of Canadian dollars to $1 U.S. per $1.2 Canadian, at which point no one could make a profit shipping basketballs across international lines and the process would cease.[4]

**purchasing-power-parity theory** A theory of international exchange holding that exchange rates are set so that the price of similar goods in different countries is the same.

The theory that exchange rates will adjust so that the price of similar goods in different countries is the same is known as the **purchasing-power-parity theory**. According to this theory, if it takes 10 times as many Mexican pesos to buy a pound of salt in Mexico as it takes U.S. dollars to buy a pound of salt in the United States, the equilibrium exchange rate should be 10 pesos per dollar.

In practice, transportation costs for many goods are quite large and the law of one price does not hold for these goods. (Haircuts are often cited as a good example. The transportation costs for a U.S. resident to get a British haircut are indeed large unless that person is an airline pilot.) Also, many products that are potential substitutes for each other are not precisely identical. For instance, a Rolls Royce and a Honda are both cars, but there is no reason to expect the exchange rate between the British pound and the yen to be set so that the prices of the two are equalized. In addition, countries consume different market baskets of goods, so we would not expect the aggregate price levels to follow the law of one price. Nevertheless, a high rate of inflation in one country relative to another puts pressure on the exchange rate between the two countries, and there is a general tendency for the currencies of relatively high-inflation countries to depreciate.

Figure 19.5 shows the adjustment likely to occur following an increase in the U.S. price level relative to the price level in Great Britain. This change in relative prices will affect citizens of both countries. Higher prices in the United States make imports relatively less expensive. U.S.

▶ **FIGURE 19.5**

**Exchange Rates Respond to Changes in Relative Prices**

The higher price level in the United States makes imports relatively less expensive. U.S. citizens are likely to increase their spending on imports from Britain, shifting the demand for pounds to the right, from $D_0$ to $D_1$. At the same time, the British see U.S. goods getting more expensive and reduce their demand for exports from the United States. The supply of pounds shifts to the left, from $S_0$ to $S_1$. The result is an increase in the price of pounds. The pound appreciates, and the dollar is worth less.

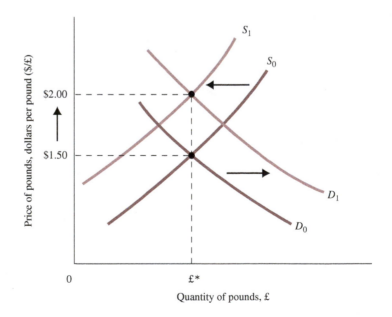

[4] Of course, if the rate were $1 U.S. to $2 Canadian, it would benefit people to buy basketballs in Canada (at $12 Canadian, which is $6 U.S.) and sell them in the United States. This would weaken demand for the U.S. dollar, and its price would fall from $2 Canadian until it reached $1.20 Canadian.

citizens are likely to increase their spending on imports from Britain, shifting the demand for pounds to the right, from $D_0$ to $D_1$. At the same time, the British see U.S. goods getting more expensive and reduce their demand for exports from the United States. Consequently, the supply of pounds shifts to the left, from $S_0$ to $S_1$. The result is an increase in the price of pounds. Before the change in relative prices, 1 pound sold for $1.50; after the change, 1 pound costs $2.00. The pound appreciates, and the dollar depreciates.

**Relative Interest Rates**    Another factor that influences a country's exchange rate is the level of its interest rate relative to other countries' interest rates. If the interest rate is 2 percent in the United States and 3 percent in Great Britain, people with money to lend have an incentive to buy British securities instead of U.S. securities. Although it is sometimes difficult for individuals in one country to buy securities in another country, it is easy for international banks and investment companies to do so. If the interest rate is lower in the United States than in Britain, there will be a movement of funds out of U.S. securities into British securities as banks and firms move their funds to the higher-yielding securities.

How does a U.S. bank buy British securities? It takes its dollars, buys British pounds, and uses the pounds to buy the British securities. The bank's purchase of pounds drives up the price of pounds in the foreign exchange market. The increased demand for pounds increases the price of the pound (and decreases the price of the dollar). A high interest rate in Britain relative to the interest rate in the United States tends to depreciate the dollar.

Figure 19.6 shows the effect of rising interest rates in the United States on the dollar-to-pound exchange rate. Higher interest rates in the United States attract British investors. To buy U.S. securities, the British need dollars. The supply of pounds (the demand for dollars) shifts to the right, from $S_0$ to $S_1$. The same relative interest rates affect the portfolio choices of U.S. banks, firms, and households. With higher interest rates at home, there is less incentive for U.S. residents to buy British securities. The demand for pounds drops at the same time the supply increases and the demand curve shifts to the left, from $D_0$ to $D_1$. The net result is a depreciating pound and an appreciating dollar. The price of pounds falls from $1.50 to $1.00.

# The Effects of Exchange Rates on the Economy

We are now ready to discuss some of the implications of floating exchange rates. Recall, when exchange rates are fixed, households spend some of their incomes on imports and the multiplier is smaller than it would be otherwise. Imports are a "leakage" from the circular flow, much like

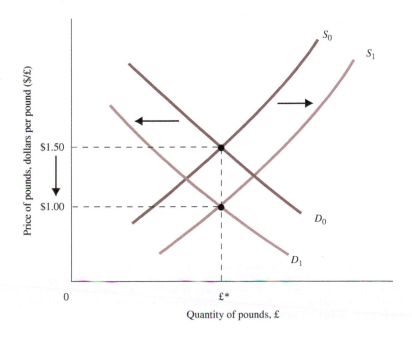

◀ **FIGURE 19.6**

**Exchange Rates Respond to Changes in Relative Interest Rates**

If U.S. interest rates rise relative to British interest rates, British citizens holding pounds may be attracted into the U.S. securities market. To buy bonds in the United States, British buyers must exchange pounds for dollars. The supply of pounds shifts to the right, from $S_0$ to $S_1$. At the same time, U.S. citizens are less likely to be interested in British securities because interest rates are higher at home. The demand for pounds shifts to the left, from $D_0$ to $D_1$. The result is a depreciated pound and a stronger dollar.

taxes and saving. Exports, in contrast, are an "injection" into the circular flow; they represent spending on U.S.-produced goods and services from abroad and can stimulate output.

### Exchange Rate Effects on Imports, Exports, and Real GDP

As we already know, when a country's currency depreciates (falls in value), its import prices rise and its export prices (in foreign currencies) fall. When the U.S. dollar is cheap, U.S. products are more competitive with products produced in the rest of the world and foreign-made goods look expensive to U.S. citizens.

A depreciation of a country's currency can thus serve as a stimulus to the economy. Suppose the U.S. dollar falls in value, as it did sharply between 1985 and 1988 and again, more moderately from 2002 to 2008 and 2012 to 2013. If foreign buyers increase their spending on U.S. goods, and domestic buyers substitute U.S.-made goods for imports, aggregate expenditure on domestic output will rise, inventories will fall, and real GDP (Y) will increase. A depreciation of a country's currency is likely to increase its GDP.[5]

### Exchange Rates and the Balance of Trade: The J Curve

Because a depreciating currency tends to increase exports and decrease imports, you might think that it also will reduce a country's trade deficit. In fact, the effect of a depreciation on the balance of trade is ambiguous.

Many economists believe that when a currency starts to depreciate, the balance of trade is likely to worsen for the first few quarters (perhaps three to six). After that, the balance of trade may improve. This effect is graphed in Figure 19.7. The curve in this figure resembles the letter J, and the movement in the balance of trade that it describes is sometimes called the **J-curve effect**. The point of the J shape is that the balance of trade gets worse before it gets better following a currency depreciation.

How does the J curve come about? Recall from Table 19.1 that the balance of trade is equal to export revenue minus import costs, including exports and imports of services:

> **J-curve effect** Following a currency depreciation, a country's balance of trade may get worse before it gets better. The graph showing this effect is shaped like the letter J, hence the name J-curve effect.

$$\text{balance of trade} = \text{dollar price of exports} \times \text{quantity of exports} \\ - \text{dollar price of imports} \times \text{quantity of imports}$$

A currency depreciation affects the items on the right side of this equation as follows: First, the quantity of exports increases and the quantity of imports decreases; both have a *positive* effect on the balance of trade (lowering the trade deficit or raising the trade surplus). Second, the dollar price of exports is not likely to change very much, at least not initially. The dollar price of exports changes when the U.S. price level changes, but the initial effect of a depreciation on the

▶ **FIGURE 19.7** **The Effect of a Depreciation on the Balance of Trade (the J Curve)**
Initially, a depreciation of a country's currency may worsen its balance of trade. The negative effect on the price of imports may initially dominate the positive effects of an increase in exports and a decrease in imports.

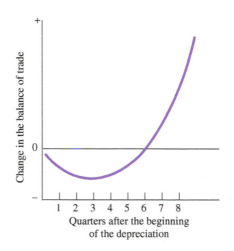

*Quarters after the beginning of the depreciation*

---

[5] For this reason, some countries are tempted at times to intervene in foreign exchange markets, depreciate their currencies, and stimulate their economies. If all countries attempted to lower the value of their currencies simultaneously, there would be no gain in income for any of them. Although the exchange rate system at the time was different, such a situation actually occurred during the early years of the Great Depression. Many countries practiced so-called *beggar-thy-neighbor* policies of competitive devaluations in a desperate attempt to maintain export sales and employment.

domestic price level is not likely to be large. Third, the dollar price of imports increases. Imports into the United States are more expensive because $1 U.S. buys fewer yen, euros, and so on, than before. An increase in the dollar price of imports has a *negative* effect on the balance of trade.

An example to clarify this last point follows: The dollar price of a Japanese car that costs 1,200,000 yen rises from $10,000 to $12,000 when the exchange rate moves from 120 yen per dollar to 100 yen per dollar. After the currency depreciation, the United States ends up spending more (in dollars) for the Japanese car than it did before. Of course, the United States will end up buying fewer Japanese cars than it did before. Does the number of cars drop enough so that the quantity effect is bigger than the price effect or vice versa? Does the value of imports increase or decrease?

The net effect of a depreciation on the balance of trade could go either way. The depreciation stimulates exports and cuts back imports, but it also increases the dollar price of imports. It seems that the negative effect dominates initially. The impact of a depreciation on the price of imports is generally felt quickly, while it takes time for export and import quantities to respond to price changes. In the short run, the value of imports increases more than the value of exports, so the balance of trade worsens. The initial effect is likely to be negative, but after exports and imports have had time to respond, the net effect turns positive. The more elastic the demand for exports and imports, the larger the eventual improvement in the balance of trade.

**Exchange Rates and Prices**   The depreciation of a country's currency tends to increase its price level. There are two reasons for this effect. First, when a country's currency is less expensive, its products are more competitive on world markets, so exports rise. In addition, domestic buyers tend to substitute domestic products for the now-more-expensive imports. This means that planned aggregate expenditure on domestically produced goods and services rises and that the aggregate demand curve shifts to the right. The result is a higher price level, a higher output, or both. (You may want to draw an AS/AD diagram to verify this outcome.) If the economy is close to capacity, the result is likely to be higher prices. Second, a depreciation makes imported inputs more expensive. If costs increase, the aggregate supply curve shifts to the left. If aggregate demand remains unchanged, the result is an increase in the price level.

**Monetary Policy with Flexible Exchange Rates**   Let us now put everything in this chapter together and consider what happens when monetary policy is used first to stimulate the economy and then to contract the economy in an open economy with flexible exchange rates.

Suppose the economy is below full employment and the Federal Reserve (Fed) lowers the interest rate. The lower interest rate stimulates planned investment spending and consumption spending. Output thus increases. But there are additional effects: (1) The lower interest rate has an impact in the foreign exchange market. A lower interest rate means a lower demand for U.S. securities by foreigners, so the demand for dollars drops. (2) U.S. investment managers will be more likely to buy foreign securities (which are now paying relatively higher interest rates), so the supply of dollars rises. Both events push down the value of the dollar. A cheaper dollar is a good thing if the goal of the Fed is to stimulate the domestic economy because a cheaper dollar means more U.S. exports and fewer imports. If consumers substitute U.S.-made goods for imports, both the added exports and the decrease in imports mean more spending on domestic products, so the multiplier actually increases. Flexible exchange rates thus help the Fed in its goal to stimulate the economy.

Now suppose inflation is a problem and the Fed raises the interest rate. Here again, floating exchange rates help. The higher interest rate lowers planned investment and consumption spending, reducing output and lowering the price level. The higher interest rate also attracts foreign buyers into U.S. financial markets, driving up the value of the dollar, which reduces the price of imports. The reduction in the price of imports causes a shift of the aggregate supply curve to the right, which helps fight inflation, which is what the Fed wants to do. Flexible exchange rates thus help the Fed in its goal to fight inflation.

**Fiscal Policy with Flexible Exchange Rates**   Although we have just seen that flexible exchange rates help the Fed achieve its goals, the opposite is the case for the fiscal authorities in normal times when there is no zero lower interest rate bound and the Fed is following the Fed rule. Say that the administration and Congress want to stimulate the economy, and they increase government spending to do this. This increases output in the usual way (shift of the *AD* curve to the right). This usual way means that the interest rate is also higher (from the Fed rule because output and the price level are higher). The higher interest rate attracts foreign investment and leads to an appreciation of the dollar. An appreciation, other things being equal, increases imports and decreases exports, which has a negative effect on output. The increase in output is thus less than it would have been had there been no appreciation. The appreciation also leads to a decrease in import prices, which shifts the *AS* curve to the right, thus decreasing the price level, other things being equal. Although the price level is lower than otherwise, output, which was the main target of the administration's policy in our example, is lower, all else equal. Flexible exchange rates thus makes the task of the fiscal authorities in their goal to stimulate the economy more difficult.

Flexible exchange rates also hurt the fiscal authorities if they want to contract the economy to fight inflation. Suppose we decrease government spending to try to reduce inflation. This shifts the *AD* curve to the left, which decreases output and the price level. The interest rate is also lower (from the Fed rule because output and the price level are lower), which leads to a depreciation of the dollar. The depreciation, other things being equal, decreases imports and increases exports, which has a positive effect on output. However, the depreciation also leads to an increase in import prices, which shifts the *AS* curve to the left, thus increasing the price level, other things being equal. Although output is higher than otherwise, inflation, which was our target, is higher than it would have been in a closed economy other things being equal. So flexible exchange rates also hurt the fiscal authorities in their goal to fight inflation.

Note that the appreciation or depreciation of the currency occurs because of the Fed rule. If the Fed does not change the interest rate in response to the fiscal policy change, either because there is a zero lower bound or because it just doesn't want to, there is no appreciation or depreciation and thus no offset to what the fiscal authorities are trying to do from the existence of flexible exchange rates.

### Monetary Policy with Fixed Exchange Rates

Although most major countries in the world today have a flexible exchange rate (counting for this purpose the eurozone countries as one country), it is interesting to ask what role monetary policy can play when a country has a fixed exchange rate. The answer is, no role.

Suppose a country fixes or "pegs" its exchange rate to the value of the dollar? In fact a number of countries do this, including countries like Hong Kong and Singapore, who are heavily reliant on their financial sectors. When a country decides to peg its exchange rate to another currency, say the U.S. dollar, it gives up its power to change its interest rate. Why? Consider a monetary authority of a pegged country that wants to lower its interest rate to stimulate the economy. The problem is that with its interest rate lower than rates abroad, people in the country will be induced to move their capital abroad to earn the higher interest rates. In other words, there will be an outflow of capital. Normally, this outflow would cause the country's currency to depreciate, but with a pegged rate, this won't happen. To keep the exchange rate from depreciating, the country's monetary authority will be forced to buy the domestic currency outflow by selling its foreign reserves. Eventually the monetary authority will run out of foreign reserves and thus be unable to support the pegged exchange rate. It is thus not feasible for the country to change its interest rate and keep its exchange rate unchanged. A commitment to peg is thus a commitment to give up one's independent monetary policy.

When the various European countries moved in 1999 to a common currency, the euro, each country gave up its monetary policy. Monetary policy is decided for all of the eurozone countries by the European Central Bank (ECB). The Bank of Italy, for example, no longer has any influence over Italian interest rates. Interest rates are influenced by the ECB. This is the price Italy paid for giving up the lira. The one case in which a country can change its interest rate and keep its exchange rate fixed is if it imposes capital controls. Imposing capital controls means that the country limits or prevents people from buying or selling its currency in the foreign exchange markets. A citizen of the country may be prevented, for example, from using the country's currency to buy dollars. The problem with capital controls is that they are hard to enforce, especially for large countries and for long periods of time.

# An Interdependent World Economy

The increasing interdependence of countries in the world economy has made the problems facing policy makers more difficult. We used to be able to think of the United States as a relatively self-sufficient region. Forty years ago economic events outside U.S. borders had relatively little effect on its economy. This situation is no longer true. The events of the past four decades have taught us that the performance of the U.S. economy is heavily dependent on events outside U.S. borders.

This chapter and the previous chapter have provided only the bare bones of open-economy macroeconomics. If you continue your study of economics, more will be added to the basic story we have presented. The next chapter concludes with a discussion of the problems of developing countries.

## — SUMMARY —

1. The main difference between an international transaction and a domestic transaction concerns currency exchange: When people in different countries buy from and sell to each other, an exchange of currencies must also take place.

2. The *exchange rate* is the price of one country's currency in terms of another country's currency.

### 19.1 THE BALANCE OF PAYMENTS   *p. 357*

3. *Foreign exchange* is all currencies other than the domestic currency of a given country. The record of a nation's transactions in goods, services, and assets with the rest of the world is its *balance of payments*. The balance of payments is also the record of a country's sources (supply) and uses (demand) of foreign exchange.

### 19.2 EQUILIBRIUM OUTPUT (INCOME) IN AN OPEN ECONOMY   *p. 360*

4. In an open economy, some income is spent on foreign produced goods instead of domestically produced goods. To measure planned domestic aggregate expenditure in an open economy, we add total exports but subtract total imports: $C + I + G + EX - IM$. The open economy is in equilibrium when domestic aggregate output (income) $(Y)$ equals planned domestic aggregate expenditure.

5. In an open economy, the multiplier equals

$$1/[1 - (MPC - MPM)],$$

where $MPC$ is the marginal propensity to consume and $MPM$ is the marginal propensity to import. The *marginal propensity to import* is the change in imports caused by a $1 change in income.

6. In addition to income, other factors that affect the level of imports are the after-tax real wage rate, after-tax nonlabor income, interest rates, and relative prices of domestically produced and foreign-produced goods. The demand for exports is determined by economic activity in the rest of the world and by relative prices.

7. An increase in U.S. economic activity leads to a worldwide increase in economic activity, which then "feeds back" to the United States. An increase in U.S. imports increases other countries' exports, which stimulates economies and increases their imports, which increases U.S. exports, which stimulates the U.S. economy and increases its imports, and so on. This is the *trade feedback effect*.

8. Export prices of other countries affect U.S. import prices. The general rate of inflation abroad is likely to affect U.S. import prices. If the inflation rate abroad is high, U.S. import prices are likely to rise.

9. Because one country's exports are another country's imports, an increase in export prices increases other countries' import prices. An increase in other countries' import prices leads to an increase in their domestic prices—and their export prices. In short, export prices affect import prices and vice versa. This *price feedback effect* shows that inflation is "exportable"; an increase in the price level in one country can drive up prices in other countries, making inflation in the first country worse.

### 19.3 THE OPEN ECONOMY WITH FLEXIBLE EXCHANGE RATES   *p. 364*

10. The equilibrium exchange rate occurs when the quantity demanded of a foreign currency in the foreign exchange market equals the quantity of that currency supplied in the foreign exchange market.

11. *Depreciation of a currency occurs* when a nation's currency falls in value relative to another country's currency. *Appreciation of a currency* occurs when a nation's currency rises in value relative to another country's currency.

12. According to the *law of one price*, if the costs of transportation are small, the price of the same good in different countries should be roughly the same. The theory that exchange rates are set so that the price of similar goods in different countries is the same is known as the *purchasing-power-parity* theory. In practice, transportation costs are significant for many goods, and the law of one price does not hold for these goods.

13. A high rate of inflation in one country relative to another country puts pressure on the exchange rate between the two countries. There is a general tendency for the currencies of relatively high-inflation countries to depreciate.

14. A depreciation of the dollar tends to increase U.S. GDP by making U.S. exports cheaper (hence, more competitive abroad) and by making U.S. imports more expensive (encouraging consumers to switch to domestically produced goods and services).

15. The effect of a depreciation of a nation's currency on its balance of trade is unclear. In the short run, a currency depreciation may increase the balance-of-trade deficit because it raises the price of imports. Although this price increase causes a decrease in the quantity of imports demanded, the impact of a depreciation on the price of imports is generally felt quickly, but it takes time for export and import quantities to respond to price changes. The initial effect is likely to be negative, but after exports and imports have had time to respond, the net effect turns positive. The tendency for the balance-of-trade deficit to widen and then to decrease as the result of a currency depreciation is known as the *J-curve effect*.

16. The depreciation of a country's currency tends to raise its price level for two reasons. First, a currency depreciation increases planned aggregate expenditure, an effect that shifts the aggregate demand curve to the right. If the economy is close to capacity, the result is likely to be higher prices. Second, a depreciation makes imported inputs more expensive. If costs increase, the aggregate supply curve shifts to the left. If aggregate demand remains unchanged, the result is an increase in the price level.

17. When exchange rates are flexible, a U.S. expansionary monetary policy decreases the interest rate and stimulates planned investment and consumption spending. The lower interest rate leads to a lower demand for U.S. securities by foreigners and a higher demand for foreign securities by U.S. investment-fund managers. As a result, the dollar depreciates. A U.S. contractionary monetary policy appreciates the dollar.

18. Flexible exchange rates do not always work to the advantage of policy makers. An expansionary fiscal policy can appreciate the dollar and work to reduce the multiplier.

## REVIEW TERMS AND CONCEPTS

appreciation of a currency, p. 367

balance of payments, p. 357

balance of trade, p. 358

balance on current account, p. 358

depreciation of a currency, p. 367

exchange rate, p. 356

floating, *or market-determined, exchange rates*, p. 364

foreign exchange, p. 357

J-curve effect, p. 370

law of one price, p. 368

marginal propensity to import (MPM), p. 361

net exports of goods and services (EX − IM), p. 361

price feedback effect, p. 364

purchasing-power-parity theory, p. 368

trade deficit, p. 358

trade feedback effect, p. 363

Equations:

Planned aggregate expenditure in an open economy:

$AE \equiv C + I + G + EX - IM$, p. 361

Open-economy multiplier =

$$\frac{1}{1 - (MPC - MPM)}, \text{p. 362}$$

## PROBLEMS

All problems are available on MyEconLab.

### 19.1 THE BALANCE OF PAYMENTS

**LEARNING OBJECTIVE:** Explain how the balance of payments is calculated.

1.1 Obtain a recent issue of *The Economist*. Turn to the section titled "Financial Indicators." Look at the table titled "Trade, exchange rates and budgets." Which country had the largest trade deficit over the last year and during the last month? Which country had the largest trade surplus over the last year and during the last month? How does the current account deficit/surplus compare to the overall trade balance? How can you explain the difference?

1.2 What effect will each of the following events have on the current account balance and the exchange rate if the exchange rate is fixed? if the exchange rate is floating?
   **a.** The U.S. government cuts taxes and income rises.

   **b.** The U.S. inflation rate increases, and prices in the United States rise faster than those in countries with which the United States trades.
   **c.** The United States adopts an expansionary monetary policy. Interest rates fall (and are now lower than those in other countries) and income rises.
   **d.** The textile companies' "Buy American" campaign is successful, and U.S. consumers switch from purchasing imported products to buying products made in the United States.

1.3 **[Related to the *Economics in Practice* on p. 360]** The United States is the second-largest oil importer in the world (just recently surpassed by China), importing an average of 5 million barrels of crude oil per day in 2014. Go to www.inflationdata.com to look up crude oil prices for the past 5 years; then go to www.bea.gov

to look up the U.S. net international investment position (NIIP) for the past 5 years. Does there appear to be a relationship between the price of crude oil and the U.S. net international investment position? Briefly explain the results of your findings.

## 19.2 EQUILIBRIUM OUTPUT (INCOME) IN AN OPEN ECONOMY

**LEARNING OBJECTIVE:** Discuss how equilibrium output is determined in an open economy, and describe the trade feedback effect and the price feedback effect.

2.1 The exchange rate between the U.S. dollar and the Japanese yen is floating freely—both governments do not intervene in the market for each currency. Suppose a large trade deficit with Japan prompts the United States to impose quotas on certain Japanese products imported into the United States and, as a result, the quantity of these imports falls.
   a. The decrease in spending on Japanese products increases spending on U.S.-made goods. Why? What effect will this have on U.S. output and employment and on Japanese output and employment?
   b. What happens to U.S. imports from Japan when U.S. output (or income) rises? If the quotas initially reduce imports from Japan by $25 billion, why is the final reduction in imports likely to be less than $25 billion?
   c. Suppose the quotas do succeed in reducing imports from Japan by $15 billion. What will happen to the demand for yen? Why?
   d. Considering the macroeconomic effects of a quota on Japanese imports, could a quota reduce employment and output in the United States? have no effect at all? Explain.

2.2 You are given the following model that describes the economy of Hypothetica.
   (1) Consumption function: $C = 80 + 0.75Y_d$
   (2) Planned investment: $I = 49$
   (3) Government spending: $G = 60$
   (4) Exports: $EX = 20$
   (5) Imports: $IM = 0.05Y_d$
   (6) Disposable income: $Y_d = Y - T$
   (7) Taxes: $T = 20$
   (8) Planned aggregate expenditure:

$$AE = C = I + G + EX - IM$$

   (9) Definition of equilibrium income: $Y = AE$
   a. What is equilibrium income in Hypothetica? What is the government deficit? What is the current account balance?
   b. If government spending is increased to $G = 75$, what happens to equilibrium income? Explain using the government spending multiplier. What happens to imports?
   c. Now suppose the amount of imports is limited to $IM = 25$ by a quota on imports. If government spending is again increased from 60 to 75, what happens to equilibrium income? Explain why the same increase in G has a bigger effect on income in the second case. What is it about the presence of imports that changes the value of the multiplier?

   d. If exports are fixed at $EX = 20$, what must income be to ensure a current account balance of zero? (*Hint:* Imports depend on income, so what must income be for imports to be equal to exports?) By how much must we cut government spending to balance the current account? (*Hint:* Use your answer to the first part of this question to determine how much of a decrease in income is needed. Then use the multiplier to calculate the decrease in G needed to reduce income by that amount.)

## 19.3 THE OPEN ECONOMY WITH FLEXIBLE EXCHANGE RATES

**LEARNING OBJECTIVE:** Discuss factors that affect exchange rates in an open economy with a floating system.

3.1 In July 2015, the euro was trading at $1.09. Check the Internet or any daily newspaper to see what the "price" of a euro is today. What explanations can you give for the change? Make sure you check what has happened to interest rates and economic growth.

3.2 Suppose the following graph shows what prevailed on the foreign exchange market in 2015 with floating exchange rates.
   a. Name three phenomena that might shift the demand curve to the right.
   b. Which, if any, of these three phenomena might cause a simultaneous shift of the supply curve to the left?
   c. What effects might each of the three phenomena have on the balance of trade if the exchange rate floats?

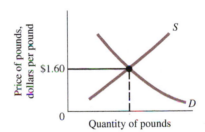

3.3 Suppose the exchange rate between the Danish krone and the U.S. dollar is 7 DKK = $1 and the exchange rate between the Chilean peso and the U.S. dollar is 650 CLP = $1.
   a. Express both of these exchange rates in terms of dollars per unit of the foreign currency.
   b. What should the exchange rate be between the Danish krone and the Chilean peso? Express the exchange rate in terms of 1 krone and in terms of 1 peso.
   c. Suppose the exchange rate between the krone and the dollar changes to 5 DKK = $1 and the exchange rate between the peso and the dollar changes to 700 CLP = $1. For each of the three currencies, explain whether the currency has appreciated or depreciated against the other two currencies.

3.4 Suppose the exchange rate between the British pound and the U.S. dollar is £1 = $1.50.

**a.** Draw a graph showing the demand and supply of pounds for dollars.

**b.** If the Bank of England implements a contractionary monetary policy, explain what will happen to the exchange rate between the pound and the dollar and show this on a graph. Has the dollar appreciated or depreciated relative to the pound? Explain.

**c.** If the U.S. government implements an expansionary fiscal policy, explain what will happen to the exchange rate between the pound and the dollar and show this on a graph. Has the dollar appreciated or depreciated relative to the pound? Explain.

**3.5** Canada is the largest trading partner for the United States. In 2014, U.S. exports to Canada were more than $312 billion and imports from Canada totaled more than $347 billion. On January 1, 2014, the exchange rate between the Canadian dollar and the U.S. dollar was 1.06 Canadian dollars = 1 U.S. dollar. On January 1, 2015, the exchange rate was 1.17 Canadian dollars = 1 U.S. dollar. Explain how this change in exchange rates could impact U.S. consumers and firms?

**3.6** The exchange rate between the U.S. dollar and the British pound is a floating rate, with no government intervention. If a large trade deficit with Great Britain prompts the United States to impose quotas on certain British imports, resulting in a reduction in the quantity of these imports, what will happen to the dollar–pound exchange rate? Why? (*Hint:* There is an excess supply of pounds, or an excess demand for dollars.) What effects will the change in the value of each currency have on employment and output in the United States? What about the balance of trade? (Ignore complications such as the J curve.)

**3.7** Do a Web search and find a Website where you can look up historical exchange rates. Find the exchange rates between the U.S. dollar and the euro, the Canadian dollar, the Japanese yen, and the Chinese yuan at the beginning of 2014 and at the end of 2014. Did the U.S. dollar appreciate or depreciate against these currencies during 2014? Go to www.census.gov and find the value of U.S. exports, imports, and the U.S. trade balance at the beginning of 2014 and at the end of 2014. Did these values increase or decrease during 2014? Explain how the changes in the exchange rates may have had an impact on the changes in U.S exports, imports, and the trade balance.

**3.8** The data in the following table represents price level changes and interest rate changes over a one-year period for three countries: Astoria, Borgia, and Calistoga. Based on the data, explain what is likely to happen to the exchange rate for Astorian asters relative to the other two countries' currencies over that one-year period. Use supply and demand graphs to support your answer, with prices listed as asters per borg and asters per cali, and quantities representing borgs and calis.

| Country/<br>Currency | Price Index<br>January<br>1, 2015 | Price Index<br>January<br>1, 2016 | Interest Rate<br>January<br>1, 2015 | Interest R<br>January<br>1, 2016 |
|---|---|---|---|---|
| Astoria/aster | 100 | 110 | 4 percent | 6 percent |
| Borgia/borg | 120 | 132 | 4 percent | 8 percent |
| Calistoga/cali | 150 | 168 | 4 percent | 6 percent |

---

# CHAPTER 19 APPENDIX

**LEARNING** OBJECTIVE

Explain what the Bretton Woods system is.

## World Monetary Systems Since 1900

Since the beginning of the twentieth century, the world has operated under a number of different monetary systems. This Appendix provides a brief history of each and a description of how they worked.

## The Gold Standard

The gold standard was the major system of exchange rate determination before 1914. All currencies were priced in terms of gold—an ounce of gold was worth so much in each currency. When all currencies exchanged at fixed ratios to gold, exchange rates could be determined easily. For instance, 1 ounce of gold was worth $20 U.S.; that same ounce of gold exchanged for £4 (British pounds). Because $20 and £4 were each worth 1 ounce of gold, the exchange rate between dollars and pounds was $20/£4, or $5 to £1.

For the gold standard to be effective, it had to be backed up by the country's willingness to buy and sell gold at the determined price. As long as countries maintain their currencies at a fixed value in terms of gold *and* as long as each country is willing to buy and sell gold, exchange rates are fixed. If at the given exchange rate the number of U.S. citizens who want to buy things produced in Great Britain is equal to the number of British citizens who want to buy things produced in the United States, the currencies of the two countries will simply be exchanged. What if U.S. citizens suddenly decide they want to drink imported Scotch instead of domestic bourbon? If the British do not have an increased desire for U.S. goods, they will still accept U.S. dollars because those dollars can be redeemed in gold. This gold can then be immediately turned into pounds.

As long as a country's overall balance of payments remained in balance, no gold would enter or leave the country and the economy would be in equilibrium. If U.S. citizens bought more from the British than the British bought from the United States, however, the U.S. balance of payments would be in deficit and the U.S. stock of gold would begin to fall. Conversely, Britain would start to accumulate gold because it would be exporting more than it spent on imports.

Under the gold standard, gold was a big determinant of the money supply.[1] An inflow of gold into a country caused that country's money supply to expand, and an outflow of gold caused that country's money supply to contract. If gold were flowing from the United States to Great Britain, the British money supply would expand and the U.S. money supply would contract.

Now recall from previously chapters the impacts of a change in the money supply. An expanded money supply in Britain will lower British interest rates and stimulate aggregate demand. As a result, aggregate output (income) and the price level in Britain will increase. Higher British prices will discourage U.S. citizens from buying British goods. At the same time, British citizens will have more income and will face relatively lower import prices, causing them to import more from the States.

On the other side of the Atlantic, U.S. citizens will face a contracting domestic money supply. This will cause higher interest rates, declining aggregate demand, lower prices, and falling output (income). The effect will be lower demand in the United States for British goods. Thus, changes in relative prices and incomes that resulted from the inflow and outflow of gold would automatically bring trade back into balance.

## Problems with the Gold Standard

Two major problems were associated with the gold standard. First, the gold standard implied that a country had little control over its money supply. The reason, as we have just seen, is that the money stock increased when the overall balance of payments was in surplus (gold inflow) and decreased when the overall balance was in deficit (gold outflow). A country that was experiencing a balance-of-payments deficit could correct the problem only by the painful process of allowing its money supply to contract. This contraction brought on a slump in economic activity, a slump that would eventually restore balance-of-payments equilibrium, but only after reductions in income and employment. Countries could (and often did) act to protect their gold reserves, and this precautionary step prevented the adjustment mechanism from correcting the deficit.

Making the money supply depend on the amount of gold available had another disadvantage. When major new gold fields were discovered (as in California in 1849 and South Africa in 1886), the world's supply of gold (and therefore of money) increased. The price level rose and income increased. When no new gold was discovered, the supply of money remained unchanged and prices and income tended to fall.

When President Reagan took office in 1981, he established a commission to consider returning the nation to the gold standard. The final commission report recommended against such a move. An important part of the reasoning behind this recommendation was that the gold standard puts enormous economic power in the hands of gold-producing nations.

---

[1] In the days when currencies were tied to gold, changes in the amount of gold influenced the supply of money in two ways. A change in the quantity of gold coins in circulation had a direct effect on the supply of money; indirectly, gold served as a backing for paper currency. A decrease in the central bank's gold holdings meant a decline in the amount of paper money that could be supported.

## Fixed Exchange Rates and the Bretton Woods System

As World War II drew to a close, a group of economists from the United States and Europe met to formulate a new set of rules for exchange rate determination that they hoped would avoid the difficulties of the gold standard. The rules they designed became known as the *Bretton Woods system*, after the town in New Hampshire where the delegates met. The Bretton Woods system was based on two (not necessarily compatible) premises. First, countries were to maintain fixed exchange rates with one another. Instead of pegging their currencies directly to gold, however, currencies were fixed in terms of the U.S. dollar, which was fixed in value at $35 per ounce of gold. The British pound, for instance, was fixed at roughly $2.40, so that an ounce of gold was worth approximately £14.6. As we shall see, the pure system of fixed exchange rates would work in a manner very similar to the pre-1914 gold standard.

The second aspect of the Bretton Woods system added a new wrinkle to the operation of the international economy. Countries experiencing a "fundamental disequilibrium" in their balance of payments were allowed to change their exchange rates. (The term *fundamental disequilibrium* was necessarily vague, but it came to be interpreted as a large and persistent current account deficit.) Exchange rates were not really fixed under the Bretton Woods system; they were, as someone remarked, only "fixed until further notice."

The point of allowing countries with serious current account problems to alter the value of their currency was to avoid the harsh recessions that the operation of the gold standard would have produced under these circumstances. However, the experience of the European economies in the years between World War I and World War II suggested that it might not be a good idea to give countries complete freedom to change their exchange rates whenever they wanted.

During the Great Depression, many countries undertook so-called competitive devaluations to protect domestic output and employment. That is, countries would try to encourage exports—a source of output growth and employment—by attempting to set as low an exchange rate as possible, thereby making their exports competitive with foreign-produced goods. Unfortunately, such policies had a built-in flaw. A devaluation of the pound against the French franc might help encourage British exports to France, but if those additional British exports cut into French output and employment, France would likely respond by devaluing the franc against the pound, a move that, of course, would undo the effects of the pound's initial devaluation.

To solve this exchange rate rivalry, the Bretton Woods agreement created the International Monetary Fund (IMF). Its job was to assist countries experiencing temporary current account problems.[2] It was also supposed to certify that a "fundamental disequilibrium" existed before a country was allowed to change its exchange rate. The IMF was like an international economic traffic cop whose job was to ensure that all countries were playing the game according to the agreed-to rules and to provide emergency assistance where needed.

## "Pure" Fixed Exchange Rates

Under a pure fixed exchange rate system, governments set a particular *fixed* rate at which their currencies will exchange for one another and then commit themselves to maintaining that rate. A true fixed exchange rate system is like the gold standard in that exchange rates are supposed to stay the same forever. Because currencies are no longer backed by gold, they have no fixed, or standard, value relative to one another. There is, therefore, no automatic mechanism to keep exchange rates aligned with each other, as with the gold standard.

The result is that under a pure fixed exchange rate system, governments must at times intervene in the foreign exchange market to keep currencies aligned at their established values. Economists define government intervention in the foreign exchange market as the buying or selling of foreign exchange for the purpose of manipulating the exchange rate.

---

[2] The idea was that the IMF would make short-term loans to a country with a current account deficit. The loans would enable the country to correct the current account problem gradually, without bringing on a deep recession, running out of foreign exchange reserves, or devaluing the currency.

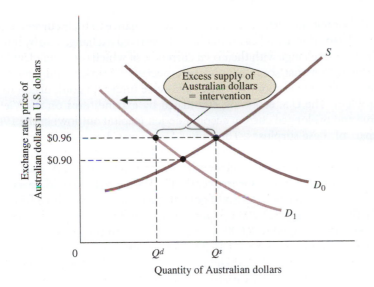

◀ **FIGURE 19A.1**
**Government Intervention
in the Foreign Exchange
Market**
If the price of Australian dollars
were set in a completely unfettered market, one Australian
dollar would cost 0.96 U.S.
dollars when demand is $D_0$ and
0.90 when demand is $D_1$. If the
government has committed to
keeping the value at 0.96, it
must buy up the excess supply of
Australian dollars ($Q^s - Q^d$).

What kind of intervention is likely to occur under a fixed exchange rate system, and how does it work?

We can see how intervention works by looking at Figure 19.A.1. Initially, the market for Australian dollars is in equilibrium. At the fixed exchange rate of 0.96, the supply of dollars is exactly equal to the demand for dollars. No government intervention is necessary to maintain the exchange rate at this level. Now suppose Australian wines are found to be contaminated with antifreeze and U.S. citizens switch to California wines. This substitution away from the Australian product shifts the U.S. demand curve for Australian dollars to the left: The United States demands fewer Australian dollars at every exchange rate (cost of an Australian dollar) because it is purchasing less from Australia than it did before.

If the price of Australian dollars were set in a completely unfettered market, the shift in the demand curve would lead to a fall in the price of Australian dollars, just the way the price of wheat would fall if there was an excess supply of wheat. Remember, the Australian and U.S. governments have committed themselves to maintaining the rate at 0.96. To do so, either the U.S. government or the Australian government (or both) must buy up the excess supply of Australian dollars to keep its price from falling. In essence, the fixed exchange rate policy commits governments to making up any difference between the supply of a currency and the demand so as to keep the price of the currency (exchange rate) at the desired level. The government promises to act as the supplier (or demander) of last resort, who will ensure that the amount of foreign exchange demanded by the private sector will equal the supply at the fixed price.

## Problems with the Bretton Woods System

As it developed after the end of World War II, the system of more-or-less fixed exchange rates had some flaws that led to its abandonment in 1971.

First, there was a basic asymmetry built into the rules of international finance. Countries experiencing large and persistent current account deficits—what the Bretton Woods agreements termed "fundamental disequilibria"—were obliged to devalue their currencies and/or take measures to cut their deficits by contracting their economies. Both of these alternatives were unpleasant because devaluation meant rising prices and contraction meant rising unemployment. However, a country with a current account deficit had no choice because it was losing stock of foreign exchange reserves. When its stock of foreign currencies became exhausted, it had to change its exchange rate because further intervention (selling off some of its foreign exchange reserves) became impossible.

Countries experiencing current account surpluses were in a different position because they were gaining foreign exchange reserves. Although these countries were supposed to stimulate their economies and/or revalue their currencies to restore balance to their current account, they were not obliged to do so. They could easily maintain their fixed exchange rate by buying up any excess supply of foreign exchange with their own currency, of which they had plentiful supply.

In practice, this meant that some countries—especially Germany and Japan—tended to run large and chronic current account surpluses and were under no compulsion to take steps to correct the problem. The U.S. economy, stimulated by expenditures on the Vietnam War, experienced a large and prolonged current account deficit (capital outflow) in the 1960s, which was the counterpart of these surpluses. The United States was, however, in a unique position under the Bretton Woods system. The value of gold was fixed in terms of the U.S. dollar at $35 per ounce of gold. Other countries fixed their exchange rates in terms of U.S. dollars (and therefore only indirectly in terms of gold). Consequently, the United States could never accomplish anything by devaluing its currency in terms of gold. If the dollar was devalued from $35 to $40 per ounce of gold, the yen, pegged at 200 yen per dollar, would move in parallel with the dollar (from 7,000 yen per ounce of gold to 8,000 yen per ounce), with the dollar–yen exchange rate unaffected. To correct its current account deficits vis-à-vis Japan and Germany, it would be necessary for those two countries to adjust their currencies' exchange rates with the dollar. These countries were reluctant to do so for a variety of reasons. As a result, the U.S. current account was chronically in deficit throughout the late 1960s.

A second flaw in the Bretton Woods system was that it permitted devaluations only when a country had a "chronic" current account deficit and was in danger of running out of foreign exchange reserves. This meant that devaluations could often be predicted quite far in advance, and they usually had to be rather large if they were to correct any serious current account problem. The situation made it tempting for speculators to "attack" the currencies of countries with current account deficits.

Problems such as these eventually led the United States to abandon the Bretton Woods rules in 1971. The U.S. government refused to continue pegging the value of the dollar in terms of gold. Thus, the prices of all currencies were free to find their own levels.

The alternative to fixed exchange rates is a system that allows exchange rates to move freely or flexibly in response to market forces. Two types of flexible exchange rate systems are usually distinguished. In a *freely floating system*, governments do not intervene at all in the foreign exchange market.[3] They do not buy or sell currencies with he aim of manipulating the rates. In a *managed floating system*, governments intervene if markets are becoming "disorderly"—fluctuating more than a government believes is desirable. Governments may also intervene if they think a currency is increasing or decreasing too much in value even though the day-to-day fluctuations may be small.

Since the demise of the Bretton Woods system in 1971, the world's exchange rate system can be described as "managed floating." One of the important features of this system has been times of large fluctuations in exchange rates. For example, the yen–dollar rate went from 347 in 1971 to 210 in 1978, to 125 in 1988, and to 80 in 1995. Those are very large changes, changes that have important effects on the international economy, some of which we have covered in this text.

---

[3] However, governments may from time to time buy or sell foreign exchange for their own needs (instead of influencing the exchange rate). For example, the U.S. government might need British pounds to buy land for a U.S. embassy building in London. For our purposes, we ignore this behavior because it is not "intervention" in the strict sense of the word.

## APPENDIX SUMMARY

1. The gold standard was the major system of exchange rate determination before 1914. All currencies were priced in terms of gold. Difficulties with the gold standard led to the Bretton Woods agreement following World War II. Under this system, countries maintained fixed exchange rates with one another and fixed the value of their currencies in terms of the U.S. dollar. Countries experiencing a "fundamental disequilibrium" in their current accounts were permitted to change their exchange rates.

2. The Bretton Woods system was abandoned in 1971. Since then, the world's exchange rate system has been one of managed floating rates. Under this system, governments intervene if foreign exchange markets are fluctuating more than the government thinks desirable.

# APPENDIX PROBLEMS

All problems are available on MyEconLab.

## CHAPTER 19 APPENDIX: WORLD MONETARY SYSTEMS SINCE 1900

LEARNING OBJECTIVE: Explain what the Bretton Woods system is.

1A.1 The currency of Atlantis is the wimp. In 2012, Atlantis developed a balance-of-payments deficit with the United States as a result of an unanticipated decrease in exports; U.S. citizens cut back on the purchase of Atlantean goods. Assume Atlantis is operating under a system of fixed exchange rates.
  a. How does the drop in exports affect the market for wimps? Identify the deficit graphically.
  b. How must the government of Atlantis act (in the short run) to maintain the value of the wimp?
  c. If Atlantis had originally been operating at full employment (potential GDP), what impact would those events have had on its economy? Explain your answer.
  d. The chief economist of Atlantis suggests an expansionary monetary policy to restore full employment; the Secretary of Commerce suggests a tax cut (expansionary fiscal policy). Given the fixed exchange rate system, describe the effects of these two policy options on Atlantis's current account.
  e. How would your answers to a, b, and c change if the two countries operated under a floating rate system?

# 20

# Economic Growth in Developing Economies

In 2000 all 189 member states of the United Nations (UN) agreed to work towards achieving a set of eight Millennium Development Goals (MDG) for the developing world by 2015. Goals ranged from eradicating hunger and achieving universal primary education to reducing child and maternal mortality to fostering gender equality and environmental sustainability. In the fall of 2015, the UN will again convene to measure progress on these goals and next steps. Although there is disagreement about how achievable some of the goals are and what strategies will be most helpful, the breadth of those goals provides us with a clear picture of on how many dimensions the developing world differs from the developed economy we have been studying in this text and how complex the process of development will be.

We will begin our discussion in this chapter with a look at some data comparing the developing and developed world. With this context, we turn to look at strategies for economic development generally and then look at evidence on some specific interventions in the developing world, largely focused on the poorest households. As part of this discussion we will touch on some methodological questions current in economics about how best to determine whether particular policy interventions work or do not work.

# Life in the Developing Nations: Population and Poverty

**20.1 LEARNING** OBJECTIVE
Discuss the characteristics of developing nations.

In 2015, the population of the world reached more than 7 billion people. Most of the world's more than 200 nations belong to the developing world, also known as the **Global South**, in which about three-fourths of the world's population lives.

**Global South** Devloping Nations in Asia, Africa, and Latin America.

In the last decade, rapid economic progress has brought some developing nations closer to developed economies. Countries such as Argentina and Chile, still considered part of the Global South, have vibrant middle classes. Russia and many countries in the former Soviet bloc have also climbed to middle-income status. China and India, while still experiencing some of the challenges of the Global South, are becoming economic superpowers. At present, China's gross domestic product (GDP) is second only in the world to the United States. Other parts of the world, most notably parts of Asia and Africa, lag behind on many of the central dimensions of well-being identified by the UN and others. A central challenge in development economics is to explain why some countries lag and whether successful strategies of the past have lessons for the countries still left behind.

Table 20.1 describes the progress of a dozen nations from 1990 to 2013 on two of the measures of human capital targeted by the MDG, child mortality younger than age 5 and literacy. As we will see in the next section, health and education are two of the lynch pins of economic development. If you think back to our discussion of economic growth in Chapter 16, you will recall the importance of human capital in promoting economic growth.

What do the data tell us? The good news is that on both measures progress has been made over the last 25 years. In all countries, developed and developing, child mortality has fallen and literacy has risen. The improvement in child mortality in China is especially notable. But the disparity between Global North and Global South remains high. In 2014 in the sub-Saharan countries 1 in 10 children die before they are five. In some of the countries in Africa, including Niger, Chad, and Central African Republic, illiteracy remains high at less than half the adult population. Moreover, even as the Global South increases its primary education levels, the Global North is providing college educations to a larger fraction of their populations. Although the countries of the developing world exhibit considerable diversity in both their standards of living and their particular experiences of growth, marked differences continue to separate them from the developed nations.

The great majority of the population in the Global South live in rural areas where agricultural work is hard and extremely time-consuming. Productivity (output produced per worker) is low in part because farmers work with little capital. Low productivity means farm output per person is barely sufficient to feed a farmer's own family. The UN figures indicate that in 2014,

| TABLE 20.1 | Comparisons of Child Mortality and Literacy: Selected Countries 1990 and 2013 | | | |
|---|---|---|---|---|
| Country | 1990: Mortality younger than age 5 | 2013: Mortality younger than age 5 | 1990: Literacy rates, ages 15–24 | 2013 Literacy rates: ages 15–24 |
| Afghanistan | 179.1 | 97.3 | Na | 47.0 |
| Angola | 225.9 | 167.4 | Na | 73.0 |
| Australia | 9.2 | 4.0 | 100.0 | 100.0 |
| Chad | 214.7 | 147.5 | 17.3 | 48.9 |
| Central African Republic | 176.9 | 139.2 | Na | 36.4 |
| China | 53.9 | 12.7 | 94.3 | 99.6 |
| Denmark | 8.9 | 3.5 | 100.0 | 100.0 |
| Guinea Bissau | 224.8 | 123.9 | Na | 74.3 |
| India | 125.9 | 52.7 | 61.9 | 81.1 |
| Niger | 327.3 | 104.2 | Na | 23.5 |
| Sierra Leone | 267.7 | 160.6 | Na | 62.7 |
| United States | 11.2 | 6.9 | 100.0 | 100 .0 |

*Source:* UN, Millennium Development Goal Data, 2015.

## ECONOMICS IN PRACTICE

### What Can We Learn from the Height of Children?

The first of the Millennium Development Goals is to substantially cut the number of households who experience extreme hunger. One of four children younger than 5 years of age in the world are characterized as stunted, extremely short because of malnutrition. Of these children, one half are in Asia and one third in Africa. For these children poor nutrition in the early years leaves a permanent mark, reflected in life span and earnings.

Recent work in economics has focused on the case of stunting in India. India's stunting rate is among the highest in the world, exceeding even that of the much poorer African nations. Moreover, despite rapid growth in the last decade, little progress has been made in reducing the stunting rate. Seema Jayanchandran from Northwestern and Rohini Pande of Harvard's Kennedy School examined several large data sets to try to understand why.[1]

The first clue comes from the pattern of India's stunting. Looking at the data, Jayannchandran and Pande learn that Indian first born sons are actually taller than their African counterparts. Stunting emerges only for later born children, and the amount of stunting increases with the number of children. Among the most disadvantaged are girls with no older brothers whose parents continue to attempt to produce a son.

The patterns that emerge from this study put a spotlight on two of the MDG concerns: hunger and gender equality. The researchers argue that India's high stunting rate is explicable by the strong son preference of Indian families and the concomitant decision to invest disproportionate family resources in the first born son to insure his survival despite the family's poverty.

#### THINKING PRACTICALLY

1. Why might growth in the overall economy not have led to more improvement in the stunting rate?

[1] Seema Jayachandran and Rohini Pande, "Why are Indian Children so Short?" Working Paper, March 2015.

870 million people, primarily in the developing world, experienced extreme hunger. In addition, many developing nations are engaged in civil and external warfare.

In recent years there has been more concern with the increased inequality that has come with development in some countries. India is on the World Bank's list of low-income countries, yet Mumbai, a state capital, is one of the top 10 centers of commerce in the world, home to Bollywood, the world's largest film industry. China with its rapid growth rates and increased affluence in urban areas still has a large agrarian population that has been mostly left behind by recent growth. Many of the specific interventions we will look at in this chapter are focused on designing strategies to bringing the households at the bottom rung of the income distribution into the mainstream economy of a country.

**20.2 LEARNING OBJECTIVE**

Describe the sources of economic development.

# Economic Development: Sources and Strategies

Economists have been trying to understand economic growth and development since Adam Smith and David Ricardo in the eighteenth and nineteenth centuries, but the study of development economics as it applies to the developing nations has a much shorter history. The geopolitical struggles that followed World War II brought increased attention to the developing nations and their economic problems. During this period, the new field of development economics asked simply: Why are some nations poor and others rich? If economists could understand the barriers to economic growth that prevent nations from developing and the prerequisites that would help them to develop, economists could prescribe strategies for achieving economic advancement.

We will see in this discussion that there is lively debate on the question of why some nations are poor and the corollary, how can we help countries get out of poverty. Ahijit Banerjee and Esther Duflo, both John Bates Clark award winners and MIT professors, on the other hand, argue in their influential book *Poor Economics*[1] that it is not really possible at this point to answer well the question of why some countries are poor and others rich and that the more relevant question is what types of policy interventions help households get out of poverty. We move to that discussion in the last section of this chapter.

## The Sources of Economic Development

Although a general theory of economic development applicable to all nations has not emerged, some basic factors that limit a poor nation's economic growth have been suggested. These include insufficient capital formation, a shortage of human resources and entrepreneurial ability, and a lack of infrastructure.

**Capital Formation**    Almost all developing nations have a scarcity of capital relative to other resources, especially labor. The small stock of physical capital (factories, machinery, farm equipment, and other productive capital) constrains labor's productivity and holds back national output.

Jeffrey Sachs, a professor at the Earth Institute at Columbia and a key economist in helping to develop the MDG, emphasizes the role of capital in moving countries out of poverty.[2] Faced with bad climates, few resources and disease, poor countries find it hard to amass the capital needed to develop. They are stuck in a "poverty trap," sometimes also called the **vicious circle of poverty**. Without investment, the capital stock does not grow, the income remains low, and the vicious circle is complete. Poverty becomes self-perpetuating.

**vicious circle of poverty** Suggests that poverty is self-perpetuating because poor nations are unable to save and invest enough to accumulate the capital stock that would help them grow.

Sachs argues that one can use foreign aid as a lever to move countries out of poverty, providing the key capital needed for both public and private investments. Indeed, Sachs estimates that $195 billion in foreign aid per year could eliminate global poverty in 20 years. Other economists are less confident that foreign aid can play this role. Both William Easterly, Director of NYU's Development Research Institute, in his book *The Elusive Quest for Growth*[3] and Dambisa Moyo, a Zambian economist, in her book *Dead Aid*[4] argue that foreign aid can actually hamper development by distorting market incentives for local entrepreneurs.

There are also questions surrounding the assumption that poor countries cannot generate capital themselves. Japanese GDP per capita in 1900 was well below that of many of today's developing nations, yet today it is among the developed nations. Among the many nations with low levels of capital per capita, some—like China—have managed to grow and develop in the last 20 years, whereas others remain behind. In even the poorest countries, there remains some capital surplus that could be harnessed if conditions were right. Many current observers believe that scarcity of capital in some developing countries may have more to do with a lack of incentives for citizens to save and invest productively than with any absolute scarcity of income available for capital accumulation. Many of the rich in developing countries invest their savings in Europe or in the United States instead of in their own country, which may have a riskier political climate. Savings transferred to the United States do not lead to physical capital growth in the developing countries. The term **capital flight** refers to the fact that both human capital and financial capital (domestic savings) leave developing countries in search of higher expected rates of return elsewhere or returns with less risk. Government policies in the developing nations—including price ceilings, import controls, and even outright appropriation of private property—tend to discourage investment. There has been increased attention to the role that financial institutions, including accounting systems and property-right rules, play in encouraging domestic capital formation.

**capital flight** The tendency for both human capital and financial capital to leave developing countries in search of higher expected rates of return elsewhere with less risk.

---

[1] Abhijit Banerjee and Esther Duflo, *Poor Economics*, Perseus Books, 2011.
[2] Jeffrey Sachs, *The End of Poverty: Economic Possibilities for Our Time*, Penguin press, NY, 2005
[3] William Easterly, *The Elusive Quest for Growth*, MIT Press, 2001.
[4] Dambisa Moyo, *Dead Aid: Why Aid is Not Working and How There Is a Better Way for Africa*, Allen Lane 2009.

Whatever the causes of capital shortages, it is clear that the absence of productive capital prevents income from rising in any economy. The availability of capital is a necessary, but not a *sufficient*, condition for economic growth. The landscape of the developing countries is littered with idle factories and abandoned machinery. Other ingredients are required to achieve economic progress.

### Human Resources and Entrepreneurial Ability

Capital is not the only factor of production required to produce output. Labor is equally important. To be productive, the workforce must be healthy. Disease today is the leading threat to development in much of the world. In 2011, almost a million people died of malaria, almost all of them in Africa. The Gates Foundation has targeted malaria eradication as one of its key goals in the next decade. HIV/AIDS was still responsible for almost 2 million deaths in 2011, again mostly in Africa, and has left Africa with more than 14 million AIDS orphans. Iron deficiency and parasites sap the strength of many workers in the developing world. Control of malaria and HIV/AIDS are one of the MDG goals for 2015.

As we saw in Table 20.1, low-income countries also lag behind high-income countries in literacy rates. To be productive, the workforce must be educated and trained. Basic literacy as well as specialized training, for example, can yield high returns to both the individual worker and the economy. Education has grown to become the largest category of government expenditure in many developing nations, in part because of the belief that human resources are the ultimate determinant of economic advance. Nevertheless, in many developing countries, many children, especially girls, receive only a few years of formal education. As technology pushes up the wage premium on skilled workers the impact of low literacy rates on a country's GDP rises.

Just as financial capital seeks the highest and safest return, so does human capital. Thousands of students from developing countries, many of whom were supported by their governments, graduate every year from U.S. colleges and universities. After graduation, these people face a difficult choice: to remain in the United States and earn a high salary or to return home and accept a job at a much lower salary. Many remain in the United States. This **brain drain** siphons off many of the most talented minds from developing countries.

It is interesting to look at what happens to the flow of educated workers as countries develop. Increasingly, students who have come from China and India to study are returning to their home countries eager to use their skills in their newly growing economies. The return flow of this human capital stimulates growth and is a signal that growth is occurring. Indeed, development economists have found evidence that in India, schooling choices made by parents for their children respond quite strongly to changes in employment opportunities.[5] The connection between growth and human capital is in fact a two-way street.

Even when educated workers leave for the developed world, they may contribute to the growth of their home country. Recently, economists have begun studying *remittances*, compensation sent back from recent immigrants to their families in less developed countries. Although measurement is difficult, estimates of these remittances are approximately $100 billion per year. Remittances fund housing and education for families left behind, but they also can provide investment capital for small businesses. In 2007, it appeared that remittances from illegal immigrants in the United States to Mexico, which had been growing by 20 percent per year, were beginning to fall with tightening of enforcement of immigration rules. Remittances fell further in 2008–2009 with the recession, but have recovered somewhat in the recent upturn.

In recent years, we have become increasingly aware of the role of entrepreneurship in economic development. Many of the iconic firms in the nineteenth century that contributed so strongly to the early industrial growth of the United States—Standard Oil, U.S. Steel, Carnegie Steel—were begun by entrepreneurs starting with little capital. In China, one of the top search engines is Baidu, a firm started in 2000 by two Chinese nationals, Eric Xu and Robin Li, and now traded on NASDAQ, as is AliBaba, an online retailer. Providing opportunities and incentives for

**brain drain** The tendency for talented people from developing countries to become educated in a developed country and remain there after graduation.

---

[5] The classic work in this area was done by Kaivan Munshi and Mark Rosenzweig, "Traditional Institutions Meet the Modern World: Caste, Gender, and Schooling Choice in a Globalizing Economy," *American Economic Review*, September 2006, 1225–1252. More recent work includes Emily Oster and Bryce Millett, "Do Call Centers Promote School Enrollment? Evidence from India," Chicago Booth Working Paper, June 2010.

# ECONOMICS IN PRACTICE

## Corruption

Many people have argued that one barrier to economic development in a number of countries is the level of corruption and inefficiency in the government. Measuring levels of corruption and inefficiency can be difficult. Some researchers have tried surveys and experiments. Ray Fisman[1] had a more unusual way to measure the way in which political connections interfere with the workings of the market in Indonesia.

From 1967 to 1998, Indonesia was ruled by President Suharto. While Suharto ruled, his children and longtime allies were affiliated with a number of Indonesian companies. Fisman had the clever idea of looking at what happened to the stock market prices of those firms connected to the Suharto clan relative to unaffiliated firms when Suharto unexpectedly fell ill. Fisman found a large and significant reduction in the value of those affiliated firms on rumors of illness. What does this tell us? A firm's stock price reflects investors' views of what earnings the firm can expect to have. In the case of firms connected to Suharto, the decline in their stock prices tells us that a large part of the reason investors think that those firms are doing well is because of the family connection rather than the firm's inherent efficiency. One reason corruption is bad for an economy is that it often leads to the wrong firms, the less efficient firms, producing the goods and services in the society.

The following chart shows the World Bank's rating of corruption levels in a number of countries in 2013. The countries are ranked from those with the strongest controls on corruption—Germany and Japan—to those with the lowest controls—Russia and Nigeria. Indonesia, as you can see, is low on the list.

### THINKING PRACTICALLY

1. As corruption falls in a country, cost of production often falls. Why?

[1] Raymond Fisman, "Estimating the Value of Political Connections," *The American Economic Review*, September 2001, 1095–1102.

**Control of corruption (2013)**

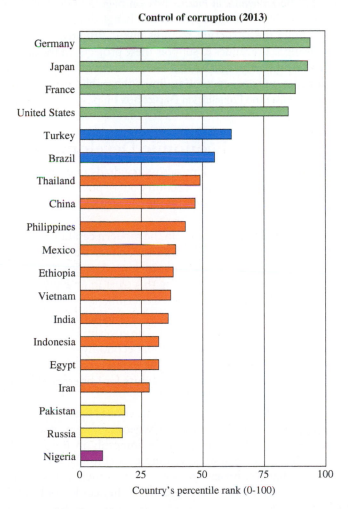

Country's percentile rank (0-100)

*Source:* World Bank, World Wide Governance Indicators Report, Policy Paper 5430, 2014.

*Note:* The governance indicators presented here aggregate the views on the quality of governance provided by a large number of enterprise, citizen, and expert survey respondents in industrial and developing countries. These data are gathered from a number of survey institutes, think tanks, nongovernmental organizations, and international organizations. The aggregate indicators do not reflect the official views of the World Bank, its executive directors, or the countries they represent.

creative risk takers seems to be an increasing part of what needs to be done to promote development. The work by Easterly and Mayo both focus on the potential for poorly-focused foreign aid to distort local entrepreneurial incentives and hamper economic growth.

**Infrastructure Capital**    Anyone who has spent time in a developing nation knows how difficult it can be to carry on everyday life. Problems with water supplies, poor roads, frequent electrical power outages—in the few areas where electricity is available—and often ineffective mosquito and pest control make life and commerce difficult.

**social overhead capital**  Basic infrastructure projects such as roads, power generation, and irrigation systems.

In any economy, developing or otherwise, the government plays an investment role. In a developing economy, the government must create a basic infrastructure—roads, power generation, and irrigation systems. Such projects, sometimes referred to as **social overhead capital**, often cannot successfully be undertaken by the private sector. Many of these projects operate with economies of scale, which means they can be efficient only if they are very large, perhaps too large for any private company or group of companies to carry out. In other cases, the benefits from a development project, although extraordinarily valuable, cannot be easily bought and sold. The availability of clean air and potable water are two examples. Here government must play its role before the private sector can proceed. For example, some observers have recently argued that India's growth prospects are being limited by its poor rail transport system. Goods from Singapore to India move easily over water in less than a day, but they can take weeks to move from port cities to supply factories in the interior. China, by contrast, spent the bulk of its stimulus money in the 2008–2009 period trying to build new transportation networks in part because the government understood how key this social overhead capital was to economic growth. The *Economics in Practice* box on page 390 describes one of the unexpected results of government infrastructure provision in Bangladesh.

To build infrastructure requires public funding. Many less-developed countries struggle with raising tax revenues to support these projects. In the last few years, Greece has struggled to repay its debt partly because of widespread tax evasion by its wealthiest citizens. In many less-developed countries, corruption limits the public funds available for productive government investments, as the *Economics in Practice* box on page 387 suggests.

## Strategies for Economic Development

Despite many studies, looking across hundreds of countries, there has emerged no consensus on the right strategy to move a country out of poverty. Nevertheless, there are several promising strategies that may prove useful at the country level in some contexts.

**The Role of Government**    In the modern capitalist world most investment capital is supplied to entrepreneurs by third parties, either through the banking system we described in previous chapters or through the stock market. For those markets to work, to enable capital to flow, requires trust. Developing this trust in an environment in which most investment is impersonal in turn requires some government oversight. Rules need to be set and enforced, governing the kinds of data reported in financial statements, and the way deposits are protected and terms of loans enforced. The government similarly plays a role in property protections needed in a modern impersonal economy. These institutions are a necessary complement to economic development. The *Economics in Practice* box on page 390 describes the way in which family loans partially substitute for impersonal loans in Bangladesh where financial institutions are less well developed.

Between 1991 and 1997, U.S. firms entered Eastern Europe in search of markets and investment opportunities and immediately became aware of a major obstacle. The institutions that make the market function relatively smoothly in the United States did not exist in Eastern Europe. The banking system, venture capital funds, the stock market, the bond market, commodity exchanges, brokerage houses, investment banks, and so on, have developed in the United States over hundreds of years, and they could not be replicated overnight in the formerly Communist world.

Similar problems exist today in the Chinese economy. Although the Chinese equity market has grown rapidly in the last decade, that growth has been accompanied by problems with weak governance and lack of transparency. These issues discourage investments by western firms.

Many market-supporting institutions are so basic that Americans take them for granted. The institution of private property, for example, is a set of rights that must be protected by laws that the government must be willing to enforce. Suppose the French hotel chain Novotel decides to build a new hotel in Moscow or Beijing. Novotel must first acquire land. Then it will construct a building based on the expectation of renting rooms to customers. These investments are made with the expectation that the owner has a right to use them and a right to the profits that they produce. For such investments to be undertaken, these rights must be guaranteed by a set of property laws. This is equally true for large business firms and for local entrepreneurs who want to start their own enterprises. China's ambiguous property rights laws may also be problematic. Although farmers can own their own homes, for example, all rural land is collectively owned by villages. Farmers have the right to manage farmland, but not own it. As a result, transfer of land is difficult.

Similarly, the law must provide for the enforcement of contracts. In the United States, a huge body of law determines what happens if you break a formal promise made in good faith. Businesses exist on promises to produce and promises to pay. Without recourse to the law when a contract is breached, contracts will not be entered into, goods will not be manufactured, and services will not be provided.

Protection of intellectual property rights is also an important feature of developed market economies. When an artist puts out a record, the artist and his or her studio are entitled to reap revenues from it. When Apple developed the iPod, it too earned the right to collect revenue for its patent ownership. Many less-developed countries lack laws and enforcement mechanisms to protect intellectual property of foreign investments and their own current and future investors. The lack of protection discourages trade and home-grown invention. For example, in late 2007, China, in recognition of some of these issues, began drafting a new set of laws for intellectual property protection.

Another seemingly simple matter that turns out to be quite complex is the establishment of a set of accounting principles. In the United States, the rules of the accounting game are embodied in a set of generally accepted accounting principles (GAAP) that carry the force of law. Companies are required to keep track of their receipts, expenditures, assets, and liabilities so that their performance can be observed and evaluated by shareholders, taxing authorities, and others who have an interest in the company. If you have taken a course in accounting, you know how detailed these rules have become. Imagine trying to do business in a country operating under hundreds of different sets of rules. That is what happened in Russia during its transition.

It is clear that economic development requires these financial and legal institutions. There is more debate about how much the lack of these institutions play a role in keeping some countries poor. Work by Acemoglu, Johnson, and Robinson looking at the history of the African nations assign a prominent role to the lack of institutions in some nations as a cause of poverty.[6] Other work suggests that institutions naturally develop along side of markets and the economy and thus their absence marks market failure rather than causing it.[7]

**The Movement from Agriculture to Industry**   Consider the data in Table 20.2. The richest countries listed—the United States, Japan, and Korea—generate much of their GDP in services, with little value contributed by agricultural production. The poorest countries, on the other hand, have substantial agricultural sectors, although as you can see, the service sector is also large in a number of these economies. The transition to a developing economy typically involves a movement away from agriculture.

Recent work has documented the higher productivity of workers in the nonagricultural sector versus the agricultural sector in developing countries. Even carefully adjusting for difference in human capital of labor in the two sectors, value added per worker is much higher in the nonagricultural sector.[8] This tells us that these countries would be better off in terms

[6] Daron Acemoglu, Simon Johnson and James Robinson, "The Colonial Origins of Comparative Development: An Empirical investigation," *American Economic Review*, 2001, 1369-1401

[7] Edward Glaeser, Rafael La Porta, Florencio Lopez-de-Silanes and Andrei Shleifer, "Do Institutions Cause Growth?" *Journal of Economic Growth* September 2004.

[8] Douglas Gollin, David Lagakos and Michael Waugh, "The Agricultural Productivity Gap," *Quarterly Journal of Economics*, 2014, 939-993

# ECONOMICS IN PRACTICE

## Who You Marry May Depend on the Rain

In Bangladesh, as in many other low-lying countries, river flooding often leaves large swaths of land under water for substantial portions of the year. By building embankments on the side of the river, governments can extend the growing season, allowing several seasons of crops. The result is a wealth increase for people living in affected rural areas. In a recent paper, several economists traced through some unusual consequences of increasing the wealth of rural populations by creating embankments.[1]

In Bangladesh marriages require dowries, paid by the bride's family to the groom. For poor families, raising these dowries can be difficult. Nor is it easy to marry now and promise a dowry-by-installment later on. Making people live up to their promises and pay debts is no easier in Bangladesh than it is elsewhere in the world! The result? In hard times and among the poorer families, people in Bangladesh often marry cousins; promises within an extended family are more easily enforced and wealth sharing inside families also more common.

Now let us think about what happens when the government builds a flood embankment, allowing farmers on one side of the embankment to till the land over most of the year, while those on the other side are faced with six-month flooding. Farmers on the flooded side of the river continue to use marriage within the extended family as a strategy to essentially provide dowries on credit. For those farmers on the more stable side of the river, cousin marriages fell quite substantially.

Because marriage of cousins can have health risks, investments in rural infrastructure can have unforeseen positive effects in an area.

### THINKING PRACTICALLY

1. What do you think happens to the overall marriage rate as a result of the embankment?

[1] Ahmed Mushfiq Mobarak, Randall Kuhn, Christina Peters, "Consanguinity and Other Marriage Market Effects of a Wealth Shock in Bangladesh," *Demography*, forthcoming 2013.

of productivity if they could more quickly move workers out of the agrarian areas and to the urban work place. Indeed, Gharad Bryan from the London School of Economics and Melanie Morton, of Stanford estimated that almost 20 percent of Indonesia's growth between 1976 and 2012 could be accounted for by the reductions in migration costs that occurred during the

| Country | Per-Capita Gross National Income (GNI) | Percentage of Gross Domestic Product | | |
|---|---|---|---|---|
| | | Agriculture | Industry | Services |
| Tanzania | $ 460 | 30 | 23 | 47 |
| Bangladesh | 570 | 19 | 29 | 52 |
| China | 3,040 | 11 | 47 | 40 |
| Thailand | 3,640 | 12 | 44 | 44 |
| Colombia | 4,640 | 8 | 35 | 57 |
| Brazil | 7,490 | 6 | 28 | 66 |
| Korea (Rep.) | 21,430 | 3 | 36 | 61 |
| Japan | 37,840 | 1 | 27 | 71 |
| United States | 47,890 | 1 | 21 | 78 |

**TABLE 20.2** The Structure of Production in Selected Developed and Developing Economies, 2008

*Source:* The World Bank.

period.[9] Similar results were found in an experiment which gave random subsidies to workers in Bangladesh to outmigrate from the farm area to the city during the lean period of the farm year.[10] This work suggests that one way to improve growth in a developing country is to invest in transportation networks or other mechanisms to reduce the costs of moving between rural and urban areas.

**Exports or Import Substitution?**   As developing nations expand their industrial activities, they must decide what type of trade strategy to pursue. Development economists discuss two alternatives: import substitution or export promotion.

**Import substitution** is a strategy used to develop local industries that can manufacture goods to replace imports. If fertilizer is imported, import substitution calls for a domestic fertilizer industry to produce replacements for fertilizer imports. This strategy gained prominence throughout South America in the 1950s. At that time, most developing nations exported agricultural and mineral products, goods that faced uncertain and often unstable international markets. Under these conditions, the call for import substitution policies was understandable. Special government actions, including tariff and quota protection and subsidized imports of machinery, were set up to encourage new domestic industries. Multinational corporations were also invited into many countries to begin domestic operations.

> **import substitution**   An industrial trade strategy that favors developing local industries that can manufacture goods to replace imports.

Most economists believe that import substitution strategies have failed almost everywhere they have been tried. With domestic industries sheltered from international competition by high tariffs (often as high as 200 percent), major economic inefficiencies were created. For example, Peru has a population of approximately 29 million, only a tiny fraction of whom can afford to buy an automobile. Yet at one time, the country had five or six different automobile manufacturers, each of which produced only a few thousand cars per year. Because there are substantial economies of scale in automobile production, the cost per car was much higher than it needed to be, and valuable resources that could have been devoted to another, more productive, activity were squandered producing cars.

As an alternative to import substitution, some nations have pursued strategies of export promotion. **Export promotion** is the policy of encouraging exports. As an industrial market economy, Japan was a striking example to the developing world of the economic success that exports can provide. Japan had an average annual per-capita real GDP growth rate of roughly 6 percent per year from 1960 to 1990. This achievement was, in part, based on industrial production oriented toward foreign consumers.

> **export promotion**   A trade policy designed to encourage exports.

Several countries in the developing world have attempted to emulate Japan's early success. Starting around 1970, Hong Kong, Singapore, Korea, and Taiwan began to pursue export promotion of manufactured goods with good results. Other nations, including Brazil, Colombia, and Turkey, have also had some success at pursuing an outward-looking trade policy. China's growth has been mostly export-driven as well.

Government support of export promotion has often taken the form of maintaining an exchange rate favorable enough to permit exports to compete with products manufactured in developed economies. For example, many people believe China has kept the value of the yuan artificially low. Because a "cheap" yuan means inexpensive Chinese goods in the United States, sales of these goods increased dramatically.

A big issue for countries growing or trying to grow by selling exports on world markets is free trade. African nations in particular have pushed for reductions in tariffs imposed on their agricultural goods by Europe and the United States, arguing that these tariffs substantially reduce Africa's ability to compete in the world marketplace.

**Microfinance**   In the mid-1970s, Muhammad Yunus, a young Bangladeshi economist created the Grameen Bank in Bangladesh. Yunus, who trained at Vanderbilt University and was a former professor at Middle Tennessee State University, used this bank as a vehicle to introduce microfinance to the developing world. In 2006, Yunus received a Nobel Peace Prize for his work.

---

[9] Gharad Bryan and Melanie Morton, "Economic Development and the Spatial Allocation of Labor: Evidence From Indonesia," Stanford Working Paper, February 2015.
[10] Gharad Bryan, Shymal Chowdhury and Ahmed Mushfiq Mobarak, "Underinvestment in a Profitable Technology: The Case of Seasonal Migration in Bangladesh," *Econometrica*, 2014.

Microfinance is the practice of lending very small amounts of money, with no collateral, and accepting small savings deposits.[11] It is aimed at introducing entrepreneurs in the poorest parts of the developing world to the capital market. By 2002, more than 2,500 institutions were making these small loans, serving more than 60 million people. Two thirds of borrowers were living below the poverty line in their own countries, the poorest of the poor.

Yunus, while teaching economics in Bangladesh, began lending his own money to poor households with entrepreneurial ambitions. He found that with even small amounts of money, villagers could start simple businesses: bamboo weaving or hair dressing. Traditional banks found these borrowers unprofitable: The amounts were too small, and it was too expensive to figure out which of the potential borrowers was a good risk. With a borrower having no collateral, information about his or her character was key but was hard for a big bank to discover. Local villagers, however, typically knew a great deal about one another's characters. This insight formed the basis for Yunus's microfinance enterprise. Within a village, people who are interested in borrowing money to start businesses are asked to join lending groups of five people. Loans are then made to two of the potential borrowers, later to a second two, and finally to the last. As long as everyone is repaying their loans, the next group receives theirs. But if the first borrowers fail to pay, all members of the group are denied subsequent loans. What does this do? It makes community pressure a substitute for collateral. Moreover, once the peer-lending mechanism is understood, villagers have incentives to join only with other reliable borrowers. The mechanism of peer lending is a way to avoid the problems of imperfect information described in a previous chapter.

The Grameen model grew rapidly. By 2002, Grameen was lending to two million members. Thirty countries and 30 U.S. states have microfinance lending copied from the Grameen model. Relative to traditional bank loans, microfinance loans are much smaller, repayment begins quickly, and the vast majority of the loans are made to women (who, in many cases, have been underserved by mainstream banks). A growing set of evidence shows that providing opportunities for poor women has stronger spillovers in terms of improving the welfare of children than does providing comparable opportunities for men. More recently small deposit savings accounts have also been introduced to the under-banked populations in the developing world. Although the field of microfinance has changed considerably since Yunus's introduction and some people question how big a role it will ultimately play in spurring major development and economic growth, it has changed many people's views about the possibilities of entrepreneurship and access to financial institutions more generally for the poor of the world.

## Two Examples of Development: China and India

China and India provide two interesting examples of rapidly developing economies. Although low per-capita incomes still mean that both countries are typically labeled developing as opposed to developed countries, many expect that to change in the near future. In the 25-year period from 1978 to 2003, China grew, on average, 9 percent per year, a rate faster than any other country in the world. Even during the 2008–2009 U.S. recession, China continued to grow, and it has continued to do so. While India's surge has been more recent, in the last 8 years, it too has seen annual growth rates in the 6 to 8 percent range. Many commentators expect India and China to dominate the world economy in the twenty-first century.

How did these two rather different countries engineer their development? Consider institutions: India is a democratic country, has a history of the rule of law, and has an English-speaking heritage—all factors typically thought to provide a development advantage. China is still an authoritarian country politically, and property rights are still not well established—both characteristics that were once thought to hinder growth. Both China and India have embraced free-market economics, with China taking the lead as India has worked to remove some of its historical regulatory apparatus.

What about social capital? Both India and China remain densely populated. Although China is the most populous country in the world, India, with a smaller land mass, is the more densely populated. Nevertheless, as is true in most developing nations, birth rates in both countries

---

[11] An excellent discussion of microfinance is contained in Beatriz Armendariz de Aghion and Jonathan Morduch, *The Economics of Microfinance*, (MIT Press, 2005.)

# ECONOMICS IN PRACTICE

## Cell Phones Increase Profits for Fishermen in India

Kerala is a poor state in a region of India. The fishing industry is a major part of the local economy, employing more than one million people and serving as the main source of protein for the population. Every day fishing boats go out; and when they return, the captain of the ship needs to decide where to take the fish to sell. There is much uncertainty in this decision: How much fish will they catch; what other boats will come to a particular location; how many buyers will there be at a location? Moreover, fuel costs are high and timing is difficult, so that once a boat comes ashore, it does not pay for the fishermen to search for a better marketplace. In a recent study of this area, Robert Jensen[1] found on a Tuesday morning in November 1997, 11 fishermen in Badagara were dumping their load of fish because they faced no buyers at the dock. However, unbeknownst to them, 15 kilometers away, 27 buyers were leaving their marketplace empty-handed, with unsatisfied demand for fish.

Beginning in 1997 and continuing for the next several years, mobile phone service was introduced to this region of India. By 2001, the majority of the fishing fleet had mobile phones, which they use to call various vendors ashore to confirm where the buyers are. What was the result? Once the phones were introduced, waste, which had averaged 5 to 8 percent of the total catch, was virtually eliminated. Moreover, just as we would have predicted from the simple laws of supply and demand, the prices of fish across the various villages along the fishing market route were closer to each other than they were before. Jensen found that with less waste

fishermen's profits rose on average by 8 percent, while the average price of fish fell by 4 percent.

In fact, cell phones are improving the way markets in less-developed countries work by providing price and quantity information so that both producers and consumers can make better economic decisions.

### THINKING PRACTICALLY

1. Use a supply-and-demand graph to show the impact of cell phones in India on prices in the fishing market.

[1] Robert Jensen, "The Digital Provide: Information Technology, Market Performance, and Welfare in the South Indian Fisheries Sector," *The Quarterly Journal of Economics*, August 2007.

have fallen. Literacy rates and life expectancy in China are quite high, in part a legacy from an earlier period. India, on the other hand, has a literacy rate that is less than that of China's and a lower life expectancy. In terms of human capital, China appears to have the edge, at least for now.

What about the growth strategies used by the two countries? China has adopted a pragmatic, gradual approach to market development, sharply in contrast to that adopted some years ago in Poland. China's approach has been called *moshi guohe*, or "Crossing the river by feeling for stepping stones." In terms of sector, most of China's growth has been fueled by manufacturing. The focus on manufacturing is one reason that China's energy consumption and environmental issues have increased so rapidly in the last decade. In India, services have led growth, particularly in the software industry. In sum, it is clear from comparing India and China that there is no single recipe for development.

# Development Interventions

**20.3 LEARNING OBJECTIVE**

Discuss the intervention methods used by development economists.

In the last 20 years, development economists have increasingly turned to much narrower, more microeconomically oriented programs to see if they can figure out which interventions do help the condition of the bottom of the income distribution in developing countries and how to replicate those successful programs. This work has in most cases taken over the field as it has moved away from a search for general recipes for growth and development.

# Random and Natural Experiments: Some New Techniques in Economic Development

Suppose we were trying to decide whether it was worthwhile in terms of student achievement to hire another teacher to reduce the student-faculty ratio. One traditional way we might try to answer that question is to find two classrooms with different enrollments in otherwise similar school systems and look at the educational performance of the students. We see comparisons of this sort everyday in newspaper discussions of policies, and many research projects take a variant of this approach. But the approach is subject to serious criticism. It is possible that differences in the two classrooms beyond the enrollment numbers also matter to performance—differences we have failed to correct in the comparisons we make. Crowded classrooms may be in poorer areas (indeed, this may account for the crowding); they may have less effective teachers; they may lack other resources. In the social sciences, it is difficult to ensure that we have comparisons that differ only in the one element in which we are interested. The fact that our interventions involve people makes it even harder. In the case of the classrooms with small enrollment, it may well be that the most attentive parents have pushed to have their children in these classrooms, believing them to be better. Perhaps the best teachers apply to lead these classrooms, and their higher quality makes it more likely that they get their first choice of classrooms. If either of these things happens, the two classrooms will differ in systematic ways that bias the results in favor of finding better performance in the smaller classrooms. More attentive parents may provide home support that results in better test outcomes for their children even if the classrooms are crowded. Better teachers improve performance no matter how crowded the classrooms are. Problems of this sort, sometimes called selection bias, plague social science research.

In recent years, a group of development economists began using a technique borrowed from the natural sciences, the **random experiment**, to try to get around the selection problem in evaluating interventions. Instead of looking at results from classrooms that have made different choices about class size or textbooks, for example, the experimenters randomly assign otherwise identical-looking classes to either follow or not follow an intervention. Students and teachers are not allowed to shift around. By comparing the outcomes of large numbers of randomly selected subjects with control groups, social scientists hope to identify effects of interventions in much the same way natural scientists evaluate the efficacy of various drugs.

The leading development group engaged in random experiments in the education and health areas is the Poverty Research Lab at MIT, run by Esther Duflo and Abhijit Banerjee. By working with a range of nongovernmental organizations (NGOs) and government agencies in Africa, Latin America, and Asia, these economists have looked at a wide range of possible investments to help improve outcomes for the poorest of the poor.

Of course, not all policies can be evaluated this way. Experimenters do not always have the luxury of random assignment. An alternative technique is to rely on what have been called **natural experiments** to mimic the controlled experiment. Suppose I am interested in the effect of an increase in wealth on the likelihood that a poor family will enroll its daughters in school. Comparing school behavior of rich and poor families is obviously problematic because they are likely to differ in too many ways to control adequately. Nor does it seem feasible to substantially increase the wealth of a large number of randomly selected parents. But in an agrarian community we may observe random, annual weather occurrences that naturally lead to occasional years of plenty, and by observing behavior in those years versus other years, we may learn a good deal. The weather in this case has created a natural experiment.

Empirical development economics thus has added experimental methods to its tool kit as a way to answer some of the difficult and important questions about what does and does not work to improve the lot of the poor in developing nations. We turn now to look at some of the recent work in the fields of education and health, focusing on this experimental work, to provide some sense of the exciting work going on in this field.

**random experiment**
(Sometimes referred to as a *randomized experiment*.) A technique in which outcomes of specific interventions are determined by using the intervention in a randomly selected subset of a sample and then comparing outcomes from the exposed and control groups.

**natural experiment** Selection of a control versus experimental group in testing the outcome of an intervention is made as a result of an exogenous event outside the experiment itself and unrelated to it.

# Education Ideas

As we suggested, human capital is an important ingredient in the economic growth of a nation. As economies grow, returns to education also typically grow. As we move from traditional agrarian economies to more diversified and complex economies, the advantages to an individual from education rises. So if we want a nation's poor to benefit from growth, improving their educational outcomes is key. This leads us to one of the central preoccupations of development economists in the last decade or so: Of the many investments one could make in education, which have the highest payoffs? Is it better to invest in more books or more teachers? How much does the quality of teachers matter? Are investments most important in the first years of education or later? In a world with limited resources in which educational outcomes are very important, getting the right answers to these questions is vital.

For most middle-class U.S. students, it may come as a surprise that in the developing world, teacher absenteeism is a serious problem. A recent study led by researchers from the World Bank found, for example, that on an average day, 27 percent of Ugandan and 25 percent of Indian teachers are not at work. Across six poor countries, teacher absences averaged 19 percent. The Poverty Research Lab has conducted a number of experiments in a range of developing countries to see how one might reduce these absences. The most successful intervention was introduced in Rajasthan, India, by an NGO called Seva Mandir. Each day when he or she arrived, the teachers in half of Seva Mandir's 160-single teacher schools were asked to have their picture taken with the children. Cameras were date-stamped. This evidence of attendance fed into the compensation of the teacher. Teacher absentee rates were cut in half relative to the seemingly identical classrooms in which no cameras were introduced.

Student absenteeism is also a problem throughout the developing world, reducing educational outcomes even when schools are well staffed with qualified teachers. Several countries, including Mexico, have introduced cash payments to parents for sending their children to school regularly. Since the Mexican government introduced these payments over time, in ways not likely to be related to educational outcomes, researchers could compare student absenteeism across seemingly identical areas with and without the cash incentives as a form of natural experiment. There is some evidence that cash payments do increase school attendance. Natural experiments have also been used to look at the effect of industrialization that improves educational returns as a way to induce better school attendance; the results have been positive.

Work using experiments, both natural and random, is still at an early stage in development economics. Although many reform ideas have proven helpful in improving educational outcomes in different developing countries, it has proven hard up to now to find simple answers that work across the globe. Nevertheless, these new techniques appear to offer considerable promise as a way of tackling issues of improving education for the poor of the developing world.

# Health Improvements

Poor health is a second major contributor to individual poverty. In the developing world, estimates are that one quarter of the population is infected with intestinal worms that sap the energy of children and adults alike. Malaria remains a major challenge in Africa, as does HIV/AIDS.

In the case of many interventions to improve health, human behavior plays an important role, and here is where development economics has focused. For many diseases, we have workable vaccines. But we need to figure out how to encourage people to walk to health clinics or schools to get those vaccines. We want to know if charging for a vaccine will substantially reduce uptake. For many waterborne diseases, treatment of drinking water with bleach is effective, but the taste is bad and bleach is not free. How do we induce usage? Treated bed nets can reduce malaria, but only if they are properly used. In each of these cases, there are benefits to the individual from seeking treatment or preventive care, but also costs. In the last several years, a number of development economists have explored the way in which individuals in developing economies have responded to policies that try to change these costs and benefits.

Intestinal worms, quite common in areas of Africa with inadequate sanitation, are treatable with periodic drugs at a relatively low cost. Michael Kremer and Ted Miguel, working with the World Bank, used random experiments in Kenya to examine the effect of health education and user fees on families' take-up of treatment of their children. Kremer and Miguel found a number of interesting results, results very much in keeping with economic principles. First, a program of charging user fees—even relatively low ones—dramatically reduced treatment rates. The World Bank's attempts to make programs more financially self-sustaining, if used in this area, were likely to have large, adverse public health effects. Elasticities were well above one. Kremer and Miguel also found that as the proportion of vaccinated people in a village grew, and thus the risk of contagion fell, fewer people wanted treatment, indicating some sensitivity to costs and benefit calculations by the villagers. Disappointingly, health education did not seem to make much difference.

As with the area of education, much remains for development economists to understand in the area of health and human behavior. Development economics continues to be one of the most exciting areas in economics.

# SUMMARY

1. The economic problems facing the Global South, the developing countries, are often quite different from those confronting industrialized nations.

## 20.1 LIFE IN THE DEVELOPING NATIONS: POPULATION AND POVERTY *p. 383*

2. The UN in its Millennium Development Goals has identified a number of areas of concern in the developing world: hunger, literacy, child mortality, maternal mortality, diseases like HIV and malaria, gender equality, and environmental quality.

## 20.2 ECONOMIC DEVELOPMENT: SOURCES AND STRATEGIES *p. 384*

3. Almost all developing nations have a scarcity of physical capital relative to other resources, especially labor. The poverty trap or *vicious-circle-of-poverty hypothesis* says that poor countries cannot escape from poverty because they cannot afford to postpone consumption—that is, to save—to make investments. There is debate as to how widespread the poverty trap is and what the right prescription is to solve the problem.

4. Human capital—the stock of education and skills embodied in the workforce—plays a vital role in economic development.

5. Developing countries are often burdened by inadequate *infrasture or social overhead capital*, ranging from poor public health and sanitation facilities to inadequate roads, telephones, and court systems. Such social overhead capital is often expensive to provide, and many governments are not in a position to undertake many useful projects because they are too costly.

6. Inefficient and corrupt bureaucracies also play a role in retarding economic development in places.

7. Moving to a sophisticated market economy requires government support and regulation of institutions of private property, the law and financial reporting to enable the allocation of capital across unrelated individuals.

8. Evidence indicates that in developing nations labor productivity is considerably higher in the industrial urban setting. Some economists suggest easing migration costs as a strategy for growth.

9. *Import-substitution* policies, a trade strategy that favors developing local industries that can manufacture goods to replace imports, were once common in developing nations. In general, such policies have not succeeded as well as those promoting open, export-oriented economies.

10. Microfinance—lending small amounts to poor borrowers using peer lending groups—has become an important new tool in encouraging entrepreneurship in developing countries.

11. China and India have followed quite different paths in recent development.

## 20.3 DEVELOPMENT INTERVENTIONS *p. 393*

12. Development economists have begun to use randomized experiments as a way to test the usefulness of various interventions. In these experiments, modeled after the natural sciences, individuals or even villages are randomly assigned to receive various interventions and the outcomes they experience are compared with those of control groups. In the areas of education and health, random experiments have been most prevalent.

13. Development economists also rely on natural experiments to learn about the efficacy of various interventions. In a natural experiment, we compare areas with differing conditions that emerge as a consequence of an unrelated outside force.

14. Many of the newer economic studies focus on understanding how to motivate individuals to take actions that support policy interventions: to use health equipment properly, to attend schools, to receive vaccinations.

# REVIEW TERMS AND CONCEPTS

brain drain, p. 386

capital flight, p. 385

export promotion, p. 391

Global South, p. 383

import substitution, p. 391

natural experiment, p. 394

random experiment, p. 394

social overhead capital, p. 388

vicious circle of poverty, p. 385

# PROBLEMS

All problems are available on MyEconLab.

## 20.1 LIFE IN THE DEVELOPING NATIONS: POPULATION AND POVERTY

LEARNING OBJECTIVE: Discuss the characteristics of developing nations.

1.1 [**Related to the** *Economics in Practice* **on p. 384**] A paper released by the World Bank in 2014 states that while economic growth is essential for reducing poverty rates, growth by itself is not enough, and efforts to reduce poverty must be complemented with programs that devote more resources to the extreme poor. According to the paper, as extreme poverty declines, growth by itself tends to be less successful at lifting additional people out of poverty because at this point, many still suffering from extreme poverty find it very difficult to improve their lives. Do you agree with this assessment? Why or why not? What fundamental economic concept seems to be at play here?

1.2 The small West African nation of Equatorial Guinea is designated as a high income country by the World Bank, with a GNI per capita of more than $22,000 when measured in U.S. dollars. Equatorial Guinea also has a poverty rate of more than 76%, one of the highest rates in the world. Life expectancy at birth is only 53 years, and the infant mortality rate is almost 10 percent. Do some research on Equatorial Guinea and try to explain the apparent discrepancies listed above for this high-income country.

## 20.2 ECONOMIC DEVELOPMENT: SOURCES AND STRATEGIES

LEARNING OBJECTIVE: Describe the sources of economic development.

2.1 For a developing country to grow, it needs capital. The major source of capital in most countries is domestic saving, but the goal of stimulating domestic saving usually is in conflict with government policies aimed at reducing inequality in the distribution of income. Comment on this trade-off between equity and growth. How would you go about resolving the issue if you were the president of a small, poor country?

2.2 The GDP of any country can be divided into two kinds of goods: capital goods and consumption goods. The proportion of national output devoted to capital goods determines, to some extent, the nation's growth rate.

a. Explain how capital accumulation leads to economic growth.

b. Briefly describe how a market economy determines how much investment will be undertaken each period.

c. Consumption versus investment is a more painful conflict to resolve for developing countries. Comment on that statement.

d. If you were the benevolent dictator of a developing country, what plans would you implement to increase per-capita GDP?

2.3 Poor countries are trapped in a vicious circle of poverty. For output to grow, they must accumulate capital. To accumulate capital, they must save (consume less than they produce). Because they are poor, they have little or no extra output available for savings—it must all go to feed and clothe the present generation. Thus they are doomed to stay poor forever. Comment on each step in that argument.

2.4 In China, rural property is owned collectively by the village while being managed under long-term contracts by individual farmers. Why might this be a problem in terms of optimal land management, use, and allocation?

2.5 An offshoot of microfinance that has grown significantly over the past few years is an idea known as crowdfunding. With crowdfunding, individuals, businesses, and communities seek monetary support for ideas or projects from other individuals, primarily over the Internet. Three of the largest and most successful crowdfunding Internet sites are GoFundMe, Kickstarter, and Indiegogo, and while the use of the term "crowdfunding" is relatively new and associated with online sites such as these, the concept has been around for many years, with projects such as the pedestal on which the Statue of Liberty resides being constructed using this style of funding. Do some research on crowdfunding and explain whether you believe crowdfunding is a viable alternative to microfinance in poor countries such as Bangladesh. Which source of peer lending, microfinance or crowdfunding, do you believe would be the most successful at reducing the problem of adverse selection? Why?

2.6 [**Related to the** *Economics in Practice* **on p. 393**] Find another example of the use of cell phones as a way to improve market functioning in a developing economy.

**2.7** [Related to the *Economics in Practice* on p. 387] Corruption in a government is often accompanied by inefficiency in the economy. Why should this be true?

**2.8** The distribution of income in a capitalist economy is likely to be more unequal than it is in a socialist economy. Why is this so? Is there a tension between the goal of limiting inequality and the goal of motivating risk taking and hard work? Explain your answer in detail.

**2.9** Although brain drain is generally associated with developing countries, the recent debt crisis in Greece has generated an exodus of highly educated human capital from this country. In Greece, college education is paid for by the government, and it is estimated that roughly 10 percent of the country's college-educated workforce have left the country, a majority of which are less than 40 years of age. What implications does this flight of human capital have on growth prospects for the Greek economy? How does the fact that the government pays for college exacerbate this problem? Do some research to find out what has happened to Greek GDP in recent years and what the forecast is for GDP in the near future, and see if this supports your answer.

**2.10** [Related to the *Economics in the Practice* on p. 390] In addition to fewer marriages within extended families, explain what other positive effects are likely to occur in the rural, flood-prone areas of Bangladesh because of increased government spending on infrastructure projects like the building of river embankments and the resulting increase in wealth of the affected rural population.

**2.11** Explain how each of the following can limit the economic growth of developing nations.
  **a.** Insufficient capital formation
  **b.** A shortage of human resources
  **c.** A lack of social overhead capital

**2.12** You have been hired as an economic consultant for the nation of Ishtar. Ishtar is a developing nation that has recently emerged from a 10-year civil war; as a result, it has experienced appreciable political instability. Ishtar has a serious lack of capital formation, and capital flight has been a problem since before the civil war began. As an economic consultant, what policy recommendations would you make for the economic development of Ishtar?

## 20.3 DEVELOPMENT INTERVENTIONS

**LEARNING OBJECTIVE:** Discuss the intervention methods used by development economists.

**3.1** As the text states, investment in human capital is an important ingredient for a nation's economic growth. The data in the following table shows the net enrollment rates in primary school as a percentage of the relevant group for 10 developing countries in 1999 and 2013. Go to *http://data.worldbank.org* and look up per capita GDP for these 10 countries for 1999 and 2013. (Search for GDP per capita [current $US] data.) Calculate the percent changes in per capita GDP from 1999 to 2013 for these 10 countries. Do the changes in per capita GDP seem to correlate with the changes in enrollment rates? What besides increased enrollment may be responsible for the changes in per capita GDP?

| Country | Net enrollment rate, primary school, percent of relevant group | | |
|---|---|---|---|
| | 1999 | 2013 | Percent change |
| Angola | 54 | 86 | 59 |
| Burkina Faso | 35 | 67 | 91 |
| Burundi | 41 | 95 | 132 |
| Chad | 50 | 86 | 72 |
| The Gambia | 74 | 69 | −7 |
| Kenya | 62 | 84 | 35 |
| Liberia | 47 | 38 | −19 |
| Mali | 47 | 64 | 36 |
| Niger | 27 | 63 | 133 |
| Tanzania | 49 | 83 | 69 |

*Source:* World Bank

**3.2** The text mentions that in the developing world, teacher absenteeism is a serious problem, averaging 19 percent across six poor countries. An article in the *Journal of Economic Perspectives* states that absenteeism of health care workers in the five of those countries where data was available averages 35 percent, or almost double the rate of teacher absence. Suggest some ways that developing countries might try to successfully reduce the high absentee rates of health care workers, and any possible problems they may encounter in implementing your suggestions.
*Source:* Nazmul Chaudhury, Jeffrey Hammer, Michael Kremer, Karthik Muralidharan, and F. Halsey Rogers, "Missing in Action: Teacher and Health Worker Absence in Developing Countries," *Journal of Economic Perspectives*, 20, no. 1, Winter 2006, pp 91 – 116.

# Critical Thinking about Research

# 21

Throughout this book we have highlighted the many areas in which economists use data and statistical methods to answer questions that are important to households, businesses, and government policy makers. Some of these questions are narrow: What happens to the sales of ketchup when the manufacturer raises its price? How much will charging a small fee for a vaccine in a developing country affect vaccination rates? Others are much broader: Will a large unexpected fall in housing prices have a substantial effect on household consumption? What happens to employment if we raise the minimum wage? These are all questions that we can begin to answer with economic theory, as you have seen in this text. But to get quantitative answers to questions like these, we need to use statistical methods to look at real world data. In this chapter we provide an introduction to the tools economists and other social scientists use to look at data. We will focus both on the standard techniques used and on some of the most common pitfalls associated with using data to answer complex questions.

The statistical tools that economists use to analyze issues are an important part of the discipline. If you go on in economics, you will learn much more about these tools. For those of you who do not continue to study economics, we hope the introduction here will allow you to be a more discriminating consumer of the economic research that you see described in the media and elsewhere.

The techniques you will learn in this chapter are used in many fields other than economics. Psychology, political science, some historical research, some sports research, and some medical research also use these techniques.

**21.1 LEARNING OBJECTIVE**

Give some examples of studies that might suffer from selection bias.

# Selection Bias

We all know that people slow down physically as they age. World records in track and field are not set by 45 year olds. Few professional baseball players continue to play after the age of 45. And yet consider this: In the 2013 Chicago marathon, the average time of the 30- to 39-age group for men was 4 hours and 17 minutes, which was essentially the same as the average time of the 40- to 49-age group for men of 4 hours and 18 minutes. What do we make of this? Should we conclude, for example, that in the marathon there is essentially no slowing down in the 10-year age interval between the mid-thirties and the mid-forties?

Or say you came across a study that randomly sampled 1,000 70-year-old men and 1,000 90-year-old men and measured their bone density. Can we compare the average bone density of the 70-year olds to that of the 90-year olds to estimate how much bone density on average declines with age?

The answer to both questions is no. There is in both cases a substantial likelihood of **selection bias**. There are many aged 30–39 ham-and-eggers running the Chicago marathon, but many fewer casual runners aged 40–49. Many people aged 30–39 run for fun, to impress a friend, or to pay off a bet. Many of these casual runners have probably selected out by age 40. Moreover, one reason people select out or stop running is that they discover they are not good runners. As a result, the average runner left in the age 40- to 49-interval is likely to be a better runner than the average runner in the age 30- to 39-interval. It is thus not surprising that there is little change in the average times between runners in the two age intervals, but this says nothing about how fast a *particular* runner slows down with age. We are in some sense comparing apples and oranges in looking at the two groups.

Selection bias would also exist in the bone density study. There are fewer 90-year-old men than there are 70-year olds. Those with lower bone density at age 70 are more likely to have fallen, broken a hip and passed away. The men left in the population age by 90 disproportionately will thus consist of those who at younger ages had higher bone densities. So it would not be sensible to compare the average bone density of the two samples. This comparison would tell us nothing about how bone density changes with age for a particular person.

The type of selection bias in these two examples is also called **survivor bias**, for obvious reasons. The more fit in the populations have survived, so there is a bias in comparing younger and older groups. Similar problems arise in financial markets when we make inferences about corporate returns in the general market from a population of firms that has survived in the market for a long period. Firms that survive are typically different, generally more successful, than the average firm. Apple, which has survived for a number of years, is surely different in its ability to deliver innovative products that people want than the average company.

The problem of selection bias pervades many studies in economics (and other disciplines). In recent years there has been considerable interest in trying to understand and improve educational outcomes in the United States. In many areas, charter schools have grown up in part to experiment with alternative educational methods. Charter schools are publicly funded, providing free education to their students, but operate independently of the traditional school district and thus have more autonomy in terms of choices around teacher selection, school hours, and pedagogy. Naturally, there has been considerable interest in how these different charter schools are performing. It might occur to you that one way to answer this question is to compare the scores of students in charter versus traditional schools in an area on the common mastery tests now given across all schools in the United States. And, indeed, we see comparisons of this sort often in local newspapers. But here too in making this comparison, you would be running into the problem of selection bias.

Where does the bias come in here? In most charter systems, students are randomly chosen to attend the school. You might think this would eliminate the selection bias problem. Unfortunately, that random choice does not fully eliminate the problem. In most charter systems, to be chosen in the lottery you must apply in the first place. But families who apply to a lottery for a charter school may well differ considerably from those who do not apply. And those differences—more attention to education, more organizational skills, and so on—are both likely to matter to educational performance and will be hard for us to observe. In other words, children who apply to a charter school may do better on the mastery tests than the average child, even if he or she does not get chosen to attend the charter! As we will see in a later section, there are ways around this selection problem but they require some ingenuity.

**selection bias** Selection bias occurs when the sample used is not random.

**survivor bias** Survivor bias exists when a sample includes only observations that have remained in the sample over time making that sample unrepresentative of the broader population.

One more example may help to show the range of the issues involved. Many studies in the medical area are aimed at helping us figure out how to live longer and healthier lives. Suppose you were interested in the effect on longevity of exercise. Luckily, you found a long-term study that tracked how often people exercised over many years and found that those people who exercised more also lived longer. Should you conclude that exercise in fact increases life span? The answer is again no. In this example we are comparing a group of people who chose to exercise with a group who chose not to. The fact that a group of people does or does not choose to exercise tells us that they likely differ on many other grounds that might independently affect life span. People who choose to exercise also likely make other healthy choices, most of which will be hard for a researcher to observe. So the longevity edge might come from the fact that one group exercised, whereas the other did not. But it might equally have arisen from the fact that the first group consists of people who make healthy choices while the second does not.

A common problem in many of these cases is that we are comparing groups who not only engaged in different activities, activities whose effect we seek to measure, but people who made different choices. To the extent that those choices reflect group differences that themselves matter to the outcomes we are measuring, we bias (or distort) our results. In the last few years, economists have become increasingly sensitive to the problem of selection bias and have engaged in many creative ways to try to eliminate the bias problem. We will describe some of the solutions to the bias problem later in this chapter. For now, we hope you will look at some of those newspaper headlines with a more skeptical eye!

# Causality

**21.2 LEARNING** OBJECTIVE

Understand the difference between correlation and causation.

As we have seen, selection bias makes it difficult to identify the effect of a treatment on a population. In other words, selection makes it hard to pin down causal effects. Identifying causality is a general issue in data analysis and goes beyond problems that arise because of selection bias. We will consider a number of causality issues in this section.

## Correlation versus Causation

Most people who have blue eyes also have light colored hair. Most people who have minivans also have children. Evidence suggests that people who are obese have a disproportionate number of obese friends. What can we conclude from these facts? Do blue eyes cause blond hair? Do minivans cause people to have children? Is obesity contagious, caught from one's friends?

When two variables tend to move together, we say they are **correlated**. If the two variables tend to move in the same direction, we say they are *positively* correlated, and if they tend to move in opposite directions, we say they are *negatively* correlated. In the examples above, the variables in each of the three sets are positively correlated. But correlation does not imply causation. It does not take a degree in biology to know that blue eyes do not *cause* blond hair. Likely evolution has selected simultaneously on these two features causing them to appear together. Dumping a bottle of peroxide on my head, although it will surely make me a blond, will not change my eye color at all! In economics, as well as in other fields, theory is often quite helpful in helping us to differentiate between correlation and causality.

**correlated** Two variables are correlated if their values tend to move together.

Minivans and children provide another example in which we need to sort out correlation and causation. In the data we see that the majority of minivan owners have children. Clearly minivans do not often cause children to be born ("Might as well have a fourth child. We already own a minivan!"). Here it is likely the causality runs in the opposite direction. Minivans are most attractive to families with children. So having children may indeed cause people to buy a minivan. Think now about why getting the causality right matters. If Japan, for example, wants to increase its very low birth rate, giving everyone a free minivan is not likely to be effective. Minivans do not by and large cause people to want children. But knowing the relationship between minivans and children is clearly relevant to automobile manufacturers who will want to exploit this relationship by focusing their marketing campaigns on families. An increase in average family size causes a shift in the demand for large minivans but the reverse is not the case.

The most complicated of the examples is obesity. Here there are theoretical arguments that support a hypothesis of causality running in both directions. Eating and exercise are social for many people, so having obese (or conversely thin) friends may well have an effect on your own weight. But in some circles at least obesity is a social stigma, and it may well be that being obese limits one's choice of friends. Thus, it is plausible that having obese friends does increase your own chances of being obese, but it is also likely that being obese increases your chances of having obese friends.

Identifying causality is critical for much policy work. Knowing that early exposure to reading is correlated with high adult incomes is interesting. Knowing that it *causes* high incomes suggests a policy intervention. Much empirical work in economics is concerned with trying to determine causality, given how important it is for policy issues. Let us consider a few ways researchers have used to identify causation.

## Random Experiments

The gold standard for empirical work is the random experiment that many of you will be familiar with from medical research. If a research team is trying to decide if a particular drug helps in treating some form of cancer, for example, a standard protocol is to randomly divide the patients afflicted with the disease into two groups, provide one group with the drug, and give the other a placebo. With a large enough group, and enough time, one should be able to tell if the drug is effective. (Of course, there is much non-human pretesting for safety reasons). Notice in this protocol that we did not select our samples by asking people to choose whether they wanted to take the drug or not (all agreed to the drug). Indeed, part of a standard medical protocol is that patients do not know which group they are in during the experiment. In this type of experiment, we have no selection issue, since there has been no user selection.

Experiments of this sort are also run in economics and are relatively prevalent in the area of economic development. To give an example, suppose we are interested in the effects of class size on educational achievement, say test scores. Comparing classes with large and small enrollments will clearly not be informative. Among other things, it is well known that classes in more affluent areas have smaller classes than those in poorer areas and that affluence will bring with it many advantages that likely lift test scores. Instead, one could run an experiment that randomly assigns students to classes that differ in enrollments and then later compare test scores for the different groups. If the assignments are truly random, there are no selection issues.

Although random experiments are common, especially in the medical field, they are not always possible to carry out. Suppose we are interested in the link between smoking and cancer. We can, of course, take a large group of mice, randomly divide them into two groups, expose one but not the other to smoke, and see whether the two groups differ in their cancer incidence. As long as our sample is reasonably large, we should be able to see a difference in cancer rates if a causal relationship between smoking and cancer exists. We have done a random experiment just as we described. Notice how this experiment differs from just comparing cancer rates of smokers to non-smokers. People who smoke have *chosen* to smoke and may well have made a number of other choices that could be unhealthy. As hard as we try to control for those smoker/nonsmoker differences, our ability to do so is limited.

For the mice there are no choice problems to worry about. But if we find that smoking causes cancer in mice, it remains to determine whether the same holds for people. Clearly, we cannot force a randomly chosen group of people to smoke and then see if their cancer rates differ from that of a control group. For many of the questions economists are interested in, it is difficult to use random experiments. Randomly exposing groups of people to something that is potentially harmful is unethical and would not pass a human subjects protocol review. Even if we are looking at interventions that have only potential benefits and no costs, we still face the problem that the randomly chosen subjects we start out with may decide not to join the study or to leave the experiment early. If this happens, the groups left will no longer be random. When there is some discretion among subjects to either take up a treatment offer or to continue in a treatment over time, selection bias will again potentially creep in to our experiment. What do we do under these circumstances?

Consider a university that has admitted 200 at-risk students from households with low incomes. It has a summer program before college begins to better help prepare such students for college life. The university wants to know if this program improves a student's four–year college performance, say measured by a student's four-year GPA. How might it proceed?

Assume that the university randomly samples 100 of the 200 at-risk students and invites them to attend the summer program at no cost. Say 60 accept the offer and take the summer program. After four years the GPAs of all the 200 students are collected and we learn that the average GPA of the 60 students who took the program was higher than the average GPA of the 140 students who did not take the course. Could you conclude from this that the program had a positive effect? No. Once again, we have a selection issue. While the 100 students offered the program were indeed a random sample, the 60 students who took up the offer were not. Maybe the 60 were on average less talented than the 40 who refused the offer and felt the need to take the program, whereas the more talented 40 did not. Or maybe the 60 were on average more serious students or more organized. However the bias runs, we cannot assume that the 60 students who accepted are a random sample of the 200 initial students. Here we are not even sure if those who accept are better or worse than the non-accepters.

But the group of the 100 students initially drawn and invited to join the program was random by design. So after four years we can compare the average GPA of the 100 students who were offered the program to the average GPA of the 100 students who were not. If the program has a positive effect, the first average GPA should be greater than the second. You might think this is an odd process for testing the efficacy of the summer program. After all, 40 of the students whose scores we are looking at did not take the program! If they did not take the program, why are they included in the average GPA along with actual program-takers? We include all students who were made the program offer in our test sample to avoid selection bias. This procedure, which is also used in medical experiments that have patient drop outs, is called **intention to treat**. But proceeding this way does have a cost.

Suppose only 10 students of the 100 took up our offer. In this case, we are comparing two random groups of students, one of which has no one taking the program and the other with 10 in the program and 90 not. With so many non-takers, it will be hard to find any gains from the program. If instead all 100 students invited to the program actually enrolled, clearly we would have more confidence that we could find an effect from the program if any existed. But whatever the case, we need to compare the performance of the 100 offered students with that of the 100 non-offered to avoid selection bias. Notice that intention to treat makes it harder to find results from a treatment and in this sense is a conservative statistical technique. The *Economics in Practice* box on page 404 describes an experiment run by the U.S Department of Housing and Urban Development (HUD) using randomly assigned housing vouchers to examine the effects of community on household well being. Here the method of intention to treat is used.

**intention to treat**  A method in which we compare two groups based on whether they were part of an initially specified random sample subjected to an experimental protocol.

## Regression Discontinuity

In many situations economists do not answer their empirical questions with random experiments, but rather try to make inferences from market data, data that come out of the everyday transactions and choices individuals make. Using market data has a number of advantages: These data reflect real choices made in everyday life by households. Much of the data are collected as a matter of course by either government or business and so are easily available to researchers. Carefully designed experiments, on the other hand, are expensive. But the fact that the data reflect individual choices, done in relatively uncontrolled settings, makes the identification of causality especially difficult. There are a number of procedures that researchers have used to try to make progress in this area.

The United States has more prisoners per capita than any other OECD country,[1] with roughly two million incarcerated. Many of those released from prison are re-arrested within a short period of time. How does what happens while someone is in prison affect the likelihood they will be

---

[1] The OECD is the Organisation for Economic Co-operation and Development. It consists largely of developed world countries, heavily weighted toward Europe.

# ECONOMICS IN PRACTICE

## Moving to Opportunity

It is well known that children who grow up in high-poverty areas on average end up as adults with lower educational attainments, poorer health, lower income levels, and a higher likelihood of being incarcerated at some point in their lives. To what extent are these results attributable to the neighborhoods in which these children grow up, and, relatedly, how much could they be changed by a locational change?

These are the very central policy questions posed by an experiment run by the U.S. Department of Housing and Urban Development in the mid-1990s and recently reevaluated by a group of economists.[1]

The Moving to Opportunity program offered to randomly selected families living in high-poverty housing projects housing vouchers that they could use to move to lower-poverty neighborhoods. The random granting of the vouchers was a direct attempt to avoid the selection bias problems found in earlier studies of housing and later outcomes. It is easy to see that if we simply look at life outcomes for children whose families move out of high-poverty areas to those who remain in those areas we will have serious selection bias issues. Moving families likely have more access to resources—perhaps ones we cannot observe—and perhaps more initiative or organizational ability than those who stay. Those differences might well have an effect on their children's outcomes independent of the gains from the move. By randomizing the voucher choice, HUD attempted to remove the choice element. Because not all families offered the vouchers moved, the researchers used the intention-to-treat methodology described in the text to control for the potential selection bias.

Early results from the experiment found little results on the economic well-being of moving families, though there were gains in mental and physical health. A longer-term, recently completed study by some of the same authors, which looked at tax data, found substantial effects on income levels of

those children who were younger than 13 years of age when their families moved, with average gains of 31 percent higher incomes for the young movers.

### THINKING PRACTICALLY

1. Some of the same researchers whose work is described also did another study looking at the outcomes of households that moved versus those that did not in the general population. To control for selection bias, the researchers compared children of different ages within families to see how much more time in the better neighborhood influenced younger versus older children. How does this attenuate the selection bias issue?

[1] Raj Chetty, Nathaniel Hendren, Lawrence Katz, "The Effects of Exposure to Better Neighborhoods on Children: New Evidence for the Moving to Opportunity Experiment," NBER working paper, May 2015.

re-arrested? Do the conditions in prison affect recidivism rates?[2] Arguments about this question have been made on both sides. Some argue that harsh conditions reduce recidivism because the worse the conditions, the more incentivized released prisoners will be to stay out of prison. On the other side, harsh prison conditions may increase a taste for violence or reduce a prisoner's future labor market value. This would suggest that harsh conditions increase recidivism.

On questions like this, it is important to bring data and evidence to the table. What happens if we just compare recidivism rates in prisoners from more or less harsh prisons? Here again, identifying causality is problematic. In general, harsher prisons house more serious criminals. So, if we see more recidivism from those coming out of harsher prisons, it could well be that the recidivist traits caused the prison choice, rather than the prison type causing the recidivist traits.

[2] This discussion is based on M. Keith Chen and Jesse Shapiro, "Do Harsher Prison Conditions reduce Recidivism? A Discontinuity-based Approach." *American Law and Economics Review* June 2007.

# ECONOMICS IN PRACTICE

## Birth Weight and Infant Mortality

Per capita health care costs in the United States are quite high, even relative to other developed countries. Much of these expenditures are concentrated on two quite different parts of the population: The very old and the very young. A central question for public policy is how effective these high expenditures are.

Medical practice often distinguishes between babies who are below 1500 grams and those above. The former are called VLBW babies, for Very Low Birth Weight, and in most hospitals these babies receive extraordinary care at birth and immediately thereafter. This extraordinary care is expensive, and there is good evidence that the hospital bills of the VLBW babies are considerably above those for infants at higher weights. But do these expenditures help?

It is, of course, quite difficult to answer this question just by comparing outcomes, like one-year mortality rates, for babies of different birth weights. We know that low-birth-weight children are at risk. So even if we found that with treatment their mortality rates were high, it would not be informative because that result would not tell us what the mortality rate would be absent extraordinary treatment. A study by Almond, et al. using the regression discontinuity procedure we discussed in the text provided a way around this problem.[1]

As indicated, the label VLBW for babies is assigned for a birth weight less than 1500 grams. Medically, this assignment is a convention and does not reflect any threshold medical condition that turns on and off at above or below this weight. But the designation does trigger a set of extraordinary treatments at most hospitals. So we have a perfect setup for a regression discontinuity study: Birth weights and medical conditions around that birth weight are continuous variables while the trigger for treatment is a fixed line. Almond

et al. examined outcomes for babies on either side of the line. What did they find? If we compare babies just below the trigger line with those just above, the babies below the line had a 1 percent *lower* one-year mortality rate than the slightly heavier babies. With a base of just over 5 percent for a one-year mortality rate, this is a substantial difference. What caused the difference? The extra medical care given by virtue of the VLBW designation!

### THINKING PRACTICALLY

1. Can you think of another medical designation for which a regression discontinuity technique might be useful?

[1] Douglas Almond, J. Doyle, A. Kowalski and H. Williams, "Estimating Marginal Returns to Medical Care: Evidence from At-Risk Newborns," *Quarterly Journal of Economics*, 2010.

Chen and Shapiro used an interesting strategy, called **regression discontinuity**, to sort out causality. The design works as follows. Once an inmate is convicted and enters the federal prison system, he is given a security score. The score predicts the prisoner misconduct and security needs. There is no personal judgment in creating this score, which simply adds up points depending on the prisoner record. The score then determines prison facility based on availability of beds. Scores of more than 6 typically go to higher-security (and typically harsher) facilities. But placement also depends on bed space, and this means that prisoners with similar scores may end up in different types of prisons. Regression discontinuity effectively compares outcomes from individuals who are close to either side of a dividing line. In this example, we are effectively comparing recidivism rates for prisoners sent to harsh versus less harsh prisons who were virtually identical on their pre-prison scores. The study in fact found that harsh prisons do not reduce recidivism, but may in fact increase it.

Similar methods have been used in other instances in which the existence of a black-and-white line based on a continuous score for individuals determines whether or not an individual is "treated." Most government programs for unemployment or insurance disability benefits have this property of setting an absolute threshold for receiving treatment, allowing a researcher to essentially use individuals very close to the threshold as a kind of control group. In the *Economics in Practice* box on this page we describe a study of birth weight and infant mortality based on this methodology.

**regression discontinuity** identifies the causal effects of a policy or factor by looking at two samples that lie on either side of a threshold or cutoff.

# Difference-in-Differences

Another interesting procedure to try to get a better handle on causality in social science studies is called the method of **difference-in-differences**.

Suppose we have a community in which a small nonprofit has run a community gardening program. The group is convinced that this program increases housing values. Someone in the group suggests that they just look at what has happened to housing values in the community in the four years since the program began as a measure of the program's success. It is easy to see that this will not work. Housing prices are quite volatile, moving with the overall level of economic activity in an area. In other words, much of the fluctuations in housing prices have nothing to do with community gardens. Another suggestion might be to compare the housing prices in this community with those in a similar neighboring community without the program. But this procedure too is problematic, as no two communities are exactly alike.

The difference-in-differences method takes a third approach that melds these two ideas. In particular, we try to relate the difference in our community's housing values over time to the difference in a neighboring community's values over the same time. (Hence the name difference-in-differences). If all of the other factors that affect housing values are the same between the two communities (that's why we have chosen a neighboring community), then this difference-in-differences procedure will show us the effect of the program.

To be clear on what the procedure does, let *pbega* and *pbegb* denote the average housing values in communities *a* and *b* before the garden project began in community *a*. Let *penda* and *pendb* denote the average housing values after four years in the two communities. Then the effect of the garden project on housing values in community *a* is estimated as:

$$effect = penda - pbega - (pendb - pbegb)$$

We take the difference in values in community *a* and subtract from it the difference in values in community *b*.

The difference-in-differences methodology is reasonably common in the social sciences. A classic example is presented in the *Economics in Practice* box on the next page, which looks at the effect of the minimum wage. But there are pitfalls as well in doing this work, pitfalls that come in part from the difficulties of identifying an appropriate comparison group.

Consider the following example: Stimulated in part by what has been happening to the cognitive functioning of aging professional athletes, especially in football, there has been growing concern among university leaders about the long-term effects of injuries in college sports. Short of banning football, which some would advocate, there have been other suggestions to reduce the incidence of injury, notably requiring better helmets and/or eliminating kickoffs (with the ball always starting on the 20 yard line).

Suppose that several years ago the Ivy League introduced such regulations and that a researcher was interested in seeing whether the regulations in fact had reduced injuries. To test whether the regulations helped, we could compare the average number of injuries per game measured in the year before the new rules, denoted *ybeg*, with injuries in the year after the new rules were instituted, denoted *yend*. But as in the case of housing values, we cannot be sure that nothing happened in the world of Ivy League football other than the rule changes over this period. Maybe the NCAA introduced other rule changes for all the colleges in the country, including the Ivy League colleges, which were designed to lessen injuries, such as telling referees to be more strict. We need a comparison group, a second set of differences.

One possible comparison group might be the PAC-12 conference. Assume that this conference did not introduce the new rules on helmets and kickoffs. Again, we collect data on the average number of injuries per game for the same two years we used in the Ivy League case for this conference, denoted *zbeg* and *zend*. We can then compare the difference between these two values and the difference between the two Ivy League values (difference-in-differences):

$$effect = yend - ybeg - (zend - zbeg)$$

By subtracting the PAC-12 difference from the Ivy difference we are controlling for country-wide changes that occurred during the two years. The variable *effect* is then the amount attributable to the Ivy League regulations only.

# ECONOMICS IN PRACTICE

## Using Difference-in-Differences to Study the Minimum Wage

There is a lively debate among economists and policy makers on the effect of the minimum wage on unemployment. Does raising the minimum wage substantially increase unemployment, particularly for the lower-skilled workers? Or can one legislate wage increases for low-wage workers without a substantial reaction from employers?

One of the first and still classic examples of the difference-in-differences technique described in the text was done by David Card and Alan Krueger in their study of state minimum wage changes.[1]

In the early 1990s New Jersey decided to raise its minimum wage. Although there is a federal minimum wage, many states adopt higher minimums for the firms employing workers within their borders. Card and Krueger decided to survey fast-food restaurants in New Jersey to determine the effect of the minimum wage increase on employment. Fast-food restaurants were an obvious target given their employment of large numbers of unskilled workers. But just looking at New Jersey would not be sufficient. Suppose employment went down after the change. One has no way of knowing what would have happened absent the rule change. After all, employment depends on a number of other factors in the economy.

Here is where difference-in-differences comes in. New Jersey is bordered by Pennsylvania, a state that made no change to its minimum wage law in the period and also has fast-food restaurants. So Card and Krueger added data from these restaurants in eastern Pennsylvania as a comparison. The key measure of effect was the difference in employment changes between New Jersey restaurants and eastern Pennsylvania restaurants over the period in question, the

difference-in–differences in short. They found no effect from the law change. Not everyone writing on the topic agrees with that conclusion, but most do agree on the usefulness of the difference-in-differences technique.

### THINKING PRACTICALLY

1. Design another experiment using difference-in-differences to understand the effect of a policy change at your college.

[1] David Card and Alan Krueger, "Minimum Wage and Unemployment: A Case study of the Fast Food Industry in New Jersey and Pennsylvania," *American Economic Review*, September 1994.

This looks neat, but there are several potential pitfalls to this research plan. Most fundamentally, we have assumed that the two-year changes absent the Ivy League regulations are the same for both conferences. But PAC-12 football is not exactly like Ivy League football (Ask any serious college sports fan!). And those differences may be important not only in starting levels (which is fine) but in changes over time (which is not fine). Because PAC-12 football is played at a higher level than the Ivy League, it could be that the change in its injuries per game over the two years is not a good approximation of what the Ivy League change would have been absent the regulations. Perhaps the PAC-12 coaches pushed their players even harder and this led to increased injuries. If the PAC-12 is not a good comparison group, then difference-in-differences will not work in this case.

One more point to reflect on in this football example. With safer helmets it could be that the players play rougher knowing that they are better protected, and playing rougher, other things being equal, increases injuries. Regulations have the potential to affect behavior in ways not anticipated by the regulators. Some of the original work documenting this effect was done by Sam Peltzman, a Chicago economist, who found that seat-belt laws might perversely encourage people to drive faster than they did without seat belts because they felt safer.[3] In the helmet case, some gains from the physical protection of a helmet might be offset by the behavioral changes it induces in the intensity of play. Economic research is not an easy task, but we hope you can see that it encourages care and creativity!

[3] Sam Peltzman, "The effects of automobile safety regulation," *Journal of Political Economy*, August 1975.

# Statistical Significance

We all know that in tossing a coin there is a 50 percent chance we will get a head. Nevertheless, it is not true that coin tosses always alternate between heads and tails. Sometimes we get two or three heads in a row before a tail shows up. How many heads would we need to get in a row before we started to think that there was something wrong with the coin?

In the coin example we answer this question by thinking about how likely it is that a fair (or normal) coin would give us head after head. Two heads in a row is relatively common, happening 25 percent of the time (0.5 times 0.5). Even four in a row sometimes happens (about 6 percent of the time). But six heads in a row happens only about one in a hundred times. At that point you may be suspicious about the coin tosser and begin to think this is not a fair coin!

In thinking about our results in empirical work in economics we use the same basic logic as we try to figure out what we can conclude from the data we have gathered and the statistical tests we have employed. The key question for the researcher is to figure out if the results he or she has found have occurred "by chance" or if they really mean something. To make that judgement researchers turn to the concept of statistical significance.

Return to the example of the summer program experiment and suppose the GPA difference observed after the program was 0.3 on a 4.0 scale. Can we conclude that the program really had a positive effect on GPA, or is 0.3 so small that it was likely due to chance. A common way of looking at this problem is to begin by assuming that the effect of whatever we are testing, here the summer program, is zero and then ask what is the probability we got the result we did if the true effect is zero. The assumption of no effect is called the *null hypothesis*. In our earlier example, our null hypothesis was that the coin was fair. Here the null hypothesis is that the summer program has no effect on GPA. We ask what is the probability we got a difference in GPA of 0.3 if the null hypothesis is true?

**p-value** The probability of obtaining the result that you find in the sample data if the null hypothesis of no relationship is true.

**statistical significance** A result is said to be statistically significant if the computed p-value is less than some presubscribed number, usually 0.05.

The probability that one got the result that one did if the null hypothesis is true can be computed given certain statistical assumptions. It is called a **p-value**. A small p-value means that the probability is small of getting the result if the null hypothesis is true. If for the 0.3 GPA difference, the p-value was 0.02, this says that there is only a 2 percent chance of getting this value if the summer program truly has no effect on GPA. The term **statistical significance** is commonly applied to a p-value of 0.05 of less. If a p-value is less or equal to 0.05, the results is said to be statistically significant.

Be clear on what we are doing here. We are starting from the premise that whatever effect we are trying to estimate does not exist (is zero). We collect our data and do our calculations to get a particular estimate of the effect we are interested in. We compute the p-value for this estimate, which again is the probability that the true effect is zero given the particular estimate that we obtained. If the p-value is small, usually taken to be less than or equal to 0.05, we conclude that our estimated effect is statistically significant. We have rejected the null hypothesis of no effect.

If you go on in statistics, you will learn exactly how p-values are computed. They depend on the variability of the population being analyzed. Consider the 200 at-risk students in the summer program experiment. Say that they are all identical, meaning that they will all get the same GPA at the end of four years if they don't take the summer program. If some do take the summer program, all those who do will get the same GPA, although this GPA will be different if the program does have a non zero effect on GPA.

We want to test whether the summer program effect is zero. We run the experiment discussed and get a difference of 0.3. Is this difference statistically significant? The answer is obviously yes. If the true effect were zero, everyone would get the same GPA whether they took the program or not, so the difference would be exactly zero. We in fact got a nonzero estimate, and so we are sure that the true effect is not zero. The p-value would be 0.00. In fact in this case we only need two students, one who took the program and one who did not. If the difference in the two GPAs is not zero, then the summer program has an effect. In this case there would be no need to use intention to treat—there are no selection problems because everyone is identical.

Now consider that there is huge variation in the population of 200 regarding what GPA they are going to achieve. Some may turn out to be stars, and some may barely make it through the four years. Whether students take the summer program or not, there will be a huge variation in

GPA scores at the end of the four-year period because of the huge variation in the population. We run the experiment and get a difference of 0.3. Is this difference statistically significant? Maybe not if the variation in the population is large. The difference of 0.3 is fairly small, and it could easily be obtained by chance. It just so happened that the particular draw of 100 students led to this outcome, but it may be that a different draw would have resulted in a difference of 0.2. The p-value that is computed for the result of 0.3 would likely be very large, perhaps close to 1.00.

The intuition to take from this discussion is that one has more confidence in results obtained from populations with low variation than from those with high variation. To get potentially significant results from a high-variation population, one needs a large sample size. If we had 2,000 at-risk students, gave offers to 1,000, and got a difference of 0.3, this might be significant. When at the end we take the average of the 1,000 GPAs, the individual student characteristics tend to cancel out in a large sample size, and we can have more confidence that the difference of 0.3 is picking up the summer-program effect. When computing p-values, the size of the sample matters as well as the variation in the population.

# Regression Analysis

**21.4 LEARNING** OBJECTIVE

Understand how regression analysis can be used for both estimation and testing.

The most important statistical tool in empirical economics is regression analysis. If you go on in economics you will see applications of regression analysis in microeconomics and macroeconomics. It can be used to forecast the effect of an increase in prices on the quantity of cat food sold in a community or the effects of a stock market decline on household consumption. Here, we provide you with a beginning sense of what regression analysis is all about.

There is evidence that the economy has an effect on votes for president in the United States.[4] If the economy is doing well at the time of the election, this may have a positive effect on votes for the incumbent-party candidate, and vice versa if the economy is doing poorly. This theory suggests that many voters reward or blame the party of the president-in-office for good or bad economic performance while that president is in office. If true, this theory suggests that, all else equal, a president who presides over a strong economy will find his or her political party doing well in the next election.

How might we test this theory using regression analysis? We first need some measure of economic performance. The growth rate of the economy is one common measure of economic strength. So we can translate our theory into a more testable form: we postulate that the growth rate of the economy in the year of the election, denoted $g$, has a positive effect on the incumbent party's presidential vote share, denoted $V$. Notice here we have chosen a specific measure of performance—the growth rate—and also a time period—the year of the election. Generally speaking, when we move in economics from a theory to a practical statistical test, we will have some choices to make. In this case, we have chosen to measure economic performance by the one-year growth rate.

We will look at the way in which the growth rate affects the vote share. In particular, we will assume that

$$V = a + bg \tag{1}$$

If $b$ is positive, this equation says that the growth rate has a positive effect on the vote share, as our theory states. Also, the relationship between $V$ and $g$ is assumed to be linear. If we take a graph with $V$ on the vertical axis and $g$ on the horizontal axis, as in Figure 21.1, the line is straight with intercept $a$ and slope $b$. The job of regression analysis is to estimate the coefficients $a$ and $b$ and to see in particular if $b$ is positive and if it "matters" in a statistical sense.

Consider how we might determine, or estimate, the values for $a$ and $b$. U.S. presidential elections are held every four years, and there are data on $V$ going back to the beginning of the country. There are also data on $g$ going back many years. If we consider the period beginning in 1916, there have been 25 presidential elections between 1916 and 2012. So we have 25 data points, or observations, on $V$ and $g$. We can plot these observations in a Figure like 21.1. In the

---

[4] See Ray C. Fair, *Predicting Presidential Elections and Other Things*, 2nd ed. Stanford University Press, 2012, for discussion of this.

**Hypothetical plot of points between the vote share and the growth rate.**

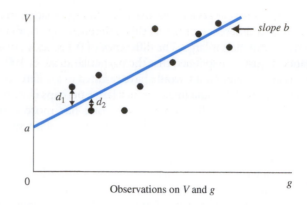

figure we have plotted 10 hypothetical points for illustration. As drawn, the figure shows that there is a positive relationship between the vote share and the growth rate. It also shows, however, that the data points are not all on the line. If equation (1) were exact, all the points would be on the straight line. In fact, in the real world equation (1) is not exact. There are other variables that affect votes for president. Some of these variables include other economic measures, such as perhaps inflation at the time of the election. Vote share may also be affected by foreign policy and personal characteristics and views of the people running for office. As a result, the points in the graph of the vote share on the growth rate are not exactly on the line. The job of regression analysis is to find values of $a$ and $b$ that provide a good fit of the data around the line. Or, in other words, to find the line that best represents the data in the figure.

How is fit determined? What do we mean by the best line? This can be seen in Figure 21.1. Draw a particular line with intercept $a$ and slope $b$. For each data point compute the vertical distance between the point and the line. We have done this for the first two points in the figure, labeled $d_1$ and $d_2$. We do this for all the points, say the 25 observations between 1916 and 2012. Some values of $d$ are positive and some are negative. The larger is the distance above or below the line, the worse does that particular point fit the line. The distances are usually called "errors" for this reason. The way the fit is determined is first to square each distance. Each squared distance is positive because the square of a negative number is positive. Then we add up all the squared distances, again in our case 25 numbers. Call this sum $SUM$. The sum is obviously a measure of fit. A small value of $SUM$ means that the points are fairly close to the line, and a large value means they are not. The fact that squared distances are used means that large outliers (distances) are weighted more than small ones in computing $SUM$.

You can think of regression analysis as doing the following, although in practice finding the right line is done more efficiently:[5] Try a million different pairs of values $a$ and $b$, and for each pair compute $SUM$. This gives us a million values of $SUM$. Choose the smallest value. The values of $a$ and $b$ that correspond to this smallest value are the best-fitting coefficients—the best-fitting intercept and slope. These estimates are called **least squares estimates** because they are the estimates that correspond to the smallest sum of the squared distances, or errors.

**least squares estimates** Least squares estimates are those that correspond to the smallest sum of squared distances, or errors.

In our theory we focused on the sign of the coefficient of the growth rate: does growth increase vote share? The size of the estimates is often also of interest. If, for example, the estimate of $b$ were 1.0, this tells us that an increase in the growth rate of 1 percentage point leads to an increase in the vote share of 1 percentage point. This would be a nontrivial effect of the economy on voting behavior. If the estimate of $b$ were instead 0.01, politicians would worry much less about how a bad economy was going to affect their votes! (In practice the estimate is about 0.67.)

Regression analysis is helpful in letting us test our theories. In our voting example, we are particularly interested in whether $b$ is zero. If $b$ is zero, this says that the growth rate has no effect on votes, and our original theory is not right. To see if we should continue to have confidence in our theory, we need to test whether $b$ is zero.

How do we test whether $b$ is zero? Here we go back to what we already know from our discussion of statistical significance and p-values. We first postulate the null hypothesis that $b$ is in

---

[5] There are many statistical programs that do this calculation with one simple command, including Excel.

fact zero. We then use regression analysis to estimate $b$, and after this is done we compute the probability (p-value) that we would have obtained this estimate if the truth is that $b$ is zero. If the p-value is low, say less than 0.05, we say that the estimate of $b$ is statistically significant. We reject the null hypothesis that the growth rate does not affect the vote share, and our confidence in the theory that economic performance affects votes is bolstered.

Most theories in economics are more complicated than simply one variable affecting another. In our voting example, as noted, inflation may also affect voting behavior. In this case two variables affect $V$: $g$ and inflation, which will be denoted $p$. In this case we could write the voting equation as

$$V = a + bg + cp \qquad (2)$$

Equation 2 has two variables that explain vote share plus a constant term. There are now three coefficients to estimate rather than two: $a$, $b$, and $c$. With more than one explanatory variable, we cannot draw a graph as we did previously. But the fitting idea we introduced works the same way when we add variables. Given observations on $V$, $g$, and $p$, you can think of the analysis as trying a million sets of values of $a$, $b$, and $c$ and choosing the set that provides the best fit. For each set of three coefficient values, the predicted value of $V$ can be computed for each observation, and the distance for that observation is the difference between the predicted value of $V$ and the actual value of $V$. We square this distance, do the same for all the observations, and then sum the squared distances. This gives us a value of $SUM$ for the particular set of the three coefficient values. We do this a million times for a million sets of three coefficient values and choose the smallest value of $SUM$. The coefficient values that correspond to the smallest value of $SUM$ are the least squares estimates of $a$, $b$, and $c$.[6] We can also test in a similar manner as discussed whether $b$ and/or $c$ are zero.

To conclude, regression analysis is used in many settings. In business, it is used to estimate the size of effects: How much do purchases of a good fall when prices rise? What is the effect of an increase in advertising on car sales? In public policy, magnitudes also matter and can be found using regression analysis: How much more will people use medical care if it is free, and how much will that help their health? How many lives are saved by reducing the speed limit on highways? These are all empirical questions in which regression analysis helps us to get at a magnitude with real consequences. With more data available every day, regression analysis has grown in importance.

---

[6] If you go on in economics, you will see that this least squares procedure has to be modified sometimes to account for various statistical problems. But the main goal of trying to find a good fit remains.

## — SUMMARY —

### 21.1 SELECTION BIAS *p. 400*

1. One example of selection bias is survivor bias, where the most fit survive. This makes it difficult to compare young and old age groups.

2. Selection bias can arise if different kinds of people select into different groups, which can bias comparisons of the groups.

### 21.2 CAUSALITY *p. 401*

3. Correlation is not the same as causality.

4. Random experiments can sometimes be used to estimate causal effects. Intention to treat is sometimes used with random experiments to deal with limited take up in an experiment.

5. Regression discontinuity and difference-in-differences methodologies are also used to identify causality in economics.

### 21.3 STATISTICAL SIGNIFICANCE *p. 408*

6. An estimated effect is said to be statistically significant if the probability is small of obtaining the particular estimate when in fact the effect is zero. A probability of less than or equal to 5 percent is commonly used.

### 21.4 REGRESSION ANALYSIS *p. 409*

7. Regression analysis is used to estimate coefficients in equations. It is used both to obtain estimates of the magnitude of effects of various economic factors and to test alternative theories.

---

**MyEconLab** Visit **www.myeconlab.com** to complete these exercises online and get instant feedback. Exercises that update with real-time data are marked with art 🔴.

# REVIEW TERMS AND CONCEPTS

correlated, *p. 401*

difference-in-differences, *p. 406*

intention to treat, *p. 403*

least squares estimates, *p. 410*

p-value, *p. 408*

regression discontinuity, *p. 405*

selection bias, *p. 400*

statistical significance, *p. 408*

survivor bias, *p. 400*

# PROBLEMS

All problems are available on MyEconLab.

## 21.1 SELECTION BIAS

**LEARNING OBJECTIVE:** Give some examples of studies that might suffer from selection bias.

1.1 Describe the selection bias likely to exist in the following situations:

a. A study of 5,000 office workers in Chicago found that those who ate fast food for lunch three or more times per week were 30 percent more likely to suffer from heart disease than those who brought their lunch to work three or more times per seek. Therefore, eating fast food three or more times per week leads to a higher incidence of heart disease in office workers.

b. A survey of senior assisted-living facilities found that 80 percent of residents are female. Therefore, as they age, men tend to need less assistance with day-to-day living than do women.

c. A study of 1,000 college graduates found that students graduating from a prestigious private university earned, on average, $40,000 more annually than students graduating from a typical public university. Therefore, an education from a prestigious private university will enhance a student's earnings.

1.2 A classic example of selection bias occurred during World War II. During the war, the British were losing many airplanes over enemy territory and therefore decided to add armor plating to their bombers. The armor was not only heavy, but also expensive, so the British decided to only add armor to the most critical areas of the planes, determined by the location of bullet holes in returning aircraft. The areas most commonly marked by bullet holes were the wings, the nose, and the tail. Before the plan was implemented, Austrian economist Abraham Wald reviewed the data and claimed that the British plan was just the opposite of what was needed, and the armor should be added to the only areas *not* designated for armor by the British plan: the body and the rudder. The British followed Wald's recommendation and as a result, many fewer planes were shot down. Explain the selection bias in the original British plan.

## 21.2 CAUSALITY

**LEARNING OBJECTIVE:** Understand the difference between correlation and causation.

2.1 Identify each of the following scenarios as examples of causation, positive correlation, and/or negative correlation, and explain your answers.

a. More attorneys own expensive foreign sports cars than do people in any other profession.

b. Most cities with an average annual rainfall of more than 40 inches have a higher propensity to flood during rainy seasons.

c. The higher a student's grade point average, the less likely he will live in a fraternity house.

d. Most men who are bald or are losing their hair also wear eyeglasses.

e. Most people who recycle their trash on a regular basis have a lower incidence of driving a large SUV than those who do not regularly recycle.

2.2 [**Related to the *Economics in Practice* on p. 404**] In a randomized one-year trial of 100 elm trees with Dutch Elm Disease, 50 are slated to receive only a fungicide treatment (we will call this Group A), and the other 50 are slated to receive the fungicide treatment and an additional insecticide treatment six months later (we will call this Group B). Assume that the insecticide treatment is ineffective in curing Dutch Elm Disease, so on average, the same proportion of trees in each group will die of the disease. In Group B, 5 of the 50 trees die in the six-month period leading up to the insecticide treatment. Of the 45 trees left, 5 die in the six months following the insecticide treatment. Since we know the insecticide treatment is ineffective, the trees in Group A will, on average, suffer the same fate as those in Group B, with 5 trees dying in the first six months and another 5 dying in the second six months.

a. For Group A, what is the rate of death due to Dutch Elm Disease?

b. If we limit the analysis in Group B to only those trees which received the insecticide treatment, what is the rate of death due to Dutch Elm Disease?

**c.** What do your answers to parts a and b suggest regarding the reduction in deaths from Dutch Elm Disease due to the addition of the insecticide treatment?

**d.** Knowing what you do about the effectiveness of the insecticide treatment, what is the problem with this analysis? How would applying the intention-to-treat method verify your answer?

**2.3** [Related to the *Economics in Practice* on p. 405] In 1991, economists Joshua D. Angrist and Alan B. Krueger published a study on the correlation between date of birth and years of schooling. The premise was that the actual amount of time an average person spends in school is tied to the time of year in which people are born. Suppose in the city of Gotham, school is mandatory for all children, and students must be 6 years old by August 31 in order to enter first grade. By law, students must stay in school until they are 16 years old, at which time they can drop out if they choose. How would you use regression discontinuity to evaluate if a person's date of birth correlates to the years of schooling the person attains in Gotham?

**2.4** [Related to the *Economics in Practice* on p. 407] The neighboring towns of East Magoo and West Magoo are divided by the Quincy River. The towns are similar in geographic size and population. The homes in both towns are powered entirely by electricity provided by Backus County Power and Light, which charges a standardized rate of $0.10 per kilowatt hour (kWh). Both East Magoo and West Magoo add on an additional $0.02 per kilowatt hour as an energy use tax. As a way to increase revenue, the mayor of East Magoo persuaded the town council to double the energy use tax on all residents, effective January 1, 2015. The average monthly energy usage per home is listed in the table below. Use the difference-in-differences method to estimate the effect of the increase in the energy use tax on the average monthly amount of energy used per home in East Magoo.

**Average Monthly Energy Use per Home**

| Town | 2014 | 2015 |
|------|------|------|
| East Magoo | 1,775 kWh | 1,917 kWh |
| West Magoo | 1,815 kWh | 2,033 kWh |

**2.5** Refer to the previous problem. At the end of 2015, the mayor of East Magoo made the following statement: "Even after we increased the energy use tax, average power consumption increased in our town. This proves that the tax increase did not cause our residents to decrease electricity use, and in fact, it appears to have encouraged them to use more electricity!" What is wrong with the mayor's logic?

## 21.3 STATISTICAL SIGNIFICANCE

LEARNING OBJECTIVE: Understand how researchers decide whether their results are meaningful.

**3.1** Of the following four scenarios, which survey results are likely to be the most statistically significant and which are likely to be the least statistically significant. Explain your answer.

*Scenario 1*: In a study to see if Yankees' fans or Astros' fans spend more on concessions at a baseball game, 20 people are surveyed as they enter Yankee Stadium in New York and 20 people are surveyed as they enter Minute Maid Park in Houston.

*Scenario 2*: 700 people are surveyed one year after completing a court-mandated defensive driving class for a study to see if their driving record improved following the completion of the class.

*Scenario 3*: 75 sophomore engineering majors at Ohio State University are surveyed for a study to see if attending a seminar on the best ways to obtain scholarship money was effective in getting additional money for school.

*Scenario 4*: 500 recently retired Pennsylvania coal miners are surveyed for a study to determine if working in the coal mines has led to a medical diagnosis of coal worker's pneumoconiosis (CWP), commonly referred to as black lung disease.

## 21.4 REGRESSION ANALYSIS

LEARNING OBJECTIVE: Understand how regression analysis can be used for both estimation and testing.

**4.1** The data in the table below was used to estimate the following consumption function: $C = 10 + 0.5Y$ On a graph, draw the consumption function and plot the points from the table. Calculate the "error" for each point in the table, and then calculate the *SUM* from your "error" calculations.

| Point | Aggregate Income ($Y$) | Aggregate Consumption ($C$) |
|-------|------------------------|-----------------------------|
| A | 10 | 13 |
| B | 20 | 23 |
| C | 30 | 30 |
| D | 40 | 32 |
| E | 50 | 33 |
| F | 60 | 44 |

**4.2** Which of the following consumption functions best fits the values in the table below?
1. $C = 6 + 0.8Y$
2. $C = 4 + 0.75Y$
3. $C = 2 + 0.6Y$
4. $C = 3 + 0.5Y$

| Aggregate Income ($Y$) | Aggregate Consumption ($C$) |
|------------------------|------------------------------|
| 5 | 10 |
| 10 | 14 |
| 20 | 23 |
| 40 | 38 |

# Glossary

**absolute advantage**  A producer has an absolute advantage over another in the production of a good or service if he or she can produce that product using fewer resources (a lower absolute cost per unit). *p. 25*

**absolute advantage**  The advantage in the production of a good enjoyed by one country over another when it uses fewer resources to produce that good than the other country does. *p. 333*

**accelerator effect**  The tendency for investment to increase when aggregate output increases and to decrease when aggregate output decreases, accelerating the growth or decline of output. *p. 290*

**actual investment**  The actual amount of investment that takes place; it includes items such as unplanned changes in inventories. *p. 147*

**adjustment costs**  The costs that a firm incurs when it changes its production level—for example, the administration costs of laying off employees or the training costs of hiring new workers. *p. 290*

**aggregate behavior**  The behavior of all households and firms together. *p. 90*

**aggregate income**  The total income received by all factors of production in a given period. *p. 141*

**aggregate output (income) (Y)**  A combined term used to remind you of the exact equality between aggregate output and aggregate income. *p. 141*

**aggregate output**  The total quantity of goods and services produced (or supplied) in an economy in a given period. *pp. 91, 141*

**aggregate production function**  A mathematical relationship stating that total GDP (output) depends on the total amount of labor used and the total amount of capital used. *p. 303*

**aggregate saving (S)**  The part of aggregate income that is not consumed. *p. 143*

**aggregate supply (AS) curve**  A graph that shows the relationship between the aggregate quantity of output supplied by all firms in an economy and the overall price level. *p. 215*

**aggregate supply**  The total supply of all goods and services in an economy. *p. 215*

**animal spirits of entrepreneurs**  A term coined by Keynes to describe investors' feelings. *p. 289*

**appreciation of a currency**  The rise in value of one currency relative to another. *p. 367*

**automatic destabilizer**  Revenue and expenditure items in the federal budget that automatically change with the state of the economy in such a way as to destabilize GDP. *p. 178*

**automatic destabilizers**  Revenue and expenditure items in the federal budget that automatically change with the economy in such a way as to destabilize GDP. *p. 276*

**automatic stabilizers**  Revenue and expenditure items in the federal budget that automatically change with the economy in such a way as to stabilize GDP. *pp. 178, 276*

**balance of payments**  The record of a country's transactions in goods, services, and assets with the rest of the world; also the record of a country's sources (supply) and uses (demand) of foreign exchange. *p. 357*

**balance of trade**  A country's exports of goods and services minus its imports of goods and services. *p. 358*

**balance on current account**  The sum of income from exports of goods and services and income from investments and transfers minus payments for imports of goods and services and payments for investments and transfers. *p. 358*

**balanced-budget multiplier**  The ratio of change in the equilibrium level of output to a change in government spending where the change in government spending is balanced by a change in taxes so as not to create any deficit. The balanced-budget multiplier is equal to 1: The change in $Y$ resulting from the change in $G$ and the equal change in $T$ are exactly the same size as the initial change in $G$ or $T$. *p. 271*

**barter**  The direct exchange of goods and services for other goods and services. *p. 188*

**base year**  The year chosen for the weights in a fixed-weight procedure. *p. 114*

**binding situation**  State of the economy in which the Fed rule calls for a negative interest rate. *p. 235*

**black market**  A market in which illegal trading takes place at market-determined prices. *p. 77*

**brain drain**  The tendency for talented people from developing countries to become educated in a developed country and remain there after graduation. *p. 386*

**budget deficit**  The difference between what a government spends and what it collects in taxes in a given period: $G - T$. *p. 164*

**business cycle**  The cycle of short-term ups and downs in the economy. *p. 91*

**capital**  Those goods produced by the economic system that are used as inputs to produce other goods and services in the future. *p. 22*

**capital flight**  The tendency for both human capital and financial capital to leave developing countries in search of higher expected rates of return elsewhere with less risk.  *p. 385*

**capital gain**  An increase in the value of an asset.  *p. 265*

**capital market**  The input/factor market in which households supply their savings, for interest or for claims to future profits, to firms that demand funds to buy capital goods.  *p. 44*

**catch-up**  The theory stating that the growth rates of less developed countries will exceed the growth rates of developed countries, allowing the less developed countries to catch up.  *p. 303*

***ceteris paribus, or all else equal***  A device used to analyze the relationship between two variables while the values of other variables are held unchanged.  *p. 8*

**change in business inventories**  The amount by which firms' inventories change during a period. Inventories are the goods that firms produce now but intend to sell later.  *p. 108*

**circular flow**  A diagram showing the flows in and out of the sectors in the economy.  *p. 94*

**command economy**  An economy in which a central government either directly or indirectly sets output targets, incomes, and prices.  *p. 36*

**commodity monies**  Items used as money that also have intrinsic value in some other use.  *p. 190*

**comparative advantage**  A producer has a comparative advantage over another in the production of a good or service if he or she can produce that product at a lower *opportunity cost*.  *p. 26*

**comparative advantage**  The advantage in the production of a good enjoyed by one country over another when that good can be produced at lower cost in terms of other goods than it could be in the other country.  *p. 334*

**compensation of employees**  Includes wages, salaries, and

various supplements—employer contributions to social insurance and pension funds, for example—paid to households by firms and by the government.  *p. 109*

**complements, complementary goods**  Goods that "go together"; a decrease in the price of one results in an increase in demand for the other and vice versa.  *p. 49*

**constrained supply of labor**  The amount a household actually works in a given period at the current wage rate.  *p. 285*

**consumer goods**  Goods produced for present consumption.  *p. 28*

**consumer price index (CPI)**  A price index computed each month by the Bureau of Labor Statistics using a bundle that is meant to represent the "market basket" purchased monthly by the typical urban consumer.  *p. 129*

**consumer sovereignty**  The idea that consumers ultimately dictate what will be produced (or not produced) by choosing what to purchase (and what not to purchase).  *p. 36*

**consumer surplus**  The difference between the maximum amount a person is willing to pay for a good and its current market price.  *p. 82*

**consumption function**  The relationship between consumption and income.  *p. 142*

**contraction, recession, *or* slump**  The period in the business cycle from a peak down to a trough during which output and employment fall.  *p. 92*

**Corn Laws**  The tariffs, subsidies, and restrictions enacted by the British Parliament in the early nineteenth century to discourage imports and encourage exports of grain.  *p. 333*

**corporate bonds**  Promissory notes issued by firms when they borrow money.  *p. 96*

**corporate profits**  The income of corporations.  *p. 109*

**correlated**  Two variables are correlated if their values tend to move together.  *p. 401*

**cost shock, or supply shock**  A change in costs that shifts the short-run aggregate supply (AS) curve.  *p. 217*

**cost-of-living adjustments (COLAs)**  Contract provisions that tie wages to changes in the cost of living. The greater the inflation rate, the more wages are raised.  *p. 252*

**cost-push, *or* supply-side, inflation**  Inflation caused by an increase in costs.  *p. 238*

**currency debasement**  The decrease in the value of money that occurs when its supply is increased rapidly.  *p. 190*

**current dollars**  The current prices that we pay for goods and services.  *p. 111*

**cyclical deficit**  The deficit that occurs because of a downturn in the business cycle.  *p. 179*

**cyclical unemployment**  Unemployment that is above frictional plus structural unemployment.  *p. 129*

**cyclical unemployment**  The increase in unemployment that occurs during recessions and depressions.  *p. 246*

**deadweight loss**  The total loss of producer and consumer surplus from underproduction or overproduction.  *p. 84*

**deflation**  A decrease in the overall price level.  *p. 93*

**demand curve**  A graph illustrating how much of a given product a household would be willing to buy at different prices.  *p. 47*

**demand schedule**  Shows how much of a given product a household would be willing to buy at different prices for a given time period.  *p. 46*

**demand-pull inflation**  Inflation that is initiated by an increase in aggregate demand.  *p. 238*

**depreciation of a currency** The fall in value of one currency relative to another. *p. 367*

**depreciation** The decline in an asset's economic value over time, or the amount by which an asset's value falls in a given period. *p. 108*

**depression** A prolonged and deep recession. *p. 91*

**desired, *or* optimal, level of inventories** The level of inventory at which the extra cost (in lost sales) from lowering inventories by a small amount is just equal to the extra gain (in interest revenue and decreased storage costs). *p. 291*

**difference-in-differences** Difference-in-differences is a method of identifying causality by looking at the way in which the average change over time in the outcome variable is compared to the average change in a control group. *p. 406*

**discouraged-worker effect** The decline in the measured unemployment rate that results when people who want to work but cannot find jobs grow discouraged and stop looking, thus dropping out of the ranks of the unemployed and the labor force. *pp. 126, 295*

**discretionary fiscal policy** Changes in taxes or spending that are the result of deliberate changes in government policy. *p. 163*

**disembodied technical change** Technical change that results in a change in the production process. *p. 308*

**disposable personal income or after-tax income** Personal income minus personal income taxes. The amount that households have to spend or save. *p. 111*

**disposable, *or* after-tax, income ($Y_d$)** Total income minus net taxes: $Y - T$. *p. 163*

**dividends** The portion of a firm's profits that the firm pays out each period to its shareholders. *p. 96*

**Doha Development Agenda** An initiative of the World Trade Organization focused on issues of trade and development. *p. 345*

**Dow Jones Industrial Average** An index based on the stock prices of 30 actively traded large companies. The oldest and most widely followed index of stock market performance. *p. 267*

**dumping** A firm's or an industry's sale of products on the world market at prices below its own cost of production. *p. 342*

**durable goods** Goods that last a relatively long time, such as cars and household appliances. *p. 106*

**economic growth** An increase in the total output of an economy. Growth occurs when a society acquires new resources or when it learns to produce more using existing resources. *pp. 10, 32*

**economic integration** Occurs when two or more nations join to form a free-trade zone. *p. 345*

**economics** The study of how individuals and societies choose to use the scarce resources that nature and previous generations have provided. *p. 1*

**efficiency** In economics, allocative efficiency. An efficient economy is one that produces what people want at the least possible cost. *p. 10*

**efficiency wage theory** An explanation for unemployment that holds that the productivity of workers increases with the wage rate. If this is so, firms may have an incentive to pay wages above the market-clearing rate. *p. 248*

**efficient market** A market in which profit opportunities are eliminated almost instantaneously. *p. 3*

**embodied technical change** Technical change that results in an improvement in the quality of capital. *p. 307*

**empirical economics** The collection and use of data to test economic theories. *p. 8*

**employed** Any person 16 years old or older (1) who works for pay, either for someone else or in his or her own business for 1 or more hours per week, (2) who works without pay for 15 or more hours per week in a family enterprise, or (3) who has a job but has been temporarily absent with or without pay. *p. 124*

**entrepreneur** A person who organizes, manages, and assumes the risks of a firm, taking a new idea or a new product and turning it into a successful business. *p. 43*

**equilibrium** The condition that exists when quantity supplied and quantity demanded are equal. At equilibrium, there is no tendency for price to change. In the macroeconomic goods market, equilibrium occurs when planned aggregate expenditure is equal to aggregate output. *p. 148*

**equity** Fairness *p. 10*

**European Union (EU)** The European trading bloc composed of 28 countries (of the 28 countries in the EU, 17 have the same currency—the euro). *p. 345*

**excess demand *or* shortage** The condition that exists when quantity demanded exceeds quantity supplied at the current price. *p. 60*

**excess labor, excess capital** Labor and capital that are not needed to produce the firm's current level of output. *p. 290*

**excess reserves** The difference between a bank's actual reserves and its required reserves. *p. 195*

**excess supply *or* surplus** The condition that exists when quantity supplied exceeds quantity demanded at the current price. *p. 62*

**exchange rate** The price of one country's currency in terms of another country's currency; the ratio at which two currencies are traded for each other. *pp. 339, 356*

**exogenous variable** A variable that is assumed not to depend on the state of the economy—that is, it does not change when the economy changes. *p. 153*

**expansion or boom** The period in the business cycle from a trough up to a peak during which output and employment grow. *p. 92*

**expenditure approach** A method of computing GDP that measures the total amount spent on all final goods and services during a given period. *p. 106*

**explicit contracts** Employment contracts that stipulate workers' wages, usually for a period of 1 to 3 years. *p. 251*

**export promotion** A trade policy designed to encourage exports. *p. 392*

**export subsidies** Government payments made to domestic firms to encourage exports. *p. 342*

**factor endowments** The quantity and quality of labor, land, and natural resources of a country. *p. 341*

**factors of production (*or* factors)** The inputs into the process of production. Another term for *resources*. Land, labor, and capital are the three key factors of production. *pp. 23, 44*

**favored customers** Those who receive special treatment from dealers during situations of excess demand. *p. 76*

**Fed rule** Equation that shows how the Fed's interest rate decision depends on the state of the economy. *p. 220*

**federal budget** The budget of the federal government. *p. 173*

**federal debt** The total amount owed by the federal government. *p. 176*

**Federal Open Market Committee (FOMC)** A group composed of the seven members of the Fed's Board of Governors, the president of the New York Federal Reserve Bank, and four of the other 11 district bank presidents on a rotating basis; it sets goals concerning the money supply and interest rates and directs the operation of the Open Market Desk in New York. *p. 198*

**Federal Reserve Bank (the Fed)** The central bank of the United States. *p. 195*

**federal surplus (+) *or* (−) deficit** Federal government receipts minus expenditures. *p. 173*

**fiat, or token, money** Items designated as money that are intrinsically worthless. *p. 190*

**final goods and services** Goods and services produced for final use. *p. 105*

**fine-tuning** The phrase used by Walter Heller to refer to the government's role in regulating inflation and unemployment. *p. 97*

**firm** An organization that transforms resources (inputs) into products (outputs). Firms are the primary producing units in a market economy. *p. 43*

**fiscal drag** The negative effect on the economy that occurs when average tax rates increase because taxpayers have moved into higher income brackets during an expansion. *p. 178*

**fiscal policy** Government policies concerning taxes and spending. *pp. 96, 161*

**fixed-weight procedure** A procedure that uses weights from a given base year. *p. 114*

**floating, *or* market-determined, exchange rates** Exchange rates that are determined by the unregulated forces of supply and demand. *p. 364*

**foreign direct investment (FDI)** Investment in enterprises made in a country by residents outside that country. *p. 306*

**foreign exchange** All currencies other than the domestic currency of a given country. *p. 357*

**frictional unemployment** The portion of unemployment that is due to the normal turnover in the labor market; used to denote short-run job/skill-matching problems. *pp. 129, 246*

**full-employment budget** What the federal budget would be if the economy

were producing at the full-employment level of output. *p. 178*

**General Agreement on Tariffs and Trade (GATT)** An international agreement signed by the United States and 22 other countries in 1947 to promote the liberalization of foreign trade. *p. 344*

**Global South** Developing nations in Asia, Africa, and Latin America. *p. 383*

**government consumption and gross investment (G)** Expenditures by federal, state, and local governments for final goods and services. *p. 109*

**government spending multiplier** The ratio of the change in the equilibrium level of output to a change in government spending. *p. 168*

**Gramm-Rudman-Hollings Act** Passed by the U.S. Congress and signed by President Reagan in 1986, this law set out to reduce the federal deficit by $36 billion per year, with a deficit of zero slated for 1991. *p. 275*

**Great Depression** The period of severe economic contraction and high unemployment that began in 1929 and continued throughout the 1930s. *p. 97*

**gross domestic product (GDP)** The total market value of all final goods and services produced within a given period by factors of production located within a country. *p. 104*

**gross investment** The total value of all newly produced capital goods (plant, equipment, housing, and inventory) produced in a given period. *p. 108*

**gross national income (GNI)** GNP converted into dollars using an average of currency exchange rates over several years adjusted for rates of inflation. *p. 117*

**gross national product (GNP)** The total market value of all final goods and services produced within a given period by factors of production owned by a country's citizens, regardless of where the output is produced. *p. 105*

**gross private domestic investment (I)** Total investment in capital—that is, the purchase of new housing, plants, equipment, and inventory by the private (or nongovernment) sector. *p. 108*

**Heckscher-Ohlin theorem** A theory that explains the existence of a country's comparative advantage by its factor endowments: A country has a comparative advantage in the production of a product if that country is relatively well endowed with inputs used intensively in the production of that product. *p. 341*

**households** The consuming units in an economy. *p. 43*

**hyperinflation** A period of very rapid increases in the overall price level. *p. 93*

**identity** Something that is always true. *p. 143*

**implementation lag** The time it takes to put the desired policy into effect once economists and policy makers recognize that the economy is in a boom or a slump. *p. 273*

**import substitution** An industrial trade strategy that favors developing local industries that can manufacture goods to replace imports. *p. 391*

**income** The sum of all a household's wages, salaries, profits, interest payments, rents, and other forms of earnings in a given period of time. It is a flow measure. *p. 49*

**income approach** A method of computing GDP that measures the income—wages, rents, interest, and profits—received by all factors of production in producing final goods and services. *p. 106*

**indirect taxes minus subsidies** Taxes such as sales taxes, customs duties, and license fees less subsidies that the government pays for which it receives no goods or services in return. *p. 109*

**Industrial Revolution** The period in England during the late eighteenth and early nineteenth centuries in which new manufacturing technologies and improved transportation gave rise to the modern factory system and a massive movement of the population from the countryside to the cities. *p. 3*

**infant industry** A young industry that may need temporary protection from competition from the established industries of other countries to develop an acquired comparative advantage. *p. 350*

**inferior goods** Goods for which demand tends to fall when income rises. *p. 49*

**inflation** An increase in the overall price level. *p. 93*

**inflation rate** The percentage change in the price level. *p. 253*

**inflation targeting** When a monetary authority chooses its interest rate values with the aim of keeping the inflation rate within some specified band over some specified horizon. *p. 242*

**informal economy** The part of the economy in which transactions take place and in which income is generated that is unreported and therefore not counted in GDP. *p. 116*

**innovation** The use of new knowledge to produce a new product or to produce an existing product more efficiently. *p. 309*

**input *or* factor markets** The markets in which the resources used to produce goods and services are exchanged. *p. 44*

**inputs *or* resources** Anything provided by nature or previous generations that can be used directly or indirectly to satisfy human wants. *p. 23*

**intention to treat** A method in which we compare two groups based on whether they were part of an initially specified random sample subjected to an experimental protocol. *p. 403*

**intermediate goods** Goods that are produced by one firm for use in further processing by another firm. *p. 105*

**invention** An advance in knowledge. *p. 309*

**inventory investment** The change in the stock of inventories. *p. 291*

**investment** The process of using resources to produce new capital. New capital additions to a firm's capital stock. Although capital is measured at a given point in time (a stock), investment is measured over a period of time (a flow). The flow of investment increases the capital stock. *p. 28*

**IS curve** Relationship between aggregate output and the interest rate in the goods market. *p. 219*

**J-curve effect** Following a currency depreciation, a country's balance of trade may get worse before it gets better. The graph showing this effect is shaped like the letter J, hence the name J-curve effect. *p. 370*

**labor demand curve** A graph that illustrates the amount of labor that firms want to employ at each given wage rate. *p. 246*

**labor force** The number of people employed plus the number of unemployed. *p. 124*

**labor market** The input/factor market in which households supply work for wages to firms that demand labor. *p. 44*

**labor productivity growth** The growth rate of output per worker. *p. 301*

**labor supply curve** A curve that shows the quantity of labor supplied at different wage rates. Its shape depends on how households react to changes in the wage rate. A graph that illustrates the amount of labor that households want to supply at each given wage rate. *p. 247*

**Laffer curve** With the tax rate measured on the vertical axis and tax revenue measured on the horizontal axis, the Laffer curve shows that there is some tax rate beyond which the supply response is large enough to lead to a decrease in tax revenue for further increases in the tax rate. *p. 322*

**laissez-faire economy** Literally from the French: "allow [them] to do." An economy in which individual people and firms pursue their own self-interest without any central direction or regulation. *p. 36*

**land market**   The input/factor market in which households supply land or other real property in exchange for rent. *p. 44*

**law of demand**   The negative relationship between price and quantity demanded: *Ceteris paribus,* as price rises, quantity demanded decreases; as price falls, quantity demanded increases. *p. 47*

**law of one price**   If the costs of transportation are small, the price of the same good in different countries should be roughly the same. *p. 368*

**law of supply**   The positive relationship between price and quantity of a good supplied: An increase in market price will lead to an increase in quantity supplied, and a decrease in market price will lead to a decrease in quantity supplied. *p. 56*

**least squares estimates**   Least squares estimates are those that correspond to the smallest sum of squared distances, or errors. *p. 410*

**legal tender**   Money that a government has required to be accepted in settlement of debts. *p. 190*

**lender of last resort**   One of the functions of the Fed: It provides funds to troubled banks that cannot find any other sources of funds. *p. 200*

**life-cycle theory of consumption**   A theory of household consumption: Households make lifetime consumption decisions based on their expectations of lifetime income. *p. 281*

**liquidity property of money**   The property of money that makes it a good medium of exchange as well as a store of value: It is portable and readily accepted and thus easily exchanged for goods. *p. 189*

**Lucas supply function**   The supply function embodies the idea that output

(Y) depends on the difference between the actual price level and the expected price level. *p. 326*

**M1, *or* transactions money**   Money that can be directly used for transactions. *p. 191*

**M2, *or* broad money**   M1 plus savings accounts, money market accounts, and other near monies. *p. 191*

**macroeconomics**   Deals with the economy as a whole. Macroeconomics focuses on the determinants of total national income, deals with aggregates such as aggregate consumption and investment, and looks at the overall level of prices instead of individual prices. The branch of economics that examines the economic behavior of aggregates—income, employment, output, and so on—on a national scale. *p. 90*

**marginal propensity to consume (*MPC*)**   That fraction of a change in income that is consumed, or spent. *p. 143*

**marginal propensity to import (*MPM*)**   The change in imports caused by a $1 change in income. *p. 361*

**marginal propensity to save (*MPS*)**   That fraction of a change in income that is saved. *p. 143*

**marginal rate of transformation (*MRT*)**   The slope of the production possibility frontier (ppf). *p. 30*

**marginalism**   The process of analyzing the additional or incremental costs or benefits arising from a choice or decision. *p. 2*

**market**   The institution through which buyers and sellers interact and engage in exchange. *p. 36*

**market demand**   The sum of all the quantities of a good or service demanded per period by all the households buying in the market for that good or service. *p. 53*

**market supply**   The sum of all that is supplied each period by all producers of a single product. *p. 59*

**medium of exchange, or means of payment**   What sellers generally accept and buyers generally use to pay for goods and services. *p. 188*

**microeconomics**   Examines the functioning of individual industries and the behavior of individual decision-making units—firms and households. The branch of economics that examines the functioning of individual industries and the behavior of individual decision-making units—that is, firms and households. *p. 90*

**minimum wage laws**   Laws that set a floor for wage rates—that is, a minimum hourly rate for any kind of labor. *p. 249*

**model**   A formal statement of a theory, usually a mathematical statement of a presumed relationship between two or more variables. *p. 7*

**monetary policy**   The behavior of the Federal Reserve concerning interest rates. The tools used by the Federal Reserve to control the short-term interest rate. *pp. 96, 162*

**money multiplier**   The multiple by which deposits can increase for every dollar increase in reserves; equal to 1 divided by the required reserve ratio. *p. 197*

**movement along a demand curve**   The change in quantity demanded brought about by a change in price. *p. 53*

**movement along a supply curve**   The change in quantity supplied brought about by a change in price. *p. 58*

**multiplier**   The ratio of the change in the equilibrium level of output to a change in some exogenous variable. *p. 153*

**NAIRU**   The nonaccelerating inflation rate of unemployment. *p. 258*

**NASDAQ Composite**   An index based on the stock prices of over 5,000 companies traded on the NASDAQ Stock Market. The NASDAQ market takes its name from the National

Association of Securities Dealers Automated Quotation System. *p. 267*

**national income and product accounts** Data collected and published by the government describing the various components of national income and output in the economy. *p. 103*

**national income** The total income earned by the factors of production owned by a country's citizens. *p. 109*

**natural experiment** Selection of a control versus experimental group in testing the outcome of an intervention is made as a result of an exogenous event outside the experiment itself and unrelated to it. *p. 394*

**natural rate of unemployment** The unemployment rate that occurs as a normal part of the functioning of the economy. Sometimes taken as the sum of the frictional unemployment rate and the structural unemployment rate. *p. 129*

**natural rate of unemployment** The unemployment that occurs as a normal part of the functioning of the economy. Sometimes taken as the sum of frictional unemployment and structural unemployment. *p. 257*

**near monies** Close substitutes for transactions money, such as savings accounts and money market accounts. *p. 191*

**net business transfer payments** Net transfer payments by businesses to others. *p. 109*

**net exports (EX – IM)** The difference between exports (sales to foreigners of U.S.- produced goods and services) and imports (U.S. purchases of goods and services from abroad). The figure can be positive or negative. *p. 109*

**net exports of goods and services (EX – IM)** The difference between a country's total exports and total imports. *p. 361*

**net interest** The interest paid by business. *p. 109*

**net investment** Gross investment minus depreciation. *p. 108*

**net national product (NNP)** Gross national product minus depreciation; a nation's total product minus what is required to maintain the value of its capital stock. *p. 110*

**net taxes (T)** Taxes paid by firms and households to the government minus transfer payments made to households by the government. *p. 163*

**new Keynesian economics** A field in which models are developed under the assumptions of rational expectations and sticky prices and wages. *p. 327*

**nominal GDP** Gross domestic product measured in current dollars. *p. 111*

**nominal wage rate** The wage rate in current dollars. is the wage rate in current dollars. *p. 283*

**nondurable goods** Goods that are used up fairly quickly, such as food and clothing. *p. 106*

**nonlabor, or nonwage, income** Any income received from sources other than working—inheritances, interest, dividends, transfer payments, and so on. *p. 284*

**nonresidential investment** Expenditures by firms for machines, tools, plants, and so on. *p. 108*

**normal goods** Goods for which demand goes up when income is higher and for which demand goes down when income is lower. *p. 49*

**normative economics** An approach to economics that analyzes outcomes of economic behavior, evaluates them as good or bad, and may prescribe courses of action. Also called *policy economics*. *p. 7*

**North American Free Trade Agreement (NAFTA)** An agreement signed by the United States, Mexico, and Canada in which the three countries agreed to establish all North America as a free-trade zone. *p. 345*

**not in the labor force** A person who is not looking for work because he or she does not want a job or has given up looking. *p. 124*

**Ockham's razor** The principle that irrelevant detail should be cut away. *p. 7*

**Okun's Law** The theory, put forth by Arthur Okun, that in the short run the unemployment rate decreases about 1 percentage point for every 3 percent increase in real GDP. Later research and data have shown that the relationship between output and unemployment is not as stable as Okun's "Law" predicts. *p. 295*

**Open Market Desk** The office in the New York Federal Reserve Bank from which government securities are bought and sold by the Fed. *p. 198*

**open market operations** The interest rate that banks pay to the Fed to borrow from it. *p. 203*

**opportunity cost** The best alternative that we forgo, or give up, when we make a choice or a decision. *p. 2*

**opportunity cost** The best alternative that we give up, or forgo, when we make a choice or decision. *p. 24*

**output growth** The growth rate of the output of the entire economy. *pp. 133, 301*

**outputs** Goods and services of value to households. *p. 23*

**per-capita output growth** The growth rate of output per person in the economy. *pp. 233, 301*

**perfect price discrimination** Occurs when a firm charges the maximum amount that buyers are willing to pay for each unit. *p. 278*

**perfect substitutes** Identical products. *p. 49*

**permanent income** The average level of a person's expected future income stream. *p. 282*

**personal consumption expenditures (C)** Expenditures by consumers on goods and services. *p. 106*

**personal income** The total income of households. *p. 111*

**personal saving** The amount of disposable income that is left after total personal spending in a given period. *p. 111*

**personal saving rate** The percentage of disposable personal income that is saved. If the personal saving rate is low, households are spending a large amount relative to their incomes; if it is high, households are spending cautiously. *p. 111*

**Phillips Curve** A curve showing the relationship between the inflation rate and the unemployment rate. *p. 253*

**planned aggregate expenditure (AE)** The total amount the economy plans to spend in a given period. Equal to consumption plus planned investment: $AE \equiv C + I$ *p. 149*

**planned investment (I)** Those additions to capital stock and inventory that are planned by firms. *p. 147*

**positive economics** An approach to economics that seeks to understand behavior and the operation of systems without making judgments. It describes what exists and how it works. *p. 7*

**post hoc, ergo propter hoc** Literally, "after this (in time), therefore because of this." A common error made in thinking about causation: If Event A happens before Event B, it is not necessarily true that A caused B. *p. 8*

**potential output *or* potential GDP** The level of aggregate output that can be sustained in the long run without inflation. *p. 226*

**price ceiling** A maximum price that sellers may charge for a good, usually set by government. *p. 75*

**price feedback effect** The process by which a domestic price increase in one country can "feed back" on itself through export and import prices. An increase in the price level in one country can drive up prices in other countries. This in turn further increases the price level in the first country. *p. 364*

**price floor** A minimum price below which exchange is not permitted. *p. 79*

**price rationing** The process by which the market system allocates goods and services to consumers when quantity demanded exceeds quantity supplied. *p. 73*

**price surprise** Actual price level minus expected price level. *p. 326*

**privately held federal debt** The privately held (non-government-owned) debt of the U.S. government. *p. 177*

**producer price indexes (PPIs)** Measures of prices that producers receive for products at various stages in the production process. *p. 130*

**producer surplus** The difference between the current market price and the cost of production for the firm. *p. 83*

**product or output markets** The markets in which goods and services are exchanged. *p. 44*

**production possibility frontier (ppf)** A graph that shows all the combinations of goods and services that can be produced if all of society's resources are used efficiently. *p. 29*

**production** The process by which inputs are combined, transformed, and turned into outputs. *p. 23*

**productivity, *or* labor productivity** Output per worker hour. *p. 294*

**productivity growth** The growth rate of output per worker. *p. 133*

**profit** The difference between total revenue and total cost. *p. 56*

**proprietors' income** The income of unincorporated businesses. *p. 109*

**protection** The practice of shielding a sector of the economy from foreign competition. *p. 342*

**purchasing-power-parity theory** A theory of international exchange holding that exchange rates are set so that the price of similar goods in different countries is the same. *p. 368*

**p-value** The probability of obtaining the result that you find in the sample data if the null hypothesis of no relationship is true. *p. 408*

**quantity demanded** The amount (number of units) of a product that a household would buy in a given period if it could buy all it wanted at the current market price. *p. 45*

**quantity supplied** The amount of a particular product that a firm would be willing and able to offer for sale at a particular price during a given time period. *p. 56*

**quantity theory of money** The theory based on the identity $M \times V \equiv P \times Y$ and the assumption that the velocity of money (V) is constant (or virtually constant). *p. 319*

**queuing** Waiting in line as a means of distributing goods and services: a nonprice rationing mechanism. *p. 75*

**quota** A limit on the quantity of imports. *p. 343*

**random experiment** (Sometimes referred to as a randomized experiment.) A technique in which outcomes of specific interventions are determined by using the intervention in a randomly selected subset of a sample and then comparing outcomes from the exposed and control group. *p. 394*

**ration coupons** Tickets or coupons that entitle individuals to purchase a certain amount of a given product per month. *p. 76*

**rational-expectations hypothesis** The hypothesis that people know the "true model" of the economy and that they use this model to form their expectations of the future. *p. 324*

**real business cycle theory** An attempt to explain business cycle fluctuations under the assumptions of complete price and wage flexibility and rational expectations. It emphasizes shocks to technology and other shocks. *p. 327*

**real interest rate** The difference between the interest rate on a loan and the inflation rate. *p. 132*

**real wage rate** The amount the nominal wage rate can buy in terms of goods and services. *p. 283*

**real wealth effect** The change in consumption brought about by a change in real wealth that results from a change in the price level. *p. 225*

**realized capital gain** The gain that occurs when the owner of an asset actually sells it for more than he or she paid for it. *p. 265*

**recession** A period during which aggregate output declines. Conventionally, a period in which aggregate output declines for two consecutive quarters. *p. 91*

**regression discontinuity** Identifies the causal effects of a policy or factor by looking at two samples that lie on either side of a threshold or cutoff. *p. 405*

**recognition lag** The time it takes for policy makers to recognize the existence of a boom or a slump. *p. 273*

**relative-wage explanation of unemployment** An explanation for sticky wages (and therefore unemployment): If workers are concerned about their wages relative to the wages of other workers in other firms and industries, they may be unwilling to accept a wage cut unless they know that all other workers are receiving similar cuts. *p. 251*

**rental income** The income received by property owners in the form of rent. *p. 109*

**required reserve ratio** The percentage of its total deposits that a bank must keep as reserves at the Federal Reserve. *p. 195*

**reserves** The deposits that a bank has at the Federal Reserve bank plus its cash on hand. *p. 194*

**residential investment** Expenditures by households and firms on new houses and apartment buildings. *p. 108*

**response lag** The time that it takes for the economy to adjust to the new conditions after a new policy

is implemented; the lag that occurs because of the operation of the economy itself. *p. 273*

**run on a bank** Occurs when many of those who have claims on a bank (deposits) present them at the same time. *p. 194*

**scarce** Limited. *p. 2*

**selection bias** Selection bias is when the sample used is not random. *p. 400*

**services** The things we buy that do not involve the production of physical things, such as legal and medical services and education. *p. 106*

**shares of stock** Financial instruments that give to the holder a share in the firm's ownership and therefore the right to share in the firm's profits. *p. 96*

**shift of a demand curve** The change that takes place in a demand curve corresponding to a new relationship between quantity demanded of a good and price of that good. The shift is brought about by a change in the original conditions. *p. 53*

**shift of a supply curve** The change that takes place in a supply curve corresponding to a new relationship between quantity supplied of a good and the price of that good. The shift is brought about by a change in the original conditions. *p. 58*

**Smoot-Hawley tariff** The U.S. tariff law of the 1930s, which set the highest tariffs in U.S. history (60 percent). It set off an international trade war and caused the decline in trade that is often considered one of the causes of the worldwide depression of the 1930s. *p. 343*

**social overhead capital** Basic infrastructure projects such as roads, power generation, and irrigation systems. *p. 388*

**social, *or* implicit, contracts** Unspoken agreements between workers and firms that firms will not cut wages. *p. 570*

**stability** A condition in which national output is growing steadily,

with low inflation and full employment of resources. *p. 10*

**stabilization policy** Describes both monetary and fiscal policy, the goals of which are to smooth out fluctuations in output and employment and to keep prices as stable as possible. *p. 591*

**stagflation** A situation of both high inflation and high unemployment. The simultaneous increase in unemployment and inflation. *pp. 98, 237*

**Standard and Poor's 500 (S&P 500)** An index based on the stock prices of 500 of the largest firms by market value. *p. 267*

**statistical discrepancy** Data measurement error. *p. 110*

**statistical significance** A result is said to be statistically significant if the computed p-value is less than some presubscribed number, usually 0.05. *p. 408*

**sticky prices** Prices that do not always adjust rapidly to maintain equality between quantity supplied and quantity demanded. *p. 90*

**sticky wages** The downward rigidity of wages as an explanation for the existence of unemployment. *p. 250*

**stock** A certificate that certifies ownership of a certain portion of a firm. *p. 265*

**store of value** An asset that can be used to transport purchasing power from one time period to another. *p. 188*

**structural deficit** The deficit that remains at full employment. *p. 179*

**structural unemployment** The portion of unemployment that is due to changes in the structure of the economy that result in a significant loss of jobs in certain industries. *pp. 129, 246*

**substitutes** Goods that can serve as replacements for one another; when the price of one increases, demand for the other increases. *p. 49*

**supply curve** A graph illustrating how much of a product a firm will sell at different prices. *p. 56*

**supply schedule**    Shows how much of a product firms will sell at alternative prices. *p. 56*

**surplus of government enterprises** Income of government enterprises. *p. 110*

**survivor bias**    Survivor bias exists when a sample includes only observations that have remained in the sample over time making that sample unrepresentative of the broader population. *p. 400*

**tariff**    A tax on imports. *p. 342*

**tax multiplier**    The ratio of change in the equilibrium level of output to a change in taxes. *p. 170*

**terms of trade**    The ratio at which a country can trade domestic products for imported products. *p. 338*

**theory of comparative advantage** Ricardo's theory that specialization and free trade will benefit all trading parties (real wages will rise), even those that may be "absolutely" more efficient producers. *pp. 24, 333*

**time lags**    Delays in the economy's response to stabilization policies. *p. 272*

**trade deficit**    Occurs when a country's exports of goods and services are less than its imports of goods and services. *pp. 338, 358*

**trade feedback effect**    The tendency for an increase in the economic activity of one country to lead to a worldwide increase in economic activity, which then feeds back to that country. *p. 363*

**trade surplus**    The situation when a country exports more than it imports. *p. 333*

**transfer payments**    Cash payments made by the government to people who do not supply goods, services, or labor in exchange for these payments. They include Social Security benefits, veterans' benefits, and welfare payments. *p. 94*

**Treasury bonds, notes, *and* bills** Promissory notes issued by the federal government when it borrows money. *p. 96*

**U.S.-Canadian Free Trade Agreement**    An agreement in which the United States and Canada agreed to eliminate all barriers to trade between the two countries by 1998. *p. 345*

**unconstrained supply of labor** The amount a household would like to work within a given period at the current wage rate if it could find the work. *p. 285*

**unemployed**    A person 16 years old or older who is not working, is available for work, and has made specific efforts to find work during the previous 4 weeks. *p. 124*

**unemployment rate**    The number of people unemployed as a percentage of the labor force. *pp. 93, 124, 246*

**unit of account**    A standard unit that provides a consistent way of quoting prices. *p. 189*

**value added**    The difference between the value of goods as they leave a stage of production and the cost of the goods as they entered that stage. *p. 104*

**variable**    A measure that can change from time to time or from observation to observation. *p. 7*

**velocity of money**    The number of times a dollar bill changes hands, on average, during a year; the ratio of nominal *GDP* to the stock of money. *p. 318*

**vicious-circle-of-poverty**    Suggests that poverty is self-perpetuating because poor nations are unable to save and invest enough to accumulate the capital stock that would help them grow. *p. 385*

**wealth *or* net worth**    The total value of what a household owns minus what it owes. It is a stock measure. *p. 49*

**weight**    The importance attached to an item within a group of items. *p. 113*

**World Trade Organization (WTO)**    A negotiating forum dealing with rules of trade across nations. *p. 344*

**zero interest rate bound**    The interest rate cannot go below zero. *p. 235*

# Index

*Notes: Key terms and the page on which they are defined appear in **boldface**. Page numbers followed by *n* refer to information in footnotes.

# Photo Credits